ADDITIONAL PRAISE FOR

WAGING

=== WAR ===

"Barron reveals, since the birth of our nation there has been a constant tug-of-war between Congress and the president. Given the current election cycle, this interesting, well written work is a worthy, timely read."

—*Booklist*

"Insightful ... a valuable work that bolsters Constitutional understanding ... Highly recommended."

—*Library Journal*

"Barron surveys the fraught struggles between presidents and congresses over their war powers since before the creation of American constitutional government in 1787 and up through the Obama administration. . . . The book should be read widely by those responsible for the development and implementation of national policies. It's a fine example of the use of history to illuminate current circumstances and to counter unsupportable claims and arguments about Congress and the president."

—*Publishers Weekly*

"As the distinguished jurist and law professor David J. Barron reminds readers in his splendid and wonderfully lucid new work, the conflict between the commander in chief and Congress to declare and wage war is truly the story of America. With a scholar's rigor and precision, a historian's hunger and curiosity, and a natural storyteller's gift for narrative and character, *Waging War* takes readers from the struggle to win and sustain independence to today's shadowy post–Cold War world, characterized by shifting global and terrorist threats and lethal new technologies. For those who care about the past and future control of the supreme power of the American state, *Waging War* is a vital and essential contribution."

—Gordon M. Goldstein, author of *Lessons in Disaster: McGeorge Bundy and the Path to War in Vietnam*, Adjunct Senior Fellow, Council on Foreign Relations

"*Waging War*, deeply researched with a compelling and exciting narrative, immerses readers in the struggles of presidents, as commanders in chief, and Congress as they walk the Constitution's high wire over when and how to wage war. With challenges to presidential powers at their zenith today, Barron offers lessons learned from George Washington to Barack Obama about a decision critical to American lives and the world at large."

—Marcia Coyle, author of *The Roberts Court*

ALSO BY DAVID J. BARRON

City Bound: How States Stifle Urban Innovation
(coauthored by Gerald Frug)

WAGING

WAR

The Clash Between
Presidents and Congress
1776 to ISIS

DAVID J. BARRON

SIMON & SCHUSTER PAPERBACKS
New York London Toronto Sydney New Delhi

Simon & Schuster Paperbacks
An Imprint of Simon & Schuster, Inc.
1230 Avenue of the Americas
New York, NY 10020

First Simon & Schuster trade paperback edition October 2017

SIMON & SCHUSTER PAPERBACKS and colophon are registered trademarks
of Simon & Schuster, Inc.

For information about special discounts for bulk purchases,
please contact Simon & Schuster Special Sales at 1-866-506-1949
or business@simonandschuster.com.

The Simon & Schuster Speakers Bureau can bring authors to your
live event. For more information or to book an event, contact the
Simon & Schuster Speakers Bureau at 1-866-248-3049 or visit our
website at www.simonspeakers.com.

Interior design by Lewelin Polanco

Manufactured in the United States of America

10 9 8 7 6 5 4 3 2 1

The Library of Congress has cataloged the hardcover edition as follows:

Names: Barron, David J., author.
Title: Waging war : the clash between presidents and Congress, 1776 to ISIS /
    David J. Barron.
Description: New York : Simon & Schuster, 2016. | Includes bibliographical
    references and index.
Identifiers: LCCN 2016025789| ISBN 9781451681970 (hardback) | ISBN
    9781451681987 (paperback)
Subjects: LCSH: War and emergency powers—United States—History. | War,
    Declaration of—United States—History. | Constitutional history—United
    States. | Presidents—United States—History. | Executive power—United
    States—History. | United States. Congress—History. | Legislative
    power—United States—History. | IS (Organization) | BISAC: POLITICAL
    SCIENCE / Political Process / General. | POLITICAL SCIENCE / Government /
    General. | HISTORY / United States / General.
Classification: LCC KF5060 .B37 2016 | DDC 342.73/0412—dc23 LC record
available at https://lccn.loc.gov/2016025789

ISBN 978-1-4516-8197-0
ISBN 978-1-4516-8198-7 (pbk)
ISBN 978-1-4516-8199-4 (ebook)

For Juliette, and our children, Cecilia, Leo, and Jeremiah

CONTENTS

Part 3
≡ *World Wars*

Part 4
≡ *Cold War and Beyond*

PREFACE

A s the British fleet reached the shores of New York City in July of 1776, the private secretary to the King's top military commander in America looked out from the deck of his anchored war vessel. The morning sun was "shining bright," affording a "beautiful prospect" that stretched as far as six miles. In the distance, Ambrose Serle could see smoke rising from the fires of the rebels' encampments.

The Americans had declared their independence a week before, but Serle was already well versed in their grievances. Months earlier, he had achieved renown for a slashing tract against their cause. He now relished the chance to crush the rebellion at its birth. Scanning the enemy forces, Serle's eyes fastened upon the "Rebel's Headquarters," and his mind turned to the man who led them: "Washington, who is now made their generalissimo with full Powers."

But is that really what General George Washington was? And is that what his successors became? More important, is that what future commanders in chief will be?

This book zeroes in on these questions by offering a new look at an old one: Who decides how America wages war? We usually think about that question by asking who has the right to start a war. For generations, the answer has been shaped by the notion of the imperial presidency. The commander in chief is said to be all-powerful in deciding whether to send troops into harm's way, while Congress is portrayed as little more than a passive bystander. But Ambrose Serle was not thinking about Washington's power to start the Revolutionary War. He was reflecting on the commander in chief's power to decide how to fight a war that was already underway.

There is no less need to reflect on that question in our own time. In the fifteen years since the Twin Towers fell and Congress authorized the president to strike back, the country has confronted a series of hard choices about how to fight this strange and still live war against Al Qaeda and its affiliates. And so, in recent years, the question of whether it is "for the president alone" to decide how to conduct a war has been at the forefront of national debate.

This book pulls back from the recent controversies over how to answer that question. It does so in order to tell the story of the clash between Congress and the president over the conduct of war from Serle's day to our own. It is a story in which presidents are not so imperial after all. Even when Congress has chosen to stay silent at the outset of an armed conflict, presidents have, time and again, met legislative resistance as the fighting has dragged on. And, sometimes, Congress has challenged the president's powers of command even in advance of the use of force, placing obstacles in his way in the event that he should choose a course of action certain to lead to war.

The result is that, for more than two centuries, presidents have found themselves mired in a swamp of statutes, both in the run up to war and in its midst. But, rather than defiantly blow past these limits, all but a few presidents have opted for a less confrontational course. Through delay, adjustment, clever argument, political calculation, and even retreat, they have worked to accommodate, if not embrace, the restrictions that Congress has placed on their power to wage war.

The story of this complicated dance between the branches is too little appreciated. But the story starts in the days before the nation was even formed—with the disputes over wartime tactics between George Washington and the Continental Congress at the outset of the war for independence. The story resumes with the similar faceoffs that took place during the nation's early entanglements with France and Britain, that broke out a half-century later at the height of the secession crisis, and that caused great drama during the Civil War and in its aftermath. The story continues with the power struggle that shaped the nation's conduct of the war in the Philippines at the turn of the century, in the two world wars that followed, and during the Cold War and its winding down. And, finally, the story concludes with the battles between the branches over how to fight the major wars of our own time, from the Iraq war to the war against Al Qaeda and ISIS, and the clashes over wartime tactics—from detention to surveillance to interrogation—that have helped to define the waging of war for the last fifteen years.

Not all of Congress's restrictions have been of equal import. But they have shaped critical wartime choices, from the threshold decision to use force at all to critical tactical judgments about the type of force to use in an ongoing military campaign. By following this single thread of history through time, it becomes clear that neither branch has overwhelmed the other in war. For good or bad, they have been enmeshed in a persistent but never-settled power struggle, in which each branch has recognized the claims of the other, even as each has sought to get its way. And, for this reason, history offers an important lesson not only for the conduct of the war in which the nation is now engaged, but also for the conduct of wars that may yet begin.

The constitutional system of checks and balances gives presidents a wide berth in war. It does not give them a blank check. Presidents have certainly tried to find ways to wage war as they wish—often through controversial interpretations of the statutory restrictions that seem to stand in their way. But the restrictions on the conduct of war that Congress has laid down have still had a disciplining effect, sometimes by encouraging presidents to exercise restraint, sometimes by spurring them to be more aggressive, and sometimes by simply causing them to put off making a decision about what to do.

For this reason, a single leader—unchecked and unstoppable—has not decided how America has waged war. And, as a result, our system of checks and balances has managed to endure even in those times when it has been under the greatest strain. In fact, our past shows that constitutional crises have erupted in war only when presidents have struck out on their own and claimed an exclusive right to decide how war should be waged. So, as much as the president's war powers have expanded over time—as they certainly have—future presidents will have to confront the same choice that those who came before them faced. They, too, will have to decide whether to embrace a too-little-known tradition of accommodation or risk the kind of wartime constitutional crisis that all but a handful of their predecessors have so skillfully managed to avoid.

But that is getting ahead of the story. We first need to turn back the clock, to the earliest days of the Revolution, when General Washington was in command, a mighty British force was poised to attack his troops in New York, and America's first commander in chief was facing an agonizing tactical choice that it was not at all clear that the Congress of his day was willing to let him make.

Part 1
FOUNDINGS

1

THE REVOLUTIONARY WAR

"I am not invested with the Powers You Suppose."

As much as Ambrose Serle had reason to wonder about the kind of rebel military leader the British were about to confront in New York, the object of Serle's gaze had plenty to occupy his own mind on that July day in the summer of 1776. The commander in chief of the Continental Army, General George Washington, was under no illusion about the threat his men faced. The Americans were badly overmatched. A fleet of more than one hundred of His Majesty's warships was massed just offshore. British general William Howe's skillful brother, Admiral Richard Howe, was in command. The rebels, by contrast, had no navy. They could barely even field an army. And so, while Ambrose Serle reflected on Washington's supposedly sweeping powers, the American general had other concerns. He was dreaming up daring plans for victory. He was also plotting his escape.

Assuming, that is, such a choice of tactics was even General Washington's to make. As a practical matter, Washington was the chief commander in the field. If he was of such a mind, he could always choose to do what he thought necessary and then dare the Continental Congress to question him after the fact. Congress was in Philadelphia, after all, and so poorly positioned to second-guess his judgment in the field. But, even at this earliest stage of American government, Washington sensed that there was peril in waging war on terms his Congress did not accept. And the instinct to stay in line with Congress would guide Washington when the time came to make the crucial tactical choice that the British assault on New York would force him to make.

* * *

If the British attack proved as ferocious as Washington expected, then he resolved, he would send his troops to safer ground. If need be, he would even direct them to abandon the city outright. In preparing for just that outcome, he had already taken the precaution of sending his personal papers—gathered in a large box, secured with nails—to Philadelphia for safekeeping. But Washington had to decide more than whether to make a last stand. He also had to decide how his men should go about withdrawing from the battle if he determined, as seemed likely, that retreat was the wiser course. That part of the decision was more complicated.

A clean retreat was certainly a possibility. It would ensure the troops could live to fight another day. It would also avoid a host of difficult judgments. But New York was no ordinary city. It occupied a vital strategic position. And it had great symbolic importance. Once in British hands, the city's loyalist leanings could make it the center of the effort to beat back the rebellion. Washington's advisors had been warning for months, therefore, that the city must not be left for the British to occupy.

As early as January of 1776—and thus well before the first British ships appeared off Long Island—the American general Nathanael Greene had implored Washington to "Burn or Garrison the City." Greene later narrowed that choice when he realized how futile garrisoning would likely be. Arson, he later explained, was Washington's only option.

There was precedent for Greene's proposal. Rebel soldiers had set fire to villages in Indian country and in Canada. It would be easy enough to do so now. Washington, as commander in chief, would order his officers to set fires strategically throughout Manhattan. The army would head for White Plains. From there, the soldiers could watch the conflagration before moving out for good.

Washington was savvy enough to foresee the controversy that might follow the execution of such a plan. The New York Convention had already inquired about a rumor that the rebels were planning to leave the city in ruins. The rump body of New York patriots assured the new commander in chief that it would "cheerfully submit to the fatal Necessity" if he deemed "it essential to the Safety of this State or the general Interest of America." But the Convention still wanted Washington's word that he would burn the city only as a last resort. The commander in chief obliged. He wrote back to the Convention straightaway, informing its members that he would take such drastic action only if circumstances would "justify me to the whole World."

Washington knew, however, that he needed to convince more than sympathetic New Yorkers or the amorphous court of world opinion. If he wished to burn the city to the ground, he also would need to persuade the institution to which he owed his command.

* * *

The Continental Congress was an unusual body—and a maddeningly disorganized one as well. Working out of a plain brick, two-story building in Philadelphia, Congress was made up of representatives from each of the newly united colonies, a collection of more than fifty people on the rare occasion when they were all assembled. A Massachusetts native, John Hancock, served as its president. But Congress could act only if a majority of its members agreed. And so, in the words of one delegate, the Continental Congress was neither fish nor fowl. It was a "deliberating Executive assembly," and it blended the functions of democratic government in one unwieldy revolutionary body.

Still, the mission of Congress was clear: to win the war for independence. Congress eventually established a rudimentary bureaucracy to aid its work. Congress would sometimes send its Board of War to the front so that its members could consult directly with General Washington. That board would even give Washington directives on the spot, a practice foreseen by the congressional order that commissioned him as the commander in chief.

The terms of that order did not grant Washington anything like the unlimited power that General Howe's secretary, Ambrose Serle, seemed to assume the top American general must have enjoyed. Congress required Washington to conduct himself "in every respect by the rules and discipline of war," and it directed him "punctually to observe and follow such orders and directions, from time to time, as you shall receive from this, or a future Congress of these United Colonies, or committee of Congress."

Washington treasured this document. He did not part with it—even in battle—during his time at the helm of American forces. But that did not mean General Washington enjoyed the tight congressional control that his commission contemplated. He could be a devastating critic of Congress's inefficiency, and an effective bureaucratic infighter if necessary. Even by the time of the crisis in New York, Washington had succeeded in convincing Congress to expand his powers in important ways. But the leash remained in place, and Washington knew it could be pulled at any moment.

* * *

By late August, the British forces had taken over Long Island. Their assault on Manhattan was imminent. The Americans' commanding general settled on a final course of action. He chose to wait before implementing it. He wanted to check in with higher authorities first. On September 2, Washington wrote to Congress with a question: "If we should be obliged to abandon this Town ought It to stand as Winter Quarters for the Enemy?"

Hancock and his fellow members of Congress were far from the battlefield when they received Washington's letter and the leading question that it posed. They knew that if New York fell, Philadelphia could be next. From their remote vantage point, there was more to consider than the struggle for terrain and temporary tactical advantage. There was also the fight for the hearts and minds of the American people and for the international standing of a government bidding for admission into the community of nations.

It was the Americans who had consistently condemned the British for burning cities—from Charlestown, Massachusetts, to Jamestown, Rhode Island. One had to look no farther than the Declaration of Independence—the very document that helped to precipitate the British attack on New York. That document listed as a leading grievance the fact that the king had "burnt our towns." More practically, the members of Congress wondered whether New York's importance actually provided a reason to spare it rather than lay it to waste. To destroy such a valuable city so early in the conflict would hardly reflect the kind of confidence in ultimate victory on which a successful rebellion depended. And what if the rebels later gained the upper hand as the war progressed? Wouldn't the rebels come to regret the destruction of their former stronghold? Hancock and the other representatives knew that if they wanted the city to survive, they needed to tell Washington right away. A courier carried Congress's response from Philadelphia the very next day. Hancock's directive instructed the commander in chief to ensure that "no damage [was to] be done" to the city, and, as Washington later recalled, "absolutely forbid" the burning.

* * *

Washington was incredulous when he received the response from Congress. But, then, the man whom Ambrose Serle had just weeks before imagined to be an all-powerful generalissimo, swiftly regained his composure. His emotions in check, Washington immediately replied with a promise to obey. "I shall take every measure in my power" to preserve the city intact, Washington explained, even though, as he later wrote to a family confidant, "this in my judgment may be set down am[on]g one of the capitol [sic] errors of Congress."

Within the fortnight, the British put Washington's promise to the test. The final British assault began on September 15. The attack was as brutal as Washington feared. The American general struggled to keep his forces intact. The British onslaught continued hour after hour. Some of Washington's men ran despite the leader's orders to stay and fight. The shells raining down from Admiral Howe's warships were more than

Washington's men could stand. With the shrieks of the frightened civilian populace adding to the frenzy, Washington at last called for a formal retreat. His men finally fled.

From his newly established position on Harlem Heights, Washington looked out upon the British encampments, much as Serle had, only a month before, surveyed the American tents arrayed across the water from his anchored British war vessel. The view was painful. New York City still stood. The congressional order had been respected. But the enemy was busy setting up quarters in the city for the bitter months ahead, and Washington's men were without their former home.

* * *

Six days later, Washington's army headed out in search of a new encampment—the beginnings of a hellish journey that would soon take the troops across the Delaware River and ultimately on to Valley Forge. As the American forces left New York, smoke could be seen rising from the city in a great plume. The fire that ran through Manhattan on September 21 destroyed hundreds of houses. Some of the British and many of the loyalists blamed Washington. They noted the town's bells had been taken and that their absence deprived the city of alarms that might have helped contain the blaze. They saw the traces of an American military plan to destroy the city in the course of the retreat. Others doubted Washington's involvement in the burning of New York. They believed the fire an accident or the work of rogue agents acting on their own.

That so much of New York survived indicated that the fire was not the result of a military plan. Surely if there had been a conscious intention to raze the city, the fire would not have been so poorly set. As for the missing bells, they were made of lead. Their disappearance was thus likely due to fleeing Americans desperate for matériel for munitions.

Washington, for his part, did not regret the burning. He later wrote that "Providence—or some good honest Fellow, has done more for us than we were disposed to do for ourselves, as near One fourth of the City is supposed to be consumed." But, by noting that the fire had resulted from efforts the rebels had been unwilling to undertake on their own,

Washington confirmed the key thing: He had played no role in bringing about the destruction. He had given his word to Hancock that he would do nothing to destroy the city that Congress wished to spare. And he had kept that promise.

* * *

New York did not mark the last time that Washington found himself at odds with Philadelphia over the conduct of the war. Nor was it the last time that he would submit to Congress in a clash over tactics in the midst of hostilities. No sooner had Washington begun to lead his men from Manhattan and eventually across the icy waters of the Delaware, than yet another conflict with Congress over tactics erupted.

This new disagreement also pitted tactical imperatives against larger strategic judgments. But now Washington favored the more humane and prudent approach, while Congress pressed hard for a more aggressive course of action.

The immediate cause of the dispute was the incautious behavior of one of Washington's fellow officers, Charles Lee. A former British solider, Lee was once a serious rival for the title commander in chief. Well schooled but slovenly, the long-faced Lee ultimately lost out to the tall gentleman from Virginia. Lee never reconciled himself to his defeat at Washington's hands. Lee's enduring envy of Washington's title as chief commander eventually led to a dramatic battlefield confrontation between the two men and, ultimately, Lee's own court-martial for misconduct. Before his shocking downfall, though, there was this earlier wartime incident, which briefly made Lee a hero and caused Washington no end of grief.

The trigger for the dispute was an unexpected American triumph. In the first true battle of the Revolutionary War, and before the rebels had even declared their independence, Washington's men had withstood a furious British assault on Boston. Those under Washington's command had performed well enough to capture hundreds of the king's soldiers. Archibald Campbell was among them. He was an officer in the 71st Regiment of Highlanders, a force of Scotsmen devoted to aiding the Crown. But the Americans were ill prepared for their unexpected victory, and they lacked a plan for quartering their newly captured prisoners. The Continental Congress stepped into the breach. Campbell and seven fellow Scotsmen were to be sent to the Massachusetts town of Reading. There they were placed in the home of an American captain, Nathan Parker, for safekeeping.

For a time, Campbell and his fellow soldiers seemed almost to enjoy the stay. Upwards of twenty servants attended to their needs. The prisoners roamed freely within a six-mile radius of the Parker homestead. Over time, however, the Americans' willingness to accommodate the "luxurious habits" of the "gay, red-coated strangers" and their "outlandish costume and music" wore thin. The guests began to "offend the frugal, self-denying farmers" of the area. Even still, things proceeded in a relatively happy fashion until the winter of 1776, when, after New York's devastating fall, American fortunes declined further. Adding to the discouraging cascade of bad news was the report that the British had made an important capture of their own.

* * *

General Charles Lee had broken camp in search of drink, and more comfortable quarters, at Widow White's Tavern in Basking Ridge, New Jersey. The enemy took Lee into custody in his dressing gown on the morning of December 13. Ignoble as Lee's capture was, his detention fast became a rallying point for rebel opposition. Rumors of his vile treatment spread with the word that the king had ordered Lee returned to England to be tried before a military tribunal. As it happened, General Howe chose to keep his prize captive on this side of the Atlantic. But that did not soothe the rebels. Calls for reprisal grew louder, if only to drown out the disappointment of the British victory in Manhattan and the string of defeats that the rebel forces endured in its wake.

Feeding off the anger, the Continental Congress stepped forward to defend American honor. The members of Congress had recently fled Philadelphia for Baltimore, in part to evade mutinous American soldiers. Before departing, the representatives had temporarily handed over full power to direct the war to Washington. But now, organized as a working body once again, the members of the Continental Congress reasserted control. Lee had been improperly denied parole and "committed to the custody of the provost," Congress declared. It was "a treatment totally unworthy of that gentleman's eminent qualifications, and his rank in the service of the United States, and strongly indicative of farther injuries to his person." To meet this outrage, Congress directed Washington to inform General Howe that, if he did not accept a prisoner exchange, Campbell and the others would be subject to the "same treatment" as had been inflicted upon Lee.

Washington did not welcome the order. He complied with it nonetheless. Perhaps he counted on General Howe to see through the political posturing. Then, six months later, Congress weighed in on the matter once again. This time, Congress ordered Campbell and the others to be put "into safe and close custody, it being the unalterable resolution of Congress to retaliate on them the same punishment as may be inflicted on the person of General Lee." By the time the new order came down, Archibald Campbell had been removed to a wooden jail—two stories high, with a four-sided roof—in Concord, Massachusetts. The sheriff of Middlesex took control.

The highest-ranking enemy officer in American custody, Campbell found his new surroundings appalling. Only days after arriving in his new locale, Campbell wrote directly to General Washington. Campbell echoed Ambrose Serle in doing so. "From the powers which I have lately understood has been reposed in y'r Excell'y as dictator," Campbell wrote, "and from the character I have always entertained of y'r generosity of sentiment, I am naturally led to use the freedom of troubling you with the complaint of an officer, who suffers at this instant a treatment more dishonorable & inhuman than has ever existed in the annals of modern war." The letter proceeded to detail the deplorable conditions: "I am lodged in a dungeon of about 12 or 13 feet square, doubly planked and spiked on every side, black with the grease and litter of successive criminals & completely hung around with cobwebs." Campbell was particularly outraged by the denial of "the attendance of a single servant on my person." The last complaint reflected how far he had fallen.

* * *

Washington was sympathetic to Campbell's plight. The chief commander believed Congress's harsh approach to the treatment of British captives would taint America's image abroad. It might also inspire retaliation against his own soldiers. And it offended his sense of decency. But Washington offered little in the way of direct help to Campbell. Washington would work to defuse the situation, but he would not defy the will of Congress. And he certainly was no dictator. Of that, he wanted Campbell to be sure.

On March 1, Washington responded in an extraordinary letter—commanding general to captured enemy prisoner. "I am not invested with the powers you suppose," Washington wrote. "It is as incompatible with my authority, as my inclination, to contravene any determination Congress may make." Washington admitted, however, that, in his view, Campbell's harsh treatment did not seem to be "required by any resolution" of Congress, as Lee had not been harshly treated. Washington informed Campbell that he had told the relevant Massachusetts officials as much. And so Washington had. The harsh treatment was not required, Washington explained, even "upon the most strict interpretation" of the congressional resolution. Lee, after all, was not being treated any worse. On that point, Washington's judgment was right—at least if one is to believe a Tory historian who researched the matter some years later. General Lee had been housed in the council chamber of New York's City Hall. He was permitted each night to order from a local public house a dinner that was big enough for six men, with liquor to boot. But still, Washington did not order anyone to do anything. Even if Campbell's treatment was wrong, Washington wanted it known, Congress's word still controlled.

The commander in chief did, however, begin pressing the Continental Congress to back off. He urged reversal of the orders of retaliation. The orders "[would] not have the desired effect . . . and will if adhered to, produce consequences of an extensive and melancholy nature." Worried about a spiral of abuse, Washington explained that retaliation was "not justified by any [mistreatment] that Genl. Lee has yet received." But here, too, Washington merely offered his views to Congress in hopes that they might influence Hancock and his men.

* * *

Two weeks later, in a letter to Washington, John Hancock responded on behalf of Congress as its president. "It was not [Congress's] intention that [Campbell] should experience any other hardship than such confinement as is necessary to his security for the [purpose of the prior retaliation resolution]," Hancock explained to his general. The assembly's sole objective was merely to ensure equal treatment—that "as severities against [Lee] were increased, the same treatment should be exercised on six Field Officers."

Washington's lobbying had plainly done some good. The Massachusetts officials placed Campbell in a room in the jailer's house. The British officer was even allowed one servant. Campbell was still not satisfied. He wrote Washington again, this time requesting a return to his former quarters in Reading. The dispute persisted into the late spring of 1777 and then the summer. General Howe upbraided General Washington along the way for keeping the British officer captive "in the jailer's house, exposed to daily insult from the deluded populace," and Washington confessed in a June letter to General Howe that "the situation of Lieutenant Colonel Campbell, as represented by you, is such as I neither wished nor approve."

The standoff did not end until mid-August of 1777—nearly a year after Washington had led the retreat from New York. Congress at last let Washington propose a prisoner swap. Nine months later, the deal was done. Lee was freed, and Campbell, too.

But while Washington was relieved to have the Campbell affair behind him, Congress remained an obstacle when it came to the treatment of enemy prisoners. Washington believed it was his duty to negotiate for the prompt release of his men as the war progressed. He also thought that obligation required him to free the British soldiers that were held by the Americans. That was the only approach likely to make such deals possible. Congress, however, sought more favorable terms than the commander in chief was willing to demand of the British. As a result, Congress scotched proposed agreements for prisoner exchanges on a number of occasions. Each time, Washington accepted Congress's right to have the final say.

It was no different no matter the tactical issue at hand. Throughout the war, the first commander in chief remained committed to the principle that the Continental Congress was supreme—so much so that he orchestrated his final day in uniform to honor that principle one last time.

* * *

By December of 1783, with the war at last won, Congress—then operating under the Articles of Confederation—had fled Philadelphia once again. Revealing the perils of independence, the members of Congress had skipped town to avoid yet another advancing band of mutinous American soldiers, this time demanding pensions.

For its new quarters, Congress had selected the senate chamber of the Maryland statehouse. It sat atop a hill in the bayside town of Annapolis. Attendance at its sessions was typically poor, but it was strong on this day—Washington's last as commander in chief.

Washington arrived in Annapolis on the afternoon of December 19. The next day, he drafted a letter to the president of Congress. It set the tone the outgoing commander wished to establish. "I take the earliest opportunity to inform Congress of my arrival in this City, with the intention of asking leave to resign the Commission I have the honor of holding in their Service," the note explained. "It is essential for me to know their pleasure, and in what manner it will be most proper to offer my resignation, whether in writing or at an Audience; I shall therefore request to be honored with the necessary information, that being apprised of the sentiments of Congress I may regulate my Conduct accordingly."

Following a dinner with the president of Congress, Washington appeared, at Congress's request, in the senate chamber the next day at noon. It was by then two days before Christmas. Upon the general's entrance, the members present uncovered their heads. They did not bow. Washington alone offered that gesture of respect. Then, after a brief and somewhat halting address, he bid "an affectionate farewell to this August body under whose orders I have so long acted." His remarks complete, Washington reached into the breast pocket of his military uniform. He drew from it his original commission—a worn piece of paper, now eight years old. It had guided his conduct throughout the conflict. He returned the commission to Thomas Mifflin, the president of Congress at the time. With that, Washington turned to the audience, bowed once more, and left. He was, at last, "translated into a private Citizen."

He would not remain one for long.

2

THE FOUNDING

"It Squints Towards Monarchy."

More than a decade after Washington stepped down, the former general took his position, in full military dress and with a sword at his side, as the first among equals at the front of Philadelphia's Independence Hall. The delegates of the seven states that made a quorum for the first real session of the Constitutional Convention had, that very day, May 25, 1787, unanimously chosen Washington to be their presiding officer. The delegates—eventually totaling fifty-five—were determined to overhaul a failing system of government. But, they worried their differences might prevent success. On one critical issue, however, consensus came early. The example that Washington had set during the war for independence helped smooth the way.

* * *

Throughout the fight against the British, Washington had followed the directives of the Continental Congress—not in an unthinking way and not without doing what he could to carve out the discretion that he thought it prudent for him to retain. But he had followed those directives nonetheless. He had done so, moreover, even when he had strongly disagreed—a point that was not lost on anyone. And, of course, Washington had then stunned the world, upon the war's conclusion, by turning in his sword at the very height of his power.

With a man like that presiding, the delegates to the Constitutional Convention did not worry all that much that a proposal to vest executive power in a single man might be a secret attempt to foist on America an Oliver Cromwell—the dreaded British exemplar of unrestrained executive power. Largely for that reason, there was shockingly little debate over the Convention's decision to create a single executive. Not that there was no disagreement or discussion. But what debate there was ended quickly.

In truth, the proposals for a plural executive—or just an assembly to lead the country—never had a chance. During the burst of state constitution making that followed the Declaration of Independence, a number of states did refuse to vest executive power in a single man. Those states concluded that an executive council, because it fragmented power, was a necessary ingredient of republican government. Despite that precedent, the Convention was content, after some debate, to consolidate executive authority in a single officer. The delegates to the Convention figured the benefits of accountability and decisive action outweighed the risks of arbitrary power. It was a calculation seemingly affirmed by Washington's presence among the delegates to the Convention—a presence that reminded them how restrained an American leader could be, even in the midst of war.

For similar reasons, there was surprisingly little debate over the actual nature of the powers this new executive should have. The fear of monarchy was pervasive. There was no chance of actually naming a king—at least not a godlike figure, whose power came from his bloodline. But there was a desire for a national executive who could lead. The ideal seemed to be some unspecified—and perhaps unspecifiable—balance. The executive (however organized or named) would have the right to "negative" the bills Congress passed. But this important veto power would be qualified: Congress would be able to override the executive's rejection of its desired laws. Beyond that carefully calibrated compromise over the extent of the executive's prerogative, however, the delegates to the Convention seemed content to leave the full extent of the executive's power to go it alone largely undefined.

Washington's presence was crucial. The delegates to the Convention—like most anyone with political sense—assumed he would be the nation's first executive. They drew comfort from that fact. With his example in mind, a surprisingly large amount of ambiguity proved tolerable.

But a proposed charter of government this cryptic was still ripe for challenge, if only because the opponents could easily exploit the ambiguities. That was especially true for the Constitution's provisions regarding the chief executive. As the months passed following the Convention's close, the opportunity grew to win over people to the opposition's side by scaring them with tales of how newfound executive powers might be stretched and abused.

The opponents of the proposed charter were gathered in the state ratifying conventions that assembled that spring and summer. By that time, those opponents had a growing sense that they might be able to stop support for this document from taking root. Of course, such a rearguard action faced real obstacles. General Washington's unimpeachable character and demonstrated respect for the power of a representative assembly—even in war—were admirable. But the opponents were beginning to realize that those very same qualities underscored a disquieting truth: There might never be another leader like him. And so the opponents tried to convince the people to look past the great man. If only the public could be convinced to think about the kind of men who might succeed Washington, the opponents thought, the people might begin to grasp just how dangerous this new Constitution—given the war powers it conferred—really was.

* * *

The anti-Federalist plea to read the draft charter with an "anti-Washington" in mind was pressed with special force in General Washington's home state, Virginia, a critical actor in the ratification process. There, two of Washington's former colleagues, Patrick Henry and George Mason, headed up the opposition to the proposed Constitution.

They were very different men. One was hotheaded and eloquent, the other gentlemanly and cerebral. In combination, they were formidable opponents of a strong executive and of ratification more generally.

Mason was known to dress in black, as if to flaunt his urbanity. His stately home at Gunston Hall—about 100 miles from the site of the Virginia ratifying convention—reinforced his image of refinement. So, too, did his highly deliberate style of argumentation. He spoke as if he had no need to impress his audience because he assumed it would hold him in high esteem. Henry, by contrast, was ever poised for verbal battle and eager to win the crowd over to his side. Known affectionately as the "Son of Thunder," the red-haired Scotsman loved to excite the audience. He also liked to play up his humble roots. He even made a show of his modest origins at the end of the state ratifying convention, performing a preposterously elaborate bow to mock a critic with a more exalted lineage. It was the kind of theater in which Henry—and his adoring fans—delighted.

For all their differences, though, Henry and Mason were united in their opposition to what the men in Philadelphia had approved. Henry was so hostile to the ideas behind the Constitution that he declined even to attend the Convention that produced it. Mason, ten years Henry's senior, went to Philadelphia at the age of sixty-two to participate in what were supposed to be secret deliberations to overhaul the Articles of Confederation. But Mason, too, was deeply opposed to the document that emerged from those meetings. He returned to Virginia as one of only three delegates to the Constitutional Convention—a fellow Virginian, Edmund Randolph, was another—who had refused to sign. Like Patrick Henry, Mason thought the final draft of the Constitution threatened liberty, both of the people and of the states.

Beyond these general objections to the tenor of the document, the two men also had more discrete concerns. High on that list—perhaps even highest—was the fact that the new constitution named the elected executive the "commander in chief."

* * *

That designation, "commander in chief," appeared in Article II of the draft constitution, the part of the document that laid out the powers of the executive. The article as a whole provided that the executive would be elected through a process designed to keep legislative influence to a minimum. That part of the document also ensured the chief executive would possess a range of important powers, including "the executive power" itself and the authority to veto bills before they became law, subject, importantly, to a supermajoritarian override by the legislature. But then, looking in the other direction, the same article seemed to pull back. It assigned the new executive the modest title "president" (rather than a more active one, like, say, "governor"). It limited his term to four years. It provided for his removal through impeachment by the House and conviction after trial in the Senate. And, finally, it required the president to ensure the faithful execution of the laws passed by Congress.

Reflecting the prevailing sensitivities about executive authority, the words of Article II were strikingly few when it came to the executive's most fearsome power: the power over war. In fact, of the more than four thousand words in the proposed charter, only thirty-five directly addressed the executive's role in war. The first thirteen formally gave the president the title of "commander in chief of the army and navy." The remaining twenty-two stated he would also serve as the commander in chief of the state militia when called into federal service. And that was it. The rest of the text said precisely nothing about what the commander in chief could or could not do.

* * *

If the face of the draft document offered little clue as to just what kind of wartime leader the delegates to the Constitutional Convention had in mind, the records of their deliberations were not much more help. The delegates clearly wanted to guarantee civilian control over the military. They ensured that result by making an elected president the nation's top military officer. But, beyond that, the records offered little insight into just what kind of military leadership they favored.

The actual phrase "commander in chief," for example, did not appear in any of the initial plans presented at the Convention. In fact, other than one early reference to the title by Charles Pinckney, a delegate from South Carolina, the phrase was apparently not heard, uttered, or seen by anyone at the Convention until early August.

The Committee on Detail did include the phrase in a near final draft of the Constitution on August 5. But the committee appears to have done so only for reasons of style. Since those words survived—with only minor fiddling—all the way to the final draft, the delegates' own understanding of what they meant is very difficult to recover.

The Convention debates do show that the delegates feared an executive with too much power over war. In making the president the commander in chief, they were not seeking to create an American king—at least not one who could on his own decide between war and peace. They seemed to think the Constitution would make war harder to carry out than was the case in England. True, they acknowledged the commander in chief would need the power to repel a sudden attack. But, otherwise, they leaned hard in Congress's favor when it came to making the crucial decision between war and peace.

The draft expressly provided that Congress could declare war, and the debates indicate the power was not thought to be a shared one. The delegates even granted Congress the power to issue letters of marque and reprisal, and these special documents authorizing the use of armed force allowed only a very limited use of military power. The idea that the president alone possessed the power to declare a more general war, therefore, seemed well outside the contemplated constitutional plan. In a similar spirit, the delegates ensured that Congress would raise the armed forces for the president and that Congress would set the rules and regulations to govern those forces. Finally, the draft charter ensured that Congress controlled the purse, and thus the legislature would have to open the till for an army or navy to exist at all.

* * *

Most of these provisions concerned the issue of who could initiate hostilities. As to what the delegates thought the commander in chief could do once war actually commenced, the evidence was murkier. The Articles of Confederation had expressly given the Continental Congress power to set rules and regulations to govern the armed forces *and* to "[direct] their operations." The final draft of the Constitution, by contrast, did not give that same power to "direct . . . operations" to the Congress that *it* created. Was that silence important? Did it show that the framers wished to reserve the power to control ongoing operations to the president alone and thus to deny the new Congress the right to limit him in the conduct of war?

Perhaps. But that was a lot to read into silence. After all, there were a number of plans presented in Philadelphia that expressly gave the executive the power to direct the conduct of war. Yet the final draft of the Constitution was completely silent on the point. And when a delegate from Maryland proposed to clarify the issue, the Convention rejected his amendment handily, preferring a final draft that said precisely nothing on the subject.

Adding to the uncertainty, the meaning of the authority to "direct" was itself not clear. True, the Virginian James Madison, as close a confidant as there was to George Washington, thought, like other delegates, that the power to direct military operations was an "executive function." The delegates thus clearly wanted the commander in chief to oversee the armed forces, and there was little doubt that supervision was a part of the executive power the new president would enjoy as top military commander. One can imagine the delegates must also have thought the president could tell the troops to move this way or that. It would mean little to place him as the chief commander unless he could issue actual commands to those forces under his charge.

But the draft Constitution also expressly gave the legislature the power to enact laws, and it imposed upon the president the duty to execute them. Among the laws Congress had been empowered to enact, moreover, were those raising the armed forces for certain purposes rather than others and those setting forth rules of conduct for the troops in the field. Adding to the uncertainty, the notes of the actual Convention debates were all but silent about what should happen in case of a conflict between the directions the president wished to give and the rules that Congress chose to lay down.

* * *

Still, there was one undeniable fact—and that was that the delegates had chosen a particular title to bestow upon the president: commander in chief. That title did have a history—and one the delegates knew.

A century or so before, "commanders in chief" had served during the reign of King Charles I. They were expressly instructed to obey the orders of Parliament. None enjoyed a right to wage war on terms Parliament ruled out.

More directly, Washington himself never enjoyed—or asserted—such a right when serving as commander in chief during the Revolutionary War. In fact, his willingness to obey the Continental Congress—even when it came to tactics—helped make him such a revered figure. The use of the well-worn title "commander in chief," then, would have been a most indirect way for the delegates to signal their desire to depart from this history and to free the president from all checks when it came to the conduct of war.

✶ ✶ ✶

For Henry and Mason, this history was of little interest. Any effort to plumb the framers' intentions—whether based on a careful parsing of the ambiguities in the document itself or guesses about what the delegates to the Constitutional Convention must have meant in choosing such language—was a wasted one. The evidence of the delegates' thinking was maddeningly inconclusive, or, at least, quite obscure. Even more important, it was not clear why anyone voting on the proposed charter of government should much care what those intentions were.

Henry and Mason were practical men. To them, what mattered was that the delegates—no matter their true intentions—had created a new structure of government. They had proposed an elected president to be the commander in chief. They had offered little clear guidance as to what his powers would be. *That* was the reality of the situation. Every actual commander in chief would be exercising power within this open-ended and highly ambiguous legal framework. That would be true for centuries to come, regardless of what those in Philadelphia might have desired at the moment they affixed their signatures to the draft charter.

The question Mason and Henry found interesting, therefore, was not what the authors of the Constitution had meant. It was what future commanders in chief would do with the opportunity to assert the power that they had been given—assuming, that is, the people chose to ratify the Convention's handiwork.

In projecting how future presidents would use their powers, the two men's own experience weighed heavily. They were war veterans, and they knew the virtues of strong executive leadership. They also knew the difficulty of restraining it, especially in war. Mason had been a colonel in the state's militia. Henry had been the commander in chief of his state's forces. He had also been Virginia's governor. He had even been accused—by no less a figure than Thomas Jefferson—of plotting to become the state's dictator during one particularly desperate phase of the Revolutionary War.

In spinning out their ominous predictions about what the constitutionally created commanders in chief would do with the opportunities to lead that they were on the verge of being given, Henry and Mason were guided by their own assessment of where danger lay. They were not especially worried that executives to come would make war on foreign countries without Congress first declaring it. Perhaps Henry and Mason figured that future presidents would need an army or a navy and that neither would emerge without Congress's blessing. Perhaps Henry and Mason believed that America's fledgling status made the prospect of executive imperialism a remote concern. But, whatever the reason, Henry and Mason did not seem to focus on that particular fear about a future defined by executive war making the world over. Instead, consistent with their commitment to states' rights and their deep love of a certain conception of liberty (albeit not one capacious enough to challenge slavery), Henry and Mason focused on the dangerous ways that the executive might conduct war at home—even if Congress authorized the use of force in the first instance.

Henry and Mason especially wanted to articulate the concern that the president, as the constitutionally empowered commander in chief, would take personal command in the field to crush a homegrown rebellion and then refuse to stand down, even after peace had been restored. Henry and Mason also gave voice to the fear that the new president might commandeer state forces and order them to and fro, across state lines, even against Congress's wishes.

Conjuring up the image of the man on horseback, bending the public to his will, Henry and Mason wished to sound the alarm. Executive wartime dominance would come, they claimed, even if no framer wished it and even if Congress tried to prevent it. The president could not be counted on to restrain himself once war was underway. The danger that Henry and Mason described was all the more frightful because the war they had in mind was likely to be carried out on American soil against Americans themselves.

* * *

Henry pressed this point in his first full address to the Virginia ratifying convention. He held forth for hours in the packed hall above Richmond's Shockoe Hill. The audience was rapt as usual when he spoke—though never more so than when, nearing the end of his oration, he took aim at the proposal to create a president. "This Constitution is said to have beautiful features; but when I come to examine these features, sir, they appear to me horribly frightful," he cried. "Among other deformities, it has an awful squinting; it squints towards monarchy."

Henry asked the delegates to think about who would come after Washington. He implored them to imagine "your American chief be a man of ambition and abilities." The army would be in his hands, and, "if he be a man of address, it will be attached to him, and it will be the subject of long meditation with him to seize the first auspicious moment to accomplish his design." Even the rules that could restrain a king would have no effect on "the president, in the field, at the head of his army." He would be able—if he wished—"to prescribe the terms on which he shall reign master, so far that it will puzzle any American ever to get his neck from under the galling yoke." The president would know that "if ever he violates the laws," his choices would be to submit to the courts or to assert his military authority. And, knowing his own guilt, who could expect him to do other than pull rank? "Can he not, at the head of his army, beat down every opposition?" Henry asked. "Away with your president! We shall have a king: the army will salute him monarch: your militia will leave you, and assist in making him king, and fight against you: and what have you to oppose this force? What will then become of you and your rights? Will not absolute despotism ensue?"

Four days later, Henry returned to this theme. In addressing the ratifying convention, he acknowledged that the Continental Congress had established "an American dictator in the year 1781" when it briefly gave great powers to General Washington. But, in that one instance, Henry explained, "America found a person worthy of that trust." For while "we gave a dictatorial power to hands that used it gloriously; and which were rendered more glorious by surrendering it up," Henry asked, "where is there a breed of such dictators? Shall we find a set of American presidents of such a breed? Will the American president come and lay prostrate at the feet of Congress his laurels? I fear there are few men who can be trusted on that head."

* * *

Mason picked up this line of argument as the day of the final vote in Virginia approached. Using his typically understated tone, and reading from carefully prepared notes, he spoke slowly but clearly to the convention. He did not quarrel with the "propriety of [the president] being Commander in Chief, so far as to give orders, and have a general superintendency." His concern lay elsewhere. "It would be dangerous to let him command in person without any restraint, as he might make a bad use of it," he said. And yet the Constitution—at least as written—allowed it.

Mason spoke from experience. He knew the delegates in Philadelphia wanted to preserve that particular executive war power. One of the first plans to create an executive—the so-called New Jersey Plan—expressly denied the president's right to take personal command of forces in the field. But the final draft did not include that restriction on the war power of the president. In fact, the Constitutional Convention overwhelmingly rejected a proposal that would have required Congress's approval before the president could take personal command.

Mason concluded his remarks by echoing Henry's point about the need to look past Washington. He reminded his audience "of what the late commander in chief might have done, from his great abilities, and the strong attachment of both officers and soldiers towards him, if, instead of being disinterested, he had been an ambitious man." After all, "so disinterested and amiable a character as General Washington might never command again." True, the Constitution did not require the president to take personal command. But "he might if he pleased; and if he was an ambitious man, he might make a dangerous use of it." It was no answer, Mason therefore explained, to say Congress would have to authorize war. Once it did, it would surely lose control. "In time of war, they must and ought to raise an army, which will be numerous, or otherwise, according to the nature of the war," Mason said. But, at that point, the president would be perfectly positioned "to command without any control."

* * *

Back in New York, one of the proposed Constitution's strongest defenders, Alexander Hamilton, was worried about the impending vote on ratification for very different reasons. He was a confidant of Washington, and he did not share the anxieties about executive authority common to his age. Perhaps that was because he had been born abroad. Perhaps, too, his utter faith in Washington helped convince him the executive would be wise. Perhaps, beyond that, he was a royalist at heart. Hamilton also was shrewd. He knew the people feared an all-powerful executive, especially in war. He worried that their fear might prevail in the ratifying debates to come.

Soon after the Convention adjourned, Hamilton, then not even forty, reflected on what might happen if its opponents won and the Constitution was not ratified. "If it do not finally obtain," he foresaw a civil war, and with the "dismemberment of the Union . . . monarchies in different portions of it may be expected." At the very least, competing republican leagues would form. That turn of events could well lead to "a reunion with Great Britain, from universal disgust at a state of commotion." The Revolutionary War would then have been won only to result in "the establishment of a son of the present monarch in the supreme government of this country with a family compact." But if, Hamilton cheered himself, the Constitution should prevail, well, then obviously "Washington will be the president of the United States." His election "will insure a wise choice of men to administer the government and a good administration"—a conclusion he no doubt reached after imagining himself among the first appointees.

"It will be Eight or Nine months," Hamilton calculated soon after the proceedings in Philadelphia came to a close, "before any certain judgment can be formed respecting the adoption of the Plan." By the spring of 1788, those months had passed. The final judgment in Virginia—perhaps the most crucial state—was fast approaching. Hamilton began to hear reports of Henry's passionate arguments. Gouverneur Morris was Hamilton's source. Morris was a friend of the new charter, and a pro-executive man himself. Morris assured Hamilton things would turn out all right. But Morris conceded his upbeat assessment owed more to a faith in reason than a sophisticated political analysis. Hamilton's concerns were not assuaged.

* * *

Hamilton got his first real feel for the substance of the objections that opponents of the Constitution like Henry and Mason would lodge from an anonymous editorial that appeared in a Virginia newspaper some months earlier. Someone using the pseudonym Tamony had penned it, a New York paper had reprinted it, and Hamilton had then come across it. Anticipating Henry and Mason, Tamony focused on the fact that the proposed charter permitted the president to take personal command of troops in the field. Tamony railed that, in practical effect, the American commander in chief, in no small part due to his possession of that one crucial power, would be more dangerous than a British king.

If Hamilton were honest, he would have admitted there was some support for monarchy among the proposed Constitution's friends; Hamilton, after all, had once expressed such support. Through the early stages of the proceedings in Philadelphia, Hamilton had kept his counsel. But when he did rise to address his fellow delegates to the Constitutional Convention—a year to the day before Mason took the floor in Virginia—Hamilton spoke at length. For six hours, Hamilton prevailed on his colleagues at the Constitutional Convention to adopt a much bolder plan. He was especially provocative in discussing the executive. He proposed a single supreme executive authority. He explained that the new executive should be called a governor, serve for life (assuming good behavior) after an election, and enjoy among his powers "the entire Direction of War when authorized or begun."

In preparing that speech, Hamilton had considered publicly endorsing his true preference: a hereditary monarch, who would "have so much power, that it will not be his interest to risk much to acquire more." But Hamilton had the good sense to hold back. Still, he could not refrain from telling his audience that he believed "an Executive for life has not this motive for forgetting his fidelity, and will therefore be a safer depository of power."

Now that the Convention was over, though, Hamilton had no reason to reprise that speech. He knew how unpopular it was when he had given it. He had even left the Constitutional Convention soon after, thereby escaping some of the harsh reaction his remarks inspired. But his immediate goal was now ratification, not vindication of his private views. For that reason, Hamilton focused on the arguments of Tamony—and, by extension, those of Henry and Mason. Hamilton resolved to meet those arguments on their own terms.

* * *

Hamilton's response—his most complete public rejoinder—took the form of the sixty-ninth installment of an anonymous series of essays he was instrumental in producing. Hamilton had collaborated with two confederates, James Madison and John Jay, to write them. Known as *The Federalist Papers*, these essays attempted to counter each and every possible objection to the Constitution its opponents put forth. Hamilton began writing these deft arguments in support of the proposed Constitution while aboard his sloop, cruising back from a visit to Albany. Hamilton worked furiously to get each installment to print, even as he attempted to carry on his thriving law practice in New York. He continued working on the project even after the ratifying conventions began to convene. He took particular responsibility for defending the executive, and his essays on that topic circulated widely. Those essays made their way to Virginia before the final vote for ratification, though the influence of *Federalist 69* on the delegates then meeting in Richmond is far from clear.

Whether or not Hamilton's analysis was much read in Virginia, the essay reveals how Hamilton thought the debate was unfolding. Hamilton used *Federalist 69* to go point by point in addressing the objections to the kind of executive the Constitution contemplated—in particular, the claim that the new president would be more powerful than the British king. Hamilton knew how potentially devastating that line of critique could be, which made the need to address it so urgent.

Both the king and the president were named commanders in chief, Hamilton explained. The similarity stopped there. The president lacked the power to declare war or to raise an armed force. The king, by contrast, enjoyed both. The president did possess command of the militia. But the president could exercise that command only when Congress provided for the militia to be called up. Thus, here, too, the Constitution had put in place an important legislative check on the president's power to take the people to war on his own. Hamilton concluded that, on any fair accounting, the president's military authority would "be nominally the same with that of the King of Great Britain but in substance much inferior to it." In the end, Hamilton explained, the American executive "would amount to nothing more" than the "first general and admiral of the Confederacy."

Alongside this careful parsing of the text, another argument ran throughout his essay. The right point of comparison was not an English king, Hamilton suggested in these passages. The real comparison should be with those chief commanders the people already knew at home. In particular, Hamilton argued, the new federal Constitution was not so different—at least when it came to the powers of the executive—from the constitution that had recently been adopted in Massachusetts. There "may well be a question," Hamilton wrote, whether the constitution of that state "confer[red] larger powers" on its chief executive than the federal one did on the president.

Hamilton had grasped, by pressing this point, the true nature of the opposition's objection. The opponents were contending that the Constitution's meaning—especially with respect to the executive and war—would emerge through practice, and that there was every reason to think that, in time, the commander in chief's powers would enlarge to the point that he would be beyond control. Assurances about the framers' intentions were, therefore, all but irrelevant to the effort to meet the paranoia of the opponents.

Whatever the framers' intentions may have been, the future, the Constitution's opponents were saying, would be the final proof of how the Constitution worked. For that reason, the opposition could only be answered by offering persuasive predictions about what would happen down the road that differed from the dark ones that the opponents were pushing. Hamilton thus held up Massachusetts as a reason to be optimistic about what lay ahead. It was a real-world counter to the prophecies of impending doom coming from the opposition. If Massachusetts had managed to create a chief executive who could be kept in check, why could the country as a whole not do the same?

* * *

The Massachusetts example was well chosen. After a bruising battle, the war-power hawks in that state—a group of North Shore wise men known to their detractors as the Essex Junto—had gotten their way. They had turned back a draft of the proposed state constitution that they believed would have enfeebled the executive, especially in war. They had thus ensured that their new governor, as commander in chief of the state militia, would be free to act with, in the words of their influential pamphlet, *The Essex Result*, the "vigour, secrecy, and dispatch" that threats to the state's security might require.

Hamilton would eventually use that same language to defend executive power in an installment of his *Federalist* essays. But the men from Essex were not interested in beating back all legislative checks—and neither was Hamilton. The Junto wanted to ensure that their leader could act quickly in times of crisis. The men in that group acknowledged—in deference to those fearful of betraying republican principles—the legislature's power to recall the troops if the governor sent them across the border. The proposed state constitution, therefore, affirmed the chief commander's significant powers of initiative. That same proposed constitution also established the commander in chief's obligation to respect the laws the legislature ultimately passed to rein him in. The start of a war would not loose him from all controls. It would merely empower him to act until the legislature prescribed what he could do.

Massachusetts adopted the Junto-backed revision in full. It listed the various powers the commander in chief would enjoy—an impressive array that plainly gave the state's leader the power to direct the forces under his command. It also provided, however, that these powers must "be exercised agreeably . . . to the laws of the land." Massachusetts was not alone. State after state employed a similar framework. Even state constitutions that were less clear about what the chief commander could do on his own expressly provided that he could do nothing the legislature actually prohibited.

It was this framework of power that Hamilton was claiming the new Constitution would track. Hamilton knew his essay could not prove the alarmists wrong. Betrayal was always possible. Paranoia might be prescient. But Hamilton did think the Massachusetts example cast doubt on the opponents' confident predictions about what the future would inevitably bring. The Massachusetts precedent suggested an all-powerful tyrant did not necessarily loom just over the horizon. It was possible to imagine a different outcome. Perhaps a popularly elected military leader could be kept under legislative control even in the midst of battle. After all, a leading state had already acted on that assumption, and other states had done the same.

* * *

Virginia ultimately ratified the Constitution. So, too, did Hamilton's New York. By then it was clear the Constitution would become law. It was equally clear that Washington would become the first to exercise the powers of the new executive office. Everyone hoped he would not also be the last. That hope underscored the point that Henry and Mason had been making all along: There would be commanders in chief *after* Washington. They and they alone would determine the worth of the assurances that Hamilton had given about Congress's power to control the commander in chief in waging war.

3

QUASI WAR

"So far and no farther he feels himself confident of his authority."

On a bright day in early March of 1797, with the air crisp and clean, the nation's political leaders gathered in Philadelphia for yet another unprecedented occasion. For the first time in nearly two decades, George Washington was not the main attraction. On this day, he was a mere witness to the main event: the inauguration of his successor.

Dressed in black velvet, the outgoing president took his place once again "as a private citizen." His seat was set to the side of the dais. In recognition of his stature, his chair had been placed just in front of the senators arranged behind him. The spectators in the gallery looked out upon a table, "round which" sat the six members of the Supreme Court. The justices faced three chairs that looked back on the overflow crowd. The man who had just been sworn in as vice president, Thomas Jefferson, occupied one of them. The secretary of the Senate held the second. The newly elected president, John Adams, took the third.

The inaugural ceremony was held in Congress Hall. It stood only a short walk from the modest structure where, a decade earlier, Washington had presided over the Constitutional Convention. Even though this transfer of power was a vindication of the work of that earlier meeting, there was little joy among those assembled—a great throng of "both sexes," the official report said. It was painful to contemplate life after George

Washington. There was an ovation when he entered the chamber. There were tears when he left. Revolutionary optimism was giving way to partisan rancor. Few thought John Adams was an inspiring substitute for the only president America had known—perhaps not even Adams himself.

Irascible, vain, easily slighted, solicitous of fame, without military experience, squat bordering on portly, Adams had been Washington's vice president and a true hero of the Revolution. But John Adams enjoyed none of his predecessor's support or respect, not even among his fellow Federalists. His own vice president, Thomas Jefferson, was the sworn leader of the opposition. His cabinet was comprised of men who owed him nothing. For all the obvious impediments to Adams's success, the fact remained that—upon taking the oath—Adams would become president. That meant he would assume the title of commander in chief. He would do so at a time as perilous for America as any since the Revolutionary War.

* * *

The source of the trouble was France. Support for declaring war against France was mounting. The most hawkish members of Adams's party, the Federalists, were enraged by stepped-up acts of French aggression. They were also ashamed by America's willingness to tolerate them. Support for the putative enemy, meanwhile, was hardening among the Republican opposition. That party was deeply suspicious of the pro-English—and supposedly protomonarchical—inclinations of the Federalists running the executive branch. Arguments for challenging the French more directly, therefore, were often understood to be part of a Federalist effort to bring America ever closer to England. Events seemed to be conspiring, then, to put the president and the Congress—given Republican (and thus pro-French) strength in the House and Federalist control of the executive—on course for an unprecedented collision over war.

It was not clear how Adams would respond to the situation. He was independent-minded and smart. He was also a loner. His plans seemed to emerge without warning. Even his friends thought him impulsive. Benjamin Franklin said he was "out of his senses." As the crisis entered its most dangerous phase, the new president was remembered for stalking about the room where his cabinet met. He berated the various department heads with obscenities, pounding his boot heels hard into the wooden floor for emphasis. The devious machinations of men supposedly charged with giving him good counsel provoked his rage. There were plenty of members of Congress who could testify to similar treatment.

Nor were the times conducive to sober reflection. The French were not letting up, and Adams was politically weak. He had won the presidency by a mere three-vote margin in the Electoral College. He could not afford to antagonize his pro-war base. He was wise to the ways of diplomacy: He had spent time with the great Benjamin Franklin while serving as an envoy to Paris. But Adams had a fondness for Britain, and no love for postrevolutionary France. Nor was he, by instinct, suspicious of executive power in the way that a man like Thomas Jefferson professed to be. Adams was even accused of supporting a hereditary monarch.

In sum, Adams was no Washington. He was not steady, prudent, wise, or committed to asserting power by disclaiming it. Adams was nearly the opposite: untested and mercurial. Nor was he above whipping up war fever. At the height of the crisis with France, Adams strode about the capital city in military costume. He sported the black cockade, by then a symbol of American resistance to France. He spent an inordinate amount of time extolling the virtues of war in his replies to the hundreds of young men who sent him letters praising his resolve. As the crisis wore on, Adams even cast doubt on the loyalty of his partisan foes. He certainly did nothing to prevent Congress from criminalizing the opposition. He went so far as to sign (though with ultimate regret) a notorious sedition law, which to this day stands as a reminder of what oppression at home during a war might look like.

There was reason to worry, then, that Mason's and Henry's dark prediction about the presidency and war might soon be proven true. Perhaps a runaway commander in chief was about to follow Washington. And yet, over the next three years, Adams did not make prophets of the two Virginian anti-Federalists. When it came to the conduct of war, the final word, Adams insisted, must remain with Congress, and he did not back away from that position during the whole of his administration. In consequence; Adams accepted a stunning degree of congressional control over his conduct of what came to be known as the "Quasi War" with France. But, by doing so, he gave himself time to find a path to peace. It was a path, it turned out, marked by a most unlikely guide: Alexander Hamilton, the man, to this day, we still think of as the most effective advocate of aggressive executive power among the founders.

* * *

Adams offered his first official comments on the growing crisis with France right after taking the oath. Those comments dominated his inaugural address and went over remarkably well. He spoke in a strong, even rousing manner. His words projected a blend of toughness and patience worthy of his predecessor. Events, however, soon forced him to strike a more aggressive—and thus more controversial—tone. French attacks on American merchant ships—eventually totaling more than three hundred, according to one report that June—continued without relent. Then came some shocking news from Paris: The French Directory had shabbily dispatched the special envoy President Washington had sent to negotiate a peaceful resolution. Adams now had no choice but to recall Congress from its customary postinaugural recess.

The special legislative session, set to begin in mid-May, would open with another presidential address. Adams consulted widely in preparation. Through that process, Alexander Hamilton became Adams's counselor, if only indirectly. Now out of office, Hamilton, who had been Washington's storied treasury secretary, was no conventional Federalist. The author of *Federalist 69* turned out to have a very different view of the crisis than many of his more hawkish fellow partisans. Where they inclined toward war, he did not. Where they emphasized the need for executive vigor, he played up the advantage of garnering congressional support.

There were ironies in Hamilton assuming an advisory role for Adams. The men barely spoke. Hamilton had tried to deny Adams the chance to succeed Washington as president. And Hamilton's devious efforts almost inadvertently threw the election to the Republicans—and thus Thomas

Jefferson ran a close second to Adams. That placement at the time made
him the president's Number Two. By the end of Adams's term, moreover,
Adams had come to think of Hamilton as a dangerous schemer, willing
to take the country to war in service of his personal ambition. Never, the
president said after one contentious meeting, had he heard a man talk
such foolishness about matters of such consequence as Hamilton.

Even more surprising than the fact of Hamilton's back-channel advisory role was the nature of the advice that Hamilton supplied. As much
as Hamilton struck a reassuring tone in *Federalist 69*, there was reason
to think he had not really meant what he had said in that ratification-era
essay about the limited nature of the powers of the commander in chief.
It was not to be assumed that, if Hamilton were whispering to Adams, he
would be counseling patience.

Hamilton had written his restrained account of the executive power in
Federalist 69, with an obvious strategic purpose: to mollify the Constitution's opponents. Read closely, the essay betrayed signs that Hamilton was
more hawkish than he was letting on. He had said, for example, that the
"direction of war"—though not the "entire direction," as he had put it in
his speech at the Constitutional Convention—belonged to the executive.
The comment hinted at a more absolutist view of executive power in war
than the essay's otherwise mild tone implied. Elsewhere in his essays on
executive power, moreover, he seemed to defend such authority at almost
every turn. His appeals to the need for "vigor" and "secrecy and dispatch"
poured forth with ease. And, if one looked back farther in Hamilton's career, the evidence of his hawkishness only seemed to get stronger. Hamilton even had flirted with the notion that America should have a king.

Hamilton also had revealed himself to be an executive partisan when
it had counted most. While serving in Washington's cabinet, Hamilton
had offered a vigorous (if anonymous) defense of the president's most
controversial assertion of independent executive authority. President
Washington's Neutrality Proclamation—issued in 1793, in the midst of
the war between France and England—technically claimed an inherent
executive authority to announce only that peace would be maintained. In
that way, it merely announced that the United States would not be taking

sides in that inter-European power struggle. But to opponents of the administration, like the estimable James Madison, it did not matter that the president was trying to keep America out of a war. A president who could choose to make peace on his own was a president who might also choose to make war by decree. By the end of Washington's administration, therefore, Hamilton stood accused of a serious offense. He was said to have laid the intellectual groundwork—through his aggressive defense of Washington's unilateral declaration of American neutrality—for a future president to make a joke of Hamilton's early assurances that the Constitution's executive possessed only limited powers of war.

But throughout April and early May of 1797, as the opening day for the special session drew near, the former treasury secretary did nothing to suggest he was the founding generation's truest champion of executive power. Hamilton was instead explaining to anyone who asked—and many did—why Congress should be allowed to shape the nation's military response to French aggression. Even more interestingly, Hamilton was doing what he could to ensure that the new president would let the legislature take the lead.

* * *

In pushing for this more restrained approach, Hamilton got access to Adams through the president's cabinet. Its key members were holdovers from Washington's final term, and they were close to Hamilton. As Adams prepared for his upcoming speech to Congress, he sent the cabinet a series of questions about what he should say in his address. The cabinet members then passed these questions on to Hamilton in hopes he would offer them helpful advice. Hamilton received the correspondence at his residence in New York, put aside the work of his law practice, and answered each letter, often at length. The cabinet members then parroted to Adams—sometimes verbatim—the lines Hamilton fed back to them. In this way, Hamilton, though no longer in government, ensured that, first the cabinet, and then the president, signed on to his plan.

The plan rested on a simple premise: The president should do nothing to provoke war on his own. Nor should Adams ask Congress to declare it—despite the general freedom to act that such a declaration could confer upon the president as commander in chief. Instead, Hamilton counseled, Adams should ask Congress for a variety of more limited and putatively defensive powers. He should do so even if there might be arguments that he could take some of those actions on his own. This prescription would give Congress—and thus the Republicans—an ongoing role in defining the terms of battle. This approach would also put off a clear choice about whether the nation should commit to all-out war.

Adams appeared before the specially called session of the Fifth Congress on May 16, 1797. In the run-up to that day, Adams—infuriated by French aggression and recalcitrance in the face of American peace offerings—considered requesting a declaration of war. But, in the end, Adams followed the unanimous cabinet recommendation Hamilton had helped to engineer. Adams would pursue a firm but measured course, one dependent on ongoing congressional involvement and support.

Central to the Adams plan was a new gambit for peace. Just as Hamilton had prescribed, Adams proposed to send yet another peace delegation of American representatives to France. But Adams was careful to pair that conciliatory gesture with a request for new legislation—again, as Hamilton had suggested. The president wanted to fortify the nation's defenses. Adams thus asked for congressional support for a slew of relatively muscular measures: from raising a multi-thousand-man "provisional" army (a carefully chosen modifier meant to address concerns about creating a standing army) to reinforcing coastal fortifications. He also explained that he wanted to enhance the nation's armed presence at sea. Each suggestion closely tracked a proposal Hamilton had identified in his own back-channel correspondence with the cabinet.

* * *

Adams assumed Congress would agree to his requests. They were, even in combination, tamer than a sweeping demand for a declaration of war. They also were more respectful of legislative power than a high-handed announcement of plans that he would undertake on his own. But the president—and thus Hamilton—had miscalculated. Congress was not the least bit charmed. The Republicans heard a "war whoop" in Adams's speech, despite his efforts to appear restrained. If heeded, the Republican congressional members feared, Adams's plan would give the president effective control over the choice between war and peace. And so, the plain building on Market Street that then housed Congress, though bearing no resemblance to the gleaming marble Capitol of today, became a site of high drama. The nation's first debate over the power to control the conduct of war was underway.

The key flashpoint—the one that dominated discussion until the session closed in July—concerned the president's request for new powers to defend the high seas. Knowing a true navy could not be "formed so speedily and extensively as the present crisis demands," Adams wanted something to fill the gap. He asked for permission to permit the arming of private vessels. That would require Congress to remove statutory strictures then in place.

Even as Adams spoke, his treasury secretary, Oliver Wolcott Jr., was adhering to a circular that had been issued by that department months before. It relied on an expansive interpretation of the neutrality law that Congress had enacted several years earlier. The circular concluded that, in that neutrality law, Congress had barred armed private merchant ships from leaving American ports for waters where French ships were likely to encounter them. It was thought such cruises could too easily touch off war by inadvertently encountering French opposition; hence the congressional prohibition and the narrow executive interpretation of its scope. Wolcott's guidance reflected the Adams administration's basic, Hamilton-inspired posture. The administration would press Congress for clear grants of warlike authority. The administration would not claim such powers unilaterally or risk skirting legislative limits then in place.

Adams also requested authority from Congress on another front. He wanted to build new national warships, and he wanted to use them more aggressively. He thought that they should be available as more than coastal defenses. They should be authorized to serve as convoys on the high seas. With those vessels, Adams explained, the fledgling American navy—long a Federalist ambition—would materialize. Those ships would in turn protect "such merchant vessels as shall remain unarmed."

By appealing to the legislature for executive powers, Adams was conspicuously not asserting the right to act on his own. But the requests were not heard that way on Market Street. Instead, the requests exposed an important constitutional fault line. Adams was asking for powers that, once given, might afford him enormous discretion—discretion the Congress had long feared the executive might somehow acquire.

* * *

From the moment Washington took office, Congress had been intent on guarding its right to declare war. Congress kept control not by legislating direct restrictions. Congress simply refused to create much of a military establishment for the executive to command. In fact, Washington left office overseeing only two light dragoon companies and four infantry regiments. The last warship, meanwhile, had been sold just before his final term ended.

This military structure—or, rather, this lack of one—ensured that Congress retained *de facto* control over the commander in chief. With no standing forces to command, the president had no choice but to seek permission to conduct any particular military operation, big or small, that he might favor. When Washington turned to the militia—as he did during his presidency, once even taking command of the troops in the field in putting down a sudden popular uprising—he was checked yet again. Often the laws authorizing him to call up the militia specified the places where they could be deployed. And when those laws did not do that, they at least set strict time limits on how long the militia could remain in service.

Adams was now putting at risk that *de facto* system of legislative control over the president's war making. True, the president and his supporters were going to Congress to start. But, in pressing for new powers, especially at sea, the administration seemed to be asking Congress to dispense with the traditional arrangement. With no standing forces, the president had no real choice but to ask for what he needed conflict by conflict. If Adams got the large-scale military establishment he was now requesting, with no clear direction on how he would be required to use it, the presidency would be a very different institution. The choice between war and peace would suddenly be in Adams's hands—in practice if not in law.

The president and his men thought they had sound reasons for making these requests and thus breaking with the normal way of doing things. They believed the old framework had already needlessly exposed the nation to constant French predations. They argued the president simply had to be given the forces up front that would permit him to protect American commerce from harassment. He also needed enough men and matériel to guard the mainland from a possible invasion or French-led insurrection. That meant he needed substantial forces in advance of an actual war, and in sufficient numbers to make an American show of resistance credible to the Directory in Paris. It did not mean Congress had no role. It was being asked to approve each request. It did mean Congress would have to give the president the tools to wage war even though war had not been declared. Deterrence required such faith in presidential judgment.

The Republicans in Congress saw things very differently. They believed that Adams was rewriting the terms of the informal constitutional deal that had been in place since Washington took office. If Congress acceded to this request for men and matériel without restrictions, only Adams's self-restraint—and not a lack of forces—would stand between war and peace. The fear, in short, was, as Hamilton once put it, that President Adams might be looking to create an "antecedent state of things"—a state of war, really—that Congress would be powerless to change.

It was a reasonable concern. In the present crisis, the power to send armed ships, private or public, into dangerous, French-infested waters was no small thing. If Adams had the power to order his captains to go out in convoys, what would stop Adams from devising missions that might goad France into responses that could touch off a full-scale war? And if France did react violently, what significance would there be in Congress formally declaring a war that had already started—and that had started because of choices that the president had made unilaterally in sending out convoys on dangerous and provocative routes that he alone had selected?

The same could be said of Adams's proposal to arm merchant ships. That proposal was defensive in concept. One could not be sure it would prove defensive in practice. Suppose a private ship, untrained and captained by a hothead, shot first. Would Adams and his partisans claim the nation was at war if the French fired back? If so, would Congress be free to disagree once the shooting had started?

* * *

These were the questions being bandied about in Congress Hall. The Republicans vowed that President Adams would not leave the special legislative session empowered to answer them on his own.

The first skirmish took place in the House. Meeting in a ground-floor room "without ventilators, more than sufficiently heated by fire, to which is superadded the oppressive atmosphere contaminated by the breathing and perspiration of a crowded audience," the House Republicans wasted little time in challenging the president. They swiftly beat back Adams's proposal to create a "provisional army." They then turned to the naval measures. They had the least trouble scuttling the president's plan to arm the merchant ships. The case against entrusting American foreign policy to a private seaman's poor judgment was relatively easy to make. It was harder to block the proposal Adams had put forward regarding the use of new national warships. There was some sense in authorizing the president to man and equip a naval fleet that could be kept close to shore. Such "wooden walls," as Adams liked to call them, might keep the French at bay. But the effort to ensure the president could not use those ships as he pleased sparked a great debate.

The standoff reached its climax in early June. The Federalists were advancing a measure to expand the naval force at the executive's discretion. John Nicholas, a Republican from Virginia, sought to curb it. He wanted to ensure that the new grant of power could not become a license for Adams's convoys. He proposed language that would limit the bill's scope. Adams could commission the new ships only "if circumstances hereafter arise [that] shall make it necessary for the defense of our seacoast." Those words suggested the new vessels would have to keep close to shore.

Another Republican member of the House, Albert Gallatin, then offered an even stricter proposal, which became the favored Republican alternative. Gallatin, a brilliant Swiss immigrant and future treasury secretary, had replaced James Madison, Hamilton's ally in writing *The Federalist Papers*, as the leader of the Republicans in the lower body—that is, to the extent they were led at all. Large nosed, balding, precocious, saddled with a strong accent that marked him as a foreigner, Gallatin's aim was simple. He vowed not to let Congress "adopt a single hostile measure" on his watch. In keeping with that commitment, Gallatin took aim at Adams's request for the right to deploy convoys. Gallatin proposed that any national warships under Adams's control be stationed only "within the jurisdiction of the United States." That would effectively bar them from cruising the high seas, where the risk of an unplanned war was great.

Tempers flared. And then, just before the matter came to a vote, Harrison Gray Otis took the proceedings to a new level.

* * *

Otis was new to Congress but not unknown. The nephew of the famed patriot James Otis Jr., who had died of a lightning strike, Harrison had attended Harvard College. There, he graduated first in his class. He went on to become a protégé of the men who comprised the notoriously pro-executive Essex Junto, which had been so successful in refashioning the Massachusetts constitution. Under their tutelage, Otis established himself as the rightful heir to the House seat of the great Federalist Fisher Ames. From that post, Otis made a name for himself as Gallatin's foil. The Adamses looked upon Otis with special fondness. But, in this instance, Otis rose to make a point that went beyond merely supporting the president's policy. He pushed a vigorous defense of the president's constitutional right to protect the nation as he saw fit—and regardless of what Congress believed. It was a position the Republicans always suspected the Federalists held.

"If a naval force was raised, it would rest with the President how it should be employed, as he was commander-in-chief," Otis asserted. "The Legislature could say whether the vessels should be employed offensively or defensively, but to say the precise place whether they were to be stationed, was interfering with the duty of the Commander-in-Chief." Congress could not, Otis argued, tell the president he could use a navy to defend the seacoast but not in the West Indies or to run convoys. The president alone had the right to choose which strategy to implement.

Otis's constitutional analysis fell flat. The House passed Gallatin's restrictive measure over Otis's objection. The focus of debate then shifted to a related bill coming out of the Senate. It proposed to give the president control of a complement of frigates already under construction. The prospect of these frigates soon hitting water made even more immediate the conflict over the convoys that Adams was asking Congress to let him deploy.

* * *

Other than a group of revenue cutters, the frigates were the only public vessels near completion. They were true warships. Their origins could be traced to a 1794 statute. Congress had passed that measure when the English and the Algerians—rather than the French—were the nation's enemies. Algiers had been using piracy to make a good income off of bribes paid by Americans. But, in keeping with the traditional arrangements regarding standing forces, the Republicans had inserted language that required construction work on the ships to stop as soon as the nation made peace with Algiers. And stop that work did when peace with Algiers finally came in 1795. Despite that restriction, President Washington was not willing to accept the outcome. He urged Congress not to let the nation's largest procurement program go to waste. Congress eventually agreed with Washington. It passed a law that let work continue on the three frigates—the *United States*, the *Constitution*, and the *Constellation*—whose hulls had already been built. The other three ships were consigned to the scrap yard.

The puny fleet that remained was hardly the stuff of which imperial presidencies are made. Hamilton had derisively referred to the frigates as "our little naval preparation." Now, a decade on, the Federalists—faced with a new foreign threat, from France—were seeking to make the most of Washington's modest victory in that earlier legislative tussle over the frigates. They were pushing to use the frigates as convoys.

Gallatin led the opposition once again. "In ordinary times," Gallatin explained, there was no need for Congress "from day to day to say how [the boats] should be employed." But now foreign hostilities were imminent. Congress was thus perfectly justified—even obliged—to direct how they should be deployed. Otherwise, Gallatin concluded, Congress would be forfeiting its right to declare war. The House Republicans backed up the argument with a proposed amendment allowing the president to use the frigates only to protect the seacoast.

The Federalists fought back hard. One Federalist member of the House even echoed Otis's constitutional speech from earlier in the debate. This member, too, claimed such a specific restriction as Congress was now considering would unconstitutionally take away the powers of the commander in chief. This renewed defense of executive absolutism fared no better than Otis's. The House adopted Gallatin's amendment: The frigates would have to hug the coasts.

The Federalists in the Senate hardened their position in response. They promised not to give in even if their obstructionism meant that the bill for funding the frigates died altogether. The nation would lose vital coastal defenses. The Federalists contended that blame for that dangerous outcome should fall on the intransigent Republicans and their unwarranted attempts to instruct the commander in chief about how to command his forces. The impasse broke only when a House member pointed out that the frigates were not as close to being ready as many had thought. Gambling that peace with France would come before Adams's frigates were built, the Republicans at last decided to back down.

* * *

The Federalist victory proved hollow. Overall, the special session had been a Republican rout. Adams's party was disconsolate, its most hawkish contingent furious. Gallatin, by contrast, was thrilled. The president had been denied his provisional army. He had been given no authority to arm the merchant ships. Congress had let him command some cutters and some frigates. But, practically speaking, the president had been given little room to employ the ships in ways that might provoke war. The same measure that funded the frigates, for example, restricted the president's use of revenue cutters to defensive purposes near the coasts. The cutters were the only vessels available for convoy duty in the near term. As if to prove a point, even the statute funding the frigates had been weighed down with an almost comically detailed set of requirements. They specified, among other things, that on Thursdays the ships' crews would receive peas. That niggling restriction made the point: This conflict would be waged on Congress's terms.

As the Federalists regrouped, Adams seemed content to pursue a more patient course. He immediately returned home to Quincy. He waited to hear from the men he had sent to Paris to negotiate a peace. A stasis set in over the whole crisis. When Congress reconvened in the fall, it did little more than argue. Its members figured that news from the envoys that Adams had recently sent to France would ultimately determine how things would unfold. As the months passed, however, Adams grew increasingly anxious that the word from abroad would be discouraging. And so, in January, he reached out to his cabinet again.

Should Adams now ask Congress to declare war? Sentiment was shifting in that direction. By early spring, even Adams's wife would favor doing so. Hamilton again went to work behind the scenes, looking for some way to prevent war from coming. He was not happy with how things had gone in the Fifth Congress, but he still advocated restraint. Go slow. Do little unilaterally. "Make a solemn and manly communication to Congress," as he put it in one letter, but under no circumstances should Adams seek a declaration of war. "It [was]," as Hamilton explained to the secretary of war, James McHenry, in response to one of McHenry's many desperate pleas for guidance, "an undoubted fact that there is a very general and strong aversion to War in the minds of the people of this country—and a considerable part of the community . . . is still peculiarly averse to a war with that Republic."

By spring, it was clear the peace mission had gone terribly. The Republicans requested that secret executive papers describing the failed diplomatic venture be shared during a closed session of Congress. The Republicans bet the disclosure would show that Adams and his administration had never really sought peace and that they had been lying about France's true posture. Once the papers leaked, though, everything changed. The papers revealed France's humiliating treatment of the American delegation. In place of negotiations, the American emissaries had been practically extorted. Republicans were suddenly on the defensive. The bombshell known as the XYZ Affair—so called for the three unnamed French intermediaries with whom the American envoys had met—severely undermined the Republican effort to check Adams. The affair suggested that the Republicans had been far too solicitous of the French and that they had been unrealistic about how intent France was on working its will against the young American nation. The XYZ Affair thus lent newfound credibility to the war hawks among the Federalist Party. France could not be trusted. Peace was but a dream.

But Congress still refused to let Adams take full command. Only now, rather than denying Adams the power that he sought to make war, Congress was the one pushing for war—faster, even, than Adams might wish.

* * *

By the end of the summer of 1798, Congress was busily enacting a repressive framework at home. It took the form most prominently of the Alien and Sedition Acts. These sweeping measures, despite the First Amendment's guarantee of free speech, made criticism of the government a crime and thus aimed to shut down pro-French sentiment in the press. Congress also gave Adams an even larger provisional army than he had sought. It was not long before the Federalists were passing legislation that came close to ordering the commander in chief to retaliate for French mistreatment of American sailors. Congress even went so far as to empower Adams to visit equivalent acts of cruelty upon Frenchmen found on American streets. Gallatin was horrified by what the legislature was doing with its power. His only solace was that Congress had left Adams some discretion as to how to use his power to retaliate. Gallatin was confident the president would use it more humanely than some in Congress hoped. The overpowering wartime executive the anti-Federalists most feared seemed to be coming into view. Ironically, he was emerging not from the executive's imperious actions but from Congress's own directives.

Still, it was at sea where the risk of the president getting ahead of Congress had always been most acute—and thus it was at sea where the risk of the president starting war on his own was greatest. Interestingly, even this new more aggressive Congress was unwilling to confer new grants of authority in that regard without limit. An act establishing a permanent navy passed by the end of April, albeit by the slimmest of margins. The new law was silent on Adams's power to set the rules of engagement. There followed, therefore, a remarkable private exchange between Hamilton and James McHenry, the ever-hapless secretary of war, over just what powers had been given to the executive.

McHenry was a soldier, not a sailor. He also had little talent for administration. But a war in fact if not in law was at hand. He knew that much. With a navy now under his control, McHenry needed to advise the president as to the instructions he should give to those who were in charge of the newly commissioned American warships. As much as McHenry could spot the problem, though, he was clueless about how to solve it. And so McHenry followed his by now standard procedure: He begged Hamilton to tell him what to say.

* * *

Hamilton's calm reply set forth a view of wartime relations between Congress and the executive far different from the one that so many now ascribe to him. Rather than counseling Adams to go it alone, Hamilton explained that the president had been given no new legislative powers of significance, even though he had received new forces to command and some greater leeway to deploy them as he wished. For that reason, Hamilton concluded, Adams should do little on his own. "In so delicate a case, in one which involves so important a consequence as that of War—my opinion is that no doubtful authority ought to be exercised by the President," Hamilton told McHenry. With "no special power . . . given by the" new statute, "it will be expedient for him, and his duty, and the true policy of the Conjuncture, to come forward by a Message to the two houses of Congress declaring that 'so far and no farther' he feels himself confident of his authority to go in the employment of the naval force," but he intends to go no further, "having no desire to exceed his constitutional limits." Hamilton added that such an approach would "remove all clouds" as to what the president's true intentions were, and that by refusing to "chicane the Constitution" he would generate the support for additional legislation that he desired.

McHenry promptly wrote to President Adams. McHenry communicated by his own hand nearly all that Hamilton had written to him—for the most part verbatim. Adams approved of McHenry's battle plan, unknowingly endorsing Hamilton's restrained counsel once again. The strategy would guide the administration's approach to the whole range of authorities that Congress conferred over the ensuing weeks and months.

"Although Congress have authorized the arming, equipping and employing a Number of Ships, an evident object of which is the Protection of the Commerce of the United States," McHenry explained, for example, to Captain Richard Dale in late May, "yet as Congress possess exclusively the Power to declare War, grant letters of Marque & Reprisal, and make Rules concerning Captures on Land and Water, and as neither has yet been done, your Operations must accordingly be partial & limited." Congress went on to pass more than twenty statutes setting the rules of engagement. Among them were new authorities not only to acquire ships but also to use them in the ways that Adams had long sought. Also included were measures that permitted the arming of merchant ships and granting Adams the power to have them capture and bring back to port French armed vessels "hovering" off the coast with hostile intent.

But important—and irritating—statutory limits remained. Adams still had not received a broad grant of power to use the merchant ships or the frigates or any other vessels to capture French ships as a general matter. Congress instead parceled out the authority to engage at sea one spoonful at a time. Each new measure added modestly to the last. Together, the new laws created an intricate legal framework of power but also constraint. Congress wanted to check French aggression. It also wanted to show respect for neutrals. And Congress was conflicted over whether it truly wanted all-out war.

* * *

Adams and his men did their best to navigate the legal maze. The new laws were sometimes literally copied the day they passed for transmission to the captains at sea. The great John Barry, for example, had barely left port aboard the frigate *United States*, in July of 1798, when a pilot tracked him down to relay a new message: "keep on & off the Capes of Delaware . . . 'til further orders . . . [as] late Acts of Congress make a variation in your instructions necessary." The directives to the merchant captains were especially emphatic. They warned them not to do more than they had been allowed by special legislative grants, lest they inadvertently cause the war Adams had yet to ask Congress to declare.

As the crisis wore on, Adams installed Benjamin Stoddert as his new, and first, secretary of the navy. Stoddert was a far more confident administrator than James McHenry. Stoddert also sometimes acted in anticipation of Congress. He advised one captain to go ahead and round up "boys" for his ship, despite the fact that Congress had not yet completed debate on the bill that would authorize him to do so. (The law giving such power passed the next day, just as Stoddert figured it would.) Later, Stoddert offered a cheeky interpretation of what constituted an "armed" French ship—thus expanding the scope of his officers' authority to engage the "enemy."

But even Stoddert—eager to make his mark—accepted the pro-Congress approach that Hamilton had promoted. In late June, with the sentiment in Congress shifting in favor of aggression, Captain Stephen Decatur—a future American naval hero—learned that a sloop controlled by mutinous "Negroes" from the Indies was hovering off the coast near Fort Mifflin. Decatur feared the ship might be trying to foment a slave uprising. The fear of such an uprising had loomed in the minds of the Federalists since the outset of the crisis. But Decatur did not know what authority he had to address such a threat. And so he called on Stoddert.

The navy secretary immediately sent Decatur a letter. It thanked him for his "Propriety and Prudence" in doing nothing precipitous. It then instructed Decatur to monitor the vessel and the men on board until "Congress determine[s] what is to be done with them." Stoddert soon followed up: Decatur should prevent the crew from landing. He should take no other measures. "Congress have the subject of these people before them," Stoddert explained, and Congress had not yet "determine[d] what shall be done with them."

Such episodes showed, as one commentator put it at the time, that "no position is more dangerous to a nation, than the awkward one between peace and war." In such circumstances, "the citizens are . . . puzzled to know what their duty is." American captains at sea certainly rued the ambiguity that Congress's half-measures created. Commodore Thomas Truxtun, in charge of the frigate *Constellation*, was especially critical. He thought the limits on his power to capture French vessels were inconsistent with the "honor of a great nation." He said he would be glad if France simply declared war so Congress could do the same in response. He did not like doing anything "by Halves."

Congress's tight control ensured that questions about the lawfulness of the Adams administration's conduct of this strange war would, in time, make their way to the Supreme Court. They did, in a series of lawsuits that challenged the legality of various seizures at sea. Adams did not seem to mind that he was presiding over a war thick with legal limits. The approach that Congress had decided upon was one that he had all but asked Congress to adopt. That approach allowed Adams to meet force with force without entering into a full-fledged war. To be sure, Adams did think about pursuing a very different course. Eventually, he openly wondered to his secretary of state, John Marshall, whether it was time to dispense with all the "restrictions and limitations" on war fighting that he had tolerated for so long. Perhaps Adams should finally press Congress for "an immediate and general declaration of war against the French Republic." But Adams never gave in to the impulse. He accepted the checks. As the crisis dragged on, and without alerting anyone to his plan—and with Hamilton himself shifting toward a far less prudent posture that

Adams thought "mad"—the president even decided to gamble for peace. Adams announced in the winter of 1799—seemingly out of the blue—that he would be sending yet another negotiator, a lone one of his own choosing, to Paris.

* * *

Hamilton was by then second in command of the army and effectively the head of the forces that Congress had made specially available for the crisis—a force that was known at the time as the Additional Army. Hamilton took full advantage of the platform that his new military post gave him. He strongly opposed Adams's new peace venture. But it was too late. Adams had gotten ahead of everyone.

With his sudden shift toward peace, Adams was now ready to clean house. He relieved Hamilton of his command. He then disbanded the recently created Additional Army. Before long, Adams also dismissed Marshall's predecessor and McHenry. He was purging the high Federalists from his administration. He craved peace, perhaps because he also craved reelection. The Republicans, led by Vice President Thomas Jefferson, were capitalizing on the disaffection of a war-weary public. And so Adams was also looking for ways to disprove the growing cries—fueled by Jefferson's camp—that the president had become the leader of a monarchical party.

Before Adams's term ended, the new round of peace talks with the enemy bore fruit. But the resulting deal, though it put an end to the crisis, came too late to do Adams much political good. Jefferson beat Adams in the election of 1800, and Adams left office embittered. He did not even attend Jefferson's inauguration. But Adams left a legacy that would appear more impressive with time. Despite the warmongering positions that had been attributed to him in the presidential campaign, Adams had actually deftly kept America out of a ruinous war. By doing so, Adams had shown that a commander in chief would follow legislative limits in conducting a war—even, that is, if his last name was not Washington.

4

THE GOOD OFFICER

"A strict observance of the written laws is doubtless one of the high duties of a good citizen, but it is not the highest."

E arly in his tenure as vice president, Thomas Jefferson broke with the Adams administration over the war and sided with the Republican opposition. But while that decision left Jefferson isolated from President Adams, he eventually used his opposition to the war to ride to the presidency. He managed to do so in large part because the nation had grown tired of that war. There was also a strong sentiment that Adams had grown too powerful during the years of fighting with France. Jefferson's fervent supporters expected that he would not only bring an era of badly desired peace. They also believed that he would restore the constitutional balance that Adams—and the Congress that aided him—supposedly had caused to tilt too far toward monarchy.

But electoral success meant that power was now in Jefferson's hands. His avowed commitment to strict construction, executive restraint, and the Republican program would no longer be a cudgel to attack a sitting president. His commitment, if honored, would be a governmental practice for which he would be responsible as president in his own right. As his antimonarchical theories confronted the realities of governance, Jefferson was unwilling to follow those theories to the letter.

Most famously, Jefferson abandoned the theory of strict construction of the Constitution in 1803 when he was offered the chance to purchase the territory of Louisiana and beyond. At first, Jefferson—almost alone among those working at the highest levels of government—thought the purchase illegal. The Constitution did not expressly authorize adding new territory to the nation. As a strict constructionist, Jefferson believed such silence was decisive: A power not expressly granted was not given. Jefferson soon got over the theory. The deal was too good to pass up. Even Congress seemed to want him to make it. In the end, he did.

Jefferson's shift in attitude was not unique to that case. It extended to views about his own powers as the chief executive. In theory, Jefferson was sympathetic to the fears about an all-powerful commander in chief that Patrick Henry and George Mason had once expressed. During the campaign for the presidency, Jefferson and his advocates had hammered Adams on that score. They accused him of using his wartime powers in ways that proved Henry and Mason had been right to sound the alarm about how the Constitution might be exploited by a power-hungry chief commander. Once in office, though, Jefferson seemed less committed to practicing restraint than his campaign might have suggested he would be. That was especially clear first in the way that Jefferson responded to a rebellion out west, and then, months later, in how he reacted when the English navy opened fire on American ships off the Virginia coast.

In struggling with the vexing constitutional issues that these crises posed, Jefferson began to see advantages in the executive possessing an uncheckable prerogative in war. But while Jefferson was willing to entertain the possibility that the chief commander could act free of Congress's restraints, he was also hesitant to embrace the exercise of unchecked executive war powers. Jefferson did his best to contain his defenses of the executive's power to ignore Congress's limits on the conduct of war in each of these episodes. He identified all manner of qualifications and caveats. He even shrouded his embrace of that power in anonymity.

* * *

In an early crisis in his administration, Jefferson had shown a keen sense of how to assert his war powers in ways that Congress could approve. His deft handling of the use of force against the Barbary States no doubt gave him confidence to act on his own in handling future threats to the nation's security. The unauthorized actions of a most unattractive person years later, however, forced Jefferson to confront the limits of executive power in war.

Often drunk, never trustworthy, always loud, James Wilkinson was famous for his bluster and poor judgment. He was also a survivor. He had served in the nation's armed forces since the Revolutionary War. Under Jefferson, he had finally risen to the top. He was now commanding general of the nation's still small army. In that capacity, he was, midway through Jefferson's second term, responsible for quelling a rebellion precipitated by none other than Aaron Burr, who, only recently, had been Jefferson's vice president. The way Wilkinson chose to go about stopping Burr, however, would provoke great controversy. Wilkinson's heavy-handed tactics would also force Jefferson into a most uncomfortable position. Jefferson would have to choose between looking feckless in the face of a threat to the national government, or supporting the notion that Congress could not place limits on the president's war powers.

The origins of Aaron Burr's rebellion were to be found in the western swing that the former vice president had taken in the spring of 1805. Burr was, by all accounts, a startling figure. His piercing gaze and elegant dress transfixed his many admirers. His transparent ambition—and charismatic manner—terrified the larger contingent that opposed him. More than a few of the nation's founders pegged him early on as an emperor in waiting. Some even named him the most dangerous American they had ever met. Burr had been Jefferson's running mate, but there had long been doubts about his loyalty. So, when Burr stepped down as Jefferson's vice president—in the wake of his infamous duel with Alexander Hamilton, which resulted in Hamilton's death—rumors about Burr's future plans immediately began to circulate.

Burr's defenders said the former vice president was merely heading

west as part of a planned expedition to capture land in Mexico—an expedition known at the time as a filibuster. Others detected a more sinister
plot. They said Burr was actually rounding up a war party to advance
on New Orleans. Burr supposedly thought the western states and territories would break from the union as soon as that city fell. And, further,
the rumor went, Burr believed that, when that city did fall, he would be
poised to lead a new, breakaway republic. Other reports were even more
sensational. One had Burr, as part of this effort to split the union in two,
planning to strike the nation's capital at a time when his confederates
would be in place to assassinate not only Jefferson but also the new vice
president and the Senate president as well.

* * *

Jefferson first started to take the Burr conspiracy seriously when, in
late October of 1806, the president received a worrisome report about
his former vice president's activities out west. Jefferson quickly convened
his cabinet for an emergency meeting. By the end of that session, he had
decided to send a number of gunboats to the mouth of the Mississippi.
Those ships would be sent to block British warships rumored to be making their way to reinforce the conspirators Burr supposedly led.

Before issuing the actual order about the gunboats, however, Jefferson
hesitated. He paused for the same reasons Adams had practiced restraint
during the Quasi War—and Washington had paused during the Revolutionary War. Jefferson, too, wanted to avoid overstepping Congress's war
powers. The president decided to ask his treasury secretary, Albert Gallatin, a staunch defender of congressional prerogatives during the Quasi
War, to confer with the secretary of the navy, Robert Smith. The two men
were charged with ensuring that existing laws authorizing naval appropriations did not prevent Jefferson's planned approach.

The key phrase in the appropriations law that applied to the proposed
gunboat mission was hardly clear. It allowed spending to cover unspecified "contingent expenses." Gallatin and Smith had been involved in
the legislative discussions that had produced that law. They had a pretty

good idea what Congress had intended. They thought there was no way to conclude, in good faith, that Congress meant to give the president a pot of funds to pay for gunboats that might fire on Americans. During the legislative negotiations, Smith had assured the appropriators that the contingent operations the administration had in mind were quite limited. Neither Gallatin nor Smith, therefore, could fail to see the problem with exploiting the looseness of that language now. The Federalist penchant for reading statutes—and especially appropriations laws—to permit assertions of executive authority that Congress had never contemplated was among the chief evils that Jefferson's men, committed antimonarchists that they claimed to be, had vowed to correct. With doubts growing about how serious the threat Burr posed really was, the legal concerns regarding statutory authorization seemed hard to ignore. Jefferson scrapped the gunboat plan the very next day.

Such prudent decision making had its costs. Two months later, with the Burr crisis heating up again, Smith lamented the consequences of the "choice" the president had made not to deploy the gunboats. He wrote to Jefferson that, if the ships had gone "as was proposed on the 24th October . . . we would at this time have nothing to apprehend from the military expedition of [Colonel] Burr." But, in light of the "limitations of existing Statutes" and "the spirit manifested by the House of Representatives at their last session," Smith reaffirmed, there really had been no choice. That was so even though, Smith concluded, "the approaching crisis will, I fear, be a melancholy proof of the want of forecast in so circumscribing the Executive within such narrow limits."

Smith did have some advice for the president about how he could best go about checking Burr. Smith told Jefferson to lay all he knew about Burr before Congress in a secret session. That way, the legislature could be convinced to suspend the great writ of habeas corpus in the inflamed western regions. Congress could then appropriate the funds needed to permit a "competent naval force" to be sent there.

Smith's suggested approach mirrored the one that the Adams administration had adopted in countering France. But Jefferson was not Adams.

Nor did he wish to be confused with him. The two men—Adams and Jefferson—had not spoken in years. They would not resume contact until long after Jefferson quit the presidency.

It was no accident that a great silence had come between them. There was, of course, the hurt that followed Jefferson's successful race against Adams in the election of 1800. There was also the fact that Jefferson wanted to break with Federalist rule. He had no political interest in keeping close to Adams. He also wanted to end federal governmental support for a substantially enhanced federal military establishment. Jefferson was leery, therefore, of any strategy for defeating Burr that would require a military expansion or the federal imposition of something like martial law—even if Congress did bless such measures in advance.

For Jefferson, as a Republican, it was not enough to touch base with Congress. He did not want to invite Congress to empower the executive unduly. Jefferson preferred a strategy that did not ask Congress to give him more federal firepower. He wanted to rely on the people out west, especially in Ohio—organized as militia if need be—to provide the main line of resistance. Such an approach would fit better with Jefferson's democratic leanings. That approach would favor liberty and local control. It could also ward off any effort in Congress to use the Burr crisis to create a standing army. Jefferson contented himself with public pronouncements that focused on what the local people, in coordination with their local rulers, could do for themselves to stop the conspirators. But the reality of the threat remained. It was not at all clear a low-key approach would prove sustainable. And, in time, that approach gave way to the one pressed by General James Wilkinson, leader of the American army.

* * *

By late November of 1806, Burr's men were said to have gathered in New Orleans. Support for the union was thought to be much weaker there than in Ohio. There was little confidence that the local populace would put up a strong defense. Adding to the concern, a large band of Burr's well-armed supporters was reportedly en route to New Orleans from Ohio.

There were also rumors that a British naval vessel, heading up from the Caribbean, was on its way to aid the rebels. The pressure for the federal army to take matters into its own hands was growing.

For months, Wilkinson had been passive in the face of the rumors about Burr. Some speculated that Wilkinson was reluctant to step in because he had been in league with Burr all along. But, with the threat posed by the former vice president so seemingly serious, Wilkinson at last roused himself—if only to prove his loyalty to the nation that he was supposedly serving.

Upon arriving in New Orleans, the general wasted little time in seizing control. He was determined to do more than merely make the federal presence known. He wanted to root out the enemy right away—to make plain that the locals could not be trusted to hold things together. He promptly asked the governor of the territory to suspend the writ of habeas corpus. That would permit the "ordinary forms of our Civil institutions," Wilkinson explained, to yield to the "Strong arm of Military Law."

The governor refused. "To violate the law is one thing," Governor William Claiborne said, "but to proclaim an intention of doing so, and under the semblance of authority is another. The one under certain circumstances is excusable nay commendable; the other, to say the least is worse than useless."

Wilkinson was not a man easily rebuffed. He knew that the law was likely against him, just as the governor had said. Wilkinson did not seem to care. Asserting his rank as commanding general of the federal army, he ordered his officers to round up Burr's confederates. He wanted the suspects placed in military custody, even though no legislature—neither the nation's Congress nor Louisiana's assembly—had sanctioned such an action. The sweep ensnared not only those directly suspected of working with Burr but also lawyers for the accused, an editor sympathetic to their cause, a local judge, and even a former senator.

Pressing the bounds of the law still further, Wilkinson directed his officers to ignore the local courts if they issued writs of habeas corpus, thereby freeing those Wilkinson had ordered to be held. The general instead directed his officers to send the most important suspects straight to the nation's capital. That way, the detainees could be kept in military detention far from those same local judges. The general even showed up in the chambers of a local judge in full military costume. Wilkinson explained he would not submit to a court he did not trust. He held fast to that position even when the federal courts tried to intervene.

* * *

Back in Washington, Wilkinson's exploits remained unknown. Everyone seemed focused on how weak the president and his administration had been. With rumors swirling about the uprising Burr was plotting out west, political points were being scored off of Jefferson's seeming nonchalance in the face of a true rebellion.

By January, news of Wilkinson's sweep had still not reached Washington. John Randolph, Jefferson's leading legislative antagonist, exploded in frustration on the House floor. Randolph was furious about the silence from the Jefferson administration. With a handkerchief covering his scalp and a bottle of ale at his side, Randolph could be an indefatigable—and intimidating—opponent in debate. He was particularly harsh on this day. He could not stand the administration's continued refusal to say what it was doing to counter Burr. Nor did Randolph have much patience with his own chamber's willingness to tolerate the lack of answers. "The United States are not only threated with external war," he raged in his address. It faced "conspiracies and treasons, the more alarming from their not being defined; and yet we sit and adjourn, adjourn and sit, take things as schoolboys, do as we are bid, and ask no questions!"

To drive home the point, Randolph introduced a resolution. It would require the president to explain his views about Burr, as well as Jefferson's plans for countering him.

But then, just days after Randolph's resolution passed, things suddenly took a very different turn. The first fruits of Wilkinson's aggressive roundup—in the form of captured conspirators—began trickling into the nation's capital. Far from seeming too passive in the face of a threat to the nation, Jefferson now stood accused of having disrespected the separation of powers. Jefferson's silence was no longer taken to be reflective of his timidity. Because Jefferson said nothing, he was accused of tacitly endorsing General Wilkinson's zealous effort to counter the at best speculative threat that Burr posed. "It is a miserable subterfuge," opponents of the administration argued, to contend that Wilkinson's "outrages" were his alone. "Wilkinson is as perfectly under the control of the executive as any clerk in one of the departments."

This charge stung. Jefferson had come to office promising to halt what his supporters thought was the creeping monarchism of a decade of Federalist rule. Jefferson's critics now claimed—after having only days before raised concerns that the president was doing too little—that Jefferson had enabled, however indirectly, that same dangerous expansion of executive authority. The opposition delighted in the irony. A Republican president, they were gloating, had seemingly overseen the imposition of martial law.

Jefferson was under great stress and not only from the mounting criticism. His head was pounding from a near debilitating headache brought on by an inflamed jaw. The pain had plagued him for some time. Some days he could barely work for more than an hour. But however much pain Jefferson was in, he now faced a stark choice. It was not one he could put off any longer. Wilkinson's controversial actions, and Randolph's aggressive resolution, had forced things into the open. Jefferson would either have to back his general's power grab or disavow it—unless, that is, he could somehow find a way of doing neither.

* * *

Jefferson was nothing if not resourceful—especially when it came to avoiding responsibility. As he contemplated the answer that he would give to Congress on January 22 in response to Randolph's resolution, Jefferson looked for something to anchor his response. He knew Wilkinson had been operating in the field, in confused circumstances, and with the seemingly admirable intention of advancing the war aims of his president.

Jefferson also knew that there was a very recent precedent that in-dicated that the public might excuse an officer's legal transgressions in the heat of battle even if, strictly speaking, they were unlawful. The trick would be to suggest that Wilkinson might deserve to be excused even if he was wrong to have used some of the harsh means he em-ployed. Or, at least, Jefferson could try to so muddy things up that it would not be entirely clear what Jefferson's view of Wilkinson's conduct really was.

The precedent for excusing Wilkinson—even if he had unlawfully seized power that was not his to seize—was a complicated one. The precedent had emerged from a judicial ruling that had come down just as Jefferson's first term was winding to a close. The Supreme Court, in an opinion by Chief Justice John Marshall, had held that an American naval captain was liable for unlawfully seizing a ship. The opinion was issued just as the Quasi War with France was fizzling to its conclusion. The captain in question, George Little, had been cruising the open wa-ters of the Caribbean. He was at the time acting under orders from Sec-retary of the Navy Benjamin Stoddert. Stoddert had made a point of sending the captain out not only with a copy of the orders themselves but also with a copy of the statutes on which those orders were based. Unbeknownst to Little, however, Stoddert had overshot the mark. Stod-dert had ordered seizures beyond those Congress had allowed. The Court had thus ruled against Little. In doing so, the Court relied on an earlier opinion written by General Washington's cousin Justice Bush-rod Washington. The conflict with France was "confined in its nature and extent," Justice Washington had concluded in that case. "[T]hose who are authorized to commit hostilities . . . can go no further than to the extent of their commission." The Supreme Court seemed to endorse that principle wholeheartedly in finding Captain Little liable for illegally seizing the ships while on patrol.

The legal principle set forth in the *Little* case was—or so it seemed—clear enough. The executive could be bound by Congress's laws, even during hostilities with a foreign nation and even as to the content of the rules of engagement that the executive could draw up for his armed forces. But if the Supreme Court had suggested that Congress might have the final word when it came to the war's conduct, it also seemed perfectly clear that the legislature could relieve Captain Little of any obligation to pay for the mistake that he had made in obeying the unlawful orders of his superior. Surely, if Congress could make its officers liable for disregarding rules it had laid down, then it could also indemnify those same officers if Congress thought they had done nothing wrong in carrying out unlawfully issued orders.

And so, soon after Chief Justice John Marshall rendered his decision in George Little's case in 1804, advocates for the captain began crafting a bill to appropriate the funds Little would need to pay his debt for extending his wartime commission too far. That bill passed both houses of Congress in the winter of 1807. It reached the desk of President Jefferson by, of all days, January 22—the very day that Jefferson was offering his public response to the news of Wilkinson's own apparent lawlessness.

The *Little* affair was in many ways a perfect precedent for Jefferson's own attempt to wriggle free from the vexing position in which Wilkinson's conduct had put him. The case of Captain Little suggested that a violation of the law—though serious—might also, on reflection, be looked upon charitably if it had been committed in the course of military operations. Little had definitely violated Congress's command, the Court had found. Congress had forgiven him nonetheless. Perhaps Wilkinson's actions, though wrong at the time, were excusable nonetheless.

But the case for excusing Wilkinson was tricky. Wilkinson was no mere captain. He was the nation's commanding general. To excuse Wilkinson on the ground that he was just doing what his superior wanted was potentially to implicate Jefferson directly as the true lawbreaker. Excusing such conduct might even suggest that, when facing a military crisis, the president was not bound by law at all, as he would be able to issue unlawful orders and then expect no consequences to follow from their execution by subordinates. Besides, Captain Little had merely been following orders that had been issued in what seemed like a good faith attempt to execute Congress's handiwork. Wilkinson, by contrast, had been self-consciously operating at the edges of the law. To forgive him would not be to excuse his misjudgment about where the legal line lay. It would be to reward his intentional lawbreaking solely because a claimed necessity demanded it.

* * *

Jefferson did his best to make his true position hard to decipher. Jefferson began his much anticipated proclamation on the Burr crisis by praising Wilkinson as a good citizen and a fine officer. Jefferson then offered a very hedged account of what the general had actually done. Of the three Burr men "the general had caused to be apprehended," Jefferson explained—using the passive voice—one had already been "liberated by habeas corpus." The other two were "those particularly employed in the endeavor to corrupt the General and Army of the United States." The description was clever: It sought to highlight the precision with which the targets had been chosen for detention and thus to downplay any suggestion of a lawless sweep.

Jefferson then added, again playing up Wilkinson's moderation, that the detainees had been taken east "probably" because of "the consideration that an impartial trial could not be expected, during the present agitations of New Orleans, and that that city was not as yet a safe place of confinement." Wilkinson was not seeking to evade legal process, Jefferson was saying. Wilkinson had actually been looking for a way to submit to it. In fact, Jefferson went on, regular order could be expected to return now that the crisis had ebbed. "As soon as these persons shall arrive," he said, "they will be delivered to the custody of the law, and left to such course of trial, both as to place and progress, as its functionaries may direct."

Jefferson concluded his reassuring message with a request that his countrymen look forward. It was as much in the interest of "the criminals" as of the "public," he explained, that the trials be held in the capital. "Being already removed from the place where they were first apprehended," Jefferson wrote, "the first regular arrest should take place here, and the course of proceedings receive here their proper direction." In short, Jefferson was telling his fellow citizens, what was done was done. There was no use dwelling on whatever illegalities may have been committed. There was every reason to believe that things would return to normal soon.

* * *

Jefferson's effort to sidestep the hard issues raised by Wilkinson's actions largely worked. The Senate liked what it heard. Within a matter of days, a bill to suspend habeas corpus for three months passed the Senate. There was hardly a dissent. The bill seemingly ensured that the captured Burrites that Wilkinson brought east still would not get a judicial forum to make their case.

But just before the Senate sent the suspension bill over to the House, the lower body adjourned for a couple of days. That brief delay proved crucial. By the time the House reconvened, emotions against Burr, and in favor of Wilkinson, had cooled in response to news reports from the field. With fear of Burr's plot subsiding, support for Wilkinson and the suspension of habeas crumbled. Randolph—hostile to Jefferson's endorsement of aggression—explained that he would not ratify illegal arrests by cutting the courts out of the picture. Such a practice was indefensible. If the Burr crisis had been as serious as Jefferson seemed to believe, Randolph argued, the president should have come to Congress and sought a suspension at the outset. He should not have participated in a plan to break the law on the expectation that he would ultimately be excused. Jefferson's own son-in-law, a representative from Virginia, did not disagree. He joined in opposition to the bill, and it promptly went down to defeat.

Throughout the suspension debate, Jefferson maintained his famously enigmatic posture. To this day, it is not known whether he favored suspension or not. But, in private, Jefferson explained his views about Wilkinson's actions in a letter he sent directly to the general in early February.

At the time, the president did not know whether Burr had been captured. The operation to put down the conspiracy was in that respect still underway when Jefferson wrote to Wilkinson. But, although the president's letter praised the general for acting "with promptitude," Jefferson wanted Wilkinson to know that he, as president, thought his general in the field had overestimated the danger. Jefferson also wanted Wilkinson to know he would not hold him responsible for any reasonable transgressions. "In approving . . . as we do approve of the defensive operations for [New] Orleans," Jefferson explained, in a phrase that left unexplained whether he believed all of Wilkinson's actions were, in fact, defensive, "we are obliged to estimate them, not according to our view of the danger, but to place ourselves in your situation and only with your information."

In this way, Jefferson circled back to the central issue. The question was not whether the general had been right or wrong. It was whether the general should be punished for what he did. To answer that question, Jefferson took refuge in the court of public opinion. His own view, he seemed to suggest, did not matter. The people would decide. They would likely support the general's decision to send true culprits east, Jefferson explained. Otherwise, he believed, the people would be skeptical of any assertion of such detention power. Jefferson thus hoped Wilkinson would "not extend this deportation to persons against whom there is only suspicion, or shades of offence not strongly marked." For if Wilkinson did that, "I fear the public sentiment would desert you; because seeing no danger here, violations of the law are felt with strength."

It was as if some amorphous entity called "the public" was the true commander in chief; it would determine the bounds of executive wartime operations, not the president. Jefferson was merely responsible for divining that public's desires and conveying them to his man in the field. In that regard, Jefferson was far more confident in the general's public vindication than he had let on to Wilkinson.

In a letter sent to Louisiana governor Claiborne about the controversy, Jefferson wrote that "we judge of the merit of our agents . . . by the magnitude of the danger as it appeared to them, not as it was known to us. On great occasions every good officer must be ready to risk himself in going beyond the strict line of law, when the public preservation requires it." For that reason, Jefferson assured Claiborne, Wilkinson's decisions "will be supported by the public approbation" irrespective of attempts by the Federalists "to make something of the infringement of liberty by the military arrest."

Still, Jefferson was trying to make sure Wilkinson knew that checks remained. He had stressed in his letter to the general that the public might excuse violations of the law, but also that it might not. If the people saw no real threat to safety, the president had informed the general, violations of the law would be "felt with strength."

If this message was Jefferson's attempt to stand up for checks and balances, it was not much of one. Even an officer as obtuse as Wilkinson could guess—without Jefferson's reminder—that he *might* face popular resistance if he decided to violate the law. Before sending the suspects to Washington, Wilkinson had the good sense to meet with the federal judge for the Orleans territory. He had asked him a simple question: Would he be hanged for what he was about to do? The judge had assured Wilkinson he would not. The notorious roundup soon followed.

Such an informal exchange, offering a seeming blanket grant of legal immunity, was hardly a substitute for an obligation to follow the law that Congress had actually laid down. In that sense, Jefferson's message, if widely known, could not have done much more than enable—and even entice—future officers to make judgments about the limits of their power on the basis of little more than a gut sense of what the people would let them get away with. Such a system for checking the commander in chief in waging war seemed to mock—rather than secure—the checks and balances that distinguished the American executive from a king. But it was a system to which Jefferson, if his private letters to Wilkinson and Claiborne were any indication, was warming.

* * *

Jefferson was about to warm to it even more. By February, Burr was in custody—his plot, whatever its aim, finally foiled. But before the year was up, the dilemma of the good officer—and the conflict between law and war that it presented—flared up again. This time the issue did not concern the actions of a single, potentially rogue general, facing what, upon reflection, increasingly looked like a pathetic, even comical, threat. The issue concerned a choice unquestionably made by the commander in chief himself, and at a time when the nation was plainly being intimidated by one of the world's great powers.

It was the summer of 1807. Congress was enjoying one of its lengthy recesses—this time brought on by the fetid June air in Washington and the ill effects that it could have on the health of the members of the House and Senate. Tensions with Great Britain had been high for some time. They were fueled by England's insistence on impressing sailors believed to have absconded to America, thus evading their obligation to serve in the Royal Navy.

At the time, the USS *Chesapeake* was moored at Hampton Roads, not far from Washington. The commanding officer of the HMS *Leopard*, an English vessel patrolling near Hampton Roads, requested the American captain, James Barron, to allow his frigate to be searched. The English officer was looking for fellow countrymen whom he believed were on board. When Barron refused the search, *Leopard* let loose an awful and wholly unexpected barrage. Twenty-two unanswered shots later, three Americans aboard the *Chesapeake* were dead. Fears of an imminent invasion of Virginia—or at least a British fleet massing on the coast that fall—were palpable.

President Jefferson scrambled to respond. His information was not much better than that of his fellow citizens. With no clear sense of what England intended, and against the advice of aides, Jefferson refused to call Congress back to Washington. He was moved by health concerns. He did not want to make the returning congressmen sick, given the perceived dangers of summer in the capital. But Jefferson was moved even more by his fear that returning members might do something rash. Jefferson did not want to take the nation to war, but the fever for it seemed dangerously high. He kept Congress away, therefore, not to make war a *fait accompli* but to prevent the people's representatives from declaring war too soon.

Jefferson's success in blocking Congress from rushing into war, however, created its own set of problems. Any response short of war would require defensive preparations. But Congress had been kept out of town. With Congress unable to pass new legislation that might be needed, Jefferson found himself inundated with the same type of vexing questions about necessity and the limits of his power as commander in chief that he had just tried to avoid answering in the Wilkinson controversy.

* * *

By this time in his presidency, Jefferson was seasoned. He seemed remarkably confident as he made his way through the legal thicket. He wasted no time in deciding, after an initial cabinet meeting, to enter into contracts for timber and saltpeter to build a fleet of gunboats. There were no appropriations for such construction, but Jefferson saw little harm in making promises in advance of Congress. Jefferson was sure the legislature would feel pressured to honor those commitments when it returned. That made Jefferson confident Congress would "sanction" the new contracts. Besides, the measures were entirely defensive in nature. Jefferson took these steps unilaterally only because the legislature was in recess. It was not as if he was plotting to take the nation to war on his own. He thus saw no real constitutional problem.

There were a host of other questions to consider as well. The sheer volume of the legal analysis Jefferson produced in the midst of the crisis was impressive. In letter after letter, Jefferson elaborated on the ideas about executive power that he had first set forth to Wilkinson in February.

Jefferson's exchange of letters with Virginia's governor was especially revealing. The governor had sent Jefferson a challenging inquiry, and the need for an answer was urgent. The governor expressed concern that strict compliance with the federal militia laws would essentially make it impossible for the state to raise the local force that the crisis demanded. Jefferson hazarded a response even though he was alone at Monticello. He was without the aid of his attorney general or any other officer of note.

Jefferson made a point of offering the governor to "participate . . .
in any risk of disapprobation to which an honest desire of furthering
the public good may expose us." Jefferson's trepidation stemmed from
his recognition of the controversial nature of the advice he was about to
give. A champion of strict construction, Jefferson would later famously
deride his Federalist nemesis Chief Justice John Marshall as a master of
"twistifications." But now, confronting a true crisis and a technical statute, Jefferson acknowledged to the Virginia governor that a law might
mean something different from what its words seemed to say. Jefferson
explained there was one law in ordinary times—what he called the law
of "*meum et tuum*"—and another in the midst of crisis. The good and
discerning officer was the one who could see the distinction. That was
especially true, Jefferson wrote, of "laws merely executive," such as those
describing the organization of the militia, where no "private right stands
in the way." If something new and unforeseen arose, it was important
not to follow such a law's "details scrupulously." Jefferson, the supposed
literalist, argued that doing so could actually frustrate Congress's intent.
Congress, after all, was trying to accomplish ends that would serve the
nation in passing laws authorizing the military to be called up. Why assume, then, Congress would have wanted to put up obstacles to those
ends being met?

But Jefferson went even further in that same letter. The militia laws, he
proceeded to explain, were intended to make it possible for men to leave
their farms and give service to their country. If Congress had said nothing about how these men were to be received into the militia, Jefferson
reasoned, the executive could obviously use the means most practicable.
Thus, if Congress had only set forth means that turned out to be unworkable, Jefferson now advised, then "the constitutional power remains, and
supplies them."

It was a potentially shocking statement. It seemed to place the commander in chief above Congress, free to disregard any statutory limit that
he deemed unworkable. But Jefferson was careful to avoid setting up such
a direct confrontation with the legislature. He explained that the details

Congress set forth in the militia laws were "affirmative merely." The words that Congress used were thus best read to create a blueprint to be followed only if workable, rather than to create a constraining structure that had to be followed no matter what. If every detail Congress specified were read to bar the executive's use of any other means, the president argued, then "the objection that our government is an impracticable one, would really be verified."

In other words, Jefferson seemed unwilling to challenge a basic point: Congress still retained the final word; Jefferson just required Congress to speak clearly. But, of course, that meant Jefferson was opening himself to the charge that he was becoming a master twistifier in his own right.

* * *

Congress returned to Washington in October. Jefferson greeted the members with a forthright admission: During its absence, he wrote in his official legislative message, he had taken a number of actions of his own accord—though seemingly none in direct violation of any statute. Jefferson had made contracts to acquire gunpowder in advance of appropriations he assumed Congress would honor. With Britain on the verge of waging all-out war, and the members of the House and Senate scattered in the several states, Jefferson thought he could hardly be faulted for that. He was confident Congress would ratify that decision, along with the others.

The president was right. A measure approving his actions passed the very next day. His actions provoked little criticism or concern—certainly none like that expressed in the earlier debate over General Wilkinson's allegedly lawless seizures in New Orleans. But Jefferson was by then confident that he knew how to deal with the tension between law and necessity in war.

The president was also confident of something else: He believed the impulse for war against England, so deeply felt after the attack in the harbor at Hampton Roads, had passed. In consequence, Jefferson concluded, an embargo on American trade with England would provide the way forward.

The Embargo Act became law that December. It set forth the policy that would define the final phase of Jefferson's presidency. It was a policy that—for all its flaws—put off a war. It thus spared Jefferson future conflicts with Congress over how war should be waged.

But the embargo was not popular. Jefferson effectively retreated to Monticello for the final year of his presidency. He was vainly trying to avoid the harsh opposition provoked by his ruinous economic policy. There were cutting accusations that he was falling back on bad habits. As Virginia's governor during the Revolutionary War, he had fled the capital as Benedict Arnold and his men led a British rout. Now, Jefferson was again retreating from a seemingly unwinnable fight.

* * *

By the fall of 1810, the crisis with England had passed. Jefferson had finally retired. Fonder memories were beginning to block out the sour finish to his presidency. His dear friend James Madison had succeeded him in a presidential election that all thought a referendum on Jefferson. With Madison's victory, Jefferson's party had been vindicated. Now past seventy, Jefferson had reemerged as a hero.

A near constant stream of admirers showed up at Jefferson's home. Some would arrive just for the privilege of peering through the windows to catch a glimpse of his family at dinner. The mail from all quarters was equally relentless—and mostly favorable.

Despite his advancing age, Jefferson spent a healthy part of each day on horseback. He took long rides to keep tabs on his several farms or just to experience the pleasure of galloping through the pines. But, as pleasant as this new life was, the reminders of his former burdens sometimes intruded. One notable intrusion occurred in mid-September. A former low-level member of his State Department crisply framed some challenging questions for the former president. They concerned General Wilkinson and his infamous roundup. The inquirer asked for the great man to offer some answers.

* * *

The author of the letter was John Colvin. A Marylander of modest means, Colvin had edited various Republican newspapers before taking a job at the State Department. While serving in that position, he had been approached by General Wilkinson. Wilkinson wanted Colvin to devote "his leisure hours"—without pay—to help him write a book that Wilkinson was planning to publish very soon.

By 1810, Wilkinson was as reviled as Jefferson was beloved. There were even calls for Wilkinson's court-martial. Wilkinson hoped the book might convince President Madison to refrain from bringing him up on charges. At the least, Wilkinson thought, the book might persuade the public of his honor. If so, the shift in public sentiment might make his acquittal more likely if charges were brought. Wilkinson especially wanted the book to counter the claim that, as commanding general, he had acted lawlessly in putting down Burr's rebellion. Wilkinson had asked Colvin to take the lead on that section of the book.

Colvin agreed. But, while researching that incident, he decided he would need the former president's help. It was for the sake of Jefferson's legacy—a legacy that Colvin was committed to preserving—that Colvin had come to Wilkinson's aid in the first place. Colvin was hopeful, for reasons both partisan and principled, that the facts about what had happened out west, once known, would vindicate his faith in Jefferson. Colvin was sure a full accounting would prove Jefferson's deep devotion to constitutional government and executive restraint in war. To make sure, Colvin needed to hear from Jefferson himself. He alone could explain what Wilkinson had done and why Jefferson had let him do it. And so Colvin reached out to his hero, confident the former president's reply would be to his liking.

* * *

Colvin explained to Jefferson that a dangerous narrative of executive overreach in New Orleans was taking hold. Colvin feared that storyline could leave a permanent stain on the "Character of republican Government." The letter Colvin sent to Jefferson, therefore, was a plea more than an inquiry. Colvin wanted Jefferson to tell him about his thinking. He seemed to assume Jefferson would be able to offer an explanation that would permit Colvin to make the case that, even in the midst of crisis, his hero had remained faithful to the principle of limited government that they both held dear. "It is of essential consequence to your good name, (so precious to the republicans of the Union)," Colvin wrote to Jefferson, "that the principles upon which you approved Gen. Wilkinson's conduct at New Orleans should not be misstated or mistaken."

In pressing for cooperation, Colvin was aware of the sensitivities. He assured Jefferson that "neither man nor woman knows of this application to you, except yourself." He then closed the letter with a pair of leading questions. Were there not times "when, in free governments, it is necessary for officers in responsible stations to exercise an authority beyond the law"? And was not "the time of Burr's treason such a period"?

In his reply, Jefferson framed the questions as if they posed the larger dilemma of what he called the "good officer"—the man in the field forced to reconcile the competing claims of law and necessity. Jefferson was conceding that neither law nor necessity was privileged. That is why Wilkinson's case was so hard. The dilemma could not be avoided by mouthing the platitudes about strict construction that Republicans, so opposed to monarchism and executive discretion, loved to recite. Neither could the dilemma be wished away by saying the law was of no importance. Such a case presented a hard choice, and it demanded a frank resolution.

It was also a choice that Jefferson had, to that point, declined to face up to directly. But now, from the quietude of his retirement, Jefferson was, in reflecting on his own legacy of power, willing to confront it. Much of what Jefferson wrote to Colvin tracked what he had already privately expressed—whether in his letter to General Wilkinson while the president feared Burr was still at large or in his correspondence with Virginia's governor in the wake of the attack on *Chesapeake*. But there were also new statements about executive prerogative, and these were a good deal stronger.

Jefferson argued over the course of several pages that the nation's chief executive, when confronted with a grave threat, was bound less by law than by his devotion to the *"salus populi"*—the good of the people.

The president could—even should—do what the public needed, even if the law forbade it. There were duties, he explained, of "higher obligation" than the "written law"—including the obligation to defeat the nation's enemies.

Jefferson was at last willing to say, straight out, that there were obligations higher than the law—and that a good president, like a good officer, was bound ultimately to live up to them. The executive might have to act "against the law" for the good of the nation, Jefferson wrote, and the situation involving Burr—at least if one looked at it through Wilkinson's eyes—was such a time, even if there were reasons to doubt the wisdom of some of the general's choices.

Jefferson knew that such a claim departed from anything Washington or Adams had publicly defended as president. It also went further than anything he had actually said publicly or done while in office. Even Louisiana had been purchased with Congress cheering him on. He also knew his new views could easily be confused with a defense of monarchical power, which his own party had supposedly been established to resist. He offered his reply, therefore, on condition that its substance would remain anonymous.

* * *

The former president had given Colvin what he needed. The portions of the book that Wilkinson had asked Colvin to write borrowed liberally from Jefferson's response—at points, parroting Jefferson word for word. But Colvin did not attribute those passages to Jefferson. Colvin kept his promise to his hero. Colvin set forth Jefferson's words as if they were his own. Jefferson's theories on a subject this delicate would not be known, even though a narrative defending his actions would now be available to the world. For years, only Colvin and President Madison's wife, Dolley— to whom Colvin had given a sneak peek—knew the exchange with Jefferson occurred.

Jefferson had once again managed to have it both ways—something that, as the slave-owning author of the opening lines of the Declaration of Independence, he was famously skilled at accomplishing. He was not publicly asserting a power to override the law. He was helping spread the word that his actions—and similar actions by future executives—could be defended on that very ground.

In time, Jefferson's reply did become known, though only after he died. Even then, the letter remained obscure for decades—lying about like a loaded weapon to be picked up and wielded in a different age, by a different president, and for purposes that might well have shocked Jefferson had he imagined them. But that view would eventually get its due. Whatever scope Jefferson had intended for this executive prerogative to have when he wrote that letter to Colvin, and however wary Jefferson was of deploying that prerogative in full, the words Jefferson used to defend that power—as with virtually everything he wrote—were undeniably eloquent. And thus, in due course, those same words, and the idea they expressed, would be impressed in service of the view that the president's power to determine the conduct of war was, necessarily, unbound by law entirely.

If, as Jefferson claimed, the people would want their president to break the law to win a war, then wouldn't the president inevitably be tempted to argue that he had not really broken the law at all? Wouldn't the president be inclined to claim that the Constitution—in making the president the commander in chief—had actually intended to permit such defiance, not as an extra-legal trump but through a grant of power to determine, as Alexander Hamilton had once said, the "entire direction of war when authorized or begun"? And if such defiance could be so easily defended as an exercise of lawful, constitutionally sanctioned wartime power, then what hope would there ever be of confining it or of convincing future chief executives of the potential peril in asserting it? It was one thing to counsel, as Jefferson had, that "violations of the law" would be felt with strength. But what disciplining effect could such a warning have if violations of the law in war were rendered impossible because an appeal to necessity could always make a hard choice legal? To be sure, presidents would still run the risk of making unpopular decisions. But would they worry anymore about paying a price for making ones that were unlawful?

Jefferson did not try to answer such questions in replying to Colvin. In fact, he did not even raise them. They were questions all the same. And while Jefferson's immediate successor did his best to avoid endorsing anything close to the position laid out in that letter to Colvin, they were questions that, within the next half-decade—especially with a civil war on the horizon—would become the subject of intense public debate.

5

THE MAN ON HORSEBACK

"The military power is clearly defined, and carefully limitted [sic], by the Constitution and laws of the United States."

Washington, Adams, and Jefferson had each been commander in chief—and each had faced military crises. But none had served during a congressionally declared war. James Madison was the first of the nation's presidents to do so, and he was a most unlikely one to have that honor.

Small of stature, often sick, bookish, he was not a military man, nor did he carry himself like one. He was derided as "little Jim"—in contrast to the taller and more vigorous man who eventually succeeded him, James Monroe. But however lacking Madison was in martial qualities, Jefferson's former secretary of state—in now leading the nation into battle after Jefferson's embargo strategy had finally failed to end the standoff with England—was as fully empowered as any commander in chief had been since the founding.

Still, Congress's decision to instruct the president, for the first time, to declare war and thus to take the fight to the enemy not by halves but in full did not fundamentally change the underlying constitutional order. Congress was still responsible for ensuring the nation was prepared to wage war. And Congress was still reluctant to provide forces adequate to the task.

Even with a declaration of war, the president had to fight with Congress for the men and matériel that would be needed to ensure the nation would emerge victorious against the British. And these fights hardly went the president's way. When controversies arose about the president's power to actually conduct the war, moreover, the old assumptions about Congress's right to define the bounds of that executive power continued to hold sway. Thus, the formal declaration of war did little to alter the by now familiar pattern. The president pushed. Congress pushed back. Neither seemed inclined to push the other too far.

True, Jefferson had flirted—as no chief executive before him had—with asserting an executive prerogative in war. And Jefferson and Madison were as intimate as brothers. But Madison showed no interest in following his predecessor's lead in stretching the president's power beyond the limits set by Congress. Madison seemed especially wary of using wartime authority to assert strong powers at home—where, as it happened, most of the fighting in the war with England would take place. Madison was so wary of wielding such powers, in fact, that he was reluctant even to ask Congress to provide them.

But, by war's end, Madison, like Jefferson, would confront the conundrum that appeals to necessity inherently presented. The precipitating event was once again a crisis in New Orleans. And the source of the controversy was once again the defiant actions of an army general—this time, one who would become a president: Andrew Jackson.

* * *

The war with England was eminently avoidable. It was also one for which the precise cause has always been hard to pinpoint.

One cause was surely Britain's impressment of suspected fugitive military men found either in the United States or on ships under the American flag. Britain took thousands of its former seamen in this fashion. America protested, but to no avail. A loud chorus thought America needed to resist the practice.

There were also deeper—and less obvious—causes. There was the festering question of just who should reign supreme in North America.

Would the United States try to wrest Canada away from England? Would England fight to keep it? There also were the ongoing economic issues concerning trade. Parliament's much-hated Orders in Council barred neutral countries from doing business with France so long as England's war with France continued. Madison had tried to get England to withdraw those trade-restraining orders, but as of the eve of war, he had failed to do so.

There was, though, another potential trigger for this war that was less tangible—but, perhaps, more important: national honor. The young nation needed to prove itself as a mature country. That felt need proved powerful—so powerful it seemed to drown out calls for restraint.

Still, while Madison led the United States into the war with England, his restrained posture was evident from the start. He rejected a proposal to deliver a war message to Congress in person, in the company of his cabinet. Madison thought such a personal appearance would imply that the legislature was passing on a decision of the president rather than deciding the question on its own. Nor would Madison ask Congress to declare war in writing. His written message to Congress in early June of 1812 merely launched a debate over the possibility of Congress making such a declaration for itself. Upon receipt of Madison's message by Congress, the galleries were cleared—even of the press. The doors were shut. The clerk then read the president's message aloud.

The message did not hesitate to say that England was in a state of war with the United States. The indignities England had visited upon its former colony in recent years were too great, the president explained, to conclude otherwise. But the message did shy away from saying that America was in a state of war with England. Such a momentous judgment, Madison wrote in his message, was not his to make. "Whether the United States shall continue passive under these progressive usurpations . . . is a solemn question, which the Constitution wisely confides to the Legislative Department of the Government," his message read. "In recommending it to their early deliberations, I am happy in the assurance, that the decision will be worthy of the enlightened and patriotic councils, of a virtuous, a free, and a powerful Nation."

＊ ＊ ＊

Madison had earlier expressed confidence that whatever decision Congress reached about declaring war would be "stamped by a unanimity." He was too optimistic. On June 18, while still meeting in secret, the Senate, in a bitterly divided vote, joined a divided House in declaring war. A jointly approved declaration was then sent to Madison for his signature, which he promptly gave.

News of the decision eventually seeped out of the secret legislative session—at last making clear the outcome of the mysterious congressional debate at which the newspapers had been guessing. A member of the Federalist Party figured out the declaration was made that same evening, but only because he noticed Republican lawmakers making their way to congratulate Mr. Madison at the weekly reception his wife, Dolley, hosted at the President's House. Otherwise, America made its decision to go to war with the people largely in the dark.

Madison was said to be "ghostly pale" upon learning of the outcome—perhaps because he doubted the legislature would really take that step. War was now at hand, and Madison was supposedly in charge. The Federalist opponents of the war emphasized Madison's leading role. They took to calling the conflict "Mr. Madison's War." It was a clever way of exploiting the public's lingering fears of executive power. It also served to distance the branch of government—Congress—in which they served from bearing responsibility for the war. But the slogan was a fiction.

＊ ＊ ＊

As much as the opposition sought to tag Madison with sole control over the war, he did what he could to resist responsibility. Madison seemed to see himself—before, during, and even after the conflict—as less the author of events than as Congress's instrument in responding to them. He may have set things in motion with his message to the Congress, but the war hawks in Congress had been responsible, too. They had demanded a declaration long before Madison. And they had confidently predicted

American forces would easily take Canada from England in the event war came. In the end, therefore, this war was no more Madison's than Congress's.

Not that Madison was a passive witness to the war. He did assert himself in various ways. He made a show of visiting all the war departments right after the declaration became known. But he would only go so far on his own. Soon after the declaration, an English representative approached Madison with a proposed deal to return the two countries to a state of peace. The president replied that he had no authority to consent to the conflict's end. The declaration of war was more than an authorization to use force if the president wished. It was, to Madison, a congressional command to prosecute hostilities to the fullest. Madison explained that he was duty bound to carry out that directive until Congress instructed otherwise.

Duty bound—but not necessarily capable of doing so. Thanks to Jefferson's successful efforts at downsizing the military in the last administration, the state of America's armed forces on the eve of this new war with England was hardly strong. The Republican hostility to standing armies and navies had left its mark. Madison struggled in the months leading up to delivering his June message to Congress to find a way to coax that body into shoring up those forces. But he joked to Jefferson in February about his lack of success. "With a view to enable the Executive to step at once into Canada," where England was thought to be most vulnerable, Madison wrote, "they have provided after two months delay, for a regular force requiring 12 to raise it, and after 3 months for a volunteer force, on terms not likely to raise it at all for that object."

Jefferson shot back—in keeping with his growing sense that a president might have to do what had to be done—with choice words about Congress's deficiencies. "I have much doubted whether, in case of a war, Congress would find it practicable to do their part of the business," he sniped. "That a body containing 100 lawyers in it, should direct the measures of a war is, I fear, impossible; and that thus that member of our constitution, which is its bulwark, will prove to be an impracticable one," given its passion for speaking rather than doing.

Madison did not, however, join in his friend's derision of the legislature. In Madison's own letter to Jefferson, the president did express frustration. But Madison also noted that Congress's halting response to his requests for more support stemmed from a "mixture of good & bad, avowed & disguised motives." During some of the worst days of the war, Madison actually seemed to take a certain pride in the nation's incapacity to fight as effectively as England. For Madison, Congress's failure to raise a force capable of taking on the English was—properly understood—less a failing of the American system than a hallmark.

Such a sentiment could sound discordant while the country was losing its battle with England. And for most of the war America was back on its heels. Still, the sentiment did fit well with the republican ideology that guided Madison. Standing armies and permanent military establishments were to be feared, not fostered. Madison was committed to the same republican principles Jefferson espoused—even though, in the heat of battle, that president had been more willing to compromise them.

* * *

That same basic restrained attitude had a certain virtue. It helped keep the president from exploiting the fissures within the American people that the war revealed. The nation was bitterly divided over the decision to go to war. The Federalists were every bit as hostile to Madison fighting the English as the Republicans had been to Adams going to battle with the French more than a decade before. But Madison, remembering the lessons of that earlier conflict, wanted no part of congressional grants of authority that would allow him to make criminals of his opponents at home. The sedition law, as he saw it, had been a stain on Adams and the nation. He thus resisted entreaties from Jefferson and even Supreme Court Justice Joseph Story to silence the war's critics, who at times seemed to be verging on treason in opposing the war. The former president had suggested tar and feathers; Justice Story, at least, was contemplating only prosecutions. Madison made clear—if only by refusing to respond—that he supported neither.

Madison's reticence did reflect prevailing sentiment about the importance of ensuring the president was restrained in his exercise of his powers. As aggressive as Story had been in urging Madison to counter his critics and show some strength, even he agreed Congress held the whip hand when it came to defining the bounds of wartime authority. The underlying declaration of war, Story explained, did not prevent Congress from shaping how those hostilities could be carried out. He made that clear from the bench in the most important Supreme Court decision addressing the scope of the president's power to conduct the war with England.

The case concerned a load of pine timber. A local official in New Bedford, Massachusetts, had seized the timber just as war was being declared. The wood was bound for London, possibly for use in assisting the enemy. The question the case presented—which the Supreme Court decided two years later, as the war was in its last throes—concerned the power of the president to seize the shipment as commander in chief.

In his decision for the Court, Chief Justice John Marshall made clear that Congress's declaration of war did not, in and of itself, shift title from all enemy property in the United States to American control. Instead, Marshall ruled, the declaration of war merely gave the American government the right to seize enemy property if it wished. The key question, therefore, concerned who spoke for the government in war. Marshall ruled that Congress did. For that reason, Marshall thought that the president could seize the timber only if Congress first passed a law expressly allowing him to do so. For without such a law, the president had no right to declare enemy property American, notwithstanding that the commander in chief was charged with winning a declared war.

Justice Story was, if anything, even more of a nationalist than Marshall. Jefferson had begged Madison not to put Story on the Court to fill the seat that came open just before the war began. Story was, Jefferson thought, too much of a "Tory" to be trusted. But a Tory's sympathies were not easy to predict when an American president was at war with England. That became clear in Story's dissenting opinion. Story did argue that the president could rely on the declaration of war to claim the timber. Story suggested that he was supportive of executive power. He also said that, even though the war declaration remained in place, Congress retained the right to tell the president "no" if it wished. In other words, even Story thought the final word remained with the legislature and not the commander in chief.

Story's notion was by no means idiosyncratic. It was, in fact, a widely held belief that Congress had the final word in war. And, not long after the war began, Madison seemed to honor that view in a difficult circumstance—and one that cut even closer to the core realm of military tactics.

* * *

The situation concerned Elijah Clark. He was an American who had made his way across the Canadian border to the United States. Clark was soon found lurking near an American military camp. His apparent aim was to report the American positions to the English forces in order to help the enemy with its planning. Clark was promptly convicted in a military court for his alleged misdeed. He was sentenced to be "hung by the neck until he be dead." But there was a question whether his status as an American citizen prevented the military from trying him. The matter was sent up to President Madison for further review.

Congress had made clear in the Articles of War that all persons not "citizens of or owing allegiance to the United States" could be convicted in military tribunals for spying. But Clark *was* an American citizen; he had been born in New Jersey. Madison thus decided Clark's residency in Canada did not suffice to give him, as the military court had ruled, a "temporary allegiance" to England. The president then ordered his War Secretary to inform the authorities of the need to remove the spy from military custody. The episode was but one of a number in which this same congressional limitation on the president's power forced the administration to undo what military commanders wished to do with suspected spies. Yet Congress refused to lift the restriction—even after an intense debate over its wisdom broke out while the war was being waged.

* * *

From the first debates over the ratification of the Constitution, the fear had been that a man of address and ambition would inevitably follow General Washington. Once the new framework for government was in place, it was said, the new president would prove impossible to control. Personally commanding his men in the field, proving his bravery, inspiring the loyalty of his troops, and emerging victorious, he would be unstoppable. An experiment in republican government would devolve into something resembling monarchy or worse.

But, as Madison's example showed, experience indicated otherwise. The nation had endured uprisings at home and a half-war with France. The United States was now engaged in a full war with England. And yet the ominous predictions about the man on horseback had not come true. Of course, there were allegations of monarchism with every new assertion of executive authority. But they were usually made even though the president was in fact acting only with the full backing of Congress.

Jefferson had come the closest of any chief executive to asserting a wartime power to trump Congress. But even he did not openly disagree with the Supreme Court's suggestion that, legally, an executive officer could go no further than a statute allowed—at least in a limited or partial war. Jefferson did argue that, in practice, an officer out in the field might act on his own in violation of the law—and that, if he did, he could appeal for forgiveness with some hope it might be given. Jefferson even suggested to his own commanding general that he would likely be sympathetic to such displays of unilateralism. But Jefferson did not contend that the president had a right to sanction, let alone to demand, such lawlessness in advance.

Even when Congress was away and a crisis was at his doorstep, Jefferson argued that the executive could take action without Congress's blessing only if the president believed the legislature would ratify such decisiveness when it returned. It was only after Jefferson had left office—and the full responsibilities of the presidency were no longer his to bear—that he had been willing to say clearly that a little lawbreaking might be necessary, even when Congress was in town and ready to entertain whatever legislative proposals the president might recommend. Even then, Jefferson took care to distance himself from that message. As difficult as compliance with legislative limits might have been, Jefferson feared that assertions of outright defiance could prove to be an even more perilous course.

But if one wanted even more conclusive evidence that Patrick Henry, George Mason, and the whole band of anti-Federalists had been wrong to predict the commander in chief would soon be beyond control, one needed only to look down the storm-beaten streets of the nation's ransacked capital on the morning of August 28, 1814. There, one could spot a smallish figure in the saddle of a horse, exhausted after riding nearly continuously since the first reports of the British advance on Washington, D.C., had reached him.

The man on horseback had come. But he was a slight-of-build sixty-three-year-old, and he had hardly come to conquer. Instead, President Madison found himself atop that horse on that street at that moment at the end of as horrible a stretch of days as any a commander in chief had yet endured—or ever would again.

* * *

That dreadful stretch of days began on the morning of August 24. After meeting with his war council, Madison rode with his attorney general, Richard Rush, from the capital to the edges of Bladensburg, Maryland. There they planned to lend direction to the volunteers and militiamen preparing for a crucial battle (should it come) with British forces. Those American troops, it was planned, would then make their way to the battlefield. That shift in location would position the troops to protect the capital from the massive British force that had finally set its sights on Washington.

Madison did not have a good feeling. Even upon setting out for Bladensburg, Madison was alarmed by the passivity of his secretary of war. Madison urged the secretary to be more forceful after the treasury secretary expressed dismay at the paltry advice his fellow cabinet member had offered during the final strategy session that had just concluded. Whatever warning signs Madison might have picked up, the true depth of the calamity that lay ahead sank in only later, when Madison finally reached the viewing point.

The president had positioned himself to take personal command of the troops in the field. No president had done so since Washington's stunning show of force in crushing the so-called Whiskey Rebellion. Then, in 1794, anger at a national tax on distilled spirits had provoked an uprising among western Pennsylvania's small farmers, whose livelihood depended upon the grain used for the now taxed whiskey. After the rebellion resulted in the torching of the tax administrator's home, President Washington, heeding the advice of his treasury secretary, Alexander Hamilton, sent more than twelve thousand troops in to quiet the rebellion. At the head of the massive force was Washington himself, atop his horse.

But Madison would not repeat that daring feat. Instead, upon reaching the destination, Madison realized how little he could profitably contribute to the fighting—and how desperate the military situation was.

With the shrieks of Congreve rockets shooting by, Madison "observed to the Secretary of War and Secretary of State that it would be proper to withdraw to a position in the rear . . . leaving military movements now to the military functionaries who were responsible for them." This the men did, and the attorney general, Richard Rush, soon joined them. And then, the president later recalled, "when it became manifest that the battle was lost," Madison and Attorney General Rush "fell down into the road leading to the city and returned to it."

In other words, the president joined in what was a tragic and full retreat. Madison hoped to make it back to Washington so he could reconnect with his beloved Dolley, who was waiting for him at the President's House. To outrun the British, she had famously begun packing up the home's treasured belongings while awaiting the commander in chief's return—gathering red curtains and silverware, securing state papers, and even ensuring that Gilbert Stuart's larger-than-life oil portrait of George Washington could be taken to a barn to prevent it from falling into the enemy's hands. But so complete was the British rout, and so fast the advance on the capital, that she had been forced to leave before Madison made it back. The president arrived at his "palace" only to find it empty. He took just enough time in his old quarters to enjoy a glass of wine and to remove the two dueling pistols he had been handed on his way to the front. Then he fled as well.

By the time the president returned to the scene days later, it was a gruesome one. The Executive Mansion had been pillaged and burned. The Capitol was a mass of charred rubble. The stench of "rotting carcasses" from animals killed during the fighting was overpowering. But amidst the destruction, Madison did his best to pull first his government, then his city, and finally his country, back together. And, by all accounts, he succeeded, with the help of a final battle in New Orleans that went America's way.

* * *

The War of 1812 had turned out to be the disaster that its opponents had predicted it would be. But the war would also be remembered, somehow, as the means by which the young nation discovered itself. It did so not with a dictator or a generalissimo, but with a distinctly American-style commander in chief—one both empowered and constrained by the Congress chosen by its people.

And yet, as Jefferson had suggested in his letter to Colvin, written back when Madison was still trying to put off the war with England, the Constitution's system of checks and balances was fragile. The notion that the commander in chief had power beyond the law—available whenever he thought necessity demanded—still lingered as a tantalizing (and terrifying) possibility. Madison did nothing to trumpet it, not even in private. But at war's end, he faced a controversy eerily reminiscent of Jefferson's involving General Wilkinson, and it, too, raised the specter of executive defiance.

The incident concerned Madison's own star general, Andrew Jackson. The forceful and daring Tennessean stood accused of acting lawlessly during the moment of America's greatest triumph in the War of 1812. In the Battle of New Orleans, the war's climactic one, U.S. forces under General Jackson's command had held off a strong British assault. By stopping the British there, the nation managed to secure a crucial victory not long after Washington, D.C., had burned. The Americans' unexpected success in New Orleans thus enabled the country to save face and claim a peace of which it could pretend to be proud.

But, in the same troublesome city where General Wilkinson had gone around the courts to snuff out Aaron Burr's supposed treason, Jackson, too, had taken liberties with the law. And, like Wilkinson, Jackson had defended his seeming lawlessness by saying necessity required that he take the law into his own hands.

In truth, Jackson had gone even further than Wilkinson. He had declared martial law outright, and he had done so with no legislative authorization. He had also extended the reach of martial law beyond the troops under his control. In sweeping fashion, Jackson had imposed martial law upon the city as a whole. Jackson then proceeded to defy not only the federal judge who tried to grant a writ of habeas corpus to one of the many men Jackson had captured but also to order and to carry out that same judge's arrest.

* * *

Upon learning of Jackson's shocking actions—including his refusal to suspend martial law even after the British had retreated to their ships— Madison was greatly troubled. The president did not, after Jefferson's fashion, send his general a secret missive approving his conduct. He did not hint to him that he understood that lawbreaking was inevitable, perhaps even warranted. Instead, the president insisted that an officer was duty bound to obey the law, no matter how intolerable its strictures might seem.

Madison used his new secretary of war, Alexander Dallas, to express to Jackson his "surprise" and "solicitude" at the reports of "certain acts of military opposition to the civil magistrate." These reports demanded "immediate attention," Dallas explained in a letter to Jackson, "not only in vindication of the just authority of the laws, but to rescue your own conduct from all unmerited reproach." Madison made sure his administration followed up when Jackson seemed unwilling to express contrition.

This new letter from Dallas, also sent at Madison's request, noted "the President would willingly abstain from any further remarks upon the subject, were he not apprehensive, that the principle of your example, and the reason for his silence, might be hereafter, misunderstood, or misrepresented." The letter went on to make clear that, in the president's view, "the military power is clearly defined, and carefully limitted [sic], by the Constitution and laws of the United States." And the letter explained that though "exigencies may sometimes arise," an "American Commander" needed to understand that if "he undertake to suspend the writ of Habeas Corpus, to restrain the Liberty of the Press, to inflict military punishments, upon citizens who are not military men, and generally to supersede the functions of the civil Magistrate," he was acting at his peril. For while a commander in the field "may be justified by the law of necessity, while he has the merit of saving his country, but he cannot resort to the established law of the land, for the means of vindication."

In short, Madison would not excuse Jackson after the federal judge he had imprisoned, Dominic Augustin Hall—the same judge whom Wilkinson had earlier defied—held Jackson in contempt. Jackson would instead be left to pay the thousand-dollar fine out of his own pocket.

* * *

As much as Madison tried to maintain a principled republican stand, the president would not press his case too firmly. Jackson was a war hero. He had done more than anyone to rally the nation after the first British attack on Washington, D.C. And so Madison said nothing in response when, at Dallas's request, Jackson finally accounted for his actions only by grudgingly forwarding to Washington, D.C., the same legal papers that he had already filed—without success—with Judge Hall. Jackson, in other words, gave no hint that he wished to make amends, and Madison gave no hint he wished to provoke a direct confrontation.

Jackson soon descended on Washington. He arrived as a beloved figure. Jackson was there chiefly to receive praise. He was also eager to make his case about his supposed lawlessness, confident that Madison would back down if the general forthrightly presented his defense of his actions in New Orleans.

The president did agree to receive the general. But he would not bless all that Jackson had done. Madison would only celebrate Jackson's recent victory. The president in this way left the more delicate matter of the sweeping show of military power for others to discuss. Still, the general felt good after leaving those meetings with Madison's underlings. Jackson would not be asked for "a further explanation," he reported afterward. There, the matter was left—a precedent of uncertain meaning, to be embraced or discarded in the face of the crises that would come in the years ahead.

6

ANTEBELLUM

"[A constitutional objection] so strange, so novel, and so important."

I n the forty years after General Washington first took command of the Continental Army, war had seemed to come to America in all its guises: uprisings, half-wars, battles at sea, skirmishes at home, and then, war in its fullest and against no less a power than England itself. But these conflicts produced little precedent to suggest the president—by dint of his title, commander in chief—enjoyed an exclusive, uncontrollable power to determine the conduct of war. The Constitution did not by terms secure it. The delegates to the Constitutional Convention did not seem to endorse it. Congress had passed laws—most especially in restricting naval movements during the Quasi War—that were predicated on the assumption that the Constitution was not intended to enshrine it. The Supreme Court issued rulings rejecting it. Presidents conducted themselves as if they did not have it.

Justice Joseph Story, writing one of the first great constitutional treatises, summed up the standard view as it stood by the century's third decade: Congress's war powers were "unlimited in every matter essential to its efficacy," including the "formation, direction, and support of the national forces." Story thought the Quasi War exemplary. It had been "regulated by the diverse acts of Congress, and of course [had been] confined to the limits prescribed by those acts."

But legal formalities aside, the idea that there was an executive prerogative "higher than law," and one that could justify executive action even though it was "against the law," had gained some ground. Or, at least, that idea had kept what ground it had always had. In fact, this prerogative had roots all the way back to John Locke, the English philosopher who greatly influenced the thinking of the American revolutionaries. That same prerogative had then been asserted in Jefferson's presidency, albeit against an easily mocked threat (posed by a power-mad and by then faintly ridiculous former vice president). Perhaps for that reason it had been advanced only in hushed tones. By the end of Madison's tenure, though, such a prerogative was associated, for the first time, with a powerful and popular man: General Andrew Jackson.

* * *

Jackson's example suggested that the executive wartime prerogative to go against the law that the legislature had laid down was a powerful one. His strong actions were widely thought to have been the means by which the country had defeated the most powerful nation on earth in New Orleans— and in a battle that ensured America's emergence as a worthy rival to its former master. Of course, one could also read that same precedent more narrowly. It was possible to think that Andrew Jackson's bold power grab was rooted in a limited claim about the legitimacy of imposing martial law on the home front in dire circumstances. But it was not obvious that those hailing Jackson as a hero were reading that precedent in that narrow way. Rather, his example seemed also to give new life to a broader notion: of an illimitable executive prerogative, one that would empower the president to do whatever he believed necessary to defeat the enemy, no matter what limits Congress had laid down.

If it was uncertain just what most people made of Jackson's triumph, it was at least clear that the intellectual journey from the first, more limited view of executive wartime prerogative to the second, much broader one was not long. After all, whatever powers to regulate the use of the armed forces in peacetime Congress might possess, "the obligation of the law," as another treatise of the era put it, is inevitably "lost in the succession of causes that prevent its operation, and the Constitution itself may be considered as thus superseding it." Necessity alone, then, might be the law in war. If so, the president need not fear punishment for doing what he believed victory demanded. Whatever he did to win would be lawful no matter what Congress's rules might be—just as Henry and Mason had predicted would inevitably prove to be the case.

* * *

Jackson's example ensured that earlier fears about the uncontrolled nature of executive war powers would not be quieted any time soon. In fact, those fears often popped up in succeeding decades thanks to Jackson himself. Each time Jackson seemed about to rise to the presidency, the old charges about his despotic ways returned. But Jackson repeatedly overcame them. And, of course, he did eventually become president, invigorating the office as never before.

Still, the thousand-dollar fine Judge Hall had imposed on Jackson—a fine President Madison had pointedly refused to excuse in any respect—was a rebuke that the hero of New Orleans never forgot. And so, three decades later, and while all but broke, the then ex-president pressed Congress to make amends. He wanted to be relieved of the obligation. The ploy touched off a thoroughly partisan debate that stretched on for nearly a year.

The debate was driven by an effort to discredit the newly ascendant, anti-executive political party, the Whigs, which had emerged as a real force in the upcoming presidential election. The Whigs fashioned themselves as opponents of the very kind of tyranny that the anti-Federalists had first predicted would flow from the creation of the American presidency. But the Whigs' true target was Andrew Jackson and all that his assertion of executive prerogative in New Orleans had seemed to bring about. And thus any effort to force the Whigs into the uncomfortable position of having to side with the British and to cast doubt on the heroics of Jackson at the end of the War of 1812 was attractive to the Democrats in Congress.

The partisan roots of that long-delayed public debate over Jackson's lawlessness in New Orleans did not, however, render it any less significant. The outcome of that debate would do more than impact the political struggle of the moment. It would potentially establish a key precedent for how executive war powers would be viewed going forward.

In the end, Jackson won his recompense—just before his death in 1845. He even recouped interest. But Jackson's victory was a cryptic one, as each pro-executive shift in the traditional balance of power in war had been to this point. The bill authorizing payment to Jackson did finally secure enough votes to pass. But the bill's supporters cobbled together their majority only after all characterizations of the goodness or badness of Jackson's actions in the field all those years ago had been stripped away from the final legislative language. Jackson would be paid, but he would not be fully absolved.

* * *

In the decade or so that followed, the power of the commander in chief to resist congressional efforts to check him became no clearer. Aside from the extended national debate over Jackson's misdeeds, there was, in these pre–Civil War years, little occasion for controversy over the relative powers of Congress and the commander in chief to determine the conduct of war. In fact, the issue came up only indirectly in connection with the actions of the remarkably assertive James Polk and his push for war in Mexico.

Congress had declared war at President Polk's insistence in 1846—after he had helped provoke the controversy by stationing American forces in the disputed territory north of the Rio Grande. Mexico claimed the positioning placed American forces on the wrong side of Texas's border with Mexico. The main war powers controversy at that time thus concerned this dispute about geography. Critics claimed the president had snookered the legislature into passing the declaration of war—by effectively invading Mexico and then claiming Mexico was actually the aggressor when it moved by force to reclaim its own land. There was little discussion of whether, in actually fighting that war, the president was free to do as he pleased or whether Congress could regulate him. The only issue seemed to be how quickly America could win it.

But the issue of whether Congress could limit the commander in chief's deployment of the troops did arise—briefly—not long after combat in Mexico had ceased. And the terms of the ensuing debate revealed how persistent the old notion of congressional control over the conduct of war remained.

During the hostilities, President Polk had diverted a regiment of riflemen to assist in his Mexican adventure. Incensed that, after the war's end, Polk had sent those returning troops to California rather than back to Oregon where Congress had first wished them to serve, the delegate from the Oregon Territory moved for a resolution. Since the troops had been raised to protect his own residents from attacks by Native American tribes, the Oregon delegate argued, Congress should pass a measure to force Polk to send the forces back there.

In the fight that followed on the House floor, one member challenged Congress's right to do so. The congressman claimed the legislature could not direct the executive's movement of troops under his command. He was soon overwhelmed by a tide of opposition. One opponent said the constitutional objection was "so strange, so novel, and so important" it could not be left unaddressed. Another added that control of the army "is altogether in the executive" but only "when legislation has done with it."

* * *

The measure passed. And there the debate seemed to come to rest as of the late 1850s. Until, that is, a different kind of war—the worst kind, really—started to come into view. With the specter of civil war real for the first time in the nation's history, the old assumptions about the relationship between Congress and the commander in chief were challenged anew. The strict vision of congressional control that had been dominant since Washington first took command would inform the actions of those called on to manage the new controversy. But that same understanding would also come under severe pressure. The union was on the verge of breaking apart. The appeal to necessity would naturally gain new adherents. And so the old debate about the need for, and the danger of, uncontrollable executive war powers was about to take a new turn. Especially since this war, if it were to come at all, would be fought at home, between brothers, and with the nation's very survival at stake.

Part 2

CIVIL WAR AND
ITS AFTERMATH

7

CONFRONTING SECESSION

"The President cannot accomplish a legal purpose by illegal means, or break the laws themselves to prevent them from being violated."

A ging, infirm, and hugely overweight, General Winfield Scott was a hero of the Mexican War. He was also, by the fall of 1860, the commanding general of the nation's army and thus not a man easily dismissed. His "views" on the subject of secession were bound to cause a sensation when news of their contents leaked. Especially given what he had to say.

Scott sent those views directly to President James Buchanan, albeit with a barely disguised eye on a wider audience. In fact, it was probably Scott's own loose talk that caused word of his thoughts about the coming crisis to hit the papers soon after they arrived on Buchanan's desk. (General Scott published them in January—with no notice to Buchanan—in the *Daily National Intelligencer.*)

The president was not pleased by what he read. Buchanan was an arrogant man—in part because he was as prepared for leadership as anyone who had ever held the office of the presidency. A former secretary of state and member of Congress, he had been raised in modest circumstances—a true log cabin in rural Pennsylvania. He was now fond of frocks and raised collars. His cabinet called him "the Old Squire" behind his back. It was a dig at his imperious manner and inflexible cast of mind.

But whatever breach of protocol was involved in General Scott's actions—including the fact he had chosen to bypass the secretary of war to get the attention of the commander in chief—the import of what Scott was saying was hard to deny. He was calling out the administration for being weak. His writings made clear that he believed secession was inevitable. So, too, he thought, was an attack on a southern fort. And yet, Buchanan and his men, from all Scott could see, were doing nothing. The most vulnerable federal military installations, whether in Florida or South Carolina, remained essentially abandoned. If anything, Scott concluded, Buchanan and his team seemed to be doing their best to keep those crucial defenses exposed.

Scott was warning the president, and he was doing so publicly. Buchanan's dithering—if not intentionally aimed at undermining the union—must end. The president needed to wrestle (*now!*) with the vexing questions of executive power that secession would inevitably present.

Those questions would be as difficult as any a president had faced in the half-century since the nation had gone to war with Europe's greatest powers, first France and then England. The president found Scott's musings distasteful. He dismissed them as unfocused, scattershot, evidencing no real plan, and, above all, dangerous. Buchanan was sure news of Scott's views would convince the most committed secessionists to strike quickly. But Scott's musings still made a point. The plan for handling an attack on a fort—and the efforts that might need to be taken in order to deter such an assault—could not be put off forever. Even if some means of forging a compromise with the South could be found, as Buchanan vainly hoped, a prudent president still needed to prepare for the worst. If he didn't, he might soon find the union dissolving before his eyes.

In time, President Buchanan realized that he did need answers to the key questions. Was secession lawful? If it wasn't, what kind of force, if any, could he use to stave it off or respond once it occurred? The answers the president eventually gave to such questions pleased almost no one. As provocative as the aggressive nature of the answers seemed to southerners, those same answers proved positively toxic in the North because of their apparent timidity. In that region, Buchanan was roundly excoriated for his unwillingness to thwart secession by unleashing the powers of the commander in chief. Surely, it was thought, a leader who wished to suppress the rebellion could.

Buchanan's seeming weakness during the crucial period between Abraham Lincoln's election in November and his inauguration in March became the object of ridicule and worse as the years passed. But, as much as Buchanan's tenure ended in failure, more than fear or arid legalism—let alone treachery—explained his limited view of his own power.

Buchanan believed, at least by the end, that he was serving the unionist cause in exercising the restraint that he thought Congress had required of him. He was also determined not to yield to those inside Congress and out who were pressing, with ever-greater vehemence, for action, the law be damned. Buchanan thought—or at least willed himself to think—that a great constitutional principle, even the separation of powers itself, was at stake in his decision not to use force without clearer evidence that Congress wanted him to do so. He believed Congress had not given such permission, and he refused to draw on General Andrew Jackson's famous example from New Orleans to bypass those limits that he believed restricted what he could do. He had, in other words, convinced himself that a commitment to principle explained his tolerance for the rebellion. Buchanan would not accede to what even General Scott would later call, in condemning the use of martial law in New Orleans, "the tyrant's plea—necessity."

* * *

The architect of President Buchanan's restrained legal approach was Jeremiah S. Black, his attorney general. Buchanan's junior by two decades, Black enjoyed a deep bond with his boss. Their ties grew from their shared Pennsylvania heritage. Their loyalty to one another was also rooted in mutual respect.

Black believed Buchanan was as fine a lawyer as he had ever known. Black was convinced the president would have been one of the great justices of the Supreme Court had his life taken a different course. Buchanan held his protégé in equally high esteem. Black's formal schooling had ended at the age of sixteen, but law and legal argument came to him naturally. He had served as chief justice of the Pennsylvania Supreme Court. Black's colleagues in the Buchanan administration referred to him simply as "Judge Black." As a measure of the president's respect, Buchanan nominated Black to the Supreme Court of the United States in the waning weeks of his presidential term. Black's chance to serve on the Court died, though, when Abraham Lincoln and the Republicans moved into the Executive Mansion that March.

Black's friends remembered him as a kindly, even sweet man. "Rumpled" and "ungainly," he was a renowned and charming talker. Conversation was said to be his "intoxicant." He also could be an imposing presence. He had thick, dark eyebrows and gray, wise eyes. He was at root a man of principle—albeit on behalf of a course of action that flouted the principle of equality. He seemed to love the law more than anything—even if the law was at odds with justice. He also had a spine of steel when he believed he was right.

In his constitutional thinking, Black was gifted but traditional—some would say wooden. He was sympathetic to the South and tolerant of slavery. He had no complaint with the established order—and the racism on which it rested. He was like Buchanan in that regard. Those views, as well as his own jurisprudential outlook, led him to have little tolerance for the appeals to higher law then popular among slavery's most fervent opponents. The abolitionists had developed these arguments to cope with the Constitution's sanction of the evil institution—"a covenant with death and an agreement with Hell," as one of them famously called the document Black revered, notwithstanding its acceptance of slavery as a lawful and protected institution. Arguments that placed the need for action, however just, above the law ran counter to everything Black believed, or so Black contended.

*, * *

As much as Black feared the "absolute despotism" he associated with appeals to higher law—a position that neatly skipped over the absolute despotism slavery made a tangible reality for millions—he was hardly reluctant to protect the executive's prerogatives when he believed Congress had gone too far. It was a pro-executive constitutional view that, in the run-up to the secession crisis in the summer of 1860, the attorney general made perfectly clear to one of President Buchanan's leading army officers. And, in setting forth that robust view of the commander in chief's powers of superintendence, Black helped the president avoid a jam that, given the rumblings of disunion, potentially spelled real trouble for Buchanan.

The dispute concerned Captain Montgomery Meigs. For some years, Meigs had been in charge of two of the most important public-works projects in the country: the construction of the Washington, D.C., aqueduct and the renovation of the Capitol Building. That latter project involved constructing two new wings to add to the main legislative chamber and refitting the great dome that remains its signature. But Meigs's combination of rigidity and vanity, unleavened by the least glimmer of humor, caused problems. It also led him to clash repeatedly with John Floyd, the newly appointed secretary of war. President Buchanan had brought Floyd into his administration largely for his southern connections, as Floyd was the recently retired governor of Virginia.

With Floyd trying to strip Meigs of authority, the irrepressible Meigs soon began lobbying Congress for protection. Meigs seemed to get the job security he sought by convincing his supporters in Congress to pass a bill. The proposed bill provided the funds that would be needed to complete the aqueduct. But the bill also expressly named Meigs the project's supervisor. The new law, if enacted, seemed sure to protect Meigs from Floyd's—and thus Buchanan's—efforts to oust him. Buchanan could not easily veto the measure. It came wrapped in a larger bill that the president needed to sign. But the president could give notice he reserved the right, as commander in chief, to transfer Meigs, a subordinate army soldier, no matter what the statute seemed to say. That is exactly what Buchanan did in late June.

Signaling his intention to act on his own power, Buchanan issued one of the nation's first signing statements, a presidential message that he appended to the bill. The statement set forth Buchanan's constitutional

concerns with the protection the new legislation gave to Meigs. The statement also announced Buchanan's intention to disregard the law—or, at
least, to read its text in ways he knew Congress could not have intended—
and thus to remove Meigs from his post. Buchanan's statement explained
that, if the president did not assert his right as commander in chief to
force Meigs into whatever new military posting the president chose, then
Congress "might upon the same principle annex to an appropriation to
carry on a war a condition requiring it not to be used for the defense of the
country unless a particular person of its own selection should command
the Army."

* * *

Secretary Floyd, who seemed more interested in directing lucrative contracts to his friends than in ensuring the public-works project's competent
completion, took full advantage of the opening that Buchanan's statement
provided. Floyd ordered Meigs removed from his present assignment.
Meigs did not go quietly. He took his case straight to Buchanan. Meigs informed the president that the recently passed appropriations law rendered
the secretary's removal order illegal. A furious Buchanan turned to Black
for advice. He wanted a legal opinion about whether Meigs could be removed, and he wanted it soon. The attorney general promptly issued one.
It blasted Meigs's insubordination and affirmed the president's authority,
as commander in chief, to assign his soldiers as he pleased, regardless of
what Congress had said.

Floyd dispensed with Meigs in October. The secretary even sent one
of his men to deliver the orders dispatching Captain Meigs—forthwith—
to a remote fort in Florida. The instructions pointedly provided no date
for Meigs's return. Buchanan was pleased with the outcome. He had worried that Floyd might resign from the cabinet if the Meigs affair dragged
on much longer. With secession sentiment growing, Buchanan badly
needed the staunch Virginian to assist in efforts to convince the leaders of
the South that they could tolerate Buchanan's administration. With Meigs
now out of the way, Buchanan could relax a bit. It seemed more likely
Floyd would continue serving.

But the Meigs matter was trivial compared to the war powers issue that Buchanan would ask Black to resolve the very next month. Its outcome, too, turned on the relative powers of Congress and the commander in chief to control the army. And, before long, with the specter of secession looming, the dispute would also involve, as with the Meigs matter, Secretary Floyd. This time, though, the stakes were immeasurably higher. They involved something more important than the president's right to make peacetime military assignments. The new matter concerned how and when the commander in chief might order the use of military force against rebellious citizens. And in this controversy, Black and Floyd would no longer be allies. Instead, they would find themselves on opposite sides—with neither man knowing which one their president was likely to favor.

* * *

By the late fall of 1860, all but the most rosy-eyed analysts realized General Winfield Scott had been right. A state was going to secede. A fort was going to be taken. Buchanan would have to decide what he should do— what he *could* do. For months, Buchanan had put off that question. But the delay in confronting the issue was becoming untenable.

Still, no resolution was readily apparent. Looking back, the constitutional process that the president was required to follow had seemed positively clear when first France, and then England, had threatened the United States. In those earlier crises, it seemed obvious to the executives then in charge that the president needed to go to Congress if he wished to use military force. Otherwise, peacetime authorities alone would have to suffice. And that is what presidents had done. Of course, when Congress was in recess and an invasion was imminent, Jefferson had indicated the Constitution must be read to permit a freer executive hand. The legislature would be unable to perform its assigned constitutional role. But, aside from that exception, and the ambiguous example of the action taken in response to the Barbary pirates, Jefferson and Adams—and, for that matter, Madison, too—had seemed content to let Congress choose whether to use armed force. Of equal import, those presidents also seemed to believe

Congress could decide whether to give such authority to the executive only in bits and pieces or, instead, all at once.

But there was no similar rulebook for responding to the threat that the South's secession posed. Secession did not involve a classic military conflict. The nation did not face a war with a foreign power. The constitutional machinery for declaring war, therefore, was not necessarily applicable.

Instead, at best, there were only vague clues as to how a president should proceed when faced with a region of the country bent on leaving the union and taking federal forts. The best clues could be found in two old statutes, one passed in 1795 and the other in 1807. But, far from giving clear guidance to Buchanan, those two federal laws only served to make the choice that he faced more difficult. The two statutes were written in general terms. The legal ambiguity made it quite unclear whether, for a president intent on following Congress's wishes, the proper course was action or inaction.

Though jealous of its right to declare war, Congress had, through those two laws, given the commander in chief a free-standing right to decide whether and when to use force. But that unusual grant of up-front power applied only in circumstances that were, in their nature, not easily defined. The measures allowed the president, under certain conditions, to call up militiamen or regulars without going to Congress for specific, advance permission. In such cases, the president needed only to decide that such force was necessary to enforce the nation's laws, suppress an insurrection, or repel an invasion. Those grants of power thus suggested the president might be confronting secession with Congress on board for him to use military force to hold the union together. On this reading of Congress's statutes, a decision by Buchanan to use force to keep the nation whole would be an execution of Congress's broad delegation of power to him and not an act of unilateral aggression.

At the same time, those two statutes were hardly clear about how they should be applied to the unusual crisis Buchanan now faced. Were they triggered when a state announced it was seceding? Only after a state (or some of its citizens) attacked a federal military post or resisted a federal court order? Or was the better view that Congress passed those laws to protect states from foreign or private threats, not to empower the president to make war on the states themselves?

* * *

There were hazards on all sides of these questions. Southern diehards were sure to cry "despotism" at the least hint of federal coercion of a seceding state. Their outrage might provoke sympathetic unionists in the Deep South—or along the border—to shift allegiance. A more cautious conclusion by the president, however, was no safer. Weakness might also encourage secessionists by emboldening them. Even if caution did not have that effect, it was sure to invite scorn from Republicans eager for the president to take on the secessionists. The Republicans were already convinced that Buchanan, along with the traitors (Floyd chief among them) allegedly serving in his cabinet, was secretly engineering the union's breakup in service of southern slaveholders. A refusal to assert the powers Congress had arguably given the president could thus itself seem like an act of defiance—and one rooted in disloyalty to the very government Buchanan headed.

Buchanan was conflicted at his core. He had strongly defended the Supreme Court's recent and notorious *Dred Scott* decision. He had done so despite the Court's absolutist language in that case denying the right of all those in bondage ever to count as citizens under the Constitution. And Buchanan had done so even though Chief Justice Roger Taney's opinion for the Court had declared unconstitutional the Missouri Compromise, which Congress had forged decades before to preclude slavery in the new territories. The Court had reached well beyond the confines of the case before it and upended what had seemed like a potentially enduring mechanism for keeping the slavery question from triggering a true sectional split. Buchanan, though, was convinced that the earlier compromise was incapable of keeping the nation whole. He thus believed, wrongly, that the Court's decision might bring harmony to the nation precisely because it was so bold. Buchanan thought the Court was establishing a much-needed, clear rule about slavery's legitimacy, once and for all. And Buchanan believed the people, committed legalists that he thought them to be, would reconcile themselves to the Court's announcement of what the law was—no matter how manifestly unjust some might think it was. In fact, Buchanan was so certain that the Court's ruling would provide resolution that he even made reference to the Supreme Court's impending settlement in his inaugural address, which preceded the Court's opinion by just a couple of days.

* * *

The president's reluctance to act swiftly and confidently against the South also owed to something else. Buchanan was certain the North was to blame for the impending crisis. In particular, he blamed the opponents of slavery. If they had been willing to let well enough alone—and to concede that territories could permit slavery—Buchanan believed there would have been no threat to the union. Instead, though, the president thought slavery's opponents had done everything to antagonize the South. They had even challenged the grounds for truce that the Supreme Court had set forth in the *Dred Scott* ruling.

Of course, a sweeping decision legitimating slavery for all time could only look like a truce for one with Buchanan's biases. His racism led him to tolerate that institution and to admire the white southern way of life. Those biases caused the president to lean toward a policy of extreme restraint and accommodation toward the secessionists. Inclining him further in that direction was something more abstract: an aversion to what he thought was a creeping defense of lawlessness, a willingness on the part of the abolitionist wing of the Republican Party to appeal to a higher law, to necessity, to anything but the positive law itself. It was a convenient concern to express for one who was partial to the South and at peace with slavery. But to Buchanan and those who thought like him, the defense of higher law did not sound like a call to freedom. Such appeals sounded like a defense of the savage brutality of John Brown and his band of abolitionists in their deadly raid on the federal arsenal at Harper's Ferry in 1859. In that raid, Brown and his men had sought to foment an antislavery uprising. Hence the danger in giving in to claims of a higher law—a law premised only on what those who marched under its banner determined to be the demand of necessity. To give in to that was to give in to the destruction of the rule of law.

Actually, though, Buchanan's thought processes were more complicated still. John Brown's raid on the federal arsenal at Harper's Ferry—and the president's unflinching decision to use military force to crush it—showed that Buchanan might actually be more willing to take on the secessionists than a quick scan of his political and ideological orientation might have suggested. Whatever his sympathies, the president of the United States was the commander in chief. In that role, Buchanan believed he was duty bound to ensure the execution of federal law. His decision to call in the troops to counter John Brown's attack on the federal arsenal at Harper's Ferry showed he might take that obligation quite seriously.

Thus, as much as Buchanan viewed the South as the aggrieved party—and as deaf as he was to the abolitionist argument—there was a chance that Buchanan might have as little tolerance for defiance when practiced by the slave states with which he sympathized as when practiced by the antislavery activists he loathed. Congress had authorized the president to use force to put down insurrections and enforce the nation's laws. In using that power to counter the secessionists, Buchanan would hardly be acting on a tyrannical claim of necessity. He might merely be doing what Congress had empowered him to do.

* * *

That November, on the day after Abraham Lincoln became president-elect, the first southern senator resigned. In response, Buchanan quickly pulled Black aside. Scott's prediction of a breakup was now coming true. The president wanted to know whether Black agreed with General Scott and his unusual views about when secession might be permissible. Did states have a legal right to secede? he asked.

Black quickly told Buchanan, "No." The union was, by its nature, "per-petual." Revolution, of course, was the right of every person; Americans knew that better than any people on the globe. But the Constitution was not a contract states could break.

Buchanan at least had that answer. With each day, though, the se-cession crisis only deepened. Buchanan would have to decide more than whether states had the right to leave. He would have to decide what *he* could do if they did. And he would have to make that position known.

If Buchanan disclaimed the power to combat secession, that would no doubt contribute to doubts about whether such power resided in the office. The president's public statement of his views about the scope of his own power, therefore, would help determine—even if no one knew exactly how—the decisions hard-core anti-unionists, as well their more loyal neighbors, would make. Or, at least, there was a good chance such executive statements might have that impact, either by inducing the se-cessionists to act quickly or by causing them to step back from the brink. And even if the traitors' calculations were immune to presidential influ-ence, Buchanan still needed to go on the record soon. Otherwise, his si-lence would be taken as acceptance of whatever treason might develop. Buchanan then would lose whatever credibility he still had with those el-ements of the country that had just elected Lincoln.

* * *

At a cabinet meeting on November 9, Buchanan laid out a plan for a compromise. It involved a proposed amendment to the Constitution that would further entrench slavery. The compromise also contemplated a program of conciliation that, absurdly, ran against the very platform on which Lincoln had just run and won.

Buchanan clung to the hope that he could broker a deal. He also heard vigorous debate from his cabinet about what he should do. Jeremiah Black argued forcefully, as Scott already had—and as even the now-exiled Montgomery Meigs did when he finally reached his new duty station in Florida—that reinforcements should be sent to the southern forts imme-diately. They should be sent especially to Charleston harbor. Black even said at one point—rebuking Secretary Floyd—that no man should serve in the federal government who believed those forts should be handed over to the secessionists.

In the days that followed, Secretary of War Floyd seemed to dawdle in putting in place the plan to reinforce those forts. Black thought Buchanan had already endorsed the plan. He could not understand why Floyd seemed to be doing nothing in response. But Buchanan eventually told Black to back off from pestering him about Floyd's recalcitrance. The president explained to Black that he was "annoyed" by his "interference in the business of another Department." Buchanan instructed Black to advise only about the extent of the president's legal power as commander in chief.

Chastened, Black met with the president. He wanted to hammer out the critical legal questions that needed to be resolved. Black wrote them out for the president's inspection. He even asked Buchanan to sign the back side of the sheet of paper on which those questions were written. Black wanted to avoid confusion. He also wanted to be clear the president had asked for the legal opinion that he was about to write. Black knew that opinion would define his reputation.

* * *

With the legal questions at last in hand—five in all—Black went to work. In a scant three days, he was done. The answers were set forth in probably the most consequential legal opinion an attorney general had ever been asked to give.

Black explained in his opinion that there was no higher law. The power of the commander in chief, he wrote, "is to be used only in the manner prescribed by the legislative department. [T]he President cannot accomplish a legal purpose by an illegal means, or break the laws themselves to prevent them from being violated." The two older statutes—the one empowering the president to call up the militia to deal with certain crises, the other allowing him to use regulars whenever the militia could be employed—set the bounds of Buchanan's power.

Black then explained how those two laws applied to the crisis at hand. They were, Black argued, much narrower than many in the North wished they were. Even though a state had no legal right to secede, Black concluded, a declaration of secession was not a declaration of war. It was an expression of defiance, with no legal force or effect under federal law. It should be met, therefore, with the continued enforcement of federal law.

Customs duties should be collected in seceding states. The federal property located there should be protected from attack. Black knew that might mean federal officers would meet resistance. A marshal's attempt to enforce a federal judge's order to pay a customs duty could be impeded by local officers. A federal fort might be assaulted. If so, Black ruled, federal military power could certainly be used consistent with the laws Congress had passed. In that event, force might be needed to ensure the execution of the laws. But, consistent with the limits set forth in the statutes, the president could direct force only against the individuals who actually impeded the execution of those laws or threatened the federal government's hold on such property. The president could not bombard the state legislature just because it had passed an ordinance of secession. States as states, in other words, could not, consistent with Congress's directions, be "coerced" into staying in the union. Congress had not conferred such power—and it was doubtful Congress even could.

Buchanan, thanks to Black, was heading into the secession winter with at least one arm—and maybe both—restrained. The president, if the attorney general was right, had no power to call up the additional forces that he might need unless Congress decided to give them. Those forces the president did command could be used—thanks to the limited nature of the Militia Act and the Insurrection Act, as Black interpreted each—only to enforce orders no federal judge was likely to be in office to issue and no federal marshal was likely to be around to execute. Once a state seceded, federal officers in that state would surely resign. They were southerners in their own right. There would be no civil enforcement of federal law to disrupt.

* * *

The criticism of Black's opinion was brutal. Senator William Seward—by then rumored for a post in Lincoln's cabinet—quipped that the administration's view was that "it is the duty of the president to execute the law—unless somebody opposes him—and that no state has the right to go out of the union—unless it wants to." That basic, mocking characterization was widely shared. Black had informed the president that secession was unlawful, it was said, but so, too, was any attempt to stop it.

Days after handing his opinion to Buchanan, Black told a friend he was proud that he "once seemed to have some portion of the public confidence." But, he knew that, by actually exercising the power conferred by that trust, his reputation would surely suffer. "It will give me far more pride for the balance of my life to remember," he explained, "that I risked and lost it in a faithful support of principles which sooner or later will be acknowledged as necessary for the preservation of the noblest political system that the world ever saw."

Even still, decades later, sitting in an easy chair on the porch of his Pennsylvania estate, looking out on the endless green fields stretched before him, Black felt terribly misunderstood. He was a wealthy man by then—one of the great lawyers the nation had produced. But he could not shake the unrelenting criticism, whether it came from Republican senators, fellow cabinet members, or even the former president of the Confederate States of America, Jefferson Davis. Each went after Black in print in the decades after the war.

There was nothing in his legal analysis that Black actually regretted. He thought not a word of the critics had come to grips with the actual legal points he had made in his opinion on secession. He noted that not even Lincoln actually questioned the conclusions—as shown by Lincoln's own cautiousness in the run-up to taking office and in the weeks before Fort Sumter came under fire. Only by willfully misreading—or by sloppily glossing over the difficult points—could one conclude that the president had a freer hand than Black had advised.

* * *

But, on reflection, Black conceded, he had made one crucial error.

Buchanan had asked Black a key question in their first conversation about the legality of secession. The president had wanted to know at that

time whether the administration should announce its position with regard to the force it could use to counter secession in a stand-alone proclamation or whether the administration should set forth its position in the
annual message Buchanan was supposed to give Congress in early December. Black answered hastily—too hastily, he thought, in retrospect—
and suggested the annual message was the better vehicle.

Looking back, Black thought he should have guessed that the president's annual message to Congress would ramble on. He should have
told Buchanan to issue a simple and forceful stand-alone proclamation
and to keep that statement separate from the more general congressional message. That approach would have made it possible for Buchanan
to announce in stark terms that the administration believed secession
was illegal. It might also have avoided the trouble that came from saying the federal government was barred from "coercing" states. In fact,
Black had, unsuccessfully, tried to get the president to remove that dread
word "coerce" from his official message. He knew it bore a legal meaning
that, however accurate, was sure to cause great political mischief if used
more loosely. The bar on "coercing" sounded like a requirement that the
president do no more than cajole the states into refraining from seizing
federal property. But Black did not tell Buchanan how to roll out the
administration's legal position. The clear and powerful demonstration
of resolve that Black thought preferable had been lost in a fog of technical legal points and ham-handed political slogans that cluttered the
rambling congressional message Buchanan actually sent. The president's
windy statement failed. It missed the chance, Black thought, to "have
stated conclusions so powerfully as possibly to have stayed the madness
of secession."

By the time Black signed off on the annual message, it was too late
for him to change the record. The secretary of state had given a copy of
Black's written legal opinion to the press right before the president delivered the official message to Congress that drew upon Black's legal reasoning. Thus, all of the rhetorical failings of that presidential message—its
seeming tolerace for the seceding states and its focus on the president's
lack of power—seemed traceable to Black and the legal advice he had

given to Buchanan. Black was the one—his opinion seemed to show—who had ruled out "coercion." His behind-the-scenes efforts to protect the forts, just like his consistent view that secession was illegal, counted for little. Black was, for many, the man behind Buchanan's treason.

* * *

As December drew to a close, the unfairness of that judgment became clearer. Black had always viewed the secession crisis through the lens of law more than statecraft. He was convinced the president was duty bound to ensure the federal government defended what it possessed. Even if the federal government could do no more than defend its possessions, it at least could do that. There was no more to it than that. That simple legal conviction pointed Black in the right direction.

The crucial test came near Christmas. South Carolina left the union on December 20. It was the first state to do so officially. A Kentucky-born federal army officer had been sent to protect the harbor in Charleston. The officer, Major Robert Anderson, was hunkered down in Fort Moultrie. Major Anderson sat just a mile across the way from the near empty Fort Sumter. Anderson was certain he could better hold the line if he could somehow make it to Sumter. But even ordinary efforts to resupply federal forts in the South—with a few arms or men—were, in that hothouse environment, provocative.

That was especially true in South Carolina, the epicenter of the drama. It was one thing to keep things as they were—with both Forts Moultrie and Sumter exposed to assault by whatever forces South Carolina's governor might deploy. It was another to improve the federal government's defenses by reinforcing Fort Sumter. That would surely be viewed in the South as a sign that the national government intended to do the very thing Black's opinion had seemed to rule out: "coerce" South Carolina into staying in the union.

For Black, the notion that a federal army officer could not choose the best defensive position to protect a federal fort was absurd. Black also thought such a notion undermined the constitutional design. South Carolina had no legal right to secede; Black's opinion in November made that clear. In Black's view, therefore, the state had no cause for complaint if Anderson moved from one federal fort to another. South Carolina had no rights over either installation.

The standoff continued for days. Then, under cover of night, on December 26, Major Anderson—on the basis only of his own judgment—made his daring journey across the harbor. Buchanan learned the news of Anderson's trip to Fort Sumter from the commissioners South Carolina had sent to the Executive Mansion to negotiate the terms of the state's separation. The president was horrified—and unprepared. He tried to keep his counsel. He pushed back against the commissioners' accusation that Anderson's alleged maneuver was performed at Buchanan's behest, and thus that the president's supposed promises to maintain the status quo had all been lies. Buchanan assured the commissioners the major must have been acting on his own discretion. But Buchanan refused to order Anderson's retreat or to condemn what Anderson had reportedly done. The president needed to know more. He would take it up with his cabinet.

* * *

The cabinet meeting that followed was tense. It lasted well into the evening. Secretary Floyd insisted that Anderson had disregarded his orders. Black knew better. The verbal instructions to Anderson had been issued two weeks before, but Black recalled that the War Department had memorialized them. In the midst of a shouting match with Floyd, Black asked for the memo setting forth the written orders to be brought to the cabinet meeting so they could be read.

The memo showed Anderson had the right to make such a move not only when attacked, but "whenever you have tangible evidence of a design to proceed to a hostile act." The record further showed that both the secretary and the president had approved the orders. Buchanan had even asked for a modest change before finalizing them. The president had wanted to make clear Anderson was not obliged to fight to "the last extremity." In addition, Black—ever the careful lawyer—had insisted that a final version of the orders be confirmed in a written message to Anderson. Black had then drafted the final orders that reached Anderson just days before his bold maneuver in Charleston. The instructions confirmed the major's "discretion" to carry out his basic obligation to "hold the possession of the *forts* in Charleston Harbor." Black had no doubt about the meaning of those words—and especially the significance of the use of the plural "forts." "Whether the president intended that the orders to Major Anderson should be so framed as to give him the right to move into Sumter I cannot say," Black later recalled. "But when I wrote the order, such was my intention, and I have no excuses to offer for that act."

In the face of such evidence, Buchanan had no choice but to agree that Anderson, acting on his own view of how best to defend the forts, committed no breach. It was less clear whether Buchanan would allow Anderson to stay at Sumter. Secretary Floyd, for his part, was convinced that Anderson must go.

When the president read the cabinet his proposed response to the commissioners, Black was crestfallen. The draft response implied the president would "negotiate" with the South Carolina commissioners—as if they were representatives of an independent nation. In Black's view, the proposed presidential message was far too accommodating. The draft response did not firmly state that Fort Sumter would be held. It also did not adhere to the basic principles Black had set forth in November about the president's legal power to counter seceding states.

* * *

While walking through the Executive Mansion with a fellow cabinet member days before, Black had suggested that, in regards to the president's team, he did not "see how we are to hold together." The divisions in the wake of the dramatic events in Charleston were too sharp. He guessed there must soon be "a general breaking up" of the cabinet. But, upon hearing how Buchanan proposed to respond to the South's concern about what Anderson had done, Black, by then secretary of state, resolved to resign.

Upon hearing the rumor of Black's impending exit, the president summoned Black to the Executive Mansion. Buchanan begged Black to stay. Too many cabinet officers had already fled. Another loss would be devastating. Black was the last man remaining in the cabinet whom the president could truly trust. Black knew how hard it would be to abandon his mentor. Still, he was prepared to resist Buchanan's efforts to convince him to stay. Black had determined that he could not remain in the administration without sacrificing his principles regarding the supremacy of the union.

Black was spared making a decision on the spot. The president—mercifully—gave him an out. Buchanan told Black he had until 6:00 P.M. to submit proposed changes to the president's draft response to the commissioners. Black rushed to the attorney general's office. It was by then occupied by his former assistant, and Lincoln's future secretary of war, Edwin Stanton. Black furiously wrote out his objections for Stanton to copy, and the memo then made its way to the president.

Confronted with Black's critique, Buchanan relented. The president's new version dropped all the troublesome points. There would be no negotiation with the commissioners. Anderson would remain in Sumter. South Carolina would have to remove him by force. Black would stay to the end.

* * *

Days after the critical cabinet meeting, Secretary Floyd announced his resignation. Black, in contrast, received fan mail from those who read of his brave defense of Major Anderson and of the "manly courage" he had displayed on behalf of the union. The pro-union faction of the cabinet was now firmly in control.

When, near New Year's Day, the customs collector in Charleston resigned, the president nominated a new one—and the nomination landed as a "thunderbolt" in the Senate. As a backup, Buchanan sought legislation to give him greater flexibility to collect the revenues at a place outside the secessionist government's control. That way, without usurping powers that Congress had not given, the supremacy of federal power—and the collection of the customs duties that fueled its operations—could be maintained. It was just the approach Black favored.

But neither the nomination of the customs collector, nor the revamped customs collection measure, gained traction. Nor did a bill to give Buchanan greater authority to call up regular troops and receive volunteers. The proposals died amidst a flurry of charges and countercharges about whether the grants of power would make Buchanan a "dictator."

Meanwhile, Buchanan continued to temporize. He refused to retaliate when a steamer sent to supply Anderson was turned away under fire. But, there were some hopeful signs for those looking for more aggression from the executive. With a new man in charge of the War Department, the administration's drift toward a more aggressive posture was evident. Montgomery Meigs was even called back from Florida to receive a gracious welcome in the capital in February. The new war secretary met with Meigs and thanked him for his letters from Florida, where Meigs had been stationed at the remote and near empty Fort Jefferson. The letters that Meigs sent from that distant locale had offered early warnings about the need to defend not only that fort but also other southern ones as well. The letters had thus helped to unmask Secretary Floyd's misleading accounts of the minimal risk that the South would seize them, the new war secretary told Meigs. In fact, the war secretary explained, the reinforcements Meigs had requested in those letters had recently been sent to his former fort.

* * *

Back in Washington, Meigs attended a reception at the Executive Mansion. There, he encountered Buchanan for the first time in months. True to form, the haughty captain cuttingly remarked on the striking shift in the fortunes of the two men. Meigs was now on the rise; Buchanan was, by then, a broken man. He had endured the endless cabinet sessions, the internal acrimony, the Hobson's choices, the constant criticism, and the stark fact that he had failed to keep the union whole. He was worn to the bone. He had a tremor in his cheek. He was gaunt. Meigs thought he looked like a cadaver. Meigs remembered the president as hollow and pale, a person for whom the only emotion one could conjure was "pity."

Black was faring only slightly better. He was worn out, too. A bout of rheumatism had felled him in January. His face was now sad and thin. He knew that, like Buchanan, failure (if not worse) was now his name. In his hometown of York, Pennsylvania, it was years before Black could restore his reputation. Buchanan guessed that his own burning effigy would likely light his way back to Wheatland, his Pennsylvania estate. Black could easily have made a similarly dark joke about what life after serving in the administration would be like for him.

Still, the two men clung to the view that the cautious strategy they had pursued was wise. Secession remained illegal as a matter of official policy. A federal flag still flew in Charleston's harbor. Virginia remained in the union—if only barely. If war came, it would not be on their watch. It would come from an act of southern aggression—unless the next president proved more foolish than they had been.

Black and Buchanan also took pride in knowing they had not used the crisis to seize dangerous executive powers. The first shot might still come. But if the South chose to take it, following the new president's inauguration in March, and with the Congress in its usual postinauguration recess, the balance of power might then be different. A president in that circumstance might be entitled to pursue a different, more aggressive course.

"Urgent and dangerous emergencies may have arisen, or may hereafter arise in the history of our country, rendering delay disastrous . . . which would for the moment justify the President in violating the Constitution, by raising a military force without the authority of law, but this only during a recess of Congress," Buchanan wrote years later, in the bitter memoir that he hoped would somehow salvage his reputation. "Such extreme cases are a law unto themselves. They must rest upon the principle that it is a lesser evil to usurp, until Congress can be assembled, a power withheld from the Executive, than to suffer the Union to be endangered."

But, Buchanan insisted, he had never been presented with that particular dilemma—and thus he had never had that historic opportunity to show his strength in defending the nation. "On the contrary, not only was Congress actually in session, *but bills were long pending before it for extending his authority in calling forth the militia, for enabling him to accept the services of volunteers, and for the employment of the navy, if necessary, outside of ports of entry for the collection of the revenue, all of which were eventually rejected,*" he wrote, pleading the limits of his own authority and his respect for the law. "Under these circumstances, had the President attempted, of his own mere will, to exercise these high powers, whilst Congress were at the very time deliberating whether to grant them to him or not, he would have made himself justly liable to impeachment. This would have been for the Executive to set at defiance both the Constitution and the legislative branch of the Government."

8

THE WAR COMES

"The evidence reaching us from the country leaves no doubt that the material for the work is abundant. . . . [I]t needs only the hand of legislation to give it legal sanction and the hand of the Executive to give it practical shape and efficiency."

I t was a beautiful April night in 1861, and the people of Quincy, Illinois, were out in force. With a gentle breeze stirring the American flag in the center of town, "The Great Union Meeting"—as the locals called it—grew too big for the local courthouse. As the gathering spilled onto the moonlit steps and out to the adjacent square, the Honorable Orville Browning held forth, defending the new president—then entering his sixth week in office—as he struggled to keep the nation from splitting in two.

The stylish and well-schooled Browning had known Abraham Lincoln for decades. They had served together in the Black Hawk War, and then again in the Illinois legislature—Browning in the senate, Lincoln in the house. Along the way, they had become friends, drawn to each other by their Kentucky roots, abiding hostility to slavery, and deep love of law. Lincoln's political career had taken off. Browning's had sputtered. That had created some distance between the two men. But the recent crisis had brought them together again, thanks to their shared conviction that the Buchanan administration's policy of accommodation must come to an end.

Browning relished the chance the Quincy rally gave him to defend his old friend's recent proclamation. The president had issued it immediately following South Carolina's shocking weekend assault on Fort Sumter. The proclamation called up seventy-five thousand militiamen. It pledged to use the new forces to retake Fort Sumter and the other federal military installations and governmental buildings that had been seized that fall and winter. It was Lincoln's declaration that the war, in effect, was on.

But Browning was a good enough lawyer—and a savvy enough politician—to foresee the controversy ahead. With coercion now the strategy, the accusations of weakness and treason that had so tarred Buchanan and his team were sure to be replaced by the charge that Lincoln was acting like a dictator. In fact, that charge was already making the rounds. In the national debate over war powers that followed, Lincoln was condemned for wielding arbitrary power and upending the Constitution in the name of saving it. Even Republicans were concerned by Lincoln's decision to all but suspend the writ of habeas corpus, eventually from Washington up to Maine.

There was, however, another side to the debate over executive war powers, and it followed a less predictable script. Here, the concern was not that Lincoln was becoming the military dictator anti-Federalists long ago predicted would emerge in the United States. The concern was that the inexperienced commander in chief would prove too timid to quash the rebellion.

Browning figured especially prominently in this turn in the conversation, both as a leading public voice and as a private confidant of Lincoln himself. Their dialogue, carried out through private meetings and sharply worded correspondence, focused on whether the war provided a valid basis for seizing and freeing the enemy's slaves and, just as important, on which branch of government was entitled to resolve that question.

Neither man showed himself to be especially loyal to his branch of government. It was Browning, by then a United States senator, who ended up arguing that the executive's war power was beyond Congress's power to control. It was Lincoln, the wartime president, who seemed eager to avoid the clash with Congress over the right tactics to deploy in defeating the enemy that his friend, Browning, thought Lincoln had a duty to provoke. To make things even more complicated, Browning mounted his defense of executive wartime prerogative chiefly in hopes of convincing Lincoln to act with restraint toward the South. By contrast, Lincoln's willingness to accept Congress's right to intervene in matters of military tactics reflected his openness to what was known as a policy of "hard war." In the context of their debate over what to do, to support Congress was to favor aggression in prosecuting the war, while to defend the prerogatives of the executive was to support a policy of caution and restraint.

While Browning and Lincoln scrambled the usual positions regarding executive war powers, the president's reluctance to challenge Congress was not born of timidity. That reluctance stemmed from Lincoln's growing realization that the struggle over war powers was not the zero-sum contest that Browning, like so many, seemed to think it was. Lincoln was coming to see it was often not clear just which branch of government was truly in charge. And so he began to appreciate that he might accomplish more by treating the war power as a shared one than by claiming it solely as his own.

* * *

Few believed Lincoln needed to wait until December to retaliate for South Carolina's attack in the Charleston Harbor. True, Congress was scheduled to be in recess until then. But, although Congress alone possessed the constitutional power to declare war, even the president's critics did not think Lincoln needed to hold his fire until the House and Senate returned as scheduled. After all, those counseling restraint did not see why the president could not call Congress back right away. At most, they argued, Lincoln would only have to wait the few weeks it would take for senators and representatives to make their way back to Washington for a special session. Congress then would be in place to bless such a momentous decision as starting a civil war.

As Lincoln's advisors gathered on the Sunday after the attack on

Fort Sumter, Secretary of State William Seward acknowledged the limits the Constitution placed on executive war making. The administration, Seward informed the cabinet, could "not levy armies and expend public money, without congressional sanction." It was a stark concession, given the sorry state of the armed forces at the time. It also raised a real question: Wouldn't Lincoln have to wait for Congress to return before making a true break with Buchanan's failed policy? How else would the new president be able to raise the forces and acquire the supplies that he would need to take the fight to the South?

Despite the legal concerns, Seward ultimately saw things differently. He warned his fellow cabinet members that Congress would not give the president what he needed in a timely fashion. That would be the case even if Lincoln did call the legislature back into session in the next few weeks. Congress would be "loyal," Seward was sure. But it was—unavoidably—a "deliberative body." His own experience in the Senate taught him that Congress was incapable of acting fast. Quoting his good friend, Thurlow Weed, Seward told the cabinet that to "wait for 'many men with minds' to shape a war policy, in the debates of an extra session, would be to invite disaster."

The president did not disagree. Lincoln chose Independence Day to start the special legislative session. The new start time was many months earlier than the House and Senate were scheduled to return. But it was also a good eighty days away. Lincoln was choosing a date for a special session that, given the imperative to act, would require him to do much on his own. The president was also picking a date that, by leaving Congress in recess for so long, allowed him to exploit the opening that Thomas Jefferson had left him half a century before.

In the *Chesapeake* affair, Jefferson did not wait for Congress's return to take steps to prepare the nation for war. Faced with a crisis and an absent Congress, Jefferson had suggested that the president had only two obligations: He must tell Congress, upon its return, what he had done while it had been away. He must also temper his actions in Congress's absence to make congressional ratification likely upon the legislature's return.

In actually asserting "extra-legal" power, however, Jefferson had been quite modest. The same could not be said for Lincoln. In the first days and weeks after the attack in South Carolina, he took a series of steps that clearly did skirt—and in some cases ignored—Congress's traditional role in war.

* * *

On April 19, Lincoln accomplished by fiat something President Buchanan had failed to convince Congress to let him do months before: shut down the Confederate ports. In effecting a blockade, Lincoln used a measure of war—a blockade being an internationally recognized tactic under the law of war—even though the branch of government constitutionally entitled to declare war was out of town.

Nearly simultaneously, the president secretly authorized a plan to purchase war supplies. The plan enlisted shadowy private men to spend federal money secretly and in a way that bypassed the regular appropriations laws. The cabinet unanimously approved the multimillion-dollar scheme despite the legal problems. The cabinet figured the bureaucracy was rife with traitors and that war preparations could not be carried out through the ordinary lawful processes.

Then, less than a week later, Lincoln took probably his most controversial action. Following another emergency cabinet meeting, this one held at the Navy Department, Lincoln issued a new proclamation. It effectively suspended the writ of habeas corpus along the military line from Washington to Philadelphia. Lincoln was trying to secure the capital after pro-Confederate riots had rocked Baltimore on April 19. With Virginia out of the union, the chaos that erupted in Maryland effectively cut off the nation's capital from the outside world. "Whoever in later times shall see this, and look at the date," Lincoln wrote in the album of a young female friend of President Buchanan who had stopped by the Executive Mansion the day of the riots, "will readily excuse the writer for not having indulged in sentiment or poetry." Instead, Lincoln continued, that same "writer" was filled with dread, as he stared fretfully out the window of his office in search of the military reinforcements he desperately hoped would soon arrive.

Even after a semblance of calm returned to Washington, Lincoln extended the initial order suspending habeas again in late April, and then again just two days before Congress returned in July. Each new proclamation brought unreviewable executive detention farther north from Baltimore—and thus deeper into territory where innocents were most likely to be arrested. The president's proclamations were sweeping where they applied. They allowed the military arrest of anyone whom commanding officers deemed threats to public safety, a category sure to pick up more than hardened combatants. The proclamations also made clear that officers should refuse to comply with judicial orders to examine the lawfulness of a detention. And refuse the officers did, even, in one instance, when the order to deliver the prisoner came from the chief justice of the Supreme Court himself.

Still, Lincoln was not through. In early May, with Congress's return another eight weeks off, he called up tens of thousands of so-called "three year men." These volunteers could serve longer than irregulars under the Militia Act. That made them especially attractive warriors. But no statute allowed the president to bring these troops on board. At the same time, Lincoln greatly augmented the regular army, and he also called up nearly twenty thousand seamen. Again, the president could not point to congressional authority for his actions. He was raising an army and a navy on his own, even though the Constitution assigned that task to Congress.

By the time Congress returned from its break, Lincoln had exercised more unilateral power in war than any president before him. Secretary Seward thought the special cabinet meeting after the riots in Baltimore had been the one that truly "put in force the war power of the government." It was at that meeting that the decision to authorize executive detention was made. But Seward also remembered that meeting for another reason. It had led the members of the cabinet down a path of extra-legal action that, as he ominously put it, "might have brought them all to the scaffold."

* * *

As Seward's remark reveals, Lincoln's team knew the dangers inherent in asserting executive war power too brazenly. Lincoln had been very aggressive in the weeks after Sumter fell, but he was wary of stepping beyond some inevitably uncertain line that the people would not tolerate. Necessity had its limits as a justification in a democracy. Jefferson made that clear at the height of the Wilkinson affair. In a pointed warning, he observed to his general in the field that "violations of the law are felt with strength." Lincoln needed no lessons on this point. He had been raised on a Whiggish distrust of executive authority. In fact, he had made a name for himself in Washington during his brief stint in Congress as a member of the Illinois delegation in the House by loudly protesting President James Polk's attempt to trick the legislature into ratifying the war with Mexico. Alarmed by the president's seemingly uncontrollable authority, Lincoln wrote to one of his colleagues, "[S]ee if you can fix any limit to his power."

Now, although Lincoln was president, his long-standing concerns about executive war had not left him altogether. In late April, even after he had suspended habeas, Lincoln shot down a plan to use the military to arrest legislators in Maryland. They were assembling to vote on secession. Some of the president's men were itching to stop them from engaging in such arguably treasonous deliberations. Lincoln claimed—in a written order to his top general, Winfield Scott—that such an assertion of executive power could not be justified in a democracy.

Only days after the attack on Fort Sumter, Lincoln turned to his attorney general, Edward Bates, for advice on another matter where Congress seemed to have hemmed him in. The president wanted to know what he could do about obstacles Congress seemed to have placed in the way of his efforts to quickly integrate the new militiamen in the existing military units. Decades before, Jefferson had faced a similar question during the *Chesapeake* crisis. Jefferson had advised then that the statutes should be read creatively to avoid hampering the war effort. Bates proved to be more of a stickler. He told Lincoln the president would need new legislation to create the special war bureaus he hoped to put in place, since Bates concluded the existing statutes barred the president's plan. The president accepted Bates's judgment, confounding supporters certain—or at least hopeful—the new commander in chief would "emulate General Jackson" and dispense with any attorney general who told him "no."

Even Lincoln's decision to delay the special session until July 4 was more than a clever ploy to ensure he could wage war as he wished without a meddlesome Congress in his way. The decision had that effect—there was no doubt. But the decision also facilitated what was shaping up to be a very shrewd legislative strategy. In particular, the delay ensured that the state Lincoln cared about most would be fully represented in the House when the special legislative session that he had called finally met.

That state was Kentucky, Lincoln's native home. Kentucky sat right on the North-South border, and, so far, it had remained loyal. Lincoln believed Kentucky, as he later put it to Orville Browning in the midst of a dispute over the president's power to use military force to free the slaves, was the "whole game." If Kentucky left the union, Lincoln was certain, the union would be lost. Maryland would then fall. That would leave the capital dangerously exposed—a prospect made terrifyingly real by the events in Baltimore of mid-April.

But Lincoln could only guarantee Kentucky's representation (and thus its affirmative support for his war plan) in the House—and Maryland's, too, for that matter—if he stalled Congress's return until at least mid-June. House member terms had expired at the end of the thirty-sixth Congress in March. A number of states had already chosen new House members the previous fall. But in fourteen states—among them Kentucky and four other states that had not yet seceded, including Maryland—new House elections were not scheduled until the late summer or fall. Those states seemingly had no representatives to seat in the House in the interim. Even worse, those states had placed restrictions on moving up Election Day. In Kentucky, for example, state law set the elections for the first Monday in August but also barred the governor from changing the date without first giving a month's notice. July 4, then, was not so far off as it seemed—not if these crucial border states were to supply the legislative support Lincoln wished to marshal to put down the rebellion.

For all of his unilateral war making, therefore, Lincoln's initial instincts were not so different from his predecessors'. Lincoln was unafraid
of war, and even welcomed it now that South Carolina had attacked. Lincoln showed no interest, however, in waging war solely by decree. Like
his predecessors, he wanted to bring the legislative branch along, through
some deft mix of aggression and restraint that would keep him in control
but not put him at odds with Congress. His plan, then, was not to seize
power for himself. It was to tell Congress what he had done in its absence
and to get its approval for those measures upon its return. Going forward,
Lincoln did not plan to conduct the war under powers solely of his own
creation. Instead, he assumed, he would wage war under the broad new
authorities the newly constituted and early recalled Congress would give.

* * *

As Independence Day approached, editorial writers were sure Congress
would help Lincoln get on with the fight. Massachusetts senator Charles
Sumner, a staunch supporter of the policy of coercion, told Lincoln's cabinet that Congress could easily wrap up its work in signing on to Lincoln's
war in ten days.

With his eye firmly fixed on Kentucky, Lincoln focused initially on securing a victory in the special House elections there. The governor had set
them for June 20 in order to accommodate the upcoming congressional
session in July. The administration's concerted efforts to woo those Ken-
tuckians still loyal to the country—and, just as important, to do nothing
that might offend them—paid off. Constantly checking in with his many
friends back home, Lincoln kept a close watch on how things were unfolding. He was thrilled to learn the Unionists won nine of the ten House
seats when the votes were finally cast. The Kentucky delegation went on to
support nearly the whole of the Lincoln program when that state's newly
elected representatives convened in Washington for the special session.

Meanwhile, Lincoln's men were busy calling in key congressional
leaders, mostly from the Senate. The administration had begun plotting
strategy for the session just a month away. Bills were lined up. Commitments were secured. Sequencing was discussed. A legislative program

began to take shape. And Lincoln turned to his next great task: writing the message he would deliver to Congress at the special session's start.

* * *

That message would account for the actions Lincoln had taken while Congress had been away. The message also would make the case for Congress to lend its support. The president spent weeks crafting the message. He worked on draft after draft to hit just the right points and just the right tone. In the final days before the session opened, Lincoln barred the usual office seekers from meeting with him. He wanted to be alone as he struggled to get the special message into final shape.

Among the chosen few allowed a sneak preview was Lincoln's old pal Orville Browning. By then, Browning's political fortunes had turned. He had been appointed to fill the remainder of the Senate term of Stephen Douglas, Lincoln's longtime Illinois nemesis, following the "Little Giant's" unexpected death in June. Browning was a calming and familiar presence in a city where Lincoln's friends were few. The president was glad to have Browning nearby. Lincoln repeatedly asked Browning to dinner during the month-long special legislative session. He even called Browning's family to the executive residence to give comfort when, later in the president's term, Lincoln's cherished son Willie passed on and his other son Tad fell terribly ill.

The bond between the two men was more than social. Back in February, Browning had shared the president-elect's train to the inauguration. Browning made it as far as Indianapolis, where Lincoln handed him a draft of his inaugural address. Lincoln made Browning promise not to show it to anyone other than Browning's wife, who also was close to the Lincolns. When Browning offered suggestions to tone down some phrasing in the address that might unduly provoke the South, Lincoln incorporated the changes in full. His friend's judgment, he knew, was good. And so now, on the eve of the special session and with the war looming, Lincoln took Browning into his confidence once again.

Browning spent most of that day preparing for his swearing-in as

Illinois's new senator. The ceremony would take place at the opening of the special session on July 4. Browning selected his seat in the Senate chamber on the morning of the July 3. That evening, Browning settled into his quarters at a boardinghouse near the Executive Mansion. Before heading to bed, though, he decided to drop in on Lincoln. When Browning arrived to find the president, he was told Lincoln was still working on the message. Rather than disturb him, Browning went to find the president's wife. But the president overheard his old friend's voice, and Lincoln called for Browning. Lincoln wanted to read Browning the near forty-page draft special message to Congress he had finally finished.

* * *

Browning was impressed by what he heard. The president's message, he recalled, was a "most admirable history of our present difficulties, and a conclusive and unanswerable argument against the abominable heresy of secession." If a disaffected minority in the South could leave because it did not get its way in an election, no republic could inspire confidence it would survive. The secessionists must be defeated so that government of the people, for the people, and by the people could endure. It was the very same argument that Browning had made to Lincoln in a letter he had sent him back in April.

Lincoln also was hoping to convey a related idea about democracy and war. He wanted to assure the people he did not believe a dictator was needed to win the war that lay ahead. A key section of the message explained that, despite Lincoln's unilateral war making during the recess, he intended to work with Congress. He further pledged to follow "the laws and the Constitution" after the war had been won.

Lincoln presented himself as an executive who, while alone in Washington, had faced a sudden and unprovoked attack from a hostile foe. He was not looking to go to war on his own. The enemy's actions triggered the executive's war power. The only question, as Lincoln framed it, was whether he acted faithfully and prudently while Congress had been away.

Here, too, Lincoln did not duck the hard questions. He said he had followed the law in calling out the militia and instituting the blockade. He rooted his power in laws Congress had passed long before but that President Buchanan had not chosen to invoke. Lincoln's case was strong. The Supreme Court later upheld the blockade as fitting within the Insurrection Act. Few could seriously dispute the argument that Browning himself had vigorously advanced at the time of the union rally in Quincy: The Militia Act amply supported the president's initial proclamation following Sumter's fall.

Lincoln was equally direct that in some cases, he had gone beyond his lawful authority. He admitted he had no legal right to raise the regulars and volunteers. But he emphasized the temporary powers he claimed were not beyond "the constitutional competency of Congress." He was only doing what he believed Congress would have done had it been around. He also made clear it was up to Congress's "better judgment" whether to fund such forces going forward, a concession to ultimate congressional control that fit the message's basic theme. "The evidence reaching us from the country leaves no doubt that the material for the work is abundant," Lincoln wrote, suggesting he believed the people were with him. "It needs only the hand of legislation to give it legal sanction and the hand of the Executive to give it practical shape and efficiency."

Still, Lincoln knew he had pushed the limits of his power to the breaking point—and, in some cases, beyond. He made no mention of the secret funding plan. Perhaps he saw no good way of defending it. He also labored to explain his decisions regarding suspending habeas. "Are all the laws but one to go unexecuted?" he asked, trying to explain his decision to deprive potential rebels of protection from arbitrary arrest. It was a direct response to Jeremiah Black, who, in the run-up to secession, had strongly advised Buchanan that the president cannot bend the laws. But Lincoln was never fully comfortable with relying on necessity alone to justify his action, knowing—and fearing—its potentially boundless quality. An early draft of his message argued that he had acted legally in empowering his officers to ignore writs of habeas corpus, not simply because of the danger to the capital but also because of Congress's absence at the time. His final message even promised a full legal opinion from Attorney General Bates to provide support for the view that the president had not acted extra-legally—at least given the unusual combination of circumstances that Lincoln faced during the recess.

* * *

With the message sent, Lincoln left it up to Congress to decide whether he had gone too far. He had defended the actions he had taken during the recess, but he was still asking Congress to give the "legal sanction" that, as he had put it in the message, only the legislative branch could give. And so, as planned, the Senate's chairman of the Committee on Military Affairs, Henry Wilson of Massachusetts, kicked off the special session with a bill to ratify all that the president had done in the previous eighty days. But, as Seward had warned back in March, getting Congress on board would be no easy task—even with a war to preserve the nation at hand.

For the first few weeks of the special session, and despite assurances to the contrary from leading senators, little of Lincoln's legislative agenda made it through. Proposals moved swiftly toward passage only to run into trouble and stall. Some members pushed measures to prod the administration into a more aggressive posture. Others offered proposals to slow things down, or to limit the significance of what Lincoln had done. There were serious efforts to bar a permanent expansion of the regular army, although those pushing for this restriction were unwilling to unwind the increase in forces Lincoln had already decreed.

Others in Congress seemed determined to press business that had nothing to do with the war. Motions were made (and debated) about whether nonwar business should be considered at all. The delays plagued even seemingly innocuous executive requests for new laws, like the one that Lincoln's team pushed to expand the War Department bureaus, an initiative made necessary by Attorney General Bates's earlier legal opinion. Everything, it seemed, was getting bottled up. Frustration was mounting.

Eventually, the dam broke. On July 29, Congress passed a bill to enhance the president's power to use militia and regulars to suppress the rebellion. On July 31, Congress cleared a bill to pay the volunteers the president had called up. Then, most crucially, on August 6, the final day of the special session, Congress passed a bill to "approve[], and in all respects legalize[] and ma[k]e valid, to the same intent and with the same effect as if they had been issued and done under the previous express authority and direction of the Congress of the United States" all those acts and proclamations that Lincoln had undertaken or announced to meet the rebellion since Congress had last been in session.

But August 6? That was more than a month after the new Congress first convened. In fact, Senator Henry Wilson's bill to ratify what Lincoln had done had been the very first measure introduced in the special session, earning it the label "S. 1." It had been no easy sell. Even die-hard Republicans were embarrassed to endorse it. Democrats challenged the constitutional theory underlining it. If what Lincoln did in April and May was legal, they taunted, there was no need for Congress to speak. And if the actions Lincoln took were not constitutional, then nothing Congress could say after the fact would make them lawful.

Habeas, in particular, proved a sticking point. The bill to ratify the president's extraordinary assertions of the power to detain fellow Americans was tabled time and time again because of its seeming sanction of his claimed right to arrest without judicial process. Thaddeus Stevens, a Republican from Pennsylvania, finally rammed the ratification measure through the House. He was not able to do so until the morning of the special session's final day. The bill had to be appended to one increasing soldier pay to get it through.

* * *

While still in Quincy, Browning had warned of the need to counter those objecting to the president's supposedly lawless conduct of the war. Such criticism, he had then feared, would sap the popular support needed to convince men to take up arms. Those urging passage of Wilson's ratification bill now pressed that same concern. Soldiers were starting to resist the call to serve, they contended, on the ground the president had no power to wage war on his own. Congress could provide the necessary assurance to new recruits, it was said, only by ratifying the earlier executive decrees.

It was an argument made all the more compelling by the union's humiliating defeat on July 21 at the Battle of Bull Run, on a field so close to the capital that Lincoln could hear the Confederate cannonade while out on a carriage ride. Making matters worse, everyone knew the administration's decision to enter that battle had not been of its choosing. Lincoln's men had been hectored into that calamitous confrontation—as General Scott sheepishly admitted to a congressman—by legislators clamoring for the army to go on the offensive before it was ready.

The disastrous outcome at Bull Run did have one good effect from the administration's point of view: It made Congress, at least for a spell, inclined to defer to executive demands. Those in Congress knew they had pressed for the Union army to start that fight—and they knew how mistaken that judgment had been. Like other crucial war measures passed around that time, the ratification measure won support less because Lincoln seemed unstoppable than because he was on the verge of losing the war before it had begun. His supporters in Congress could not afford to weaken him further.

* * *

Lincoln had come through the special session largely unscathed. It had not been easy. Even Browning had grown disillusioned with his branch's conduct by session's end. He had watched as the man who had sworn him in, Senator Lyman Trumbull, claimed powers for Congress that Browning thought the commander in chief alone possessed. He thought Trumbull's resolutions ordering Lincoln to take Richmond "before July 20" "absurd" and "dangerous." Those measures had failed to win support, but the distractions they caused, the resistance to Lincoln's plan they represented, and the pressure they exerted, shook Browning. So, too, did the measures that actually passed. "Our Legislation has been hasty, and in some instances crude and ill considered," he reflected the night before the session's final day. "I am not as hopeful of the future as I was when I came here."

Orville Browning was seeing firsthand that the power struggle between Congress and the commander in chief was no simple tug-of-war. The mighty executive was not always striving to grab more and more wartime power; the legislature was not honorably trying to rein him in. Energy might also run the other way. The "radicals" in Congress—the most antislavery and pro-war Republicans—might press for aggressive action. The president, attuned to the need to hold the border states, might assume the temporizing role.

This dynamic was most evident in the debate over the root cause of what Seward earlier called the "irrepressible conflict." Lincoln had been careful—exceedingly so—in both his inaugural address, and then again in his Fourth of July message to Congress, to ensure that the war for union would not be mistaken for an effort to free the slaves. He framed his message around the need to defend democracy itself. But if the president stuck to that message, Congress was a cacophony.

There were bills to establish the war was for union alone, and they fared well. Browning even signed on to them. But there were also bills to make inroads on the evil institution that Lincoln, like his fellow Republicans, viewed as a stain on the nation they loved. The fight over that legislation—a fight that extended well into the next year and eventually pitted Browning and Lincoln against one another—became the focal point for the struggle to control the conduct of the war.

* * *

As early as April, Browning had foreseen how the issue would arise. In a letter sent from Illinois on April 30, he had pushed Lincoln to fight hard and to widen the conflict. "March at once, with all the power you can command, upon the rebel states, and retake all the places which have fallen," he urged, "and crush all rebel forces that can be found." But, he had also noted that "whenever our armies march into the Confederate states, the negroes will, of course, flock to our standards. . . . This is inevitable." And because it was inevitable, Browning had further added, "the question arises, and we are bound to consider and decide it, 'What is to be done with them?'"

Within a month, that question confronted the administration head-on. In late May, three slaves fled their masters. They sought refuge with General Benjamin Butler's forces at Fortress Monroe in Virginia. Butler decided on the spot he would not return them. The eventual head of the Army of the Potomac, General George McClellan, had made an opposite promise to southern masters. He promised to follow the Fugitive Slave Act, despite the armed conflict underway. But Butler reasoned that a commander in the field could seize the enemy's property for military purposes. He also noted it was well accepted that a commander could deny the enemy use of property in the war itself. He did not see, therefore, why he could not keep enemy slaves for some length of time—even if, strictly speaking, they were not property—thereby treating them as if they, too, were "contraband," subject to seizure in the midst of war.

Butler's logic—which tore a hole through the Fugitive Slave Act in union-occupied territory in the South and potentially in border areas, too—captured the North's imagination. It was also quickly endorsed in Washington. On May 30, Secretary of War Simon Cameron, after a cabinet meeting, wrote Butler to say that he could refuse to return slaves (including their wives and children) who "come within your lines," even though he could do nothing to interfere with slavery otherwise. Left vague was when, if ever, the enslaved people might be returned.

* * *

Soon enough, Congress stepped in to make this ad hoc policy, born in the field, a binding rule for the war's conduct. The author of the key legislation was none other than Lyman Trumbull, the senior Illinois senator whom Browning had viewed so warily in July. Trumbull had introduced what became known as the First Confiscation Act soon after the special session opened. Browning supported the measure, as did all good Republicans, and it had passed near session's end. But that was largely because the act posed no real challenge to Lincoln's command. The new law basically tracked Butler's policy. It did not try to give enslaved people permanent freedom. The new law just endorsed Butler's intuition that any slaves used by the enemy in the war effort—as those who sought Butler's protection had been used—need not be returned to the enemy to be placed in service against the union.

Butler's background, as a Democrat committed to union but sensitive to the danger of acting too aggressively, had helped him craft a challenge to slavery that seemed like it was actually little more than a military tactic in an ongoing war—a veneer that made the approach more palatable to those wary of taking on slavery directly. The Executive Mansion buzzed with appreciation for Butler's skill in upending the fugitive slave laws in the most noncontroversial manner possible. But not all of Lincoln's officers were so subtle. Soon after Congress closed out the special session, the supremely confident Major General John Frémont, from his headquarters in St. Louis, made clear he was no Butler. His actions would soon cause Lincoln and Browning—as well as the branches of government each represented—to diverge.

* * *

Frémont was determined to strike a blow for freedom. Having already declared martial law in Missouri—an act that occasioned outrage among the Democrats still in Congress—Frémont followed up by issuing an even more controversial decree in August. Frémont's announcement provided that "all persons who shall be taken with arms in their hands, within these lines, shall be tried by Court Martial, and, if found guilty will be shot." But he also added that "the property, real and personal, of all persons in the State of Missouri who shall take up arms against the United States, or who shall be directly proven to have taken active part with their enemies in the field, is declared to be confiscated to the public use, and their slaves, if any they have, are hereby declared freemen."

Lincoln was appalled. All the caveats in Butler's position on fleeing slaves were missing from Frémont's approach. So, too, was any acknowledgment of the limitations built into the First Confiscation Act. Most notably, there was no reference to the requirement that earlier law had set forth requiring a judge to find a slaveowner treasonous prior to allowing the confiscation of the owner's slaves. Frémont was claiming an executive power to free virtually all slaves within the field of his occupation pure and simple. He was also asserting the right to remove them from bondage permanently—not just for the duration of the war or for so long as military necessity demanded.

The president was convinced the proclamation was illegal. His most trusted political scouts were also advising him that Frémont's move was sure to push Kentucky into the South's column. Lincoln asked Frémont to withdraw the order. But Frémont declined, after considering the request for an insultingly long week and even sending his wife to personally lobby the president to back him up.

Put off by a midnight, face-to-face challenge to his authority from Jessie Frémont, the problematic general's wife, Lincoln finally countermanded the order. But the president did not stand on his constitutional authority as commander in chief. Lincoln wrote that he was "cheerfully" trimming the emancipation order to "conform to, and not to transcend," the limits Congress had so recently established in the First Confiscation Act.

The president's rebuke left Frémont rejected and embarrassed. His supporters, of whom there were many, were furious. They were shocked at the president's disregard of the rights of the enslaved. They thought Lincoln's legalistic outlook—and his attention to Congress's prerogatives—ridiculous. And Frémont's supporters were, as ever, disdainful of Lincoln's solicitude for the border states.

* * *

Among the angriest was Orville Browning. Fort Sumter's fall had temporarily inflamed Browning, who, moderate by nature, was always sure to calibrate his reactions to the prevailing popular mood. Browning had also apparently come under Frémont's spell—enticed, perhaps, by the prospect of munitions contracts for Quincy. Frémont dangled them before Browning when they met in St. Louis days after the special session ended. Eager for Frémont to succeed, Browning had immediately written to Lincoln that "Frémont's proclamation was necessary, and will do good," while noting his concern about rumors that the cabinet disapproved. Then, six days later, upon learning Frémont's order had been reversed by the president, Browning wrote Lincoln to express his displeasure.

Browning set forth a constitutional theory sweeping in its view of the executive's war power. Frémont was pursuing the enemy as a commanding officer in the field. The president, Browning argued, should have let his general prosecute the war as he wished. "It is true there is no express, written law authorizing it," Browning wrote in a follow-up letter, "but war is never carried on, and can never be, in strict accordance with previously adjusted Constitutional and legal provisions." Lincoln thus had no cause to suggest there had been any "collision" with Congress or that Congress had any role in a military decision of this kind. The First Confiscation Act was, to Browning, irrelevant. Congress could fiddle with the laws all it wished outside a war, Browning believed, but the war should be fought by the executive on any terms that the laws of war allowed and that the commander in chief thought wise.

Lincoln fired back. He professed to be "astonishe[d]" by Browning's criticism. Within weeks, Lincoln reminded his friend, Browning had gone from supporting Congress's right to pass a confiscation act to denying Congress's right to determine the commander's authority to accept slaves at all. The president was hinting that his old friend had let the excitement of the moment get the better of his legal judgment. It was an especially loaded charge. Browning had recently but unsuccessfully lobbied Lincoln to appoint him to the Supreme Court. That effort involved an embarrassingly pleading letter from Browning's wife to Lincoln that, like Browning's own letter on the same subject, had gone unanswered.

General Frémont's action, Lincoln wrote, was "purely political; without the savor of military law about it." Lincoln even dismissed Frémont's action as "simply 'dictatorship.'" "I do not say Congress might not with propriety pass a law, on the point, just such as General Frémont proclaimed," Lincoln explained. "I do not say I might not, as a member of Congress, vote for it. What I object to is, that I as President, shall expressly or impliedly seize and exercise the permanent legislative functions of the government." Then, echoing his earlier message to Congress and challenging a free-floating defense of necessity, Lincoln wrote that Frémont was hardly "saving" the government. "Can it be pretended," he asked, in words that would soon enough be hard to square with his own actions, "that it is any longer the government of the U.S.—any government of constitution and laws,—wherein a General, or a President, may make permanent rules of property by proclamation?"

Browning did not give up. He followed Lincoln's reply with a thirteen-page rejoinder. It challenged the claim of dictatorship on the ground that the executive would merely be following the international laws of war. But Lincoln did not answer. He instead left Browning to absorb the silence.

* * *

When the new legislative session convened in December, the president and his cabinet took a meeting with congressional heavyweights. They promptly dressed down the executive and his men for their torpor. Lincoln could barely contain himself, but it was just the beginning of Congress's effort to assert control. That same month, Congress formally established the Joint Committee on the Conduct of the War. Its "greatest purpose seems to be to hamper my action and obstruct the military operations," Lincoln complained.

In truth, Lincoln, too, was frustrated by the slow pace of the fighting. He confided at one point to Browning that he was thinking of taking personal command in the field. He described to his friend in a private meeting his imagined schemes of destruction, backed by displays of massive force. At the same time, Lincoln was wary of the mounting interest in using the war to bring about emancipation. Thanks to Frémont's actions, and Lincoln's reversal of them, there was now a wedge between the president and his officers in the field over that issue. Congress would soon exploit it.

Senator Lyman Trumbull, upon Congress's return, began pressing a measure to codify Frémont's policy, just as Trumbull had used the First Confiscation Act to codify Butler's. The ensuing debate over the Second

Confiscation Act proved tortuous. Innumerable versions of the measure appeared over the better part of a year. The proposed law took on Lincoln's apparent war strategy. It also gave rise to the most extensive debate over Congress's authority to direct the commander in chief's waging of war that the nation had yet seen. Browning took center stage as the law's chief opponent.

* * *

To "insure the speedy termination of the present rebellion," as the final language of Trumbull's Second Confiscation Act read, Congress had imposed on the president a "duty . . . to cause the seizure" of a vast array of rebel property. The measure included a separate emancipation provision. It declared the slaves of rebels in occupied territory, whether they came within Union lines or not, forever free. Critically, the sweeping provision applied whether the masters had impressed their slaves into serving the war effort or not. The masters' rebel status alone sufficed to make the slaves free under the new law—something the earlier confiscation measure, like General Butler's initial policy, had been careful not to do.

Going into the fight over the proposed law, Browning had good reason to think he had won back Lincoln's confidence. In a meeting at the Executive Mansion days before the new legislative session opened, the two men discussed the virtues of a gradual plan for compensated emancipation, with newly freed slaves ultimately being colonized in Africa. "There was no disagreement in our views upon any subject we discussed," Browning noted.

Browning also had begun to reconsider the wisdom of what Frémont had done—and thus the wisdom of the recent congressional attempts to mandate that Lincoln endorse it. Browning had grown fearful of what passage of the new confiscation law would mean for Republican fortunes, including his own. There was already growing anger at the suspension of habeas corpus. Browning was certain this new measure would compound the problem among the wavering unionists. He also saw his own reelection prospects dimming with the administration's turn to harsher war measures, especially since the battlefield gains seemed so meager.

There was also, to Browning's mind, a constitutional principle at stake. It was the same one Browning had articulated to Lincoln before—and one that, at first blush, there was little reason for Lincoln to reject. Browning drew on the logic that had earlier led him to counsel Lincoln to stand with Frémont. It was not for Congress to say how the president should treat the enemy. Such matters, under the Constitution, were for the commander in chief alone to resolve. Congress, therefore, had no right to impose a duty on the commander in chief to free enemy slaves.

The twists and turns in Browning's position—leaning in favor of Frémont's nascent experiment with emancipation months before, recoiling from it now—reflected the senator's view of which tactic would work best at these different stages of the war. The Constitution, Browning believed, was designed to give the commander in chief just this flexibility over tactics. Browning saw no contradiction in his defense of executive prerogative—even if it meant that he once had counseled Lincoln to assert such power in order to engage in a vigorous executive prosecution of the war, and that he now advised Lincoln to unsheathe those same unlimited powers in order to maintain a more restrained approach than Congress wanted to require the president to pursue. Simply put, Browning thought that the president should not allow himself to be boxed in by a statute dictating the terms of battle. A wise commander needed to keep his options open.

* * *

With the legislative debate coming to a head, Browning spoke against the Second Confiscation Act for nearly three hours on the Senate floor. There was some sympathy in the Senate and the House for the concern he was raising about Congress overstepping its powers. Competing versions of the confiscation bill had consciously sought to avoid requiring the president to do anything. These proposals merely authorized the president to make the judgment about military necessity on which the fateful determination to confiscate the slaves would turn. But those efforts at moderation were not winning the day. Fast moving toward passage was a measure that would require the president to issue a proclamation warning the South that if the rebellion did not end within a certain time, slaves would be taken by operation of law.

Browning's allies were few in his effort to thwart the Radical Republican effort to make the war about ending slavery. But Browning was a powerful enough voice to draw concerted opposition from those who, by this point, saw nothing wrong with Congress seizing control.

Senator Charles Sumner of Massachusetts rose to make clear he believed "Congress may make all laws to regulate the duties and the powers of the Commander-in-Chief." Jacob Howard of Michigan contended it was absurd to suggest, as Browning had, that the commander in chief could wage war free from congressional control. The Continental Congress had constantly checked George Washington, Howard noted. Nor had Howard found "in the Federal Convention, [or] in any State convention, one word, intimation, or hint, from any speaker in any one of those numerous bodies, affording a shadow of support for the claim now set up."

Browning read the history differently. He saw in the shift from a commander in chief appointed by the Continental Congress under the Articles of Confederation to one elected by the people under the Constitution a crucial reallocation of authority. That change, Browning argued, was evidence the founders wished to free the executive from legislative control in the prosecution of a war. It was clear, Browning thought, that "active operations in the field" were off limits to Congress. Browning also thought it was clear Congress could not "direct the movements of the Army," just as Congress could not possibly have the right to regulate which enemy property a commander must or must not take. That decision was the president's alone to make.

Howard agreed that it would be absurd in most cases for Congress to try to dictate what should happen on the field of battle. Howard did not think that meant Congress was powerless to make such judgments as a legal matter. "Should the President, as Commander-in-Chief, undertake an absurd and impracticable expedition against the enemy, one plainly destructive of the national interests and leading to irretrievable disaster, or should he basely refuse to undertake one, or, having undertaken it, insist upon retreating before the enemy, and giving over the war to the manifest prejudice of the country, or should he treacherously enter into terms of capitulation with the manifest intent to give the enemy an advantage," Howard asked of Browning, "would the Senator rise in his seat here and insist that Congress has no power to interpose by legislation and prevent the folly and the crime?" Howard could not imagine that Browning would be willing to follow the logic of his position and "exclaim, 'the country is without remedy; Congress is powerless; the Constitution furnishes no means to arrest the approaching ruin; we must not travel out of the Constitution; and we must submit our necks to the yoke. It is the will of the Commander-in-Chief, and that, and that only, in such a case is the Constitution.'"

While Browning praised his adversary for "meet[ing] the question in the most direct and manly terms," he did not back down. The legislature, he claimed, was constitutionally required to make an all-or-nothing choice. It must disband the army or leave it to the commander in chief to decide how to use it when fighting was underway. "When the Army is raised, when the Army is supported, when it is armed, when we are engaged in war, and it is in the field marshaled for the strife," Browning said, "I deny that Congress, any more than the humblest individual in the Republic, has any power to say to the President, do this or do that; march here or march there; attack that town or attack this town; advance to-day and retreat tomorrow; give up a city to be sacked and burned; shoot your prisoners."

* * *

Lincoln, for the most part, kept his counsel. Still, he maintained close relations with Browning through the whole of the legislative battle. One evening, after Browning had spent the day on the Senate floor blasting the bill and standing up for the president's prerogatives, the two friends met back at the Executive Mansion. They amused themselves by reading poems from their youth. Finally, Lincoln concluded he could no longer hold off the crowd "buzzing" at the door, ready to subject him to what he called the "harassments" that came with the office, and their time together ended.

But try as Browning did to stop the bill in the Senate, he had no luck. The radicals were too strong. The last hope for common sense to prevail, he concluded, lay with Lincoln himself.

On Sunday, July 13, with the bill having passed the Senate, Browning met with Seward to make his case against the radicals' confiscation plan once more—this time hoping to convince the administration to support a veto. "His general views coincide with my own," Browning recalled of Seward's thoughts. The meeting ended with Seward promising to "have a conversation with [the President] upon the propriety of vetoing it." The next morning, Browning went to the Executive Mansion with a copy of the bill in hand. He met with Lincoln and expressed "very freely my opinion that it was a violation of the Constitution and ought to be vetoed." Browning explained that he believed his old friend from Illinois "had reached the culminating point in his administration, and his course upon this bill was to determine whether he was to control the abolitionists and the radicals, or whether they were to control him."

By this time, however, Lincoln was seeing his power through a different lens. The Second Confiscation Act was not, he was beginning to think, a threat to his authority as commander in chief. It was, in key respects, a permission slip. The risk to the border states of precipitous action remained. But the gains from making this war about slavery were greater— and Congress was giving every indication it wanted the president to make emancipation the goal. If Lincoln wished to support emancipation, he realized, now was the time. Congress was all but imploring him to act. Lincoln issued a tame message about the bill. The message sought tweaks to address concerns about the bill operating as a bill of attainder. When Lyman Trumbull addressed those concerns in a last-minute resolution, Lincoln offered his support for the law. The president signed the measure that Browning had warned him would forever give Congress the upper hand in how the war would be waged.

* * *

The very morning before Browning had pressed Lincoln to veto the Second Confiscation Act, the president, during a carriage ride with his secretary of the navy, Gideon Welles, first let slip his plan to free the slaves. In other words, at the very moment Browning was imploring Lincoln not to let Congress run roughshod over him with the Second Confiscation Act, the president was actually plotting how he could take advantage of that same law to make his boldest single move as commander in chief.

Lincoln explained to Welles during that carriage ride that emancipation was "a military necessity absolutely essential for the salvation of the union. . . . We must free the slaves or be ourselves subdued." Lincoln's long-held view that the border states must be accommodated so that their unionist instincts might spread southward no longer seemed right. It was becoming increasingly clear to the president that an opposite strategy was more likely to succeed. With slavery uprooted in the South, the evil practice would inevitably lose its grip in the border regions as well. And with slavery no longer in place, the cause for rebellion would be lost. Hence, the conclusion: Emancipation was a necessary step in the path toward victory.

Given this course of thinking, there was no dissonance in the unusual confluence of events of July 13, 1862: Lincoln resolving that day to take charge as commander in chief even as he also resolved to refuse to veto the most intrusive measure Congress had yet passed regarding the conduct of the war. The war was now more than a year old. There had been a constant back and forth between the president and the Congress, each branch asserting itself at different moments. By this time, it was hazy just who was leading whom: Congress or the commander in chief?

It was also no longer clear that Lincoln was assessing the situation in such simplistic terms. There was a war to be won. There was a principle about freedom to be vindicated. If the president could draw strength from Congress's own actions in serving those now mutually reinforcing ends, then he was hardly the weaker for accepting the legislature's right to have a say. But, as well, and controversially, if Lincoln could accomplish Congress's true objective only by going further than Congress had pushed him, there was no constitutional problem with that course either.

Lincoln issued the preliminary emancipation proclamation on September 22. Lincoln did so only after waiting long enough for a union victory so that he would not seem desperate in taking such a strong action
against slavery. The delay, taken at Seward's suggestion, had attracted
great criticism. Commentators and newspapers even argued that, by refusing to issue the proclamation sooner, Lincoln was all but defying the
will Congress had expressed in the confiscation law he had just signed.
Not surprisingly, then, when Lincoln finally did issue his historic proclamation, he made a point of wrapping himself in the language of the
Second Confiscation Act.

The proclamation's first references to abolition were revealing. They
did not cast the president's intended emancipatory actions as a unilateral
display of executive force. They referred instead to a legislative request he
soon planned to make to give financial aid to those "slave states, so called,"
that ceased rebelling and have adopted "immediate or gradual abolition
within their respective limits." The preliminary proclamation went on to
promise that the famous emancipation proclamation would come on January 1. But it then immediately stated that "attention is hereby called" to
the Second Confiscation Act. Congress had instructed that he warn Confederate slaveholders that, unless they lay down their arms, their slaves
would soon be deemed forever free. The preliminary emancipation proclamation then quoted in full the three key sections of the act, and, for
good measure, the president "enjoin[ed] and order[ed]" all those under
his command to follow "the sections above recited." The president, in
other words, was now carrying out Congress's directive. The final proclamation also invoked the act's language in its final paragraph: The standard
of judgment for ultimate emancipation would be the one that Congress
had already decreed—military necessity.

But, of course, the president was not only relying on Congress's backing. He intermixed his references to the recent legislation with assertions
of his independent powers as the commander in chief. Such assertions
were necessary. The Emancipation Proclamation did not perfectly track
the confiscation law. It claimed broader powers to free the slaves than

Congress had claimed in the painfully complicated verbiage of the Second Confiscation Act itself. But if, at an earlier moment in the war, Lincoln had read Congress's rules for confiscating the enemy's slaves as a limitation on what a commander in the field could do—and as rules that could not be "transcend[ed]" by an officer fighting a war, as he had written in overturning General Frémont's earlier unauthorized emancipation decree—Lincoln no longer did. The president now saw in Congress's actions acquiescence, even authorization, for his effort to move the nation further toward freedom.

Browning was sure the president's action in signing the Second Confiscation Act was a grave strategic and constitutional error. He insisted it was one Lincoln could have avoided. He should have, in Browning's view, more firmly resisted Congress's efforts to take charge of the war's conduct. The president would then have avoided being pressed to the wall as he now was. But Lincoln saw things otherwise. He was happy for people to conclude that his boldest assertion of the war power—the Emancipation Proclamation—bore Congress's stamp. He knew, as time passed, it would also be remembered as an "act of justice." And Lincoln knew as well that the author of that act would be forever known as the president and the president alone.

9

THE WAR ENDS

"They cannot, perhaps, authorize an officer to command the Commander-in-Chief, but they can direct any officer what to do. That I hold very distinctly is the power of the people; and gentlemen mistake when they suppose that because the President as a matter of military rank is head of the Army it is out of the power of Congress to say what the head of the Army shall do, or shall not do."

After years out of the limelight, Jeremiah Black was back in its glare. It was March 6, 1866. The Supreme Court was assembled in its new home—an ornate, two-story room, bathed in natural light from above. The Senate had used this chamber for four decades before abandoning it for larger surroundings two years prior to the outbreak of the Civil War. But now the actual waging of the war was over. Reflecting this shift, the landmark case that Black was arguing drew special significance from its connection to a larger power struggle between the president and Congress over the proper conduct of this new and final phase of the war.

Much of what Black said to the Court that day echoed themes that he advanced years before, just weeks after Lincoln had been elected president but months before the new president had taken office as the new commander in chief. At that time, while serving as President Buchanan's outgoing attorney general, Black had made the legal case for limiting the federal army's power to "coerce" the seceding states. He had emphasized, in a much-derided legal opinion, that the commander in chief had an obligation to obey the limits Congress had laid down. Now, Black was again seeking to restrain the president's war power. He was calling on the Court to prevent the executive from using a military commission to try an American—charged with siding with the enemy—for a capital offense. But this time, in asserting limits on the executive's war powers, Black was hardly taking Congress's side. In fact, Congress was perhaps more eager than even the president for the Court to bless this unusual system of military justice.

The reason that Black's arguments now had such a different valence was simple. Andrew Johnson was president—the first Democrat president since James Buchanan had slinked away in disgrace. Thus, Johnson, like Black, hailed from a party opposed to the Republican-led Congress's plan for remaking the South known as Reconstruction. That legislative plan depended heavily on using the military to bring order to the South. It was thought that only such a federal military presence would protect the newly freed slaves. Republican leaders thus feared the potential consequences of a Supreme Court ruling in the military commission case that took the side Black was arguing. These leaders worried that Black might convince the justices to strike down the military commissions and thereby hand the new president a perfect excuse to give substance to his southern sympathies and pull the federal army from the former Confederate states.

But while the Court's decision about military commissions would surely impact the power struggle over Reconstruction between Congress and President Johnson, the Court would not actually resolve it. Instead, in the wake of the Court's ruling, new clashes between Congress and the president over Reconstruction and the military's role in implementing it began exploding on a variety of fronts. The most serious one erupted the next winter. The controversy concerned President Johnson's right to control the nation's highest-ranking army officer, the Republican war hero Ulysses S. Grant. With Congress committed to doing everything it could to frustrate the president in his dogged efforts to sideline Grant, this clash would soon lead to a final constitutional showdown. The clash would take place not far from where Black had made his case to the justices—in the Senate's new chamber, the site of the historic impeachment trial of President Andrew Johnson.

* * *

The spark for this unprecedented period of conflict was Lincoln's death. He died eleven months before Jeremiah Black made his argument to the Supreme Court. Only five weeks before the president's assassination, the nation's capital city had been readying itself for Inauguration Day. Lincoln seemed eager to start his second term. Johnson, as his late-breaking choice for the reelection ticket, was looking forward to serving as the great man's vice president.

Together, the two men from opposite parties were prepared to present a unified front. They would stitch the nation back together following the peace that seemed finally to be at hand. In fact, that peace would be officially concluded just days before Lincoln was shot. Sensing the war's end, Lincoln had already begun implementing an executive-led approach to what was being called "reconstruction." Lincoln's plan was surprisingly lenient in its treatment of the former rebels. Due to the good will the president had earned, however, that plan was proving fairly popular in not only the South but the North as well.

But now, with Lincoln gone, there was great unease. How would the new president govern in this twilight period between war and peace? Andrew Johnson lacked Lincoln's unique capacity to instill confidence that he was making decisions with the nation's best interests—and highest ideals—in mind. Johnson was also a southerner and a Democrat. Those features of his biography automatically made him suspect in the eyes of many Republicans. That Johnson had made a fool of himself at his post-election debut added to the doubts. While Lincoln was preparing to deliver his famous second inaugural address, Johnson was drinking one too many whiskeys. He had to be hurried from the stage at the end of his embarrassing vice presidential speech.

But the responsibility suddenly thrust upon Johnson seemed to change the new president. Johnson carried himself amazingly well in the

weeks that followed the assassination. He projected a straight-back so-
briety that matched his black hair. He had the good sense to keep the
now-deceased president's cabinet intact. For a while, Johnson convinced
Lincoln's men, including many in Congress, that he actually was on their
side. In Johnson's most striking act, he personally dispatched General
Ulysses S. Grant to the South. Johnson directed Grant to reverse a peace
agreement that had been reached by a different general on terms Johnson
agreed were too generous to the former Confederates. Johnson's strong
show of federal power—and his seeming alliance with Grant—was widely
praised.

With his popularity soaring, Johnson's improbable political rise
seemed all the more remarkable. In a little more than two decades, he had
gone from poor, illiterate tailor's apprentice in a small Tennessee town (he
did not learn to write until he was twenty), to local alderman, to governor,
to famously unionist senator (the only one from the South to maintain
his Senate seat during the war), to military governor of his native state, to
Lincoln's candidate for vice president during the reelection run. And then,
finally, Johnson had become, amazingly enough, a take-charge and widely
admired commander in chief.

But by the spring of 1866, just as Black's case about the military commissions was coming to the Supreme Court, Johnson was starting to assert himself as more than a stand-in for a deceased hero. That new way
of presenting himself was causing trouble. Johnson's tendency toward rigidity and hardheadedness did not help. Neither did his inflexible states'
rights views about constitutional law or his overt racism. He also displayed flashes of venom and vitriol that did less to overwhelm his opponents than to cement their hostility.

The real problem for Johnson stemmed from his views about Reconstruction. Those views were becoming better known, and Lincoln's followers did not like them. Those followers also still controlled Congress.
Johnson's views did have a following of their own, especially among the
rebels rushing back to a Democratic Party whose ranks had been depleted
by secession. In fact, a Democratic Party stalwart had urged Jeremiah
Black, months before, to return to Washington. Andrew Johnson, the

friend explained, was back to his "true fold." Lincoln's reign was finally over. The capital was once again home to some who, like Black, had never reconciled themselves to the Republican takeover.

* * *

To judge only from what Jeremiah Black said to the justices during the oral argument on that March day in 1866, though, it hardly would have seemed like Black and Johnson were allies. Black was contesting the federal government's plan to kill an Indiana man, Lambdin Milligan. It was Johnson, as the leader of that same government, whom Black was asking the Court to stop. Indeed, it was the military, of which Johnson was the chief commander, that had charged and then convicted Milligan of a capital offense. The alleged crimes included Milligan having plotted, while serving as the leader of a renegade group known as the Knights of the Golden Circle, break-ins at Union prison camps. The plot sought to help liberate Confederate prisoners of war. After prosecuting those charges, the military had then, in its own special tribunal, sentenced Milligan to death and set his hanging for May of 1865. Thus, while the commission's sentence had come down during Lincoln's administration and been delayed only to permit the legal challenge to continue, it was Johnson's administration that had taken up the government's side of the case. Johnson's appointees even invoked the president's expansive war powers in defending the right to execute Milligan through the use of this special military court. Thus, Johnson seemed very much on the federal army's side—and Johnson very much seemed Jeremiah Black's opponent before the Supreme Court.

In taking on the president and his war powers, moreover, Black was unsparing. In a presentation to the Court that lasted more than two hours, Black argued—unaided by a single note—that the justices' ruling would determine far more than Milligan's fate. Depending on the outcome of the case, Black warned, the United States would choose the path of either law or lawlessness in resolving a civil war that had already, in Black's view, seen the federal government stretch the Constitution past the breaking point.

The executive suspension of the Great Writ of Habeas Corpus had long been a source of concern for Democrats and even moderate Republicans. Black was making the point that even after passage of the new Habeas Corpus Suspension Act in 1863—which had curbed some of the army's excesses—the federal government continued to use military force to imprison and try countless citizens captured far from any active battlefield. Thus, the question, as Black framed it for the Court, was simple: Could the current administration continue the extraordinary practice that had prevailed during the war, even though the South had now surrendered? If so, Black contended, then the Constitution's basic guarantees would be subject to suspension at a president's whim.

By all accounts, Black's argument to the Court was masterful. It reached for something grand and timeless: a call to the justices to honor basic principles, to vindicate the historic right to trial by jury, to ensure that no captured citizen could be put to death by other than a civilian proceeding, and to put an end to the continued use of military justice to preserve order. Orville Browning, whom Johnson would soon pluck from his thriving Washington law practice to serve as his secretary of the interior, was in the courtroom when Black made his case. Browning swooned at Black's torrent of words, remembering them as among the "most magnificent" he had ever heard a lawyer speak.

Meanwhile, a Kentucky visitor who had mistakenly stumbled upon the Court's session was equally impressed. As Black proceeded to regale the justices with another supporting tale from history about how "the people rose in their wrath, smashed down the whole machinery of oppression, and drove out into innermost shame, king, dogs and strumpet," the visitor suddenly rushed out of the Court's session to find his home-state congressman. The man located the House chamber, made his way past the doorkeeper, and pulled at the tail of his representative's coat while he was still mid-address. And then, in words that spoke for many a white southerner eager to put an end to federal control, the visitor yelled out: "Wind her up, Bill! Wind her up, and come over here and listen to old Jerry Black giving 'em hell!"

* * *

If one grasped the broader political context, though, it was evident that Black was not really trying to rein in a runaway commander in chief. Despite what Black seemed to be saying to the justices, he well knew that, by the spring of 1866, Andrew Johnson had swung back to embrace the tenets of the Democratic Party. The president was by then making it well known that he shared that party's long-standing hostility to federal coercion of the states and that party's support for white rule. Perhaps it should have been no surprise, then, that on the eve of the Court's ruling, and less than two weeks after Black's pitch to the Court, Andrew Johnson all but threw the case of Lambdin Milligan.

In a sweeping proclamation, Johnson stated that "there no longer existed any armed resistance of misguided citizens or others to the authority of the United States in any or in all the States before mentioned, excepting only the State of Texas." The president's announcement suggested peace was officially at hand—even in the Deep South—notwithstanding the terror then being visited on newly freed men and women who had been enslaved. As if to further undermine the government's case, the president's proclamation also went on to say that, in consequence of the end of hostilities, "the laws could be sustained and enforced in the several States before mentioned . . . by the proper *civil* authorities, State or Federal."

With statements like that coming from the president, it was clear that Black, in railing against the expansive use of war powers, was not actually challenging the authority of the current president. Black was challenging the power of Congress. It was the Republican-run legislature, led by men like Thaddeus Stevens and Charles Sumner, that actually favored the postwar form of Reconstruction that depended upon military enforcement. It was the Republicans who wanted to deploy the army to enforce the end of slavery, dismantle the Confederacy, and bring about the new birth of freedom that Lincoln promised at Gettysburg. In attacking the military tribunal's constitutionality, then, Black was challenging these legislators—the same ones Black had taken on six years before in suggesting Buchanan was limited in what military force he could use to fight secession.

But because Black was taking on the Republicans in Congress, he was in effect siding with President Johnson. The new commander in chief, after all, was in conflict with the leaders in Congress, too. In truth, then, Black's presentation to the Court was more than a constitutional challenge to the use of this military commission. It was also a sketch of the argument for federal military restraint that Johnson himself would soon make in fending off congressional efforts to force him to implement a more aggressive form of Reconstruction.

* * *

The Court announced its judgment in *Milligan* on April 3, 1866. The ruling drew howls from the Radical Republicans in Congress and their supporters in the press. They saw the Court's action as a badly disguised attempt to outlaw the Republican form of Reconstruction. That approach depended upon the military, which, the Republicans believed, alone had the capacity to suppress the remnants of the Confederacy and to protect the rights of the newly freed slaves. Yet the Court announced that it had decided to strike down the tribunal that had convicted Lambdin Milligan on broad constitutional grounds. That decision inevitably put martial law in doubt not only in Indiana but everywhere, including the South.

The Court's ruling alarmed Chief Justice Salmon Chase. He had served in Lincoln's cabinet as the treasury secretary. He had then been appointed chief justice (the only office besides president that he desired) as Lincoln's first term was coming to an end. Chase was also a well-known supporter of black suffrage. But he was a complicated figure. He had a Democratic pedigree deep in his past. He also had his eye forever on a presidential run. His main goal during this uncertain period thus seemed to be to keep his—and his country's—options open.

For that very reason, though, Chase saw little wisdom in his brethren's broad constitutional decision outlawing military tribunals. The majority had held that, under the Constitution, Milligan must be tried before a jury of his peers. He was a citizen, and the regular courts were open. That was, for the majority, the end of the matter. Chase, by contrast, based his separate concurring opinion solely on the Habeas Corpus Suspension Act of 1863. He held the statute, though permitting military detention and trial in some cases, did not allow the government to use a military tribunal in the special circumstances of the case at hand. He thus sought to find a way to preserve Congress's power to authorize military commissions in the future by avoiding a constitutional ruling of any kind.

But, in protecting Congress's interests, Chase still did his best to keep close relations with President Johnson. The two met frequently. Chase served as an informal advisor to Johnson, even while Chase served as chief justice. In keeping with that posture, Chase declined, in his separate opinion in *Milligan*, to champion legislative power without limit. In a passage of his opinion that offered no citation to any prior decision of the Court and that, if anything, seemed at odds with earlier rulings, Chase wrote that Congress could not restrict the president in his role as commander in chief in the "conduct of campaigns."

It was not entirely clear what that phrase meant. Chase was definitely saying that there *were* limits on Congress's power to force the commander in chief to heed its wishes—at least in circumstances Chase did not define. That assertion left much uncertain about just how limited Congress's powers were in war. It also put Congress on notice. Was Chase signaling he might side with President Johnson if Congress pressed its challenge to the powers of the commander in chief too far?

* * *

By the following winter, the limits on Congress's power to control the commander in chief were, at least in President Johnson's eyes, becoming clearer. The object of the president's attention was Ulysses Grant. The president focused on the efforts by the Republicans in Congress to insulate the nation's top general from Johnson's oversight. The Republicans were trying to do so as part of their increasingly aggressive efforts to force through their preferred approach to Reconstruction.

Grant was, by that time, clearly the president in waiting—or at least the one Republican capable of claiming Lincoln's mantle. At the same time, Andrew Johnson was still the commander in chief. Grant, as the highest-ranking military officer in the country, formally answered to Johnson. But, by the time the Court's opinion came down in *Milligan*, Grant had decided to break with Johnson. It was a painful decision. Grant had begun to fear, though, that, in the growing battle between Johnson and Congress over Reconstruction, Johnson was acting illegally. Grant was also becoming worried that Johnson might continue down that path to the point where the separation of powers itself would be at risk. "We are fast approaching the point where he will want to declare the body itself illegal, unconstitutional, and revolutionary," Grant wrote privately to a friend about Johnson's attitudes toward Congress. In response, Grant had even begun to take precautions. He went so far as to order his officers to move army weapons in the South to the North. He worried the president might otherwise commandeer the weapons for his own nefarious purposes.

Still, Grant was too circumspect—or too clever—to make his break with the president conclusive. Grant was also too desirous of preserving his own power—and thus his presidential prospects—to step down as the nation's top general. But that did not mean that Grant was willing to conform his views to those of his president—or that he would do nothing to undermine him.

* * *

The first sign of Grant's break came in October. The president was trying to control the federal military presence in the South. Johnson had received reports that his top general was passing instructions to his officers that conflicted with Johnson's own view that only a limited military presence was proper. The president decided, therefore, to send Grant out of the country so that he could replace Grant with a more compliant general in Washington, D.C. Specifically, Johnson planned to request that Grant join a diplomatic mission to Mexico. But Grant, counseled by Republican allies, decided he would not give up his spot in Washington, fearing that his absence would allow Johnson to take control over the military aspect of Reconstruction.

Grant's refusal—made in the middle of a cabinet meeting, from which he would ultimately walk out—shocked Johnson. But Grant would not back down. He was going to keep his position in Washington. He beat back the president by arguing that a military officer need not follow a presidential directive on a matter of diplomacy.

The standoff revealed a breakdown within the military chain of command. Republicans in Congress soon moved in to exploit the rift—and to shore up Grant's position, now that they saw how eager the president was to go around him. But, interestingly, the first prod to protect Grant came not from the legislature but from within Johnson's own administration.

Concerned by Johnson's efforts to consolidate his power, Edwin Stanton, the only Lincoln appointee still left in Johnson's cabinet, decided to engage his allies on the Hill. Stanton thought that with their help he might be able to thwart the president's effort to assert control. Stanton was Johnson's secretary of war, but he was a Lincoln man through and through. He felt obliged to prevent Johnson from forging the peace on his terms, especially since Stanton believed those terms would betray the Union victory. And that meant Stanton felt obliged to do something to secure Grant's standing.

* * *

"I received a note from Mr. Stanton asking me to meet him at the War Office with as little delay as might be practicable," Massachusetts congressman George Boutwell later wrote, recalling the events that had transpired upon his December return to Washington for the new legislative session. The two men soon repaired to the secretary's office, after Boutwell showed up at the War Department. There, Stanton laid bare his fears.

Stanton relayed that he "had been more disturbed by the condition of affairs in the preceding weeks and months than he had been at any time during the war." Stanton explained the situation to Boutwell as follows: "Orders had been issued to the army of which neither he nor General Grant had any knowledge." Worse, echoing Grant's own private concerns, Stanton explained that he feared President Johnson was about to attempt "to reorganize the Government by the assembling of a Congress in which the members from the seceding states and the Democratic members from the North might obtain control through the aid of the Executive."

Stanton was warning Boutwell that an executive coup might be at hand. Stanton was also suggesting that the ordinary chain of command had been corrupted. So corrupted, in fact, that Stanton himself might not

know if a presidentially led coup was underway. As a result, Boutwell remembered, Stanton "thought it necessary that some act should be passed
by which the power of the President might be limited." And so, "under
[Stanton's] dictation," Boutwell began writing down the terms of the law
that Stanton wanted the congressman to introduce.

The measure Stanton came up with would amend the pending army
appropriations bill. It would ensure the headquarters of the general of the
army—the title then held by Grant—would be "fixed at Washington," unless those headquarters were moved with the consent of the general or
the Senate. Further, the law would make it "a misdemeanor for any officer
to obey orders issued in any other way than through the General of the
Army, knowing that the same had been so issued." In short, Johnson was
being stripped of his power to push Grant to the side, and this flank attack
was being carried out by the hand of the president's own cabinet officer,
who was authoring the unprecedented legislation on the sly.

* * *

The extraordinary bill, known as the Command of the Army Act, went
before Congress right away. For some, the bill demonstrated how badly
things were out of kilter. If the ordinary operations of the government—in
which the commander in chief stood atop the military hierarchy—had to
be deformed to compensate for an untrustworthy president, then perhaps
the constitutional system would be best served simply by impeaching
Johnson. True, impeaching a sitting president might have its own dangerous precedential effects, especially since the grounds for removal would
be essentially political and policy-based. But, at least impeachment, if successful, would ensure the government would not have to be remade in
ways that, even if strictly speaking constitutional, were as dysfunctional
as those under consideration.

At the time, though, impeachment was a very remote possibility. Congress took up the measure that Boutwell, with the hidden assistance of the
secretary of war, had put on the floor. The back and forth over the bill's
legality was most extensive in the Senate. There, the relatively moderate

William Fessenden, a Republican from Maine, took the lead in defending the law in late February. "The Commander in Chief of the Army of the United States is subject to the power of the people, to be exercised by Congress," Fessenden explained. "They cannot, perhaps, authorize an officer to command the Commander-in-Chief, but they can direct any officer what to do. That I hold very distinctly is the power of the people; and gentlemen mistake when they suppose that because the President as a matter of military rank is head of the Army it is out of the power of Congress to say what the head of the Army shall do, or shall not do."

Reverdy Johnson, a Democrat from Maryland and former counsel for the slave owner in the *Dred Scott* case, led the opposition. The issue was not sovereignty. The issue was the separation of powers, the people having delegated their authority to three distinct branches of the government. "I understand the honorable member virtually as saying that it would be in the power of the Congress of the United States to conduct a military campaign in a time of war, to provide by legislation where the fleets of the United States are to go, to send commissioners to head the armies, as was done by France during the Revolution, and to control the military officers in command," Reverdy Johnson said in challenging Fessenden. But that view was clearly contrary to the Constitution. Johnson claimed the founders created the Constitution on the basis of their experience of their own Revolution and "for the very purpose of escaping from the interference of Congress in the management of the armies of the United States, as far as the command was concerned."

Never for a moment, Reverdy Johnson added, would such a law have been passed if Lincoln were still alive. Nor would it have been passed if a president was in office who had not so lost the confidence of the Congress as Andrew Johnson had. But distrust of the president was no justification for passing such a law now. "Suppose the President of the United States should be satisfied that the presence of General Grant was necessary in the case of an invasion or outbreak again in some other place than Washington, and he should order him there, and he should say 'No, I will not go,'" Reverdy Johnson noted. "If Grant could take that position, and back it up with an appeal to this statute," then the president's constitutional right to command had been "denied."

Fessenden disagreed. The president did not enjoy "absolute power to do as he pleases with our armies because he is Commander-in-Chief." The notion that "when we have raised an Army and get it into the field, we have no further power over it, cannot direct its operations in any way, cannot direct against whom its operations shall be carried, and cannot make any rules which regulate it in actual service" would mean, Fessenden said, "we are at the pleasure of a military despot at any time who may happen to be Commander-in-Chief of the Army of the United States."

There were efforts to narrow the disagreement. One senator rose to point out that the bill would not dictate what Johnson could order the army to do. The bill regulated only how such orders, whatever their substance, must be made: through Grant, who must remain in Washington. So understood, the senator observed, there was good reason to pass the bill. He had learned from Grant himself, while conferring with him on other matters, that "it has been the practice for orders to go out concerning military affairs without ever passing through him at all, and consequently the public business of that character has been transacted to some extent without the coherence and consistency that it should be transacted with."

But "coherence and consistency" was a euphemism. That phrase covered over the chaos. Congress, the military establishment, and the president did not agree about how the army should be used. Nor did they share similar views about the future direction for the nation. The problem was not a bureaucratic one. It was a political and moral one. And each side was determined to win.

* * *

As the appropriations bill hurtled toward passage, Congress was also rushing to pass the Reconstruction Act of 1867. The bill sought to erase the last traces of Andrew Johnson's preferred brand of Reconstruction. The proposed law effectively supplanted the Southern governments that had been established by the president. In their place, the new law set up a system of military receivership, overseen, of course, by the army's top officer. In other words, the new law would make Grant an even more crucial actor in defining the postwar world.

No one doubted that Johnson would find Congress's newly minted approach unacceptable. On March 2, he made that clear. With Jeremiah Black's help, the president wrote a stinging veto message. Reflecting Black's influence, the message quoted liberally from the Court's majority opinion in *Milligan*. It gleefully cited the opinion's most strident passages about the dangers of unrestrained presidential power to determine which citizens were actually wartime enemies. At last, Black's winning argument before the Supreme Court—an argument rooted in distrust of executive authority—had been turned against Congress directly.

General Grant was repulsed. He wrote a friend that the Black-Johnson collaboration produced the most "ridiculous" veto message any president had ever issued. Wryly commenting on Black's role in writing it, Grant also remarked that it was "a fitting end to all our controversy that the man who tried to prove at the beginning of our domestic difficulties that the nation had no constitutional power to save itself is now trying to prove that the nation has not the power, after a victory, to demand security for the future."

Grant's jab at Black reflected a common concern among Republicans. They feared the world was going back in time, to Buchanan's day, as if all the errors of that administration had been forgotten. But the coda that Grant added to the letter he had sent his friend reflected Grant's recognition of how badly the government was now broken. "Do not show what I have said on political matters to anyone," Grant wrote. "It is not proper that a subordinate should criticize the acts of his superiors in a public matter."

* * *

As much as Andrew Johnson hated the new Reconstruction Act, he could not figure out how to stop it from becoming law. Any more than Johnson could figure out how to stop the Command of the Army Act—or seemingly anything else Congress wanted to do. Massive gains in the midterm elections had ensured Republicans now enjoyed huge majorities. The Republicans could work their will. Johnson settled on signing the Command of the Army Act and issuing a statement in protest. It blasted the law's supposedly unconstitutional incursion on his prerogatives as commander in chief.

Things deteriorated quickly. Congress passed the Reconstruction Act of 1867 over Johnson's veto. The president did his best to undermine the new law. Johnson considered firing the military leadership posted in the South so he could install generals more inclined to his view of how to make peace. In aid of those efforts, Johnson's attorney general issued opinions construing the newly enacted reconstruction law narrowly, thus making way for Johnson to assert control. The Republicans, though, contended the interpretations were unjustified and thus that the president was acting lawlessly. Grant even advised his officers that the attorney general's legal opinions were not "orders," thus effectively freeing his men to act as they chose. Consistent with that resistance, the Republicans in Congress also enacted new statutes that sought to clarify what Johnson's lawyers had claimed had been left unclear. The inconsistency and incoherence only worsened.

Throughout these months, President Johnson chose not to challenge Grant directly. The general was too popular. Johnson thought Grant might even be useful if he could somehow be kept neutral. But Secretary of War Stanton was a different matter. He was dangerous to be sure. He was also a far more inviting target than Grant. Stanton was not a political man, and there was no question of Johnson forging a tenuous alliance with him. To fire him, though, would be no easy matter. The Command of the Army Act had insulated Grant. The recently enacted Tenure in Office Act had done the same for Stanton.

* * *

That latter act made it a crime for Johnson to remove his war secretary absent Senate consent. Johnson saw no alternative. He was convinced that Stanton was daily conspiring with his Republican friends in the House and Senate to oust the president. Against the advice of Grant, much of his cabinet, and even Chief Justice Chase, Johnson moved the following winter, on February 21, to notify the Senate of his intention to remove Stanton. In doing so, Johnson doubled down on his earlier decision to suspend Stanton during the Senate's recess.

By then it had been more than a year since Stanton had first warned Boutwell that the president might be planning to take over the government. Similar rumors of such a takeover began to take on new life the day after Johnson notified the Senate that he intended to fire Stanton without the Senate's blessing.

The immediate trigger for the speculation that the president might be about to assert control in drastic and unprecedented ways was a meeting that Johnson had requested that morning with William Emory, the major general in command of the Military District for Washington. Upon being summoned to the president's office, Emory came over right away. Emory found the president alone at the Executive Mansion at about noon. The meeting did not last long, but word of it quickly made its way to the House. The scuttlebutt was that Johnson had brought Emory in for the purpose of conspiring with him—in direct violation of the Command of the Army Act—to bypass Grant and plot the military takeover that Stanton had long feared. At a minimum, the story went, the two men were working up a plan to cut out Grant so that they could deploy the army to assist Johnson militarily in forcing Stanton from office.

In response to these reports, Thaddeus Stevens pushed his House committee to vote for impeachment immediately. The vote was taken that very day, even though no formal articles of impeachment had yet been drawn up against the president. But, days later, the full House voted impeachment on eleven articles, the ninth of which was the so-called Emory article. It stated that Johnson had, "in disregard of the Constitution, and the laws of the United States duly enacted," instructed Emory that the key part of the Command of the Army Act was "unconstitutional, and in contravention of the commission of said Emory." The article went on to charge that Johnson had informed Emory of the law's unconstitutionality so that Emory could help Johnson to frustrate the execution of the Tenure in Office Act and thus unlawfully remove Stanton.

Johnson received the news of the House's dramatic action that evening. He supposedly took it "very calmly," confident that "many of those
who had voted for impeachment felt more uneasy as to the position in
which they had thus placed themselves than he did as to the situation in
which they had put him."

* * *

Weeks later, the Senate gathered for the impeachment trial of the president. Chief Justice Chase presided over the proceedings as the Constitution required. The first real bombshell came when Emory appeared as a
witness. If there was direct evidence that Johnson was plotting an executive takeover, Emory could supply it. But instead, in offering his much
anticipated testimony, Emory invoked the Command of the Army Act as
a shield against that very charge.

According to Emory, Johnson had called on him out of fear the military might be rising up against the president. Johnson, in other words,
had reached out to Emory. But Johnson had not done so to enlist Emory
in a plot to oust Congress. Johnson had instead reached out to Emory to
get information about any unusual troop movements that might suggest
an anti-Johnson uprising was at hand. Emory reported that he told Johnson he knew nothing of that and that, in light of the Command of the
Army Act, any such plans would have to go through Grant. As the military leader in Washington, Emory further explained, he would certainly
have known of any such orders coming from Grant.

Emory reported that Johnson expressed shock upon hearing about
this law restricting his powers of command: "Am I to understand that the
President of the United States can not give an order except through the
General of the Army? Or General Grant?" But Emory recalled that he had
reminded Johnson that he had signed that very act, and that orders had
even been issued under the president's name instructing army officers to
follow it. The text of that order and of the Command of the Army Act
were then brought into the president's office. That way, Johnson could
read them himself.

Emory added that he told Johnson that, like other army officers, he had consulted lawyers—including Reverdy Johnson—to get advice about his obligation to follow the act's requirements. The lawyers had told the officers they were all bound to obey orders, and thus to accept the act's prohibition against the president giving orders directly to them. At that point, Emory recalled, President Johnson remarked simply: "The object of the law was evident," as, at that moment, it must certainly seemed to have been.

Emory's no-nonsense testimony confirmed that Johnson had told him that the restriction on his powers of command was unconstitutional. But Johnson had already made that view known when he issued the statement saying as much upon signing the Command of the Army Act into law. Far more significant, Emory had dispelled any suspicion that President Johnson was trying to get around the act and enlist an army general in some sort of an executive coup. The president, in other words, had not defied Congress. According to Emory, Johnson accepted Emory's insistence that Congress's intrusive legislation controlled what he could do. It seemed, for the first time since the House had voted to impeach, that Congress's effort to oust Johnson might fail.

* * *

Johnson was ultimately acquitted by a single vote. There were many reasons for that result besides Emory's testimony. High on the list were several key evidentiary trial rulings by Chief Justice Chase. The rulings reflected Chase's concern that Congress had overstepped by going after the commander in chief. It was a concern Chase had first signaled in his concurrence in *Milligan.*

But Chase was hardly alone in taking that view of Congress's over-reaching ways. The story of this broader power struggle is now usually remembered in much the way that Chase saw it then: as an example of Congress taking things too far. In the decades after the trial, the story of congressional overreach burrowed into the national memory, assisted by generations of historians (many southern) portraying Johnson as a hero for resisting the Radical Republican Reconstruction plot.

Alongside that favorable political account came a wave of supporting constitutional opinion. Treatise writers and constitutional scholars took turns in the next decades elaborating on Chase's sentence in his concurring opinion in *Milligan* about the president's inviolable right to determine the "conduct of Campaigns." Thus, for the first time in the nation's history, there was a respectable constitutional treatise clearly teaching that Congress could not limit the president's powers of command, and the treatise did so in terms that went far beyond the strict words that Chase had used.

The old fears that had caused George Mason and Patrick Henry to plead for some limitation on the president's unchecked right to take command of troops in the field no longer seemed to have the same resonance. The salient image was no longer that of the man on horseback, immune to legal control. It was of a Congress so seized by its own power that it had practically divested the commander in chief of his power to command.

The unusual battle lines that had been drawn in the struggle between Andrew Johnson and Congress made this new image of legislative tyranny easier to conjure. In the fight over Reconstruction, the partisans of an unrestrained executive war power had been against the aggressive use of military force. The supporters of congressional control of the commander in chief had been committed to using military force to keep the citizenry in check. The whole episode seemed to confound traditional assumptions about where the risk of uncontrolled power lay—and thus to create room for new defenses of the unrestricted powers of the commander in chief as a check on military dictatorship.

* * *

By the time the century came to a close, this story of congressional overreach had become the conventional wisdom.

As such, it made a lasting impression on an enterprising political science professor from Virginia. Woodrow Wilson had imbibed this story of Reconstruction as a youth, and he soon made his name by attacking the system of what he called "congressional government." Wilson's scholarly positions nearly tracked the pro-Johnson narrative even if they were not, strictly speaking, offered for that purpose.

But there was another lesson to be gleaned from the battle for control of the army that had defined Johnson's presidency. Johnson had survived in office, to be sure, but only in a much weakened state. He was in no position to challenge Congress directly in the last nine months in office that he had secured by winning acquittal at his impeachment trial. Moreover, in the next election, Grant replaced Johnson. Congress thus got the chief commander it had favored all along. Finally, Grant, upon taking office, assured the country in his inaugural address that he would enforce the laws Congress passed, making a pointed effort to distance himself from the defiant pose of his predecessor.

Congressional government, in other words, was powerful in fact no matter how problematic it might be in theory. For that reason, no president—no commander in chief—could safely assume otherwise. That did not mean, though, that none would be willing to test the proposition in the future.

"Great as the provocation has been in dealing with foes who habitually resort to treachery, murder, and torture against our men, nothing can justify or will be held to justify the use of torture or inhuman conduct of any kind on the part of the American Army."

T he failed effort to impeach President Andrew Johnson touched off what turned out to be nearly a decade of partisan strife. But conflict-weary Americans found reason for hope in the election of Grover Cleveland, who took the presidential oath in March of 1885. He promised order, stability, and a return to an earlier time—before the great trauma that the country had just endured. There was, if Cleveland could live up to his promise, little chance that the constitutional system that had been stressed and strained from the secession winter through Reconstruction would be put to the test again.

A Democrat from upstate New York, Cleveland had won with a bipartisan coalition. It was hostile to immigration and enthralled by civil service reform. Consistent with that inward-looking platform, Cleveland's inaugural address was a modest call for unity and good government. So far from his mind were foreign affairs that his speech barely touched on the principles that would guide him as commander in chief. To the extent that the speech did, it sounded notes that were designed to diminish any

concern that the constitutional separation of powers was going to be put
through its wartime paces yet again.

"The genius of our institutions, the needs of our people in their home
life, and the attention which is demanded for the settlement and development of the resources of our vast territory dictate the scrupulous avoid-
ance of any departure from that foreign policy commended by the history,
the tradition, and the prosperity of our Republic," Cleveland explained
in announcing that he favored preserving American "neutrality, rejecting
any share in foreign broils and ambitions on other continents and repel-
ling their intrusions here." He then added that, like George Washington,
he would seek "peace, commerce, and honest friendship with all nations;
entangling alliances with none."

But within the decade, Cleveland's earnest but unambitious approach
to foreign policy was under serious assault. With that challenge came renewed struggles over the balance of power, provoked—for the first time
in the nation's history—by a swelling movement in favor of the aggressive
projection of American military force abroad. That movement eventually
had a champion in the commander in chief. It also sparked a counterrevolution that drew its strength from citizen-activists and an ever-growing
contingent of supporters in Congress.

The result was a sharp shift over the next many decades in the terms
of the debate about the powers of the commander in chief. The focus
would no longer be on the imperatives (or dangers) of executive aggression in protecting America from foreign predations, as it had been in
the earlier debates over whether the nation should remain neutral in the
face of the threats posed by France and then England. Nor would the
focus be on the scope of the power of the chief commander to manage
a civil war in which the enemy was as American as the army that he
led—a focus necessitated by constitutional crises that had brought the
system almost to collapse during the Civil War. Instead, the focus would
turn to whether the president had the right to use military force abroad
and not for—strictly speaking—defensive purposes but to claim foreign
territory. The ensuing debate, which turned as much on whether the
constitutional plan contemplated the government as a whole acting like

an empire as on what the president had the right to do, would at points become quite sharp. The result was as much a philosophical clash as a constitutional one. But, at the height of the executive-led effort to promote an American empire, Congress did assert itself, less by passing new laws to check the president than by using its power of oversight to shame him into obeying the ones that were already on the books.

* * *

Leading the expansionist crusade was an impressive cadre of intellectual and political leaders. Foremost among them was a fireball of energy and action named Theodore Roosevelt. A New Yorker himself, he would, after the turn of the century, make it all the way to the presidency after the Republican leader that he briefly served as vice president was shot dead early in his second term. Aiding Roosevelt at every step was his dear friend, one-time Harvard historian, and eventual coauthor, Henry Cabot Lodge, the stern and uncompromising Republican senator from Massachusetts.

Together, the two men would work to make space for a newly aggressive executive, one less interested in keeping America out of war than in ensuring America would win wars of its choosing. Adherents referred to the approach to foreign affairs championed by Roosevelt, Lodge, and others of their mindset as the "large policy." Opponents derided that approach as "imperialism"—a label chosen to make the point that this "large policy" was antithetical to the American idea.

In time, the debate over this new vision of America's role in the world—and the conception of the commander in chief that it entailed—would become hopelessly tangled. Imperialists like Lodge would, in the decades that followed Roosevelt's ascension to the Presidency, morph into what critics would call isolationists. They earned this moniker due to their hostility to the internationalist vision promoted by Woodrow Wilson, the first Democrat to become president since Cleveland. Some former anti-imperialists, by contrast, would be derided as internationalists, charged with being overly eager to enter into entangling alliances with European powers that risked committing America to enter European wars it had no independent interest in fighting.

But there was no debating that, in consequence of the aggressive stances taken by men like Roosevelt and Lodge, a new concern about the danger posed by an out-of-control commander in chief had emerged. Neither George Mason nor Patrick Henry, focused as they were with protecting domestic liberties and the rights of the states, had really contemplated what later commentators would refer to, in a nod to Roosevelt's time in office, as the imperial president. But, after Roosevelt, fears of a commander in chief hell-bent on committing the nation to foreign wars were ever present. If there was a single armed conflict that cemented the concern about what such an imperial presidency might look like, it was the war in the Philippines. Roosevelt was the commander in chief. Lodge was his valiant defender in the Senate, working furiously to fend off a relentless congressional investigation aimed at proving that the executive war power had indeed run amok.

* * *

The path that brought Roosevelt and Lodge together was a long one. They first met at the St. Botolph Club in Boston in the late 1870s. They joined forces politically soon thereafter. The connection between them was deep. Lodge reported in 1884 that "Theodore is one of the most lovable as well as one of the most cleverest and most daring men I have ever known. The more I see him, as the fellow says in the play, 'the more & more I love him.'" Later, Lodge would even write to his friend that it was as if there was a "telepathy" between them.

Together, Roosevelt and Lodge led a movement for a far more expansionist view of American power. Inspired by Darwinist theories of social progress, concerns about the closing of the American frontier, and an almost mystical attachment to notions of manliness and racial supremacy, this large policy was not focused merely on defending America from foreign threats. The approach sought instead—and to an unprecedented degree—to promote the need for the country to take new territory abroad.

Critical to the success of that mission, Roosevelt explained in his glowing 1890 review of Alfred Mahan's classic history of the importance of sea power, was the need for America to build "a fighting-fleet." Within the decade, thanks to Lodge's well-placed assistance, Roosevelt would find himself perfectly positioned to help the country do just that, setting him on a course that would end with Congress attempting to micromanage his control of that fleet during his last days as president.

* * *

The president when Theodore Roosevelt first came to Washington was William McKinley. He had brought Roosevelt's and Lodge's Republican Party back to power in the election of 1896. He had done so by defeating Grover Cleveland, who was seeking reelection after serving an unprecedented second but nonconsecutive term. Although hailing from a different political party than Cleveland, McKinley shared his same basic outlook on foreign policy. Cleveland had spent his last year in office doing what he could to put off a war with Spain. McKinley followed suit. He announced in his inaugural address that "we want no wars of conquest. We must avoid the temptation of territorial aggression."

But the pressure for McKinley to take the fight to Spain was intense, fueled by reports of abuses by Spain of its subjects in Cuba and by the uprising then underway in that country. Leading the effort to push America to challenge Spain and force it out of Cuba were Roosevelt and Lodge. By then a senator from Massachusetts, Lodge had spoken for both men in addressing his twenty-fifth Harvard reunion class in 1896. With Roosevelt looking on approvingly, Lodge had told his former classmates that "this great democracy is moving onward to its great destiny. Woe to the men or to the nations who try to bar its imperial march."

Although McKinley did not share Lodge's outlook in foreign affairs, the two men were close. And so the president eventually gave in to the senator's persistent requests to hire Lodge's friend, Roosevelt, as assistant secretary of the navy. The new man, a known wild card, quickly made an impact in Washington. He was tireless in bending the naval bureaucracy to his will. He took great advantage of his immediate superior's extended absence from the Navy Department. He also gave one incautious speech after another in which he extolled the virtues of making war.

Remarkably, after only a little more than a year of work, Roosevelt

had managed—with Lodge assisting from the Senate and the yellow press
working the public into an anti-Spanish frenzy—to help steer the nation
toward a head-on collision with Spain, not only in the Caribbean but in
the Pacific, too. The tipping point for going to war with Spain occurred in
February of 1898. That was when the American warship *Maine* exploded
in Havana harbor.

* * *

The cause of the explosion was almost certainly an accidental coal fire. It
did not matter. Roosevelt and others effectively portrayed the tragedy as
one that Spain had engineered. From that moment on, the country was
going to war. McKinley finally gave in and asked Congress to declare war
on Spain in April of 1898.

For Roosevelt, the conflict with Spain was not necessary merely to
defend the dignity of the Cuban colonists. The fight with Spain was, in
his mind, part of a much needed strategic shift. He wanted Spain out of
the Americas, and he wanted the United States to seize control of Spain's
holdings in the Pacific, too. America would then have the territories beyond its borders that he believed that it deserved to control. And so, no
sooner had Congress voted for war than Roosevelt announced—to the
amazement of the secretary of the navy—that he was quitting his post
and leaving the Navy Department for good. He did not want to be a mere
witness to the war that he had dreamt of for so long. He left Washington,
D.C., for Texas to prepare to lead a group of volunteers into battle.

Exchanging letters with Lodge from his military outpost in Texas,
Roosevelt made clear where he hoped things were heading. Lodge had
informed Roosevelt just the day before—"in confidence but in absolute
certainty"—that "the administration is grasping the whole policy at last."
Battleships were already en route to the Philippines to challenge Spanish
rule there, too, Lodge disclosed. The administration "mean to send not
less than twenty thousand men" to that far-flung second front in the bud-
ding war with Spain. As for Cuba, Lodge excitedly noted, "they intend to
put one hundred thousand men" into the island "so as to sweep the whole

thing up at one quick stroke." And he assured his friend that "Puerto Rico is not forgotten and we mean to have it." Summing up, Lodge could barely contain himself: "Unless I am utterly and profoundly mistaken the administration is now fully committed to the large policy that we both desire."

Heartened by Lodge's news, Roosevelt bragged in his return letter about the quality of the troops under his command. He was readying them for battle "in Camp near San Antonio." The men comprised "as typical an American regiment as ever marched or fought," Roosevelt reported. He assured Lodge that "you would enjoy seeing the mounted drill, for the way these men have got their wild half horses broken into order is something marvelous."

More broadly, Roosevelt told his friend that he and his men "most earnestly hope we can be sent to Cuba, and if for any reason Cuba should fail, then to the Philippines—anywhere so that we can see active service." And then, expressing the cocksure attitude that had coursed through his writings for decades and that had sustained his breakneck pace at the Navy Department, he offered one last wish: "I earnestly hope that no truce will be granted and the peace will only be made on consideration of Cuba being independent, Porto Rico ours, and the Philippines taken away from Spain."

* * *

The Spanish-American War—at least in its initial phase—was a smashing success for Roosevelt. His regiment assisted in the American invasion of Cuba. He was even crowned a war hero by the press for his daring exploits on San Juan Hill. Meanwhile, the American "fighting-fleet" that Roosevelt had helped build destroyed the Spanish navy in a battle in Manila Bay. There was no longer any doubt about America's status as a world power. Just as Lodge and Roosevelt had hoped, Cuba, Puerto Rico, the Philippines, and the island of Guam to boot were now all controlled by America. A peace treaty that the United States signed with Spain in Paris that December made America's heightened power clear.

Roosevelt was ascendant. The reputation he had earned from leading the Rough Riders—as his regiment was known—propelled him almost immediately to the governorship of New York. And then, in what seemed like the blink of an eye, he was put on the ticket with McKinley in his successful campaign for reelection. All of which meant that when an assassin gunned McKinley down in the fall of 1901, Roosevelt, at the age of only forty-two, was suddenly the commander in chief—and at a most challenging time to hold that title, given how things were unraveling half a world away.

* * *

Roosevelt had lustily supported the original plan to kick the Spanish out of the Philippines. His navy had then routed the enemy just as he had predicted it would. But if Roosevelt's policy toward the Philippines was consistent with his overarching views about the need to assert American power, the people of the Philippines were not as willing to accept foreign rule as the new president might have wished. The insurrection that ensued occasioned a reaction in Congress.

Spearheading this revived legislative effort to challenge the president's power of wartime command were those senators who had opposed imperialism all along. They spoke for that considerable chunk of the country that remained sympathetic to the older, less ambitious vision of foreign affairs that Cleveland had succinctly articulated a decade or so earlier. To the anti-imperialists, as they called themselves, Roosevelt and company were leading America—inevitably—to a reckoning that they were too shortsighted to see. The clearest signs of that reckoning were the insurrection in the Philippines and the president's chosen means of suppressing it.

The political danger for Roosevelt grew as the anti-imperialists successfully used the Senate Committee on the Philippines, created in 1899, to take on Roosevelt and his men for their conduct in countering the uprising. At first, Roosevelt's supporters were not overly worried. The committee was firmly controlled by Roosevelt's side. Lodge even served as the committee's chair. But, as the insurrection persisted, reports of abuse by American troops steadily increased, sometimes brought to light through the committee's own efforts. The reports then spurred Roosevelt's opponents on the committee to demand yet further investigations of how this "war" was being run. Finally, the pressure for the Senate to undertake a more focused inquiry into possible war crimes became too great for the president's team to resist.

Lodge's Senate committee would undertake a separate inquiry into the alleged misdeeds. That separate inquiry—with Lodge still in charge—began in January of 1902, just months after McKinley's September death and Roosevelt's unexpected ascension to the presidency.

The Lodge committee's investigation into these abuses was an immediate object of public attention. The anti-imperialists viewed the hearings as their best chance to make their case. Lest anyone doubt the need for such an inquiry or the righteousness of the challenge to continued American control of the Philippines, the anti-imperialists contended, one needed only to read an internal administration report about army abuses of the local population that had recently been uncovered by the commanding general of the United States Army, Nelson Miles.

* * *

Despite having led the nation's army in the Spanish-American War, Miles was reportedly planning to run as a Democrat in the upcoming presidential election. The rumor was that he would do so as, of all things, an anti-imperialist candidate. So, the tensions between the commander in chief and his commanding general were high when Miles showed up at a White House reception in early January 1902 to clear up some remarks that he had made to the press.

Miles had criticized the administration's limited response to reports of abuses by American troops in the Philippines, and his remarks had been poorly received. Miles was hoping to use the spur-of-the-moment appearance to make amends with the president for having publicly taken him to task. He had miscalculated. He soon found himself face-to-face with a furious commander in chief. Roosevelt shot the general down before he could even express regret. The president went so far as to say, with a full crowd of onlookers present, that the general's earlier public comments had made him worthy of censure.

Miles retreated until that spring, when he got his first chance for a measure of revenge. Congress, pressed by the administration, was considering an important piece of legislation to reorganize the army. The proposed bill sought to abolish the office of the commanding general and to vest more power in the secretary of war. Roosevelt's team figured that the public would support a measure that would enhance civilian control. But Miles upended that assumption. The general testified against the bill. He framed the proposed reform as a step toward dictatorship. He explained that he would resign rather than give in to the White House's "despotism." The bill went down to defeat—at least on this first go-round. Headlines followed, with one writer celebrating the defeat of "an Act to make the President of the United States a military dictator."

Then Miles struck again in April.

* * *

The general had come across a secret administration report about army abuses that seemed to confirm the worst of the anti-imperialist suspicions about what the war in the Philippines had led the American army to do in the nation's name. The existence of the so-called Gardener Report had been the subject of rumors for weeks thanks to Miles's skillful leaking to the press. Lodge felt that he had no choice but to have his committee publish the report.

Released on April 10, 1902, the report was a bombshell. Major Cornelius Gardener, the civil governor of the Philippine province of Trabayas, had written the report in December. He had then sent it to the governor-general of the archipelago, William Howard Taft, a close friend of the president, a former federal judge, and, of course, a future president.

Back in February, Taft had appeared as the very first witness before the special inquiry into army abuses in the Philippines undertaken by Lodge's Senate committee. But Taft had made no mention of the Gardener Report in his testimony at that time, even though a number of the committee members had squarely raised the issue of abuses by the troops. Thus, once the report was out in the open, the administration was on the defensive, not only for what it had said but also for seeming to mislead Congress.

The report explained that the local people had initially welcomed the American presence in the archipelago. The report then described how the locals had turned against the United States due to their unconscionable treatment at the hands of U.S. forces. The report explained that "of late by reason of the conduct of the troops, such as the extensive burning of the barrios in trying to lay waste the country so that the insurgents cannot occupy it, the torturing of natives by so-called water cure and other methods, in order to obtain information, the harsh treatment of natives generally, and the failure of inexperienced, lately appointed lieutenants commanding posts, to distinguish between those who are friendly and those unfriendly and to treat every native as if he were, whether or no, an insurrecto at heart, this favorable sentiment above referred to is being fast destroyed and a deep hatred toward us engendered." The report concluded that the means the Americans were using to suppress the insurrection were "sowing the seeds for a perpetual revolution against us," with the consequence that "we are daily making permanent enemies."

* * *

When the legislative hearings resumed in the wake of the Gardener Report's release, Lodge gamely tried to explain that the War Department had quite reasonably kept the report secret in order to avoid unfairly tarring the army officers named in it. But there was more to come that would aid the administration's opponents in Congress in their efforts to paint the strategy of expanding the nation's footprint through the acquisition of territory as one at odds with American values. And thus Lodge's efforts to protect Roosevelt would be tested severely.

Two days after the release of Major Gardener's report, another army major, C.W. Waller, testified in Manila at his court-martial for war crimes. He explained to the court that General Jacob H. Smith had ordered him as follows: "I wish you to kill and burn. The more you kill and the more you burn, the better you will please me." Waller then went on to explain that the general had clarified that he "wanted all persons killed who were capable of bearing arms." In a devastating coda, Waller added that when he inquired whether there was any age limit he should respect, the general had simply said: "Ten years."

The news of this testimony traveled quickly, and the revelations at the Senate hearings did not stop. Egged on by Lodge's Senate counterpart from Massachusetts, George Hoar, the anti-imperialists suddenly seemed to have the upper hand. First one Senate committee witness and then another gave detailed—and chilling—accounts of the use of the so-called water-cure by American forces. The detainee "is simply held down, and then water is poured onto his face, down his nose and face from a jar," testified one witness, explaining to the committee how he had seen the tactic used. "That is kept up until the man gives some sign of giving in or becomes unconscious, and when he becomes unconscious he is simply rolled aside and he is allowed to come to."

Lodge and other supporters of the administration did their best to deflect the unrelenting criticism of the army's harsh conduct of the counterinsurgency. If they could just wait out the criticism, they wagered, the defeat of the insurrection would quiet the critics for good. But the president was taking a beating from the continued congressional hearings, as was the whole expansionist project. The anti-imperialist senators were not so subtly making the case that the effort to acquire new territory in distant locales was destined to dishonor the country. Their questioning of administration witnesses was designed to show that there was only one way to end the disgrace that the war was becoming: America needed to give up the Philippines and to recognize that all people should be permitted to exercise the right to self-government.

* * *

With the president's command authority and his foreign policy under daily challenge in the Senate, Roosevelt realized that he was facing a true crisis. In mid-April, after a particularly bad day for the administration in Congress, the president called an emergency cabinet meeting. He wanted to discuss the allegations of brutality and what his response should be. His team had spent months essentially dismissing the criticism of the war's conduct. Roosevelt now believed that it was time to shift course. There was too much talk that the Philippines might be *the* issue in the 1904 presidential election. The president could not afford to seem indifferent to revelations that were discrediting the "large policy" that he had helped legitimate.

Through his secretary of war, Roosevelt made it known to the press that he was ordering a thorough investigation of all charges of brutality. "Great as the provocation has been in dealing with foes who habitually resort to treachery, murder, and torture against our men," Secretary Elihu Root explained in a public statement he issued on the president's behalf, "nothing can justify or will be held to justify the use of torture or inhuman conduct of any kind on the part of the American Army."

Still, the revelations kept coming. Each day seemed to beget new allegations. Allies of the president were starting to soften in their support for his policy in the Philippines. His staunchest opponents were pressing to expand the Senate investigation. There was growing concern that defections within the Republican congressional contingent might lead to the defeat of the president's planned legislation to place the Philippines under American civilian control.

Lodge offered a stern defense of the Philippines venture. Senator Hoar gave back just as good. In a brutal speech on the Senate floor, he accused Roosevelt, through his "practical statesmanship," of "converting a people who three years ago were ready to kiss the hem of the garment of the American and to welcome him as a liberator . . . into sullen and irreconcilable enemies, possessed of a hatred which centuries cannot eradicate."

* * *

Roosevelt decided to speak out. In a fiery speech, he accused his opponents of a dangerous naïveté. He hinted that they were disloyal. Surely they must know, the president said, that it was better for America to defeat the insurrectionists than to lose to them. But while Roosevelt's strong defense of his command did help to sway popular opinion, the

Senate hearings continued, with yet more awful revelations pouring forth. And, then, at last, in late June, Lodge gaveled the special inquiry to a close.

The final report of the Lodge inquiry was more than three thousand pages long. It was a depressing chronicle of a war gone wrong. But the insurrection was in its last throes, and three days after Lodge shut down the proceedings, Roosevelt announced that the war in the Philippines was finally over. In a proclamation that he signed on July 1, the president ordered a return to complete civilian control—albeit under American direction. He was able to do so because he had managed to ram through the civilian government act for the territory. Hoar turned out to be the only Republican defector. The United States would thus continue to run the Philippines.

The president did gesture toward those who had been so loudly calling on the administration to recognize the right to self-government of the Filipinos. Those calls had captured the public's imagination. The aggressive congressional challenge to the executive's seeming tolerance of the use of illegal tactics in gaining control over a foreign population was damaging the president politically. In a nod to the strength of the claims they were making on behalf of the principle of self-government, Roosevelt changed the date on the proclamation that declared that the war was over: He chose instead July 4.

* * *

As much as Roosevelt and the Senate had been at odds over the Philippines, the clash was noteworthy as much for what it exposed about differing visions of America's place in the world as for the shared legal premise on which it proceeded. The two sides sharply diverged when it came to the underlying view about whether America should be using military force to acquire territory abroad. However, they agreed that there were legal limits to what the president could authorize his troops in the field to do to defeat the enemy. They agreed, too, that those limits could take the form of congressionally enacted laws that could result in the criminal prosecution of the troops who violated those criminal prohibitions. Roosevelt never contemplated asserting a constitutional right as commander in chief to permit his forces to engage in torture. There was no suggestion that Congress lacked the power to declare certain tactics in war beyond the pale.

If anything, the shared understanding that torture and its cousins were illegal practices, and that Congress could make them so, helped ensure that the torrent of revelations of American abuse was especially damning for Roosevelt and his administration's "large policy." The critics asked fairly: If that policy led to such rampant illegality, then how could such a policy be consonant with the American system of constitutional government? The constitutional balance, in that basic sense, had not been upended, even if the pursuit of the large policy inevitably raised questions about how this age-old balance would fare if such a policy—or some variant of it—eventually took root and was pursued in some form in the years to come.

The congressional hearings—and the headlines that they generated—had punctured the expansionist bubble. But if Roosevelt was eager to put the war in the Philippines behind him, he did not retract his belief that America needed to maintain a strong presence abroad. In the years that followed, Roosevelt oversaw the construction of numerous battleships. And then, famously—in the midst of his second term—he sent his newly constructed "Great White Fleet" on an unprecedented 'round-the-world cruise. He sought to show the world the extent of America's military prowess and to gin up popular support for the construction of yet more battleships.

True to past pattern and practice, the president's planned imperial cruise was not cheered unconditionally. It stoked concern in Congress and thus touched off a new round of thrusts and parries between the branches over just which one would control the great fleet that was Roosevelt's pride. There were particular worries that the cruise might touch off a war with Japan. Tensions between the two countries were high. The public's appetite for more war was no longer as great as in the headiest days of the large policy. A Maine senator went so far as to threaten legislation that would deny Roosevelt the funds to send the ships across the globe.

It was to no avail. Roosevelt shot back. He already had the money he needed for his cruise, and he was not about to give it back.

But if Roosevelt came out ahead in that round, he was not the victor for good. His aggressive brand of executive leadership presaged what was to come. But he had not fundamentally challenged the basic understanding of who had the final say when it came to the powers of the commander in chief. In fact, he had not even really tried to bring about such a transformation. In the last year of his final term, Roosevelt even found himself countermanded by Congress on a military matter near to his heart: his authority to determine the type of officers who would be permitted to serve on the great fleet that he had devoted his life to creating.

* * *

With his days in office winding down, Roosevelt issued an executive order to ensure that the navy's ships would be manned solely by the navy itself. Marines would be barred from serving on them because they would be confined to onshore service. It was a reform much in keeping with the president's earlier effort to reform the army. He wanted to rid the armed forces of antiquated structures that were keeping it from meeting its full potential as a fighting force. The reform also reflected his pro-navy inclinations.

The order went over poorly in Congress. News spread that the president's order to expel the marines from the ships was part of a larger presidential plan to fold the marines into the army. An amendment was quickly put forward in the House. The proposed law would have required that at least 8 percent of the officers on any ship were marines.

The nation was not then at war, and there was an abstract quality to the debate that followed in the Senate over the constitutionality of this legislation. But there was a deep point of principle at issue, and the senators knew it. Lodge—reprising the role that he had played in overseeing the Senate investigation into the Philippines insurrection—did his best to provide cover for the administration. He insisted that there was no need to resolve the ultimate constitutional question of where final power resided.

His colleagues were not so sure. A proponent of the bill put the point in simple and stark constitutional terms. Could it really be that once the president had been given a navy to command, Congress had no power to direct how he would be permitted to use it? "Suppose upon the occasion of a doubtful presidential election, in which the incumbent was a candidate, he saw fit to order 50,000 men to the capital: does the Senator doubt the power of Congress by law to say that they should be ordered elsewhere?" Senator Augustus Octavius Bacon, a Democrat from Georgia, asked. "If so, we have very little barrier between ourselves and despotism whenever a bad man happens to be President."

Idaho senator William Borah—a reform Republican who sided with Roosevelt but would emerge as a leading voice for maintaining American neutrality in the decades ahead—offered the only rejoinder that could have any force: "The fathers who framed the Constitution did not seem to know whether the men would be in Congress or in the presidential chair." For that reason, Borah concluded, impeachment was the proper remedy to rely upon if Congress found itself facing off with a president with despotic tendencies.

This extended constitutional debate over the legislature's right to check the commander in chief ultimately concluded no differently from others that had been held on the floor of Congress. The measure passed. And the president signed it, on his next-to-last day in office.

* * *

The marines-on-ships bill was, by design, not intended to take effect until Roosevelt's successor took office. (Roosevelt himself did not order any marines back onto naval ships.) But that new president, William Howard Taft, raised no objection to the legislative override of Roosevelt's executive order once he took office. In fact, Taft's attorney general, George Wickersham, concluded in a formal opinion that he had "no doubt of the constitutionality of the provision." He explained: "Inasmuch as Congress has power to create or not to create, as it shall deem expedient, a marine corps, it has power to create a marine corps, make appropriation for its pay, but provide that such appropriation shall not be available unless the marine corps be employed in some designated way."

In a later opinion, though, the attorney general backtracked a bit. He made clear that there might still be limits to what Congress could do to restrain the commander in chief in "an emergency making such action imperative for the protection of the interests of the Government, such as might arise in time of war or public danger." It was a position that Taft himself, writing as a Yale law professor two years after he left the White House, seemed to embrace. He explained that it is the president "who is to determine the movements of the army and of the navy" and that Congress could not "themselves, as the people of Athens attempted to, carry on campaigns by votes in the market-place." Reinforcing the point, Taft explained in a published version of his lecture that "when we come to the power of the President as Commander-in-Chief it seems perfectly clear that Congress could not order battles to be fought on a certain plan, and could not direct parts of the army to be moved from one part of the country to another."

* * *

Perhaps not. But soon enough, the constitutional debate over Congress's power to set limits on the power of the commander in chief to wage war would resume in earnest. War was breaking out in Europe. The old worries about unchecked executive war powers, first surfaced by Patrick Henry and George Mason before there even was a Constitution, were front and center. But, as had long been true, the battle lines over war powers turned out to be more crooked than straight.

With the new Democratic president, Woodrow Wilson, a most reluctant warrior, and his Republican opponents in Congress aghast at his seeming refusal to assert American power as fully and as unilaterally as they thought proper, there followed a sharp interbranch clash. The fight, though, was more about the president's right to dictate the terms on which the war would be fought than about the wisdom in going to war at all. In consequence, the president found himself challenged by those in Congress who were committed to blocking his efforts to wage war on terms that he was determined to make more internationalist than his opponents were willing to countenance. The result was that, paradoxically, some who were most eager for Wilson to take the nation to war at the outset were, by the end, handmaidens of an isolationist vision that would create all sorts of obstacles when, decades later, another president confronted the prospect of a world war erupting due to German aggression.

Part 3
WORLD WARS

≡ 11 ≡

THE GREAT WAR

"I wish to feel that the authority and the power of the Congress are behind me in whatever it may become necessary for me to do. We are jointly the servants of the people and must act together and in their spirit."

H e Kept Us Out of War." It was the key slogan in Woodrow Wilson's 1916 reelection campaign. The keenest political minds thought the message might strike a special chord with mothers, as women had recently been given the vote in a number of western states. If so, there was a chance the propeace reminder of what their president had done to keep the peace could make the difference in what was expected to be a close contest. The anti-imperialist—some said "isolationist"—outlook had gained traction over the last decade. There was a renewed attraction to neutrality. Given that turn in public opinion, Wilson's team thought that the president's election-year slogan would help him expand his electoral base beyond traditionally Democratic territory. Most observers, though, were dubious. The constant attacks on the president's refusal to stand up to the Germans, coupled with the news reports of the Germans' continued intransigence, made Wilson's political position vulnerable. There were signs his aggressive program of presidentially led domestic reform had run its course.

On election night, a resigned Wilson gathered with his family at his private estate in New Jersey. There, the group received initial, unfavorable reports. With the mood glum, a serene but dejected Wilson went to bed, fully expecting to wake to news of his defeat. He had even vowed privately to aides that he would immediately resign his post, rather than leave the nation with a defeated lame duck for the four months until the new president would take office. Wilson was thus delighted when, the next morning, he learned that women voters out west had likely put him over the top. They were apparently fearful Wilson's Republican opponent, the former Supreme Court justice, Charles Evans Hughes, would send their sons to die in the Great War in Europe. Days later, when the last votes came in from California's mountain towns, it was clear the mothers had indeed come through for the man who promised continued peace.

Woodrow Wilson, against all odds, would be serving four more years—years that, sadly, would all but break him. During his second term, Wilson would not bask in a worldwide peace of his own creation as he had hoped and promised. He would be forced to test his novel theories of executive government in the crucible of a world war, during a time when political opponents controlled the Congress that it had long been Wilson's mission to overcome. It was a mission Wilson was not able to accomplish.

* * *

The president was always peripatetic, and he had no intention of slowing down now that he had been given another term. Even before his second swearing-in, Wilson—still the tall, thin, vigorous, if slightly stiff man with the spectacles of a scholar that he had been when first elected—resolved to offer nothing less than an unprecedented plan to ensure "the future security of the world against wars."

To make good on that commitment, the president appeared before a specially called legislative session on January 22, 1917, more than a month before the scheduled congressional recess was set to end. From the House chamber, amidst continuing attacks on his strength of character, Wilson gave a strong speech—his diction soaring and his voice, as always, gripping in its depth. He refused to back down from his previous commitments to forge a peace that would end the bloodshed "over there." Wilson proposed a "Fourteen Point plan" to secure a comprehensive European "peace without victory." Its centerpiece was a newly proposed League of Nations. Members would agree to subject their power to go to war to the votes of other members. America, Wilson made clear, would be a founding participant.

Prominent observers hailed the speech, but the reviews were not all glowing. Wilson had won the White House, but the Republicans had done well in the congressional elections. And members of the opposition party—like Wilson's great rival, Theodore Roosevelt—were not shy about mocking the address's dreamy tone. The Republicans were put off by Wilson's decision to give this peace sermon after German U-boats had taken out cruise liners, some with American passengers on board.

Even more worrisome, the speech was received poorly by America's European allies. They feared Wilson's sunny sentiments would only encourage Germany to think that America's president, evidently looking to cut a deal, would cave if pressured. Less than ten days after Wilson's address, the Germans seemed to prove those skeptics right. Rather than making an overture, the Germans served notice: Beginning the very next day, the Germans announced, they would use "every available weapon" to interdict all sea traffic around Great Britain, France, Italy, and the eastern Mediterranean—a listing that made American merchant ships targets, too.

* * *

Wilson's grand hopes for world peace seemed dashed by Germany's latest moves, before the president even had been in a position to give those hopes substance. Still, one might have been excused for thinking that the president saw opportunity in the apparent setback. Wilson was less a creature of government than a man with ideas about how to organize it. He was no lover of war. But he did believe in the untapped potential of the assertive exercise of executive power. And, from his studies, he knew how advantageous military action could be for a president determined to expand the influence of the executive office.

Wilson had risen to the presidency as no man had before: as a political scientist by trade and a politician only by serendipity. Since his days as a doctoral student, Wilson had been convinced that, at least in the

modern world, America could no longer afford for the legislative branch
to be the locus of policy-making power. That old system, which Wilson
derisively called "congressional government," was intolerable now that
America had become a great power, with a modern economy and a fate
deeply entwined in world affairs.

In his academic writings, Wilson argued for what he eventually called
"constitutional government"—in contrast to its nemesis, "congressional
government." In this new model, the president would take the lead role
in giving direction to the nation's affairs, at home and abroad. By guiding
and directing Congress, openly and transparently, the president would
ensure the two branches worked hand in hand to implement the executive's, and thus the nation's, program.

As president, Wilson had achieved much domestically in his first term
by putting those theories into action. But conditions were more favorable
during those years, what with large Democratic majorities in each chamber. It would not be so easy now. That made all the more significant Wilson's observation as a scholar that, historically, it was war that provided
about the only means by which presidents managed to loose themselves
from the grip of Congress's control.

Of course, war could not automatically imbue the presidency with
strength. Madison's example a century earlier in the war with England
made that clear. But keying off of Lincoln's stunning example during
the Civil War—which Wilson identified as the ideal of constitutional
government—the Princeton professor had famously remarked that the
presidency was only "as big" as the man in office chose to make it. Now, im-
probably, that choice was his to make, thanks to an unlikely rise to power
and the sudden turn in world affairs. In what seemed like a flash, Wilson
had zoomed from a controversial tenure as Princeton's president, to the
governorship of New Jersey, to the White House. Wilson's confidence—
some might say his narcissism—had been nourished (or indulged) along
the way. But this head-spinning journey made it most unlikely Wilson
would squander the moment history had given him. All his life, it seemed,
had prepared Wilson to take maximum advantage of this historic chance
to make the presidency as big as he could.

* * *

Wilson was not clear, however, about how best to proceed. He was terribly conflicted about war, and this potential war with Germany most particularly, as the whole reelection campaign had made perfectly clear. Throughout his first term, Wilson consistently reminded his advisors that he had known war as a young boy in the South. The experience of the Civil War—or, perhaps, the southern version of the history of that war—had inspired within him a deep sympathy for the conquered. It also gave him an aversion to vengeance. An accommodating peace, even with a party responsible for a war, was hardly dishonorable in his southern-bred eyes. It was also what he had promised the American people.

Wilson's initial inclination in the face of German aggression, then, was to step forward gingerly, committing the nation to nothing until there was no other choice but war. But even in this tentative mode—one aimed at respecting Congress's prerogatives when it came to making the decision between war and peace—Wilson encountered legislative resistance. Congressional government, it turned out, was a force he would have to reckon with no matter how antiquated he believed it was.

As the German U-boat campaign accelerated, the president's cabinet struggled with the knotty questions of neutrality that had tied up Wilson's predecessors—first Adams, then Jefferson—during earlier European wars. At a cabinet meeting on February 13, 1917, Treasury Secretary William McAdoo—by then Wilson's son-in-law—insisted Wilson place naval gun crews on merchant ships. McAdoo forcefully argued that America needed to do at least that much to protect its commercial interests from Germany. Wilson had been pondering a policy of "armed neutrality," and his secretary of state, Robert Lansing, formerly the Department of State's top lawyer, assured him it would be neither an act of war nor a violation of international law. But, Wilson worried, such an approach would be perceived as forcing Congress's hand on the question of war—if not preempting Congress's deliberations altogether—given the risk that fire might be exchanged on the high seas.

With the situation worsening, the cabinet gathered again ten days later, with the pressure growing on Wilson to act more forcefully. One participant remembered the meeting as "one of the most animated sessions of the Cabinet that I suppose has ever been held under this or any other President." This time, McAdoo was even more emphatic about the need to arm the merchant ships. Wilson admired his son-in-law's talents, but the president thought he lacked vision. He thought McAdoo saw only what was right in front of him, not the larger canvas Wilson was always scanning. And here, Wilson believed, the bigger picture concerned power and who possessed it in war. Seen this way, armed neutrality was not a mere temporary tactic. It was a first step toward full-on war. Hesitant to enter this war, Wilson did not see how he could take even this measure, given all that it could lead to, without support from Capitol Hill. "The government would continue to be one of law," he pointedly informed his cabinet. The better course, therefore, was to seek specific legislative authorization, even if, as McAdoo assumed, such approval was not required.

The next day, Wilson drafted a two-paragraph version of his ideal legislation. Then, on Monday, February 26, he appeared before yet another specially requested joint session of Congress. In making his case for legislative support, Wilson was careful not to suggest he was completely dependent upon Congress: "No doubt I already possess [the] authority" to arm merchant ships "without special warrant of law, by the plain implication of my constitutional duties and powers." Still, Wilson insisted that "I prefer . . . not to act upon general implication." "I wish to feel," Wilson explained, "that the authority and the power of the Congress are behind me in whatever it may become necessary for me to do. We are jointly the servants of the people and must act together and in their spirit."

* * *

Congressional sentiment seemed on the surface to be running strongly in Wilson's favor. Front-page reports the next day revealed the Germans had recently sunk the British liner *Laconia*, en route from New York to Ireland, and that two female American passengers had perished from exposure in lifeboats. The House of Representatives quickly passed a version of Wilson's legislation. It seemed Wilson was making headway, driving his agenda, forcing Congress to go along with each step he took. But time was running out. The final session of the sixty-fourth Congress would end at noon that coming Sunday. In the ordinary course of events, the new Congress would not convene for many months after the break.

The final weekend of the sixty-fourth Congress found Washington deluged by a cold, driving rain. With the House's work done, only the Senate remained to be convinced of Wilson's plan. But Senate rules of that era allowed senators to filibuster indefinitely, and a handful of senators—some hostile to war, others courting it, neither camp willing to empower Wilson to be the ultimate decision maker—seemed determined not to allow a vote on the legislation to authorize arming the merchant ships.

As Saturday came and went, the recalcitrant senators blocked each and every motion to proceed to a vote. Wilson was a firsthand witness to the final debacle. Just before noon on Sunday, Wilson had settled into the President's Room of the Capitol, located just outside the Senate chamber. Wilson had made unprecedented use of this room in his campaign to reverse the flow of power in the executive's favor. His sweeping domestic reforms had come to fruition through those lobbying efforts. But, on this day, the president was there for a special reason. Wilson was waiting for Chief Justice Edward White to administer the oath of office for his second term. It would be a private ceremony, scheduled to occur on the constitutionally appointed day and time. Wilson would retake the oath publicly the next day, after the Sabbath had ended and a full-dress inauguration could be staged.

Wilson fitfully waited, until, finally, the word from the Senate came: The session was gaveled to a close with no new legislation concerning the merchant ships having passed. Wilson was furious—and disgusted. After taking the oath four minutes later, he rushed back to his study in the White House. There, he hurriedly drafted a statement lambasting the Senate. The statement was mimeographed and rushed to the press that evening. Wilson's statement accused a "little group of willful men, representing no opinion but their own," of "render[ing] the great Government of the United States helpless and contemptible," even though, "as a matter of fact, the nation and the representatives of the nation stand back of the Executive with unprecedented unanimity and spirit."

The *New York Times* reported Wilson's close friends were certain he would now act on his own, in accord with McAdoo's long-standing suggestion that the president should order the navy to furnish guns to the merchant ships. But there was a catch—and one that exposed the difficulties in making the shift away from congressional government that Wilson was supposedly so eager to make.

* * *

The first hint of a problem came in an addendum to the administration's earlier press statement blasting the Senate. This new "Supplementary Statement" explained that the Senate's action had made the situation "even more grave than it had been supposed that it was." That was due, the statement explained, to the "discovery that, while the President under his general constitutional powers could do much of what he had asked the Congress to empower him to do, it had been found that there were certain old statutes as yet unrepealed which raised insuperable practical obstacles and virtually nullified his power." Then, even more unusually, several hours later, the White House issued a third statement. This one made the president's legal position more equivocal: The "old statutes" at issue, the new version read, "*may* raise" insuperable practical obstacles and "*may* nullify" the president's power to arm the ships.

The "discovery" of the "old statutes" came from an examination of the transcript of a colloquy on the Senate floor, which had occurred near the end of the congressional session. The back and forth had involved Republican Minority Leader Henry Cabot Lodge, the revered Massachusetts Senator. He had supported the armed neutrality legislation in the debates on the Senate floor. He had also explained, though, that statutory authorization was necessary because a long-forgotten statute, enacted in 1819, "expressly provide[d]" that merchant vessels must not use force to defend themselves against the armed ship of a nation with which the United States was "at amity."

The mention of the old statute in that colloquy unnerved the president and his men. It was one thing to call Congress back and demand its support for legislation. It was another for Wilson to act unilaterally if Congress chose to keep silent. It was something altogether more problematic—something not even the strongly pro-executive Wilson could support—to defy a statutory bar that Congress had placed in the president's way.

Wilson immediately consulted with Secretary Lansing. He informally advised the president that, at least on first impression, he disagreed with Lodge's reading of that old statute. Before departing for the ceremonial inaugural events on March 5, though, Wilson turned to his attorney general, Thomas Gregory. Wilson asked Gregory for an answer to this late-breaking legal question within twenty-four hours.

With news of the obstacle out, legal scholars jumped into the fray. Former attorney general George Wickersham sent off a long, rambling letter to the *New York Times* counseling that "the only really effective method of dealing with the situation" was for Wilson to convene Congress anew and obtain authorizing legislation. The president clearly needed an answer to the legal question. He got it the next morning. Attorney General Gregory formally concluded that the problematic statute did not apply. Secretary Lansing concurred. The president's men had found a "more or less technical" way out. They concluded that the old law, styled as a grant of authority, was not clearly intended to prohibit anything. In any event, they determined, that law seemed to apply against nations "in amity with the United States," a category that hardly covered Germany, even if it was not yet an enemy.

Wilson could now move forward. The president announced the action from his sickbed, having caught a terrible cold from the windy inauguration ceremony. He told the nation he intended to order that arms be furnished to American merchant ships right away.

* * *

Wilson's strategy of "armed neutrality" seemed to work politically. Even senators initially opposed to his requested legislation saw that the president, clearly scrambling to stay right with Congress, was not trying to act in a high-handed manner. Wilson, though, remained cautious. If the Germans did not relent, Wilson knew war could not be put off for long. The onset of outright hostilities would bring new challenges in managing Congress.

Before too long, the Germans pressed the conflict into a new phase. Their submarines began sinking U.S. vessels. Wilson once more addressed an extraordinary joint session of Congress. His former posture of neutrality, armed or otherwise, was no longer tenable. Explaining that it would be "neither right nor constitutionally permissible" for him to make the "very serious" decision to go to war unilaterally, given what a "fearful thing to lead this great peaceful people into war, into the most terrible and disastrous of all wars, civilization itself seeming to be in the balance," Wilson put the decision to declare war in Congress's court.

Wilson made sure to impress upon Congress that once it took the first step of recognizing the state of war, he expected to determine how the military effort should be run. "I shall take the liberty," Wilson announced, "of suggesting, through the several executive departments of the Government, for the consideration of your committees, measures for the accomplishment of the several objects I have mentioned." As Wilson saw it, these were not to be mere suggestions. "I hope that it will be your pleasure," he pointedly added, "to deal with them as having been framed after very careful thought by the branch of the Government upon which the responsibility of conducting the war and safeguarding the nation will most directly fall."

Wilson did not waste time making good on his commitment to take the lead. Before Congress declared war, he was busy drafting a self-styled "Programme" to be sent to the legislature for its approval. And, as soon as Congress made the requisite declaration of war, Wilson sprang into action, sending a stream of bills down Pennsylvania Avenue for urgent consideration. The legislation dealt with a wide range of matters. It included Wilson's infamous Espionage Act, as well as strict export controls and a notorious censorship regime. It also called for the creation of an administration empowered to regulate food production and consumption; the requisitioning of railroads for military use; various maritime regulations, including authority to seize interned enemy ships; and emergency appropriations of all kinds.

Still, Wilson had not shed the instinct against war that had for so long led him to counsel peace. And that instinct would color how he would assert his powers now that war had been declared. Wilson would use those powers in ways that would run counter to the typical image of the president as war leader.

* * *

Wilson resolved that if this war with Germany had to be fought, he would not fight it to advance American interests alone, or even those of its Allies. He certainly would not do it in the name of vengeance. He would wage war to usher in a new international legal order that, through the League of Nations, would bring about an enduring world peace. In other words, at least in Wilson's mind, the Fourteen Point plan (and its centerpiece, the League of Nations) was hardly dead—no matter that Germany had continued its campaign of aggression or what his Republican critics might have thought. Through war, the president would bring "peace without victory" to life. But, in pursuing his own unique vision of wartime leadership, Wilson would find himself plunging into a struggle with Congress. For while Congress was happy to lend its aid in going to war, Congress also remained quite concerned about what seemed to be the president's unconventional conception of what would count as victory. No matter how hard Wilson pushed Congress to let him fight the war his way, and for the ends that he defined, the Republican opposition—and, on occasion, even members of his own party—refused to get out of his way.

Some of the resistance simply stemmed from a turf struggle. On points large and small, many in Congress saw Wilson's assertiveness in stark, constitutional terms. Even members of the president's own party shared the concern that Wilson was acquiring too much authority. In fact, Military Affairs Committee Chairman Hubert Dent, a powerful fellow southern Democrat, went so far as to vow that he would resign before he would accept "the argument . . . that, in time of war the executive department shall draft its legislation and send it to Congress, and Congress shall not exercise the right to cross a 't' nor dot an 'i.'"

But the opposition—the Republicans most especially—was also driven to take on Wilson by a very different vision of what the war was all about. Peace without victory, the president's opponents continued to believe, was not a worthy goal for a commander in chief. The pursuit of peace without victory was instead a surefire way to court defeat. And thus, with Theodore Roosevelt still active after all these years, and as nationalistic as ever, goading them on, the opponents were loath to give Wilson an unfettered hand. They would do what they could to force him to fight on their terms and thus to ensure victory was the final outcome.

* * *

The first real sign of the fight to come concerned the centerpiece of Wilson's wartime "Programme": the proposal for a comprehensive military draft. Wilson had effectively won a consensus on the need to conscript. But that did not end the debate.

As House and Senate prepared to go to conference to reconcile their competing conscription bills, attention centered on a provision in the Senate measure that the House had left out. The Senate version authorized the president to raise and maintain up to four infantry divisions of *volunteers*, in addition to the divisions of conscripted personnel. Everyone knew this volunteer provision was designed to allow the former president of the United States, Theodore Roosevelt, to organize and command troops, including a cavalry in France. Everyone also knew it was the last thing Wilson wanted Congress to include in legislation authorizing the draft.

Roosevelt had been lobbying to reprise his role as leader of the Rough Riders since before Wilson had even decided to ask Congress to declare war. While clamoring for the "big war" and spreading word about his doubts about Wilson's courage, Roosevelt had filed an "application" with the War Department to raise an infantry division. Roosevelt had even informed Secretary of War Newton Baker in early February that he would cancel his scheduled sail to Jamaica for a month's vacation if Baker expected war to begin imminently, so that he could saddle up right away.

Baker brushed Roosevelt off as politely as he could. But the awkward correspondence continued as tensions with Germany intensified. In one exchange, Baker informed Roosevelt that, in the event of a war and the use of any volunteer forces, all volunteer officers would be drawn from the regular army. Roosevelt "respectfully" pointed out to Baker in a written response that as a "retired Commander-in-Chief of the United States Army," he was "eligible" to command any U.S. troops.

Baker could barely believe what he was reading. He sent Roosevelt's response to the president, who wrote Baker back to say: "This is one of the most extraordinary documents I ever read! Thank you for letting me undergo the discipline of temper involved in reading it in silence!"

Meanwhile, Roosevelt was busy recruiting his band of volunteers. Applications poured in from all over the country, including from many famous military figures and descendants of Civil War heroes (and a young lieutenant from Kansas, Dwight David Eisenhower). Roosevelt was also rapidly raiding the ranks of younger officers from the army itself. "So far as I am able," he wrote to a friend, "I shall endeavor to free this country from the disgrace of seeing it embark in a war without fighting, for such a war can only be ended by a peace without victory"—a sneering reference to Wilson's hoped-for resolution of the Great War.

* * *

With the war finally declared, Roosevelt decided to take his case for leading the troops into battle straight to the White House. He popped in unannounced on April 10. Wilson had little choice but to welcome Roosevelt into the Green Room. The two men, archrivals who had squared off against one another in the 1912 election, had rarely met in person. This was only the second time they had encountered one another since 1905. Each was certain that he and he alone knew what it took to lead the nation to victory. But during the twenty-five minutes they were together, Wilson warmed up; the two men even exchanged a bit of laughter.

Even so, Wilson was not moved by Roosevelt's case. Wilson feared—
with cause—that Roosevelt would hardly be amenable to Wilson's strategic plans for Europe. The president worried Roosevelt might well ally with
those Europeans calling for vengeance rather than for the just and lasting
peace Wilson still envisioned. The last thing the president needed was an
uncontrollable, demagogic figure riding roughshod in France. Roosevelt's
expeditionary force would inevitably divert critical officers and resources
from the military, just at the time when the armed forces were most in
need of expansion and strengthening.

Henry Cabot Lodge assigned Senator Warren Harding to manage the
effort to secure votes for the Roosevelt volunteer provision. "There is but
one Theodore Roosevelt in the world," Harding said on the Senate floor,
claiming that just the sight of the former Rough Rider at the helm "would
put new life in every allied trench and a new glow in every allied camp fire
on every battle front of Europe." Lodge chimed in with still more florid
defenses of Roosevelt—"He is known in Europe as no other American is
known"—that were unmistakably, if indirectly, critical of Wilson.

The bill went to conference. Wilson and his allies managed to force
through a conscription bill free from what the president called "any feature that would embarrass the system of draft upon which it is based."
But Roosevelt and his allies pushed back. Using the lateness of the hour
to their advantage, they secured enough votes in the House to revive
the measure favoring Roosevelt. The ex-president's rejuvenated friends
in the Senate rose once more to extol his "tenacity" and "courage"—the
"red blood in his veins"—and so, to great fanfare, both houses approved
the conscription bill, *including* the volunteer provision. "Roosevelt Wins
Army Bill Point," blared the headline in the *New York Times* the next
morning.

* * *

Roosevelt immediately sent a telegram to Wilson seeking permission to
raise two divisions for service at the front—or even four divisions, if the
president so desired. Wilson found a way to wriggle free. The controversial provision had been written in permissive, not mandatory, terms. And

thus, with his back against the wall, the president exercised the discretion Congress had quietly afforded him.

Wilson knew full well he was bucking the expectations of most, if not all, of the legislators who had fought so strenuously for the "Roosevelt Amendment." Wilson released a statement to the *New York Times*. The statement acknowledged that the provision in question was added "with a view to providing an independent command for Mr. Roosevelt," so that the former president's "vigor and enthusiasm" could be used on the Western Front. Wilson feigned that it "would be very agreeable to me to pay Mr. Roosevelt this compliment." But then he countered that to send Roosevelt to France "would seriously interfere" with the primary aims of the legislation "and would contribute practically nothing to the effective strength of the armies now engaged against Germany." Accordingly, Wilson would "not avail [him]" of the authorization Congress had just given him.

A day later, Wilson sent a telegram to Roosevelt to soothe him. A bitter Roosevelt, meanwhile, wrote a public letter to the thousands of volunteers he had assembled. Roosevelt addressed them as "the men who have volunteered for immediate service on the firing line in the divisions which Congress authorized." But, in the end, Roosevelt regretfully concluded, "the only course open to us is forthwith to disband and to abandon all further effort in connection with the divisions." After all, "as good American citizens we loyally obey the decision of the Commander-in-Chief of the American Army and Navy."

* * *

Roosevelt's deferential statement notwithstanding, the legislative resistance to Wilson's efforts to ensure that the war would be fought as he wished did not let up. Just three days after Congress declared war in April 1917, Republican senator John Weeks offered a resolution to create a special congressional joint committee, composed of members of both houses, to "make a special study of the problems arising out of the war, [and to] confer and advise with the President of the United States and the heads of the various executive departments." Senator Weeks deliberately modeled

his proposal on the Joint Committee on the Conduct of the War that had
bedeviled Lincoln during the Civil War. The committee would, for example, have virtually unlimited subpoena and investigative powers. And the
committee also was designed to "furnish a direct connecting link between
the executive and the legislative branches of the Government."

Wilson wanted no part of it. He wrote to the manager of the bill to
which the rider would be attached that the joint committee would "render my task of conducting the war practically impossible." The President
added that "the constant supervision of executive action which it contem-
plates would amount to nothing less than an assumption on the part of
the legislative body of the executive work of the administration." Senator
Robert Owen, an influential Democrat, tried to smooth things over. He
proposed limiting the committee's jurisdiction to expenditures and contracts relating to the conduct of the war, but not the conduct of the war
more broadly. Owen respectfully urged Wilson to embrace the proposal.
Owen stressed that the committee would be under the control of his fellow Democrats. In making the case, Owen invoked Wilson's own famed
philosophy of "common counsel" between the president and his allies in
Congress. "We are jointly the servants of the people," Owen said, quoting Wilson's own words back to him, "and must act together and in their
spirit."

Wilson would not yield. The supercommittee would inevitably have
only the function of "criticism and publicity," Wilson wrote to Owen. But
such an arrangement "would produce discussion and not efficiency." With
support from Democrats in the House, Wilson kept the initiative at bay.
By doing so, he spared himself the kind of supervision to which Lincoln
had been subjected.

* * *

The congressional effort to seize control of the war's conduct would not
sputter out so quickly. It got new wind in the spring of 1918, following
a controversy concerning the Aircraft Production Board and its failure
to provide a single combat plane for deployment despite the government
having spent about half a billion dollars on the effort. With rumors of graft

flying, Democratic senator George Chamberlain, chair of the Military Affairs Committee and previously a staunch opponent of the attempts to create a special investigative committee, flipped his stance. Chamberlain now offered a resolution to empower the existing Senate Military Affairs Committee (rather than a new joint committee) to inquire into not only aircraft production but also "any other matters relating to the conduct of the war."

Once again, Wilson tried to gather his loyal congressional troops. "These are serious times," the president wrote a senator, in a letter the White House distributed to the *New York Times*. "It is absolutely necessary that the lines should be clearly drawn between friends and opponents," for the Chamberlain proposal "would constitute nothing less than an attempt to take over the conduct of the war, or, at least so superintend and direct and participate in the executive conduct of it as to interfere in the most serious way with the action of the constituted Executive."

Fearing Wilson would lack the necessary support, the president's advisors hatched an ingenious idea. The president would assign former Supreme Court justice Charles Evans Hughes, Wilson's vanquished opponent in the 1916 election, to spearhead a Department of Justice investigation into the Aircraft Production Board, under the nominal direction of the attorney general.

Hughes's presence would assure the public that the investigation would not be a whitewashing. But Hughes was also an effective defender of executive prerogatives in wartime. In fact, Hughes had recently given a major public speech at the annual meeting of the American Bar Association on "War Powers under the Constitution." He argued that the Constitution does not contemplate "that the command of forces and the conduct of campaigns should be in charge of a council or that as to this there should be a division of authority or responsibility."

When Hughes called upon Senator Chamberlain to back down, the president's opponents accused Hughes of being a "damned piker" for having effectively muted the Senate initiative. But Wilson's appointment of the esteemed former justice met with acclaim in the press, and Chamberlain did back down.

* * *

Wilson still faced one more congressional attempt to challege his running of the war. The winter of 1917–1918 was not a good one for the Allies' war efforts. The Germans continued to gain ground on the Western Front. The entry of the United States did not appear to be improving the situation in any great respect. The American effort, such as it was, was hamstrung by a woeful lack of arms and ammunition. Back in the States, meanwhile, the conditions in army encampments were also bleak. There was a lack of heating, blankets, winter clothing, sanitation, and medical necessities. The situation only became graver when record cold temperatures swept the nation that winter. Press and congressional investigations revealed mismanagement, graft, and corruption, resulting in widespread suffering; an acceleration of diseases such as scarlet fever, meningitis, and diphtheria; and alarming death rates among the troops.

Members of both parties, and virtually the entire media, scathingly criticized the War Department, helmed by Wilson's confidant Secretary Baker. Former president Roosevelt led the charge, stirring up a vociferous public campaign to condemn Wilson's war efforts and warning ominously of ignominious defeat unless radical changes were made. Within Congress, Chamberlain again led the effort to challenge the administration and its wartime leadership. Determined to strip Newton Baker of his authority as secretary of war, Senator Chamberlain proposed legislation to create a new cabinet officer, the secretary of munitions. This new officer would be responsible for virtually all weapons and related war contracts and manufacture, as well as the direction and coordination of all other industrial resources in the war effort. The Chamberlain bill would have transferred a substantial percentage of the War Department's jurisdiction to the new munitions department.

Republicans were thrilled. They saw the Chamberlain initiative as a means by which they could counteract Wilson "upon high patriotic grounds." Chamberlain and a colleague met with Wilson in the White House to persuade him of the virtues of this proposal. But Wilson responded in a letter—a copy of which he distributed to the press—claiming that his judgment was "decidedly that we would not only be disappointed in the results, but that to attempt such a thing would greatly embarrass the processes of coordination and of action."

Still, Chamberlain would not blink. In mid-January of 1918, he introduced yet more legislation, this time to create a "War Cabinet," consisting of "three distinguished citizens of demonstrated ability to be appointed by the President." This brand new war troika would have virtually complete control over all war-related matters, in effect relegating the War and Navy Departments to ministerial functions. In a speech defending this proposal to two ultrapatriotic groups in New York, Chamberlain alleged that the military establishment of the nation had broken down entirely and that there was "inefficiency in every bureau and every department of the United States government."

There was no doubt that the bill was designed, at the very least, to embarrass Wilson and Baker. Perhaps Chamberlain actually wanted to reorganize the executive machinery of the war, but he had gone about it in a way that would make it much more difficult for Wilson to direct the war as he saw fit. As a result, Wilson was furious. The secretary of the navy observed in his diary that "the President has his blood up" and "has all the nerve any man needs." Taking on Chamberlain in personal terms, and all but threatening a veto of his proposed bill, Wilson effectively killed the Chamberlain proposals before they could come to a vote.

Using the scandals and perceived inefficiencies in the War Department as the occasion for proposing his own law—one that would involve a vast delegation of authority to the president himself—Wilson decided to turn the tables. "Senator after Senator has appealed to me most earnestly to 'cut the red tape,'" Wilson wrote in March 1918. "I am asking for the scissors."

The president's critics were incredulous, expressing "frank amazement" at the audacious sweep of the proposed measure. Senator Gilbert Hitchcock, one of Chamberlain's closest allies, said that if Congress approved Wilson's proposed delegation legislation, it would be "an abdication by Congress of its lawmaking power." But in May, Congress enacted a law giving the president virtually unfettered authority to transfer

functions among executive agencies as he deemed appropriate for purposes of prosecuting the war and to redirect virtually all appropriations
dedicated to the war effort.

A newly triumphant Wilson paid a visit to a joint session of Congress
at the end of that same month. There he received a standing ovation from
both sides of the aisle. He praised "the way in which the two houses of
the Congress have co-operated with the Executive," which he described
as "generous and admirable." His speech then implored Congress to put
partisan considerations aside for the good of the nation, in the singular service of the unified war effort. "The consideration that dominates
every other now," he said, "and makes every other seem trivial and neg-
ligible, is the winning of the war." "We must meet [our duty] without
selfishness or fear of consequences," Wilson famously urged. "Politics is
adjourned."

He could not have been more wrong.

* * *

The triggering event for the resumption of partisan hostilities was, ironically, the first clear indication of American success in battle. The stronger
the American military position, the more likely the Germans would seek
peace. It would be the terms of peace that would expose the long-standing
fissures between the parties—and thus the branches—over the very purpose of the war that Wilson had been so reluctant to enter.

In early October, the newly appointed German chancellor decided to
test the waters for a possible negotiated armistice. The first German peace
note to the American president purported to embrace the "Fourteen
Point" program for peace that Wilson himself had announced the previous January. Encouraged, Wilson responded cautiously but hopefully. He
was open to doing business with the Germans, as a prelude to his long-
term objectives for securing peace through a new international order.

Republican leaders were horrified. They had long feared a peace negotiated by the famously internationalist Democratic president. They suspected Wilson's eagerness to establish the capstone of his Fourteen Points
program, a "general association of nations," would lead him to give away

too much. The opponents seized on Wilson's perceived softness and in-
veighed against the "Abyss of Internationalism."

Indiana senator Harry S. New warned that negotiations with the
Germans could not be entrusted "to the dreamers, the social uplifters,
the pacifists, and the bolshevists . . . who appear prominently among the
President's chief advisors." Former president Theodore Roosevelt, declaring on the hustings that "we are not internationalists—we are American
nationalists," quipped that "professional internationalism stands toward
patriotism exactly as free love stands toward a clean and honorable and
duty-performing family life." The Senate minority leader, Henry Cabot
Lodge, warning of Germany's "poisonous peace propaganda," offered his
own ten-point program for peace, one predicated upon unconditional
German surrender, with no mention of a League of Nations.

* * *

On October 24, Teddy Roosevelt published a telegram to Senate leaders. It
preemptively and derisively urged the leaders to thwart Wilson's prospec-
tive peace efforts. "Let us dictate peace by the hammering guns and not
chat about peace to the accompaniment of the clicking of typewriters," he
declared.

Recognizing the dangerous situation he faced with the midterm elections less than a month away, Wilson did his best to fight back. The very
evening Roosevelt sent his telegram, Wilson repaired to his study in the
White House. There, he put the finishing touches on an unusual partisan
appeal to the American electorate. Wilson had been drafting the statement
for weeks, unbeknownst to most of his closest advisors. Earlier drafts were
marred by an unseemly, acerbic bitterness. The president was angry and
flustered, and it showed in his writing. The president's final written appeal, though milder, retained a distinct air of petulance and desperation.

The slashing appeal appeared in many of the nation's newspapers the
next morning. The upcoming election, Wilson wrote, would "occur in the
most critical period our country has ever faced or is likely to face in our
time." The president then moved right into his unadorned partisan plea:
"If you have approved of my leadership and want me to continue to be

your unembarrassed spokesman in affairs at home and abroad," Wilson wrote, "I earnestly beg that you will express yourselves unmistakably to that effect by returning a Democratic majority to both the Senate and the House of Representatives." Invoking the need for "unity of command," Wilson cited the European war in his warning that "if the control of the House and Senate should be taken away from the party now in power, an opposing majority could assume control of legislation and oblige all action to be taken amidst contest and obstruction." The Republican leaders, Wilson explained, although "unquestionably pro-war," had also been "anti-administration": "At almost every turn, since we entered the war, they have sought to take the choice of policy and the conduct of the war out of my hands and put it under the control of instrumentalities of their own choosing."

Wilson's October appeal fell on deaf ears. In November, the electorate delivered both houses of Congress to Republican majorities. The Democrats even blamed the president's tone deafness for their poor showing. Wilson's adversaries, meanwhile, quickly characterized the midterm elections as a referendum on the manner in which the balance of control had shifted concerning the conduct of the war over the preceding two years. Writing to Lord Bryce, the former British ambassador to the United States, just a few days after the 1918 election, Henry Cabot Lodge, the incoming Senate majority leader, called the Republicans' electoral mandate "one of the worst mid-term defeats that any president ever received, and such a defeat never happened before in time of war. It came from the popular uprising against his attempt to order a Congress as he would order a dinner, and the people saw in it instinctively the beginning of a dictatorship and went against it."

* * *

Wilson was in a much weakened position at home. He would not let his dream of a certain kind of peace die. He headed to Europe to negotiate a peace on his terms, confident he could force the Europeans to accept it. He told himself he would reach a separate deal with the Germans if the Allies proved too obstinate. He could then sell it to his countrymen.

Wilson returned to America in July of 1919, a copy of the treaty in his pocket. He prepared to make his case first to the Senate and, if need be, the American people as a whole.

In the end, Wilson failed spectacularly, all but killing himself in the vain effort to sell the Treaty of Versailles. He barnstormed the country that September, despite his failing health, traveling nearly eight thousand miles in less than a month, attending forty rallies and leading parades, pressing his case for his peace plan and his League of Nations to all who would listen. The plan would not win the Senate's approval. Wilson, a hero and, for a time, a truly dominating figure, would be remembered by most as a frail and defeated man who could not get the Senate to accept either his vision of the war, or the peace he had done so much to win. Congressional government, as Wilson had long counseled, was a remarkably persistent force.

══ 12 ══

PREPARING FOR WORLD WAR II

"The ruling was that he could go as far as Congress authorized and no farther. This seems hardly 'autocracy,' 'arbitrary' or 'dictatorial,' such eminent authority notwithstanding."

By the summer of 1939, Adolph Hitler was on the march, and Franklin Roosevelt—canny, idealistic, pragmatic, and supremely confident—was pushing hard to send arms to England and France. But, as the president neared the end of his second term, he kept running into statutes that blocked his way. Years earlier, Roosevelt had signed into law some of these same measures—while seeking to keep America neutral in any new European war. Germany's recent advance had not dampened support for keeping America out of a second European war in a generation. That made it nearly impossible for Roosevelt to convince Congress to roll back the existing neutrality rules, some of which were criminal prohibitions.

After months of ineffective legislative lobbying by the administration, the vice president, John Nance Garner, floated a provocative way forward on July 1. He told Roosevelt that "the President should not be bound at all by [this] legislation as such legislation offends his constitutional powers." Harold Ickes, the president's most combative cabinet member, agreed. He advised that same day that Roosevelt "would be amply justified in taking the position that the constitution gives the Executive power to conduct foreign affairs." Ickes even wondered, Roosevelt noted, whether it would be a mistake to continue to ask Congress for relief, as doing so might only bolster "the claims of the Congress to power that it does not have."

Roosevelt was intrigued enough by Garner's suggestion that he decided to seek advice from his attorney general, former Detroit mayor Frank Murphy. Roosevelt had lured Murphy to the Justice Department by dangling the prospect of eventually naming him secretary of war. "If we fail to get any Neutrality Bill," the president asked Murphy that afternoon, "how far do you think I can go in ignoring the existing act—even though I did sign it?"

The president put the question in a way that betrayed his concern about defying Congress. But his willingness to ask showed that he thought America's place in the world had changed and, with it, potentially, the scope of the president's power. America was now, as Roosevelt's secretary of state Cordell Hull remarked, "a great nation in a world of nations." In such a dangerous and complicated world, in which the president commanded a standing (though still poorly prepped) army and a significant (if still too small) navy, technology was shrinking the distance between countries, and dictatorships were gaining, perhaps America could no longer afford to let Congress control the president when it came to the nation's security and its relations with foreign powers.

Neither Garner nor Ickes offered a fully worked-out constitutional theory in opening the door to a new brand of executive unilateralism. But they were suggesting that the president enjoyed extravagant powers in matters of war and peace. Roosevelt was willing to explore the possibility that Garner and Ickes were right.

As the crisis in Europe grew worse, and the statutory limits on Roosevelt's power continued to frustrate the administration, the temptation to defy Congress only became greater. The question whether Roosevelt would claim such a prerogative—and break with a century and a half of constitutional practice—loomed over the critical choices facing him in the run-up to America's entry into this new and total war.

Those choices would also be influenced by what Roosevelt's lawyers would be willing to approve—and, in particular, by what Robert Jackson, who in short order would take Frank Murphy's place as attorney general, would feel comfortable concluding that the commander in chief could do on his own.

The entwinement of law and politics was tight. Roosevelt would be influenced by the legal advice he received. In turn, he would exert influence on that advice. Not in the crude sense that Roosevelt would demand legal opinions that conformed to his desires. The influence would be more subtle. In legal terrain as uncertain as this, and in times as tense as these, a close question would surely look different if the president seemed determined to press forward out of fear that the nation's security would be harmed than if the president seemed content to sit back and let time pass before sending further assistance abroad.

Roosevelt also knew that, in a country this steeped in the language of constitutional law, political judgments about war and peace were shaped by popular understandings about the importance of checks and balances and fears of presidential power spinning out of control. Whatever the merits of a military aid policy might be, Roosevelt intuited that, as his hero Jefferson had observed long before, "violations of the law are felt with strength"—at least in the absence of a clear and convincing show of necessity.

Roosevelt's own sense of how hard to push, therefore, would be shaped by his sense of how plausible the legal argument for action would seem to the public that he would need to convince. Whatever course Roosevelt would pursue in the fraught months that followed—and as the prospect of German dominance became terrifyingly real—would be marked at each turn not only by what he believed would best protect the nation but also by what his lawyers advised. Together the president and his lawyers would seek a way forward—preferably one that the public, and their representatives in Congress, could abide.

* * *

To answer Roosevelt's pending question about the limits of his power, Frank Murphy sought help from some of the best lawyers in the Justice Department. Their answer was not encouraging. "In this instance the President could not safely rely on a claim of constitutional right to justify a disregard of the Neutrality Act as a matter of law," the lawyers wrote to the attorney general on July 8. "To act without authority of Congress in the field of foreign relations is one thing," but "to disregard an express enactment of Congress . . . is quite another thing."

"Apart from the legal side of the question," the lawyers added, it was "doubtful whether public opinion would support . . . an attitude" of unrestrained authority. Echoing Jefferson's admonition to General Wilkinson more than a century before, the lawyers noted that public support was crucial "in the successful assumption by the President of the right or duty to act where legal authority is wanting or doubtful." For that reason, the lawyers warned Murphy, "in the present circumstances, independent action by the President might be viewed also, or pointed to, as evidence of dictatorial tendencies and purposes."

The advice was sound, especially given the times. Roosevelt had assumed office at a time of great economic crisis. He had asserted leadership as no other president had. He had made Woodrow Wilson's vision of a strong president, leading Congress, a reality—and in the name of the very reformist brand of governance Wilson had championed. But Roosevelt had overreached in the wake of his overwhelming re-election in 1936. He had challenged the one institution that seemed determined to prevent the emergence of the new America he was bent on fashioning. The Supreme Court had frustrated Roosevelt (and the Congress he dominated) again and again. Roosevelt had decided to frustrate the Court in return. Roosevelt launched, after secret preparations, a bill to expand the Court's size and remake it in his image.

The so-called Court-packing plan imploded in 1937. There followed growing concerns about the emergence of fascist dictators abroad and the Democrats' poor showing in the midterm elections. Those developments combined to create a most inhospitable climate for aggressive executive action. This was no time for a president to be thinking about asserting a sweeping prerogative to aid a warring party abroad on whatever terms he pleased and with no regard to the criminal statutes that Congress had placed in the president's way. That was especially so because these criminal prohibitions had been signed into law by Roosevelt's own hand, as the president had pointedly noted, and because the president had tried, repeatedly and unsuccessfully, to convince Congress to repeal them.

No one could doubt that Roosevelt was a forceful leader. It was well known that he had little patience with "legalism" or technical concerns that stood in the way of experimentation. That was in part why his opponents were able, at times effectively, to cast him as a nascent dictator. But, at the same time, much of Roosevelt's success stemmed from his uncanny sense of timing, his innate feel for public opinion, and his unusually high level of comfort with ambiguity and uncertainty. That comfort afforded him room to maneuver. He rarely foreclosed options that he might want to avail himself of if circumstances, and popular opinion, changed.

At this particular moment, therefore, Roosevelt decided not to commit himself to the view that he was legally entitled to do as he wished. A show of defiance when it came to the neutrality laws, he thought, was doomed to fail. Or, at least, it was bound to stir up more trouble than the policy of lending aid to Europe was worth. Why, then, claim a constitutional power that it might be imprudent to exercise?

Roosevelt decided not to press the matter. Instead, he kept pushing Congress to unwind the Neutrality Act of 1937. Secretary of State Hull was by then calling that law a "wretched little bob-tailed, sawed-off domestic statute" that "conferred a gratuitous benefit on the probable aggressors." To Hull, it was "just plain chuckle-headed" for Congress to leave the restrictions in place. But as much as Hull was eager to see these laws repealed, he doubted he ever would.

* * *

Congress finally relented that September. The new statutory regime Congress put in place tracked the one that Roosevelt had proposed during the special congressional session he had convened—for the first time in his presidency—right after Poland fell to the Nazis.

The president initially wanted the outright repeal of the problematic strictures. He knew that Congress would not stand for it. In keeping with the prevailing politics, the president had tempered his request. He pitched his proposed reforms as a way to ensure that the United States would remain on the sidelines, rather than as an effort to increase American involvement abroad. The president reconciled himself to the only offer on the table: a modest relaxation of the existing constraints.

Soon, though, Roosevelt and his team found themselves pressing against the limits of their newly acquired powers, as they worked furiously to shore up friendly defenses abroad. Over the course of the next year, administration lawyers had little choice—if the aid was to be sent—but to fall back on the same stratagems that they had relied upon before the new legislative reforms went into effect. The lawyers spent countless hours crafting imaginative ways to get around (while technically complying with) the statutory limits still in place. "In carrying out our neutrality laws," Ickes recalled the president instructing, "we would resolve all doubts in favor of the democratic countries."

The White House's aggressive approach did encounter internal resistance. The War Department remained headed by an unapologetically isolationist secretary. The underlying war bureaucracy also worried about giving up badly needed arms and shipping them abroad. Even Attorney General Frank Murphy thought there was only so much room to maneuver. He encouraged his lawyers "to err on the side of safety" in resolving close questions of neutrality law.

At a November cabinet meeting, the attorney general personally spoke up against a plan to transfer American ships to European allies through Panama. Such an approach would hide the ships' true country of origin. But Murphy objected that the scheme was "untimely and unwise" and that the public would see the maneuver for the unlawful evasion he thought it was.

Roosevelt backed down in that particular case. But the president proved relentless over time. He fought off all manner of legal and policy objections from within the bureaucracy. Planes and other matériel—including even some boats—made their way, at times circuitously, to the democracies Hitler threatened. Still, the requests for assistance kept coming all through the winter and spring of 1940—and they were getting harder and harder to meet.

* * *

In the middle of May, Britain's new prime minister, Winston Churchill, took office. He followed Neville Chamberlain, who was ushered out of the official residence at Downing Street once his initially popular assurances about Hitler's limited ambitions proved dangerously naïve. By then, German forces had moved deep into the interior of France, and they were heading for Paris. Fearing the French defenses would soon collapse, Churchill begged his American counterpart—with whom he had been surreptitiously communicating for some time prior to his ascension to prime minister—for immediate help.

Churchill wanted Roosevelt to send England fifty of America's old destroyers. The prime minister also asked for a complement of smaller, faster craft, known variously as mosquito boats or torpedo boats. Noting that the "scene has darkened swiftly," Churchill warned that, without this support, Germany might soon occupy France *and* control the English Channel. "You may have a completely subjugated, Nazified Europe established with astonishing swiftness."

The president quickly answered Churchill's cabled May 15 plea, but not favorably. Roosevelt said he would need more "specific authorization from Congress" to send the destroyers. Privately, the president feared the politics of handing over such a large set of warships while pushing Congress to build up defenses at home. It would not look good. Roosevelt also worried that Germany might overwhelm England, seize the destroyers, and use them to attack the United States. That, of course, would look even worse. Unless Congress signed off, Roosevelt was not willing to help with the destroyers, no matter how desperate Churchill was.

The mosquito boats were different. They were smaller, and they were not yet in the navy's possession. That made handing them over somewhat easier, politically and, potentially, legally. By the end of May, with Germany then in control of France and readying to attack London, Roosevelt decided to make an agreement with the private company making the smaller boats. He arranged for the Electric Boat Company to defer the mosquito boats' delivery to the navy and instead to send them on to England, all pursuant to a creative reading of the government's existing statutory authority to modify contracts.

Churchill was pleased with this development but hardly satisfied. He still wanted the destroyers. As he continued to push for them, rumors of a secret deal with the president began to spread.

* * *

Picking up on news reports about what Roosevelt might be up to, the Senate Naval Affairs Committee announced on June 13 that it would begin a formal investigation into the propriety of any possible transfer. Fearing what might come out, the acting navy secretary called up the committee's chair the next day. In that conversation, the acting secretary told Massachusetts Democratic senator David Walsh about the mosquito boats deal that was by then already in the works.

Walsh was furious. His Senate committee convened that same afternoon. There had been conflicts before over Roosevelt's efforts to sidestep the neutrality rules. The last great blowup was over the massive but hidden effort to sell warplanes to France. Now, Roosevelt seemed to be extending his reach into the navy. He was doing so even though Congress had reformed the neutrality laws in his favor but still had declined to include any new grant of power that would seem to bless the mosquito boats deal.

At the hearing, outraged senators listened to Navy officials explain the administration's various statutory theories justifying the decision to provide the aid that had already been quietly sent and the future transfers that were about to be consummated. Walsh was shocked at how effectively the administration had exploited ambiguities in the neutrality laws. He was also incredulous at the scale of the operation. He and others began drawing up legislation to plug the loopholes and to put a stop to the impending transfer of mosquito boats. It went without saying that, in shoring up these limitations, the committee assumed any deal to send the destroyers would be barred as well.

* * *

Meanwhile, Roosevelt's new attorney general, Robert Jackson, was starting to have doubts of his own about the mosquito boats deal. Jackson became the nation's top lawyer after Frank Murphy was confirmed to the Supreme Court. Jackson had held a variety of high positions in the Justice Department, including solicitor general. He was a brilliant man, and a self-taught one. He had risen from small-town roots in New York to national prominence, thanks to a long association with the current president. The president invited him along on fishing trips on several occasions—even delaying the start of one to accommodate Jackson's attendance at his son's high-school graduation. It was rumored Roosevelt looked upon Jackson as a worthy successor, assuming one believed the president would not run for a third term.

At a key White House meeting in early June, Roosevelt told his cabinet—with Jackson at the table—that the attorney general had signed off on the mosquito boat deal. That announcement silenced the top navy lawyers, who had been raising serious objections for weeks. But Roosevelt, it turned out, was wrong. The president had misunderstood what his attorney general had told him when they had lunched together—as they often did—before the key cabinet meeting. In truth, Jackson had not looked into the matter at all—a point he made known to some of his fellow cabinet members when the session broke up.

Jackson now had no choice but to dig in to the issue. He turned to Newman Townsend, one of the same Justice Department lawyers who had advised Frank Murphy that Roosevelt could not defy the Neutrality Act of 1937. Word soon came back from Townsend that this time, too, the legal risks were real. Townsend thought the mosquito boats deal likely violated the Espionage Act of 1917 and potentially a criminal neutrality law that dated all the way back to 1794.

With the controversy over the deal escalating on the Hill, Jackson informally notified the cabinet on June 20 that the proposed transfer was illegal. The decision caused some concern, leading Roosevelt's aides to scurry in search of a way out of a potentially embarrassing diplomatic development.

Roosevelt's right-hand man, Harry Hopkins, suggested the British should simply inform the navy that England did not want the ships anymore. In the end, though, Jackson only days later gave the navy a more formal, though unpublished, version of the same legal judgment. Roosevelt did not object, and the White House issued a statement that cited the attorney general's legal objection as the only reason for the cancellation. By that time, Senator Walsh had already informed his committee that the deal was dead.

* * *

Roosevelt might have put a stop to the mosquito boats deal even if Robert Jackson had found legal support for it. The president could read a hostile Congress as well as anyone. But, as a result of Jackson's decision, there was now something beyond the shifting legislative mood that stood in the way of Roosevelt's inclination—tentative though it was—to meet Churchill's desire with respect to the destroyers. There was a binding legal pronouncement from the administration's top lawyer that made clear earlier neutrality laws limited the ships that could be sent. Senator Rush Holt said upon learning the president had scrapped the deal on the basis of the attorney general's advice, "I am glad that Bob Jackson looked up the law on the subject."

Jackson, in other words, had clarified the legal lines—something at which Roosevelt, who thrived on improvisation and ambiguity, chafed. Jackson was now seemingly on record (if not in a public writing) about the correct meaning of a pair of old neutrality laws—one of which dated to the eighteenth century Quasi War with France and the other of which was a provision of the World War I–era Espionage Act. By their terms, those two laws seemed to apply to warships generally, not only small ones. On its face, then, Jackson's rationale seemed to cover not just the mosquito boats but the destroyers as well. The destroyers were clearly vessels of war. Besides, it would be strange to think that Congress, in an effort to keep the nation neutral, intended to permit the president to transfer large destroyers but not small mosquito boats.

Adding to the impact of Jackson's ruling was the fact that it made some high-level members of the administration—and Secretary of the

Treasury Henry Morgenthau in particular—newly skittish about testing legal limits. The experience of watching their clever but secret reading of a criminal statute exposed to public light, mocked in Congress, and then overruled by the attorney general, was unsettling. Some of these officials even feared they might have exposed themselves to criminal liability— as conspirators—in the course of searching for a way around Congress's words. The appetite for pushing statutory boundaries was no longer quite what it had been.

Even worse, whatever instinct for risk that remained would now also have to overcome the new statutory obstacle Senator Walsh had rammed through, as an appropriation rider, on June 28. This measure initially sought to bar the transfer of any matériel that could be "use[d]" by a belligerent. But even in the watered-down form in which the restriction finally passed, it was a formidable barrier. It barred the government from sending "in any manner" any "military or naval" matériel "to which the United States has title . . . unless the Chief of Naval Operations in the case of naval material, and the Chief of Staff of the Army in the case of military material, shall first certify that such material is not essential to the defense of the United States."

Then, in early July, Representative Carl Vinson of Georgia added one more check. This new provision appeared to allow the administration to send navy ships to England only if the navy first certified the vessels were no longer "fit" for use. Vinson's addition had this consequence because it seemed to identify the discrete statutes the administration could rely upon in transferring any portion of its fleet. Those statutes, on first glance, imposed this additional certification requirement about whether the ships were "fit."

If the attorney general thought even the mosquito boats could not be sent before the Senate had weighed in with these new restrictions, how could he possibly think the answer would be different when it came to the destroyers? If anything, the legal path was now much rockier than it had ever been.

* * *

As bleak as the legal landscape was, Britain's situation was getting bleaker. By July, London was being bombed, sometimes fiercely. The prospect of England falling was real. The prime minister had already warned in mid-June (as he had earlier done in May) that, without the ships, his country might have no choice but to cut a deal with Germany—if, that is, Churchill was cast out of power and a less determined government took over.

The president's newly appointed war secretary, the seventy-three-year-old Henry Stimson, was rattled to the point of sleeplessness throughout much of that sweltering July. Reflecting the growing sense that England's plight was truly desperate, Harold Ickes advised early that month that Roosevelt should get Churchill the destroyers by "hook or crook."

Churchill, for his part, refused to let up in the campaign to enlist America. All through July, Churchill barraged Roosevelt and his men with a steady stream of urgent requests, demands, and pathetic pleas—anything that might make the difference. Finally, on the last day of the month, the prime minister put the request for the destroyers as forcefully and directly as he could. "In the long history of the world," Churchill implored in a cable, "this is a thing to do now."

Roosevelt knew Churchill needed the ships. But the president was still not prepared to give them—at least not without Congress expressly signing off first. On top of the continuing legal concerns, there was also a new political development that contributed to this hesitance.

In mid-July, Roosevelt began preparing to announce at the upcoming Democratic Convention that he would run for a third term. In making that decision, Roosevelt would be exposing his policy of aiding England to the rigors of a campaign for reelection. That alone made the president cautious about pushing too hard. Roosevelt would also be breaking the custom established by George Washington, and followed by every chief executive since, of serving no more than two terms. That might make it seem Roosevelt was seeking to be the kind of "strong-man" no constitutional republic should tolerate.

Roosevelt was sufficiently concerned about seeming like a dictator-to-be that he reached out in mid-July for reassurance from Felix Frankfurter, the Harvard Law School professor and New Deal architect he had appointed to the Supreme Court in 1939. From his perch as justice, Frankfurter advised in a private memo that Roosevelt would be doing nothing wrong in running for a third term. But Frankfurter did tell the president he should simply portray himself as a humble patriot, trying to fulfill a public duty in a time of crisis.

Thus, however much Churchill might want the ships, and however much Roosevelt might want to give them, Roosevelt was in no mood to do anything that might make it seem like he was trying unilaterally to commit the nation to a war he was not sure the people would support. Or, at least, he was not willing to take such a step until he had a better feel for the electorate's mood.

And yet, at the very same time Frankfurter was advising Roosevelt on the virtues of presenting himself as a reluctant wartime leader, the justice was also advising a former student, Benjamin Cohen, who was then working in the administration on a memo that pushed in nearly the opposite direction. Far from counseling Roosevelt to be wary of seeming to lust for power, Cohen's memo instead sketched an argument for why Roosevelt would be justified in transferring the destroyers without getting Congress's express consent. And, in time, and with Frankfurter's encouragement, that memo would become public, thus thrusting the "strong-man" charge to the very center of the national political debate.

* * *

An anonymous but superb administration lawyer, and one seemingly without portfolio, Cohen was working out of the Interior Department at the time. The journalist Joseph Alsop—rather than anyone actually in the government—had first prodded Cohen to take on the assignment of crafting an argument for why Roosevelt could send the destroyers to England if he wished. Alsop was a leading member of an influential group of internationalists. They had been reading about the struggles over the destroyers and were convinced the survival of democracy might depend upon their timely delivery. Alsop and his like-minded members of the Century Group were thus searching for some way to move past the legislative logjam. Cohen was their latest instrument for doing so.

Cohen knew he would need a legal theory that somehow showed respect for Congress's role. He did not rely on the constitutional powers of the commander in chief over war or foreign affairs. Nor did he counsel an appeal to presidential prerogative or the assertion of a right to defy a slow-moving legislature. Cohen slalomed through the various statutes that stood in the way of the destroyer deal until he came to rest at the conclusion that Congress had already provided the authority Roosevelt needed. Or, more precisely, Cohen concluded that, in light of the president's obligation to protect the nation, there was no reason to assume Congress meant to leave him no room for escaping the seeming statutory constraints.

Cohen's key insight concerned Walsh's amendment. The statute forbade delivering the destroyers unless the chief of naval operations determined that they were not "essential" to the nation's security. That officer, unfortunately, had already told Congress the ships were too important to scrap. But Cohen did not see that earlier testimony as a bar. The judgment that needed to be made now was between keeping the destroyers in the American naval fleet and sending them to England, not between maintaining them and scrapping them altogether. Thus, the judgment of the destroyers' national security significance could only be made, Cohen thought, after one considered the use England would make of them. It was, as Jackson later put it, a "relative" rather than an "absolute" assessment that was required. If Churchill could successfully deploy the destroyers to delay Germany's advance, then they would be doing more for the United States' safety and security in England's hands than America's. For that reason, it would not be "essential" to keep them under the navy's control. In fact, the exact opposite would be true.

As for the neutrality laws that Jackson had concluded barred the mosquito boat deal, Cohen saw an escape route there, too. In fact, he saw many—his always active mind burst with creative possibilities. But Cohen argued most ingeniously that the statutes only barred sending ships built at the specific direction of the belligerent nation receiving them (something true of the still-under-construction mosquito boats but not of the already completed World War I–era destroyers).

Cohen's memo changed the terms of the debate. Roosevelt could act without having to endure the delay that would inevitably attend passage of new legislation, and he could do so without first defying any statutes Congress had already enacted. Cohen was raising the possibility that the president might provide the requested assistance to England without provoking a constitutional showdown. While the present Congress surely would not have been willing to bless this subtle interpretation, neither did it have the will definitively to reject that reading with a new and clarifying law. Instead, the legal provisions Cohen had to make sense of were far from clear. Nor had they been written to categorically hem the president in, even though Congress surely could have used words to that effect if it had wished.

* * *

Cohen sent his analysis to the White House in late July, with Icke's blessing. Cohen made sure to include a cover note emphasizing that he knew "congressional opinion" mattered. He wanted the president to know this advice was practical and politically attuned.

Roosevelt was impressed but dubious. The president was skeptical anyone in need of convincing—and especially the chief of naval operations, who would have to provide the certification under Walsh's amendment—would buy the argument. The whole point of Walsh's amendment had been to block the transfer.

By early August, the situation in England had deteriorated greatly. Roosevelt, for that reason, at last concluded that America should send Churchill the destroyers. His conviction was bolstered by secret discussions that had been ongoing between the new navy secretary and Britain's ambassador about sweetening the prime minister's request. Perhaps, it was suggested, the destroyers could be swapped for some English military bases in the Caribbean. That, Roosevelt thought, might be enough to make the case that the transfer of destroyers was essential, given how good the deal would be for the nation's security.

At a cabinet meeting held on the afternoon of August 2—after what Secretary of War Henry Stimson called one "of the most serious and important debates" he had ever witnessed but also one that he thought "too serious" even to describe in his private diary—the cabinet agreed the destroyers should be sent. The prospect of a true exchange—the ships would be given in return for the important defensive outposts in the Caribbean that England possessed—was critical.

Even with that change in the terms of the deal, neither the president nor his team yet saw how the ships could lawfully (or politically) be sent unless Congress first expressly approved. The cabinet thus resolved to begin a renewed legislative push for authorization. The administration would reach out to the new Republican presidential nominee, Wendell Willkie. Emissaries would see if, with Willkie's blessing, some Republicans in Congress might move toward the president's position. "The matter involves legislation," Stimson cryptically wrote in his journal the night of the cabinet meeting, "and legislation involves probably, in order to be successful, a union in recommendation of the two candidates—the President and Mr. Willkie."

It was not to be. By the middle of the month, the legislative outlook was still discouraging. Willkie had said nothing definitive. The word on the Hill, as one senator put it in confidence to Stimson, was that "there was no chance" of getting the repeal.

* * *

By then Cohen's self-initiated effort to identify a way around Congress had gained a second life. Felix Frankfurter, with whom Cohen was in regular contact, had urged his former student to send the memo, which had gained little traction within the administration, to Dean Acheson. A respected Washington lawyer and former Roosevelt administration official, Acheson was a committed internationalist. He also had wide connections in the press and a strong reputation as a man of integrity. He had even resigned from the Roosevelt administration years before, after the president disregarded his legal concerns about a proposed Treasury Department policy.

Acheson immediately saw promise in Cohen's draft. After a trip to New York, and some editing in Cohen's apartment there, the memo was reconstituted for public use. It now took the form of a lengthy opinion piece that appeared in the *New York Times* on August 11. Acheson and a number of top members of the private bar signed on. (Cohen remained, as always, in the background, presumably because he still worked in the government).

Reflecting the increasing pressure on Roosevelt to act on his own, a Chicago lawyer wrote to the president the very next day. He echoed the defiant constitutional position Ickes had urged the president to take the prior summer. "The enclosed idea may have a germ of value and if so I hope you will avail of it in any way with or without my name," Murry Nelson wrote. "The constitution is the Supreme Law, under it the executive power is reposed in the President who by this Supreme Law is commander-in-chief of the Army and Navy. If in his discretion it appears vital to the United States to use military or naval equipment in cooperation with or as a donation to another government, there is no statutory bar which could limit his constitutional discretion."

Even Roosevelt's secretary of war, Henry Stimson, now wanted the president to act on his own. Stimson was a Republican. He was not an isolationist. William Taft's secretary of war and Herbert Hoover's secretary of state, Stimson had been brought in to Roosevelt's cabinet to help smooth the way with Republicans in Congress as the administration pushed to get military aid to England. But, during his few months in office, Stimson began to sour on working with Congress. He thought the focus on national defense was being lost in a fog of legal technicality and constitutional concern.

The following January, Stimson went so far as to embrace defiance. He urged Roosevelt to reject a proposed statutory limitation on his right to deploy military convoys in the Atlantic Ocean. Stimson said it was an unconstitutional incursion on the powers of the commander in chief. Stimson did not have to go that far when it came to providing counsel about the destroyers. He could take comfort in the editorial that he had just read in the *New York Times*—the one laying out Cohen's clear legal analysis. It had, Stimson thought, thrown "a little speck of light" on an otherwise "gloomy" situation.

* * *

With momentum building for Roosevelt to act without express congressional support, Acheson and Cohen called the attorney general while he
was away on a family camping trip and urged him to reconsider his legal
opinion about the mosquito boats. Meanwhile, Frankfurter was telling
Stimson how credible he found the rationale sketched in *The New York
Times*, a view Stimson made sure to pass on to Roosevelt.

Shifting the legal course would not be easy. Jackson had already taken
a firm position by rejecting the mosquito boats deal. Ickes had also told
Cohen in late July that "in view of the Jackson opinion the President could
not now reverse himself." Jackson would thus have to find some new line
of argument to explain why the destroyers could be sent. On first read,
he was not sure that the Cohen-Acheson collaboration identified such a
path. Their write-up in the *Times* seemed not very different from the early
draft of the memo that Cohen had sent Jackson weeks before—a draft
Jackson had not found all that convincing.

Plus, at that time, it had seemed to Jackson that Roosevelt took some
comfort in standing on Jackson's prior ruling and passing on responsibility to Congress for America's delay in coming to England's aid. "I think he
feared possible embarrassment as much from having a power he did not
think it expedient to use," Jackson recalled of the president's first reaction
to Cohen's analysis, "as from finding that he was without it."

The pressures, though, were different now. Roosevelt and the cabinet
were in agreement that the destroyers should be sent. The public discussion of the president's unilateral legal power had been joined. England's
predicament was worse than ever.

Looking for help, and perhaps assurance that a shift in judgment would
not be a capitulation to presidential desire, Jackson once again sought out
Newman Townsend, a "hardheaded" and "conservative" Justice Department lawyer in whom Jackson had great confidence. In a memo sent two
days after the Acheson piece appeared in the *Times*, Townsend, who had
hardly been generous in his prior interpretations of executive authority,
largely came down on Cohen's side.

Walsh's amendment, Townsend agreed, was no bar, given the defense
benefits America would reap from England deploying the destroyers

against Germany. Townsend was also willing to endorse Cohen's reading of the Espionage Act and its eighteenth-century counterpart. Those laws could be read, Townsend agreed, to permit the transfer of warships built decades earlier, even if they barred sending vessels that, like the mosquito boats, were built to assist in the war then underway. That was especially true if the destroyers could be delivered in a way that would keep them out of combat until they reached an English port. Townsend thought Jackson could approve the destroyers' exchange without taking back his earlier advice—and thus without relitigating the earlier collision with Congress over the mosquito boats.

There was one possible hitch. Vinson's July amendment seemed to require the government to rely on the powers granted in certain specific statutes. Those statutes were not the ones on which Cohen and Acheson had relied in their analysis. Under the applicable laws, moreover, the navy would be required to strike ships from its registry and to declare them unfit for use before they could be transferred. It seemed hard to say that the destroyers were useless given that England desired them so badly.

* * *

Jackson was not concerned. Though he was still not convinced a swap of boats for money would be enough to justify the certification under Walsh's amendment, Jackson knew that the deal was likely to be considerably more favorable to American interests than it once had seemed it would be. England would be giving up the Caribbean bases for the destroyers. That kind of deal was one Jackson had no qualms about approving. He was also confident the navy would make the necessary certification to satisfy the laws that Vinson's amendment required the government to rely upon. Besides, as Townsend had noted, those laws did provide the president with the power to waive certain requirements in writing. Jackson let the president know he now saw a way forward.

Roosevelt, masterful as always at not boxing himself in, informed Churchill on August 13 that at long last "it may be possible" to provide for the "immediate" delivery of destroyers, assuming they were delivered in return for the bases. For England, that was progress enough. After

nearly three months of begging, and after a good eight weeks of intensive internal legal analysis and debate, Churchill and his team finally
believed the Americans had found a viable route for navigating the statutory shoals.

* * *

Until, that is, things fell apart again days later. The chief of naval operations was willing to say the destroyers were not "essential" to the nation's
defense, so long as Jackson would back up that judgment with a formal
opinion emphasizing the import of the destroyers-for-bases exchange.
But the navy would not certify the destroyers were unfit for use. That
became clear at a tense meeting Jackson held with naval officials in the
attorney general's grand conference room at the Justice Department. Roosevelt took in the bad news. He also made it known he wanted a solution.

Back at the Justice Department, the pressure on Jackson to find that
solution was immense. Consideration was given to asserting an executive prerogative of the kind Roosevelt had asked Murphy about a little
more than a year before. An early draft opinion prepared for Jackson's use
(though not drawn up by the attorney general himself) began by baldly
asserting: "In view of your constitutional power as Chief Executive and as
Commander in Chief of the Army and Navy, many authorities hold that
the Congress could not by statute limit your authority in this respect."

Ultimately, though, Jackson opted for a different approach. "The
opinion—not rest on Stimson ground inherent power . . . Statutory
only . . . Domestic law—not go on inherent powers—no danger," Jackson
later noted of his thinking at the time. Jackson chose to rely on a question-
able statutory claim to get around the certification problem. Congress,
Jackson informally concluded, had actually authorized the president to
issue a written waiver of the requirements that would otherwise force the
navy to strike a ship from the registry and deem it unfit for use before
transferring it.

By August 16, the president was willing to share his plan for the exchange with his cabinet. Jackson spoke at the meeting. He made a "very
good" statement, Stimson recalled, about why "the consent of Congress is

not necessary." Roosevelt then discussed the possible terms of the deal at a news conference. By then, as Stimson recalled, it was finally "out in the open."

There was still some concern about how best to avoid a congressional uproar, especially if Churchill would not be willing to call the swap of bases for destroyers a true deal. Churchill would give up the bases. He would accept the destroyers. But the prime minister had expressed concern almost from the start about making the transaction a quid pro quo. Churchill had his own domestic politics, and the terms were too favorable to the Americans.

Faced with the continuing British reluctance to call it a deal, Jackson hosted a meeting in his conference room on August 21. It was suggested the ships be sent to Canada rather than to England directly. That would add a measure of legal cover. Secretary Stimson was in attendance. He was fed up with the continuing legal machinations. He forcefully objected to the proposed Canadian plan. He said it was nothing more than a transparent reflection of a lack of confidence in the legal grounds for going forward that Jackson had laid out to the cabinet. Stimson's statement carried the day. Even still, Stimson thought the fact that the proposal "should actually have been put forward was an evidence of how technical stupidity can get into these pleasant people."

The rejection of the Canadian solution, though, did nothing to ensure Churchill would come around. Roosevelt had been assured by the Senate Republican leader and vice presidential candidate, Charles McNary, in confidence, that he would support the transfer only if a "plausible" legal basis could be found. Jackson and his lawyers had managed to come up with one, precisely because there was a meaningful quid pro quo. But Churchill seemed unwilling to budge on that point. He did not want to admit there was a destroyers-for-bases deal. The British intransigence left Roosevelt exposed, both legally and politically.

To iron things out, Roosevelt set up a phone call with himself, Jackson, and the prime minster. At the president's prompting, the attorney general explained why American law—and Walsh's amendment in particular—required a quid pro quo exchange. Churchill replied that empires

did not bargain. Jackson supposedly shot back that republics did. Churchill advised Roosevelt to find a new lawyer. But although the call ended
without a resolution, the air had been cleared. Lawyers at the State Department soon worked with Britain's ambassador to forge a compromise.
Certain bases would be exchanged. Others would be simply given. The
deal was complete within days.

* * *

Jackson signed his formal opinion ratifying the deal on August 27. The
opinion would be sent to Congress. Jackson then met with the president
so Roosevelt could personally edit the opinion line by line.

An earlier version had adverted to a prerogative to defy Congress. But
the final version did not touch on such provocative legal territory. Instead,
Jackson's opinion read: "So far as concerns this statute, in my opinion it
leaves the President as Commander in Chief of the Navy free to make
such disposition of naval vessels as he finds necessary in the public interest, and I find nothing that would indicate that the Congress has tried to
limit the President's plenary powers to vessels already stricken from the
naval registry. The President, of course, would exercise his powers only
under the high sense of responsibility which follows his rank as Commander in Chief of his nation's defense forces." And, to emphasize the
modesty of Roosevelt's claim in this case, the final draft went on to say: "I
find in no other statute or in the decisions any attempted limitations upon
the plenary powers of the President as Commander in Chief of the Army
and Navy and as the head of the State in its relations with foreign countries to enter into the proposed arrangement for the transfer to the British
Government of certain over-age destroyers and obsolescent military material except the limitations recently imposed by section 14(a) of the act
of June 28, 1940, c. 440, 54 Stat. 681." And yet that statute was no obstacle,
the opinion explained, because "this section, it will be noted, clearly rec-
ognizes the authority to make transfers and seeks only to impose certain
restrictions thereon."

Wendell Willkie expressed mild support for the deal when Roosevelt announced the "fait accompli" in a hastily called press conference in early September. The Republican presidential nominee said he approved of the substance of the exchange. He only lightly rebuked the administration for not having gone back to Congress for clearer authority (refusing to admit that Congress would hardly have been receptive or quick in providing such approval).

Under pressure from his political supporters, however, Willkie soon went on the attack. Within days, he claimed that "the method by which that trade was effected was the most arbitrary and dictatorial action ever taken by any president in the history of the United States." Willkie was not alone. In newspapers and on the floor of Congress, similar sentiments were expressed.

The famous Princeton historian Edward Corwin summed up that line of critique in a lengthy editorial in *The New York Times* that appeared later in the fall. Corwin decried Roosevelt's lawlessness. He derided in particular what he believed was the opinion's implicit reliance on the prerogative power that Roosevelt had first asked Frank Murphy about nearly a year before. For that reason, Corwin described Jackson's opinion as "an endorsement of unrestrained autocracy in the field of our foreign relations." Corwin even wrote that "no such dangerous opinion was ever before penned by an Attorney General of the United States."

* * *

Acheson found all of this legalistic hand-wringing tiresome. Despite pockets of criticism, the truth was that the general public reaction had been very favorable and the congressional resistance minimal. "I have very little patience with people who insist upon glorifying forms on the theory that any other course is going to destroy our institutions," he concluded. "The danger to them seems not in resolving legal doubts in accordance with the national interest but in refusing to act when action is imperative."

Henry Stimson, who recognized early on what a serious step it would be to send the destroyers without clearer congressional consent, was also dismissive of the constitutional complaints. He had long believed the president, given the national security needs, had a "duty" to act without Congress if he could do so lawfully. Too much was at stake for Roosevelt to cave to politics and refuse to exercise power that existed. He was also convinced that Congress was acting unwisely in trying to pin the president down. Stimson thus had little patience with those who counseled a rigid reading of the laws. "The chief hold of the Congress on the Executive is their ability to vote or to refuse to vote supplies for an Army or their right to raise and support armies in the Constitution," Stimson noted in his diary just weeks after the destroyer controversy. "The more I run over the experience of the summer, the more I feel that that ought to be substantially the only check; that these other little petty annoying checks placed upon the Commander-in-Chief do an immense amount more harm than good and they restrict the power of the Commander-in-Chief in ways in which Congress cannot possibly wisely interfere. They don't know enough."

But this growing contempt for legal niceties, and this gathering disdain for Congress's role, was not the only ground on which one could rebuff critics like Willkie and Corwin. Nor was it the ground that Jackson chose—at least not when he sat down to tell his version of the story years later.

* * *

Jackson, like Acheson and Stimson, thought Willkie's and Corwin's constitutional complaints absurd. But Jackson shared this view because he did not see how—given all the meetings he had sat through, all the legal wrangling he had engaged in, all the theories he had seen rejected, and all the revisions to the final deal that had been made—anyone could possibly think Roosevelt had simply done as he pleased. The whole object of the months-long exercise, Jackson thought, was to honor the "forms" Acheson derided. It was by showing respect for them, in Jackson's view, that congressional and popular support for the transfer had been secured. Jackson's final opinion had even reaffirmed that the mosquito boats could not be sent, and, indeed, they had been held back, prompting a weeks-long campaign by Churchill to convince Roosevelt to send them. (A substitute was eventually found).

Jackson was not denying that the president and his team wanted to aid England from the start. But they had gotten their way only after much delay and bargaining. The result was a deal that had evolved over time. America was getting more for giving up the destroyers than had been contemplated from the start. This was not government by fiat. Churchill for one could attest to how inefficient the process had been. But Jackson saw a virtue in the tortured process he had just endured. It reflected his understanding of how a democracy should work.

"The fact was that the opinion expressly avoided reliance for its conclusion on inherent, implied, or independent constitutional powers of the presidential office," Jackson wrote in a draft manuscript that he never published but in which he sought to explain what he had done. "Instead, it expressly rested upon the effect of a series of interrelated Acts of Congress held to authorize him to dispose of the destroyers but not to authorize him to dispose of the mosquito boats. The ruling was that he could go as far as Congress authorized and no farther. This seems hardly 'autocracy,' 'arbitrary' or 'dictatorial,' such eminent authority notwithstanding."

* * *

Roosevelt continued to promise—overtly and emphatically—that he would not get the country into another war. As he famously put it while on the campaign trail in October, "Your president says this country is not going to war." He maintained that posture while seeking more authority to send arms to Europe, pressing after long hesitation for a (defensive) draft, and sending forces to Iceland (albeit in keeping with statutes ensuring they never got too far forward). Still, the destroyers transaction was, as Stimson told Roosevelt and the Canadian prime minister at a private meeting on a train car on August 18, "the turning point in the tide of the war." America was now supporting the enemies of the Axis powers. Jackson and the president had, together, paved the way for America's entry into World War II, whether they had intended to or not.

On the heels of that historic transaction, and in the face of continuing legal obstacles, and still more advice from Newman Townsend that congressional restrictions prevented this or that proposed aid transaction from being carried out in a straightforward manner, Roosevelt finally sought the true reform of the neutrality laws that he had wanted all along. Congress approved the sweeping law he proposed—the Lend Lease Act— after a lengthy debate that was littered with charges Congress would be making Roosevelt a dictator by law.

The new measure expanded the logic of the destroyers deal. The new law conceived of all of America's armaments as potentially most useful to the nation's defense if sent to Europe. That continent was no longer so far away. It was the front line of the war and possibly the last line of resistance before America's own coasts. The new law thus gave Roosevelt great and totally unprecedented freedom to provide military aid to the European democracies. It was only a matter of time before the United States would become a recognized belligerent in its own right.

* * *

That the war to come would be largely waged abroad, and only after America had been attacked on its own soil, ensured that Congress would give Roosevelt great leeway as commander in chief once the war had been declared. But the fact the fighting would occur in a new era of what was being called "total war" also meant that Roosevelt—backed by a broad congressional declaration of war—would be wielding the war power in striking ways at home.

Even before war was declared, and during the post-destroyers-deal mobilization effort, Roosevelt had authorized (with Jackson's blessing) the seizure of an airplane factory in California in order to prevent a labor strike from disrupting the production of bombers. It perhaps should have been expected, then, that, in response to the Japanese attack on Pearl Harbor in December of 1941, the president would not be inclined to show restraint.

In the wake of the Japanese bombing raid, there were additional industrial seizures. The president also declared martial law in Hawaii, and he kept that order in place long after the imminent threat passed. The following spring, he began forcibly relocating nearly a hundred thousand Japanese Americans then living on the West Coast—a shocking exercise of power unprecedented in its infringement on liberty. They were sent to army-run internment camps. For the most part, Congress supported the commander in chief, passing a measure making it a crime to disobey the relocation orders of the army.

The more the war touched the home front, and the longer it went on, the more the prospect of a fresh clash with existing statutes came into view. In the summer and fall of 1942, that clash was at hand. With the arrest of two groups of suspected Nazi saboteurs along the East Coast and growing worries about the war's devastating effect on the economy, there were new temptations for Roosevelt to assert the power to conduct this war on his terms, no matter what Congress might have said. And with that temptation came new worries that, if he did so, the older notions of checks and balances would not survive the war against dictatorship that America was by then fully committed to trying to win.

TOTAL WAR

"[The Supreme Court not only does not] need to go, but should not go, into inherent constitutional power of [the president], which neither Congress nor the Court can limit."

I t was the spring of 1942. Robert Jackson, fresh off his successful tenure as attorney general, was approaching the end of his first full term as a Supreme Court Justice. He was already frustrated. With the nation's war on the Axis powers raging, Jackson worried his new posting at the Court amounted to little more than an embarrassingly inconsequential "back eddy." Former South Carolina senator James Byrnes had taken his seat on the bench the same day as Jackson. He shared Jackson's disillusionment. He even referred privately to the Court as the "marble mausoleum." The U.S. war effort was entering its fifth month. All the action was in the two branches of government that these men had just left. They were growing terribly restless.

For a time, Justice Byrnes coped with the lack of "excitement" by providing informal advice to the Roosevelt administration. He even quietly helped the president's men draft wartime legislation, writing his confidential strategy memos on Supreme Court letterhead. Byrnes soon realized that such moonlighting was no answer. He had lost interest in the work of the Court. That fall, at Roosevelt's request, Byrnes left for good so that he could work full-time for the White House's team.

For his part, Jackson had actually tried to beat Byrnes to the door.

During an April visit with Roosevelt at presidential advisor Pa Watson's farm in Charlottesville, Virginia, Jackson took his former boss aside. The former attorney general explained to the president that "there were a good many men who were entirely capable of performing the function on the Court with satisfaction, and if there was anything in the war effort he thought I could be more useful in, I would be quite ready to resign and take it on."

Roosevelt told Jackson to stay put. "The work on the Court had permanent importance," the president said, "even though temporarily it did not seem to be important." Roosevelt even hinted the chief justiceship might be Jackson's if he waited. While that promotion never came, Jackson did soon find himself grappling with a question of undeniably "permanent importance," thanks to a case about the war that had reached the Supreme Court that July.

* * *

The case concerned the fate of a small group of alleged Nazi saboteurs who had been rounded up by the FBI in New York and Chicago in late June and then handed over to the military. In July, the case was before the Court, with the saboteurs challenging the president's right to try them for war crimes before a military commission that the president had specially convened in Washington, D.C. The case thus hearkened back to the Civil War and the great case of Lambdin Milligan, in which the Court had ruled that the Constitution barred the president from using his power as commander in chief to bypass the civil courts.

The saboteurs' case also raised a question that was less about civil liberties than the proper allocation of constitutional power: Did Congress or the commander in chief control the conduct of war? Jackson had deftly helped Roosevelt to avoid resolving that same question in the controversy over sending the destroyers to England. But Jackson was no longer the president's lawyer, and the country was now officially at war. Each man thus had reason to rethink where he thought the ultimate balance of power lay. Each man also knew the dangers of coming to a definitive conclusion on such a fundamental matter.

The traditional lines between the home front and the fighting front were blurring. Technological advances made it possible to send bombers across the ocean. The demands of industrial war production—and concerns about civil defense—combined to ensure that whole populations were mobilized for battle. A president who enjoyed an absolute power to determine the "conduct of campaigns" might reign supreme far beyond the conventional battlefield in this new era of total war, in which everything that the government did could arguably be tied to the conduct of the war.

By late September, as the Supreme Court was preparing its final opinion in the case of the Nazi saboteurs, it was very clear that these concerns about constitutional executive war powers were not merely theoretical. There was suddenly a lot of talk about Roosevelt invoking his wartime authority as commander in chief to claim vast and unchecked powers over the entire domestic economy. This talk had been fueled by White House hints that the president might defy restrictions in the Emergency Price Control Act of 1942 as part of his assault on inflation, which Roosevelt feared would cripple the war effort if rising prices were not brought under control.

* * *

This brewing constitutional controversy over price controls would be very much on the justices' minds as they considered the basic question of the limits of presidential war powers that the Nazi saboteurs' case had forced them to confront. The war was being felt at home—and on a variety of fronts. In ruling on the saboteurs' claims, Jackson and his fellow justices realized they might be deciding much more than a single case. They might be committing themselves—if they were not careful—to a broader view about the separation of powers in an age of total war, and at a moment when Congress and the commander in chief were heading toward a showdown over that very issue.

The constitutional danger signs were flashing. That did not mean there was a consensus about the need for the president to proceed with caution. Everyone serving in the government—the president and his aides and lawyers, the senators and representatives and their staffs, the justices and their clerks—understood the argument for breaking with traditional understandings of the relationship between the commander in chief and Congress. With the war going badly, the country fully committed to victory, the stakes of losing unfathomably grave, and the nature of modern warfare all encompassing, there was a case to be made for freeing the president—now well into an unprecedented third term—from customary legal restraints. That way, Roosevelt could prosecute this war as fully as his less restrained counterparts in Germany, Japan, and Italy. The summer and fall of 1942 presented the case for permitting a quasi-dictatorship to take hold as starkly as at any time since the early days of the Civil War.

In such circumstances, there seemed little chance that the Court would actually prevent the president from bringing the alleged Nazi invaders to justice as he saw fit. Roosevelt certainly believed the justices would not dare to challenge him so frontally. He had appointed more than half of them to the Court. But on what terms would the justices rule for him? The answer was far less certain. As the justices (including Roosevelt's own picks) dug into the saboteurs' case, the broader ramifications of a pro-Roosevelt ruling came into view. And, as those consequences became clearer, divisions began to emerge within the Court. Was this the moment to call into question the received wisdom about the whole system of checks and balances? Or was this instead a time to leave a decisive resolution about the scope of Congress's power to control the conduct of war for another day?

* * *

The first four German operatives had come ashore on a moonless evening in mid-June. They hit the sand at Amagansett Beach on Long Island sometime after midnight. The next four saboteurs arrived days later, also by U-boat. They landed at Ponte Vedra Beach in Northern Florida.

Carrying large amounts of cash, explosives, and civilian clothes—into which they changed after burying their sea-soaked German military uniforms in the sand—the two gangs of trained saboteurs slowly made their way to the nearest cities. They were tasked with blowing up aluminum plants, energy facilities, and transportation networks throughout the country. If time permitted, they were also supposed to terrify the civilian population by bombing targets in popular, crowded areas, like the "Jewish-owned" Macy's department store in Manhattan.

As fearsome as the initial news reports made the intruders seem, the specially chosen German operatives—each had lived in America at some point—proved to be quite hapless. By the end of June, amidst a nationwide manhunt, one of the saboteurs called the Federal Bureau of Investigation and exposed the sensational plot.

Once the men were in federal custody, the FBI, at the president's direction, handed them over to the military. The army then charged them as war criminals under the laws of war. They were to be tried before the secret military commission that was about to get underway in the nation's capital.

The defendants did not submit quietly to this strange new tribunal. Through their army-appointed defense counsel, Lieutenant Colonel Kenneth Royall, they filed an extraordinary petition with the Supreme Court. At first, their legal challenge seemed quixotic. Royall failed in his initial stab at getting the Supreme Court involved. He went to the home of the only justice he believed was still in town during the Court's summer recess in hopes of convincing him to get the Court to take the case. The Justice brusquely turned Royall away. That member of the Court wanted nothing to do with a request to review the actions of the commander in chief in the midst of an ongoing war. Through persistence, though, Royall eventually convinced some of the other justices to take the petition seriously. Chief Justice Harlan Fiske Stone in particular was interested. He took the lead and scheduled a special summer session—the first the Court had held in more than seventy years.

The last one had occurred in the aftermath of the Civil War. At that time, the Court had also met in July. It had done so for the same reason: to hear an emergency legal challenge to a presidentially established military commission about to issue a death sentence. Andrew Johnson was president then. With the war won, Johnson had seemed remarkably unconcerned by the Court's possible intervention in a military trial that had been initiated under his predecessor. In fact, he seemed to welcome a loss as a useful means of helping him return the country to what he believed was an acceptable peace.

But, this time the war was just getting underway, and there was no doubt about where the president stood. Roosevelt had personally suggested the government use a military commission to try these defendants. He let it be known, according to a message the justices received through back channels, that he had no intention of releasing the captured Germans to a federal marshal waving a federal court order. Roosevelt even hinted in private that he might carry out the executions no matter what the Supreme Court did. It was a prospect that filled Chief Justice Stone with dread.

* * *

The military commission met in a good-sized, high-ceilinged office on the fifth floor of the Justice Department's massive building on Pennsylvania Avenue. The trial was thus held halfway down the corridor from the grand suite that housed the office of the attorney general, which was by then occupied by Francis Biddle.

Most recently the solicitor general and before that a wealthy Philadelphia lawyer, Biddle came from a distinguished family with ties to the country that dated back to the Revolution. His great-great-grandfather was Edmund Randolph, the nation's first attorney general. Born of privilege, Biddle had a healthy self-regard, a taste for fancy white suits, and a reputation as a staunch defender of civil liberties. He was also strongly supportive of the decision to try these defendants as war criminals.

Biddle came to that view after having been advised that it would be hard to make out a standard federal criminal case against the alleged saboteurs. Even if a regular prosecution succeeded, he had been informed, it would likely yield a modest sentence. By contrast, a successful military prosecution—based on the surreptitious invasion—would be easy to secure. A conviction for violating the laws of war could also, according to the administration's view, support the death penalty. "Hanging would afford an efficacious example to others of like kidney," a close Roosevelt aide noted on the day the president signed the order creating the commission.

Biddle was well aware, though, of the Court's decision in *Ex Parte Milligan* seventy-five years before. There, the Court had ruled the Constitution guaranteed a citizen, even one suspected of aiding the enemy in the Civil War, a right to be tried by a regular jury so long as the civilian courts were open. In reaching that conclusion, the Court noted the defendant in that case, Lambdin Milligan, had been captured in Indiana, a place far from any live battlefield and where the regular courts were up and running. For that reason, the Court ruled the president could not bypass the protections that those courts offered by instead using a military commission.

That same logic conceivably could be used to help the alleged saboteurs, especially the one defendant with the strongest claim to being an American citizen. After burying their sabotage materials on the beach, the men had melded into ordinary American urban life for more than a week: lunching at automats, dropping in on old loves, hanging out at bars, shopping for clothes. They were then whisked off the streets of New York and Chicago and thrown into a secret system of army justice, a mile or so from a fully functioning federal courthouse. If they could be treated like this, couldn't any American?

To take the sting out of that objection, Biddle had advised the president to issue a special proclamation narrowing his power. It stated the president would use a military commission only for those citizens and residents of a country at war with America who "during time of war enter or attempt to enter the United States . . . through coastal or boundary defenses, and are charged with committing or attempting or preparing to commit sabotage, espionage, hostile or warlike acts, or violations of the law of war." In other words, the president announced he was targeting only enemy invaders who were violating the laws of war—not those

Americans who, like Milligan three generations earlier, were already in the country and were at most collaborating with the enemy.

Nor in seeking to keep the civilian courts on the sidelines was Roosevelt trying to, Lincoln-like, suspend habeas corpus by fiat. In fact, when Kenneth Royall decided that, as a matter of conscience, he had no choice but to challenge the commission's authority before the Supreme Court, Biddle did not object to the Court's right to hear the case. Roosevelt did not mind Biddle giving in on that point. The merits were a different matter. Roosevelt was not about to lose this case—or to have the justices tell him how to run the war. The president agreed when the attorney general asked to be named the prosecutor in the war crimes trial. "We have to win the Supreme Court, or there will be a hell of a mess," Biddle had explained in making the case that he, rather than an army officer, should be given the prosecutorial reins. Roosevelt told Biddle to clear it with Secretary of War Stimson. Then the president flashed a mischievous grin: "You're damned right there will be, Mr. Attorney General."

* * *

The Court sat for two days of argument. Justice William Douglas had to fly in from the west and was late making it to the bench. Justice Frank Murphy recused himself altogether, on account of his status as an active-duty army officer. Two other justices, Felix Frankfurter and Jimmy Byrnes, were in frequent contact with Roosevelt and his administration throughout the period. Byrnes even advised the president on the scope of his war powers—concerning a separate matter—just days before the case was heard. Neither man declined to hear the case.

The arguments were held before a packed courtroom and a crowded press gallery. The proceedings began at noon and ran until 5:00 P.M. References to "total war" peppered the justices' back and forth with counsel.

The justices seemed convinced that, with bombers and paratroopers, submarines and aircraft carriers the new instruments of war, this armed conflict would not be fought in marked-off fields. It would be waged everywhere and at every moment. No part of any country was truly safely outside the theater of operations.

The justices seemed less clear as to what this shift might mean for traditional understandings of executive war powers. Was there any facet of American life beyond the president's reach as commander in chief? Might an American citizen be subject to prosecution in a military commission for merely leading a strike at an arms factory? If so, could the president now rely on the law of war to exercise total control over anything he thought would interfere with the effort to win the war—a war for which there was no clear end in sight?

The justices made a point of asking Attorney General Biddle these questions. They wanted to make sure that, in ruling for him, they were not signing on to a momentous change in the constitutional balance. But they actually did not seem too worried that would happen. These German saboteurs were, as Robert Jackson noted at the argument's outset, "an invading force." That fact made this case an easy one. Since the saboteurs had come to America's shores on a German war submarine, the justices' questions indicated, the saboteurs had effectively brought the war with them. The saboteurs seemed in principle no different from paratroopers dropping behind enemy lines or bomber pilots flying over New York City.

Kenneth Royall gamely tried to make the case seem more difficult. He denied the saboteurs were engaged in combat when they first landed on the beaches. But his efforts to distinguish the accused from paratroopers and bombardiers fell flat. He argued the defendants had hit the shore unarmed, carrying no guns, and showing no indication that they wished to engage in combat. Under Jackson's questioning, Royall had to admit that the men were holding crates of explosives. The courtroom erupted in laughter at the concession.

Nor did the justices seem concerned about whether they might have to overrule *Milligan* to find for Roosevelt in this case. Biddle made clear he thought the Court could rule for Roosevelt without touching a "hair" of the *Milligan* precedent. The justices seemed to think he was right.

One question was more troubling: Even if the President had a right to try these men outside the regular courts, what rules would constrain him in the new military forum he preferred? Rules that Congress set or ones the president would himself make up?

* * *

Under the Articles of War, Congress had seemed to require unanimity before a military tribunal could order a death sentence. That requirement was not to be found in the rules the administration had come up with for this military commission. Those rules seemed to allow a death sentence to be imposed by a two-thirds vote. Nor did the commission require the president to hear from the judge advocate general before approving a conviction, even though the Articles of War seemed to make that a precondition for the president imposing a sentence.

Biddle tried to argue the commission's procedures fit comfortably within the Articles of War, just as he had done in his brief. But on the second day of his presentation, he added the suggestion—for the first time—that it might not matter. Even if there were a conflict between the executive order and the Articles of War, Biddle explained, the president might still be entitled to insist upon his own rules "in the exercise of his great authority as the Commander-in-Chief during the war and in the protection of the people of the United States."

Chief Justice Stone was taken aback. He cut Biddle off. The chief wondered why the Court should entertain an argument for unchecked executive war power. Biddle agreed the Court "[did] not have to come to that." But a bit later, after Biddle seemed to suggest the tribunal's procedures *could* be "modified by Congress," he corrected himself when Justice Frankfurter pressed on whether he really wanted to make that concession. "Perhaps I narrowed that too much," Biddle explained. "I have always claimed that the President has special powers as Commander-in-Chief. It seems to me, clearly, that the President is acting in concert with the statute laid down by Congress. But . . . I argue that the Commander-in-Chief, in time of war and to repel an invasion, is not bound by a statute."

Biddle, like the justices, was torn. There had to be a way to decide the case without discussing first principles and making grand statements about the president's powers in war. But, if those principles had to be confronted, Biddle wanted the Court to know he would not shy away. "The Commander in Chief . . . is not bound by a statute." It was a bold statement. Biddle was daring the Court to announce the true allocation of authority once and for all. And yet, the more Biddle pressed the point, the more resistance he encountered.

* * *

The next day, the Court issued a short *per curiam* opinion. It said almost nothing about the Court's legal thinking. It was entirely silent about whether the commission's procedures complied with Congress's dictates. The brief opinion simply announced the judgment denying the alleged saboteurs' petition on the merits.

Roosevelt was "not surprised." He could not imagine the Court would interfere with his prosecution of such a matter and at such a time. He now hoped the commission would soon order the death penalty. In short order, the commission did convict the accused, condemning all eight to death by electric chair. (Roosevelt then commuted the sentences of the two who had helped blow the plot's cover; one would serve life and the other thirty years.).

But, as had been the case in *Milligan*, this initial opinion would not be the Court's last word. Chief Justice Stone announced the Court would issue a full opinion explaining its reasoning at the start of its next regular session in October. The Court's unanimous judgment, issued just days after the argument, gave no sign of the coming struggle over what that fuller opinion would say. But that struggle would be significant. It would also play out against the backdrop of a recently concluded constitutional showdown between Congress and the commander in chief. And, in the eyes of many, that controversy raised the specter of a truly fundamental reordering of established understandings of the separation of powers in a time of war.

* * *

That second power struggle unfolded over the course of many months. Its origins could be traced back to January 30 of that same year. That was the day Roosevelt signed the Emergency Price Control Act of 1942. This new statute gave Roosevelt many tools he believed he needed to keep inflation

under control. But, in the view of the president and his team, the new statute did not go nearly far enough, as the president had noted at the time.

By April, prices were rising fast, and the law's shortcomings were becoming more obvious and less tolerable. Roosevelt decided to take his
concerns to the people. The result was a seven-pronged blueprint for future legislative action that he unveiled late that month. The most contentious piece of the plan involved the president's request for new statutory
authority to impose controls on farm prices.

In a lengthy message to Congress, and in an accompanying radio
speech to the country, Roosevelt attacked the current price control law
for giving what amounted to a huge gift to the large commercial farmers.
By ensuring the government had no power to bring farm prices as low as
they had been at their peak a generation earlier, the president argued, a
law supposedly aimed at licking inflation actually locked it in.

The fight over farm prices was not just a battle over economics. It
was also about how best to run the war and over who had the final say on
such a matter. "The president did not consider inflation to be a strictly
domestic matter," Samuel Rosenman, Roosevelt's eventual legal counsel,
recalled. "He looked upon it as something inseparably bound up with
winning or losing the war. This was a point he always stressed whenever
he talked about inflation, privately or publicly."

Roosevelt was thinking not only of "the greatly increased cost of war
and the heavier debt burden which would result from inflated prices."
Roosevelt worried "even more [about] the immediately devastating effect of inflation on the energies and morale of the American people." As
Rosenman remembered, the president also "was thinking of inflation's
impact on wages and wage earners, of the vastly increased possibility of
strikes, of the great diversion of energy from war production to the personal problems of making both ends meet. Nothing worried him more
than the possibility of unrestrained inflation, and no nonmilitary problem took so much of his time and thought."

Despite these concerns, Roosevelt initially resisted his aides' pleas to
go to Congress to change the troublesome farm price formula. The farm
lobby's influence and the upcoming midterm elections led the president

to conclude that no amendment could get through the House and Senate. If Congress rebuffed him, Roosevelt further calculated, the ripple effects would be awful. A failure to convince Congress to side with him in controlling farm prices might give labor an excuse to oppose his efforts to promote wage stabilization. Union leaders would ask why they should make concessions on wages when producers were not similarly doing their part to keep prices low. Better, Roosevelt figured, to avoid a fight with Congress on this issue than to risk losing labor's support for his efforts to keep wages in check as well.

Eventually, though, Roosevelt gave in to the economic arguments of his team. Pressed hard by his closest aides, he relented when his flamboyant director of the Office of Price Administration, Leon Henderson, weighed in at the end of the deliberations. Henderson argued that the current price control system was certain to touch off the dangerous inflationary spiral Roosevelt feared. By April, the stage was set for a battle with Congress—one the president believed was as vital to the war effort as any he would wage.

* * *

The president tried that summer, albeit halfheartedly, to convince Congress to move in his direction. As with the president's efforts years before to roll back the Neutrality Act, he had little success in getting the Emergency Price Control Act changed. And so, by that summer, Roosevelt decided he could not wait anymore, just as he had decided in the late summer of 1940 that Churchill's requests for the destroyers had to be met. But, as had been true then, Roosevelt knew the difference between deciding something must be done and figuring out how best to do it.

The president had resolved to make his proposed course of action known to the public on Labor Day. The details of how he would secure the necessary power over farm prices would matter, however, and he still had no clear idea of what those details were. The days leading up to the deadline were filled with tension, indecision, and intensive internal lobbying. Through late August and early September, Roosevelt turned the issue over in his head again and again as he made his way between the White House,

Hyde Park, and his retreat in Shangri-la, located in the mountains near Washington, D.C. The president was searching, often alone, for a way through a crisis that, due to the date he had set forth as the deadline, was in some respects of his own making and in others all too real.

In one camp were those aides pressing Roosevelt to go it alone. They urged him to issue a sweeping executive order that would implement the basics of the April plan, including the strategy for stabilizing farm prices. They counseled him to rely on the clearest source of authority for such a bold decision: his war powers as commander in chief.

Of course, there would be loud protests from Congress. But, as his speechwriter Robert Sherwood explained, one had to realize how disingenuous such criticism would be. "There were unquestionably many Congressmen who fervently hoped that he would do it this way and thereby absolve them from all responsibility for decision on such a controversial issue," Sherwood believed, adding: "It was an ironic fact that many of the Congressmen who were loudest in accusing Roosevelt of dictatorial ambitions were the most anxious to have him act like a dictator on all measures which might be unpopular."

Other aides argued—just as aggressively—that a unilateral approach would be unnecessarily, even dangerously, provocative. Roosevelt should instead demand Congress pass legislation on his terms, using the upcoming elections as pressure. On this view, wavering senators and representatives would be moved by the commander in chief blaming them for imperiling the war effort. They would not gamble they could survive an encounter with the voters without having first given Roosevelt what he said he needed to defeat the enemy.

* * *

Initially, Sherwood recalled, the president "was in favor of an arbitrary Executive Order to achieve stabilization, and his speech was at first written as a proclamation and explanation of that." The president would give a radio speech to the nation from Hyde Park in the evening. The speech would follow a Labor Day message he would send Congress "possibly announcing a proposal to solve the problem of mounting prices by an

Executive Order." Reflecting the gravity of the issue, the president's secretary, William Hassett, explained that "all of this deals with, perhaps, the most important phase of the war since Pearl Harbor. If the fight against inflation at home is not won, the global war is as good as lost and the President fully realizes it."

But this first outline of the president's plan for acquiring new powers was still tentative. Even as Sam Rosenman was working "hard" to finalize the draft executive order, he told Hassett on August 29 that "the President [was] still undecided as to his proposal to Congress." By September 3, things had not seemed to become much clearer. The president, Harry Hopkins, Sherwood, and Rosenman all headed out from Washington that evening. The speech was still not written. The plan was for the president to go with those aides to Hyde Park and give "a weekend consideration of the whole problem of inflation, or, as he likes to call it, the stabilization of the cost of living." As Hassett put it, "The Boss still seeking guidance from all sources on an issue which reaches every American home—the biggest since Pearl Harbor and the toughest."

Upon settling into his childhood estate in the Hudson Valley, the president decided he would not come back to Washington before the plan had been announced. Whatever his decision would be, he would make it known from there, "with no announcement in advance" or indication from where he was speaking. Extra stenographers and telegraph operators were thus brought in to help with the "huge task" that remained.

* * *

With two days left before the scheduled Labor Day announcement on September 7, the press was predicting the course the president would choose. The president grew irritated by that morning's papers, which were filled with "elaborate forecasts" of what he was supposedly sure to do.

The reports were "virtually unanimous in saying he would handle the whole problem through an Executive Order which would prescribe a limit on wages, salaries, and farm prices," Hassett recalled. These stories were almost certainly based on leaks coming from those working in the White House. The reports were mistaken. "The president told me a number of orders had been drafted, none of them approved, and all of them definitely abandoned," Hassett noted in his diary that day. "[He] said he had decided against an Executive Order before leaving Washington. This leaves the Washington correspondents very far out on a limb which the Boss will saw off in his message to the Congress Monday."

Roosevelt had been moved off of the unilateral approach by the arguments of his close aide Harry Hopkins and by the price administrator Leon Henderson. They had "strongly recommended that he put the issue up to Congress in the form of an ultimatum—'you act before October 1st or I will'—and their arguments finally prevailed." These aides were influenced by a deep sense that no system of price controls could be effective unless it was believed to be legitimate—a belief that congressional support could help engender. Or, at least, these aides were convinced that feeling would be more likely to take hold if Congress was not constantly screaming that the whole enterprise was illegal.

That Sunday, Roosevelt finished editing the speech, saying that, after seven drafts, "he didn't want to see it again." He then spent the evening playing solitaire, knowing "the faces of the correspondents will be red when they receive the texts. They will then learn there is no Executive Order."

* * *

Roosevelt, as was so often the case, had picked a less than straightforward means of acting boldly. But his ultimatum was still startling. As much as he had given Congress time to meet his demands, and in that sense shown restraint, he had also left no doubt that he believed he could act on his own. And, it seemed, from both his address to the nation over the radio and his congressional message, that he was resting his right to act alone in setting prices solely on a shockingly sweeping view of his authority as the nation's constitutionally designated commander in chief.

That understanding of the president's ultimatum set off immediate charges of dictatorship, most prominently from his Republican nemesis Senator Robert Taft, son of the former president who had been governor of the Philippines during an earlier Roosevelt's clash with Congress over war policy. "The doctrine that is asserted leaves Congress as a mere shell of a legislative body," Taft told the Senate in a floor speech given immediately after the president's address. The assertion of power was "so dangerous and so revolutionary" it made the rumors that the president might be planning to postpone the midterm legislative elections newly plausible. If Roosevelt could impose price controls by executive order, and trump a statute in doing so, Taft explained, than what was to stop the president from instituting a draft or imposing new tactics by similarly unilateral means?

There was a predictably partisan quality to the criticism. Even some of Roosevelt's supporters worried, however, about the constitutional precedent the president seemed to be setting. "It came as a shock to many of us in [the Office of Price Administration]," Thomas Emerson, then a young New Deal lawyer in the agency, recalled. Emerson surmised that Leon Henderson and the agency's general counsel had to have known about the plan in advance, and so he went to the top lawyer to express his "shock that the president was taking matters so far into his own hands." But the lawyer "only smiled and said, 'Well, probably it will never get to an issue.'"

What Roosevelt actually believed about his right to defy Congress was not entirely clear. Hassett, who was as close to Roosevelt as anyone, seemed to think the president was claiming unchecked constitutional powers to run the economy as he thought necessary in order to win the war. Certainly, Roosevelt had done much to give that impression.

"The President has the powers, under the Constitution and under Congressional Acts," Roosevelt explained in his broadcast, "to take measures necessary to avert a disaster which would interfere with the winning of the war." The president then went on to make clear that this general power took on special meaning in this "total war, with our fighting fronts all over the world," for it "makes the use of the executive power far more essential than in any previous war."

To further drive home the point, the president explained to the millions listening at home that it was quite obvious that "if we were invaded, the people of this country would expect the President to use any and all means to repel the invader." But while "the Revolution and the War between the States were fought on our own soil," the enemy need not actually reach America's shores for the president to be looked upon to act. "I cannot tell what powers may have to be exercised in order to win this war," he said, somewhat ominously. But whatever those powers might be, Roosevelt wanted his audience to know three things: "that I will use my powers with a full sense of responsibility to the Constitution and to my country"; "that I shall not hesitate to use every power vested in me to accomplish the defeat of our enemies in any part of the world where our own safety demands such defeat"; and that "when the war is won, the powers under which I act will automatically revert to the people of the United States—to the people to whom those powers belong."

For all the atmospherics of a president claiming unprecedented and seemingly limitless war powers, though, the truth, as usual, was much more complicated. Roosevelt had been careful to note in his speech that he had authority "under the Constitution *and under Congressional Acts*," and it appears that he never actually intended to rest his executive order on his constitutional powers alone. Instead, as in the destroyers controversy, the draft executive order was premised all along on a close reading of Congress's own handiwork.

* * *

That reading could be found in an elaborate legal opinion signed by Francis Biddle. It drew in turn on a series of memos from Oscar Cox, a top lawyer in the solicitor general's office. Cox believed deeply that, as he explained in a speech he gave while crafting the theory the administration would ultimately rely upon, "the responsibility of the government lawyer in time of war is, above everything else, the affirmative one of finding ways and means by which the decisions of the policy-makers can be most promptly and effectively fulfilled." That did not mean the lawyer should "countenance shady evasions nor dishonest shortcuts to a desired end." But the good executive branch layer did have to keep in mind that "quibbling over legalistic niceties may as decisively sabotage some aspect of the war effort as a sit down strike on an assembly line." The task, in the end, was to remain true to "the fundamental concepts of our law, our democratic processes, and the social and human values we are fighting to preserve," a task that fortunately could be carried out because "the fact remains that our legal framework allows far more latitude for administrative action than is popularly supposed."

The latitude in this case was to be found in a quirk of the statutory language contained in a measure known as Title III of the Second War Powers Act. This recently passed update of the prior war powers law had been enacted *after* the Emergency Price Control Act of 1942. The new measure added a key phrase to the prior version. It thus seemed to give the president some flexibility to address some of that price control statute's shortcomings, or so the secret memos explained.

The path to that conclusion was not a simple one. In July, Cox began sketching out a legal theory that might allow the president to revise the Price Control Act's farm price formula on his own. He even confidentially ran it by Justice Byrnes—then still on the bench—just a week before the Court was set to hear the argument in the saboteurs' case.

By early August, a presidential decree that would simply announce a new and lower farm price ceiling—and thus cap the legal sales price in direct violation of the act—seemed out of the question. Such an exercise of power, though clean and direct, would, everyone seemed to agree, conflict directly with the Price Control Act and thus go beyond the powers of the commander in chief. As Byrnes wrote in an August 8 letter, summing up the emerging consensus, he did "not believe that the President could either violate or evade the law in a matter where the Congress has affirmatively acted," as it had done on farm prices in setting the high ceiling. "If he does, he cannot expect compliance by the average citizen."

But the Second War Powers Act, Cox discovered, could be read to trigger the president's right to establish an allocation program to address wartime shortages, and then to set conditions on the things allocated as part of the war effort. After all, the Second War Powers Act had expressly added this new language about setting "conditions" on allocations, and it had done so in the wake of the Price Control Act's passage. Cox thus figured Congress must have been giving the president an out if the war demanded price controls different from those specified in the price control law itself.

To implement this approach, Cox concluded, the president needed to create a "Stabilization Administrator" who would then "promulgate a program of allocation and impose price conditions." By doing all of this under the Second War Powers Act, Roosevelt could solve the inflation problem and avoid the consequences of an attempted exercise of the war power in a manner contrary to statutory enactment.

It was a clever and aggressive solution—and possibly (though by no means definitely) wrong. The theory arguably converted a statute intended to confer the power to engage in wartime rationing into a means of addressing the danger posed by inflation. But if Cox was right about the power that Second War Powers Act gave to Roosevelt, then he was likely also right that the Emergency Price Control Act was no bar to using it. True, Roosevelt would be doing what appeared to be the very thing Congress had supposedly prevented him from doing: stabilizing farm prices. But just as he had found a way to use existing legislative grants of power to get the destroyers to England—despite statutes passed on the assumption he did not have such power—he had found a work-around. Congress may have been trying to help the farmers, but they had left Roosevelt an opening. He was going to run with it. It was just the kind of legislative loophole that Roosevelt had been exploiting for the better part of two years.

* * *

When Roosevelt last pulled such a maneuver, with the destroyers, he made a point of ensuring that Robert Jackson's legal opinion would accompany his announcement. He had even gone over it line by line and joked with Jackson that the careful legal analysis was sure to attract all the hostile fire. The disclosure of the legal rationale had helped soothe those in Congress who might have been alarmed by a more forthright claim of unchecked authority.

In this standoff with Congress, however, Roosevelt was not looking to counteract the suspicion that he was a dictator in waiting. The president openly courted the view that he was prepared to govern the country under emergency powers that he would seize on his own if Congress refused to act. It was as if he needed Congress to believe he was willing to go that far in order to get it to come his way. He did nothing to trumpet the carefully worked out statutory argument.

This strategy proved a winning one. However sound the technical statutory argument for unilateral action may have been—and it took a fair amount of concentration to follow its winding path—the threat of the president claiming a constitutional power to wage war beyond Congress's power spurred legislative action. In the congressional debate that followed, member after member rose to explain how the president had to be given what he wanted precisely because he might otherwise grab the power for himself in violation of the law. The resulting precedent such unilateralism would set, these defenders of congressional prerogative emphasized, would prove far more dangerous to democracy than the momentary political victory that Roosevelt might secure if Congress blinked. In the politics of the moment, in other words, the surest way to keep Roosevelt in check suddenly seemed to be to give him what he wanted. To cap off the bold move, Roosevelt named Justice Byrnes the stabilization czar.

* * *

Just as Roosevelt's Labor Day threat to seize power was heard with alarm in Congress, it also made an impression on the Court. But if the threat motivated Congress to affirm Roosevelt's authority, it seemed to have just the opposite impact on the justices. Questions about the president's power to defy Congress in running the war were very much on the Court's mind that September, thanks to the unfinished business left over from the saboteurs' case. The Court had affirmed the military commission's authority to conduct the trial. The Court had not yet written its opinion justifying that result. The task of writing it soon exposed fissures on the Court about the fundamental question of whether Congress could check the president in the midst of war.

The internal debate began in earnest less than three weeks after the president's speech about the farm prices. On September 25, Chief Justice

Stone apprised his colleagues of his great struggles in writing the final opinion about the fate of the saboteurs. "Just how the opinion in these cases should deal with the [statutory questions] raised by petitioners . . . is a question of some delicacy and difficulty," Stone explained in the memorandum he circulated that day to the Court. As Stone saw things, there were only two options, and "in the present posture of the case the adoption of either [alternative] involves the Court in some embarrassment to which I invite your attention."

Stone first explained the difficulties with saying the Court had no more information about what had actually occurred at the trial than it had in July and thus that the Court was, for that reason, leaving unaddressed again that issue of whether the procedures used were the ones that Congress expected the executive to use. Such an approach, Stone thought, risked making the Court look foolish—and cruel. Soon enough "the fact" of how the military commission had actually conducted the trial would be known. At that point, the two saboteurs whose lives had been spared could be expected to seek relief if the commission's procedures did actually diverge from those seemingly required in the Articles of War. The Court would then be forced to confront the issue, leaving it "in the unenviable position of" having to concede that it had "stood by and allowed six men to go to their death without making it plain to all concerned— including the President—that it had left undecided a question on which counsel strongly relied to secure petitioners' liberty."

The other option was not much better. If the Court tried to resolve whether the procedures were the right ones in its final opinion, then the Court would run headlong into the hard fact that, as Stone put it, the "proposition of law [was] not free from doubt." For another thing, the Court really did not have much more information than it had in July. The Court would thus be offering what Stone called an "advisory opinion." The Court would be merely guessing about whether there really had been any deviation from the Articles of War in the commission's proceedings.

It was an awkward time for Stone to be suggesting the Court needed to come to grips with this potential conflict between Congress and the commander in chief over the proper conduct of the military tribunal's proceedings. On the one hand, the war was going badly. The Germans had won a crucial battle in North Africa just days before the saboteurs had been discovered. The justices surely had no desire to hand Hitler a propaganda victory, which any suggestion that Roosevelt had acted illegally would surely do.

At the same time, this was hardly a propitious time to be coming down unreservedly in favor of executive war power. The president had just seemingly told the nation—in addressing the farm prices crisis—that he believed that in this total war his powers might be truly, if temporarily, limitless. Unless someone could figure out how to explain away the seeming conflict between the commission's procedures and those that Congress had required in the Articles of War, the Court might have to give support to that notion and rule the president had the sole power, in a time of war, to determine how best to defeat the enemy.

* * *

For Robert Jackson, Stone's concern was misplaced. Jackson was convinced that Congress did not want to tie the president's hands in a case like this one. He could not believe the procedural protections that Congress had provided in the Articles of War were intended to protect anyone other than American servicemen and those civilians subject to martial law in case of an occupation. He certainly could not believe these procedural safeguards were meant to benefit enemy invaders who were seeking to bring the war directly to America's cities. But Jackson had to admit the Articles of War did not directly limit their reach in the way that he assumed Congress must have intended. In fact, as Stone's memo indicated, the statutes setting forth the procedural protections were in some respects more naturally read to apply generally to all military tribunals, including those set up to try the enemy.

For that reason, Jackson proposed that the Court rely on an argument he had been loath to advance while advising Roosevelt as attorney general. Jackson suggested the Court rely on the long-standing presumption that Congress never intended to place a limit on the president that would run afoul of the Constitution. By doing so, the Court could bolster its defense of a narrow reading of the Articles of War and thus uphold the president's right to use special procedures for the commission.

For that argument to work, though, the Court would have to be willing to sign on to the view that Congress probably had no power to limit the commander in chief's right in an ongoing war to treat the enemy as he saw fit. Only then would there be a potentially serious constitutional question to avoid. And thus only then could a statute—the Articles of War—that seemed to prescribe certain procedures be justifiably read not to have done that at all.

Jackson was perfectly willing to adopt that view. He circulated a draft separate opinion on October 16 that made that point. "We should not only be slow to find that Congress unwittingly had done such a thing," the draft read in explaining that Congress could not have meant to restrict the president's power to set procedures as he pleased, "but even if it had clearly done so we would have a serious question of the validity of any such effort to restrict the Commander in Chief in the discharge of his constitutional functions." To make clear the breadth of the argument, Jackson even offered the example of a president potentially needing to visit cruel treatment on the enemy in order to a convince a warring party to release captured American soldiers. Surely, he indicated, Congress would have no right to interfere.

The draft quickly set off alarms in the other chambers. Hugo Black was a former Alabama senator and an early Roosevelt appointee to the Court. He was also the justice who had turned away the military defense counsel who had first brought the petition to his attention in July. In that encounter, Black had immediately shown Kenneth Royall the door to his home after expressing incredulity that anyone would think the Court should interject itself into such a matter. In response, Royall had offered only three words before leaving Black's house: "You shock me."

Now that the case was actually before the Court, though, Black believed there were certain constitutional principles that had to be respected. Black was happy to rule for Roosevelt. He was not about to sign off on an opinion that seemed to give the president carte blanche. As Black's law clerk explained in a memo to his boss that strongly urged him to refrain from endorsing Jackson's suggestion about the president's unchecked power, Jackson's latest draft seemed to be pushing the Court to write just such a blank check.

Jackson's proposition seemed "completely and outrageously wrong," Black's clerk wrote of the proposed language about the president's exclusive wartime powers. "It is precisely the sort of loose reasoning that the Administration was relying on in the farm price fight. It is what the Attorney General was trying to get out of this court—an expression of complete executive authority." If Black and the Court joined Jackson on that point, the clerk continued, "the President's position as Commander in Chief gives him authority to over-ride express acts of Congress, it would be construed without question as a complete blessing of the President's position on farm prices, and would be a complete green light to the executive for the future."

Others on the Court had similar misgivings. Frankfurter remained devoted to Roosevelt, and he was in frequent contact with him. The two men traded letters joking about Roosevelt's public relations skills and how the president could likely write better (or at least more dramatic) opinions than the Court. Frankfurter had even sent the president a note on September 8 praising his Labor Day address to the nation on the farm prices, noting that "merely because some of the matters dealt with in your Fireside Chat last night were outside my area of free opinion, is no reason why I should not tell you how very much I liked those as to which I have no judicial lockjaw."

But the president's discussion in that Labor Day speech about the scope of his power to act unilaterally had been a subject about which Frankfurter most certainly did have "judicial lockjaw." He was well aware of the dangers of the Court seeming to weigh in on that issue. He thus sent around a brief memo, apparently to Black, emphasizing that he, too, believed the Court not only did not "need to go, but should not go, into inherent constitutional power of [the President], which neither Congress nor the Court can limit."

* * *

Frankfurter soon followed up with another circulation to the full Court. He urged his brethren to follow his instincts and avoid getting into a matter of such ultimate authority. Frankfurter laid out an elaborate explanation of how the Articles of War could be read to give the president far more procedural leeway than the counsel for the defense had suggested. Frankfurter concluded his efforts to forge a compromise by circulating a remarkable memo to his fellow justices that he titled "F.F.'s Soliloquy."

Frankfurter began by trying to make sense of the continuing disagreement between Chief Justice Stone and Justice Jackson over how best to write the opinion. Frankfurter explained that he "could not for the life of me find enough room in the legal difference between them to insert a razor blade." And yet, it soon became clear, he did grasp the constitutional principle at the heart of the dispute Jackson was tempting the Court to resolve. Jackson was pressing for a statement acknowledging the president's exclusive right to make determinations about how to treat the enemy. Stone, like many of his colleagues, was reluctant to get anywhere near a statement that suggested the commander in chief was beyond Congress's power to control. In Frankfurter's judgment, it was time for the two contending sides to back down. They needed to do so for the sake of their fellow countrymen, and, particularly, for the sake of those then fighting abroad.

"It requires no poet's imagination to think of their reflections if the unanimous result reached by us in these cases should be expressed in opinions which would black out agreement in result and reveal internecine conflict about the manner of stating that result," Frankfurter wrote his colleagues. "I know some of these men very, very intimately. I think I know what they would deem to be the governing canons of constitutional adjudication in a case like this. . . . They would say something like this but in language hardly becoming a judge's tongue."

Frankfurter closed with an imagined plea from America's fighting forces to the divided Court he was hoping to bring together. "What in hell do you fellows think you are doing?" Frankfurter's fictional soldier asked. "Haven't we got enough of a job trying to lick the Japs and Nazis without having you fellows on the Supreme Court dissipate the thoughts and feelings and energies of the folks at home by stirring up a nice row as to who has what power when all of you are agreed that the President had the power to establish this Commission and that the procedure under the Articles for War for courts martial and military commissions doesn't apply to this case. Haven't you get any more sense than to get people by the ear on one of the favorite American pastimes—abstract constitutional discussion [?]"

That last question was meant to answer itself, but Frankfurter added one last piece of advice from his imagined man on the front lines. "Just relax and don't be too engrossed in your own interest in verbalistic conflicts because the inroads and energy and national unity that such conflict inevitably produces, is a pastime we had better postpone until peacetime."

Frankfurter got his wish. Stone's final opinion was a haze of obfuscation. But the new draft opinion convinced the Court to suppress its disagreement over the president's power to overrun Congress amidst a war. The opinion made no reference to the dangerous doctrine that Jackson had tried to get the Court to endorse. The Court instead unanimously declared that its earlier *per curiam* judgment was amply justified, either because the statutes requiring certain procedures actually had not been intended to apply or because they could be read to give the president discretion Roosevelt lawfully exercised.

With that, the debate over the outer limits of the executive's power to conduct war was, for the moment, put to rest. The Court had sanctioned Roosevelt's rushed form of wartime justice. It had given him no basis on which to build an argument for the kind of novel wartime powers he had so recently served notice he might be forced to claim in the name of ensuring victory.

* * *

The fall of 1942 had been a time of great crisis, but it passed with the constitutional structure—at least in form—unchanged. No new precedent declared Congress lacked the power to control the president in waging war. The old cases upholding legislative restrictions—including one from the Quasi War with France—remained in place. They could be read, if one wished, to be limited by the ambiguous words from Chief Justice Chase's Civil War–era concurrence in *Milligan*. That opinion had suggested there *were* limits on the constraints Congress could place on the actual conduct of a military campaign. But there was nothing in the Court's latest decision to suggest Chase's view had prevailed in this new age of total war and thus that the old notion of congressional control was antiquated.

Nor had the president's own actions during this frenzied period led to any new and striking constitutional precedent about the unlimited nature of the executive's wartime power. Roosevelt had not actually acted in direct defiance of Congress. He had instead been marvelously unclear about just what kind of power he planned to exercise during the standoff over farm prices. And his bluff had worked. Fearful of inviting Roosevelt to create the kind of precedent that might legitimate a commander in chief's right to take over Congress's traditional power to manage the economy, the House and Senate had hurriedly acted to give the president something very close to the power he had wanted. Thus, what threatened to be a new precedent for expanded presidential power could be assimilated quite comfortably to the tradition of accommodation between the branches that stretched all the way back to Washington and the Revolutionary War.

But, given all that had occurred in that first year of American involvement in this new world war, there was a real question whether it was only the "forms" of constitutional law that had been honored. It was not hard to tell a story in which the actual balance of power had swung wildly in the president's favor. Roosevelt had been pushing since well before the attack on Pearl Harbor to enter into an alliance with England, by then a belligerent in a foreign war. Roosevelt had managed to accomplish that objective without Congress specifically signing off.

Similarly, when the war finally came, Roosevelt had been far from restrained. He had established a military commission on domestic soil for the first time since the end of the Civil War, and he had done so without asking for Congress's special blessing. He had also pressed Congress to the wall in a game of constitutional chicken over price controls, and he had won by confidently asserting that he had the power to do what he wished whether or not Congress cleared the way. And, of course, Roosevelt had asserted—and exercised—the power to force tens of thousands of Japanese Americans from their West Coast homes, relocating them in internment facilities that bore an eerie resemblance to the concentration camps constructed by America's enemy.

* * *

Still, the "forms" did seem to matter—and not just to punctilious legalists who had no real influence on how such high-stakes decisions were made. Those forms also seemed to matter to those who were involved in making the actual decisions about how the war should be waged. The administration lawyers had hardly viewed the legal arguments as mere window dressing. They had instead declined to baldly assert the president alone could make these calls in a time of war. They struggled mightily to explain how the statutes then in place created room for the commander in chief to carry on the war in the manner he had chosen, and the president had not for a moment questioned the technical limits on his means of controlling prices that their legalism required him to accept.

The justices had been no different. They had refused to write an opinion about the president's war power that called *Ex Parte Milligan* a dead letter or that embraced a sweeping view of the president's right to have the final word in war. And they had declined to do so precisely because of their concerns about what such a doctrine, when laid down in black and white, might do to the delicate balance between Congress and commander in chief that would still have to play itself out for the war's duration. Far from thinking these abstract views about constitutional structure were a sideshow, such views had in fact been the only subject of intense disagreement on the Court in the saboteurs' case. No one doubted the president's right to use an army tribunal to mete out justice to German soldiers who had slipped behind coastal lines via a U-Boat that Adolph Hitler had personally sent to wreak havoc on America's wartime production system. There were doubts, though, about whether the commander-in-chief could try them on terms Congress ruled out.

The members of the House and Senate, too, seemed to feel strongly that a power exercised pursuant to a grant of statutory authority would do much less damage to the system of checks and balances than one the president asserted under his own power and in outright disregard of statutory checks Congress had imposed. For that reason, the members of Congress had scrambled to give Roosevelt the powers he demanded rather than watch him take the political risk—alone—of acting in defiance of legal limits. And, in the wake of the president's victory, the legislators had returned to their old process of bargaining with the administration—refusing to grant his request for the power to cap all salaries at $25,000 a year and even eventually driving Leon Henderson from office because of concerns about his policies.

Virtually no one in a position of authority, in other words, was willing to breach the forms that were so easily dismissed as meaningless. Even the internment of the Japanese Americans came to an end when, on the eve of the Court's announcement of its twin opinions ruling on the legality of those measures, the military issued an order renouncing its authority to intern loyal citizens. That order thus accommodated in advance the Supreme Court's possible judgment the next day that the president's exercise of such a power would run afoul of the statute that Congress had passed two years earlier ratifying, subject to limits, the initial army relocation order.

Despite the crisis of war, the relevant actors, time and again, chose not to push the confrontation to the limit. Instead, they did what they could to find ways of stretching and bending the powers that statutes already gave—reflecting an embrace of creativity, pragmatism, and, to the most cynical, a certain tolerance for lawlessness. In this way, and by these means, however much authority Roosevelt was acquiring, and however much the system of checks and balances was tilting in his favor (as it most certainly was), the system retained influence forcing arguments, delays in action, second-guessing, cajoling, justifications, alterations—in short, forcing a process of accommodation and mutual concession that, even in the midst of total war, seemed to the leaders of all three branches a crucial foundation of the constitutional democracy that they claimed to be committed to preserving.

Part 4

COLD WAR AND BEYOND

KOREA AND ABSOLUTE WAR POWERS

"The whole business of trying to prescribe by law the movements of military forces which are carried out in order to build up a force to prevent war is not a sensible thing to do."

T he end of World War II marked the start of the atomic age. It also sparked a Cold War. Together, these developments put great pressure on traditional understandings of separation of powers— and called into question whether the age-old respect for the "forms" of constitutionalism continued to make any sense. The task of adjusting to this new world—and deciding whether those forms were worth honoring, especially if reality suggested the chief executive had to be free to protect the national security in a way he had never been free before—initially fell to a leader who seemed wholly unprepared to handle it.

Harry Truman was an accidental president. He hailed from a small Missouri town. He went on to become a popular but hardly dynamic senator. Franklin Roosevelt then plucked him from Congress to serve as his running mate in the race for the president's fourth and final term. But though Truman had risen to vice president, he was never invited into the White House's inner circle. His involvement in the great man's wartime decisions was embarrassingly slight. He also had no executive experience of his own.

Still, once president, Truman surprised in his new role. He was a self-taught student of the past. His voracious reading as a youngster had convinced him that individual leaders could shape history. A former senator with deep reservoirs of good will in Congress, he turned out to be committed to defending the prerogatives of his new office. He also proved to be quite comfortable exercising them.

* * *

The early days of Truman's presidency were heady ones. Truman was behind the desk when Japan surrendered. He presided over the nation's final victory in World War II. His popularity soared. It was as if his every move was wise and well timed. He fast developed a reputation for decisiveness, even courage.

But it was in the years that followed that Truman made his most significant mark in the nearly two-century-old conversation about the powers of the commander in chief. After he had been elected in his own right, his administration took a series of steps that launched a new phase in that conversation. Up to that point, its cadence had barely changed. From George Washington's time forward, presidents had worked to find language to defuse confrontations over the conduct of war. Even Franklin Roosevelt had stepped back from the brink. With the singular exception of Reconstruction, Congress had tried to answer in kind, avoiding the strident tone that might set off a constitutional showdown with the commander in chief. The Supreme Court, meanwhile, seemed basically happy to listen. It said the president lacked an unlimited power to wage war *and* that there were certain lines Congress could not cross. The Court had been careful not to say much more.

Under Truman, circumspection gave way to blunt talk—and cruder formulations of the executive's war power. The Truman administration was convinced that the isolationists in Congress threatened the nation's security. The Democratic Party establishment had lost patience with Republican arguments for legislative rights. The constitutional complaints of men like Republican senator Robert Taft seemed less like principled defenses of the rule of law than covers for the same worldview that favored appeasement—"silly or cynical" "window dressing," as Truman's secretary of state put it.

A growing concern about the dangers of atomic weapons also influenced administration thinking. There was much worry about America looking weak in the high-stakes game of chicken then underway with the Soviet Union. From that concern flowed a new theory of executive authority. The president must be able to deploy armed force exceedingly swiftly. The enemy could inflict so much destruction so fast that the commander in chief must not be forced to wait for Congress's blessing before sending armed forces abroad. Once the president committed the nation's prestige militarily, moreover, he could not afford to let Congress weaken his hand. Otherwise, the president would lack credibility in the next round of brinksmanship with the Communists. The emerging argument for unchecked war powers thus justified itself: The president must have a free hand at the outset of a crisis, and, for that reason, Congress had no right to impose checks. Otherwise, the new thinking went, the president's ability to project strength at the outset would lack credibility over time.

This turn in the conversation led, in time, to a significant expansion of the commander in chief's power. All through the postwar decades presidents sent troops into harm's way without first getting clear congressional support. Slowly, executive branch lawyers expanded past precedents in ways that, to many, left them hard to recognize. In Korea, Truman even went so far as to start, for the first time in the country's history, a full-blown foreign war. He did so on the basis of nothing more than his own say-so and the blessing of the United Nations.

But the president was not solely responsible for this break with the old way of doing things. Congress's reluctance to challenge the new security logic helped as well. Even staunch defenders of the war powers of Congress, like Senator Edwin Johnson of Colorado, started to shift their thinking. Soon after Japan surrendered, during the debate over the implementation of the treaty committing the United States to join the United Nations, Johnson explained the reasons for his shift toward a more pro-executive position. In objecting to a proposal to legislate a cap on the number of troops the president could commit on his own to a UN mission, Senator Johnson explained to his colleagues that, in light of the development of atomic weapons, it was dangerous to restrict the commander in chief up front. "Nations not set to get underway trigger-quick," he said, "will get whipped before they start."

Still, the growth of the executive's war power was not linear. In the midst of the Korean War, Truman suffered as embarrassing a rebuke from the Supreme Court as any commander in chief had ever received. The justices—and Justice Robert Jackson most especially—seemed eager to defend Congress's important wartime role. The judicial opinion Jackson wrote in that case became the singular Supreme Court statement of the dangers of a president waging war on terms Congress had ruled out.

Truman's time in office was notable, therefore, less for his administration's success in actually securing absolute executive war powers than for its willingness to assert them in stark terms. But, as much as these sweeping claims created space for more aggressive executive war making—as they surely did—they also provoked unease. The result was the start of a cycle of constitutional crises and reaction over executive war powers and their limits that would continue for decades.

* * *

In a moment of endearing candor, Truman said he felt as if the "moon, the stars, and all the planets" had come crashing down on his shoulders when Roosevelt died. Who could blame him? The responsibility thrust upon him was immense. No sooner had Truman sworn to counter enemies foreign and domestic—at a hastily called ceremony in the Oval Office, with Roosevelt's timeworn effects still cluttering the room—than Henry Stimson pulled the new commander in chief aside. The secretary of war wanted to set a time to give his new boss some sobering news.

Specifically, Stimson wanted to arrange a private meeting to brief the president on a secret weapons project. Truman had heard rumors about it while serving in the Senate. At that time, he had even pressed Stimson for more information. But, when Stimson brushed him back in stern terms, Truman, the senator, said he understood the need for White House secrecy. Now, though, Truman was the president. Stimson needed him to know—and soon.

Within the week, Stimson brought the key briefing papers to Truman.

Stimson laid them before the president in the Oval Office. They detailed the country's still secret efforts to build an atomic bomb. Truman was wide-eyed. He believed he knew what this information meant. The war with Japan might soon be over—if, that is, he was willing to give the order to deploy the bomb.

At a deeper level, Stimson was telling Truman something more profound. The new president, Stimson was saying, now had access to unfathomably great power. So great, in fact, that Stimson was torn by the ethical questions such power raised. The bomb frightened Stimson. Its killing power was almost too horrifying to contemplate. Yet the tactical advantage it offered could not be denied. And, besides, America's enemies might soon acquire their own bomb. If the president did not use it, an opposing leader surely would.

Harry Truman did not hesitate. His certainty revealed that he was either a man of unusual self-confidence or one of great caution. Perhaps his calculus stemmed from a mix of these dispositions. To decide against using the bomb would have been to buck the near uniform view of the council of advisors the White House had assembled and that Stimson oversaw. The council was charged with advising Truman on whether and how to use the weapon. In a final memo sent to the president in the summer of 1945, that council explained its thinking. The atomic bomb should be used when ready. To shock Japan into submission, the first blow needed to be sudden, unexpected, and devastating. The target should be a city central to Japanese war production. (Stimson struck Kyoto from the target list only because he personally admired the place.)

The two resulting blasts killed more than a hundred thousand people. Most were civilians. The president never specifically signed off on the second target. His initial order instead gave the military the power to make that choice. But, as striking as it was for one man to have the power to destroy a city (and then to delegate the power to decide to destroy another), virtually no one suggested Truman had abused his powers as commander in chief. He had acted wholly on his own and in secret. His choice to wipe out two urban centers was widely seen as nothing more than a tactical decision. It was made in the course of an ongoing war that Congress had already declared. The decision was thus understood to have been his to make.

* * *

Richard Russell, a senator from Georgia and later the Democratic chair of the Senate Armed Services Committee, sent Truman a telegram soon after the first explosion. Far from raising a ruckus about the threat to the constitutional system posed by a single president's secret decision to deploy a weapon more destructive than any previously known to man, Russell urged Truman not to stop at Hiroshima's near total obliteration. "If we do not have available a sufficient number of atomic bombs with which to finish the job immediately," the telegram read, "let us carry on with TNT and fire bombs until we can produce them." Russell added he hoped Truman would "issue orders forbidding the officers in command of our air forces from warning Jap cities," as he believed such "showmanship can only result in the unnecessary loss of many fine boys in our air force" and risk the lives of those Americans being held as prisoners of war. Russell feared the Japanese would bring the prisoners to the target cities upon being apprised of an impending attack.

Still, some did see—and worry about—the ramifications of leaving a decision about this weapon solely in the hands of the commander in chief. Could it really be that the constitutional system left it to one man to make a judgment that could result in such destruction so quickly? Even Truman had his doubts. In a conversation with Stimson right after he received news of the first detonation, the president reflected on the "terrible responsibility that such destruction" placed on him. And, in replying to Russell, Truman seemed to want to distance himself from the remorseless approach the senator advocated. Truman closed his own telegrammed response to Russell by stating that while his object was to save as many American lives as possible, he also had "a humane feeling for the women and children in Japan." He thus would not continue "wiping out whole populations" unless he believed it "absolutely necessary," pointedly noting how little he thought of Russell's implicit suggestion that because the

Japanese behaved "like beasts" in warfare, "we should ourselves act in the same manner."

In fact, with Stimson's backing, Truman and his administration had been planning for some time to introduce framework legislation governing the "use of the atomic bomb." The new law they were working on would ensure some legislative involvement in future judgments. Stimson spoke with Truman about how the draft bill was coming along in his very first telephone call with the president after the bomb hit Hiroshima.

Before too long, that legislation passed. But even under the new law, the president kept the power to deploy the bomb on his own command. Congress did not try to take it away. Hiroshima and Nagasaki were now precedents for future presidential decisions. The commander in chief had done what George Washington had refused to do in the early days of the Revolutionary War in New York: order an entire city laid to waste. But Truman, unlike Washington, had not been told by Congress to hold his fire.

* * *

If the specter of the bomb's future use made the commander in chief appear more powerful than ever, Truman was not as much in control as it may have seemed. By 1949, the Soviets had manufactured an atomic bomb of their own. That resulted in a strategic logic no president could easily challenge, especially not when Congress subscribed to that logic so strongly.

It was no real surprise, therefore, that Truman, after receiving the nonbinding recommendations of the statutorily established Atomic Energy Commission, decided in early 1950 that he would green-light efforts to develop the so-called Super—the hydrogen bomb. That choice was driven as much by lobbying from Capitol Hill, and perceived strong support there, as by the new commander in chief's sense of prerogative or personal desire.

Some of Truman's closest aides doubted the wisdom of going ahead with such a catastrophically destructive weapons program. The Super was orders of magnitude more powerful than its predecessor. The president's advisors thought no other option was viable. Such were the realities of

Soviet aggressiveness and congressional politics. "Even if the Soviet Union refrained from undertaking a thermonuclear program as the result of our refraining—a non-existent prospect—the Administration would run into a Congressional buzz saw and the proposal . . . would be still born," an aide recalled, recounting the political thinking behind the final internal recommendation to develop the Super.

Truman did not take terribly long to act on the recommendation to go forward in developing the Super—seven minutes, in fact. In response to the question "Can the Russians do it?" the assembled advisors all nodded their heads in the affirmative. "What the hell are we waiting for?" the president responded. "Let's get on with it."

* * *

The nuclear arms race shadowed all the military decisions that followed. The most consequential was the one Truman made two years after he was elected president.

Reports of the new crisis, this time in Asia, came in over the weekend in late June of 1950. Truman was out of town. South Korea was at risk of falling to Communist invaders from the north. Truman, urged on by his secretary of state, Dean Acheson, committed the nation to what amounted to a war in Korea. He did so by sending in thousands of American troops. Rather than first going to Congress, Truman relied solely on a fast-tracked resolution of the Security Council of the United Nations, whose proceedings the Soviet Union was boycotting at the time.

Once again, Congress expressed little concern about Truman acting on his own. The need to counter the Communists was widely accepted on the Hill. The only real objection came from a small group of Republicans, the most vocal of whom was Senator Robert Taft. Even Taft agreed with the president on the merits of making a show of force. One senator whom Truman conferred with in early July told him not to worry. He assured the president that "most of the members of Congress were sick of the attitude" Taft expressed. Within days, Congress did quietly appropriate funds that would be needed for fighting the battles ahead; the appropriations bill also extended the draft.

Nonetheless, in a nod to the constitutional objection Taft had raised, some of Truman's advisors did suggest, in the first days after the deployments to Korea, that it would be wise for the president to go to Congress for more direct congressional approval. Legislative support, even after the fact, would reduce the risk of Truman becoming a victim of his own unilateralism in the event the war went badly.

Truman saw little upside in that approach. Most important, he saw no need to get a formal declaration of war. "They are all with me," the president said at the time, describing the sentiments of his former colleagues. There was some concern about Taft's contention that Truman had violated the United Nations Participation Act. Truman had signed that measure years before. His men had assured Congress at the time that the law was a check against the president using the United Nations to make an end run around Congress in committing the country to a war.

As with so many statutes that appeared to regulate decisions about war and peace, this one, too, had its limits. The law required the president to get specific congressional approval of any "special agreements" he forged with the United Nations under Article 43 of the UN charter. Such agreements obliged a country that entered into such agreements to lend military support to a United Nations force. But, Truman had not reached any "special agreement" with the UN regarding Korea. The Security Council, at America's request, had merely recommended under Article 39 that the United States assist in defending against the Communist invasion.

In other words, Truman was not compelled to help the UN save Korea. He was merely permitted to assist in the defense of that country if he chose. Technically, then, the United Nations Participation Act—and its requirement of congressional approval—had not been triggered.

The legal distinction was a fine one, but it was sound. The Security Council resolution meant that Truman was acting lawfully—violating neither international law nor congressional statutes—so long as he was not flouting Congress's constitutional power to declare war. Truman and his team were convinced the president was not doing that.

* * *

In a press gathering in late June, Truman called the initial deployment of air and sea power a mere "police action" aimed at suppressing "bandits." That characterization was initially widely accepted, even though, by early July, Truman had sent in two army divisions—some hundred thousand soldiers in all. There were reasons why there was a general aversion to calling what was happening a "war" that had nothing to do with skirting the Constitution. The truth was that Truman's advisors, both in and out of Congress, feared the symbolic fallout of asking for a declaration of war and then succeeding in getting it.

The last thing Truman wanted to do was suggest that the United States, so soon after concluding a second world war, was embarking on a third. The aim was to proceed as if the country was engaged in a far more limited action—something much less threatening than the kind of total war that had just concluded and that, with the bomb now at the forefront of everyone's consciousness, conjured up fears of the gravest sort.

A war declaration would run counter to all of that. It might cause alarm among the public. It could also provoke the new Communist regime in China, and potentially the Soviets as well, to enter the conflict out of a mistaken belief that America was intent on starting something larger. In December, Truman went on national television to dispel the brewing sentiment for a wider war. At that time, some members of Congress were advocating atomic strikes outside Korea. The president—in his typical monotone, and speaking too fast to inspire—made the case for keeping the conflict in Korea limited. He warned his countrymen that if a more general war began, people should expect "many atomic bombs to be dropped on American cities."

Of course, Truman could have gone back to Congress for something more modest—say, the right to act only after providing a formal report on the situation. His secretary of state began pushing him to do just that in the first days after the initial deployments to Korea. But it was not clear what Truman would be asking of Congress if he were not asking it to declare war. That lack of clarity, in turn, could be problematic. It might cause Congress to push back, sparking what could be a weeks- or months-long debate over the respective roles of the two branches. Truman and others thought that could be extremely harmful to the morale of American fighting forces in Korea.

If the administration tried to jam Congress into saying Truman had done everything right in not declaring war, Truman doubted his old colleagues would sign on. Such an attempt might have the opposite effect. It might force those in Congress to stand up for their own constitutional authority. The president agreed with those advisors who suggested he should avoid a confrontation. Those advisors included the key congressional leaders Truman had consulted. They counseled silence, too. Truman chose to do nothing that might stir up a Congress that, for now, seemed content to watch from the sidelines. The president declined even to give a speech to the public, fearing that a so-called fireside chat, by directly addressing the people about why he had acted on his own, would make him look high-handed. He emphasized to those at the meeting that he must do nothing that would make him "appear to be trying to get around Congress and use extra-constitutional powers."

That did not mean Truman was blind to the risks of not seeking formal support on the Hill. He ended this internal debate—which at times grew tense—on a dark note. After hearing what the proposed congressional resolution would say, he remained committed to keeping Congress out of it. A senator in attendance assured Truman he was making the right choice. The senator added that "he did not think Congress was going to stir things up." Truman quickly shot back: "This depends on events in Korea." It was an accurate assessment. Truman knew how quickly Congress might turn on a president waging an unpopular war.

* * *

The first sign things might not be simple came in the late fall of 1950—after months of setbacks in Korea and, most concerning, the entry of the Chinese Communist army into the conflict. The dustup arose from a casual comment Truman made to the press. If things got really bad, Truman noted to a clutch of reporters on November 30, he was better positioned than prior commanders in chief had been. He had special weapons at his disposal. The use of atomic weapons, he confirmed, had been "under

active consideration." Responsibility for making any tactical decision
about which weapons to use, he explained, would reside with the theater
commander. In other words, he seemed to be saying, the haughty and
hard-to-control General Douglas MacArthur was empowered to decide
whether to deploy the bomb if he wished.

Truman was oblivious to how his off-the-cuff remarks would be heard.
The power Truman invoked did nothing to calm the nerves of those harboring doubts about the war's outlook. The effect was precisely the opposite. Both at home and abroad, there was immediate alarm at the prospect
of Truman, in the midst of fighting a losing war that he had started by
decree (despite his risible efforts to cast it off as a mere "police action"),
causally leaving it to a general in the field to touch off a nuclear firestorm.

An administration spokesman assured the press the president had
been misunderstood. Truman was not saying that atomic weapons *would*
be used. He was just saying their use—like the use of any weapon—was
a possibility. In any event, no decision to use the bomb could be made
without his assent as commander in chief.

Still, almost as soon as word of the president's incautious comments
reached the floor of Parliament, England's prime minister, Clement Attlee,
announced he would go to Washington to make known his concern. Upon
arriving in D.C., Attlee sought assurances Truman would not act alone.
When Truman told his aides he had privately given that promise during
his meeting with Attlee at Blair House (the temporary quarters Truman
used during the White House's renovation), the president inadvertently
caused a problem on a separate front. In trying to keep the war limited, the
president had raised concerns among Republicans. After initially berating
Truman for going it alone, they now objected that the president, by seeming to promise England he would seek its approval before doing anything
rash, was being too weak. Reflecting their hostility to any notion America
might make its national security hinge on a secret pact with Europe, twenty-four Republican legislators had even signed a resolution objecting in
advance to any secret deal Truman and Attlee might reach.

Truman's aides scrambled to clean up the mess. They feared a leak
might disclose that the president had promised to keep the atomic bomb

under wraps unless England agreed to its use. The aides drew up new and vague language for a joint communiqué with Attlee. It said the president had no intention at present of using atomic weapons and that he would let England know if circumstances began to change. In other words, Truman reserved his right to act on his own if he felt it necessary to do so.

* * *

The episode revealed the practical limits of the new power that the commander in chief had been given. Popular and congressional opinion would shape the administration's views as to what it could and could not do with a weapon that dangerous. But that reality also underscored the dangers the country faced now that its chief rival had weapons of the same basic type.

Truman thus found himself betwixt and between. He was armed with more power than any president had ever been. He faced a foe that possessed a similarly destructive capability. Truman was politically obliged (many thought) to match shows of force with shows of force. Any other course might give the Soviets encouragement to use the weapons first. And yet, the end goal of avoiding nuclear destruction necessarily restricted Truman's capacity to use his full armament to check the enemy. Even the threat of doing so, he had just learned, could provoke a backlash. But then so, too, could a commitment to refrain from giving the green light to the use of such destructive power.

Inevitably, the administration came to think, the nation's security would have to be enforced by soldiers no matter how many atomic bombs America produced. Thanks to the shift in the strategic landscape—a shift partly caused by the advent of nuclear weapons—those troops would have to be used in connection with a far more proactive and even preemptive military strategy than America was used to implementing.

Attacks had to be deterred, not merely answered in this new age. The strategy thus seemed to require the United States to extend its military commitments well beyond Korea. Specifically, it was decided, the United States needed a round-the-clock protection force—and thus a hedge against Communism's advance—in the heart of Europe, where it was feared that the Soviets next might extend their influence.

* * *

It took no special political savvy to see that controversy would attend a unilateral executive effort to stand up such a force in Europe. It was one thing to have a standing army at home. It was another to let the president set one up anywhere he wished—let alone in a part of the world that might touch off a war with Russia.

In the winter of 1950, a half-year after Truman had first publicly committed to sending U.S. air, naval, and ground forces to assist South Korean forces, the dispute over the use of ground troops elsewhere broke out into the open. The immediate provocation was an announcement that Truman had made in early September.

Without congressional authorization for his plan, Truman unveiled it anyway. He would send four army divisions to reinforce the forces already serving in Europe under the recently created North Atlantic Treaty Organization. The Soviet threat was already gathering. That meant an additional hundred thousand Americans would be going to the volatile region, with no upper bound on how many more might follow. In defending this approach, Truman said that, as commander in chief, he could "send troops anywhere in the world" without consulting Congress.

With the events in Korea as a backdrop, the claim set off an extended discussion in the Senate. It lasted more than three months. The so-called Great Debate laid bare the new doctrine of absolute war powers that Truman and his men seemed eager to advance.

The site of the starkest defense of that position was a grand Senate hearing room. It was just a few days into February 1951. The Armed Services and Foreign Relations Committees had convened for an unusual joint hearing. The key witness was Harry Truman's secretary of state.

* * *

With his patrician bearing and jaunty mustache, Dean Acheson was not a man lacking in self-confidence. As a private citizen, he had taken the lead in pushing Roosevelt to send Churchill the destroyers in the run-up to World War II. Nor did Acheson have much doubt about the greatness of the president whom he now served. Hard decisions did not scare Truman, and Acheson admired his new president's simple, straightforward strength.

Acheson also had personal reasons for his loyalty to Truman. The president had helped Acheson ascend to the height of power, after years of service in the government as a lawyer and a counselor. Truman had appointed him to the cabinet at a time when Acheson was mired in the doldrums of private law practice and doubting the meaning in his work.

Even more significant, Truman had stood by Acheson earlier that year when he had come under intense fire. Republicans in both the House and Senate had passed resolutions calling for his ouster. Their hostility had much to do with Acheson's seeming contempt for them. The push to drive Acheson out of office also stemmed from the devastating—and wholly shocking—Chinese rout of American troops in Korea earlier in the year. Acheson's stubborn refusal to turn his back on his good friend Alger Hiss, who had been convicted of spying for the Communists, added to the congressional opposition. More than a few Democrats had come to regard Acheson, given his high-handed manner, as a political liability. Truman would not budge. He would stand by his secretary of state.

For all of these reasons, Acheson was more than happy to use his testimony to the Senate to make the case for the robust internationalist policy of the Truman administration. He was not only there to defend foreign policy positions that he believed to be correct. He was also looking to mix it up with Congress on behalf of his boss.

At the time, the president's standing in the polls was sinking. His political exposure was great. In time, the polls would show that more than three-quarters of the American public disapproved of his performance. Things were going very badly in Korea. China's entry into the war had created panic. Many Americans began to fear that the nation was on the precipice of a third world war. In response, some members of Congress were already calling on Truman to use atomic weapons to suppress the Chinese offensive and spare American soldiers the risks of going to war.

At the same time that Truman was being criticized for being too weak, he was also under assault for being too high-handed, as his proposed troop deployment to Europe appeared to many on the Hill to demonstrate.

Acheson was not one to back down from a fight. He was more than willing to push for sending more troops—without congressional support. Acheson told the Senate that Truman was perfectly entitled to send an *additional* four army divisions to Korea without consulting Congress. And, Acheson explained, he was equally sure of the president's right to send troops to Europe on his own say-so. Such action was necessary to support the Western alliance there against rumblings from the Soviet Union.

* * *

As Acheson saw things, the world had been reordered in the wake of the defeat of Hitler and the Japanese military leader, Hideki Tojo. Through the treaties creating the UN and the North Atlantic Treaty Organization, America was firmly enmeshed in the first international security system. The president was no longer the military leader of just his own country. He was the leader of the free world. Hadn't the Senate wanted a strong president when it had ratified these treaties? Hadn't it known those treaties signaled a shift toward the executive in international and military affairs?

Acheson wasn't finished. Out of the wreckage of World War II, Acheson and his allies had made something good, something lasting. He was not about to let an incoherent mix of anti-Communist and isolationist dogma steal that future. And so, Acheson explained to the members of Congress, the point was not just that the president could act first in committing the nation's military abroad. He also could keep those armed forces there as long as he wished—even if Congress, responding to public pressure against military commitments that seemed too costly, wanted to bring them home. Once the troops had been sent, Acheson explained, Congress was powerless to recall them. Such judgments were—at least in this new and dangerous world—for the president alone to make.

"Not only has the President the authority to use the Armed Forces in carrying out the broad foreign policy of the United States and implementing treaties," Acheson's State Department had argued in a submission to the Senate back in January, "but it is equally clear that *this authority may not be interfered with by the Congress in the exercise of powers which it has* under the Constitution." In a follow-up memorandum submitted to the Senate after Acheson's February testimony, the administration argued that because "the direction of the armed forces is the basic characteristic of the office of the Commander in Chief, the Congress cannot constitutionally impose limitations upon it."

It was a striking position, and Acheson knew it. He made some attempts to soften his tone. He argued that "trying to split legal hairs" over constitutional powers was a terrible waste of time. All that really mattered was that Congress and the president were united in the felt need to bolster Europe's defenses in the name of America's national security. "We are in a position in the world today where the argument as to who has the power to do this, that, or the other thing," Acheson said, "is not exactly what is called for from America in this very critical hour, and if we could all agree on the fact that something should be done, we will perform a much greater role in the world, than by quarreling about who ought to do it."

Acheson was not being entirely straight. He had told the Senate that "the whole business of trying to prescribe by law the movements of military forces which are carried out in order to build up a force to prevent war is not a sensible thing to do." As he put it, "The idea that all of this thing has to be legislated by the code, and you look up in the book to see 'May I send a company!' 'No; section 357 says I can't do that,' that is not the way to carry on this great task."

Acheson was doing more than calling for unity. He was defending the president's legal right to commit the nation militarily—and in circumstances that could certainly be provocative to the Soviet Union—and explaining that Congress should have no right to object. That was his bottom line. In fact, the hearing had been framed as a consideration of a resolution proposed by Senator Kenneth Wherry of Nebraska, one of the few members of Congress who had raised constitutional concerns at the outset of the Korean crisis. Wherry's proposed resolution sought to limit ground troops from going to Europe absent Congress's consent. The resolution that ultimately passed did not much matter. Acheson had by then made clear that it was his view—and that of the administration—that Congress had no power to do more than register a complaint. The president would be the final voice as to whether that complaint would be heeded.

* * *

The Acheson testimony expressed an attitude toward executive war powers that did more than justify a strategy of Communist containment. It also reflected an attraction to unchecked power. The very next year, that same attitude would provoke a true constitutional crisis. It was born of a claim to executive war power untempered by any of the nuance or subtlety characteristic of the approaches of past presidents.

For months, Truman had put off the decision to seize the nation's steel mills in order to end a nationwide steel workers' strike. The president had delayed any such decision despite mounting concern the work stoppage threatened the war effort in a grave way. The army needed steel, but the strike seemed to prevent it from being processed. Nothing Truman tried did anything to put an end to the standoff—including a plea to Congress for new authority to resolve it. None of it worked. The order to seize finally went out. The administration justified the decree as the prerogative of a commander in chief in dire need of steel for the troops fighting in Korea under his direction.

When pressed at a news conference whether the president's logic implied that he also could seize newspapers if he thought that necessary to win the war, Truman wouldn't say "no." The uproar was intense. To be sure, some opponents were archenemies of labor; others were champions of the press. But that was not the whole of it. The president's claim to expansive—seemingly limitless—war power was making a lot of people uneasy.

To calm things down, the president eventually said he would accept the Supreme Court's review of his seizure of the mills. It seemed like a concession to checks and balances. The statement helped bring him back in line with his predecessors. But, in a federal district court in Washington, the Justice Department seemed to be saying the opposite. Echoing

Acheson's idea of the president's unchecked power over the armed forces, Homer Baldridge, the lawyer making the case for seizing the mills on behalf of the United States, defended the seizure by saying the commander in chief could do whatever he thought necessary to address the emergency. When Judge David Pine asked whether that meant the courts "cannot even review whether it is an emergency," Baldridge replied simply: "That is correct."

Pine ruled the government's position "alien" to the constitutional system. The case then moved to the Supreme Court. At a specially called emergency session, the Court sided with Judge Pine. In probably the most famous war powers opinion ever written, Justice Robert Jackson explained why in a separate and eloquent concurrence. Truman kept saying Congress could stop him if it wished. Jackson countered that the president had failed to see that Congress had already—in effect, if not in clear language—told him to back down. Jackson explained the president could not simply seize a company to end a labor standoff on terms favorable to workers, not even by invoking his powers as commander in chief. Congress had given him other means—the power to enjoin the strike among them. The commander in chief would thus be acting contrary to Congress's direction in taking the mills; he would not merely be taking advantage of Congress's failure to address the issue at all.

To drive home the point, Jackson referred in a footnote to his own opinion from his days in the Roosevelt administration. In his infamous opinion on the destroyers-for-bases deal, Jackson had denied the commander in chief the power to send Churchill mosquito boats because Jackson had found that a statute stood in the way. Jackson seemed pleased to have the occasion to affirm the same principle again—that the powers of the commander in chief, at least on the matter at hand, were not beyond legislative control.

Jackson was hardly pure on that issue. He had, in private negotiations with his fellow justices, taken a much stronger stand in favor of the commander in chief during the debate over the trial of the Nazi saboteurs. At that time, he had suggested Roosevelt enjoyed an absolute power to disregard the rules for the military tribunal that Congress had set forth. He had argued then that it was absurd to think that a president should be tangled up in arcane procedures of Congress's making. He needed the freedom to visit harsh justice on an invading force on the home front.

But there was so much about the steel seizure case that was different. The president was leveraging a war of his own creation rather than one Congress had declared. He was asserting his military authority upon American factory owners and in favor of striking laborers. He was not, like Roosevelt, using his military power to repel an invading enemy force. Nor was he addressing directly Congress's power to control the president's use of combat forces in foreign fields. In fact, Jackson noted that "I should indulge the widest latitude of interpretation to sustain his exclusive function to command the instruments of national force, at least when turned against the outside world for the security of our society."

Jackson was happy to concede: There was anything but clarity for those searching for past precedents that would set out the president's power to conduct a war in a manner contrary to Congress's direction. The legal precedents on the subject were as hard to make sense of as the "dreams Joseph was called to interpret for Pharaoh," he wrote with his flair for the arresting phrase. Jackson also had no doubt that if Truman could take his administration's expansive views of the executive power as commander in chief and use them in this way, the Constitution would be badly deformed. An affirmation of the president's seizure of the mills would validate the very fears that had first led Patrick Henry and George Mason, during the ratification debates in Virginia, to object to the Constitution's naming of the president the commander in chief.

* * *

Truman was surprised by the Court's final decision—a decisive, though not unanimous, rejection of his action. He had been privately assured the case would come out all right by Chief Justice Fred Vinson, his good friend and a man he had tried to recruit to run for president as his successor. But, eventually, Truman got over the setback. He even agreed to join the justices for a glass of bourbon at the home of Supreme Court Justice

Hugo Black. The justice had extended the invitation to help clear the air after the Court had rebuffed Truman so clearly.

Still, the extreme nature of Truman's position was not easily forgotten. It brought together in one concrete example all the concerns that the opponents of the New Deal had been identifying. Here, at last, seemed tangible evidence of the dictator come to life: siding with one sector of American society over another, seizing property to aid the specially chosen side, and doing so in the name of war powers triggered solely because the president decided to trigger them. The nation had been blanketed with newspaper editorials framing Truman's actions in just such frightening terms. A key member of his team resigned in apparent protest.

The electorate replaced Truman with a military hero in the presidential election of 1952. It was an election Truman decided to sit out. He knew how unpopular he had become. But the new leader was a military officer himself: Dwight D. Eisenhower, the man who had led the American forces at D-Day and thus the man who had done as much as anyone to defeat Hitler and win World War II.

The new president was determined to project a more prudent face of power. Truman had caught the drift of public opinion too late. He spent the last weeks on the stump on behalf of the Democratic nominee, making a fool of himself. He warned that General Eisenhower was another Cromwell, about to bring military dictatorship to the republic, seemingly oblivious to how much his own overreach had helped make Eisenhower's more moderate tone attractive.

The ploy did not work. Eisenhower beat his Democratic opponent, Illinois senator Adlai Stevenson, in a landslide—thus resulting in the ascendance to the nation's highest office of a military general in a race in which, as one senator put it, the "usurpations of the executive" and the "trends to socialism" were definitely on the ballot.

* * *

Once in office, Eisenhower aimed, as he often told his aides, to be a "constitutional" president. It was a none-too-subtle put-down of his predecessor. The phrase reflected Eisenhower's low opinion of Truman's power grabs—most especially the steel mills seizure, which Ike likened to the fascist displays of power he had fought against at D-Day. It was not simply a post-hoc characterization.

On the same day Secretary of State Dean Acheson had testified to the Senate about Congress's utter powerlessness to check a president committed to sending troops abroad in the name of protecting national security, Eisenhower sounded a very different note. Testifying as a top military commander of American NATO troops, Eisenhower was asked by the committee to appear as the lead-off witness. Eisenhower was careful to say he did not believe the Constitution ousted Congress from the picture—even if others in the administration might think otherwise.

The general explained that, while Congress should avoid putting the executive in a box, "I do think that the Congress of the United States ought to see a respectable, reasonable approach, and the second they see anything to be, let's say, cockeyed and crazy, to get into the thing with both feet." For while "I should like to see a certain degree of flexibility in this particular problem," Eisenhower assured the committee that "long before [the president] could transfer to France what anybody such as this would consider an inordinate amount of strength, you can step in, and when common sense has been violated, certainly it is within the power of Congress to bring us back to our normal senses." It was the kind of measured—analytically muddled but practically sensible—accounting of the separation of powers that presidents had been mouthing for more than a century.

* * *

Once in the White House, Eisenhower had trouble proving he was no Truman. Truman's own aggressive actions had polarized the country on issues of war, peace, and national security. Certain positions became associated with executive overreach, no matter whether they actually required a president to be defiant to adopt such a view. Internationalism in general had acquired the taint of executive power run amok. But Eisenhower, for all of his Republican support and all of his not-so-subtle efforts to associate himself with the anti-executive critique of Truman, was a much more committed internationalist than many of his most fervent voters. He was thus bound to disappoint them. And he did. He was most disappointing to the Truman and Roosevelt haters who had supported him because he refused to rip up the post–World War II agreements with Russia and others that those Democratic presidents had signed to settle the peace after that great armed conflict.

Still, Eisenhower was no Truman. Rather than sending troops here and there, or starting small wars to counter Soviet advances, Eisenhower implemented his internationalist agenda, and Cold War strategy, chiefly through stealth. He saw in covert operations—run out of the secret agency Truman did so much to establish—a way of winning the Cold War that would avoid a catastrophic conflict with the Soviets. He also saw in such operations an attractive means of avoiding the constitutional face-offs with Congress and the Court that Truman's more confrontational approach had invited. And so, while Eisenhower was quite aggressive in secret, the constitutional crises with the Court and Congress that had defined Truman's presidency seemed to be at an end. Until, that is, they started up again. They were provoked most strikingly a decade after Eisenhower stepped down, by a president who was attracted to even cruder assertions of wartime prerogative than Truman had been willing to make, and who was serving at a time when Congress's trust in the clandestine national security apparatus was starting to erode.

15

WAR IN INDOCHINA AND CONGRESSIONAL RESURGENCE

"[T]he President does not need the approval of Congress to do what he is doing in Cambodia. . . . [A]t the same time, Congress retains the authority to determine where and for how long the U.S. can wage war. So, it can say the U.S. will NOT fight in Cambodia."

In May of 1970, a young but startlingly influential White House lawyer named Tom Huston sent a memo to the chief of staff and other top advisors to the president. The subject line: "The Assault on the Constitutional Powers of the Presidency."

Huston wrote, in unusually blunt terms, that Congress would soon begin an all-out effort to rein in the president's war powers. He counseled the administration to launch a counterattack. Otherwise, Huston warned, the Democratic opposition would take control of the war in Vietnam that was—depending on how one counted—already in its sixth year.

For much of the country, the contents of Huston's memo—had they been known—would have been infuriating. They also would have confirmed a long-held view. It was an article of faith among many opponents of the Vietnam War that the White House—and its present occupant in particular—believed that decisions about war and peace were the commander in chief's alone. For that reason, it was thought, President Richard

Nixon believed he was entitled—even obliged—to wage a military campaign against Communist forces, whether the public wanted him to or not, so long as he thought the nation's security required it.

But, as much as the Huston memo would have fed the image of a White House seized by power and gripped by Cold War thinking, the memo also would have contained a surprise. The memo showed the administration was actually quite worried—and growing ever more so—about its ability to make war in the face of determined popular resistance at home.

The Nixon administration had worked hard to project an aura of invincibility—from making a point of playing "Hail to the Chief" whenever the president entered a public event to outfitting the White House guards with epaulets fit for a monarch's protectors. As Huston's words revealed, the truth was otherwise. The memo showed that, to the men around the president, it would not take much for Nixon to lose the upper hand. Congress would need only to shake off its decades-long slumber and reassert its constitutional power to limit the commander in chief.

Huston's memo, then, neatly captured two polar ideas, each of which gained traction as the Vietnam War entered its climactic phase. Just as Huston predicted, the ensuing years saw the rise of a resurgent Congress, committed to forcing the president to bring the troops home from Vietnam and newly skeptical of the national security expertise that had sustained executive power in the decades after World War II. But this period also crystalized an opposite idea—and one very much to Huston's liking. This idea was, ironically, pressed hard by the war's opponents. It was also nurtured by the White House as part of its effort to maintain its posture of total control. The idea portrayed the commander in chief as an all-powerful force that, in this new and dangerous nuclear world, could overwhelm any legislative effort to stop him.

These years thus gave birth, simultaneously, to two conflicting accounts of how the separation of powers works in war. The one stressed how a powerful Congress could bring the commander in chief to heel, even with troops in the field, if only the Senate and the House could muster the will to mount a challenge to his authority. The other was summed up by an evocative phrase, "the imperial presidency," coined just a few years after Huston sent his memo. The phrase was used to underscore the dangers of runaway executive power. It also suggested the president had become uniquely powerful in the last half-century and that, because Congress would not dare to take him on, he would likely remain unstoppable for decades to come.

This last idea—that the constitutional balance had tilted decisively and perhaps irrevocably in the president's favor—would eventually capture the public's imagination. The story of these years, then, obscured just how fragile the chief executive's grip on the war power truly had been in the final stages of the conflict in Indochina. The new story instead cemented in the public's mind the idea that the modern president could inevitably work his will when it came to war, as if the notion that Congress could check him was only a quaint memory from a much earlier time in the nation's history.

* * *

At first, the American presence in Vietnam consisted of only the small complement of military advisors that President John F. Kennedy had sent to that part of the world near the beginning of his brief time in office. Soon enough, the size of the force deployed in that early Cold War effort to insulate Asia from further Communist influence had increased dramatically.

At its height, the nation's commitment in Vietnam engaged more than half a million troops. Even after the most recent round of withdrawals that President Nixon had ordered, there were still more than four hundred thousand soldiers in the field. Meanwhile, the casualties kept mounting: By the spring of 1970, the killed and wounded totaled in excess of forty thousand on the American side, and the bombing of the enemy—and thus the deaths of countless civilians who found themselves in harm's way—continued without relent.

The war seemed to go on no matter the president—whether Kennedy's successor, Lyndon Johnson, who first ramped up the deployments; or

Richard Nixon, the former Republican nominee who had lost to Kennedy in 1960 but had mounted an improbable reinvention and was now midway through his second year in office.

After Johnson decided not to run again, Nixon had won the presidency in 1968. Nixon's second run for the White House had succeeded in part because he had promised, Eisenhower-like, to bring an end to what was looking like another unpopular Asian war that a Democratic president had started.

Upon taking office, though, Nixon turned out to be a staunch advocate for the war's vigorous prosecution. In his first year alone, there were ten thousand American casualties, proof that Nixon was not looking for a quiet or quick exit.

There were also reports that Nixon had ordered a secret, expanded military campaign in Laos. And, thanks to a leaked report in *The New York Times* that appeared in May, there was growing concern that Nixon was pursuing a similar expansion into Cambodia.

For many—including members of the Democratic establishment at first hopeful Nixon might secure a final peace—the president's aggressive approach to fighting the war was a source of great disappointment. In time, that disappointment turned to anger, even rage.

Nixon was drawing down the troops as part of his so-called Vietnamization strategy. The idea was to slowly shift the burden of the fighting to the people of South Vietnam. But Nixon refused to commit to pulling American forces out altogether. And, it was fast becoming clear, whatever he called the strategy, he was going to end the war—if at all— only after first fighting it very, very hard. That was the only way, Nixon believed, that America could secure the kind of peace of which it could be proud, and thus that was the only way that Nixon was going to wage this war.

If once hopeful opponents of the war were starting to realize they could not count on Nixon to stop the killing, they had no reason to believe Congress would force him to do so. The push to stop the war had led to severe unrest on college (and even high school) campuses. There were regular demonstrations in Washington. At one point, a nationwide moratorium drew millions into the antiwar effort.

Through it all, Congress, save for some inconsequential stirrings, seemed content to remain a spectator. Even at this late date, and despite the years of intense opposition, the most significant legislation Congress had passed about the unpopular war consisted of measures that, collectively, gave the president the right to do pretty much whatever he pleased. Most important in that regard was the open-ended grant of authority to repel "aggression" contained in the still unrepealed Gulf of Tonkin Resolution from 1964. But that sweeping law had been followed in the years since by a steady stream of appropriations measures. In combination, the legislation had ensured that Congress supplied the funding to support a wide array of presidentially initiated military operations throughout Indochina. If the war was ever going to end, therefore, it would only do so if the president would decide for himself to end it—and not because Congress would force Nixon to end the hostilities and accept a competing, post–Cold War vision of America's proper role in the world.

* * *

Nevertheless, by the spring of 1970, Tom Huston, all of twenty-nine years old and a native of Indiana, was convinced that this conventional assessment of the politics of the war—in which Congress would deflect all responsibility and the course of the war would be determined by Nixon and Nixon alone—was wrong. Huston had picked up signs of an important shift in the attitude toward presidential power among the liberal intelligentsia, which, after nearly a decade of Democratic control of the White House, found itself out of power. Huston was convinced that this crucial component of the foreign policy establishment—long committed to the view that Congress had no business interfering with the president's judgments about how best to lead the free world—was starting to rethink its constitutional premises. Huston thought that this shift in the thinking of these elite figures would inevitably seep into the popular consciousness and alter the mood on Capitol Hill, where Democrats held substantial majorities in both chambers. Huston thus warned that one could not count on the continuation of the last two decades of congressional deference to the commander in chief, rooted in the unhappy memory of isolationist opposition to Franklin Roosevelt and sustained by the fact of nuclear weapons and a strong, bipartisan consensus about the need to contain the Communist threat. Instead, Huston argued, the long era of legislative passivity was about to come to an end.

The specific impetus for Huston's dire prediction in his May 3 memo was the congressional reaction to a speech the president had given just days earlier. Seated at his desk in the Oval Office, and aided by maps poised on a nearby easel, President Nixon gave a prime-time, televised address on April 30. He announced a major American military incursion into Cambodia. It was his latest move in his larger gambit to use greater and greater force to bring about a negotiated peace.

Nixon knew that by publicly ordering substantial numbers of American ground forces into combat in a new country he was courting a popular rebellion. Members of his cabinet opposed the move for just that reason. And, for months, similar concerns had led the president to take extraordinary steps to keep secret the bombing raids that he had already ordered in Cambodia. Nixon had even ensured that the pilots of the B-52s flying those missions did not know their true targets in order to reduce the risk of leaks.

Some of the secrecy was intended to placate the Cambodian government. It had agreed to look the other way so long as the rest of the world did not know what was happening. Nixon had also taken these precautions—or, as critics would later say, facilitated such deception—in order not to provoke a new round of public protests against the administration's supposedly illegal war making. Nixon was certain he could never convince North Vietnam to believe he was willing to do whatever it would take to crush the enemy—what he had earlier told his chief of staff was his "madman theory" of waging the war—if the nightly news was broadcasting images of his own citizens massing in the streets to block him from doing just that.

By April, though, the protests against the war were gaining strength again. Nixon and his team decided that it was time to take their lumps in the press and on the campuses. The administration would make known its intent to pursue an even more aggressive war effort in Cambodia than the one it had been pursuing in secret. That way the administration could finally come clean, as the president put it in his 9:00 P.M. speech to the country, about its belief in the need to "go to the heart of the trouble . . . [and] clean[] out major North Vietnamese and Vietcong occupied territories—these sanctuaries which serve as bases for attacks on both Cambodia and American and South Vietnamese forces in South Vietnam."

* * *

The president's speech was direct and uncompromising. "If the North Vietnamese . . . continue to escalate the fighting when the United States is withdrawing its forces," he pointedly promised, "I shall meet my responsibility as Commander in Chief of our Armed Forces to take the action I consider necessary to defend the security of our American men." Nixon made clear he would conduct the war the way he thought most likely to bring what he called a "peace with honor" or, as he sometimes incautiously suggested, "victory." Just as significantly, Nixon let it be known this approach, in order to succeed, would require stepped-up bombing raids and an expansion of the field of battle beyond the territorial limits of Vietnam.

The president's forceful statement of his intentions pushed the war's opponents in Congress to make a choice. They would have to commit to countering the commander in chief or, Nixon seemed to be signaling, he would treat their silence as acquiescence in the war widening on several fronts. The president's tough talk thus had an unanticipated and unwelcome effect. It went over well with the general public, but it galvanized not only the usual critics—reporters and television commentators, academics and students—but also, for the first time, the kind of legislative resistance that Huston's soon-to-be-sent memo foresaw.

* * *

For years, Congress had been fairly effective in shielding itself from blame for the policies that presidents had pursued in Vietnam. Legislative silence, far from being read as tacit approval for executive war making, had been the predicate for the antiwar crowd's legal challenge to the president's authority to step up the pace, or expand the scope, of the fighting. The war's critics argued with special force that Nixon was making a shambles of the Constitution—deploying combat forces to neutral countries, without ever asking, let alone getting, Congress to declare war.

To those of a more sophisticated and perhaps cynical bent, the constant focus on Congress's failure to declare war had an unfortunate and distorting effect on the public debate. It served only to cover up Congress's real failing: its refusal to place any direct limits on what Nixon could do. After all, if Congress really believed Nixon was acting against its wishes, then why should its silence be excused? Why was it not making its opposition clear?

The lead editorial in the March 3, 1970, *The Harvard Crimson*—speaking at that moment for a student body that was at the forefront of the antiwar effort and that had gone on strike in opposition to the war the year before—nicely made the point. There was no use harping on Congress for never having declared war, the editorial explained. The truth was that "the Gulf of Tonkin Resolution fulfilled all the constitutional niceties. By expressing the sense of Congress, it eliminated the need for a declaration of war."

Thus, according to the editorial, the real problem was not that the president was exploiting Congress's silence for his own ends. The real problem was that Congress had, in actual fact, handed the president broad war-making power in all of Southeast Asia years earlier and then done nothing to limit him as first Johnson and now Nixon expanded the country's military commitment. "At any time then or later," the editorial noted, "the Senate could have chosen to pit its will against the President's or submit his facts to closer scrutiny." But it hadn't. "Instead, the Congress gave the President carte blanche authority to do whatever he likes in Southeast Asia. Vietnam indicates a failure of will, not a failure of constitutional mechanisms."

Having placed the blame squarely on Congress, though, the editorial closed on a hopeful note. The bipartisan foreign policy consensus that had for so long produced a culture of deference to the president's strongly anti-Communist foreign policy—and even more to Defense Department decisions aimed at destroying the North Vietnamese—was showing cracks. As it began to break apart, the editorial said, a new spirit of "legislative independence" could be discerned.

Which, of course, is precisely what so worried Tom Huston.

* * *

Surveying the last several decades of elite thinking, Huston explained in his memo that he, too, thought Congress was not likely to stay quiet much longer. "For the first time since 1940, the vocal intellectual establishment is united in opposition not merely to American involvement in foreign wars," Huston explained, "but to the institutionalized power of the President to conduct the foreign relations of the United States."

Noting that "learned opinion in this country is virtually unanimous that Presidents have been usurping the power of Congress," the young lawyer from Indiana urged his seniors to think beyond this "limited revolt against Cambodia" and to see it for what it was: "a major revolution against the foreign policy powers of the Presidency." Huston wanted the higher-ups to grasp that "ideas have consequences." If they doubted that, he told them, then they had forgotten their recent history. "Those who believe that Presidents can always do what they wish in foreign policy without regard to the operations of Congress and the people should take a look at the experience of Franklin Roosevelt from the adoption of the First Neutrality Act in 1935 to the attack on Pearl Harbor in 1941," Huston wrote. "It can happen again, and the consequences could be fatal."

Huston was without peer when it came to espousing extreme views about the president's war powers. Even as he claimed that a dangerous constitutional revolution against the president was brewing in Congress, he was, within the month, sending around what became known as the Huston plan.

Formulated at the president's request, the plan did not come to light until years later. When the memo did surface, it met with outrage. The plan called for a series of steps to turn domestic intelligence operations against various administration opponents, especially those hostile to the war. FBI director J. Edgar Hoover and Attorney General John Mitchell teamed up to quash it—in part because it threatened Hoover's control. But while they succeeded in getting the president to withdraw his initial approval, the spirit behind the plan lived on in the machinations of G. Gordon Liddy and the so-called Plumbers. That was the band of shadowy Nixon operatives who ultimately were responsible for the break-in at the Democratic Party headquarters at the Watergate apartment complex that eventually led to the president's downfall and his resignation from office.

Outrageous as the Huston plan was, it did reflect a working assumption among at least some important White House players. As Huston later put it, the executive could do what was necessary to protect the nation from internal security threats. John Ehrlichman, a top Nixon aide, would later testify before the Senate to that same view in the course of defending the seemingly indefensible: a White House–approved break-in of the psychiatrist's office of Daniel Ellsberg, the former administration official who had leaked the secret Defense Department history of America's involvement in Vietnam known as the Pentagon Papers. And Nixon himself would later seem to confirm his own belief in such unlimited national security power. In a post-resignation interview, he defended the propriety of his own conduct by saying: "When the President does it, that means it's not illegal."

For all of this radical talk about the commander in chief's unlimited power, Huston was not being paranoid in laying out the danger to the presidency he saw coming from Capitol Hill. If the idea took hold that Congress had the right to challenge the commander in chief over the war's conduct, then the president would be in real trouble. Once Congress got a taste of its ability to assert control, there was little reason to think Congress would restrain itself. Not with the antiwar sentiment running so hot. Huston therefore urged Nixon's men to put together a team that could campaign to rekindle the spirit of Truman and Acheson, great advocates of presidential power in the national security realm and Democrats to boot.

Through this outreach effort, Huston thought, the White House might succeed in de-legitimating the increasingly mainstream notion that Congress had the right to tell the commander in chief how to fight an ongoing war. If such an effort succeeded, it might give Nixon's legislative opponents pause before they asserted their right to tie the president's hands. Even if this educational campaign did not have that effect, the effort would at least prepare the public for the executive defiance in which Nixon might have to engage. For without such defiance, Huston was warning, Nixon might find himself unable to prevent Congress from dictating how this war would end.

* * *

Three days after Huston's memo made its way around the West Wing, Bryce Harlow, one of the president's top aides, received another missive. It seemed to confirm Huston's worst fears.

The memo Harlow received had been sent by longtime Nixon confidant and future White House counsel Leonard Garment. A copy of the memo was also sent to the president's chief of staff, Bob Haldeman. The memo summarized the views of the renowned Yale constitutional scholar Alexander Bickel. Garment had reached out to Bickel in hopes of getting some advice about the constitutional issues raised by the Cambodia controversy.

Bickel was clear, Garment reported, that the "President does not need the *approval* of Congress to do what he is doing in Cambodia." But, Garment added, that was no longer the real issue. What really mattered, Garment explained, was Bickel's striking conclusion that, "at the same time, Congress retains the authority to determine where and for how long the U.S. can wage war. So, it can say the U.S. will NOT fight in Cambodia."

Along the same lines, and at about the same time, soon-to-be Supreme Court justice William Rehnquist, then serving as an assistant attorney general for the Office of Legal Counsel in the Department of Justice, came close to reaching the same conclusion. In a secret opinion signed a week earlier, Rehnquist had examined whether the president could constitutionally go after the sanctuaries in Cambodia (where Congress had thus far remained silent) and Laos (where, notwithstanding Congress's intervention, the use of air power had not been made illegal).

The president, Rehnquist concluded, could continue the operations in both countries so long as Congress took no further action—in other words, even if the president received no clear authorization from Congress to proceed. That conclusion once would have given the administration great confidence in its legal position. Too much noise was now coming from Congress about its interest in passing laws that would cut off funds for any such missions. Rehnquist thus also had looked at what might happen if Congress did intervene to block the president from pursuing these missions. Like Bickel, Rehnquist was far from sure Nixon would be on firm legal ground in forging ahead.

In testimony to the House, Rehnquist agreed there had to be some limit on Congress's right to dictate tactics. If it intervened too specifically, that could present a serious constitutional problem. As Rehnquist later testified, Congress could not tell the president he could not take a particular hill. Short of that kind of extreme intrusion, Rehnquist seemed to be saying, Congress's authority to limit or even to stop a war in progress was, from the perspective of the Nixon White House, distressingly wide.

The White House team was coming to realize that the constitutional ground was shifting. Nixon and his team had grown comfortable asserting the president's right to act on the basis of the authorities Congress had given him. Nor did they mind relying on claims about the president's constitutional powers when Congress watched silently. But the new battle to maintain control over the war, it seemed, might soon turn into a much more difficult one. The administration might well have to make the case that the commander in chief could constitutionally disregard a congressional effort to curb his right to wage war. Yet word kept coming back that support for that view might be hard to find. No matter how one thought about the proposed restrictions making their way through Congress, therefore, they were a cause for concern. The president had been operating freely for years. That freedom was now at risk.

* * *

Of the antiwar bills then pending, the most problematic was known as Cooper-Church. It took the form of a proposed amendment to the Foreign Military Sales Act. It was not like the one earlier restriction that Congress had passed. That one had been written in conjunction with the White House, and it merely confirmed Nixon's already publicly stated intention to send no ground troops into Laos. This one, by contrast, was designed to veto the mission the president had just ordered, not to ratify its parameters. As proposed, the measure would have barred all further combat activity—on land and in the air—in Cambodia.

The sponsors of this potentially explosive restriction were an odd pair. John Cooper was a tall, thin Kentucky Republican, an elder statesman of a moderate to liberal bent. Frank Church, by contrast, was a publicity-loving, increasingly liberal Idaho senator who, after more than a decade in the Senate (he was elected at the age of thirty-two), was just beginning to find his voice. But, while Cooper was an absolutely crucial partner, it was Church who would become the true leader of the legislative effort to rein in Nixon.

Church had won his seat in a squeaker the same year Eisenhower had won his second term. Of late, though, Church had allied himself with the antiwar left. And while it was far from clear that his constituents at home shared that viewpoint, Church had been pushed firmly into that camp by Nixon's speech on Cambodia.

"Unctuous," Church let out upon hearing Nixon's cloying close to his April 30 speech about the new plan to bomb Cambodia. Listening to Nixon's words with an aide at a local NBC affiliate, Church was "seething" by the end. And then, while leaving the station, he overheard a television reporter praise Nixon's "great" speech and comment on his just concluded interview with the vice president, Spiro Agnew. Church turned to his aide and told him that he expected Agnew's response to the president's speech was probably "*Sieg Heil.*"

Still fuming on May 1, Church took the Senate floor to challenge the White House. "If the executive branch will not take the initiative, then the Congress and the people must." He announced Cooper-Church would soon be introduced.

Meanwhile, the president was not backing down. During a confidential military briefing at the Pentagon that same day, the president blurted out: "I want to take out all those sanctuaries. Knock them all out!" When Nixon was told why, for technical reasons, that might not be possible, he would have none of it. "You have to electrify people with bold decisions," he shouted. "Bold decisions make history. . . . Let's go blow the hell out of them!"

* * *

The makings of a true constitutional confrontation were all there. Assuming, that is, that Church and his sober ally, John Cooper, could find the votes to tee it up. Church, for all his bluster, was a notorious trimmer. That caused some suspicion among the most committed opponents of the war. It also meant the young senator—dismissed by some as the "boy orator"—was keenly aware of where the votes were. Thus, whether out of timidity or calculation, Church had consciously framed his first significant antiwar measure as a moderate alternative to the more extreme ones that were also being put forth around this time.

The earliest of those measures had been introduced in the fall of 1969. It was one of eleven antiwar measures that had been introduced in the span of several weeks. It called for a complete end to the war in Vietnam, tempered only by the proviso that the president should first be permitted to ensure that American prisoners of war be returned.

Church correctly judged that such a frontal attack on the war was doomed to fail, just as it had failed to that point. Nixon privately dismissed such measures as "bugout resolutions," suggesting the line of attack that any such congressional effort to force a quick end to American fighting would face.

Church believed the only hope lay in coming at the president from the side: building on the momentum from the Laos restriction to choke off Nixon's efforts to make the war a regional one. Cooper-Church would do just that: limit the president's ability to engage in combat operations in Cambodia while saying nothing about Nixon's freedom of action elsewhere.

But Church's middle way created a serious problem of its own. If the North Vietnamese did in fact wish to set up Cambodian "sanctuaries," as the administration called them, then how could Congress legitimately preclude the president from going after them? To let North Vietnam set up enemy bases just over the border all but ensured soldiers still fighting on America's behalf in Vietnam would never succeed. What was the sense in permitting the war to go on while preventing the president from fighting the enemy where they were?

Nixon previewed that concern at a tense meeting with the Senate Foreign Relations Committee on May 6. Asked by one senator how Congress "could 'properly manifest [its] will,'" Nixon was happy to advise. He pointed out that Congress could always declare war, though he thought that "would be a great mistake" given the delicate negotiations with the enemy then underway. He also said another meaningless antiwar resolution would serve no purpose. But he did concede a point that his administration would soon question. Congress, he said, could assert control through the appropriation process. If it did, though, Nixon wanted to make clear, Congress had better think twice. "I will protect our men in Vietnam unless Congress hamstrings me," Nixon said. "If it does that, then you will have to take the responsibility for American lives."

* * *

The president's challenge at that meeting framed the next several months of debate over Cooper-Church—the longest sustained debate over a measure seeking to tell the commander in chief how to conduct a war since the one over the Second Confiscation Act during Lincoln's tenure. Again and again, opponents of the measure—led by the Kansas Republican senator Bob Dole—pressed Church and his allies to answer the same key questions: Didn't the president have the constitutional right to protect the lives of American soldiers? If he did, then how could Congress possibly pass a measure that seemed to take it away?

Church and his supporters bobbed and weaved in response. Their favored formulation was near impenetrable. It seemed like they were saying the president, if need be, should just do what he thought necessary. At least that way, Congress could not be charged with lending its blessing if he overreached.

The muddled response suggested the unanswerable nature of this basic challenge to Congress's attempt to define how the commander in chief should fight. The critics charged Church and company with endangering the lives of American soldiers by barring Nixon from protecting them from the enemy. The bill's opponents pressed to gut the measure by amending it.

The simple change the opponents offered was clever. The tweak would ensure that the restriction on combat in Cambodia applied unless the president determined American forces were in jeopardy. In other words, the amendment ensured that the ban would not apply at all since Nixon's professed reason for going into Cambodia was to wipe out the sanctuaries endangering American troops across the border.

Remarkably, though, Church and his supporters managed to beat back the language. Trust in the president had reached a low point. "The dispatch of American troops into Cambodia, though presently limited in scope, could easily become the first step toward committing the United States to the defense of still another government in Southeast Asia," Church told the Senate two weeks into the debate. "Sobering as this specter should be, in light of our experience in Vietnam, it nonetheless presents Congress with a historic opportunity to draw the limits on American intervention in Indochina." One could credibly argue, it now seemed, that no matter how reasonable the administration's request for flexibility might seem in theory, it was sure to be exploited and manipulated in unforeseen ways that would only expand the war.

Cooper-Church also began to take on symbolic status. It represented an end to congressional acquiescence and thus a validation of the popular opposition to the war. The convulsive reaction touched off by Nixon's announcement of the Cambodian effort emboldened Congress. Or, at least, the popular uprising against the bombing gave antiwar senators no room to back down from their challenge to Nixon. With campuses inflamed— and the situation worsened by the shootings by national guardsmen of four students at Kent State—the country literally seemed to be coming apart. Supporters presented Cooper-Church, therefore, as more than a statement of preferred war tactics. They suggested the bill offered a way to bring the country back from the brink by restoring constitutional processes.

* * *

Still, the president and his supporters retained a strong hand. So strong, in fact, that Church conceded in the course of the seemingly interminable debate that the president must have the right to follow the enemy over the border to stop raids against the American fighting forces in Vietnam. Having conceded that much, though, it was not the least bit clear how Cooper-Church could make it through the legislative process intact.

The flat ban on the use of combat forces in Cambodia seemed to give the president no wiggle room at all. That was intentional. Church did not see how, in the current climate, he could risk giving Nixon an inch. Nixon would almost certainly use such leeway to pull America into a full-fledged war to prop up the Cambodian government and ward off Communist control. But that assessment did not make the danger that the proposed law posed to the American troops any less real. And that posed a real conundrum for Church and the rest of his coalition.

The solution to this dilemma took the form of obfuscation. A new pro-administration amendment gained support. It affirmed, in simple terms, that Cooper-Church did not take away any of the president's "constitutional power and authority," and it passed overwhelmingly. Church himself supported it.

But this language, though vague, did threaten to render the basic restriction on combat in Cambodia meaningless. After all, what was the scope of Nixon's constitutional authority? And didn't it at least include the power to protect American troops in danger? Senator Jacob Javits was so concerned about this potential loophole that he tried to save face for Congress and the antiwar faction within it with a symmetrical amendment. Javits's amendment provided that nothing in Cooper-Church took away any of the prerogatives of *Congress*.

This language also passed, as did the bill, in a surprisingly strong Senate vote. But Nixon's team had gotten through the debate seemingly unscathed. His team even claimed, at first, that Nixon had actually pulled out a last-minute victory. The final language of Cooper-Church, by endorsing the president's constitutional powers, made the restriction hard for Nixon to overstep and easy for his lawyers to maneuver around.

* * *

A student of Huston's memo would have found little reason to cheer in the administration successfully securing that technical escape hatch. The real news of this debate was not how much Nixon had managed to preserve. The news was that the old consensus in favor of executive war making—one sustained by the Democratic Party and now embraced by a Republican president—was crumbling. "The pattern was clear," a top Nixon aide later recalled. "Senate opponents of the war would introduce one amendment after another, forcing the Administration into unending rearguard actions to preserve a minimum of flexibility for negotiations."

That January, Cooper-Church finally passed through Congress—having, remarkably, won support in the House. Its final terms were far less sweeping than the original—targeting the use of ground forces and including slippery language limiting air power to missions unrelated to protecting the Cambodian government. But it was a constraint nonetheless. The president pulled out the last ground troops from Cambodia just in time to meet the statutory deadline.

Even more important, Cooper-Church was a precedent. Congress had shown that it could challenge Nixon and his war, at least at the edges. That victory gave the antiwar contingent in Congress confidence to do more.

Not long after Cooper-Church became law, Congress at last repealed the Gulf of Tonkin Resolution. And though Nixon's landslide reelection victory less than a year later might have suggested otherwise, it was clear before Nixon had even taken the oath for a second time that the bipartisan elite consensus in favor of executive powers was in tatters.

THE IMPERIAL PRESIDENCY AND
THE END OF THE PRESIDENT'S WAR

"In the last half century, international crises, genuine, contrived, or imagined have at last given presidents the opportunity to exercise . . . almost royal prerogatives. This is the story of the imperial presidency."

The winter that followed Richard Nixon's overwhelming reelection brought a round of shocking reports about the president's most recent action in the war—a massive bombing campaign in North Vietnam. The stories were spread across the front page of every newspaper. They stirred up a new round of antiwar activism. The hostility was rooted as much in moral revulsion at the killing being done in America's name as in a desire to spare American blood and treasure.

In response, the old liberal establishment, through its most articulate spokesman, began the process of formally repudiating its long-held belief—dating back to FDR—that a near unfettered presidential power over war and foreign affairs was a necessity in the modern world. That spokesman was Arthur M. Schlesinger Jr., a Harvard historian famous for his role in championing Franklin Roosevelt's legacy and the virtues of strong presidential leadership in taking on foreign threats. He was also a former political advisor to both Truman and Kennedy, whose administration had been responsible for initially committing the country to a military role in Vietnam.

Schlesinger had long voiced doubts about the war, but, upon reading the reports of the so-called Christmas bombings—furious in their intensity and reaching deep into North Vietnam—he resolved to make a lasting point. He wanted to do more than criticize the president's latest tactic or urge Nixon to bring the troops home. He wanted to suggest that what was happening under Nixon was a threat to the foundations of the constitutional system, and he wanted to help that system right itself.

* * *

Just days after Nixon won his second term, Schlesinger wrote to Arthur Goldberg, a former Supreme Court justice and an ambassador to the United Nations during the war's early stages. Schlesinger asked him if he could "remember a crowd more insensitive to constitutional prescription"? Then, a few days before New Year's Day, Schlesinger wrote in his journal about the consequences of the president's seeming disdain for the separation of powers. "The year comes to an end in great gloom," he explained. "Nixon's resumption of the obliteration of North Vietnam is the most shameful and tragic thing in American history."

Earlier that same morning, Schlesinger spoke with Clark Clifford. Late of the Johnson administration and a former counselor to President Truman, the long and lean Clifford was a pillar of the Democratic establishment. Like Schlesinger, he, too, was deeply troubled by recent reports of the bombing campaign in North Vietnam. Clifford doubted Nixon would relent. He had seen the same arrogance in Franklin Roosevelt. As a young White House aide, Clifford had watched that president up close after his landslide reelection in 1936. Besides, Clifford observed, Nixon wanted to show the world he was one "tough hombre."

To stop Nixon, the wise man counseled, Congress would have to be far more aggressive. But, Clifford added, Congress would never summon the needed courage without a "drumfire of pressure."

* * *

Clifford's remarks greatly impressed Schlesinger. Eager to get the drumfire rolling, he jotted down some thoughts about their conversation. He noted to himself that he was working on an essay that he planned to publish very soon. It appeared in *The New York Times Magazine* the first Sunday in January under the provocative headline "Presidential War," and it began with this sweeping claim: "For war at Presidential pleasure, nourished by crises of the 20th century, waged by a series of activist Presidents and removed from processes of Congressional consent, has by 1973 made the American President on issues of war and peace the most absolute monarch (with the possible exception of Mao Tse-tung of China) among the great powers of the world."

Schlesinger admitted that Nixon had not "invent[ed]" what the historian was now calling "presidential war." Nixon had drawn support from precedents and theories that had been "defended in general terms by many political scientists and historians, this writer among them." Schlesinger did not believe that history made Nixon blameless. Instead, Schlesinger used the balance of the essay to excoriate the sitting president for twisting these prior understandings in dangerous and unprecedented ways.

Schlesinger assured his readers the founding fathers would never have approved of Nixon's unilateral war making. He explained that they feared entrusting such power to a single man, which is why they gave *Congress* the power to declare war. But Schlesinger was a devoted New Dealer, who believed the Constitution was a living thing. So, for him, the real problem was not that Nixon was breaking faith with the founding generation. It was the lack of precedent in the whole sweep of American history for what Nixon was doing.

True, Lincoln had responded unilaterally to the attack on Fort Sumter. But he was facing a civil war and at a moment when Congress was out of town. And while Truman had admittedly pushed things pretty far in Korea, he, too, had confronted a true emergency, given the prospect of a Chinese invasion. He had also acted under the auspices of a treaty, which meant, at least, the Senate had signed off. Other presidents, in Schlesinger's telling, had either sought Congress's approval before committing forces abroad or sent small complements of troops here or there, usually in order to protect Americans in distress. They had never unilaterally waged full-scale foreign war in a circumstance like this one—and certainly not in a manner this brazen.

Schlesinger wanted his readers to grasp that Nixon was not just like all the rest. He had already—and secretly—extended the war to Laos and Cambodia. Now he was going it alone in escalating it still further in North Vietnam. And because the Gulf of Tonkin Resolution offered only the thinnest congressional support for widening the war in these ways, Schlesinger went on, the president had resorted to justifying his power grab by asserting his constitutional prerogatives as the commander in chief. He was thus all but "claiming the unlimited right of the American chief executive to commit American forces to combat on his own unilateral will." If he succeeded in that effort, Schlesinger warned, every president would feel free to start a war on his own. The result would be a system of government the framers would not recognize and that no prior president had dared to bring about.

Schlesinger blamed Nixon's character. He lacked, in the professor's judgment, a basic understanding of American history and its nuances. He did not appreciate the "unwritten checks" that had long restrained presidential war. Public opinion. A strong cabinet. International sentiment. The press. These were just obstacles—maybe even enemies—in Nixon's distorted mind. He did not grasp that they were vital restraints that encouraged presidents, as Schlesinger later put it, to "organize consent." And so Schlesinger suggested that Nixon had seen in earlier examples of presidential assertiveness only what he wished to see: precedents for the exertion of executive power. The result was that America now had something new: a president convinced he had the right to start an all-out war whenever and wherever he wished and regardless of what others thought.

There remained the question why Congress had not tried to stop the president. Schlesinger admitted that Congress had been "impotent." He concluded his article with a call for legislative action. Drawing on Clifford's advice from the week before, Schlesinger even raised the prospect of impeachment. It was a remarkable suggestion. The president would be sworn in for a second time in two weeks. He had just won a landslide victory over an opponent vowing to bring Americans home. Schlesinger was unfazed. The stakes were too high to be polite. Congress, he had decided, needed to be prodded.

* * *

Richard McAdoo, Schlesinger's longtime editor, loved the piece. Two days after reading it, he made a pitch to Schlesinger from his office at Houghton Mifflin. He knew the bespectacled, bow-tied professor could write as quickly and as bracingly as anyone around. He also knew the question of the president's constitutional power to wage the Christmas bombing campaign was "the only [thing] that a thoughtful person can think about these days." And so, even though Schlesinger's in-box was overflowing, in part with requests from McAdoo himself, he asked Schlesinger to make time for a new project: a "brief, hard-hitting book" expanding on the essay.

McAdoo did not want Schlesinger just to make the constitutional case against Nixon's recent actions. With the Watergate scandal erupting, McAdoo urged his prized writer to think more broadly. He should place the current constitutional crisis in its full context—"to discuss not only the war-making power, but . . . the long-run consequences when the balance is changed, even for good ends by the good guys." That last phrase—about the potential complicity of the "good guys" and the kind of runaway presidency they had wrought in the service of progressive ideals—mattered most.

In choosing Schlesinger, McAdoo was picking the perfect person to defend executive restraint. Liberals were just becoming comfortable with their rediscovery of its virtues. Schlesinger was a liberal himself. But he was not just any liberal. He was also a bona fide hawk, and one who had done more than any historian of his era to breathe life into the activist vision of executive power. Equally important, Schlesinger understood—and admired—the "good guys" McAdoo suggested were Nixon's true ancestors.

Schlesinger had already written an acclaimed book celebrating President Kennedy's first thousand days. At that very moment, he was working on a new volume eulogizing the late president's fallen brother. Together, these works would make fitting complements to his brilliant works about Franklin Roosevelt's forceful crisis leadership, and his Pulitzer Prize–winning account touting Andrew Jackson as the patron saint of the aggressive modern executive. Schlesinger, in short, all but owned the argument that America was at her best when led by presidents who asserted their power in bold and novel ways. He had also done more than anyone to fuse progressivism with aggressive executive action. For that reason, McAdoo knew the public would take note if Schlesinger sounded the alarm that the presidency had grown too powerful.

Always attracted by the limelight, and eager to cleanse his pro-executive views of the taint of Nixon and of Vietnam, Schlesinger signed on right away. "In short, I am interested," he wrote McAdoo the next day from his Manhattan apartment. "We may be getting into a constitutional crisis; the political and public interest should be considerable."

* * *

There remained the issue of what the book would say. Schlesinger agreed that he should do his best to avoid an all-out, anti-Nixon screed. The historian had been a scholarly champion of executive power, it was true, but he also had been a famously loyal defender of Democratic presidents. Roosevelt. Truman. Kennedy. These were his men—especially the first and the last. He had even served in Kennedy's administration. A book that attacked Nixon as a unilateral warmonger but exonerated each of his

Democratic predecessors—given their own hawkish acts, from Korea to the Bay of Pigs—would surely be dismissed as little more than a partisan hatchet job. That was especially true because the roots of Vietnam could be traced to Kennedy.

Schlesinger needed an angle that would inoculate him from such criticism, and McAdoo's brief pitch offered a solution. McAdoo was inviting Schlesinger to admit it was "the good guys" working for "good ends" who had truly changed the constitutional balance—and well before Nixon had come on the scene. All that the Democrats' in-house historian needed to do, therefore, was to confess that the presidents he most admired had paved the way for Nixon's power grab.

It would not be easy for Schlesinger to follow McAdoo's advice. The differences between Nixon and the other presidents, despite their seeming similarities, had been the central point of Schlesinger's recent essay on presidential war. But, by portraying Nixon as a symptom rather than a cause, the professor would free himself to rise above the partisan fray. He could describe the true depth of the constitutional crisis—a crisis that he was beginning to believe was much bigger than any one president. As Schlesinger noted in his diary in the midst of campaigning for George McGovern in the presidential contest with Nixon in 1972, the attitudes Schlesinger had espoused on behalf of the presidency in the 1950s were, at long last, "coming home to roost"—a tacit admission that he had been playing with fire all along.

The line between what Nixon was doing in North Vietnam and what President Lyndon Johnson had done in sending hundreds of thousands of Americans to fight in Indochina without a declaration of war was hardly crystal clear. An approach that lumped all modern presidents together therefore had integrity. It would also enable Schlesinger to mark the end of an era, one he had helped create and had come to regret. Liberal hostility to the isolationist Congress of the interwar years was yielding to a profound skepticism about the executive's role in promoting foreign intervention. Schlesinger's book could mark the culmination of that intellectual journey—one that tracked his own disillusionment following Bobby

Kennedy's assassination in the midst of his campaign to end the war that Nixon was now widening.

* * *

By the end of March, Schlesinger was fully engaged in telling a story very different from the one he had been telling for most of his career. But he was still no closer to settling on a title for it. For weeks he traded letters with his friends in his quest to find the right one.

"The Almighty Presidency, The Royal Presidency, The Magic of the Presidency, The Mystique of the Presidency, The Myth of the Presidency, The Prodigal Presidency, the Hyperbolical Presidency?" It was late March 1973. By then, Schlesinger had floated each of these possible titles to his former Harvard colleague and fellow Kennedy confidant John Kenneth Galbraith, a gifted writer with a proven talent for the graceful turn of phrase.

At times, Schlesinger toyed with using other, very bland options. At others, he considered punchier ones: "The Omnipotent Presidency," "The Runaway Presidency." He ultimately rejected these as well. He thought they were either fatally inaccurate (in the case of the first) or too anti-Nixon (in the case of the second). Then, nearly four months after signing on to McAdoo's proposal, he hit upon the one that still lives on.

Schlesinger seemed to come upon *The Imperial Presidency* as if by accident. He floated it to McAdoo in an April letter that listed it as but one of a number of possibilities. It quickly became the book's organizing theme—and, ultimately, its legacy.

The Imperial Presidency followed McAdoo's brief template beautifully. It pulled back from the immediate controversies over Vietnam and Watergate to offer a sweeping account of the root cause of modern executive abuse, picking up on a phrase that harkened back to the turn in American foreign policy that Teddy Roosevelt had occasioned.

America's rise to power in the wake of World War II, Schlesinger explained, tempted *all* modern presidents to seize the power to start wars on their own—each president building on more modest precedents that had been accumulating since Jefferson. Modern presidents had been moved to do so by the very real threats they faced during the Cold War and by the strength they felt they needed to project even when those threats were illusions. Schlesinger also wanted people to know that Congress had aided and abetted this de facto transfer of power. America's ongoing contest with the Soviets—and the ever-present prospect of nuclear catastrophe—had induced the legislative branch to give away too much, whether because it feared being perceived as weak or because it lacked confidence in its ability to second-guess the executive during such a perilous time.

Schlesinger did not stop there. The power to decide whether to use military force was so consequential, Schlesinger argued, that its capture by the commander in chief had not only led the country to the quagmire in Vietnam. It had remade all aspects of the modern presidency. Once presidents believed they possessed this singular power to take the country to war, Schlesinger contended, they naturally began to think there were few, if any, powers they lacked.

The shocking executive abuses coming to light in the investigations into Watergate, therefore, were not as surprising as they might seem. Not if one knew the broader history. A president entitled to start a war on his own, Schlesinger was saying, was a president sure to abuse his power more generally. Nixon's apparent pattern of executive lawbreaking in the name of national security was thus in fact best understood as the predictable byproduct of the trend Schlesinger identified. What began with a claimed right to start a war had soon, Schlesinger was arguing, morphed into a broader right to wage it on whatever terms the president thought necessary.

* * *

That Nixon wasn't the outlier many liberals thought was the real news of Schlesinger's book. It was a nonpartisan concession reviewers praised him for making, particularly those inclined to dismiss him as little more than a Kennedy lover. In Schlesinger's hands, Nixon was not a runaway Republican dishonoring the legacy of Democrats like Roosevelt and Kennedy. He was but the latest modern chief executive to take advantage of the opportunities for aggrandizement afforded by the new age of presidential war. "In the last half century, international crises, genuine, contrived, or imagined have at last given Presidents the opportunity to exercise . . . almost royal prerogatives," Schlesinger wrote some years later, conspicuously joining all modern presidents together in one continuous narrative. "This is the story of the imperial Presidency."

Schlesinger did worry that his readers might conclude the imperial presidency had become a fixed—and thus irreversible—feature of modern American governance. The kinds of forces he blamed for its rise were, by his own account, extremely powerful. Every modern president in his story had embraced presidential war to some degree.

Schlesinger's alter ego, the Amherst historian Henry Steele Commager, had endorsed this pessimistic view only a year before. Dreading Nixon's impending election in the fall of 1972, Commager sent his long-time academic ally an anguished letter. He assured his friend that he felt "no more embarrassment about my support of ex[ecutive] power under FDR and Truman and my hostility to it now than you do," notwithstanding that Nixon was "a master of deceit and trickery" and thus was making their earlier defenses look naïve. But Commager still thought that in a democracy there was no avoiding the need to trust executives who might betray such trust. "Only the solution of the problem of Cold War," Commager therefore concluded, "could abate executive authority, or the misuse of it."

Schlesinger rejected such fatalism. A reformer at heart, he wanted to awaken the American people to how badly things were off track. He filled his book's final chapter with procedural proposals for stopping presidents from starting wars on their own. He peppered his narrative with passages renouncing constitutional positions he had once confidently advanced. In 1951, he had publicly defended Truman against the charge—pressed by leading historians of the day—that the so-called "police action" in Korea had usurped Congress's right to declare war. Now, writing with the conviction of a convert, he admitted his defense of Truman had gone too far. It was something that even in January he had been unwilling to concede in his essay for *The New York Times*.

Try as Schlesinger might to put the genie back in the bottle, though, it was not clear he could. His book might have been aimed at putting an end to the imperial presidency. But there was always the danger that his book was announcing its birth. Schlesinger completed the final draft of the book in June after six intense months of work—labor that he viewed as partial atonement for prior sins. The cover note to the final manuscript he sent to Commager read simply: "For Henry—cherished colleague in high-flying and repentance[.]"

* * *

The old idea on which presidents had counted in pursuing the fight against Communism was under assault, just as Tom Huston had predicted three years before. And, because ideas do matter, much as Huston thought, the president did now find himself under constant challenge from Congress.

In fact, by the time Schlesinger had finished his manuscript, it was already clear that the Nixon White House could not stem the tide that Huston had seen coming. The legislature had shed its spectator role and begun to define the scope of executive war powers.

In June and July, Congress passed a series of sweeping funding cutoffs. They effectively locked in the president's peace accord with North Vietnam that the administration had forged that summer in Paris. Congress had waited for that peace deal to be signed before writing into law that the president no longer had the right to use armed force in the region. That delay was hardly evidence of legislative timidity. Instead, these measures showed just how much control Congress exerted. Fearful that Nixon would use a breach in the agreement as the predicate for renewed bombing campaigns—a fear Nixon had all but promised to make real—the new laws were imposed over his objection. They would deprive him of the money that would be needed to pay for combat operations "in or over" in effect the whole of Indochina. Once again, Nixon was forced to wrap up a piece of the military campaign on a schedule he did not control.

In April, faced with a North Vietnamese offensive against Laos and clear signs that the peace deal was not being honored, the administration began considering a new bombing campaign. But, by the end of that month, with the Watergate scandal closing in on Nixon, it was clear the president had no power to proceed as he wished. "My problem is I don't see how we can get anything done in this climate," Nixon's national security advisor, Henry Kissinger, concluded. "I mean supposing we start bombing. This will crystalize all the Congressional opposition."

That fall, Congress went further still in asserting itself. It passed the War Powers Resolution over Nixon's veto, leaving the president able only to issue a statement echoing Acheson's constitutional vision and implicitly rejecting both Bickel's and Rehnquist's.

The new law required the president to consult with Congress before introducing armed forces into hostilities and placed what amounted to a ninety-day limitation on the nation's continued engagement in them. Nixon thought the new law was a usurpation of his basic power. But he could not stop it from becoming law.

Congress kept up the pressure, right through Nixon's resignation the following year and straight into 1975. Congress renewed the funding limits, effectively barring all further combat operations in all the relevant theaters. But because Congress had been focused on ending combat activities, it had given little thought to whether the terms of these prohibitions fully accounted for the challenges that winding down the war would bring. It would thus be left to Nixon's successor to deal with the messy and unprecedented task of implementing a congressional dictate to end a war.

Even worse, the new president would have to meet that challenge at a time when, ironically, the concerted effort to stop Nixon's war had given rise to a new conventional wisdom. Ever since World War II, Schlesinger had helped teach the country, modern presidents had defined their strength chiefly by waging war without the slightest concern for what Congress thought. As a result, the new president would find himself engaged in an excruciating balancing act, with the charge of weakness, on the one hand, and imperialism, on the other, certain to be lodged against every military decision he would have to make.

≡ 17 ≡

"I made the very accurate comment that the Ford Administration is not an imperial presidency. We don't have the ceremony and pomp and the dictatorial attitude. . . . The White House performs the function that was set up in the Constitution. And we believe that an imperial presidency is not in conformity with what I think our Founding Fathers believed."

Gerald Ford had received his political education in Congress, and he had learned well. For a quarter century, he represented Grand Rapids, Michigan. He rose from obscure, junior congressman to Republican leader of the House. But his deep roots in Congress did not make him a reflexive partisan for legislative power. Even as a representative, Ford spotted problems with Congress's repeated efforts to check the commander in chief. He vigorously opposed the War Powers Resolution as an impractical infringement on the president's constitutional authority. He also saw danger in the recently passed restrictions on the conduct of the war in Indochina. Echoing the Nixon White House view, Ford raised the concern that these limits might prevent the president from fulfilling a basic duty of his office: rescuing Americans from enemy hands.

But now that Richard Nixon had resigned in disgrace, Ford was president in his own right. As the man charged with actually running the war, or at least winding it down, he would soon have to deal with the practical consequences of this supposed congressional overreach. This shift in perspective did not, however, make Ford partial to Nixon's uncompromising view of executive authority. Ford had moved to the Oval Office less than a year after he had been named vice president. He knew he had made that once unfathomable leap only because his predecessor had badly overstepped the limits of his power. Ford also knew that, in consequence, the nation was still very hostile to executive power.

In a hopeful moment, a close aide had dubbed Ford "Eisenhower without medals." The description spoke to the new president's unusual place in history. He was coming to office as the foil to a man many believed had acted like a dictator. Eisenhower had taken power under analogous, though by no means identical, circumstances, having entered the White House in Truman's wake. Ford, like Eisenhower, believed he had a responsibility to show the public that the presidency was not the dangerous institution many were starting to believe it was.

But Ford, unlike Ike, did not have a massive electoral win to propel him to success in that effort. Ford was instead taking over in a remarkably weakened state. There was as much risk, then, that Ford would be a mere witness to the legislature's domination of the presidency as that he would overreach.

* * *

By personality, Ford was well matched to the moment. He was no war hero. But, like Ike, he was instinctively attracted to understatement. He shed the trappings of the imperial presidency, not only to make a point, but also because he had no use for the accoutrements of power. He banned the playing of "Hail to the Chief" when he entered a room. He rechristened the Executive Mansion with the more modest, "the Residence." By then, the epaulets that Nixon had ordered placed on the uniforms of the White House guards had been removed. In that same spirit, Ford seemed committed to following the lead of earlier commanders in chief in how he dealt with Congress.

Confronted with legislative limits on their war powers, those presidents had looked for ways to accommodate the restrictions. They had rarely chosen to bring the confrontation to a head. Nixon's contrasting approach stood out as an aberration. The nation's experience with Nixon's brand of leadership had spawned an extreme narrative of ever increasing executive hubris, and Schlesinger's dramatic account of the rise of the imperial presidency had done so most especially. Obscured was the more temperate story of how executives had behaved during the nation's wartime past.

Ford seemed to embody that older, more restrained tradition. He operated as if the war powers restrictions that he confronted were simply a fact of life. That did not mean Ford welcomed those limits. Nor did it mean that he was unaware of the political danger that might come with showing respect for them. He knew, of course, that, given Nixon's disgraceful tenure, he needed to prove that he was not an imperial president. And thus he understood the dangers of defiance. But he also realized the public was schizophrenic when it came to presidential power. There was a great fear that such power could not be checked. But there were also many who doubted whether a truly great leader would shrink from asserting the powers of the office to their fullest. As one columnist put it in the early months of Ford's tenure, "It's hard for politicians who remember the 'total presidencies' of the last 10 years to accept so restricted a definition of presidential leadership," one that the commentator dubbed a plebeian presidency. Ford knew he would be subject to criticism for being too strong and and also that he was at risk of condemnation for being too weak.

* * *

Ford's effort to strike the right balance was tested most severely in the spring of 1975, a season that spanned his first months in office. Throughout March and April, the president was consumed by the efforts to evacuate Americans from first Cambodia and then Vietnam, as the now deeply unpopular war came to an end. Ford groped for a way to carry out those operations on his own terms, without provoking a confrontation with Congress. The severe restrictions on the use of military force by then in place made that task unimaginably hard.

It had been clear for some time that Cambodia was all but lost. For that reason, it was no shock to anyone that a plan for getting the remaining Americans out of that country might have to be implemented soon. But there was also a new source of concern. This one came as a most unwelcome surprise. All through that spring, the military situation in Vietnam seemed to be getting desperate, too.

The North Vietnamese continued to advance. They were now not far from Saigon, the capital of South Vietnam. That was so despite the Paris peace accords.

Nixon and Kissinger had sealed that agreement with a secret promise to the South Vietnamese leadership. The president and his top national security advisor had vowed—in private—that the United States would use military force to enforce the deal's terms. In other words, Nixon and his team had made clear that, if the Communists continued to push to take over South Vietnam, the United States would use military force to push them back.

That covert commitment meant that the peace deal in Paris did not actually guarantee peace. The agreement just put the fighting on hold. But, even though North Vietnam was, by the spring of 1975, breaching the Paris agreement on a daily basis, the American promise to restart the war in such circumstances turned out to be an empty one. Whatever that president may have secretly said, Congress had passed measures in the interim that all but ensured the promise could not be kept by the one now in office.

Or, at least, that was how the administration saw things. To the White House, blame for South Vietnam's impending fall was easy to place: Congress was responsible. It had tied the president's hands with the sweeping funding cutoff. The North Vietnamese could work their will, confident that there would be no price to pay. As that reality set in, the White House began to face up to a hard fact: America's next major military operation in South Vietnam would likely be the nation's last in the now decade-old war.

That operation would not focus on saving South Vietnam. It would focus on evacuating those Americans still left in that country.

* * *

The president and his team took up the prospect of an evacuation at a small meeting on April 9. By then, there were only fifty Americans still left to yank from Cambodia's capital, Phnom Penh. Kissinger (serving President Ford as both national security advisor and secretary of state) started the meeting by conceding defeat in Cambodia. Absent Congress providing military assistance for that country in the next couple of days, Kissinger explained, the president should just pull the remaining Americans out. Cambodia was lost.

But, Kissinger continued, Vietnam was a different story. There was a case to be made that Ford should simply lead the "way out" of Vietnam, just as Kissinger was counseling him to do in Cambodia. Ford could seek more humanitarian aid for South Vietnam from Congress. He could then try to forge a negotiated settlement with North Vietnam. And he could say he intended to use just enough military force to take the rest of the Americans out of South Vietnam if the North would not agree to a settlement.

Kissinger did not, however, actually advocate that approach. He knew Ford did not either. Ford certainly did not want to "bug out," using Nixon's favored term for tagging Congress with cowardice when it had first tried to legislate the war's end. Ford was eager to hear what Kissinger thought past presidents engaged in Vietnam would have done. Nixon, Kissinger said, would probably bomb: "He was vicious in these things." Kennedy would probably bug out, while pretending not to. Lyndon Johnson would stay the course, while being urged by aides to do the opposite.

Ford chose the Johnson model, though he did so with his advisors' backing. Ford wanted to press Congress for more military assistance. He still hoped South Vietnam could somehow be kept stable. There was also a more subtle reason for standing firm. Ford, like Kissinger, felt America had a moral obligation to more than its own people still left in Vietnam. As many as a quarter-million South Vietnamese had helped the

American effort to hold off the attacks by the North. Some lists of those South Vietnamese in need of protection reached one million. As a matter of honor—and as a matter of America seeming strong in the world—the United States needed to help these people get out of the country safely if the end was truly at hand.

To get the South Vietnamese out safely, though, would not be easy. The United States could not seem to be waving the white flag too soon. Panic was sure to set in at the first hint of the White House giving up.

At the same time, the president did not like the idea of acting solely on his own authority in this last delicate stage in the war. Ford wanted to pressure Congress to back his efforts to prop up the government in South Vietnam. He also wanted to make sure he could get Congress to give him some flexibility to use military force if an evacuation became necessary.

* * *

As President Ford listened to his advisors discuss the estimated scale of the evacuation at a National Security Council meeting the next day, he grew concerned. "Would that not require violation of the law or the agreement of Congress if we need to use force?" he asked. Kissinger thought it might. "You would have to ask Congressional authority to take forces in." Unlike the evacuation in Cambodia, Kissinger explained, this operation "will last longer. Even if we have the consent of the [government], we will have to fight the Vietnamese. If that is your decision, this will require U.S. forces."

Ford's secretary of defense, James Schlesinger, did say the president had the "innate" authority to protect Americans. Kissinger thought Schlesinger was wrongly focused on the War Powers Resolution. He was not grasping where the real legal difficulty lay. The War Powers Resolution recognized the president's constitutional authority, and so it seemed, as its legislative history showed, that the president probably did retain the power to rescue Americans. But the real problem, Kissinger explained to Schlesinger, was "the Indochina Restrictions, where the issue becomes more difficult. Elsewhere it would appear to be easy to use U.S. Forces for this purpose." The legislature's distrust of the executive after years of secret bombings and unknown pacts had resulted in a law with, seemingly, no escape hatch.

So far, those restrictions had been manageable. The massive Danang sealift, which spirited Vietnamese refugees out of coastal seaports under assault from Communist forces and relocated them in safer locales, was undertaken successfully in mid-spring. The military pulled it off under strict orders that naval vessels stay clear of possible hostilities. They "would lie offshore so that the refugees could be ferried out from the beaches." The whole operation was characterized as a "humanitarian" rather than a combat one. All these steps were aimed at avoiding a confrontation with Congress.

A final evacuation of American personnel from South Vietnam would pose far greater challenges. Ford asked hopefully about which restriction was the last one that Congress had enacted: the War Powers Resolution or the funding cutoffs on combat activities? He seemed to be thinking that, ironically, the War Powers Resolution, by recognizing the president's constitutional authority, could be read to have restored the war-fighting authority to save Americans that the Indochina restrictions' blanket ban seemed to have taken away.

* * *

Kissinger quickly dispelled the notion. He explained that even the Nixon administration had already concluded otherwise. Besides, the real question "is whether it would be politically acceptable." The president agreed. "It's great for people to say this . . . to the effect that we can go ahead. But, of course, if it does not it is we who are in trouble."

Kissinger reinforced the point. He noted that the evacuation would be very hard to justify legally because it would involve rescuing South Vietnamese citizens. There might be a legal argument for using force to rescue Americans, notwithstanding the funding cutoff. Such a power arguably inhered in the president. Congress might be powerless to take it away. Or, perhaps, there was an argument that Congress would never have meant to trump such authority and that Congress's restrictions should be read narrowly to preserve such executive authority.

Either way, it would be hard to extend that argument to justify a combat operation to save citizens of South Vietnam. If the president could evade Congress's seeming ban on combat even for that reason, then couldn't he also use force to prop up South Vietnam as a whole? Such an action also would be aimed at saving the citizens of South Vietnam. Simply put, it was one thing to read an implicit constitutional exception into the funding cutoff to permit the president to save his own countrymen from the enemy in the midst of a war. It was another to read the statute to permit the president to save any South Vietnamese he deemed worthy. There were limits to what creative lawyering might allow. Those limits seemed to make a rescue of South Vietnamese citizens a nonstarter—unless Ford was willing to suggest that his constitutional powers to keep the war going were essentially beyond Congress's power to curb.

* * *

"I think that we should ask for a change in the law that we can use certain resources that we need for evacuation," Ford finally concluded. "If we have a disaster, Congress will evade the responsibility. Let us get some language. I am sick and tired of their asking us to ignore the law or to enforce it, depending on whether or not it is to their advantage."

But how to ask? If Ford settled only for what Congress wanted to give him in terms of humanitarian aid to South Vietnam, and perhaps some added power to immediately pull out Americans, then he would not get what he really thought he needed. Instead, he would simply get just enough support to fund and authorize the very "bug out" that Ford disdained. And yet, if Ford asked for all that he wanted—military assistance and a broader power to do the evacuation on his terms—he might get nothing at all. Then, even to evacuate the Americans, he would have to act in a way that the statute seemed to forbid.

In the end, Ford resolved to ask for the full amount of military assistance for South Vietnam that his advisors said would be needed to help keep the government in place from falling: $722 million in all. Ford further resolved to request that Congress provide the assistance by May. He addressed the nation on the urgent need for help from Congress that next night.

* * *

The following afternoon, Ford was again huddled with his top military advisors and also the White House counsel. This time the focus was on Cambodia. Operation Eagle Pull, the code name for the emergency evacuation of Americans from that country, was set to begin. It was scheduled to last less than two hours and to involve more than thirty helicopters.

The president wanted to know if the odds of any fighting breaking out were less than 50 percent. He also wanted to know "by what authority this is being done." He was told that "the rescue operation is to protect American lives, any fire is to protect American lives and Khmer evacuation is incidental to the American evacuation." The White House counsel chimed in: "Yes," he assured everyone, "the Khmer evacuation is incidental."

There was real concern about just how true that was. Kissinger thought the administration should admit it was "stretching the law" and that it was doing so to remain faithful to the president's policy announced in his speech the night before. A top aide, Donald Rumsfeld, expressed concern about the word "incidental." The Khmer being airlifted outnumbered Americans nearly twenty to one. The word "incidental," Rumsfeld thought, would just be thrown back at Ford as evidence of his continuation of Nixon's deceptive ways. The secretary of defense admitted: "It is there we might be vulnerable."

That night, Ford reported the evacuation operation to the Hill. Somewhat miraculously, the evacuation ended with little controversy. There turned out to be no need to engage American armed forces in hostilities. In fact, civilian aircraft had been used to get the people out. That approach helped avoid any conflict with either the War Powers Resolution (Ford's decision to give notice of the operation to Congress helped in that regard, too) or any of the related laws restricting American combat operations in the region that had been passed over the last couple of years.

* * *

Ford was not by any means free of the difficulties the war's end presented. The following week, on April 14, at another meeting with his top national security team, Ford returned to the situation in Vietnam. By then, the Senate Foreign Relations Committee had all but rejected the president's funding request. It had done so even after a meeting with Ford and Kissinger and other national security aides at the White House.

During that meeting, Kissinger explained that the administration believed it had authority to get the Americans out under the War Powers Resolution but the White House was unsure of its power under the other laws. Kissinger added that the administration believed it lacked the power to evacuate the South Vietnamese. That is why Congress needed to help.

The plea seemed to go nowhere. Senator Jacob Javits bluntly said he would give "large sums for evacuation but not one nickel for military aid" for the South Vietnam leadership. Frank Church was less accommodating. He was happy to help with "getting the Americans out," and he was sure that could be "worked out." The South Vietnamese evacuees were a different matter. "Clearly there is no legal inhibition to bringing some out along with Americans," he explained "but 175,000 [South Vietnamese], with American troops involved, could involve us in a very large war. This raises the specter of a new war, thousands of American troops holding on in an enclave for a long period."

The president explained that prolonged fighting was not "envisaged." His audience did not buy that assurance. "I feel put upon in being presented an all or nothing number," said Senator Joe Biden, one of the new class of young, post-Watergate Democrats. "I am not sure I can vote for an amount to put American troops in for one to six months to get the Vietnamese out. I will vote for any amount for getting the Americans out. I don't want it mixed with getting the Vietnamese out." And Senator John Glenn—the former astronaut—summed up the thinking of the group: "The idea here is very different from what I envisioned. I and most Senators thought of a surgical extraction, not of a ten-day to two-week operation with a bridgehead. This is a re-entry of a magnitude we have not envisioned."

* * *

Resigned to the fact that Congress was rejecting his request, Ford laid out for his team the options about how best to respond. "We can reiterate our previous request and say anything less is more harmful," he said, "or just let the Congress work its will." Kissinger argued for not giving an inch. "My experience on Vietnam is when we compromised we usually lost. We usually held tough until the last minute. The record shouldn't show we collaborated." The deeper point was this: "There is no longer any chance for Vietnam in Congress." Kissinger thought that meant there was no reason for the president to cave.

The president agreed. "I don't think they will pass anything," Ford said, "so we ought to do what is right." And so, Ford concluded, "we will signal we want what we ask for and let it go at that." But Ford's tough talk was not really as tough as it sounded. He was talking about what he would ask Congress to do. There was no talk of the president using force if Congress would not sanction it.

Earlier in the spring, Ford had tried to devise a series of military measures to show American resolve. The list was notable mainly for how tame it was. It was designed to avoid introducing American forces into hostilities. It involved the repositioning of ground troops and the use of reconnaissance flights. There would be no bombings from above or raids on the ground. Even then, Kissinger found that the Department of Defense was reluctant to implement the measures, so worried were its officials about how Congress might react.

Evacuation, therefore, seemed almost inevitably to be the next move. Ford and his team were reduced to debating how best to make the argument that would convince Congress to give him the power he needed to carry it out as he wished. The talk of strength and resolve had to be understood in the context of the president's greatly weakened position.

* * *

Eventually the president made his case for getting help in a special legislative session. He asked for a new law that would remove the restrictions
on combat then in place. The Democratic leadership—and a good chunk
of the Republicans—feared clearing the way for a weeks-long operation
that could precipitate a full-fledged war with North Vietnam. Interbranch
distrust, fostered over a decade of secrecy, deception, and a demoralizing
war, was too great. So, too, was the scale of the possible evacuation. It involved potentially thousands of Americans. If the administration had its
way, tens and perhaps hundreds of thousands of South Vietnamese would
be involved as well.

The risk of the rescue operation escalating into a full-fledged battle
with the North Vietnamese terrified those in Congress who had been
working for years to end the war. The administration might restart the
conflict under cover of a federal statute that, though intended to confer
limited power, would inevitably be written in ways vague enough to permit the mission's creep. Unable to find legislative language to thread the
needle, Congress chose to remain silent. The evacuation would have to be
shoehorned into the narrow box of authority that remained open—a box
that put a premium on rescuing Americans.

The solution Ford's team came up with was ingenious. The South
Vietnamese could be spirited away but only so long as their rescue was
"interwoven," as the State Department's legal advisor later put it, with the
evacuation of the Americans. The safe extraction of the Americans depended on not creating panic among the South Vietnamese also looking
to leave. Such panic could be avoided only by assuring the South Vietnamese they might be entitled to leave as well. The president was not
claiming any power to protect the South Vietnamese alone. He was only
claiming a right to help them that was incidental to his authority to rescue
his own countrymen.

Such a strategy required, however, that the evacuation be drawn out.
Otherwise, the deserving South Vietnamese would never make it—for
the simple reason that, Kissinger thought, "Congress would surely cut off
all funds with the departure of the last American." The pace of the withdrawal became a source of tension.

Congress had established the framework within which the operation would be drawn up. The president and his men did what they could to maneuver within it. Congress kept pressing the administration to make the evacuation go faster, even as Ford instructed his team to carry it out as slowly as possible.

Finally, on the evening of April 29, Lieutenant General Brent Scowcroft, a top White House national security aide, popped into a meeting on energy policy. He whispered to Ford that two marines had just been killed in a rocket attack on the airport in Saigon. Ford whispered instructions back. In hours, the national security team was meeting to game out "the final American withdrawal from Vietnam."

* * *

The president still wanted to move cautiously. He went to the Residence, had a martini, and later a full dinner, with black cherry Jell-O for dessert. The president wanted to stick to the plan. The military should rely on fixed-wing aircraft for the pullout for as long as circumstances permitted. The White House even refused to allow Air Force escort planes to protect the C-130s that were being used to get people out. That order reflected a great fear of the hostile congressional reaction that would attend such a show of force. The top echelons of the Pentagon were furious. Such restraint, they thought, posed a grave danger for those in the field.

As the night progressed, the long-feared panic on the ground in Saigon started to set in. With Ford's approval, the administration eventually moved to what was known as option four: The rest of the evacuation would be carried out by helicopter alone. The president went to bed around one thirty in the morning. Kissinger told him there was nothing more for him to do.

By late the next morning, Ford learned that the operation had gone much better than at times it had seemed it would. He told his cabinet he was proud. "The fact is we did not panic and we handled it carefully. . . . We came out of a very difficult situation better than we had any right to expect."

But the windup of a decade-old war was not something that could be neatly scripted. The Americans could control an evacuation of their own people, though, even then, the operation had been chaotic. Its final frantic hours were marked by harried phone calls and desperate helicopter lifts. The crisis that soon followed, therefore, was sure to be even more difficult to manage.

* * *

The president received the news about the urgent situation in Cambodia just weeks after the last helicopter had flown out of Saigon. His national security advisor informed him that the Cambodians had seized an American merchant vessel, the *Mayaguez*, and its crew of thirty-nine men.

Ford's national security team gathered around lunchtime on May 12 to digest the terrible news. Secretary of Defense James Schlesinger made clear at the outset that the options for using force that he was laying out "would have to be scrutinized by the Congress because, while you have inherent rights to protect American citizens, you would soon run into the" Cambodia restrictions. Ford wanted to know how the military options "would be hamstrung" by the limits on warmaking Congress had put in place. But he would not be boxed in. "I can assure you that, irrespective of the Congress, we will move," he told his aides, now asserting a confidence about his authority that he had been unwilling to express in the deliberations over how to evacuate non-Americans from Saigon.

As the discussions continued over the next couple of days, Schlesinger continued to raise the concern about Congress. So, too, did White House Counsel Phil Buchen. Kissinger had little patience with this law talk. He counseled defiance. Ford took it all in. He said that he and Buchen had been arguing for years about the effect of the congressional restrictions. Buchen sheepishly replied: "I have to state the problems that we face."

In the end, Ford—after asking Buchen to reveal what the law required— told his men he wanted to inform Congress he would act. He was happy to set a precedent that the War Powers Resolution would not be ignored (even if, in the aftermath of the crisis, there would be recriminations about the president's decision to inform rather than truly consult with Congress about what to do). Ford also designed a rescue mission that, though some-what broader than a by-then chastened Defense Department had advo-cated, was much narrower than the blunderbuss Kissinger advocated.

In thinking through how best to proceed, Ford drew upon his knowl-edge of the Hill. As a congressman, Ford had pressed for a clarification of the measure banning combat in Cambodia from its sponsor in the House. He had asked what might happen if American civilians or soldiers were in danger. The bill's House sponsor had explained that a protective mission was different. So, when White House Counsel Phil Buchen raised this re-striction once more at the final planning meeting for the operation to free the captives aboard the *Mayaguez*, Ford responded with confidence: "We cannot be that concerned in this instance." He knew that Congress would never contend its sweeping combat ban should be read literally—and certainly not so literally that the president could blame Congress for a decision to do nothing to save Americans taken hostage by the enemy. But there would be no thoroughgoing attack on Cambodia. Ford even declined to use B-52s—a restrained decision crafted to bolster the case that the mission was fundamentally protective in nature, a point he em-phasized in his memoirs.

* * *

The actual rescue operation was carried out while Ford, in full tux-edo, was hosting a state dinner for the Dutch prime minister. Distracted throughout, Ford was "annoyed" by his guest's intolerance for his repeated departures from the table to consult with aides about what was happening half a world away. Ford finally received good news at eleven o'clock that night.

The American captives had been located and were waving white flags. They were now safely in American control. Ford let down the receiver from his phone in the Oval Office. He let his emotions flow. "It went per-fectly," he told those in earshot. They promptly erupted in cheers.

Many in Congress, however, saw things differently. They attacked Ford for a Nixon-like readiness to go it alone in using force. Ford had no use for such critics. His final act before going to bed the night of the operation was to write the letters to Congress required by the War Powers Resolution, despite his doubts that it applied. He had hardly used the crisis to restart the fight with the Khmer Rouge. The critics, Ford thought, were "hopelessly naïve."

In one sense they were. The public's willingness to support a presidential use of military force remained. Even around Ford there was a sense that the *Mayaguez* incident slew the Nixon demon. "Damn, it puts the epaulets back on," one aide remarked, alluding back to the pomp associated with Ford's predecessor. Another said: "By God, we've got ourselves a president," as if only such a show of force could credibly enable one to claim that title. Reflecting that political reality, Ford's political team was, as a testament to the public's appetite for strength, touting his resolve in the *Mayaguez* incident as "proof that he is that 'strong president' that all of Washington believes America wants."

* * *

Ford's balancing act in coping with the Nixon legacy involved more than winding up the war in Vietnam. Ford also had to respond to a flood of proposals aimed at limiting his covert national security powers. Their expansive use was also part of the legacy of distrust that Nixon had bequeathed.

Spurred by Nixon's abuse of those powers, a number of congressional investigations had, by 1974, uncovered transgressions that reached back to Eisenhower and before. The investigations indicated that, through secret surveillance and covert operations, including even political assassinations, the national security apparatus had spun out of control. Perhaps most troubling, the operations were not strictly illegal. The legislative proposals to make them so came fast and furious.

Ford tried to head them off with self-limiting executive orders—including the one banning assassinations that remains in place to this day. Ford also went further. A proposal to place limits on one of the most troubling features of the whole Watergate affair, the executive's surveillance of Americans, was gaining steam. Congress wanted to require judicial approval of national security wiretaps of Americans. Ford's national security advisors—Kissinger, Brent Scowcroft, and others—lined up against it. Another young assistant attorney general for the Office of Legal Counsel—who, like Rehnquist, would go on to become a Supreme Court justice—Antonin Scalia, seemed to agree. Ford's White House lawyer Phil Buchen was of the same view.

But the internal opposition to the legislation faced a formidable opponent: the attorney general of the United States. Edward Levi was a former dean of the Chicago Law School. Ford had sought him out to become the nation's top lawyer despite misgivings on the Hill. Some feared he was a liberal academic with no sense of the real world. The president was convinced, however, that he needed someone in that office who could restore the public's confidence that the executive believed in the rule of law. Thus, Levi came to his new post with a mission untethered to any narrow aim of advancing the powers of the president he served.

* * *

Levi strongly believed that the surveillance power should be brought within a legislative framework that would require judicial approval. He had even drawn up a proposed statute. Each time a memo went over to the president laying out the constitutional arguments against the bill, Levi ensured his contrary view was noted.

The attorney general ultimately won the bureaucratic battle. Appearing before the Senate Judiciary Committee in 1976, Levi offered a stark contrast to John Ehrlichman's uncompromising testimony before the Senate Watergate Committee. When asked if Congress could define the extent of the president's surveillance powers, Levi seemed to think the answer obvious: "Oh yes, I think in effect the bill does it." Levi knew this statement was a major concession to congressional power, a point he wryly noted. "Now . . . if you would wish me to be a proper Attorney General, always supporting the ultimate in Executive power, I may retreat from my statement," Levi said. "But I have tried to give you what I regard as really

the most thoughtful and accurate statement of what I think it should be.
. . . I think there is an area where the Congress can establish procedures to
govern the exercise of [presidential] power and I think this bill does that."

* * *

And Ford was content with such a view. At a press conference just weeks
before the election for what would be his first true term, Ford recalled
that he had been asked the night before about "the difference between
the Ford Administration and the Nixon Administration, and I made the
very accurate comment that the Ford Administration is not an imperial
presidency. We don't have the ceremony and the pomp and the dictatorial
attitude. . . . The White House performs the function that was set up in
the Constitution. And we believe that an imperial Presidency is not in
conformity with my own personal ideas, nor is it in conformity with what
I think our Founding Fathers believed."

Ford was describing a different, and older, way of understanding the
presidency. He was suggesting, in response to the narrative of the imperial presidency that Arthur Schlesinger had helped create, that this way
of thinking about the presidency was not a novel one. It was instead the
norm—a norm, he wanted to explain, that Nixon had breached and that
he had helped to reestablish. The commander in chief was not beyond
control—not even in conducting a war.

But there was a certain naïveté in Ford's own assessment of his tenure—as if one president could really exorcise Nixon's legacy and convince
the public that the imperial presidency was no more. Some years later,
after the surveillance bill that Levi had championed was signed into law
by Ford's successor, Jimmy Carter, Ford gave Levi credit. Ford recalled that
Levi had, with the president's full support, "cooperated with the Senate
Judiciary Committee in drafting legislation that struck a balance among
the need for secrecy, citizen privacy, the requirements of national security,
and the reassurance afforded by judicial review of such operations." Ford
went on to say that Levi "deserve[d] major credit . . . for the legislative
effort that has made electronic surveillance for national security purposes
virtually noncontroversial."

But the era of the imperial presidency had not come to a close. The appeal of executive defiance remained for many who surrounded Ford. And some of them would go on to serve his successors. In fact, nearly thirty years later, that very surveillance law—and questions about whether it could limit the commander in chief in a time of war—would occasion as dramatic a constitutional war powers showdown as there has been in our history, one that erupted amidst a war unlike any that had been waged since Washington's day.

≡ 18 ≡

POST-COLD WAR

"We have had two Presidents in a row who are willing to cede power, and I think that is good."

T he twin traumas of Vietnam and Watergate had stripped the sheen off the executive's assertion of unchecked national security powers—powers that both parties had defended for decades. But the shadow cast by Nixon's lawlessness also began to fade over the course of the next four presidencies. Not entirely, of course. The term "imperial presidency" remained an epithet. The charge that a president's assertion of unilateral executive war powers might plunge the nation into a new Vietnam still had resonance. During these years, only one president committed the nation to war on a scale at all comparable to Vietnam: President George Herbert Walker Bush in the first Gulf War. But Bush sought—and received—express legislative authorization before actually going to battle.

Still, each of the four presidents who served between 1974 and 2000—Jimmy Carter, Ronald Reagan, Bush, and Bill Clinton—did, at some point in their tenure, unilaterally send troops into harm's way. The first and the last of those presidents were more guarded in asserting their constitutional power to do so than were the two in between. The willingness of each to lay claim to such authority, however, reflected a simple fact. The memory of the Nixon years was receding.

For the most part, these presidents' unilateral assertions of war powers did not lead to dramatic constitutional showdowns with Congress, save for one exception. The Cold War was winding down during these years. By the early 1990s, the fall of the Soviet Union brought it to a close. The only unilateral military operations that these presidents initiated—with limited exceptions—aimed less at demonstrating American dominance over a threatening rival than at lending American assistance to multilateral efforts to contain local conflicts before they morphed into wider wars.

That did not mean that these humanitarian and peacekeeping missions were without risk. Nor did it mean that they were popular. It did mean that when these operations turned bloodier and more difficult to carry out than first anticipated, the executive was not inclined to press on with the mission at all costs. The strategic logic of the Cold War—in which victory was the only option—no longer controlled. The need to show strength seemed to give way to a new imperative: to ensure that America would not be ensnared in another costly and unpopular foreign adventure in which the nation's interests were far from clear.

The result was that presidents during these years—ones in which the military was now an all-volunteer force, the draft having ended in 1973— seemed quite willing to back down when Congress, fearful that things might spiral out of control, moved to cut the missions short or, at least, to establish certain parameters regarding duration or tactics. The twilight of the Cold War, in other words, led to an interbranch détente. Presidents, at first tentatively and then more boldly, did lay claim to unilateral constitutional war powers. But, in response, Congress pressed its right to check those powers in ways that presidents saw no need to defy.

For the most part, this uneasy truce held until, after the century's turn, a new type of national security threat emerged, ushering in a new strategic logic shaped by the unique nature of the terrorist threat. Only then did the unsteady, post–Cold War equilibrium between Congress and the commander in chief come undone, as the long-smoldering tensions between the branches turned white-hot.

* * *

On the day that Gerald Ford left the White House, a renewed war powers clash between Congress and the president seemed most unlikely. Ford
knew the legacy of the imperial presidency was an electoral drag. He
had tried to avoid its taint, in ways large and small: most dramatically by
agreeing to testify before Congress—the first time that a sitting president
had ever agreed to do so—to defend his pardon of Nixon.

Further seeming to push the imperial presidency into the background, Ford lost his bid to win the presidency at the ballot box in
1976 to a little-known former Georgia governor, James Earl Carter. The
victor took advantage of a swooning economy and rising inflation. He
also framed his winning electoral message around the notion that he,
not Ford, was the true antidote to the scheming, secretive, power-mad
Nixon. In keeping with that message, Carter made it known that he intended to pursue a foreign policy that no one could confuse with an
imperial one.

The word "humble" or a variant appeared more than once in Carter's inaugural address. He seemed eager to show that America no longer
wished to engage the world as a warring force. Consistent with the theme
of peaceful restraint and plain-mannered honesty, Carter got out of the
presidential limousine and, hand-in-hand with his wife, Rosalynn, and
young daughter, Amy, walked the mile-and-a-half inaugural parade route
down Pennsylvania Avenue. "They're walking. They're walking!" some
among the 350,000 spectators shouted as they watched the unprecedented
stroll in amazement.

That modest gesture was one of many that Carter made in an attempt
to restore trust in the presidency. In keeping with a campaign promise, he
signed a new law, the Independent Counsel Act, that institutionalized the
position of special prosecutor. That position had played a critical role in
exposing executive branch lawbreaking during Watergate and, ultimately,
calling Nixon to account. By virtue of this new legislation, any such prosecutor who would be appointed in the future would be even less in the
president's control.

Carter also sent a strong signal that, though a former naval officer, he did not believe his war powers were beyond Congress's power to restrict. Soon after taking office, he told CBS Radio that the War Powers Resolution's ninety-day limit on unilateral commitments of force imposed an "appropriate reduction" in the president's power—a position that a formal legal opinion from Carter's Justice Department also set forth.

Finally, to end the era of abusive secret intelligence operations, Carter gave his blessing to the Foreign Intelligence Surveillance Act. The new law required the use of a court-ordered warrant for national security wiretaps, even in wartime.

Ford's attorney general, Ed Levi, had first championed that bill. Carter was well into his presidency when the law actually made it to the chief executive's desk. By that time, it was clear that Carter would sign the bill without reservation. His top constitutional lawyer had already testified to Congress that the new surveillance measure was lawful.

Carter's folksy attorney general, Griffin Bell, testified similarly. A Southerner through and through, Bell charmed Congress with his testimony in support of the bill. "We have had two Presidents in a row who are willing to cede power," he explained, "and I think that is good."

* * *

Even still, there were signs that support for Congress's assertion of tight control over national security matters was not universally supported. Not even in Congress.

The FISA bill got to Carter's desk only after a tough legislative battle over its constitutionality. Several conservative members of the House contended that the proposed legislation should be amended to clarify that the president would retain his constitutional prerogatives, particularly during war. The Illinois Republican Henry Hyde made the case succinctly, arguing that such an amendment would "recognize[] that we know the Constitution has given the President some power that we cannot deprive him of."

But although the House approved that limit on the new bill's sweep, the Senate members of the conference committee were not willing to make such a concession. They eventually got their way. The bill's final version specifically removed a provision that preserved the president's constitutional authority during wartime. Instead, the final bill included language dictating that FISA and specific provisions of the criminal code were to be the "exclusive means by which electronic surveillance . . . may be conducted," including in wartime.

* * *

A little more than a year later, the political need for Carter to distance himself from Nixon was no longer the imperative it had once been. The economy was in the doldrums. The Soviet Union was newly aggressive. The president that July had even given a remarkable televised address in which he reflected on what he conceded was the nation's "crisis of confidence."

Then, that fall, Carter's presidency received a new blow that seemed to confirm the critics' contention that the nation was in a dangerously weakened condition. On November 4, 1979, with the next presidential election just a year away, Islamic revolutionaries in Iran seized the American embassy in Tehran and took more than fifty hostages. The ensuing standoff would define the rest of Carter's time in office.

As the hostage ordeal entered its fifth month, the president finally decided that he needed to take the offensive. He ordered the use of force for the first time as commander in chief—and he did so unilaterally and secretly.

The military plan called for a rescue mission to free the hostages, with helicopters landing in the desert before making their way to Tehran. But the plan failed miserably, and the helicopters never made it to the city.

Few concluded, however, that this disastrous covert operation—undertaken without the president having first given notice to Congress—confirmed that presidents should not use force on their own. Rather, to many, the blown rescue effort revealed only the depths of American powerlessness.

* * *

By Election Day 1980, a year and counting into the hostage crisis, it was clear to everyone but the First Lady that Carter would not win a second term. When the returns finally came in, he was swept from office so decisively that he gave the earliest concession speech in three-quarters of a century. The polls had not even closed in California when Carter appeared in front of a ballroom of devastated fans. "I promised you four years ago that I would never lie to you," Carter told them, reaching back to his campaign commitment to bring about a new, less cynical, less out-of-control era of executive leadership. "So I can't stand here tonight and say it doesn't hurt."

The president spent his last forty-eight hours in the White House holed up in the Oval Office. For much of it, he was stretched out on the sofa, his legal counsel similarly positioned on the opposite couch. They were desperately awaiting word of a pre-inaugural release of the hostages. None came. And none would, it became clear, until the new president formally took the oath.

All through the White House were signs that a new crowd was taking over. They would be on the watch when the hostages were finally handed over. Vigorous, confident, victorious, the newcomers projected an aura of success. Among their number were quite a few who believed that Griffin Bell's earlier testimony to Congress about the virtues of ceding executive power was wrong in every respect.

* * *

The lead incoming staffer for the new president was James Baker: a Texan, an oil industry lawyer, a key campaign aide, a consummate tactician, and the new chief of staff. The incoming president, Ronald Reagan, was the former governor of California and a one-time insurgent conservative hero. He had mounted a serious challenge to Gerald Ford during the Republican nomination contest in 1976 and, in the years that followed, seized control of his party.

Now that Reagan had won the presidency and asked Baker to helm his staff, Baker wanted advice from the last person to oversee White House operations for a Republican president: Richard Cheney. He was serving in the House of Representatives as the congressman from Wyoming. By then fifty years old—sixteen years removed from his appointment, at the remarkably young age of thirty-four, to be chief of staff to Gerald Ford— Cheney still carried the memory of serving in a White House besieged by a resurgent Congress.

Like many of President Ford's top aides, Cheney had left the White House deeply concerned that the presidency, post-Nixon, was in a dangerously diminished state. He worried, in particular, that the commander in chief, hemmed in and back on his heels, was no longer positioned to project the strength needed to protect the nation.

Baker used a yellow notepad to record Cheney's advice. At the very top of that pad, Baker wrote: "Restore power & auth to Exec Branch— Need strong ldr'ship. Get rid of War Powers Act—restore independent rights.****** Central theme we ought to push."

* * *

Implementing Baker's advice proved difficult in President Reagan's first real clash with Congress over war powers. The mission that touched off the confrontation exemplified the kind of military operation that would define the post-Vietnam period. It aimed less at preserving America's standing in the Cold War than in mediating a regional conflict that threatened to spin out of control.

The mission began in late August of 1982, about midway into Reagan's first term. It followed the Israeli invasion of Lebanon. Reagan sent a significant contingent of troops to that country to join a multinational peacekeeping force. The dangers were obvious; the exit strategy was not. But the mission was not an offensive one. Nor, even, was it one aimed at countering a specific enemy. Instead, by design, America was aiming to enforce a peace between two warring parties, neither of which was portrayed as posing a threat to the United States.

Given the limited nature of the projection of force abroad, the admin-istration concluded that the War Powers Resolution—and its ninety-day clock—did not apply. The thinking was that the law had been enacted in response to Vietnam and was thus meant to curtail presidentially initi-ated "hostilities." Since Lebanon was a peacekeeping mission, the think-ing continued, the mission did not seek to thrust American troops into "hostilities." It merely inserted those forces between two hostile parties in order to prevent war breaking out.

Over time, though, that legal position proved hard to defend. In April of 1983, terrorists bombed the American embassy in Lebanon. In August, two Marines were killed in a firefight. Congress, by then, had had enough of a so-called peacekeeping mission that it had never formally voted to approve and that was now almost a year old. Congress wanted the Amer-ican forces to come home—right away. And it seemed that there might be enough votes in the Senate and the House to order the president to bring them back.

Fearing an embarrassing funding cutoff, the Reagan administration brokered a compromise. Congress passed a joint resolution declaring that "hostilities" were underway. The new law thus made clear that, contrary to the administration view, the War Powers Resolution clock had been triggered.

Congress did agree, however, to extend the timeline for ending the mission or securing new legislative authorization to eighteen months. But Congress was not content to let the president use the troops as he wished for the next year and a half. The new statute ordered the president to en-sure that the mission be confined to the "defensive" one that the adminis-tration had been saying it was committed to all along.

The president signed the bill. He also issued a signing statement. It addressed his constitutional concerns with the legislative restrictions in language that only a lawyer could love. "Impermissibl[e] infringements" of the president's war power, the statement said, were . . . well . . . imper-missible.

In truth, Reagan had no more desire to commit the nation to a hopeless war in the Middle East than did Congress. As U.S. forces took more fire in the months that followed, Reagan agreed to authorize more aggressive military strikes to back them up. But he was worried about where things were headed. He seemed to have little appetite for facing off with Congress over whether he was respecting the limits on the mission that had been imposed by statute.

In his diary on September 11, 1983, Reagan wrote about the dilemma. "Our problem is do we expand our mission to aid the Lebanese Army with artillery and air support?" the president noted. The problem with that approach, though, was that it "could be seen as putting us in the war." He acknowledged that he had "ordered the use of naval gunfire." But, the president concluded, such a limited use of firepower did not cross the line. "My reasoning is that this can be explained as protection of our Marines hoping it might signal the Syrians to pull back."

Eight days later, Reagan wrote more about his concern: "N.S.C.: Our Navy guns turned loose in support of the Lebanese Army fighting to hold a position on a hill overlooking our Marines at the Beirut airport." Nonetheless, the president jotted down that his national security team had assured him that even this increased use of force "still comes under the head of defense."

Then, in late October, a car bomb went off outside the American barracks in Beirut, killing more than two hundred marines. Congress moved to require an immediate withdrawal of U.S. forces from Lebanon. Reagan condemned the legislation. Congress agreed to hold off, at least for the moment.

* * *

Just two days after the barracks bombing, in a striking show of force, the president ordered the invasion of the tiny Caribbean nation of Grenada. The administration defended the operation, as a legal matter, in modest terms. The administration portrayed the deployment as a rescue mission to save American medical students endangered by the Marxist government that had taken over the country.

Still, the invasion was the most substantial unilateral use of military force—now calling on volunteer troops—by a president since the failed Iranian hostage rescue mission. And because the Grenada invasion succeeded, it was also the first unilateral use of force that could be counted as a victory since the *Mayaguez* incident. In this case, though, the president had not sent troops abroad—as Ford had felt he had to do—to facilitate an ignominious American exit from a conflict gone wrong. Reagan had sent them to underscore the influence that the nation wielded in its own hemisphere.

Reagan knew that he was taking a risk in conducting the Grenada invasion in total secrecy, thus leaving Congress in the dark. But he worried that news of the operation would be leaked by members of Congress eager to warn the public of the dangers of "another Vietnam." Convinced that the nation should not be "spooked" by that history into forgoing uses of force that could be contained, Reagan decided that it was important not to let anyone in Congress have a chance to say "no."

Grenada, in other words, was intended to be a precedent and thus, perhaps a harbinger. Judging from the tepid legislative criticism, there was reason to think that there was a shift back toward older, Cold War understandings of the constitutional balance. But there was also reason to doubt that was the case, as events in Lebanon were making plain.

* * *

With the sudden fall of the Lebanese government in February, the president knew that the "defensive" mission in that country was over. Dramatically, and with little warning, Reagan announced that American troops were withdrawing to ships just off the coast. So as not to project weakness, he did change the rules of engagement, allowing a substantial artillery attack from offshore.

Congress was relieved. The mission was coming to an end. By late March, the marines were out—well before the congressionally imposed eighteen-month deadline had expired.

Looking back on Lebanon, soon after he had left office, Reagan laid out principles for the use of force going forward. Among them was this: "Before we commit our troops to combat, there must be reasonable assurance that the cause we are fighting for and the actions we take will have the support of the American people and Congress. (We all felt that the Vietnam War had turned into such a tragedy because military action had been undertaken without sufficient assurances that the American people were behind it.)" Baker's earlier advice about the need to restore executive authority, in other words, no longer sounded quite as compelling.

* * *

There was no significant showdown over the projection of American military forces abroad during Reagan's second term—the first second term, as it happened, that a president had managed to serve in full since Eisenhower. But that did not mean there was no conflict over the president's unilateral exercise of national security powers.

The chief source of friction was a secret executive branch effort to fund rebel forces, known as Contras, who were fighting the Soviet-aligned government in Nicaragua. The scandal came to public light in August of 1985. As details emerged, it became clear that the funding effort had been carried out in seeming violation of restrictions that Congress had enacted to stop such covert assistance. The secret program also seemed to have involved trading arms for hostages with Iran—with proceeds from the deal funneled to rebel groups in Central America that Congress had wanted the United States not to assist.

The resulting uproar led to the appointment of a special prosecutor, various indictments of top executive branch officials, and dramatic congressional investigative hearings that echoed those of Watergate. But, the Iran-Contra Affair turned out to be a strange kind of precedent. It clearly revealed a breakdown in the system of congressional oversight of executive branch–run covert operations—a persistent problem since Truman's day. It also highlighted the potential for a secret national security operation run out of the White House to go rogue. Reagan himself, however, seemed to have little interest in claiming the activities of his own National Security Council were extensions of his own constitutional authority. If anything, he seemed most committed to disclaiming any knowledge of what had been going on.

But Richard Cheney, working from his position as a member of the joint House-Senate committee assigned to investigate the scandal, had no doubt about the need to claim all that had transpired as a precedent. And ironically, given the branch in which he was seated, the precedent that he wished to cement was one that favored unchecked presidential authority.

When a bipartisan majority report was issued challenging the legality of the secret program, Cheney fired off a blistering dissenting report. Most but not all of his fellow Republican committee members signed on. Among the positions that the dissenting report set forth was the following: "Congressional actions to limit the president in this area therefore should be reviewed with a considerable degree of skepticism. If they interfere with core presidential foreign policy functions, they should be struck down."

* * *

Superficially, the administration of George H. W. Bush adopted the same hard line reflected in Cheney's minority legislative report. In fact, with Cheney serving as secretary of defense for President Bush, it seemed that virtually no statute purporting to restrict the commander in chief was immune from constitutional objection.

A slew of signing statements registering the president's constitutional objections to each of these measures poured forth. These statements objected to all manner of peacetime limitations on the size and placement of forces. Bush, like Reagan in Grenada, also unilaterally ordered an invasion: an operation in Panama that led to the arrest and ouster from office of the dictator Manuel Noriega.

But the noise that the Bush administration made about the need for an unfettered commander in chief—and the signals that it sent claiming that the War Powers Resolution was a constitutional nullity—were less significant than its most significant judgment about the extent of the president's unilateral power to wage war. When faced with the biggest military decision of his tenure, the decision to send hundreds of thousands of troops to evict Iraq from Kuwait, Bush sought and received, by a narrow margin in the Senate, an authorization from Congress.

The president was fully prepared to act on his own to drive Iraq out of Kuwait, even if Congress refused to give him authority. That was a prospect that he privately feared would almost certainly lead to an effort to impeach him. But, in the end, the president was not willing, Truman-like, to proceed without first at least putting Congress to the test. Too much history had intervened. He chose not to defy the War Powers Resolution, a measure with which Truman did not have to contend. Instead, President Bush would make the senators and representatives vote—just as the War Powers Resolution seemed to require. That choice paid off: The president got legislative validation up front, and Desert Storm proved to be a total victory. The president's approval rating soared into the low nineties, the highest ever recorded for a sitting president.

* * *

Despite Bush's success in Iraq, a military intervention that finally ended what had been referred to as the Vietnam syndrome, Bush left office after only one term. The truth was that, with the Soviet Union dissolving as it did on Bush's watch, there was no longer a single national security conflict around which national strategy could be organized. There were instead only ad hoc crises to be managed.

On Bush's way out, just such a crisis flared up. The departing president thus handed his successor responsibility for a foreign military deployment that, though styled as a noncombat, humanitarian mission, would, in short order, come to look very different and eventually provoke fierce congressional opposition. In the last months of the Bush administration, and thus after that president had lost his reelection bid, President Bush had ordered a deployment of troops to take part in a multilateral, UN force marshaled to address a humanitarian crisis that had arisen in Somalia, that swiftly imploding East African nation. Bush concluded that it was best for him to order the deployment, so as not to relieve the incoming president from having to make that choice so soon after entering office.

The Bush administration did reach out to the president-elect's team about the deployment. "I'm not asking you; we're going to do this," Bush's national security advisor, Brent Scowcroft, told Sandy Berger, his then-counterpart from the incoming Clinton administration. "You don't have to worry about it, because they will be out of there by inauguration day."

But if Scowcroft had ultimately come to that view, he had earlier expressed concerns about the absence of any viable exit strategy. At one planning meeting, he had remarked, "We can get in . . . but how do we get out?"

By design, the troops were supposed to serve purely in a peacekeeping role. The American forces were not to take part in combat; they would serve as part of an international force. So, once again, as with Lebanon, the executive branch took the view that the ninety-day War Powers Resolution clock had not been triggered—meaning that, legally, the troops could stay until Congress took some new action to force them to leave.

* * *

The Clinton administration's incoming national security aide, Sandy Berger, had a bad feeling about the situation in Somalia from the start. Was this Lebanon all over again? The event that suggested an affirmative answer to Berger's question was the deadly battle for Mogadishu. It broke out in early October of President Clinton's first year.

The horrific images of American soldiers under attack—eighteen of them were killed—sent the administration reeling and Congress into a frenzy. The new commander in chief had come to office with governmental experience limited to state electoral politics in Arkansas. He now faced a major military crisis in Africa.

The president sent his secretaries of state and defense to meet with over two hundred members of Congress in order to calm them down. The two men offered no firm commitment to withdraw American forces from Somalia by a certain date. The meeting did not go well. "The people who are dragging American bodies don't look very hungry to the people of Texas," Senator Phil Gramm, a Texas Republican, told the *New York Times* that day. "Support for the president in the country and Congress is dying rather rapidly."

Gramm's assessment was widely shared by his colleagues on the Hill. His implicit warning about dwindling legislative support had teeth. Under the terms of a nonbinding resolution passed in September, Congress had mandated a vote by mid-November "to authorize the mission or force a pullout." It now seemed unlikely that the vote would go well for the president—if, that is, he wished to keep Americans forces in that country.

During the campaign, the president had made facilitating American participation in UN-led humanitarian missions of just this kind an important part of his foreign policy platform. But, confronting this crisis, he agreed to withdraw all American forces by March of the next year. Congress codified that commitment by passing a measure that cut off all funding for the mission as of that date.

* * *

Somalia and missions like it dominated American foreign policy debates for the remainder of Clinton's time in office: Haiti, Bosnia, Kosovo. In each case, as in Lebanon, Congress made known its concerns about mission creep as presidentially initiated peacekeeping operations, often carried out in conjunction with the UN, morphed into efforts to oust hostile governments.

In response, Congress enacted statutes setting timelines and limiting the scope of each mission. Clinton, upon signing these restrictive measures into law, did attach hard-to-decipher statements preserving some unknown quantum of executive flexibility—usually, it appeared, in order to carve out a right to withdraw with honor and to ensure the safe exit of all Americans. But there were no defiant claims building on Acheson's legacy or bids to make Cheney's vision a reality.

In fact, by the end of Clinton's term, the strongest assertion of executive constitutional war powers in the teeth of legislative resistance did not come against the War Powers Resolution. Nor did Clinton take aim at the various laws limiting military missions that came in its wake. The president instead targeted a proposed law that purported to restrict his right to place U.S. forces under UN command, a reprise of the isolationist effort to enforce neutrality in an earlier era but now applied in a humanitarian context.

But while President Clinton would challenge that law's constitutionality on paper in direct terms, he would not actually defy it. In fact, he had accepted a provision in the law ending the mission in Somalia that barred him from placing those forces under UN command prior to the pullout. Concerned about congressional opposition, he also scuttled a National Security Council strategy document that had long been in preparation and that seemed to view such UN-controlled missions as a tactic of choice in future missions.

* * *

From the aborted Iranian rescue mission to Grenada to the Balkans, these post-Nixon presidents—two Democrats and two Republicans—had been willing to send troops abroad without getting congressional support in advance. But none had seen the need to challenge, as Truman and Nixon had done, Congress's power to define the scope and duration of those military missions as they dragged on. The last of them, Clinton, found himself fighting with Congress on especially limited terrain. He asserted his authority to organize the internal administration of peacekeeping missions that the president had all but conceded Congress could control—whether by prohibiting the use of ground troops (as in Bosnia) or by setting deadlines for ending deployments (as in Somalia).

Such executive assertiveness was real, in other words. But it was a far cry from the bold revival of "strong executive leadership" that Cheney had counseled Baker to claim a decade and more before. Not long after Clinton's successor took office, however, the defense of that more aggressive approach to executive war powers reappeared. And, by virtue of his new position in the executive branch, Cheney was well placed to help the new president champion its return.

≡ 19 ≡

THE GLOBAL WAR ON TERRORISM

"These decisions, under our Constitution, are for the President alone to make."

For most of the day, the president said little publicly. In the morning, he did make some cursory remarks to reporters while he was stuck at the same Florida elementary school he had been visiting when he had heard the first reports of the awful events unfolding. He had penned them with a Sharpie on a yellow notepad, and he delivered them in the school gymnasium right before he left the Sunshine State on *Air Force One*. This brief news conference offered little insight into how the president—then less than a year in office—planned to respond to what had just occurred.

That night, George W. Bush spoke to the nation more formally. Broadcast from the White House at 8:30 P.M., the speech explained that the military was on high alert, that law enforcement was working hard to track down those responsible for the attacks, and that these "evil, despicable acts of terror" would not go unanswered. The president closed with a quotation from the Lord's Prayer. He said little that foreshadowed what might come next.

By the next evening, the president was finally ready to be more definitive. He settled into the chair behind his desk in the Oval Office at 6:00 P.M. for his second televised address since the Twin Towers had fallen, the

Pentagon had gone up in flames, Flight 93 had crashed in a rural field in Pennsylvania, and his presidency had changed forever. This speech, too, was brief. It ran less than five minutes. But the president was now ready to make clear that the previous morning's attacks were not merely acts of terror.

They were, he said for the first time, "acts of war."

With these three words, the president effectively committed the country to a new phase in American war making: what he would call the global war on terror. In this new kind of war, the old struggles over the president's right to take the nation to war on his own—fights that, from Korea to Vietnam, had bookended the Cold War—would no longer be the central focus of constitutional debate. Instead, the battle lines with Congress would be drawn over how, rather than whether, this new war should be fought.

* * *

The shift in the terms of debate was not immediately apparent in the wake of the terrible destruction that had occurred in New York and Pennsylvania and Washington, D.C. Still attuned to the constitutional concerns raised by Arthur Schlesinger and others in the twilight years of the Cold War, senators and representatives were on alert for what they had been conditioned to look out for. They wanted to ensure President Bush's commitment to launch a sweeping global war on terror was not going to result in a reprise of the imperial presidency's signature claim: that the president possessed an absolute right to choose to go to war.

At first, there seemed little reason to worry that the president had any such plan in mind. Bush's televised statement calling the attacks "acts of war" was dramatic. But he had not mentioned his constitutional role as commander in chief. He had not suggested he would use military force precipitously or unilaterally. He had instead promised patience, committed himself to working with allies around the world, and warned of a long struggle to come. He even thanked Congress for its early expressions of unity and support—support that included a resolution that

Congress had passed earlier that day endorsing the nation's right to respond militarily.

Consistent with this cooperative posture, the president had quickly dispatched a team of lawyers to begin negotiating with congressional leaders and their staffs so that they could jointly hammer out a legislative measure to authorize the use of force. The legislative leaders seemed eager to help. They agreed to bypass the usual congressional committee process. The talks were conducted by representatives of the president and the top leaders from each party in both the House and the Senate: Senate Majority Leader Thomas Daschle and House Minority Leader Richard Gephardt for the Democrats, and Senate Minority Leader Trent Lott and Speaker of the House Dennis Hastert for the Republicans. An impressive cadre of lawyers and policy aides assisted with the technical issues.

The White House started the talks by submitting its own proposal for a force authorization measure. The administration did not seek a formal declaration of war, which would have automatically triggered a large array of statutory executive authorities that go into effect only upon such a declaration. The administration told legislative negotiators that such authorities "were unnecessary and even undesirable."

But the administration's proposal was very broad, and it definitely raised concerns. The administration's bill authorized the president to use force not only against those nations and entities responsible for the September 11 attacks but also "to deter and pre-empt any *future* acts of terrorism and aggression against the United States." In other words, the proposed measure did not attempt to identify the enemy. It simply gave the president the authority to do whatever he deemed necessary to keep the nation safe.

The legislative negotiators were prepared for a bold executive first move, a traditional opening gambit in such high-stakes negotiations. But the White House's request was "particularly breathtaking," one of the principal congressional negotiators recalled. As he and the other legislative actors immediately recognized, the Bush draft "would have authorized the President to use force not only against the perpetrators of the

September 11 attacks, but also against (at least arguably) anyone who might be considering future acts of terrorism, as well as against any nation that was planning 'aggression' against the United States."

If Congress signed on to the draft, it would be handing the president a blank check. "Given the breadth of activities potentially encompassed by the term 'aggression,'" as one of those involved in the negotiations later put it, "the President might never again have had to seek congressional authorization for the use of force to combat terrorism."

* * *

A major concern on the Hill was that the proposed bill would make the War Powers Resolution a dead letter, at least with respect to the major national security challenges of the day. Congress had enacted that measure in 1973, over President Nixon's veto. The War Powers Resolution aimed to prevent the sort of unilateral presidential initiatives that had expanded the Vietnam War to Laos and to Cambodia without congressional knowledge, let alone direct approval. That law had not, in practice, prevented presidents from unilaterally committing troops abroad to military engagements. But it had set down an important marker.

Since its passage nearly forty years before, Congress had expressly authorized the only Vietnam-scale commitment of force in which the nation had engaged: the first war in Iraq, back in the early 1990s. To be sure, Presidents had used force unilaterally many times during the decade that followed passage of the War Powers Resolution. From the failed rescue of the hostages in Iran during Jimmy Carter's presidency, to the invasion of Grenada under Ronald Reagan, to the assault on Panama under the first President Bush, to the air campaign during the Balkans War under President Clinton, presidents had hardly been timid about striking out on their own. Still, these operations were limited ones.

There was still a sense, then, that, in the aftermath of Vietnam, a kind of truce had been reached between the branches. Relatively small-scale, short-term commitments of troops were tolerated—and, actually, sometimes even encouraged—by those in Congress, even when the president did not seek true consultation in advance. Larger and more enduring commitments of force—ones comparable to President Truman's wager in Korea—were not pursued by the executive without full congressional backing. The first Gulf War, in 1991, was carried out under the auspices of a bipartisan, congressional authorization to use force that the first President Bush pressed for at some political risk—in part out of a constitutional concern about proceeding otherwise.

This tacit pact was as much a political as a legal one. No president wished to enter into a failed war of real scale without having forced Congress to sign on first. But, thanks to the War Powers Resolution, even small-scale, executive-led military missions were at least on the clock. The resolution barred the president from committing troops to "hostilities" for longer than sixty days (or ninety days in emergency situations), unless the president first received congressional approval to extend the conflict beyond that period. And, despite debate about just what counted as "hostilities," presidents in practice honored that timing rule, perhaps because it captured the point at which the public's patience might begin to run out on a military venture that was not coming to a quick and victorious end.

Against this background legislative negotiators worried that the Bush White House's proposal for responding to the recent attacks would, in practical effect, make the War Powers Resolution's clock irrelevant. The measure seemed to give the president carte blanche for any mission aimed at countering something as amorphous as "terrorism" or as hard to define as "aggression." It was as if the White House was probing to see whether the politics of war making were shifting in the face of the most deadly attack at home since Pearl Harbor. Perhaps the post-Vietnam wariness about presidents taking the nation to war on their own was waning. Perhaps now Congress was willing to let go of the reins, however loosely it had been holding them.

* * *

The congressional leadership doubted that voters would have much patience for a protracted lawyerly squabble over the branches' respective war powers, let alone for arcane disputes over the wording of a law authorizing the use of force. There was great anxiety in Congress nonetheless, and on both sides of the aisle.

To give the president the sole power to determine the countries and groups that the United States could attack in the name of "pre-empting" all terrorism and possible "aggression" would have been no small step. Was the war on terrorism to be a war against Al Qaeda and the perpetrators of the 9/11 attacks? Or was it to be a broader war on a whole range of terrorist groups and supporting governments—from Hamas to Hezbollah—that could thrust the United States into a conflict with countries throughout the Middle East? And what about the myriad countries with some possible connection to terrorists, from Iran to Iraq? Was the president being given the power to attack them, too?

For many involved in the deliberations on the Hill, those questions seemed like just the kind the founding fathers intended the legislature to resolve when they gave Congress the power to declare war. The ever-present ghost of Vietnam—and the Gulf of Tonkin Resolution, which gave formal legal support to that war—also hung over the negotiations.

So, soon after word of the Bush proposal leaked out, a group of senators told reporters they were determined, as the Vietnam War hero and Republican senator John McCain put it, to ensure that the new statute would not be "another Tonkin Gulf Resolution." Whatever the nation's response to the terrorists' "acts of war" would be, the legislators vowed, there would be no confusion this time about which military actions Congress was blessing and which it was not.

* * *

The congressional negotiators quickly turned their attention to suggesting ways of narrowing the White House's proposed text. Perhaps surprisingly, the White House gave ground. The administration did not appear to be looking for a fight. The resulting compromise did much to ease the minds of those who feared Congress would cede its war powers in one incautious swoop.

The final negotiated text of the Authorization to Use Military Force—or the AUMF, as it has come to be known—authorized the president to use all "necessary and appropriate" military force but only against those persons and groups (and countries that harbored them) that the president deemed "responsible" for the September 11 strikes. The Senate majority leader would later write that "with this language, Congress denied the president the more expansive authority he sought and insisted that his authority be used specifically against Osama bin Laden and al Qaeda."

The new law did not directly forbid the president from expanding the field of battle to all terrorist groups within global reach. But if the president wanted to widen the war on terrorism dramatically on his own—and the prospect of war against Iraq was on the minds of many even at that early date—he presumably would have had to seek further congressional approval, just as the War Powers Resolution contemplated. Indeed, if he were to go further on his own, he would have a difficult time explaining why Congress's narrower grant of authority in this AUMF did not preclude such unilateral war making. At least, that was the understanding at the time.

The limits did not sit well with some of the president's congressional defenders. For Representative Lamar Smith, a Republican for Texas, this was hardly the right moment to be denying the executive any war powers. "This resolution," he later railed, "ties the President's hands."

But Smith's was a relatively lonely voice in Congress. To most of his colleagues, the final bill was a success precisely because of how balanced they thought it was.

In speech after speech on the floor of Congress after the proposed force authorization was put up for a vote, the nation's elected representatives rose to reassure their constituents. The president had been given the powers he needed, they said, but he could not widen the war on terrorism without first coming back to Congress. They had done their constitutional duty, they explained. Another Gulf of Tonkin Resolution had been avoided—and, with it, another Vietnam-like quagmire.

* * *

Before Congress could vote on the bill, though, the White House made one last effort to expand the scope of the president's authority. And that effort offered the first sign of the true constitutional clashes to come.

Just as Senator Daschle headed to the Senate floor to introduce the new legislation on Friday morning, the White House Counsel's Office rushed over an eleventh-hour amendment for the senator's personal consideration. The last-minute language proposed that the words "in the United States" be inserted into the AUMF to spell out the sort of "necessary and appropriate force" that the president would be authorized to use.

Senator Daschle and his colleagues were, in his words, "dumbfounded." But the White House's last-minute proposal revealed a fundamental difference in the mindsets of the executive and legislative negotiators.

The congressional representatives started from the premise that the president lacked the constitutional power to engage, unilaterally, the United States in a substantial and long-term military conflict. To them, the negotiations were principally about how much authority Congress should affirmatively provide the president—without which he would be powerless to act—to undertake a military action of that potential scale.

But the Bush advisors, as would soon become apparent, were not overly concerned about securing congressional support to use substantial force abroad to respond to the events of 9/11 and strike at the terrorist leaders still plotting future operations. Given the recent attacks, they were confident they would get that. What concerned them more was the raft of statutory *limitations*—the details and scope of which executive branch lawyers were only just beginning to grasp—that were already on the books and that might threaten the government's ability to stave off what the administration most feared: another round of domestic terrorist strikes, the so-called second wave.

The plan for the terrorist attacks may have originated in the outer reaches of Afghanistan, but foreigners who had unobtrusively resided in the United States for months in advance had carried them out here at home. There was, accordingly, a palpable fear of additional sleeper cells, any one of which could be the leading edge of the second wave. And to interdict this threat, the administration thought it likely that the president would have to use some forms of military force—including surveillance—*inside* the United States, where, not surprisingly, many of the existing statutory limitations on executive authority had their strongest bite. Hence, the motivation for the White House's last minute proposal to amend the AUMF that so shocked Daschle.

* * *

The concern about these existing statutory limits was shared by some of the administration's most stalwart legislative defenders. The whole point of the bill then making its way through Congress, explained House Speaker Dennis Hastert, was not simply to give the president the power to go to war. Rather, the point was to "clear away [the] legal underbrush" that might tie his hands in fighting it.

Some of the savvier members of Congress who were of a more civil libertarian bent also recognized this looming issue. They feared that the courts might interpret the new law to have just the kind of ground-clearing effect Speaker Hastert favored. They wondered whether the broad language in the White House's initial version was intended to be a wolf in sheep's clothing: a minideclaration of martial law within the United States masquerading as an authorization to bomb Afghanistan.

Those harboring such concerns—however unfounded—made a point of filling the congressional record with much narrower descriptions of the legislation's aim. They argued that the new law would do little more than authorize the use of military force. They stressed that it certainly was not intended to change the existing rules of the road in any meaningful way. If changes were needed—such as to the powers of the government to gather intelligence or to act covertly within the United States—they would have to be approved by Congress one by one in the weeks and months to come.

As the week wore on, the administration, aware of the doubts being expressed on the Hill about the authorization's reach, had grown less content to leave things murky. They worried that in a close case the courts might not give the president the benefit of the doubt if other laws barred the actions he claimed the new force authorization measure granted. Thus, the administration's late-breaking Friday-morning pitch to Senator Daschle to pencil in the phrase "in the United States." If he agreed to make that change, the domestic implications of the bill would be undeniable. The authorization would then unmistakably authorize the use of military force at home to counter the terrorist threat, and seemingly on the same terms and to the same extent that such force could be used abroad.

But Daschle refused. "The shock and rage we all felt in the hours after the attack were still fresh. America was reeling from the first attack on our soil since Pearl Harbor. We suspected thousands had been killed, and many who worked in the World Trade Center and the Pentagon were not yet accounted for," he recalled. "Even so, a strong bipartisan majority could not agree to the administration's request for an unprecedented grant of authority."

Once again, the administration backed down. It was Friday. No one wanted the public to see the White House and Congress fighting during the very first weekend after the September 11 attacks.

* * *

That morning—September 14, while buses lined up at the base of the Capitol steps to take politicians to the National Cathedral for a special memorial service at which the president himself would speak—Senator Daschle formally asked his colleagues to approve Senate Joint Resolution 23, the Authorization to Use Military Force in Response to the Attacks of September 11, 2001. The bill authorized the president to use "all necessary and appropriate force" but only against specified enemies—"those nations, organizations, or persons he determines planned, authorized, committed, or aided the terrorist attacks that occurred on September 11, 2001, or harbored such organizations or persons"—and then only in the service of specified objectives: namely, "in order to prevent any future acts of international terrorism against the United States by such nations, organizations or persons."

The AUMF—which remains to this day the closest thing to a formal declaration of war in the "war on terrorism"—sailed through. All ninety-eight senators present voted "aye." Later that day, the House passed an identical version with only a solitary dissent.

The president signed the bill on September 18, a week to the day after the attacks that had killed more than three thousand Americans. His official signing statement heralded what looked to be a new era of good feelings and bipartisan cooperation. "Both Houses of Congress have acted wisely, decisively, and in the finest traditions of our country," the president wrote. "I thank the leadership of both Houses for their role in expeditiously passing this historic joint resolution. I have had the benefit of meaningful consultations with members of the Congress since the attacks of September 11, 2001, and I will continue to consult closely with them as our Nation responds to this threat to our peace and security."

So far as one could tell, things were following the text of a high-school civics course. The president had asked Congress for permission to respond militarily before acting on his own. Congress had answered by authorizing him to send American troops into harm's way in a "necessary and appropriate" manner, for specified purposes and against particular enemies deemed to be responsible for the 9/11 attacks.

"Ambition must be made to counteract ambition," Madison explained in defending the constitutional structure of divided powers. That centuries-old framework seemed to have earned its stripes. To all outward appearances, signs of the imperial presidency that Arthur Schlesinger had described and lamented were curiously absent from the scene.

Reflecting on his involvement in the legislative deliberations over the AUMF, David Abramowitz, chief counsel to the Democrats on the House Committee on International Relations, was encouraged. He characterized the back and forth as "part of an ongoing dialogue between the executive and legislative branches on the exercise of their various powers." And he concluded on a note of pride that the imperial presidency had not proved dominant: The fact that "this dialogue continued even at the onset of the

current crisis reflects well on the continuing vitality of the Founders' vision of a government characterized by branches with separate and distinct
powers."

* * *

There were, however, signs that a clash between the branches might lie
ahead. The first real hint that this might be the case came in a nationally
televised interview with the vice president, Richard Cheney.

Appearing from Camp David on a special edition of *Meet the Press*
on September 16—just two days before the president signed the Authorization to Use Military Force into law—Cheney explained the kind of
national response that would be needed. "We also have to work, though,
sort of the dark side, if you will," the vice president said in a somber but
forceful tone. "We've got to spend time in the shadows in the intelligence
world. A lot of what needs to be done here will have to be done quietly,
without any discussion, using sources and methods that are available to
our intelligence agencies, if we're going to be successful. That's the world
these folks operate in, and so it's going to be vital for us to use any means
at our disposal, basically, to achieve our objective."

The show's host, Tim Russert, a lawyer by training and a Senate aide
during the post-Watergate decade of reform, knew there might be existing statutes that could get in the way of doing what Cheney was saying
needed to be done. "There have been restrictions placed on the United
States intelligence gathering," he reminded Cheney, "a reluctance to use
unsavory characters, those who violated human rights, to assist in intelligence gathering.

"Will we lift some of those restrictions?" Russert asked the vice president.

"Well, I think so," Cheney quickly replied. "It is a mean, nasty, dangerous dirty business out there, and we have to operate in that arena. I'm
convinced we can do it; we can do it successfully. But we need to make
certain that we have not tied the hands, if you will, of our intelligence
communities in terms of accomplishing their mission."

The vice president did not explain *who* would free the intelligence community from its shackles. Would Congress do so by passing new laws repealing the old statutory limits? Would the president take the lead by asking Congress to lift them? If Congress refused to go along, or it seemed unlikely to comply with the executive's requests, would the president simply defy the laws and assert a constitutional power as commander in chief to ignore them?

Earlier in the interview, Russert asked whether international law would permit the United States to kill Osama bin Laden. The vice president declined to offer a final view, noting that he would "have to check with the lawyers on that, obviously." But, he added that while "lawyers always have a role to play, one of the intriguing things here is the way in which people have rallied around, other governments have rallied around this notion that, in fact, this is a war."

* * *

In the days that followed the AUMF's passage, President Bush continued to outwardly praise Congress for its cooperation and to praise the constitutional system of divided powers. At a press conference on September 19, while standing alongside the congressional leadership, he stressed that "this government, working with Congress, [is] going to seize the moment." And, in his dramatic address to a joint session of Congress and the American public the following evening, he began by thanking Congress for its "leadership at such an important time."

But six days later, on September 25, the administration issued an elaborate internal legal memorandum, which would not become public for another two years. This memo was, in retrospect, the opening salvo in what would turn out to be the most significant constitutional showdown over war powers since the 1970s—one that would dramatically shift the focus of the more than two-century-old debate over our constitutional system of war powers.

Drafted by a deputy in the Department of Justice's Office of Legal Counsel, the twenty-six-page memo was addressed to Alberto Gonzalez, the White House counsel and thus the president's most intimate legal advisor. The bulk of the memorandum focused on what one scholar has called "the ultimate question of law" when it comes to war powers: "Whom does the Constitution authorize to commit United States troops to military hostilities?" The memo offered a ringing defense of presidential authority to initiate military conflicts, even going so far as to conclude that as commander in chief the president could initiate a "full-scale war" without Congress's prior involvement.

But now that the AUMF had passed, the real import of the memorandum could be found in its final two sentences. The administration's constitutional reasoning on this score was uncompromising. Neither the War Powers Resolution nor the Authorization to Use Military Force—nor, impliedly, any other statute—"can place any limits on the President's determinations as to any terrorist threat, the amount of military force to be used in response, or the method, timing, and nature of the response." The memorandum concluded that "these decisions, under our Constitution, are for the President alone to make."

* * *

The president was conducting a new kind of war—a war on terrorism. Congress had authorized him to do just that only a few days before. In the view of the administration's lawyers, however, that was just the beginning of his power in the war. Sure, Congress had authorized him to fight this war. But, equally important, they believed, Congress could not now handcuff him in carrying it out. No Congress had a right to do that. Once the war began, the president and the president alone was in charge.

In October of 2001, a memo to the White House counsel and the general counsel of the Defense Department relied on this sweeping claim about the chief commander's unchecked power to defend the lawfulness of using the military to combat terrorist activity within the United States. In November, an opinion from another deputy in the office referenced the same broad constitutional claim in discussing the president's constitutional power to use military commissions in ways that might conflict with statutory limits. In March 2002, a memorandum from the head of the Office of Legal Counsel to the General Counsel of the Defense Department invoked the argument while defending the president's power to use rendition, whereby terrorist suspects would be captured and delivered to other countries for questioning.

In June two more opinions sounded the same theme. The first suggested that a statute passed in response to the internment of the Japanese Americans and prohibiting the detention of American citizens outside civil processes might infringe on the commander in chief's constitutional authority in prosecuting the war on terrorism. The second defended his constitutional authority to override two-century-old statutes restricting his power to board and search "foreign vessels on the high seas." And there were other opinions of this ilk, including two that questioned the constitutionality of statutes barring torture and cruel treatment.

A little less than one year after the passage of the AUMF, the assistant attorney general for the Office of Legal Counsel explained the administration's constitutional view further. "Congress can no more interfere with the President's conduct of the interrogation of enemy combatants than it can dictate strategic or tactical decisions on the battlefield," the assistant attorney general wrote, in a pithy summation of what became the administration's new constitutional credo. "Just as statutes that order the President to conduct warfare in a certain manner or for specific goals would be unconstitutional, so too are laws that seek to prevent the President from gaining the intelligence he believes necessary to prevent attacks upon the United States."

* * *

This doctrine guided the administration through many of its most critical choices about which tactics to use to counter the terrorist threat. Through a series of memos and legal opinions, the administration had argued that key aspects of the response to 9/11 by the military and intelligence agencies—from the assessment of the threat to the amount of armed force—was beyond Congress's control or regulation as a constitutional matter.

From an operational perspective, this legal theory mattered greatly. The primary obstacle to the use of what the Central Intelligence Agency had decided were necessary tactics in interrogating Al Qaeda detainees was a federal criminal statute that categorically prohibits torture outside the United States. The military faced an equally severe obstacle, however, since the Uniform Code of Military Justice is a congressional statute that prohibits military personnel from using assaults, threats, and cruelty or maltreatment against detainees under their control.

One of the August memos from OLC purported to address the first concern by contending that if the torture prohibition applied to the planned interrogations of enemy combatants, then it unconstitutionally impinged upon the executive's tactical judgment as to how best to defeat the enemy. The Pentagon applied that same reasoning to the UCMJ, with the support of OLC memorandum issued in March 2003.

Behind the debate over interrogation methods, therefore, was the administration's initial determination that the president's commander-in-chief authority "could render specific conduct, otherwise criminal, *not* unlawful." Indeed, the president issued a statement suggesting as much in 2005 in the course of signing into law legislation that banned the use by all U.S. officials of "cruel, inhuman, and degrading" treatment or punishment of individuals in their custody or physical control.

The same dynamic played out over surveillance. Through a classified memorandum issued less than two months after the 9/11 attacks, the Department of Justice ruled that a secret surveillance program did not violate the Foreign Intelligence Surveillance Act (FISA), because the post–September 11 AUMF authorized such surveillance. In light of Senator Daschle's refusal to approve the last-minute amendment authorizing the president to conduct military operations within the United States, the administration bolstered its statutory contention with a constitutional argument. It concluded internally that FISA would raise serious constitutional questions under the commander in chief clause if it were construed to bar the president from authorizing such surveillance without court approval. And the memo went even further by concluding that, if the AUMF could not be so construed, the president had the constitutional power to ignore FISA's prohibitions.

* * *

It was as if the administration and the outside world of presidential observers, commentators, and scholars lived in parallel universes. In the wake of Vietnam, the general view had been that congressional abdication put the constitutional order out of balance by permitting an imperial presidency to rise unrivaled. The blame was said to rest as much with Congress as with the president.

But while commentators lamented Congress's failure to impose limits on the president's national security powers and called for an ever-expanding list of so-called framework statutes to restore checks and balances, the administration in September of 2001 was looking out on what seemed to be an entirely different world. Faced with as grave a national security crisis as there had been since the end of the Cold War, the commander in chief seemed to be bumping up against statutory limitations at every turn. Within the administration, then, a simple narrative took hold early on.

The president was being "strangled by law." Congressional responses to national security abuses—egged on by the aggressiveness of a whole school of international law theorists that was antagonistic to American foreign policy objectives—had left the president encased in a web of statutory restrictions that imperiled the nation. Even worse, many of the statutes that regulated detention, interrogation, and surveillance took the form of criminal laws, subjecting violators to severe penalties.

Officers in the Central Intelligence Agency, the Department of Defense, and elsewhere were understandably reluctant to engage in action that arguably fell within or came close to infringing on such a criminal prohibition. They wanted substantial assurances that they would have airtight defenses against any future prosecution. They might well conclude that creative statutory interpretation was not enough—that they needed the imprimatur of a constitutional presidential "override" to establish a complete defense.

Administration lawyers believed that Congress, by passing these criminal bars, had baited the president into confronting a question that in earlier years was easily avoided: whether the executive had the constitutional power to defy a statute regulating the conduct of war even if it plainly applied. In the past, presidents had seemingly tamed applicable statutory limits by means of creative—in some cases, perhaps, even tendentious—statutory interpretation. But now, it seemed, the ultimate question of constitutional power could not be avoided. And when the administration confronted that question head-on, the lawyers concluded, again and again, the president's constitutional war powers won out.

* * *

As the war continued, the Supreme Court and Congress did step in, asserting some control over who could be detained and how detainees could be treated in this new kind of war. In the most important war powers case since President Truman lost his battle over the steel mills, a former naval officer in World War II, Justice John Paul Stevens, affirmed Congress's power to do so. He declared the president's military commissions did not conform to the statutes Congress had properly passed, and he emphasized that this meant the president would be powerless to continue the commissions without major changes. Just as important, Justice Stevens explained that a crucial portion of the Geneva Conventions applied to the battle with Al Qaeda: namely, the one banning cruel treatment. That ruling triggered yet another statutory limitation, the War Crimes Act.

Now challenged, some of the president's top officials advised Bush not to back down. They were proposing a one-page bill to strip the Supreme Court of its jurisdiction in this area. But, at a meeting in the Oval Office, the president made clear he was "not going to overrule the Supreme Court."

The Bush administration, like Truman's, walked back from its defiant posture—if not in theory then in practice. The administration announced that it would comply with the Court's ruling and work with Congress on new military commissions and detainee legislation. The sweeping claim of a power to interrogate the enemy in any manner that the commander in chief deemed fit—which, years earlier, had been the legal predicate on which the interrogation program had been designed—was no longer the conversation-stopper it had once seemed it might be.

IRAQ

*"I cannot believe the President of the United States will not
pay attention."*

R ight alongside this newly authorized war on terror, a more conventional war was also being waged. Here, too, a similar dynamic
took hold: The president operated relatively freely at first only to
run into legislative resistance over time.

The enemy this time was not a shadowy network of nonstate terrorists. It was the well-armed Iraqi army and its leader, Saddam Hussein. But
as distinct as this second war was, its origins, too, could be traced to the
terrorist strikes of September 11, 2001.

* * *

Right after those attacks, President Bush had made his way back to the
White House. Following a highly classified meeting about how to respond
to the attacks, in which much of the focus was on bin Laden and Al Qaeda,
the president pulled his closest counterterrorism advisors into the Situation Room. There, he engaged them in a brief but urgent conversation.

No effort had yet been made to get authorization from Congress to
strike at the Taliban in Afghanistan and to hunt down Osama bin Laden.
The president wanted to know whether there might be any link between
the recent strikes on America and Saddam Hussein.

In time, that initial inquiry would lead to a massive ground war in Iraq that Congress would overwhelmingly back—through a formal grant of authority to use force. But despite the strong up-front show of legislative support for this second war, Congress's willingness to back the president would, over time, ebb. After years of fighting this second war—with concerns about executive overreaching in the conduct of the military campaign against Al Qaeda kicking into overdrive, as reflected by the Court's rebuke to the president in the military commissions case—a new battle between the president and Congress over the waging of war erupted over Iraq.

By the end of 2007, the president was well into his final term in office. A presidential election loomed. One of the most prominent contenders for the opposing party's nomination, Illinois senator Barack Obama, had opposed the war while he was still a state legislator. The willingness to challenge the president about Iraq was greater than it had ever been. The nation soon found itself as near to a reprise of the age-old debate about presidential war and the legislative power to end it as at any time since Frank Church and his Kentucky ally, John Cooper, had notched their first victory in the effort to bring President Nixon's war in Indochina to a close.

* * *

From the very moment of the president's election, a powerful contingent within the administration was convinced that the tenuous situation in Iraq that had prevailed in the decade following the end of the first Gulf War was unsustainable. A no-fly zone had been in place over Iraq since the end of the first war in Iraq. The result was a persistent, low-level, but at times intensive and certainly financially costly air campaign in Iraq. Nominally, in other words, the Gulf War that had ended more than a decade before continued in diminished form.

Many of the most influential foreign policy and military experts within the Bush administration believed that this status quo could not be permitted to continue. Those already eager for a more aggressive campaign against Iraq perceived in the events of September 11 a new and urgent reason to change the dynamic in the Iraqi-American conflict: the now manifest danger posed by terrorists.

On this view, the attacks in New York, D.C., and on the plane that crashed in Pennsylvania taught a simple lesson: Don't wait. Offense beats defense. Hussein had used chemical weapons against his own people—albeit years earlier, in the war between Iraq and Iran. To many in the administration, therefore, there was no question but that the Iraqi dictator currently maintained a major program for weapons of mass destruction. And since Hussein sought to acquire the capacity to hit his enemies with chemical, biological, and, in the worst case, nuclear weapons, Iraq necessarily presented a clear and present danger. Anyone who understood that the threat matrix had changed in the wake of 9/11 would have to acknowledge the potential threat Iraq posed.

The president's national security advisor, Condoleezza Rice, put the point succinctly in a speech she gave in late January of 2002. By then the administration was getting ready to ask the House and Senate to vote on an authorization to use force in Iraq. The president had prepared the ground for that request with an aggressive State of the Union address. Rice now amplified that message. "As the President said," she told the conservative activists arrayed before her, "we must not and we will not wait on events while dangers gather."

This emerging conviction about the need to act encouraged a view of the president's decisive role in making the decision to go to war that some thought hearkened back to what Arthur Schlesinger had dubbed the imperial presidency. The chief executive, many inside the administration believed, was once again being forced to make the hard call to go to war to stave off a nuclear threat—though this time not one arising out of a Cold War standoff. Reflecting the belief that only the president could make a decision that tough and that necessary, the administration had come up with the perfect name for the plan to go to war in Iraq without the backing of any European allies, a possibility that those inside the White House dreaded but that they also did not necessarily reject out of hand. They called such a plan to go it alone "the Imperial Option."

* * *

The skeptics, including some within the administration itself, were formidable. As a group, they doubted that a new war on Iraq made any sense. They thought Iraq's connection to the terrorist attacks of September 11 was loose at best. To them, there certainly was no evidence supporting the idea that a war in Iraq was some necessary imperative in the way that the mission in Afghanistan was. In fact, the doubters believed, an invasion of Iraq would only divert attention from the one truly imminent threat the country faced: the one posed by Al Qaeda.

This concern, that the president might be committing the country to a campaign in Iraq that could not possibly end well, was voiced by influential figures within both parties. In an editorial that appeared in early August, Brent Scowcroft, who had served the first President Bush as national security advisor during the first Gulf War (following his earlier service advising President Ford during the last days of the Vietnam War), questioned the case for a preemptive attack and all-out invasion of Iraq.

It was clear that popular backing for this campaign would be less complete than it had been for the use of force in Afghanistan and against Al Qaeda more broadly. The invasion force the president was contemplating was going to be a massive one, at least in comparative terms, no matter how successful the Pentagon was in devising a strategy that would keep troop levels to a minimum. Only the first Gulf War was of a similar scale. In the wake of Vietnam and the War Powers Resolution, there was no realistic argument that such a campaign could be waged without first getting Congress to formally sign on to it legislatively.

White House lawyers did make clear that, in their view, the president had the constitutional authority to invade Iraq unilaterally. But the president told his top people in the fall of 2002 that he wanted to get authority from Congress. That meant that he would have to find a way to bring the House and Senate along.

* * *

In the congressional debate that ensued, those opposed to war emphasized over and over that the planned invasion ignored the lessons of Vietnam. As if speaking lines already written for them in battles over that earlier quagmire, the critics questioned the seriousness of the threat and challenged the administration's true motivation for pushing for war. In an impassioned floor speech in the midst of the debate over the vote to authorize the war in Iraq, Senator Edward Kennedy took issue with the whole notion of preemption that the administration had been pushing.

That idea, the senator roared, was "a call for 21st century imperialism that no other nation can or should accept."

But, over time, the president did manage to get Congress to approve the mission. His administration lined up key European allies, Britain most especially. And the president ignored the internal advice given by his most hawkish advisors to avoid seeking a resolution from the United Nations Security Council. With the UN resolution in hand, the president and his team slowly but surely crafted an argument that attracted support.

The only way to get Saddam Hussein to come clean about his WMD program, the administration argued, was to make a credible threat that the United States would invade Iraq. That argument proved to be a winning one. Wavering members of Congress eventually assured their constituents that they were not actually voting for the measure because they wanted the president to start the war. They explained that they wanted only to ensure that he would have all the support he needed to convince Hussein that he would have to renounce his weapons program before the world in order to avoid war.

In the end, Congress approved a broad authorization for the president to use military force in Iraq. The measure passed by margins far larger than those that the president's father had secured from Congress when he sought legislative authorization to use force in the first Gulf War. But even if the vote to authorize the use of force was a contingent one, aimed at getting Saddam to bend more than giving a green light to Bush to invade, it was a key step in a march that, once it reached a certain point, could not easily have been stopped even by a president harboring second thoughts.

American credibility was on the line. More than a hundred thousand troops were positioned, and allies were publicly signing on in support of taking action. There would soon come a point when, absent some major turn of events such as Hussein voluntarily leaving, war was going to start.

Congress had given the president the power to use force. Polling showed large majorities thought the administration had made a convincing case. It was now up to the president to decide how to use the power that he had been given.

On March 19, 2003—less than two years from the date the president

first asked top aides whether Saddam was responsible for the attacks of
9/11—Bush informed the nation: The war on Iraq had begun.

* * *

In waging this new war, the president found that Saddam Hussein was not
hard to defeat. Baghdad was actually taken with stunning speed. But the
fall of Iraq's capital was only the beginning. America was soon fending off a
full-fledged insurgency—not unlike the one that had caused such problems
for America in the Philippines. As the effort to quell the uprising stalled
and sputtered, so, too, did support back home, just as it had back then.

The president was now engaged in wars on three fronts, each one
distinct. There was the ongoing and deeply frustrating effort to stabilize
Afghanistan. There was the faltering effort to do the same in Iraq. And
there was the increasingly controversial effort to wage a new kind of war
against Al Qaeda and its offshoots, involving means of interrogation and
surveillance that were provoking sharp battles over the limits Congress
could place on the president's power to wage war.

There had been warnings from the get-go that the war in Iraq might
not go as planned. The promised support from the Iraqi people might not
materialize. The much-vaunted Iraqi WMD program might turn out
not to exist. Getting out might prove harder than going in. Those who
sounded such warnings made clear that Congress and the public might
then turn on the war they had once seemed more than willing to bless.

The war was coming up on its fifth year—and the president on his last in
office. There were thousands of dead American soldiers. Iraq itself seemed to
be in a state of chaos, with increasing signs that Al Qaeda—which had had no
presence in Iraq before the invasion—was now making inroads. It was no longer clear the choice about what to do in Iraq would be the president's to make.

Just before the midterm elections, the president met with a senator
from his own party. The senator told Bush that Iraq might cost the Republicans control of the Senate. The president asked what the senator wanted
him to do. "Mr. President, bring some troops home from Iraq," the senator
reportedly said during the Oval Office meeting. The president responded:
"I will not withdraw troops unless military conditions warrant." By 2007,

though, the Democrats had in fact taken control of both houses of Congress, in large part because of the public's souring mood on Iraq.

* * *

The president announced he was undertaking a full-fledged strategy review. He ultimately decided to break with the advice he was getting from many military officials—as well as many of his top national security officials. Rather than reducing the American presence in Iraq and all but conceding defeat, he would back a surge in forces, aimed at reclaiming some semblance of American control over the situation—his own effort to secure the peace with honor that had proved elusive in Vietnam.

On January 10, in a televised address, hurriedly scheduled just two weeks before his State of the Union, the president announced the planned surge. He called for committing more than twenty-one thousand additional troops to Iraq. The president tried to strike a conciliatory tone, impliedly acknowledging that he needed Congress's help. "I respect you and the arguments you've made," the president said. "We went into this largely united in our assumptions and in our convictions. And whatever you voted for, you did not vote for failure. Our country is pursuing a new strategy in Iraq, and I ask you to give it a chance."

The call for a surge provoked the most intensive clash between Congress and the president over ending a war since Vietnam. There had been earlier post–Cold War skirmishes over Congress's power to end a war. Congress had all but ordered President Clinton to get American troops out of Somalia, after his predecessor's limited intervention there resulted in a horrifying attack on American forces soon after the new president took office. Congress later restricted President Clinton's use of ground troops in the Balkans and then refused to authorize continued air strikes in Kosovo even though the ninety-day war powers clock was about to turn—leading the administration to scramble to justify the campaign on the basis of the continued appropriations. But the clash over the surge in Iraq was more serious, given how substantial the troop commitment to Iraq already was and the undeniable strategic ramifications of a defeat in that military effort.

Within days of the president's speech announcing the surge, members of

Congress, including some from the president's own party, sponsored a spate of proposals to challenge the president's war plan. The proposals with the best shot were nonbinding resolutions that directly expressed disapproval of the decision to send in more troops. One of them passed the House with relative ease, after an extended debate in which more than three hundred members took to the floor to make their position, for or against, in five-minute speeches.

But the effort to take on the president's plan stalled in the Senate, despite intensive efforts by Joseph Biden to team up with a moderate Republican senator from Virginia, John Warner. They tried to come up with a text for a resolution that could actually get voted on and win in the Senate. Biden took flak from those who argued these nonbinding resolutions were toothless. There were proposals on offer, after all, that went a good deal further. The leading Democratic contenders—Hillary Clinton and Barack Obama—each introduced their own binding measures that in one form or another sought to cap troop levels at their existing level absent express congressional authorization to send in more.

Biden believed, though, that the Senate's passage of even a nonbinding resolution, when paired with similar action in the House, would send a strong message. "I cannot believe the President of the United States will not pay attention." If Bush did not pay attention, then Biden planned to find a binding way to affect the president's policy in Iraq.

Biden's less confrontational strategy also reflected a keen sensitivity to the political risks of challenging the president in the midst of a war over how to fight it. Like many of his colleagues, he was quite aware of the political dangers of any suggestion that the opposition party might be trying to cut off funding to troops in the field. Nancy Pelosi, the newly elected Democratic speaker of the House, had already vowed "never to cut off funding for our troops when they are in harm's way." And while polls showed strong support for directly challenging the president, they did so only so long as there would be no funding cut off.

* * *

The president made clear that he had no intention of backing down in the face of the mounting legislative resistance. He said even a nonbinding resolution of disapproval was "too extreme," and his spokesperson made clear that the administration's position was that, while Congress surely had a right to weigh in, ultimate responsibility rested with the commander in chief. Vice President Cheney reinforced the point. The pending resolutions "won't stop us," Cheney said in a cable news interview right after the president's address.

The president's Senate supporters successfully maneuvered to make sure that no bill of disapproval, binding or not, was put up for a vote. The surge went ahead as planned, ultimately meeting with more success than the critics had predicted. But even though the president had succeeded in getting his way for the moment, the war in Iraq was no longer one that enjoyed the support it once had.

In April, the Senate and the House attached a rider to the war-spending bill that would require a troop withdrawal by 2008. The president vetoed the measure, but it was clear that any president who continued to push for substantial military commitments was sure to find Congress standing in the way from this point forward. As a result, there were increasingly serious concerns that congressional support to fund the war might not last through the fall. There were urgent White House discussions that summer about whether a proposed timetable for withdrawal had to be floated with Congress, lest it abandon the president altogether.

That November, the presidential election was won by Barack Obama, the candidate who was most identified with opposing the Iraq War. And so, just as had happened in the wake of Truman's initial defiant assertions during Korea in the early days of the Cold War, a new administration took over that was committed to making a break with the predecessor's war making and that promised, Ike-like, to restore a constitutional presidency.

But that new president would not be operating on a clean slate. Just as the Cold War had not ended with the election of Truman's successors, neither had the wars of the present time ended with the conclusion of the Bush administration. In fact, President Obama would be coming to office with the wars in Afghanistan and Iraq still very much underway, and the war on terror still to fight. His campaign promises to restore the balance would now be tested—and while America remained very much at war.

EPILOGUE

"[T]he sweeping assertions in the opinions above that the President's Commander in Chief authority categorically precludes Congress from enacting any legislation concerning the detention, interrogation, prosecution, and transfer of enemy combatants are not sustainable."

I joined the Obama administration on its first day: January 20, 2009. I was returning to the office in the Department of Justice where I had first worked as a young lawyer in the Clinton administration, the Office of Legal Counsel. It was an obscure office when I had last left it. Most people back then just assumed it was in the White House, and they were usually vaguely disappointed—and somewhat mystified—when they learned that it wasn't.

But the office was not obscure any more. Not after all the controversy that had been stirred up by the positions it had taken about the president's unchallengeable constitutional power to interrogate, detain, and wiretap.

I had been a law professor when the memos setting forth those constitutional positions had first appeared. I had spent the better part of three years working with a colleague on a long pair of scholarly articles that tried to show that American history offered little support for a sweeping view that Congress had no right to check the president's conduct of war.

But now I was walking down Constitution Avenue, with what seemed like a million people lining the Washington Mall for the inauguration, as I headed in to begin running the office. I would be the office's acting assistant attorney general until the president's nominee for the permanent position could get confirmed—something, as it turned out, that never happened. And that meant I was likely to find myself, over the course of the next eighteen months until I stepped down, addressing many of these basic questions about who controls the conduct of war—not in the abstract, but for real.

A key question—and one that the lawyers for the president-elect had been struggling with throughout the transition, in which I had also served—concerned what should be done about all the controversial legal positions that had been taken in the prior administration. The president could criticize the policies that had been implemented in consequence of them, as he had done as a candidate. And now that he was the president, he could on his own commit to changing interrogation practices, limiting surveillance approaches, and even to closing the detention facility at Guantanamo. But his success in making these changes still might depend on the cooperation of Congress. For what was the new president to do if he were confronted with an effort by Congress to block his favored way of conducting an ongoing war? Would he, too, contend Congress had no right to do so? And if he wouldn't, then what would he do? Those questions were not in the forefront of my mind on that first day. But, if history was any guide, they were sure to arise.

* * *

The clashes with Congress to come were not obviously on the horizon at first, certainly not when it came to the authority to continue the war on Al Qaeda and its offshoots. There was good reason to think that this new president, like his predecessor, would have great support in using military force to pursue this aspect of the nation's counterterrorism strategy.

America was not fighting an ideological threat that manifested itself in proxy wars between superpowers over strategic predominance abroad or the stockpiling of nuclear weapons in a race for supremacy. Instead, the enemies of the moment were more tangible. They were organized, nonstate terrorist organizations from the Middle East, committed to carrying out terrorist attacks against Americans on American soil.

With that enemy front and center, the specter of imperialism that shadowed all of the old Cold War battles no longer loomed as large as it once did. The result was a seemingly strong consensus, at least among the political branches, about the need for the president to use military force.

That stark reality did not mean, though, that the new president would be altogether free to decide how to prosecute this war on Al Qaeda and its affiliates. Eisenhower had managed to avoid a constitutional conflict with Congress in conducting his version of the Cold War largely by relying on stealthy means of using force. He was a great fan of the secret services. But he was operating in an era in which the secret uses of armed force were subject to much less scrutiny than any current president (or any lawyer advising him) could prudently expect in the wake of Vietnam and the Church Committee. And that scrutiny was sure to be trained on the new president at some point.

As much as Obama had come to office having criticized the claimed excesses of his predecessor, he, too, believed that the terrorist threat was real. He had made that clear during the campaign. Inevitably, then, this new president was going to find himself confronting some novel question about the use of armed force in this strange war that might require him to decide whether Congress had meant to bar its use—and, if he concluded that Congress had, he would then have to decide what he was willing to do in response.

There was also another reason to think that this new president might find himself in a clash with Congress over the proper tactics to use in the conduct of this war. Even if the new president might find ways to avoid pressing the fight against the enemy more aggressively than existing statutes had necessarily contemplated, he also would be seeking to find ways to scale back some of the means that had been used before. He had committed to doing so as a candidate. If he carried through on that commitment, though, there was the very real possibility that those efforts could put him at odds with Congress.

Even presidents wary of fighting a hard war have confronted legisla-

tures eager to stop the commander in chief from treating the enemy with
what some of their members considered kid gloves. Lincoln found himself
hounded by a Congress that believed he was too timid in his conduct of
the Civil War. Andrew Johnson was almost impeached for what the Congress of his day thought was a similar sin when it came to the use of the
army in that war's aftermath. And Congress repeatedly pressed Woodrow
Wilson to give up on an approach to war making that his congressional
enemies thought an oxymoron: peace without victory.

Thus, while the campaign of Barack Obama was all about change and
the need for it, his oft-stated claim that he aimed to restore the rule of
law was not merely an important part of his appeal to many of his supporters. That commitment was also a potential source of tension with the
legislature, which, when faced with an effort by the executive to roll back
national security policies that were then in place, might be none too eager
to do so.

* * *

Over the course of the new president's time in office, Barack Obama
would find himself at odds with Congress in fighting his version of the
war on terror on both fronts—for being too aggressive and for not being
aggressive enough.

Like Ike after Truman, the president found that many of his most fervent supporters in the campaign soon took to criticizing him for being
too much like his predecessor. Yes, he had issued an executive order that
subjected all interrogations to the *Army Field Manual.* Yes, he had barred
the black sites. Yes, he had told the courts to look to the laws of war, and
not away from them, in determining the scope of his detention powers.
Yes, he had shepherded through a revised military commissions system
that narrowed its differences with the criminal justice system—though
not nearly enough in the eyes of critics.

But still, there were signs—too many, the critics thought—that Obama
was willing to continue the same war against Al Qaeda that had been
going on for years. There were reports he was even stepping it up—and,
in doing so, using force in novel ways that Congress had, some claimed,

meant to foreclose. And so, with respect to the use of drones, surveillance, and detention, he was accused of breaching limits on the conduct of war that Congress had put in place.

The line thus soon became a standard one. Obama had continued "virtually" all of the Bush practices. And it was not only the means of force Obama was using in the war against Al Qaeda that was causing concern about presidential war powers getting beyond congressional control. Even as the public's willingness to back a continuation of the war in Iraq had seemed to run its course, there remained the reality that the much less hotly disputed war against Al Qaeda was continuing, and the enemy was morphing seemingly by the month into new incarnations.

In response, a president who had signaled as a candidate his wariness about engaging in unilateral executive war making would, by the end of his second term, find himself accused of doing just that. The president relied on the original 2001 Authorization to Use Military Force that was understood to justify the initial invasion of Afghanistan in order to justify attacks in a number of countries against a number of new terrorist organizations. He relied on the AUMF, too, to justify renewed operations in Iraq in order to destroy the Islamic State in Iraq and Syria (or, as it soon became known to the world, ISIS). Critics claimed he was stretching the AUMF beyond recognition, though Congress did little in response.

The Senate and the House, however, were less wary of challenging the president for waging military missions not directly tied to counterterror operations. As a result, the president found himself running into strong congressional headwinds both for his limited and controversial campaign in Libya—based on constitutional power alone—and for his aborted mission to enforce a red line against Syrian leader Bashar Al-Assad.

After running up against the 90-day War Powers Resolution clock during his campaign in Libya, a controversy erupted over the president's contention that he was not in breach of the statute because, though his administration did not challenge its constitutionality, the repeated air strikes did not actually constitute the kind of "hostilities" that triggered the clock in the first place. And when it came to Syria, the president first signaled an intent to use air power there to challenge that governing regime's reported use of chemical weapons but then pulled back when the president decided he should not go forward without congressional backing.

As it happened, the president eventually would pursue military operations in Syria. By then, though, as with his stepped-up campaign in Iraq following his declared end to the combat mission there, he based his authority on the fact that the mission was to defeat ISIS. The administration dubbed ISIS a cobelligerent with Al Qaeda and thus an enemy covered by the original AUMF passed in mid-September 2001. Such contentions fueled the criticism that the president was a unilateralist after all.

But as much as the president's aggressiveness occasioned critique, there was an irony in what some pointed to as the clearest proof that the new president was no different from the last: Guantanamo remained open. It was Congress, after all, that had made a nullity of the commander in chief's inaugural-week executive order to close the facility within one year. Through a series of legislative restrictions—that, together, were both detailed and comprehensive—Congress greatly limited his ability to transfer detainees to foreign countries or to the United States, not even for criminal prosecution.

* * *

Against this background, the relevant precedents about the president's powers as commander in chief in this new age of American warmaking are not to be found in the much-scrubbed history that shows how Congress stopped declaring war and how presidents started striking out on their own to make it. Rather, the history that matters is to be found in the much less well-known, centuries-long history of prior fights between Congress and the commander in chief over the conduct of war.

The guidance that history offers on this score is hardly crystal clear. Justice Robert Jackson, while writing his famous concurring opinion in the steel seizure case, reflected back on his time as attorney general. In doing so, he remarked on how little help past precedents offered on the great question of what a wartime president could do when confronted with a legislative check.

In writing those passages of his opinion, Jackson was clearly thinking back to those months, years before, when he had been under great pressure to find some lawful way for Roosevelt to send destroyers to England despite the various statutes that had seemed to block the president from pursuing that course. Those tense days in the Justice Department were well in Jackson's past by the time he found himself writing his opinion in the steel seizure case. But you could almost see him grimace as, in crafting his concurrence, he recalled the "poverty of useful" assistance to be found in the precedents, both in the courts and out, which had accumulated over more than a century and a half of American wartime history.

All but fed up, Justice Jackson finally sighed in his concurrence that if an answer was to be found at all, it "must be divined from materials almost as enigmatic as the dreams Joseph was called up to interpret for Pharaoh." Obscure as those dreams were, Jackson tried to make sense of them as best he could. And, in the case of Truman's seizure of the steel mills, just as in the case of the destroyers-for-bases deal, Jackson turned away from the idea that the president had an absolute power to fight a war on his own terms.

Such a sweeping view of presidential power in war might sound appealing, especially to one accustomed to advising the president how he could accomplish his ends. It might even be a position one could credibly defend with this piece of history or that snippet of Supreme Court dicta, or even with a bit of logic. But, Jackson ultimately concluded, it was a dangerous idea and one that a fair reading of the past suggested presidents had consistently shied away from making.

* * *

The Bush administration, of course, had interpreted the signals from the past very differently. Choices about how to fight the war were, opinion after opinion from the prior administration had said, for the president alone.

That view was not without a pedigree. One could find statements that had a similar flavor over the course of the many post–Cold War presidencies. In fact, when I had worked in the Office of Legal Counsel in the Clinton administration, it, too, had suggested, in this context or that, that a certain statute, if applied in a certain way, might infringe on the

constitutional prerogatives of the commander in chief. That administration had been especially wary of the Republican-controlled Congress's
attempts to micromanage its various efforts to engage with the United
Nations in various so-called peacekeeping efforts. And there had been
particular controversy over a series of appropriations riders that sought
to prohibit the president from placing any U.S. armed forces under the
control of a United Nations commander.

But those skirmishes had been fought on the edges. They did not get
at the heart of where the balance of power lay when it came to the conduct of war. They were nothing like the head-on confrontations that had
defined the constitutional battle between the branches for the last many
years. Jackson's opinion offered counsel about how to handle a confrontation like that. A showdown should be avoided. The president would be
wise to find some workable alternative path forward, no matter that it
might take some time to discern the route and no matter that the way
forward might end up being a less straightforward and smooth one.

As it turned out, that same view was shared by a number of people
within the Bush administration, as I would learn as soon as I took up my
new duties.

* * *

It was both startling—and not surprising at all, given our nation's history—to find on my first day in the Office of Legal Counsel as its new
head what would turn out to be inside the plain manila envelope awaiting
me. My outgoing predecessor had left the envelope there. And he had
made clear he wanted me to see it. Inside, there was a then-still-secret
memorandum that this outgoing official had prepared. He had signed
it during his last week in the department. And the memo came down
squarely on Justice Jackson's side.

The memorandum was clearly the product of a lot of work. It zeroed
in on what it identified as a critical aspect of the prior administration's potential constitutional legacy. It explained why it was a legacy that needed
to be rejected—and that the Bush administration had itself disclaimed
that legacy midway through its time in office.

"The purpose of this memorandum," the document began, "is to confirm that certain propositions stated in several opinions issued by the Office of Legal Counsel in 2001–2003 respecting the allocation of authorities between the President and Congress in matters of war and national security do not reflect the current views of this Office." The memo went on to explain that the office had "previously withdrawn or superseded a number of opinions that depended upon one or more of these propositions," but that the office had never said why. "For reasons discussed herein," the memo said, "we explain why these propositions are not consistent with the current views of OLC, and we advise that caution should be exercised before relying in other respects on the remaining opinions identified below."

The memo noted that the opinions being repudiated had been "issued in the wake of the atrocities of 9/11, when policy makers, fearing that additional catastrophic terrorist attacks were imminent, strived to employ all lawful means to protect the Nation." And the memo explained that "in the months following 9/11, attorneys in the Office of Legal Counsel and in the Intelligence Community confronted novel and complex legal questions in a time of great danger and under extraordinary time pressure."

These pressures "perhaps" had led the opinions to depart from "this Office's preferred practice of rendering formal opinions addressed to particular policy proposals and not undertaking a general survey of a broad area of the law or addressing general or amorphous hypothetical scenarios involving difficult questions of law." But "mindful of this extraordinary historical context," the memo concluded, "we nevertheless believe it appropriate and necessary to confirm that the following propositions contained in the opinions identified below do not currently reflect, and have not for some years reflected, the views of OLC."

Over the course of eleven single-spaced pages, the memorandum recited the passages from more than a dozen different Justice Department legal opinions—touching on all the most contentious issues of the war on terror—in which in one way or another the administration had "advanced a broad assertion of the President's Commander in Chief power that would deny Congress any role in regulating the detention, interrogation, prosecution, and transfer of enemy combatants captured in the global War on Terror." In going through these opinions one by one, the memorandum quoted the sweeping assertions of absolute executive wartime power that the administration had previously set forth and then explained that although "the President certainly has significant constitutional powers in this area . . . the assertion in these opinions that Congress has no authority under the Constitution to address these matters by statute does not reflect the current views of OLC and has been overtaken by subsequent decisions of the Supreme Court and by legislation passed by Congress and supported by the President."

The memo did not give up entirely on the idea of an unchecked executive power to conduct war. "A law that is constitutional in general may still raise serious constitutional issues," the memo noted, "if applied in particular circumstances to frustrate the President's ability to fulfill his essential responsibilities under Article II." But even still, the memorandum concluded, "the sweeping assertions in the opinions above that the President's Commander in Chief authority categorically precludes Congress from enacting any legislation concerning the detention, interrogation, prosecution, and transfer of enemy combatants are not sustainable." In other words, even the administration that had been the most forceful defender of the defiant view of the president's power to conduct war on his own terms was now retreating from it.

* * *

The young Nixon White House lawyer Thomas Charles Huston insisted forty years before that ideas matter when it comes to presidential war powers. At the root of each of the most controversial aspects of the first phase of the war on terror—from interrogation, to surveillance, to detention— was an idea. General Washington's acceptance of his Revolutionary-era Congress's limitations on the conduct of war was quaint. Wartime decisions, the first commander in chief in our longest war asserted, were now for the president alone.

But once that idea—and the consequences that it produced—had come to light, it had not fared well. Nor should it have been surprising that it did not. The idea that the president is really not bound by Congress in war runs against the grain of history.

In truth, commanders in chief have found themselves mired in statutory restrictions in every prior phase of American war making, from the Revolutionary War, to the early wars with France and England, to the Civil War and its aftermath, to the specter of total war culminating in World War II, to the Cold War itself. And thus presidents have throughout our history had to figure out how best to respond to these restrictions.

In crafting their responses, defiance has rarely been their strategy of choice. Presidents have, with remarkably few exceptions, struggled to find ways to cope with these restrictions or to find creative ways around them that might prove tolerable to Congress. That last memo from the Bush administration was reflecting that history. It was saying that presidents should be required to do no less in this new war—one that is already more than a decade old and that shows no signs of coming to a sudden end.

* * *

Of course, a president could abandon the sweeping idea that choices about the conduct of war are his alone to make without thereby agreeing to be the pawn of Congress. Presidents and their lawyers are expert at finding ways to read statutes that reveal loopholes and gaps where it might seem Congress intended to establish a clear bar. The process by which executive branch lawyers go about interpreting these statutes to find some way for the president to accomplish his ends might all be dismissed as an elaborate show. The legal escape routes that lawyers help find for their presidents can always be characterized as little more than fig leaves for lawbreaking. And sometimes, no doubt, such criticism is fair.

But while any process may be abused, there is a difference between a president feeling bound to account for the views of Congress and a president not feeling bound in that way at all. The felt sense that Congress may have the last word creates a dynamic the virtues of which are too easily discounted. The specter of lawbreaking slows things down, forces deliberation, and points up the political risks of taking a given action that rubs up against a legal line that might otherwise not fully come into view. The group think that can easily set in within any administration—especially one that finds itself in the midst of a war—is less likely to take hold when the general sense is that the president is not simply able to fight the war on his terms and his alone.

We cannot know—and I cannot prove—that we are the better for the fact that for most of our history our presidents have chosen not to assert a sweeping power to run the wars in which they have led the country however they have seen fit. The line between cynicism and naïveté is a thin one. Even the Bush administration's last memo, a cynic might say, shows only that an outgoing president of one party wanted to tie the hands of an incoming president of another party. But as hardheaded as it may seem to read our past with a cynic's eye, presidents simply have not been willing to claim the unchecked powers we often assume they think they have. Instead, presidents have time and again recognized the danger to themselves—and to our constitutional system of checks and balances— that inheres in the idea that decisions about the conduct of war are theirs alone to make. And so they have struggled to find ways to conduct war that have not depended on the view that they possess uncheckable wartime powers.

That does not mean that a president who wants to demonstrate respect for our system of separated powers, and the checks and balances it establishes, will ensure that the excesses of war will be avoided. Our constitutional system—and the history of accommodation between the branches that underlies it—does not ensure us the conventional happy ending that those fierce critics of the imperial presidency seem to promise will result from a return to what they contend are our nation's true founding principles.

The truth is that Congress is sometimes more willing to favor an aggressive approach to the conduct of war than the president. A president committed to avoiding a clash with Congress, therefore, is not necessarily a leader who will exercise restraint in battle. As much as the detainees at Guantanamo have become for many a symbol of what happens when a wartime president becomes convinced that decisions about how to fight are his alone to make, they remain there in part because a president who asserted his power to close that facility has found himself effectively countered by a Congress determined to stop him from doing so.

All of which is to say that presidents repeatedly have faced the same hard question: Can they find a way to wage war without claiming that decisions about the conduct of war are the commander in chief's alone to make? It is a question that has been with us since George Washington first took on the British in the early days of the Revolutionary War. It is one that we should hope presidents never feel entitled to stop asking. Their felt need to answer it has been a key reason why our system of checks and balances, for all its limitations, has managed to endure even when America is waging war.

NOTES

Preface

xi   **"shining bright. . . beautiful prospect"**: Ambrose Serle, "Journal Entry: July 12, 1776," in *The American Revolution: Writings from the War of Independence, 1776–1783* (New York: Literary Classics of the United States, Inc., 2001).

xi   **"generalissimo with full Powers"**: Ibid.

xii   **"for the president alone"**: John C. Yoo, "The President's Constitutional Authority to Conduct Military Operations Against Terrorist Organizations and the Nations that Harbor or Support Them" (September 25, 2001), available at: www.justice.gov/sites/default/files/olc/opinions/2001/09/31/op-olc-v026-p0188-0.pdf.

Chapter 1
☰ *The Revolutionary War*

3   **epigraph:** George Washington to Archibald Campbell, March 1, 1777, reprinted in Charles H. Walcott, *Sir Archibald Campbell of Inverneill: Sometime Prisoner of War In the Jail at Concord, Massachusetts* (Boston: Beacon Press, 1898), p. 37.

3   **A fleet of more than one hundred:** Edward G. Lengel, *General George*

Washington: A Military Life (New York: Random House, 2005), pp. 135, 137–41; David McCullough, *1776* (New York: Simon & Schuster, 2005), p. 157.

4 **In preparing for just that outcome:** Lengel, *George Washington*, pp. 139–40.

4 **New York was no ordinary city:** Lengel, *George Washington*, p. 129. **Washington's advisors had been warning:** Benjamin L. Carp, "The Night the Yankees Burned Broadway: The New York City Fire of 1776," *Early American Studies* (Fall 2006), p. 491.

4 **"Burn or Garrison":** Nathanael Greene to Samuel Ward, Sr., January 4, [1776], quoted in Carp, "The Night the Yankees Burned Broadway," p. 491; Nathanael Greene to George Washington, September 5, 1776, reprinted in Philander D. Chase and Frank E. Grizzard, Jr., eds., *The Papers of George Washington, Revolutionary War Series*, vol. VI, pp. 222–24.

4 **Rebel soldiers had set fire:** Carp, "The Night the Yankees Burned Broadway," pp. 492–93. **army would head for White Plains:** Nathanael Greene to George Washington, September 5, 1776, reprinted in Chase and Grizzard, eds., *Papers of George Washington*, pp. 222–24.

5 **savvy enough:** Carp, "The Night the Yankees Burned Broadway," p. 494; **"cheerfully submit . . . general Interest of America":** Abraham Yates, Jr., to George Washington, August 22, 1776, reprinted in Chase and Grizzard, eds., *Papers of George Washington*, p. 108; **"justify me":** George Washington to the New York Convention, August 23, 1776, reprinted in ibid., p. 114.

5 **"deliberating Executive assembly":** Thomas Burke to the North Carolina Assembly, August 1779, reprinted in Edmund C. Burnett, ed., *Letters of Members of the Continental Congress*, vol. IV (Washington, D.C.: Carnegie Institution of Washington, 1928), p. 367; Jack N. Rakove, *The Beginnings of National Politics: An Interpretive History of the Continental Congress* (New York: Alfred A. Knopf, 1979), p. 383.

5 **Congress would sometimes send:** Jay Caesar Guggenheimer, "The Development of the Executive Departments, 1775–1789," in J. Franklin Jameson, ed., *Essays in the Constitutional History of the United States in the Formative Period, 1775–1789* (Cambridge, MA: Riverside Press, 1889), pp. 118–26; Abraham D. Sofaer, *War, Foreign Affairs and Constitutional Power: The Origins* (Cambridge, MA: Ballinger Publishing, 1976), pp. 20–21, 388 n.76; Francis D. Wormuth and Edwin B. Firmage,

To Chain the Dog of War: The War Power of Congress in History and Law (Urbana, IL: University of Illinois Press, 2d ed., 1989), pp. 108–09; Logan Beirne, "George vs. George vs. George: Commander-in-Chief Power," *Yale Law and Policy Review* 26 (2007); Worthington Chauncey Ford et al., eds., *Journals of the Continental Congress, 1774–1789*, vol. V, pp. 605–06 (Washington, D.C.: GPO, 1906); Joseph J. Ellis, *His Excellency: George Washington* (New York: Alfred A. Knopf, 2004), p. 93.

6   **"in every respect by the rules and discipline":** Congress to George Washington, June 17, 1775, reprinted in Worthington Chauncey Ford et al., eds., *Journals of the Continental Congress, 1774–1789* (Washington, D.C.: GPO, 1905), vol. II, p. 96.

6   **Washington treasured this document:** William M. Fowler, Jr., *American Crisis: George Washington and the Dangerous Two Years After Yorktown, 1781–83* (New York: Walker & Co., 2011), p. 234.

6   **British forces had taken over Long Island:** Carp, "The Night the Yankees Burned Broadway," p. 493; Nathanael Greene to George Washington, September 5, 1776, reprinted in Chase and Grizzard, eds., *Papers of George Washington,* p. 222; George Washington to John Hancock, September 8, 1776, reprinted in ibid., pp. 140–48. **"If we should be obliged":** George Washington to John Hancock, September 2, 1776, reprinted in Carp, "The Night the Yankees Burned Broadway," pp. 495–96.

7   **"burnt our towns":** The Declaration of Independence (U.S., 1787). **"no damage":** John Hancock to George Washington, September 3, 1776, reprinted in Dorothy Twohig, ed., *Papers of George Washington* (1994), vol. VI, p. 207. **"absolutely forbid":** George Washington to Lund Washington, October 6, 1776, ibid., p. 493.

7   **Washington was incredulous:** John Ferling, *The Ascent of George Washington: The Hidden Political Genius of an American Icon* (New York: Bloomsbury Press, 2009), p. 113. **"I shall take every measure":** George Washington to John Hancock, September 6, 1776, reprinted in Twohig, ed., *The Papers of George Washington,* vol. VI, p. 207. **"this in my judgment":** George Washington to Lund Washington, October 6, 1776, ibid., p. 493; Carp, "The Night the Yankees Burned Broadway," pp. 496–97.

7   **The final British assault began on September 15:** Ferling, *Ascent of George Washington,* pp. 111–14; Ellis, *His Excellency,* pp. 92–96; Lengel,

George Washington, pp. 149–55; David Hackett Fischer, *Washington's Crossing* (New York: Oxford University Press, 2004), pp. 81–114; McCullough, *1776*, pp. 210–14.

8   **Some of the British and many of the loyalists:** Carp, "The Night the Yankees Burned Broadway," pp. 504–05; entry for September 21, 1776, reprinted in Ambrose Serle, *The American Journal of Ambrose Serle, Secretary to Lord Howe, 1776–1778* (San Marino, CA: The Huntington Library, 1940; reprinted Arno Press, 1969), pp. 110–11; Lengel, *George Washington*, 157–58; McCullough, *1776*, pp. 221–24.

8   **As for the missing bells:** Carp, "The Night the Yankees Burned Broadway," p. 479.

8   **"Providence—or some good honest Fellow":** George Washington to Lund Washington, October 6, 1776, reprinted in Carp, "The Night the Yankees Burned Broadway," p. 497.

9   **Well schooled but slovenly:** Ellis, *His Excellency*, pp. 80–82.

9   **Those under Washington's command:** Walcott, *Sir Archibald Campbell*, pp. 9, 20–22.

10   **Campbell and seven fellow Scotsmen:** Archibald Campbell to George Washington, February 14, 1777, James Murray Robbins Family Papers.

10   **"luxurious habits . . . self-denying farmers":** Walcott, *Sir Archibald Campbell*, pp. 22–23; Archibald Campbell to James Bowdoin, April 13, 1777, reel 48, box 55, Massachusetts Historical Society, Bowdoin and Temple Papers.

10   **The enemy took Lee into custody:** McCullough, *1776*, pp. 264–66. **rallying point . . . this side of the Atlantic:** Walcott, *Sir Archibald Campbell*, pp. 23–24.

11   **"committed to the custody . . . same treatment":** *Orders of Congress*, January 6, 1777 & February 20, 1777, reprinted in Walcott, *Sir Archibald Campbell*, pp. 24–25.

11   **"into safe and close custody":** *Order of Congress*, February 20, 1777, reprinted in Walcott, *Sir Archibald Campbell*, p. 25. **By the time the new order came down:** Ibid., pp. 26–27.

11   **Campbell found his new surroundings appalling:** Archibald Campbell to General William Howe, February 14, 1777, Call number MSN801, James Murray Robbins Family Papers. **"From the powers which I have lately understood . . . servant on my person":** Archibald Campbell to

George Washington, February 4, 1777, reprinted in Walcott, *Sir Archibald Campbell*, pp. 31–35.

12 **Washington was sympathetic:** Walcott, *Sir Archibald Campbell*, pp. 36–38.

12 **"I am not invested . . . required by any resolution":** George Washington to Archibald Campbell, March 1, 1777, reprinted in Walcott, *Sir Archibald Campbell*, p. 37. **"upon the most strict interpretation":** George Washington to James Bowdoin, February 28, 1777, quoted in ibid., p. 36. **Lee, after all, was not being treated:** Archibald Campbell to William Heath, May 16, 1777, reels 4–7, 9, Massachusetts Historical Society, William Heath Papers. **He was permitted each night:** Walcott, *Sir Archibald Campbell*, pp. 44–45.

12 **"[would] not have the desired . . . Lee has yet received":** Letter to Congress: George Washington to Congress, March 1, 1777, reprinted in Walcott, *Sir Archibald Campbell*, p. 38.

13 **"It was not . . . on six Field Officers":** John Hancock to George Washington, March 17, 1777, reprinted in Jared Sparks, ed., *Correspondence of the American Revolution: Being Letters of Eminent Men to George Washington, From the Time of Taking His Command of the Army to the End of His Presidency* (Boston: Little, Brown & Co., 1853), vol. I, pp. 356–57.

13 **Washington's lobbying had plainly done some good:** Walcott, *Sir Archibald Campbell*, p. 40. **He wrote Washington again:** Archibald Campbell to James Bowdoin, April 13, 1777, reel 48, box 55, Massachusetts Historical Society, Bowdoin and Temple Papers; Archibald Campbell to James Bowdoin, April 17, 1777, reel 48, box 55, Massachusetts Historical Society, Bowdoin and Temple Papers; Walcott, *Sir Archibald Campbell*, pp. 40–41. **"in the jailer's house":** William Howe to George Washington, May 22, 1777, quoted in Walcott, *Sir Archibald Campbell*, pp. 42–43. **"the situation of":** George Washington to William Howe, June 10, 1777, reprinted in Walcott, *Sir Archibald Campbell*, p. 50.

13 **standoff did not end:** Walcott, *Sir Archibald Campbell*, pp. 50–51; Betsy Knight, "Prisoner Exchange and Parole in the American Revolution," *William and Mary Quarterly* (April 1991), pp. 204–16.

13 **As a result, Congress scotched:** Knight, "Prisoner Exchange and Parole," pp. 204–216.

14 **Revealing the perils of independence:** Letter from George Washington

to Joseph Reed, March 3, 1776, reprinted in John Fitzpatrick, ed., *The Writings of George Washington* (Washington, D.C.: GPO, 1931–44), vol. IV, p. 367.

14 **"I take the earliest opportunity":** George Washington to the President of Congress, December 20, 1783, reprinted in Fitzpatrick, ed., *Writings of George Washington*, vol. XXVII, pp. 277–78.

14 **"an affectionate farewell":** Address to Congress on Resigning His Commission, December 20, 1783, reprinted in Fitzpatrick, ed., *Writings of George Washington*, vol. XXVII, pp. 284–86 & n.68. **His remarks complete:** Ellis, *His Excellency*, p. 146; Ferling, *Ascent of George Washington*, pp. 243–44; Fowler, *American Crisis*, pp. 234–40.

15 **"translated into a private citizen":** George Washington to James McHenry, December 10, 1783, reprinted in Fitzpatrick, ed., *Writings of George Washington*, vol. XXVII, p. 266.

Chapter 2
≡ *The Founding*

17 **epigraph:** Speech of Patrick Henry in the Virginia Ratifying Convention, June 5, 1788, reprinted in William Wirt Henry, *Patrick Henry: Life, Correspondence, and Speeches* (New York: Charles Scribner's Sons, 1891), vol. III, p. 451.

18 **With a man like that presiding:** Donald L. Robinson, "Inventors of the Presidency," *Presidential Studies Quarterly 13* (Winter 1983), pp. 8–9, 20, 23.

18 **During the burst of state constitution making:** Ray Raphael, *Mr. President: How and Why the Founders Created a Chief Executive* (New York: Alfred A. Knopf, 2012), p. 40.

18 **actually naming a king:** Eric Nelson, *Royalist Revolution: Monarchy and the American Founding* (Cambridge, MA: Harvard University Press, 2014), pp. 210–11. **the delegates to the Convention:** Raphael, *Mr. President*, p. 63.

19 **two of Washington's former colleagues:** Henry, *Patrick Henry*, vol. II, p. 350.

19 **they were formidable opponents:** Thomas S. Kidd, *Patrick Henry: First Among Patriots* (New York: Basic Books, 2011), pp. 193–211.

20   **Mason was known to dress in black:** Hugh Blair Grigsby, *The History of the Virginia Federal Convention of 1788* (Richmond, VA: Virginia Historical Society, 1890), vol. I, p. 4 n.6. **"Son of Thunder":** Richard Beeman, *Plain, Honest Men: The Making of the American Constitution* (New York: Random House, 2009), p. 396. **He even made a show of his modest origins:** Harlow Giles Unger, *Lion of Liberty: Patrick Henry and the Call to a New Nation* (Cambridge, MA: Da Capo Press, 2010), pp. 237–39.

20   **For all their differences:** Beeman, *Plain, Honest Men*, pp. 395–99; Unger, *Lion of Liberty*, pp. 210–40. **Henry was so hostile to the ideas:** Patrick Henry to Edmund Randolph, February 13, 1787, reprinted in Henry, *Patrick Henry*, vol. II, p. 311. **He returned to Virginia:** Robinson, "Inventors of the Presidency," p. 12.

21   **other than one early reference:** Max Farrand, ed., *The Records of the Federal Convention of 1787* (New Haven, CT: Yale University Press, 1911), vol. I, p. 23 and vol. III, p. 595, 599; Raphael, *Mr. President* pp. 3–4, 91.

22   **But the committee appears to have done so:** Charles C. Thach, Jr., *The Creation of the Presidency 1775–1789: A Study in Constitutional History* (Baltimore, MD: Johns Hopkins Press, 1922), pp. 112–16.

22   **The Convention debates do show:** Jack N. Rakove, *Original Meanings: Politics and Ideas in the Making of the Constitution* (New York: Alfred A. Knopf, 1996), p. 257; Raphael, *Mr. President*, p. 55. **True, they acknowledged:** Thach, *Creation of the Presidency*, p. 127.

22   **"[direct] their operations":** Articles of Confederation, art. IX, para. 4.

23   **the framers wished to reserve the power:** Oversight Legislation: Hearings Before the Select Comm. on Intelligence, 100th Cong. 179–81 (1987) (written response of Charles Cooper, Assistant Att'y Gen., Office of Legal Counsel); Richard Hartzman, "Congressional Control of the Military in a Multilateral Context: A Constitutional Analysis of Congress's Power to Restrict the President's Authority to Place United States Armed Forces Under Foreign Commanders in United Nations Peace Operations," *Military Law Review* 162 (1999), pp. 72–76.

23   **there were a number of plans presented:** Rakove, *Original Meanings*, p. 269; Jack N. Rakove, "Taking the Prerogative out of the Presidency: An Originalist Perspective," *Presidential Studies Quarterly* 37 (March 2007), pp. 93–94; Raphael, *Mr. President*, pp. 67–68, 91–92; Farrand, *Records of the Federal Convention*, vol. I, pp. 64–66, 70, 88–89, 97 (Virginia

Plan); ibid., pp. 242, 244 (New Jersey Plan); ibid., p. 292 (Hamilton's Plan).

23 **"executive function":** Madison Convention Notes, reprinted in Thach, *Creation of the Presidency*, p. 127; Farrand, *Records of the Federal Convention*, vol. II, p. 319. **The delegates thus clearly wanted:** Rakove, *Original Meanings*, p. 263; Raphael, *Mr. President*, p. 99.

24 **A century or so before:** David J. Barron and Martin S. Lederman, "The Commander in Chief at the Lowest Ebb—Framing the Problem, Doctrine, and Original Understanding," *Harvard Law Review*, vol. 121 (2008), pp. 772–73; Charles M. Clode, *The Military Forces of the Crown: Their Administration and Government* (London: John Murray 1869), vol. I, pp. 425–29; Rakove, *Original Meanings*, pp. 245–48; **The use of the well-worn title:** Francis D. Wormuth, "The Nixon Theory of the War Power: A Critique," *California Law Review* 60 (1972), pp. 623, 630; Commission to General Monck as Commander-in-Chief (Jan. 26, 1659), reprinted in *The Clarke Papers* (C.H. Firth ed., 1901), vol. IV, pp. 137–39; William C. Banks and Peter Raven-Hansen, *National Security Law and the Power of the Purse* (New York: Oxford University Press, 1994), pp. 11–17.

25 **It was what future commanders in chief:** Henry, *Patrick Henry*, vol. II, pp. 385, 387; Rakove, *Original Meanings*, pp. 272–274; Donald L. Robinson, "Inventors of the Presidency," *Presidential Studies Quarterly* 13 (Winter 1983), p. 23.

25 **Henry had been the commander in chief:** Kidd, *Patrick Henry*, pp. 103–116, 129–50. **He had even been accused:** Ibid., pp. 132–33.

25 **Henry and Mason focused on the dangerous:** Henry, *Patrick Henry*, vol. II, pp. 384–85, 401; Woody Holton, *Unruly Americans and the Origins of the Constitution* (New York: Hill and Wang, 2007), pp. 247–48; Virginia Convention Debate, June 5, 1788, reprinted in John P. Kaminski and Gaspare J. Saladino, eds., *The Documentary History of the Ratification of the Constitution: Ratification of the Constitution by the States* (Madison, WI: The State Historical Society of Wisconsin, 1990), vol. IX, pp. 951–68 (Henry); ibid., June 18, 1788, vol. X, pp. 1378–79 (Mason).

26 **He held forth for hours:** Hugh Blair Grigsby, *The History of the Virginia Federal Convention*, vol. I, p. 67. **"This Constitution . . . towards monarchy":** Virginia Convention Debate, June 5, 1788, reprinted in Kaminski

and Saladino, eds., *Documentary History*, vol. IX, p. 963; Speech of Patrick Henry in the Virginia Ratifying Convention, June 5, 1788, reprinted in Henry, *Patrick Henry*, vol. III, p. 451.

26   "your American chief . . . despotism ensue": Speech of Patrick Henry in the Virginia Ratifying Convention, June 5, 1788, reprinted in Jonathan Elliot ed., *The Debates in the Several State Conventions on the Adoption of the Federal Constitution* (New York: Burt Franklin Press, 1888), vol. III, p. 60; Henry, *Patrick Henry*, vol. III, p. 452; Virginia Convention Debates, June 5, 1788, reprinted in Kaminski and Saladino, eds., *Documentary History*, vol. IX, p. 964; George F. Willison, *Patrick Henry and His World* (Garden City, NY: Doubleday and Co., 1969), pp. 425–26.

27   "an American dictator . . . can be trusted on that head": Speech of Patrick Henry in the Virginia Ratifying Convention, June 5, 1788, reprinted in Henry, *Patrick Henry*, vol. III, p. 485; Virginia Convention Debates, June 9, 1788, reprinted in Kaminski and Saladino, eds., *Documentary History*, vol. IX, p. 1058.

27   "propriety . . . might make a bad use of it": Virginia Convention Debates, June 18, 1788, reprinted in Kaminski and Saladino, *Documentary History*, vol. X, p. 1378.

27   the Constitutional Convention overwhelmingly: Rakove, "Originalist Perspective," pp. 93–94; Farrand, *Records of the Federal Convention*, vol. I, p. 242, 244, and vol. III, pp. 217–18.

27   "of what the late . . . without any control": Virginia Convention Debates, June 18, 1788, reprinted in Kaminski and Saladino, eds., *Documentary History*, vol. X, p. 1378–79.

28   "If it do not finally obtain . . . a good administration": Alexander Hamilton, Conjectures about the New Constitution, September 17–30, 1787, reprinted in Harold C. Syrett and Jacob E. Cooke, eds., *The Papers of Alexander Hamilton* (New York: Columbia·University Press, 1962), pp. 275–77.

29   "It will be Eight or Nine months . . . adoption of the Plan": Alexander Hamilton, Conjectures about the New Constitution, September 17–30, 1787, reprinted in Syrett and Cooke, eds., *Papers of Alexander Hamilton*, pp. 275–77. **Hamilton began to hear reports:** Gouverneur Morris to Alexander Hamilton, June 13, 1788, reprinted in Syrett and Cooke, eds., *The Papers of Alexander Hamilton* vol. V, p. 7.

29   **Someone using the pseudonym Tamony:** Tamony, "To the Freeholders of America," Virginia Independent Chronicle, Virginia, January 9, 1788, reprinted in Kaminski and Saladino, eds., *Documentary History*, vol. VIII, pp. 286–88; Rakove, *Original Meanings*, p. 272.

29   **If Hamilton were honest, he would have admitted:** Thach, *Creation of the Presidency*, p. 52; Raphael, *Mr. President*, p. 73. **But when he did rise to address:** Rakove, "Originalist Perspective," pp. 93–94; Raphael, *Mr. President*, pp. 68–72.

30   **"the entire Direction":** Alexander Hamilton, *Propositions for a Constitution of Government*, June 18, 1787, reprinted in Henry Cabot Lodge, ed., *The Works of Alexander Hamilton* (New York: G. P. Putnam's Sons, 1904), vol. I, p. 348.

30   **"have so much power":** Raphael, *Mr. President*, pp. 71–72. **"an Executive for life":** Alexander Hamilton, *Propositions for a Constitution of Government*, June 18, 1787, reprinted in Lodge, ed., *Works of Alexander Hamilton*, vol. I, p. 392.

31   **"be nominally the same . . . admiral of the Confederacy":** Alexander Hamilton in Clinton Lawrence Rossiter, ed., *The Federalist Papers*, No. 69 (New York: Signet Classic, 2003), p. 416.

31   **real comparison should be with those:** Barron and Lederman, "Commander in Chief at the Lowest Ebb," pp. 780–85, 781 n.299. **"may well be a question . . . larger powers":** Alexander Hamilton in Rossiter, ed., *Federalist Papers*, p. 417.

32   **The Massachusetts example was well chosen:** Thach, *Creation of the Presidency*, pp. 43–48; Lawrence Friedman and Lynnea Thody, *The Massachusetts State Constitution* (New York: Oxford University Press, 2011), pp. 9–10; David H. Fisher, "The Myth of the Essex Junto," *William and Mary Quarterly* 21 (April 1964); Ronald M. Peters, Jr., *The Massachusetts Constitution of 1780: A Social Compact* (Amherst, MA: University of Massachusetts Press, 1978), pp. 30–31; Samuel Eliot Morison, *A History of the Constitution of Massachusetts* (Boston: Wright & Potter Printing Co., 1917), pp. 16–18. **They had thus ensured that their new governor:** *Result of the Convention of Delegates Holden at Ipswich in the County of Essex* (Newbury-Port, MA: John Mycall, 1778), pp. 36, 58–59.

32   **Hamilton would eventually use that same language:** Rossiter, ed., *The Federalist Papers*, No. 70 (Alexander Hamilton) (New York: Signet

Classic, 2003), p. 423; Robert A. Ferguson, *Reading the Early Republic* (Cambridge, MA: Harvard University Press, 2004), pp. 76–77.

33 **"be exercised agreeably"**: Massachusetts Constitution of 1780, ch. 2, sec. 1, art. VII, reprinted in Peters, *Massachusetts Constitution of 1780*, p. 212. **Massachusetts was not alone**: Lynnea Thody, *The Massachusetts State Constitution* (New York: Oxford University Press, 2011), pp. 10–11; Barron and Lederman, "The Commander in Chief at the Lowest Ebb," pp. 780–85.

Chapter 3
≡ Quasi War

35 **epigraph**: Alexander Hamilton to James McHenry, May 17, 1798, reprinted in Harold C. Syrett and Jacob E. Cooke, eds., *The Papers of Alexander Hamilton* (New York: Columbia University Press, 1974), vol. XXI, pp. 461–62.

35 **"as a private citizen . . . round which"**: *Annals of Congress*, March 4, 1797.

35 **The inaugural ceremony**: David McCullough, *John Adams* (New York: Simon & Schuster, 2001), pp. 467–69. **It was painful to contemplate life**: Alexander DeConde, *The Quasi-War: The Politics and Diplomacy of the Undeclared War with France, 1797–1801* (New York: Charles Scribner's Sons, 1966), p. 14; JA to AA, March 17, 1797, reprinted in John Adams, *Letters of John Adams Addressed to His Wife* (XXX), vol. II, p. 252 ("All of the federalists seem to be afraid to approve any body but Washington."); Jean S. Holder, "The Sources of Presidential Power: John Adams and the Challenge to Executive Primacy," *Political Science Quarterly* 101 (1984), p. 605.

36 **Irascible, vain, easily slighted**: Stanley Elkins and Eric McKitrick, *The Age of Federalism: The Early American Republic, 1788–1800* (New York: Oxford University Press, 1993), pp. 531–37; DeConde, *Quasi-War*, pp. 3–5; McCullough, *John Adams*, pp. 18–20.

36 **The source of the trouble**: Elkins and McKitrick, *Age of Federalism*, pp. 537–38; DeConde, *Quasi-War*, pp. 17–24; McCullough, *John Adams*, pp. 473–79; George C. Daughan, *If by Sea: The Forging of the American Navy—From the American Revolution to the War of 1812* (New York: Basic Books, 2008), pp. 303–05.

36   It was not clear: DeConde, *Quasi-War*, pp. 3–5; Elkins and McKitrick, *Age of Federalism*, pp. 531–37. "out of his senses": Benjamin Franklin, quoted in James Schouler, *History of the United States of America Under the Constitution* (Washington, D.C.: W. H. & O. H. Morrison, 1880), vol. I, p. 497.

37   He berated the various department heads: Joseph J. Ellis, *American Sphinx: The Character of Thomas Jefferson* (New York: Alfred A. Knopf, 1997), pp. 187–88. was even accused: David McCullough, *John Adams*, pp. 375–380.

37   The French were not letting up: McCullough, *John Adams*, p. 471, 484; Holder, "Sources of Presidential Power," pp. 602–03; Ian W. Toll, *Six Frigates: The Epic History of the Founding of the U.S. Navy* (New York: W. W. Norton & Co., 2006), pp. 79–80. Adams had a fondness for Britain: DeConde, *Quasi-War*, pp. 5–6, 379 nn.5–9.

37   Nor was he above whipping up war fever: DeConde, *Quasi-War*, pp. 80–84, 403 n.18; Elkins and McKitrick, *Age of Federalism*, p. 589; John Ferling, *John Adams: A Life* (Knoxville: University of Tennessee Press, 1992), p. 356. He went so far as to sign: Elkins and McKitrick, *Age of Federalism*, 590–93. Jay Winik, *The Great Upheaval: America and the Birth of the Modern World, 1788–1800*. New York: HarperCollins, 2007), 539–41.

38   by doing so, he gave himself: DeConde, *Quasi-War*, pp. 6–7, 380 n.10.

38   Adams offered his first official comments: Charles Francis Adams, ed., *The Works of John Adams* (Boston: Little, Brown and Co., 1854), vol. IX, pp. 105–11; DeConde, *Quasi-War*, pp. 14–15; Elkins and McKitrick, *Age of Federalism*, p. 542; McCullough, *John Adams*, pp. 467–70. French attacks on American merchant ships: Timothy Pickering to John Adams, June 21, 1797, reprinted in *Naval Documents Related to the Quasi-War Between the United States and France: Naval Operations from February 1797 to October 1798* (Washington, D.C.: US GPO, 1935), vol. I, p. 6; Daughan, *If by Sea*, p. 304. Adams now had no choice but to recall Congress: Elkins and McKitrick, *Age of Federalism*, pp. 550–52; DeConde, *Quasi-War*, pp. 16–17.

38   Where they inclined toward war: Elkins and McKitrick, *Age of Federalism*, pp. 544–54.

38   There were ironies in Hamilton: DeConde, *Quasi-War*, pp. 6–7; Elkins and McKitrick, *Age of Federalism*, pp. 539–40, 547, 864 n.40.

39   **the president said after one contentious meeting:** Daughan, *If by Sea*,
      p. 339; Elkins and McKitrick, *Age of Federalism*, pp. 599–606; DeConde,
      Quasi-War, pp. 121–23;

39   **"direction of war":** Clinton Lawrence Rossiter, ed., *The Federalist Pa-
      pers*, No. 74 (Alexander Hamilton) (New York: Signet Classic, 2003),
      p. 446. **"entire direction":** Alexander Hamilton, Propositions for a
      Constitution of Government, June 18, 1787, reprinted in Henry Cabot
      Lodge, ed., *The Works of Alexander Hamilton* (New York: G. P. Put-
      nam's Son's, 1904), p. 348; Charles C. Thach, Jr., *The Creation of the
      Presidency 1775–1789: A Study in Constitutional History* (Baltimore,
      MD: Johns Hopkins Press, 1922), p. 52; Ray Raphael, *Mr. President:
      How and Why the Founders Created a Chief Executive* (New York: Al-
      fred A. Knopf, 2012), p. 68–73; Jack N. Rakove, "Taking the Prerog-
      ative out of the Presidency: An Originalist Perspective," *Presidential
      Studies Quarterly* 37 (March 2007), pp. 93–94. **"vigor . . . secrecy and
      dispatch":** Rossiter ed., *The Federalist Papers*, No. 70 (Alexander Ham-
      ilton), p. 423, 425.

39   **While serving in Washington's cabinet:** Pacificus No. I, June 29, 1793,
      reprinted in Syrett and Cooke, eds., *The Papers of Alexander Hamilton*,
      vol. XV, pp. 33–43; Pacificus No. VII, July 27, 1793, reprinted in ibid., pp.
      130–35; Alexander Hamilton and Henry Knox to George Washington,
      May 2, 1793, reprinted in ibid., vol. XIV, pp. 367–96; Alexander Hamil-
      ton to George Washington, May 2, 1793, reprinted in ibid., pp. 398–408;
      Elkins and McKitrick, *Age of Federalism*, pp. 336–41.

40   **key members were holdovers:** DeConde, *Quasi-War*, pp. 7–8, 18–19,
      22–23; Elkins and McKitrick, *Age of Federalism*, pp. 544–53, 631–62;
      McCullough, *John Adams*, pp. 471–72, 494–95; Holder, "Sources of
      Presidential Power," pp. 605–08; Ferling, *John Adams*, pp. 332–47;
      James McHenry to Alexander Hamilton, April 14, 1797, reprinted in
      Syrett and Cooke, eds., *Papers of Alexander Hamilton*, vol. XXI, pp. 48–
      49; ibid., April 19, 1797, pp. 51–52; Alexander Hamilton to James
      McHenry, April 1797, ibid., pp. 72–75; ibid., January 27–February 11,
      1797, pp. 341–46.

41   **Adams appeared before the specially called session:** John Adams to
      Congress, May 16, 1797, reprinted in *Annals of Congress*, vol. VII, pp.
      54–59; Adams, *Works of John Adams*, vol. IX, pp. 111–20. **Hamilton had**

helped to engineer: DeConde, *Quasi-War*, p. 23; Elkins and McKitrick, *Age of Federalism*, pp. 552–53; Ferling, *John Adams, A Life*, pp. 332–48; Winik, *The Great Upheaval*, 518–19.

41   **Just as Hamilton had prescribed:** DeConde, *Quasi-War*, pp. 10–11; Elkins and McKitrick, *Age of Federalism*, pp. 544–45. **Adams proposed to send yet another peace delegation:** DeConde, *Quasi-War*, pp. 18–19, 28–29; Elkins and McKitrick, *Age of Federalism*, pp. 555–58. **Adams was careful to pair that conciliatory gesture:** DeConde, *Quasi-War*, pp. 25–30; Elkins and McKitrick, *Age of Federalism*, pp. 552–53; McCullough, *John Adams*, pp. 483–86.

41   **Congress was not the least bit charmed:** DeConde, *Quasi-War*, pp. 26–28; Elkins and McKitrick, *Age of Federalism*, p. 552; McCullough, *John Adams*, pp. 483–85.

42   **"war whoop":** McCullough, *John Adams*, p. 485. **Republican congressional members feared:** DeConde, *Quasi-War*, p. 34.

42   **key flashpoint:** DeConde, *Quasi-War*, p. 31. **"formed so speedily":** Adams, ed., *Works of John Adams*, vol. IX, p. 116.

42   **Even as Adams spoke:** Circular to the Collector of Customs, April 8, 1797, reprinted in *Naval Documents Related to the Quasi-War*, vol. I, pp. 4–5; Syrett and Cooke, eds., *The Papers of Alexander Hamilton*, vol. XXI, pp. 47–48 n. 2.

42   **authorized to serve as convoys:** John Adams to Congress, May 16, 1797, reprinted in *Annals of Congress*, vol. VII, pp. 54–59; Elkins and McKitrick, *Age of Federalism*, p. 553.

43   **"such merchant vessels as shall remain unarmed":** Adams, ed., *Works of John Adams*, vol. IX, p. 116.

43   **From the moment Washington took office:** David J. Barron and Martin S. Lederman, "The Commander in Chief at the Lowest Ebb—A Constitutional History," *Harvard Law Review*, vol. 121 (2008), pp. 955–964; Allen Millet, Peter Maslowski, and William B. Feis, *For the Common Defense: A Military History of the United States from 1607–2012* (New York: The Free Press, 2012), p. 95.

44   **Republicans in Congress:** James Madison to Thomas Jefferson, April 15, 1798, reprinted in James Madison, *Letters and Other Writings of James Madison* (Philadelphia: J. B. Lippincott & Co., 1867), vol. II, pp. 134–37; DeConde, *Quasi-War*, pp. 25–27, 80–81, 88–89. **"antecedent state of**

things": Pacificus No. 1, June 29, 1793, reprinted in Syrett and Cooke, eds., *The Papers of Alexander Hamilton*, vol. XV, p. 42.

45 **"without ventilators":** Samuel Eliot Morison, *The Life and Letters of Harrison Gray Otis, Federalist, 1765–1848* (Boston: Houghton Mifflin Co., 1913), vol. I, p. 60. **They swiftly beat back:** *Annals of Congress*, vol. VII, pp. 283–95, 359–409; Elkins and McKitrick, *Age of Federalism*, p. 555, 581; DeConde, *Quasi-War*, pp. 31–35. **"wooden walls":** John Adams to Boston Marine Society, September 7, 1798, reprinted in Adams, *Works of John Adams*, vol. IX, p. 221.

45 **Federalists were advancing a measure:** *Annals of Congress*, vol. VII, p. 283 (statement of Rep. Smith). **Nicholas . . . sought to curb it:** *Annals of Congress*, vol. VII, p. 286 (statement of Rep. Nicholas).

46 **offered an even stricter proposal:** *Annals of Congress*, vol. VII, pp. 287–89 (statements of Rep. Gallatin).

46 **a brilliant Swiss immigrant:** Daughan, *If by Sea*, pp. 306–07. **"adopt a single hostile measure":** Albert Gallatin to James Nicholson, May 26, 1797, reprinted in Henry Adams, *The Life of Albert Gallatin* (Philadelphia: J. B. Lippincott & Co., 188), p. 184. **"within the jurisdiction":** *Annals of Congress*, vol. VII, p. 289 (statement of Rep. Gallatin).

46 **Tempers flared:** *Annals of Congress*, vol. VII, pp. 360–66.

46 **Otis was new to Congress:** Samuel Eliot Morison, *Harrison Gray Otis, 1765–1848: The Urbane Federalist* (Boston: Houghton Mifflin Co., 1969), pp. 1–82, 102, 190–92; Samuel Eliot Morrison, *Letters of Harrison Gray Otis*, vol. I, pp. 1–72.

46 **"If a naval force was raised":** *Annals of Congress*, vol. VII, p. 290 (statement of Rep. Otis).

47 **The House passed:** *Annals of Congress*, vol. VII, p. 297. **focus of debate then shifted:** *Annals of Congress*, vol. VII, pp. 19–22, 359–60.

47 **Other than a group of revenue cutters:** Michael A. Palmer, *Stoddert's War: Naval Operations During the Quasi-War with France, 1798–1801* (Columbia, South Carolina: University of South Carolina Press, 1987), p. 15. **The other three ships:** Toll, *Six Frigates*, pp. 40–43, 62.

47 **"Our little naval preparation":** Alexander Hamilton to Theodore Sedgwick, January 20, 1797, reprinted in Syrett and Cooke, eds., *The Papers of Alexander Hamilton*, vol. XX, p. 473.

48 **"In ordinary times":** *Annals of Congress*, vol. VII, p. 363 (statement of

Rep. Gallatin). **House Republicans backed up the argument:** *Annals of Congress*, vol. VII, p. 365 (statement of Rep. Giles).

48   **Federalists fought back hard:** *Annals of Congress*, vol. VII, pp. 360–67. **take away the powers:** Ibid., p. 363 (statement of Rep. Sewall); ibid., p. 367 (statement of Rep. Kittera). **House adopted Gallatin's amendment:** *Annals of Congress*, vol. VII, p. 365.

48   **The Federalists in the Senate hardened their position:** *Annals of Congress*, vol. VII, pp. 28–31. **impasse broke:** Ibid., pp. 407–10.

48   **special session had been a Republican rout:** Elkins and McKitrick, *Age of Federalism*, pp. 555, 581; DeConde, *Quasi-War*, pp. 31–35.

49   **specified, among other things:** Act Providing for Naval Armament, July 1, 1797, reprinted in *Naval Documents Related to the Quasi-War*, pp. 7–9.

49   **He immediately returned home to Quincy:** DeConde, *Quasi-War*, p. 35. **the men he had sent to Paris:** Ibid., pp. 59–62. **in January, he reached out:** Ibid., pp. 63–65; Questions to Cabinet, reprinted in Adams, ed., *Works of John Adams*, vol. VIII, pp. 561–62.

49   **Sentiment was shifting:** McCullough, *John Adams*, p. 504. **"solemn and manly communication":** Alexander Hamilton to Theodore Sedgwick, March, 1798, reprinted in Lodge, ed., *Works of Alexander Hamilton*, p. 278. **"an undoubted fact . . . war with that Republic":** Alexander Hamilton to James McHenry, January 27–February 11, 1798, reprinted in Syrett and Cooke, eds., *Papers of Alexander Hamilton*, vol. XXI, p. 342.

50   **Once the papers leaked:** DeConde, *Quasi-War*, pp. 72–76; Elkins and McKitrick, *Age of Federalism*, pp. 588–89, 593; Daughan, *If by Sea*, pp. 310–12; Toll, *Six Frigates*, pp. 90–91; Ferling, *John Adams*, pp. 354–55.

50   **summer of 1798:** Elkins and McKitrick, *Age of Federalism*, pp. 588–95; DeConde, *Quasi-War*, 98–103; Daughan, *If by Sea*, pp. 314–18. **Congress also gave Adams:** Act of May 28, 1798, ch. 47, § 1, 1 Stat. 558; Act of July 16, 1798, ch. 76, § 2, 1 Stat. 604; Act of March 2, 1799, ch. 31, §§ 1, 6–9, 1 Stat. 725–26. **Congress even went so far:** Act of May 28, 1798, ch. 48, 1 Stat. 561; Act of July 9, 1798, ch. 68, § 1, 1 Stat. 578; Act of June 28, 1798, ch. 62, § 1, 1 Stat. 574.

51   **act establishing a permanent navy:** Daughan, *If by Sea*, pp. 312, 314–15.

51   **little talent for administration:** DeConde, *Quasi-War*, pp. 7, 90; Palmer,

Stoddert's War, pp. 7–8; Elkins and McKitrick, *Age of Federalism*, p. 630. **He begged Hamilton to tell him:** James McHenry to Alexander Hamilton, May 12, 1798, reprinted in Syrett and Cooke, eds., *The Papers of Alexander Hamilton*, vol. XXI, pp. 459–60.

51 **"In so delicate a case . . . chicane the Constitution":** Alexander Hamilton to James McHenry, May 17, 1798, reprinted in ibid., pp. 461–62.

52 **"Although Congress have authorized . . . be partial & limited":** James McHenry to Richard Dale, May 22, 1798, reprinted in *Naval Documents Related to the Quasi-War*, vol. I, p. 77; Palmer, *Stoddert's War*, pp. 15–16. **Congress went on to pass:** DeConde, *Quasi-War*, pp. 90–106, 126–27; Elkins and McKitrick, *Age of Federalism*, pp. 588–93; Palmer, *Stoddert's War*, p. 16.

53 **laws were sometimes literally copied:** James McHenry to Captain Richard Dale, May 22, 1798, reprinted in *Naval Documents Related to the Quasi-War*, p. 77; ibid., July 13, 1798, p. 204; An Act More Effectually to Protect the Commerce and Coasts of the United States, May 28, 1798, ibid., pp. 87–88; Instructions to commanders of armed vessels, May 28, 1798, ibid., p. 88; James McHenry to Captain Thomas Truxton, May 30, 1798, ibid., pp. 92–94; An Act Further to Protect the Commerce of the United States, July 9, 1798, ibid., pp. 181–83; Instructions of Secretary Stoddert, 10 July 1798, to commanders of United States armed vessels, ibid., p. 187; Benjamin Stoddert to Captain Stephen Decatur, July 11, 1798, ibid., pp. 192–93; Benjamin Stoddert to Captain James Sever, July 11, 1798, ibid., pp. 193–94. **"keep on & off":** Benjamin Stoddert to Captain John Barry, July 3, 1798, ibid., pp. 161–62; ibid., July 7, 1798, p. 174; ibid., July 11, 1798, pp. 189–91; Tim McGrath, *John Barry: An American Hero in the Age of Sail* (Yardley, PA: Westholme Publishing, 2010), pp. 459–60.

53 **Adams installed Benjamin Stoddert:** DeConde, *Quasi-War*, p. 90; Palmer, *Stoddert's War*, pp. 7–10; Daughan, *If by Sea*, pp. 313, 319–24. **advised one captain to go ahead:** Benjamin Stoddert to Captain Stephen Decatur, June 21, 1798, reprinted in *Naval Documents Related to the Quasi-War*, p. 127. **Stoddert offered a cheeky interpretation:** Benjamin Stoddert to Willings & Francis, Agents for U.S. Ship Ganges, October 9, 1799, reprinted in *Naval Documents Related to the Quasi-War*, vol. IV, p. 270; Palmer, *Stoddert's War*, p. 141.

54 **"Propriety and Prudence . . . done with them"**: Stoddert to Captain Stephen Decatur, June 28, 1798, reprinted in *Naval Documents Related to the Quasi-War*, vol. I, pp. 149–50.

54 **"no position is more dangerous . . . what their duty is"**: The Minerva, Dedham, MA, August 2, 1798, p. 3. **"by Halves"**: Captain Thomas Truxton to Benjamin Stoddert, February 10, 1799, reprinted in *Naval Documents Related to the Quasi-War*, vol. II, p. 327.

54 **"restrictions and limitations . . . against the French Republic"**: John Adams to John Marshall, September 4, 1800, reprinted in Adams, *Works of John Adams*, vol. IX, p. 81. **accepted the checks**: Message to Both Houses of Congress; On the State of Affairs with France, June 21, 1798, reprinted in ibid., pp. 158–59; Daughan, *If by Sea*, pp. 326–29, 338–39; Elkins and McKitrick, *Age of Federalism*, pp. 599–618; DeConde, *Quasi-War*, pp. 181–85; Ferling, *John Adams*, pp. 372–86.

55 **"mad"**: John Adams to Harrison Gray Otis, undated, quoted in Morison, *Letters of Harrison Gray Otis*, p. 162; DeConde, *Quasi-War*, p. 171. **seemingly out of the blue**: Message to the Senate; Nominating an Envoy to France, February 18, 1799, reprinted in Adams, ed., *Works of John Adams*, vol. IX, pp. 161–62.

55 **Hamilton was by then second in command**: Elkins and McKitrick, *Age of Federalism*, pp. 599–618; Daughan, *If by Sea*, pp. 327–30, 338–39.

55 **his sudden shift toward peace**: Daughan, *If by Sea*, pp. 330, 340–42; Holder, "Sources of Presidential Power," pp. 612–14; DeConde, *Quasi-War*, pp. 187–96.

55 **Before Adams's term ended, the new round**: Daughan, *If by Sea*, pp. 340–45. **He did not even attend**: McCullough, *John Adams*, pp. 564–65.

Chapter 4
≡ *The Good Officer*

57 **epigraph**: Thomas Jefferson to John Colvin, Paul Leicester Ford, ed., September 20, 1810, reprinted in *The Works of Thomas Jefferson* (New York and London: G.P. Putnam's Sons, 1904–05), vol. XII, pp. 146–50.

57 **Most famously, Jefferson abandoned**: Thomas Jefferson to John

Dickinson (Aug. 9, 1803), reprinted in Ford, ed., *The Works of Thomas Jefferson*, vol. X, pp. 28–30; Robert J. Delahunty and John C. Yoo, "Dream on: The Obama Administration's Nonenforcement of Immigration Laws, the Dream Act, and the Take Care Clause," *Texas Law Review*, vol. 91 (2013), pp. 812–14.

58   **almost alone among those working:** Jon Meacham, *Thomas Jefferson: The Art of Power* (New York: Random House, 2012), pp. 389–93.

58   **During the campaign for the presidency:** David McCullough, *John Adams* (New York: Simon & Schuster, 2001), pp. 536–38, 544–46.

59   **Jefferson had shown a keen sense:** Meacham, *Art of Power*, pp. 364–66.

59   **Often drunk, never trustworthy:** John Colvin to Thomas Jefferson, February 4, 1811, reprinted in J. Jefferson Looney, ed., *The Papers of Thomas Jefferson: Retirement Series*, (Princeton: Princeton University Press, 2004), vol. III, pp. 359–60; James E. Savage, "Spaniards, Scoundrels, and Statesmen: General James Wilkinson and the Spanish Conspiracy, 1787–90," *Hanover Historical Review*, vol. XI, available at http://history.hanover.edu/hhr/98/hhr98_1.html; Meacham, *Art of Power*, pp. 419–20. **Wilkinson's heavy-handed tactics:** Robert Allen Rutland, *James Madison: The Founding Father* (Columbia, MO: University of Missouri Press, 1997), pp. 220–21.

59   **Burr was, by all accounts:** Nancy Isenberg, *Fallen Founder: The Life of Aaron Burr* (New York: Viking, 2007), p. 1. **His transparent ambition:** Ibid., p. 300; Meacham, *Art of Power*, pp. 292–93; Joseph J. Ellis, *American Sphinx: The Character of Thomas Jefferson* (New York: Alfred A. Knopf, 1997), pp. 174–75. **More than a few of the nation's founders:** Alexander Hamilton to James A. Bayard, August 6, 1800, reprinted in Syrett and Cooke, eds., *The Papers of Alexander Hamilton* (New York: Columbia University Press, 1977), p. 25; Buckner F. Melton, Jr., *Aaron Burr: Conspiracy to Treason* (New York: John Wiley & Sons, Inc., 2002), pp. 24–26. **So, when Burr stepped down:** Meacham, *Art of Power*, pp. 331, 419–20; Ellis, *American Sphinx*, pp. 174–75.

59   **Burr's defenders:** Meacham, *Art of Power*, pp. 419–20; Isenberg, *Fallen Founder*, pp. 300–01.

60   **One had Burr, as part of this effort:** Henry Adams, *History of the United States of America During the Administration of Thomas Jefferson* (New York: C. Scribner's Sons, 1921), vol. II, p. 239.

60 **Jefferson first started:** Adams, *History of the United States*, vol. II, pp. 279–80.

60 **Jefferson, too, wanted to avoid:** Adams, *History of the United States*, vol. II, p. 280. **president decided to ask:** Thomas Jefferson, Informal Memorandum, October 24, 1806, reprinted in Ford, ed., *The Works of Thomas Jefferson*, pp. 402–03.

60 **"contingent expenses":** *Annals of Congress*, vol. XV, p. 998. **They had a pretty good idea:** Robert Smith to Thomas Jefferson, December 22, 1806, reprinted in Adams, *History of the United States*, vol. II, p. 331.

61 **Smith had assured:** Report of the Secretary of the Navy Robert Smith, April 18, 1806, *Annals of Congress*, vol. XV, p. 1021. **Neither Gallatin nor Smith:** Henry Adams, *The Life of Albert Gallatin* (Philadelphia: J.B. Lippincott & Co., 1880), pp. 180, 299; Speech of John Randolph, *Annals of Congress*, vol. XV, p. 1063. **With doubts growing:** Adams, *History of the United States*, vol. II, pp. 280–81.

61 **"as was proposed . . . within such narrow limits":** Robert Smith to Thomas Jefferson, December 22, 1806, reprinted in Adams, *History of the United States*, vol. II, p. 331.

61 **"competent naval force":** Robert Smith to Thomas Jefferson, December 22, 1806, reprinted in Adams, *History of the United States*, vol. II, p. 331.

62 **Jefferson preferred a strategy:** Thomas Jefferson's Proclamation of November 27, 1806 reprinted in Ford, ed., *Works of Thomas Jefferson*, vol. X, pp. 301–02; Isenberg, *Fallen Founder*, pp. 314–15.

62 **By late November of 1806:** Andro Linklater, *An Artist in Treason: The Extraordinary Double Life of General James Wilkinson* (New York: Walker, 2009), pp. 228, 258–59; Adams, *History of the United States*, vol. II, pp. 323–25.

63 **Wilkinson had been passive:** Adams, *History of the United States*, vol. II, p. 332.

63 **"ordinary forms":** James Wilkinson to William Claiborne, Dec. 6, 1806, reprinted in William Charles Cole Claiborne, *Official Letter Books of W.C.C. Claiborne 1801–1816*, Dunbar Rowland, ed. (Madison, WI: Democrat Printing Co., 1917), vol. IV, pp. 46–47.

63 **"To violate the law":** Claiborne to Wilkinson, December 17, 1806, ibid., pp. 63–64; Adams, *History of the United States*, vol. II, p. 318.

63 **Asserting his rank as commanding general:** Adams, *History of the*

United States, vol. II, pp. 318–20. **The sweep ensnared:** Francois-Xavier Martin, *History of Louisiana: From the Earliest Period* (New Orleans: A.T. Penniman & Co., 1829), vol. II, p. 286.

63   **Wilkinson directed his officers to ignore:** James Ripley Jacobs, *Tarnished Warrior: Major General James Wilkinson* (New York: The Macmillan Company, 1938), p. 234; **the General instead directed:** Stephen I. Vladeck, *The Detention Power* (New Haven, CT: Yale *Law & Policy Review*, 2004), vol. 22, p. 159. **general even showed up:** Jacobs, *Tarnished Warrior*, p. 234.

64   **news of Wilkinson's sweep:** Adams, *History of the United States*, vol. II, pp. 335–36. **With a handkerchief:** Anthony S. Pitch, *The Burning of Washington* (Annapolis, MD: Naval Institute Press, 1998), p. 14; **"The United States are not only . . . no questions":** Adams, *History of the United States*, vol. II, pp. 335–36.

64   **Randolph introduced a resolution:** Ibid., pp. 335–36.

64   **days after Randolph's resolution:** Ibid., pp. 336–38. **"It is a miserable . . . in one of the departments.":** "Extract from a letter from New Orleans to Editor of Baltimore American, December 17, 1806" in *New York Commercial Advertiser* (January 23, 1806).

65   **Jefferson was under great stress:** Meacham, *The Art of Power*, pp. 421–423, 430.

65   **As he contemplated the answer:** Thomas Jefferson to James Wilkinson, Feb. 3, 1907, reprinted in Andrew A. Lipscomb and Albert Ellery Bergh, eds., *The Writings of Thomas Jefferson* (Washington, D.C.: Thomas Jefferson Memorial Association of the United States, 1905), vol. XI, p. 149.

66   **Supreme Court, in an opinion:** *Little v. Barreme*, 6 U.S. (2 Cranch) 170 (1804); Frederick C. Leiner, "The Seizure of the Flying Fish," *The American Neptune*, vol. 56 (1996), pp. 131–43. **He was at the time acting:** "Circular Instructions to the Captains & Commanders of Vessels in the Service of the United States," March 12, 1799, reprinted in *Naval Documents Related to the Quasi-War Between the United States and France: Naval Operations* (Washington, D.C.: US GPO, 1935), p. 447; Michael A. Palmer, *Stoddert's War: Naval Operations During the Quasi-War with France, 1798–1801* (Columbia, SC: University of South Carolina Press, 1987), pp. 91–94. **"confined in its nature . . . extent of their commission":** *Bas v. Tingy*, 4 U.S. (4 Dall.) 37 (1800).

67   advocates for the captain began crafting a bill: 16 *Annals of Congress*
      259–60 (1807) (Congress's vote); "Indemnity Made to an Officer for Re-
      sponsibility Incurred in the Execution of His Instructions," February 20,
      1805 (requesting indemnification); Leiner, "Seizure of the Flying Fish,"
      pp. 131–43. **bill passed both houses:** *Annals of Congress*, vol. XXVI,
      (1807), pp. 32, 260–61. Leiner, "Seizure of the Flying Fish," pp. 138, 138
      n.57.

67   **He was the nation's commanding general:** George M. Dennison, *Mar-
      tial Law: The Development of a Theory of Emergency Powers*, 1776–1861
      (Philadelphia: *American Journal of Legal History*, 1974), vol. 18, pp. 56–
      57. **Wilkinson, by contrast:** Dumas Malone, *Jefferson the President*
      (Charlottesville: University of Virginia Press, 1974), vol. V, p. 266.

68   **"the general had caused . . . of the United States":** Thomas Jefferson,
      Special Message to Congress on the Burr Conspiracy, January 22, 1807,
      Annals of Congress, vol. XVI, Appx., pp. 39–43.

68   **"the consideration that . . . as its functionaries may direct":** Ibid.

68   **"the criminals . . . receive here their proper direction":** Ibid.

69   **Jefferson's effort to sidestep:** Adams, *History of the United States*, vol. II,
      pp. 338–39.

69   **hostile to Jefferson's endorsement:** Speech of John Randolph, January
      26, 1807, *Annals of Congress*, vol. XV, pp. 416–424. **Jefferson's own son-
      in-law:** Adams, *History of the United States*, vol. II, p. 39.

70   **"with promptitude . . . only with your information":** Thomas Jefferson
      to James Wilkinson, Feb. 3, 1807, reproduced in Lipscomb and Bergh,
      eds., *Writings of Thomas Jefferson*, vol. XI, pp. 147–50.

70   **"not extend this . . . felt with strength":** Thomas Jefferson to James
      Wilkinson, Feb. 3, 1807, reproduced in ibid., pp. 147–50.

70   **"we judge of the merit . . . by the military arrest":** Thomas Jefferson
      to Governor William Claiborne, February 7, 1807, reprinted in H. A.
      Washington, ed., *The Writings of Thomas Jefferson*, (New York: Riker,
      Thorn & Co., 1854), vol. 5, pp. 40–41.

71   **Jefferson was trying:** Thomas Jefferson to James Wilkinson, Feb. 3,
      1807, reproduced in Lipscomb and Bergh, eds., *Writings of Thomas Jef-
      ferson*, vol. XI, pp. 147–50.

71   **Before sending the suspects:** Martin, *History of Louisiana*, vol. II,
      p. 266.

71 **Burr was in custody:** Linklater, *Artist in Treason,* p. 273.

72 **Congress was enjoying:** Thomas Jefferson to Barnabas Bidwell, July 11, 1807, reprinted in Ford, ed., *Works of Thomas Jefferson,* vol. X, pp. 455–59.

72 **USS *Chesapeake*:** Meacham, *Art of Power,* pp. 425–27. **Fears of an imminent:** Spencer C. Tucker and Frank T. Reuter, *Injured Honor: The Chesapeake-Leopard Affair,* June 22, 1807 (Annapolis, MD: Naval Institute Press, 1996), p. 125.

72 **Jefferson scrambled:** Tucker and Reuter, *Injured Honor,* p. 125; Meacham, *Art of Power,* p. 425. **no clear sense:** Tucker and Reuter, *Injured Honor,* p. 126. **He was moved by health concerns:** Thomas Jefferson to Barnabas Bidwell, July 11, 1807, reprinted in Ford, ed., *Works of Thomas Jefferson,* vol. X, pp. 455–59.

73 **He wasted no time:** Meacham, *Art of Power,* p. 426; Tucker and Reuter, *Injured Honor,* p. 126. **"sanction" the new contracts:** Thomas Jefferson to Barnabas Bidwell, July 11, 1807, reprinted in Ford, ed., *Works of Thomas Jefferson,* vol. X, pp. 455–59.

73 **governor had sent:** Thomas Jefferson to William H. Cabell, August 11, 1807, reprinted in Ford, ed., *Works of Thomas Jefferson,* vol. X, pp. 440–43.

74 **"any risk of disapprobation . . . details scrupulously":** Thomas Jefferson to William H. Cabell, August 11, 1807, reprinted in ibid., pp. 440–43.

74 **"twistifications":** Thomas Jefferson to James Madison, May 25, 1810, reprinted in J. C. A. Stagg et al., eds., *The Papers of James Madison: Presidential Series* (Charlottesville, VA: University Press of Virginia, 1999), vol. II, pp. 356–57; Andrew Burstein and Nancy Isenberg, *Madison and Jefferson* (New York: Random House Trade Paperbacks, 2010), p. 505. **"meum et tuum . . . details scrupulously":** Thomas Jefferson to William H. Cabell, August 11, 1807, reprinted in Ford, ed., *Works of Thomas Jefferson,* pp. 440–43.

74 **"constitutional power remains":** Ibid.

75 **"affirmative merely . . . would really be verified":** Ibid.

75 **Congress returned to Washington:** Act of Mar. 3, 1809, ch. 28, §1, 2 Stat. 535, 535; Thomas Jefferson, Annual Message to Congress (Oct. 27, 1807), in *Annals of Congress* vol. 17, pp. 14–17 (1807). **He assumed**

Congress: Thomas Jefferson, Informal Memorandum, July 28, 1807, reprinted in Ford, ed., *Works of Thomas Jefferson*, vol. I, p. 415.

75   **measure approving his actions:** Act of March 3, 1809, ch. 28, §1, 2 Stat. 535, 535; Thomas Jefferson, Annual Message to Congress (Oct. 27, 1807), in *Annals of Congress* vol 17, pp. 14–17 (1807).

75   **He believed the impulse for war:** Thomas Jefferson to Albert Gallatin, August 11, 1808, reprinted in Ford, ed., *Works of Thomas Jefferson*, vol. XI, pp. 41–42.

76   **Embargo Act became law:** Ellis, *American Sphinx*, pp. 237–38.

76   **embargo was not popular:** Meacham, *Art of Power*, pp. 432–33. **As Virginia's governor:** Michael Kranish, *Flight from Monticello: Thomas Jefferson at War* (Oxford: Oxford University Press, 2010), pp. 181–83.

76   **dear friend James Madison:** Meacham, *Art of Power*, pp. 433–34.

76   **near constant stream of admirers:** Ibid., pp. 451–52; 463–65; Ellis, *American Sphinx*, pp. 232–33.

76   **pleasant as this new life was:** Meacham, *Art of Power*, pp. 452–55. **One notable intrusion:** John Colvin to Thomas Jefferson, September 14, 1810, reprinted in Looney, ed., *Papers of Thomas Jefferson*, vol. III, pp. 78–79.

77   **author of the letter:** John Colvin to Thomas Jefferson, September 14, 1810, reprinted in ibid., pp. 78–79. **Marylander of modest means:** John Colvin to Thomas Jefferson, December 21, 1814, reprinted in ibid., *Papers of Thomas Jefferson*, vol. VIII, p. 151. **"his leisure hours":** John Colvin to Thomas Jefferson, September 14, 1810, reprinted in ibid., vol. III, p. 78; Jeremy D. Bailey, *Thomas Jefferson and Executive Power* (Cambridge, MA: Cambridge University Press, 2007), p. 252 n.100.

77   **convince President Madison:** Linklater, *Artist in Treason*, pp. 290–92; Robert Allen Rutland, *James Madison: Founding Father* (Columbia, Curators of the University of Missouri First University of Missouri Press, 1997), pp. 220–21. **Wilkinson especially wanted the book:** John Colvin to Thomas Jefferson, September 14, 1810, reprinted in Looney, ed., *Papers of Thomas Jefferson*, vol. III, pp. 78–79; Jeremy David Bailey, "Executive Prerogative and the 'Good Officer' in Thomas Jefferson's Letter to John B. Colvin," *Presidential Studies Quarterly*, vol. XXXIV, pp. 734–35.

77   **Colvin agreed:** John Colvin to Thomas Jefferson, September 14, 1810, reprinted in Looney, *Papers of Thomas Jefferson*, vol. III, pp. 78–79;

Bailey, "Executive Prerogative," pp. 734–35. **Colvin was hopeful:** Ibid., p. 734.

77 **"Character of republican . . . misstated or mistaken":** John Colvin to Thomas Jefferson, September 14, 1810, reprinted in Looney, ed., *Papers of Thomas Jefferson*, vol. III, p. 78.

78 **"neither man nor woman . . . treason such a period":** John Colvin to Thomas Jefferson, September 14, 1810, reprinted in Looney, ed., *Papers of Thomas Jefferson*, vol. III, pp. 78–79.

78 **"good officer":** Thomas Jefferson to John Colvin, September 20, 1810, reprinted in Ford, *The Works of Thomas Jefferson*, vol. XII, pp. 146–50.

78 **"*salus populi* . . . written law":** Thomas Jefferson to John Colvin, September 20, 1810, reprinted in ibid., pp. 146–50.

79 **"against the law":** Thomas Jefferson to John Colvin, September 20, 1810, reprinted in ibid., pp. 146–50.

79 **He offered his reply:** Ibid.

79 **portions of the book:** General James Wilkinson, *Memoirs of My Own Times* (Philadelphia: Abraham Small, 1816); John Colvin to Thomas Jefferson, September 14, 1810, reprinted in Looney, ed., *Papers of Thomas Jefferson*, vol. III, p. 78; Bailey, *Jefferson and Executive Power*, p. 252 n.100. **Only Colvin and President Madison's wife:** John Colvin to Thomas Jefferson, February 4, 1811, reprinted in Looney, ed., *Papers of Thomas Jefferson*, vol. III, p. 359–60.

79 **slave-owning author:** Charles Burleigh Galbreath, *Thomas Jefferson's Views on Slavery* (Columbus: Library of Congress, 1925), p. 201.

80 **In time:** Bailey, *Jefferson and Executive Power*, p. 252 n.100.

80 **"entire direction of war":** Alexander Hamilton, Propositions for a Constitution of Government, June 18, 1787, reprinted in Henry Cabot Lodge, ed., *The Works of Alexander Hamilton* (New York: G. P. Putnam's Son's, 1904), vol. I, p. 348.

Chapter 5
≡ *The Man on Horseback*

83 **epigraph:** Alexander J. Dallas to Andrew Jackson, July 1, 1815, reprinted in John Spencer Bassett, ed., *Correspondence of Andrew Jackson* (Washington, D.C.: Carnegie Institution, 1927), vol. II, pp. 211–13.

83 **Small of stature, often sick:** Hugh Howard, *Mr. and Mrs. Madison's War* (New York: Bloomsbury Press, 2012), pp. 28, 63–65; Andrew Burstein and Nancy Isenberg, *Madison and Jefferson* (New York: Random House Trade Paperbacks, 2010), pp. 14–15, 470. **"little Jim":** Howard, *Mr. and Mrs. Madison's War*, pp. 143–44.

85 **nation needed to prove itself:** A.J. Langguth, *Union 1812: The Americans Who Fought the Second War of Independence* (New York: Simon & Schuster, 2006), pp. 79–80; Walter R. Borneman, *1812: The War that Forged a Nation* (New York: Harper Perennial, 2005), pp. 49–50.

85 **war message to Congress:** reprinted in William S. Dudley, ed., *The Naval War of 1812: A Documentary History* (Washington, D.C.: Naval Historical Center, 1985), vol. I, p. 73. **The clerk then read:** Borneman, *War that Forged a Nation*, pp. 49–50.

85 **"Whether the United States shall continue passive":** President James Madison to Congress, June 1, 1812, reprinted in Dudley, *Naval War of 1812*, vol. I, p. 80.

86 **"stamped by a unanimity":** see Gaillard Hunt, ed., *The Writings of James Madison* (New York: G. P. Putnam's Sons, 1908), vol. VIII, p. 83. **bitterly divided vote:** Anthony S. Pitch, *The Burning of Washington* (Annapolis, MD: Naval Institute Press, 1998), p. 16; Borneman, *War that Forged a Nation*, pp. 49–51. **jointly approved declaration:** An Act Declaring War Between the United Kingdom of Great Britain and Ireland and the Dependencies Thereof and the United States of America and Their Territories, June 18, 1812, United States Statutes at Large, vol. II, p. 755.

86 **News of the decision eventually seeped:** Robert Allen Rutland, *The Presidency of James Madison* (Lawrence, KS: University Press of Kansas, 1990), pp. 102–03.

86 **"ghostly pale":** David S. Heidler and Jeanne T. Heidler, *Henry Clay: The Essential American* (New York: Random House, 2010), p. 98; Borneman, *War that Forged a Nation*, p. 51; Rutland, *Presidency of James Madison*, pp. 102–03. **"Mr. Madison's War":** John Lowell, "Mr. Madison's War," *Evening Post* (July 31–August 10, 1812); Rutland, *Presidency of James Madison*, p. 129; Irving Brant, *James Madison: Commander in Chief*, 1812–1836 (New York: The Bobbs-Merrill Company, Inc., 1961), p. 31; Howard, *Mr. and Mrs. Madison's War*, p. 45.

86 **set things in motion:** Pitch, *Burning of Washington*, pp. 13–16; Rutland, *Presidency of James Madison*, pp. 95–97; Burstein and Isenberg, *Madison and Jefferson*, pp. 499–503.

87 **visiting all the war departments:** Brant, *Commander in Chief*, p. 22. English representative approached Madison: Ibid., pp. 33–34.

87 **Thanks to Jefferson's successful efforts:** Borneman, *War that Forged a Nation*, pp. 45–46. "With a view to enable": James Madison to Thomas Jefferson, February 7, 1812, reprinted in J. C. A. Stagg et al., eds., *The Papers of James Madison: Presidential Series* (Charlottesville, VA: University Press of Virginia, 1999), vol. IV, pp. 168–69.

87 **"I have much doubted":** Thomas Jefferson to James Madison, February 19, 1812, reprinted in Stagg, eds., *Papers of James Madison*, vol. IV, pp. 195–96.

88 **"mixture of good & bad":** James Madison to Thomas Jefferson, February 7, 1812, reprinted in Stagg, eds., *Papers of James Madison*, vol. IV, pp. 168–69.

88 **nation was bitterly divided:** Borneman, *The War that Forged a Nation*, pp. 48–49; Rutland, *Presidency of James Madison*, pp. 102–07, 126–32; Brant, *Commander in Chief*, pp. 13–32; Burstein and Isenberg, *Madison and Jefferson*, pp. 507–11. former president had suggested: Thomas Jefferson to James Madison, June 29, 1812, reprinted in Stagg, eds., *Papers of James Madison*, vol. IV, p. 519; Burstein and Isenberg, *Madison and Jefferson*, pp. 511–12. Madison made clear: Brant, *Commander in Chief*, p. 24; Burstein and Isenberg, *Madison and Jefferson*, p. 512.

89 **made that clear from the bench:** *Brown v. United States*, 12 U.S. (8 Cranch) 110 (1814).

89 **The case concerned:** *Brown v. United States*, 12 U.S. (8 Cranch) 110 (1814).

89 **Jefferson had begged:** Thomas Jefferson to James Madison, October 15, 1810, reprinted in Stagg, eds., *The Papers of James Madison: Presidential Series* (Charlottesville, VA: University Press of Virginia, 1999), vol. II, pp. 580–81; Burstein and Isenberg, *Madison and Jefferson*, p. 505. Story's dissenting opinion: *Brown v. United States*, 12 U.S. (8 Cranch) 110, 129 (1814) (Story, J. dissenting).

90 **situation concerned Elijah Clark:** "Case of Clark the Spy," *The Military Monitor and American Register* (Feb. 1, 1813), pp. 121–22; Jan Ellen

Lewis, "Defining the Nation: 1790 to 1898," in Daniel Farber, ed., *Security v. Liberty: Conflicts between Civil Liberties and National Security in American History*, Daniel Farber, ed. (New York: Russell Sage Foundation, 2008), p. 134; Brant, *Commander in Chief*, p. 233; *The Documentary History of the Campaign Upon the Niagara Frontier in the Year 1812* (E. Cruikshank, ed.), pp. 294–95. **"hung by the neck":** Ingrid Brunk Wuerth, "The President's Power to Detain 'Enemy Combatants': Modern Lessons from Mr. Madison's Forgotten War," *Northwestern Law Review*, vol. 98 (2004), pp. 1583–85.

90   **"citizens of or owing":** Articles of War, reprinted in Isaac Maltby, *A Treatise on Courts Martial and Military Law* (Boston: Thomas B. Wait & Co., 1813), p. 35. **Clark *was* an American:** "Case of Clark the Spy," pp. 121–22; Wuerth, "President's Power to Detain," pp. 1583–85; Lewis, "Defining the Nation," p. 134; Brant, *Commander in Chief*, p. 233.

92   **spot a smallish figure:** Howard, *Mr. and Mrs. Madison's War*, pp. 194, 210–11; Borneman, *War that Forged a Nation*, pp. 228–29; Brant, *Commander in Chief*, p. 308.

92   **Madison found himself:** Donald Dewey & Barbara Bennett Peterson, *James Madison: Defender of the American Republic* (New York: Nova Science Publishers, 2011), pp. 189–90; Howard, *Mr. and Mrs. Madison's War*, pp. 194, 210–11; Borneman, *War that Forged a Nation*, pp. 228–29; Brant, *Commander in Chief*, p. 308.

92   **After meeting with his war council:** Memorandum, August 24, 1814, reprinted in Gaillard Hunt, ed., *The Writings of James Madison* (New York: G. P. Putnam's Sons, 1908), vol. VIII, pp. 295–96; George Campbell to Congress, December 7, 1814, reprinted in *American State Papers: Military Affairs* (Washington, D.C.: Gales and Seaton, 1832), vol. I, pp. 597–99; Borneman, *War that Forged a Nation*, pp. 226–29.

92   **Madison was alarmed by the passivity:** Memorandum, August 24, 1814, reprinted in Hunt, ed., *Writings of James Madison*, vol. VIII, pp. 294–96; George Campbell to Congress, December 7, 1814, reprinted in *American State Papers*, vol. I, pp. 597–99; Brant, *Commander in Chief*, pp. 298–301.

93   **No president had done so:** Joseph J. Ellis, *His Excellency: George Washington* (New York: Alfred A. Knopf, 2004), pp. 224–26.

93   **"observed to the Secretary of War . . . and returned to it":** Memoran-

dum, August 24, 1814, reprinted in Hunt, ed., *Writings of James Madison*, vol. VIII, p. 297; Borneman, *War that Forged a Nation*, p. 227.

93 **she had famously begun packing:** Howard, *Mr. and Mrs. Madison's War*, pp. 190–95; Borneman, *War that Forged a Nation*, p. 230; Rutland, *The Presidency of James Madison*, p. 164.

94 **arrived at his "palace":** Samuel Eliot Morison, "Our Most Unpopular War," *Proceedings of the Massachusetts Historical Society*, vol. 80, p. 40; Burstein and Isenberg, *Madison and Jefferson*, p. 547.

94 **By the time the president returned:** Borneman, *War that Forged a Nation*, pp. 231–33; Rutland, *Presidency of James Madison*, pp. 163–65; Brant, *Commander in Chief*, p. 310; Howard, *Mr. and Mrs. Madison's War*, pp. 210–11, 214.

94 **forceful and daring:** Dewey and Peterson, *Defender of the American Republic*, pp. 199–200; Howard, *Mr. and Mrs. Madison's War*, pp. 266–71; Borneman, *War that Forged a Nation*, pp. 290–92; Rutland, *Presidency of James Madison*, p. 185–87.

95 **declared martial law:** Jackson's order to D.A. Hall, March 11, 1815, reprinted in Bassett, ed., *Correspondence of Andrew Jackson*, vol. II, pp. 189–90; James Parton, *Life of Andrew Jackson* (Boston: Houghton, Mifflin and Company, 1885), vol. II, pp. 311–313; George M. Dennison, "Martial Law: The Development of a Theory of Emergency Powers 1776–1861," *American Journal of Legal History*, vol. XVIII (1974), pp. 61–62; Brant, *Commander in Chief*, pp. 363, 383; Matthew Warshauer, "The Legacy of the Battle of New Orleans," *A Companion to the Era of Andrew Jackson*, Sean Patrick Adams, ed. (Malden, MA: Wiley-Blackwell, 2013), pp. 85–88.

95 **"surprise . . . from all unmerited reproach":** Alexander J. Dallas to Andrew Jackson, April 12, 1815, reprinted in Bassett, ed., *Correspondence of Andrew Jackson*, vol. II, pp. 203–04; Brant *Commander in Chief*, pp. 383–86.

96 **"President would willingly . . . means of vindication":** Alexander J. Dallas to Andrew Jackson, July 1, 1815, reprinted in Bassett, ed., *Correspondence of Andrew Jackson*, vol. II, pp. 211–13.

96 **Madison would not excuse Jackson:** John Henry Eaton, *The Life of Andrew Jackson* (Philadelphia: Samuel F. Bradford, 1824), p. 419; James Parton, *Life of Andrew Jackson* (Boston: Houghton, Mifflin and Company, 1885), vol. II, p. 319; Dennison, "Martial Law," vol. XVIII, p. 63.

96   **Madison said nothing:** Andrew Jackson to Alexander J. Dallas, May 23, 1815, reprinted in Bassett, ed., *Correspondence of Andrew Jackson*, vol. II, pp. 206–07.

97   **Jackson soon descended on Washington:** Parton, *Life of Andrew Jackson*, vol. II, pp. 334–35; Andrew Jackson to John Coffee, Dec. 4, 1815, reprinted in Harold Moser et al., eds., *The Papers of Andrew Jackson*, (Knoxville: University of Tennessee Press, 1991), vol. III, pp. 394–95. **eager to make his case:** Matthew Warshauer, "The Legacy of the Battle of New Orleans," *A Companion to the Era of Andrew Jackson*, Sean Patrick Adams, ed. (Malden: Wiley-Blackwell, 2013), pp. 86–87.

97   **general felt good after leaving:** Andrew Jackson to John Coffee, Dec. 4, 1815, reprinted in Moser, *Papers of Andrew Jackson*, vol. III, pp. 394–95; Parton, *Life of Andrew Jackson*, vol. II, pp. 334–35. **"a further explanation":** Ried to John Coffee, Nov. 21, 1815, reprinted in Moser, *Papers of Andrew Jackson*, vol. III, pp. 395 n.5.

Chapter 6
≡ *Antebellum*

99   **epigraph:** Mr. Dunham, *Cong. Globe*, 32d Cong., 1st Sess. (1852), p. 517.

99   **"unlimited in every matter . . . prescribed by those acts":** Joseph Story, *Commentaries on the Constitution of the United States* (Boston: Hillard, Gray & Co., 1833), vol. III, pp. 62, 68.

100   **"higher than law . . . against the law":** Thomas Jefferson to John Colvin, September 20, 1810, reprinted in Paul Leicester Ford, ed., *The Works of Thomas Jefferson* (New York and London: G.P. Putnam's Sons, 1904–05), vol. XII, pp. 146–50. **True, this prerogative:** John Locke, *Two Treatises of Government*, Peter Laslett, ed. (Cambridge, UK: Cambridge University Press, 1960), pp. 383–84; David J. Barron and Martin S. Lederman, "The Commander in Chief at the Lowest Ebb—A Constitutional History," *Harvard Law Review*, vol. 121, no. 4 (February 2008), pp. 745–47.

100   **"the obligation of the law":** William Rawle, *A View of the Constitution of the United States of America* (Philadelphia: H.C. Carey & I. Lea, 1829), pp. 153–54.

101   **Each time Jackson seemed about to rise:** Harold Moser et al., eds., Andrew Jackson to Samuel Swartwout, March 25, 1824, reprinted in *The*

Papers of Andrew Jackson, (Knoxville: University of Tennessee Press, 1991), vol. V, p. 90; Matthew Warshauer, "The Legacy of the Battle of New Orleans," *A Companion to the Era of Andrew Jackson*, Sean Patrick Adams, ed. (Malden: Wiley-Blackwell, 2013), p. 90. **of course, he did eventually:** Jon Meacham, *American Lion: Andrew Jackson in the White House* (New York: Random House, 2008), p. 28; Arthur M. Schlesinger, Jr., *The Age of Jackson* (Boston: Little, Brown and Company, 1945), pp. 42–44.

101 **three decades later:** Matthew Warshauer, *Andrew Jackson and the Politics of Martial Law* (Knoxville: University of Tennessee Press, 2006), pp. 170–74.

101 **Whigs fashioned themselves:** Meacham, *American Lion*, pp. 288–89.

102 **Jackson won his recompense:** Warshauer, *Politics of Martial Law*, p. 177.

102 **Congress had declared war:** *Cong. Globe*, 29th Cong., 1st Sess. (1846), pp. 795–805. **Critics claimed:** Abraham Lincoln, Speech of January 12, 1848, *Cong. Globe*, 30th Cong., 1st Sess. (1848), pp. 94–95.

103 **During the hostilities:** *Cong. Globe*, 32d Cong., 1st Sess. (1852), p. 507; David J. Barron and Martin S. Lederman, "The Commander in Chief at the Lowest Ebb—Framing the Problem, Doctrine, and Original Understanding," *Harvard Law Review*, vol. 121 (2008), pp. 991–92; Robert Marshall Utley, *Frontiersmen in Blue: The United States and the Indian, 1848–1864* (Lincoln: University of Nebraska Press, 1981), p. 104 n.34.

103 **"so strange, so novel":** *Cong. Globe*, 32d Cong., 1st Sess. (1852), pp. 507–509, 517–20.

Chapter 7
Confronting Secession

107 **epigraph:** Jeremiah Black, "Opinion of Jeremiah Black to James Buchanan, Power of the President Executing the Laws," Opinion of the Attorney General, (November 20, 1860), vol. 9, p. 516.

107 **Aging, infirm, and hugely overweight:** Wayne Fanebust, *Major General Alexander M. Mccook, USA* (Jefferson, NC: McFarland & Company, Inc., 2013), pp. 32–33. **His "views":** Winfield Scott, "General Scott's Views," *Daily National Intelligencer*, issue 15 (January 18, 1861), p. 113.

107 **Scott sent those views:** George Ticknor Curtis, *Life of James Buchanan: Fifteenth President of the United States* (New York: Harper & Brothers,

1883), vol. II, pp. 297–302, 365–68, 416–17. **Scott even published them:** Scott, "Scott's Views," p. 113.

107 **The president was not pleased:** Curtis, *Life of James Buchanan*, vol. II, pp. 301–02. **former secretary of state and member of Congress:** Jean Baker, *James Buchanan* (New York: Henry Holt and Company, 2004), p. 9. **He was now fond of:** Ibid., pp. 47; Adam Goodheart, *1861: The Civil War Awakening* (New York: Alfred A. Knopf, 2011), pp. 78–79. **called him "the Old Squire":** William Norwood Brigance, *Jeremiah Sullivan Black: A Defender of the Constitution and the Ten Commandments* (Philadelphia: University of Pennsylvania Press, 1934), p. 72.

108 **But whatever breach of protocol:** Scott, "Scott's Views," p. 113; Brigance, *Jeremiah Sullivan Black*, p. 83; Curtis, *Life of James Buchanan*, vol. II, pp. 302–07.

108 **questions would be as difficult as any president:** Baker, *James Buchanan*, pp. 108–112; Steven G. Calabresi and Christopher S. Yoo, "The Unitary Executive during the Second Half-Century," *Harvard Journal of Law and Policy*, vol. 26 (Cambridge, MA), pp. 709–710. **Scott's views:** Brigance, *Jeremiah Sullivan Black*, p. 83; Curtis, *Life of James Buchanan*, vol. II, pp. 302–04; Scott, "Scott's Views," p. 113.

108 **President Buchanan realized:** Elbert B. Smith, *The Presidency of James Buchanan* (Lawrence, KS: University Press of Kansas, 1975), pp. 143–44; Curtis, *Life of James Buchanan*, vol. II, pp. 303–05, 334–35.

109 **Buchanan . . . willed himself:** Smith, *Presidency of James Buchanan*, pp. 143–45, 182, 189; Philip Shriver Klein, *President James Buchanan: A Biography* (University Park, PA: The Pennsylvania State University Press, 1964), pp. 363–64; Goodheart, *1861*, p. 82. **He believed Congress had not given:** James Buchanan, *Mr. Buchanan's Administration on the Eve of the Rebellion* (New York: D. Appleton and Company, 1866), pp. 125–27, 129–31. **"the tyrant's plea":** Winfield Scott, *Memoirs of Lieut.-General Scott, LL. D.* (New York: Shelton & Company, Publishers, 1861), p. 267.

109 **architect of President Buchanan's:** Chauncey F. Black, *Essays and Speeches of Jeremiah S. Black: With a Biographical Sketch* (New York: D. Appleton, 1885), p. 8; Francis Newton Thorpe, "Jeremiah S. Black," *Pennsylvania Magazine of History and Biography*, vol. 50, no. 3 (July 1926), pp. 117–133; Phillip Gerald Auchampaugh, *James Buchanan*

and His Cabinet on the Eve of Secession (Lancaster, PA: Private, 1926), pp. 99–101, 139.

109 **Black believed Buchanan:** Joseph Carson, "Book Review: Jeremiah Sullivan Black, by William Norwood Brigance." *University of Pennsylvania Law Review*, vol. 83, issue 4 (February 1935), p. 546. **Buchanan held his protégé:** Black, *Essays and Speeches*, pp. 24–25; Auchampaugh, *Buchanan and His Cabinet*, pp. 99–101, 139; Curtis, *Life of James Buchanan*, vol. II, p. 325; Brigance, *Jeremiah Sullivan Black*, p. 72. **Black's formal schooling:** Black, *Essays and Speeches*, pp. 2–5; Carson, "Book Review," p. 545; Mary Black Clayton, *Reminiscences of Jeremiah Sullivan Black* (Christian Publishing Company, 1887), pp. 17–20. **served as chief justice:** Thorpe, "Jeremiah S. Black," pp. 125–26. **"Judge Black":** Curtis, *Life of James Buchanan*, vol. II, p. 382, 400, 522, 530, 558, 639. **Black's chance to serve on the Court:** Black, *Essays and Speeches*, pp. 24–25.

110 **"Rumpled . . . ungainly":** Brigance: *Jeremiah Sullivan Black*, p. 5. **"intoxicant":** F. Black, *Essays and Speeches*, p. 30. **He also could be:** Brigance, *Jeremiah Sullivan Black*, p. 5; Clayton, *Jeremiah Sullivan Black*, pp. 132–33. **at root a man of principle:** Black, *Essays and Speeches*, pp. 30–31; Auchampaugh, *Buchanan and His Cabinet*, pp. 101–02, 114, 139; Clayton, *Jeremiah Sullivan Black*, pp. 25–26, 139.

110 **In his constitutional thinking:** Curtis, *Life of James Buchanan*, vol. II, pp. 326–28.; Brigance, *Jeremiah Sullivan Black*, p. 78. **abolitionists had developed:** Ibid.; Jeremiah Black, "Mr. Black to Mr. Wilson," *Galaxy*, vol. 11, issue 2 (February 1871), p. 262; Frank Burr, "Judge Black's Answer," *Philadelphia Weekly Press* (September 13, 1883). **"covenant with death":** William Loyd Garrison "New England A.S. Convention," reported by I. M. W. Harington, in *The Liberator* (Boston: June 15, 1855). **Arguments that placed the need:** Curtis, *Life of James Buchanan*, vol. II, pp. 326–28; Brigance, *Jeremiah Sullivan Black*, p. 78.

110 **"absolute despotism":** Jeremiah Black, "Senator Wilson and Edwin M. Stanton," *Galaxy*, vol. 9, issue 6 (June 1870), p. 817. **he was hardly reluctant:** Black, "Mr. Black to Mr. Wilson," pp. 265–67; Burr, "Judge Black's Answer."

111 **dispute concerned:** Russell F. Weigley, *Quartermaster General of the Union Army* (New York: Columbia University Press, 1959), pp. 61–63, 77–78; Sherrod E. East, "The Banishment of Captain Meigs," *Records of*

the Columbia Historical Society (1940), pp. 99–100. **But Meigs's combination:** Ibid., pp. 101–05; Auchampaugh, *Buchanan and His Cabinet*, p. 92; Weigley, *Quartermaster General*, pp. 79–112, 115, 129; William C. Dickinson, Dean A. Herrin, and Donald R. Kennon, eds., *Montgomery C. Meigs and the Building of the Nation's Capitol* (Athens, OH: Ohio University Press, 2001), p. 174.

111 **With Floyd trying to strip:** Weigley, *Quartermaster General*, pp. 102–04; Dickinson et al., *Montgomery C. Meigs*, p. 177, East, "Banishment of Captain Meigs," pp. 99–108; Weigley, *Quartermaster General*, pp. 102–04; Brigance, *Jeremiah Sullivan Black*, pp. 69–70; Harold K. Skramstad, "The Engineer as Architect in Washington: The Contribution of Montgomery Meigs," *Records of the Columbia Historical Society* (1970), pp. 268–71, 276. **president could give notice:** Weigley, *Quartermaster General*, p. 104; East, "Banishment of Captain Meigs," pp. 129–31.

111 **Signaling his intention to act:** Weigley, *Quartermaster General*, p. 104; East, "Banishment of Captain Meigs," pp. 99–100, 106–08. **"might upon the same principle":** James Buchanan, "Special Message to the House of Representatives: June 25, 1860," The American Presidency Project, available at: http://www.presidency.ucsb.edu/ws/index.php?pid=68444.

112 **Floyd ordered Meigs removed:** "Memorial of Captain Meigs," *Opinion of the Attorney General* (1860) vol. 9, pp. 462–71; Weigley, *Quartermaster General*, pp. 104–12. **furious Buchanan:** East, "Banishment of Captain Meigs," pp. 127–31; "Memorial of Captain Meigs," pp. 468–69.

112 **instructions pointedly provided:** William C. Dickinson et al., *Montgomery C. Meigs*, pp. 177–79; East, "Banishment of Captain Meigs," pp. 131–36; "Memorial of Captain Meigs," pp. 462–71.

113 **By the late fall:** Buchanan, *Buchanan's Administration*, pp. 99–101; Curtis, *Life of James Buchanan*, vol. II, p. 313, 325, 342.

114 **at best, there were only vague:** "An Act to Provide for Calling Forth the Militia to Execute the Laws of the Union, Suppress Insurrections, and Repel Invasion; and to Repeal the Act now in Force for Those Purposes" (February 28, 1795), 1 Stat. 424; "An Act Authorizing the Employment of the Land and Naval Forces in Cases of Insurrections" (March 3, 1807), 2 Stat. 443; Buchanan, *Buchanan's Administration*, pp. 125–126; Smith, *Presidency of James Buchanan*, pp. 147.

114 **Though jealous of its right to declare war:** "An Act to Provide for

Calling Forth the Militia to Execute the Laws of the Union, Suppress Insurrections, and Repel Invasion; and to Repeal the Act now in Force for Those Purposes" (February 28, 1795), 1 Stat. 424; "An Act Authorizing the Employment of the Land and Naval Forces in Cases of Insurrections" (March 3, 1807), 2 Stat. 443.

115 **hazards on all sides:** Buchanan, *Buchanan's Administration*, pp. 128–31.

115 **Buchanan was conflicted:** Auchampaugh, *Buchanan and His Cabinet*, pp. 30–31, 146. **Buchanan was so certain:** Buchanan, *Buchanan's Administration*, p. 48; James Buchanan, "Inaugural Address" (March 4, 1857), http://www.presidency.ucsb.edu/ws/?pid=25817.

116 **They had even challenged:** Buchanan, *Buchanan's Administration*, pp. 65–69.

116 **biases caused the president:** Auchampaugh, *James Buchanan and His Cabinet*, pp. 14–15; Buchanan, *Buchanan's Administration*, pp. 62–65. **to Buchanan and those who thought like him:** Scott, *Memoirs*, vol. II, pp. 609–11; Auchampaugh, *Buchanan and His Cabinet*, pp. 62–63.

117 **Buchanan's thought processes:** Chester G. Hearn, *Six Years of Hell: Harper's Ferry During the Civil War* (Baton Rouge, LA: LSU Press, 1999), pp. 17, 22, 29–40; Curtis, *Life of James Buchanan*, vol. II, pp. 322–23, 554.

117 **decision to use military:** Daniel A. Farber, *Lincoln's Constitution* (New York: Harper & Brothers, 1883), pp. 75–76; Eric Foner, *Free Soil, Free Labor, Free Men: The Ideology of the Republican Party Before the Civil War* (New York: Oxford University Press, 1995), p. 131, 177; Douglas R. Egerton, *Year of Meteors: Stephen Douglas, Abraham Lincoln, and the Election that Brought on the Civil War* (New York: Bloomsbury Press, 2010), pp. 225–26.

117 **That November, on the day after:** Bruce Catton, *The Coming Fury* (Garden City, NY: Doubleday & Company, 1961), pp. 123–24. **president wanted to know:** Ibid., pp. 123–25; Curtis, *Life of James Buchanan*, vol. II, pp. 315–19.

118 **Black quickly . . . "no":** Burr, "Judge Black's Answer"; Catton, *Coming Fury*, pp. 125–26; Curtis, *Life of James Buchanan*, vol. II, pp. 319–24. **union was . . . "perpetual":** Burr, "Judge Black's Answer"; Smith, *Presidency of James Buchanan*, p. 146; Catton, *Coming Fury*, pp. 125–26; Buchanan, *Buchanan's Administration*, p. 122; Curtis, *Life of James Buchanan*, vol. II, pp. 319–24.

118   cabinet meeting on November 9: Brigance, *Jeremiah Sullivan Black*, pp. 82–83; Catton, *Coming Fury*, pp. 123–25, 128; Auchampaugh, *James Buchanan and His Cabinet*, pp. 130–32, 146. compromise also contemplated: Curtis, *Life of James Buchanan*, vol. II, pp. 308–09, 359, 412.

118   Buchanan clung: Catton, *Coming Fury*, pp. 123–28; Brigance, *Jeremiah Sullivan Black*, pp. 82–83; Scott, "Scott's Views," p. 113; Weigley, *Quartermaster General*, p. 125. reinforcements should be sent: Brigance, *Jeremiah Sullivan Black*, pp. 75, 82–83; Catton, *Coming Fury*, p. 124; Curtis, *Life of James Buchanan*, vol. II, p. 385; H. Jefferson Powell, *The Constitution and the Attorneys General* (Durham, NC: Carolina Academic Press, 1999), p. 167; Auchampaugh, *Buchanan and His Cabinet*, pp. 132–34.

119   days that followed: Auchampaugh, *Buchanan and His Cabinet*, pp. 132–34; Burr, "Judge Black's Answer." "annoyed": Henry Wilson, "Jeremiah S. Black and Edwin M. Stanton," *Atlantic Monthly*, vol. 26, issue 157 (October 1870), pp. 471–73.

119   Black met with the president: James Buchanan to Jeremiah Black, Requesting Attorney General's Opinion (November 17, 1860), in Curtis, *Life of James Buchanan*, vol. II, p. 319. Black wrote them out: Ibid., pp. 319–24; Black, "Opinion of Jeremiah Black," pp. 516. He even asked Buchanan: Brigance, *Jeremiah Sullivan Black*, p. 84. He also wanted to be clear: Burr, "Judge Black's Answer"; Black, "Mr. Black to Mr. Wilson," pp. 264–65; Auchampaugh, *Buchanan and His Cabinet*, pp. 134–35.

119   legal questions at last in hand: Curtis, *Life of James Buchanan*, vol. II, pp. 319–24; Auchampaugh, *James Buchanan and His Cabinet*, pp. 134–35.

119   "is to be used only in the manner": Black, "Opinion of Jeremiah Black," vol. 9, p. 516; Curtis, *Life of James Buchanan*, vol. II, pp. 319–24; Auchampaugh, *James Buchanan and His Cabinet*, pp. 134–35; Brigance, *Jeremiah Sullivan Black*, p. 78. two older statutes: "An Act to Provide for Calling Forth the Militia to Execute the Laws of the Union, Suppress Insurrections, and Repel Invasion; and to Repeal the Act now in Force for Those Purposes" (February 28, 1795), 1 Stat. 424; "An Act Authorizing the Employment of the Land and Naval Forces in Cases of Insurrections" (March 3, 1807), 2 Stat. 443; Black, "Opinion of Jeremiah Black," vol. 9, p. 516; Burr, "Judge Black's Answer"; Curtis, *Life of James Buchanan*, vol. II, p. 322.

119   Black then explained: Black, "Opinion of Jeremiah Black," vol. 9, p. 516;

Curtis, *Life of James Buchanan*, pp. 319–24; Powell, *Constitution and the Attorneys General*, p. 167; Burr, "Judge Black's Answer"; Black, "Mr. Black to Mr. Wilson," pp. 264–66.

120 **Customs duties should be collected:** Black, "Opinion of Jeremiah Black," vol. 9, p. 516; Curtis, *Life of James Buchanan*, vol. II, pp. 319–24. **"coerced":** "Opinion of Jeremiah Black," vol. 9, p. 516; Burr, "Judge Black's Answer"; Black, "Mr. Black to Mr. Wilson," pp. 264–66.

120 **Buchanan, thanks to Black:** Black, "Opinion of Jeremiah Black," vol. 9, p. 516; "An Act to Provide for Calling Forth the Militia to Execute the Laws of the Union, Suppress Insurrections, and Repel Invasion; and to Repeal the Act now in Force for Those Purposes" (February 28, 1795), 1 Stat. 424; "An Act Authorizing the Employment of the Land and Naval Forces in Cases of Insurrections" (March 3, 1807), 2 Stat. 443; Curtis, *Life of James Buchanan*, vol. II, pp. 319–24. **Once a state seceded:** Ibid., p. 323.

120 **criticism of Black's opinion:** Wilson, "Black and Stanton," p. 468; Black, "Mr. Black to Mr. Wilson," pp. 259, 264–65; Curtis, *Life of James Buchanan*, vol. II, pp. 325–29; Brigance, *Jeremiah Sullivan Black*, pp. 84–90. **"It is the duty of the president":** Walter Stahr, *Seward: Lincoln's Indispensable Man* (New York: Simon & Schuster Paperbacks, 2012), p. 211. **basic, mocking characterization:** Brigance, *Jeremiah Sullivan Black*, pp. 84–90.

121 **"once seemed . . . that the world ever saw":** Auchampaugh, *Buchanan and His Cabinet*, p. 109.

121 **Even still, decades later:** Burr, "Judge Black's Answer."

121 **nothing in his legal analysis:** Burr, "Judge Black's Answer"; Black, "Mr. Black to Mr. Wilson," p. 264.

121 **But, on reflection:** Burr, "Judge Black's Answer."

121 **Buchanan had asked Black a key question:** Auchampaugh, *Buchanan and His Cabinet*, pp. 101–02; Burr, "Judge Black's Answer"; Black, "Mr. Black to Mr. Wilson," p. 264.

122 **might also have avoided the trouble:** Auchampaugh, *Buchanan and His Cabinet*, pp. 75, 138; Brigance, *Jeremiah Sullivan Black*, pp. 86, 99–102; Buchanan, *Buchanan's Administration*, p. 129; Curtis, *Life of James Buchanan*, vol. II, pp. 381–82. **"have stated conclusions":** Burr, "Judge Black's Answer."

122 **By the time Black:** Brigance, *Jeremiah Sullivan Black*, pp. 86–87; Curtis,

Life of James Buchanan, vol. II, pp. 333, 399; Auchampaugh, *Buchanan and His Cabinet*, pp. 137–41; Buchanan, *Buchanan's Administration*, p. 109. **Black was, for many:** Burr, "Judge Black's Answer"; Wilson, "Black and Stanton," pp. 463–75.

123 **December drew to a close:** Gaillard Hunt, "Narrative and Letter of William Henry Trescot, Concerning the Negotiations Between South Carolina and President Buchanan in December, 1860," *American Historical Review*, vol. 13, no. 3 (April 1908), p. 533; Brigance, *Jeremiah Sullivan Black*, p. 78.

123 **crucial test came near Christmas:** Brigance, *Jeremiah Sullivan Black*, p. 94; Auchampaugh, *Buchanan and His Cabinet*, pp. 75, 154–55; Smith, *Presidency of James Buchanan*, p. 143, 176. **Anderson was certain:** Smith, *Presidency of James Buchanan*, p. 169; Curtis, *Life of James Buchanan*, vol. II, pp. 358, 366; Smith, *Presidency of James Buchanan*, pp. 13–15; Brigance, *Jeremiah Sullivan Black*, p. 94.

123 **For Black, the notion:** Brigance, *Jeremiah Sullivan Black*, pp. 98–101. **In Black's view, therefore:** Smith, *Presidency of James Buchanan*, p. 177; Black, "Opinion of Jeremiah Black," vol. 9, p. 516.

124 **under cover of night:** Smith, *Presidency of James Buchanan*, pp. 178–81; Goodheart, *1861*, pp. 13–15; David Detzer, *Allegiance* (New York: Harcourt, Inc., 2001), p. 113; Hunt, "Narrative and Letter," pp. 545–50. **president was horrified:** Smith, *Presidency of James Buchanan*, pp. 179–81; Auchampaugh, *Buchanan and His Cabinet*, pp. 96–97; Goodheart, *1861*, pp. 13–15, 136–37; Detzer, *Allegiance*, pp. 77–78, 137–48; Brigance, *Jeremiah Sullivan Black*, pp. 94–95.

124 **cabinet meeting that followed:** Smith, *Presidency of James Buchanan*, pp. 179–80; Auchampaugh, *Buchanan and His Cabinet*, pp. 96–98; Black, *Essays and Speeches*, p. 12.

124 **"whenever you have tangible evidence":** Curtis, *Life of James Buchanan*, vol. II, p. 376. **"the last extremity":** Buchanan, *Buchanan's Administration*, pp. 165–67; Curtis, *Life of James Buchanan*, vol. II, p. 376; Brigance, *Jeremiah Sullivan Black*, pp. 94–96. **"discretion . . . hold the possession":** George Congdon Gorham, *Life and Public Services of Edwin M. Stanton* (Boston and New York: Houghton, Mifflin and Company, 1899), vol. 1, pp. 131–33. **"Whether the president intended":** Burr, "Judge Black's Answer."

125 **When the president read:** Brigance, *Jeremiah Sullivan Black,* pp. 94–96; Smith, *Presidency of James Buchanan,* pp. 179–80; Auchampaugh, *Buchanan and His Cabinet,* pp. 96–98; Black, *Essays and Speeches,* p. 13.

125 **"see how we . . . general breaking up":** Burr, "Judge Black's Answer"; Auchampaugh, *Buchanan and His Cabinet,* p. 120. **Black resolved:** Burr, "Judge Black's Answer"; *The Philadelphia Weekly Press* (September 13, 1883); Gorham, *Life and Public Services,* vol. 1, pp. 146–47.

125 **rumor of Black's impending exit:** Auchampaugh, *Buchanan and His Cabinet,* pp. 110–11; Burr, "Judge Black's Answer"; Gorham, *Life and Public Services,* vol. 1, pp. 146–47; Smith, *Presidency of James Buchanan,* pp. 180–82; Curtis, *Life of James Buchanan,* vol. II, pp. 381–83.

126 **Black was spared making a decision:** Gorham, *Life and Public Services,* vol. 1, pp. 146–47; Auchampaugh, *Buchanan and His Cabinet,* pp. 110–11; Burr, "Judge Black's Answer"; Smith, *Presidency of James Buchanan,* pp. 180–82.

126 **Confronted with Black's critique:** Auchampaugh, *Buchanan and His Cabinet,* pp. 110–11; Burr, "Judge Black's Answer"; Smith, *Presidency of James Buchanan,* pp. 180–81.

126 **Days after the critical cabinet meeting:** Gorham, *Life and Public Services,* vol. 1, p. 145; Curtis, *Life of James Buchanan,* vol. II, p. 410. **"manly courage":** C.J. Wood, *Reminiscences of the War: Biography and Personal Sketches of all the Commanding Officers in the Union Army* (1863), p. 155.

126 **"thunderbolt" in the Senate:** Mark J. Stegmaier, ed., *Henry Adams in the Secession Crisis: Dispatches to the Boston Daily* (Baton Rouge, LA: LSU Press, 2012), p. 81. **As a backup, Buchanan:** Buchanan, *Buchanan's Administration,* p. 159; Curtis, *Life of James Buchanan,* vol. II, pp. 482–83; Auchampaugh, *Buchanan and His Cabinet,* p. 175. **That way, without usurping:** "An Act Further to Provide for the Collection of Duties on Imports" (1833), 4 Stat. 632. "An Act Authorizing the Employment of Land and Naval Forces in Cases of Insurrections" (March 3, 1807), 2 Stat. 443; **just the approach Black favored:** Black, "Opinion of Jeremiah Black," vol. 9, p. 516.

127 **neither the nomination:** Buchanan, *Buchanan's Administration,* pp. 159–60; Representative Bingham, Proposed Bill H.R. 910 (December 31, 1860), 36th Congress, 2nd Session; Senator Collamer, Proposed Bill S. 545, "In relation to the Collection of Duties on Imports" (January

23, 1861), 36th Congress, 2nd Session; Senator Collamer, Proposed Bill S. 545 (amended by Senator Fessenden), "In relation to the Collection of Duties on Imports" (February 4, 1861), 36th Congress, 2nd Session; Senator Collamer, Proposed Bill S. 545 (amended by Senator Hemphill), "In relation to the Collection of Duties on Imports" (February 6, 1861), 36th Congress, 2nd Session; Senator Collamer, Proposed Bill S. 545 (amended by Senator Collamer), "In relation to the Collection of Duties on Imports" (February 6, 1861), 36th Congress, 2nd Session. **Nor did a bill to give:** Representative Reynolds, Proposed Bill H.R. 968 (January 30, 1861), 36th Congress, 2nd Session; Representative Stanton, Proposed Bill H.R. 1003 (February 18, 1861), 36th Congress, 2nd Session.

127 **Buchanan continued to temporize:** Stegmaier, *Adams in the Secession Crisis*, p. 89; Baker, *James Buchanan*, p. 115; Curtis, *Life of James Buchanan*, vol. II, pp. 374–75; Buchanan, *Buchanan's Administration*, p. 189. **Meigs was even called back:** Weigley, *Quartermaster General*, pp. 129–30. **new war secretary told Meigs:** Weigley, *Quartermaster General*, pp. 127–29; Baker, *James Buchanan*, p. 115. **letters had thus helped to unmask:** Weigley, *Quartermaster General*, pp. 120–21; David W. Miller, *Second Only to Grant* (Shippensburg, PA: White Mane Books, 2000), pp. 76–78.

127 **Back in Washington:** Weigley, *Quartermaster General*, pp. 129–30. **He was worn to the bone:** Baker, *James Buchanan*, p. 130. **"pity":** Weigley, *Quartermaster General*, pp. 129–30; Baker, *James Buchanan*, p. 130.

128 **Black was faring:** Auchampaugh, *Buchanan and His Cabinet*, pp. 112–13. **His face was now sad:** Ibid., pp. 112–13; Clayton, *Jeremiah Sullivan Black*, pp. 114–15; Black, *Essays and Speeches*, pp. 24–25. **Buchanan guessed that his own burning:** Clayton, *Jeremiah Sullivan Black*, pp. 116–17; Black, *Essays and Speeches*, pp. 24–25.

128 **Still, the two men:** Auchampaugh, *Buchanan and His Cabinet*, pp. 108–09, 230; Burr, "Judge Black's Answer"; Black, "Mr. Black to Mr. Wilson," 257–76. **Virginia remained in the union:** Curtis, *Life of James Buchanan*, vol. II, pp. 306, 312.

128 **"Urgent and dangerous . . . to be endangered":** Buchanan, *Buchanan's Administration*, p. 161.

128 **"On the contrary . . . legislative branch of the Government":** Buchanan, *Buchanan's Administration*, p. 161.

Chapter 8
≡ *The War Comes*

131 **epigraph:** Abraham Lincoln, "Special Session Message" (July 4, 1861) in James D. Richardson, ed., *A Compilation of the Messages and Papers of the Presidents*, vol. VII–VIII, pp. 3221–32.

131 **beautiful April night:** Orville Hickman Browning, 1861, reprinted in Theodore Calvin Pease, ed., *The Diary of Orville Hickman Browning* (Springfield, IL: 1925–1933), vol. I, pp. 463–64. **"Great Union Meeting":** Henry Asbury, *Reminiscences of Quincy, Illinois: Containing Historical Events, Anecdotes, Matters Concerning Old Settlers and Old Times, Etc.* (Quincy, IL: D. Wilcox & Sons, Printers, 1882), p. 144.

131 **stylish and well-schooled:** Maurice Baxter, "Orville H. Browning: Lincoln's Friend and Critic," *Indiana Magazine of History*, vol. 53 (December 1957), pp. 431–35; David Herbert Donald, *We Are Lincoln Men: Abraham Lincoln and His Friends* (New York: Simon & Schuster, 2007), pp. 103–05, 114. **they had become friends:** Maurice Baxter, "Lincoln's Friend and Critic," pp. 437–38. **recent crisis:** Ibid., pp. 444–46; Donald, *We Are Lincoln Men*, pp. 103, 111–12.

132 **Browning relished:** Abraham Lincoln, *Special Session Message* (July 4, 1861), James D. Richardson, ed., *A Compilation of the Messages and Papers of the Presidents* (New York: Bureau of National Literature, Inc., 1917), vol. VII–VIII, pp. 3221–32; "An Act to Provide for Calling Forth the Militia to Execute the Laws of the Union, Suppress Insurrections, and Repel Invasion; and to Repeal the Act now in Force for Those Purposes" (February 28, 1795), 1 Stat. 424; Donald, *We Are Lincoln Men*, pp. 112–13.

132 **Browning was a good enough lawyer:** Donald, *We Are Lincoln Men*, pp. 113–15. **coercion now the strategy:** Orville Hickman Browning, *1861*, reprinted in Pease, ed., *Diary of Orville Hickman Browning*, vol. I, p. 503; Bruce Tap, *Over Lincoln's Shoulder: The Committee on the Conduct of War* (Lawrence, KS: University Press of Kansas, 1998), pp. 14–16. **Even Republicans were concerned:** *Cong. Globe*, 37th Cong., 1st Sess. (1861) pp. 336–42; O. H. Browning, "The Quincy Herald and the President's Proclamation," *The Quincy Daily Whig Republican* (April 18, 1861), p. 2.

132 **there was another side:** *Cong. Globe*, 37th Cong., 2d Sess. (1862), pp. 501–17.

132 **Browning figured especially prominently:** Donald, *We Are Lincoln Men*, pp. 114–20.

133 **"hard war":** James M. McPherson, *Tried by War* (London: Penguin Books, 2008), pp. 103–05.

133 **Few believed Lincoln needed to wait:** Abraham Lincoln, "Special Session Message," July 4, 1861, available at: http://www.fordham.edu/halsall/mod/1861lincoln-special.asp; McPherson, *Tried by War*, pp. 22–25; "The Thirty-Seventh Congress: Already Elected: States to Elect," *Chicago Tribune* (March 5, 1861); "Congressional Elections," *Vincennes Gazette* (March 23, 1861). **At most, they argued:** "Thirty-Seventh Congress."

133 **As Lincoln's advisors gathered:** Walter Stahr, *Seward: Lincoln's Indispensable Man* (New York: Simon & Schuster Paperbacks, 2012), pp. 260–62. **"not levy armies":** William Henry Seward and Frederick William Seward, *Autobiography: Seward at Washington, as Senator and Secretary of State, A Memoir of His Life, with Selections from His Letters, 1846–1861* (New York: Derby and Miller, 1891), pp. 544, 592.

134 **Despite the legal concerns:** Doris Kearns Goodwin, *Team of Rivals* (New York: Simon & Schuster, 2005), pp. 340–42; Seward, *Autobiography*, p. 544; Stahr, *Seward*, pp. 265–72. **"deliberative body . . . to invite disaster":** Seward, *Autobiography*, p. 544.

134 **president did not disagree:** McPherson, *Tried by War*, pp. 18–20; Lincoln, "Special Session Message," July 4, 1861; Charles W. Ramsdell, "Lincoln and Fort Sumter," *Journal of Southern History*, vol. 3 (August, 1937), pp. 287–88. **president was also picking a date:** Thomas Jefferson, "Seventh Annual Message to Congress," The American Presidency Project (October 27, 1807), available at http://www.presidency.ucsb.edu/ws/index.php?pid=29449; David J. Barron and Martin S. Lederman, "The Commander in Chief at the Lowest Ebb—Framing the Problem, Doctrine, and Original Understanding," *Harvard Law Review*, vol. 121 (2008), pp. 974–75.

134 **In the *Chesapeake* affair:** Jefferson, "Seventh Annual Message to Congress" (October 27, 1807); Barron and Lederman, "Commander in Chief at the Lowest Ebb," pp. 974–76; William C. Banks and Peter

Raven-Hansen, *National Security Law and the Power of the Purse* (New York: Oxford University Press, 1994), pp. 37–39.

134 **"extra-legal" power:** Barron and Lederman, "Commander in Chief at the Lowest Ebb," pp. 974–76. **same could not be said:** Ibid., pp. 976, 1001; *Cong. Globe*, 37th Cong., 2d Sess. (1861), p. 2383; McPherson, *Tried by War*, pp. 14–20.

135 **Lincoln accomplished:** Michael Burlingame and John R. Turner Ettlinger, eds., *Inside Lincoln's White House*, "November 1861" (Southern Illinois University Press, 1999), pp. 32; Goodwin, *Team of Rivals*, pp. 351–52; McPherson, *Tried by War*, pp. 23.

135 **Nearly simultaneously, the president:** Barron and Lederman, "Commander in Chief at the Lowest Ebb," pp. 1001–03; *Cong. Globe*, 37th Cong., 2d Sess. (1862); McPherson, *Tried by War*, p. 24.

135 **less than a week later:** Stahr, *Seward*, pp. 283–84. **"Whoever in later times . . . sentiment or poetry":** Abraham Lincoln to William Seward, April 19, 1861, reprinted in Roy P. Basler, ed., *Collected Works of Abraham Lincoln* (New Brunswick, NJ: Rutgers University Press, 1953), vol. IV, p. 339.

136 **semblance of calm:** Abraham Lincoln, Executive Order to the Commanding General of the Army of the United States, Apr. 27, 1861, reprinted in Richardson, ed., *Papers of the Presidents*, vol. VII, p. 3219; Abraham Lincoln, *The Lieutenant-General Commanding the Armies of the United States*, June 20, 1861, reprinted in ibid., vol. VII, p. 3220; Abraham Lincoln, *The Commanding General, Army of the United States*, July 2, 1861, reprinted in Richardson, ed., *Papers of the Presidents*, vol. IV, p. 3220. **refuse the officers did:** *Ex Parte Merryman*, 17 F. Cas. (C.C.D. Md.) 144 (1861).

136 **Still, Lincoln was not through:** McPherson, *Tried by War*, pp. 30–35; Ron Field, *Lincoln's 90-Day Volunteers 1861: From Fort Sumter to First Bull Run* (Oxford: Osprey Publishing, 2013); D. Reid Ross, *Lincoln's Veteran Volunteers Win the War* (Albany, NY: State University of New York Press, 2008), p. 25.

136 **"put in force . . . all to the scaffold":** Stahr, *Seward*, p. 284.

137 **Lincoln had been very aggressive:** Louis P. Masur, *Lincoln's Hundred Days* (Cambridge, MA: The Belknap Press of Harvard University Press, 2012), p. 21; Adam Goodheart, *1861: The Civil War Awakening*

(New York: Alfred A. Knopf, 2011), pp. 136–50; McPherson, *Tried by War*, pp. 23, 38–41; Field, *90-Day Volunteers*; Ross, *Veteran Volunteers*, pp. 21–37. "violations of the law": Thomas Jefferson to Albert Gallatin, January 4, 1807, reprinted in Paul Leicester Ford, ed., *The Works of Thomas Jefferson* (New York and London: G.P. Putnam's Sons, 1904–05), vol. X, p. 336. "[S]ee if you can fix": Abraham Lincoln to William H. Herndon, February 15, 1848, reprinted in John G. Nicolay and John Hay, eds., *Abraham Lincoln: Complete Works, Comprising His Speeches, State Papers, and Miscellaneous Writings* (New York: The Century Co., 1920), vol. I, p. 111–12; Abraham Lincoln, Speech of January 12, 1848, *Cong. Globe*, 30th Cong., 1st Sess. (January 12, 1848), pp. 94–95.

137   **In late April:** Abraham Lincoln, Executive Order to the Commanding General of the Army of the United States (April 27, 1861), Richardson, ed., *Papers of the Presidents*, vol. VII, p. 3219; Abraham Lincoln, Proclamation (May 10, 1861), ibid., vol. VII, p. 3217–18; Abraham Lincoln, Executive Order to the Commanding General of the Army of the United States (July 2, 1861), ibid., vol. VII, p. 3220; Stahr, *Seward*, p. 221, 240, 286–87. **Lincoln claimed:** Abraham Lincoln to Winfield Scott, April 25, 1861, reprinted in Andrew Delbanco, ed., *The Portable Abraham Lincoln* (New York: Penguin Books, 2009), pp. 237–40; Abraham Lincoln to Winfield Scott (April 25, 1861), in Richardson, ed., *Papers of the Presidents*, vol. VII, pp. 3215–3219.

137   **Only days after the attack:** Edward Bates, Opinion of the Attorney General, July 5, 1861, reprinted in *House Documents*, vol. 156 (U.S. Government Printing Office, 1861), pp. 101–12. **Decades before, Jefferson:** Jefferson, "Seventh Annual Message to Congress" (October 27, 1807); Thomas Jefferson, Informal Memorandum, July 28, 1807, reprinted in Ford, ed., *Works of Thomas Jefferson*, vol. I, p. 415; Banks and Raven-Hansen, *National Security Law*, pp. 37–39. **"emulate General Jackson . . . no":** "The News in Washington; The Excitement at the Capital . . . The President's Proclamation. The Unanimity of the Cabinet," *New York Times* (April 15, 1861), available at http://www.nytimes.com/1861/04/15/news/washington-excitement-capital-dispatches-president-creditability-telegrams.html?smid=pl-share.

138   **Even Lincoln's decision:** Thomas Speed, *The Union Cause in Kentucky, 1860–1865* (New York: G. P. Putnam's Sons, 1907), pp. 88, 94–95;

McPherson, *Tried by War*, p. 23; Lincoln, "Special Session Message," July 4, 1861; Ramsdell, "Lincoln and Fort Sumter," pp. 287–88.

138 **state was Kentucky:** Harold D. Tallant, *Evil Necessity: Slavery and Political Culture in Antebellum Kentucky* (Lexington, KY: University Press of Kentucky, 2003), p. 218; "Judge Robertson on the Crisis," *Louisville Journal* (June 7, 1861). **"whole game":** Abraham Lincoln to Orville Browning, September 22, 1861, reprinted in Basler, ed., *Works of Abraham Lincoln*, vol. IV, p. 531–33.

138 **Lincoln could only:** Horace Greeley, *The American Conflict: A History of the Great Rebellion in the United States of America* (Hartford, CT: O.D. Case & Company, 1864), p. 555; "Thirty-Seventh Congress"; McPherson, *Tried by War*, p. 23; "Judge Robertson on the Crisis." **Those states:** Ibid.; "Congressional Elections," *Vincennes Gazette* (March 23, 1861); "Thirty-Seventh Congress"; Speed, *Union Cause in Kentucky*, pp. 94–95.

139 **As Independence Day approached:** "Congress and the Country," *New York Times* (June 9, 1861), available at: http://www.nytimes .com/1861/06/09/news/congress-and-the-country.htm; "Notes of the Rebellion: Martial Law. Some Points Suggested for the Consideration of Chief Justice Tancy," *New York Times* (June 8, 1861), available at: http://www.nytimes.com/1861/06/08/news/notes-rebellion-martial -law-some-points-suggested-for-consideration-chief.html.

139 **eye firmly fixed:** "Judge Robertson on the Crisis"; Abraham Lincoln to Orville Browning, September 22, 1861, reprinted in Basler, ed., *Works of Abraham Lincoln*, vol. IV, p. 531–33. **governor had set them:** Speed, *Union Cause in Kentucky*, pp. 88, 94–95. **administration's concerted efforts:** Lowell Harrison, *The Civil War in Kentucky* (Lexington, KY: University Press of Kentucky, 2010), pp. 11–12; Lowell Harrison, *Lincoln of Kentucky* (Lexington, KY: University Press of Kentucky, 2000), pp. 143–45.

139 **Meanwhile, Lincoln's men:** Douglas L. Wilson, *Lincoln's Sword: The Presidency and the Power of Words* (New York: Alfred A. Knopf, 2006), pp. 71–104; Goodwin, *Team of Rivals*, p. 366.

140 **message would account:** Wilson, *Lincoln's Sword*, pp. 71–104; Harry V. Jaffa, *A New Birth of Freedom: Abraham Lincoln and the Coming of the Civil War* (Lanham, MD: Rowman & Littlefield, 2000), pp. 357–64. **final days before the session:** Wilson, *Lincoln's Sword*, pp. 101–02.

140 **Among the chosen few:** Ibid., p. 102; Orville Hickman Browning, 1861, reprinted in Pease, ed., *Diary of Orville Hickman Browning,* vol. I, pp. 475–76. **He had been appointed:** Ibid., pp. 475–76; John V. Denson, *A Century of War* (Austria: Ludwig von Mises Institute, 2006), p. 83; Tony Wolk, *Abraham Lincoln: A Novel Life* (Portland, OR: Ooligan Press, 2004), p. 224; Donald, *We Are Lincoln Men,* pp. 113–20. **Browning was a calming:** Ibid., pp. 114–120; Orville Hickman Browning, 1861, reprinted in Pease, ed., *Diary of Orville Hickman Browning,* vol. I, pp. 475–76; Denson, *Century of War,* p. 83; Ramsdell, "Lincoln and Fort Sumter," pp. 286–88. **even called Browning's family:** Orville Hickman Browning, 1861, reprinted in Pease, ed., *Diary of Orville Hickman Browning,* vol. I, p. 530; Donald, *We Are Lincoln Men,* p. 120.

140 **bond between the two men:** Orville Hickman Browning, reprinted in Pease, *Diary of Orville Hickman Browning,* vol. I, pp. 453–56. **When Browning offered suggestions:** Ibid., pp. 455–56; Donald, *We Are Lincoln Men,* pp. 113–20. **now, on the eve:** Orville Hickman Browning, reprinted in Pease, ed., *Diary of Orville Hickman Browning,* vol. I, pp. 475–76; Wilson, *Lincoln's Sword,* p. 102; Donald, *We Are Lincoln Men,* pp. 113–20.

140 **Browning spent most of that day:** Orville Hickman Browning, reprinted in Pease, ed., *Diary of Orville Hickman Browning,* vol. I, pp. 475–76; Denson, *Century of War,* p. 83; Ramsdell, "Lincoln and Fort Sumter," pp. 286–88; p. 117; Donald, *We Are Lincoln Men,* pp. 113–17.

141 **"most admirable history":** Orville Hickman Browning, reprinted in Pease, ed., *Diary of Orville Hickman Browning,* vol. I, p. 475; Donald, *We Are Lincoln Men,* p. 114. **If a disaffected minority:** Abraham Lincoln, Special Session Message (July 4, 1861), reprinted in Richardson, ed., *Papers of the Presidents,* vol. VII–VIII, pp. 3221–32. **same argument:** Orville Hickman Browning, reprinted in Pease, ed., *Diary of Orville Hickman Browning,* vol. I, pp. 462–67; Donald, *We Are Lincoln Men,* pp. 113–14.

141 **Lincoln was also hoping:** Wilson, *Lincoln's Sword,* pp. 78–79, 103. **key section of the message:** Abraham Lincoln, Special Session Message (July 4, 1861), Richardson, ed., *Papers of the Presidents,* vol. VII–VIII, pp. 3221–32.

141 **Lincoln presented himself:** Abraham Lincoln, Special Session Message

(July 4, 1861), Richardson, ed., *Papers of the Presidents*, vol. VII–VIII, pp. 3221–32.

142 **Here, too, Lincoln:** Abraham Lincoln, Special Session Message (July 4, 1861), ibid., vol. VII–VIII, pp. 3221–32. **The Supreme Court:** *Prize Cases*, 67 U.S. (2 Black) 635, 665–74 (1863); Orville Hickman Browning, 1861, reprinted in Pease, *Diary of Orville Hickman Browning*, vol. I, pp. 463–464.

142 **"competency of Congress . . . shape and efficiency":** Abraham Lincoln, Special Session Message (July 4, 1861), Richardson, ed., *Papers of the Presidents*, vol. VII–VIII, pp. 3221–32; Wilson, *Lincoln's Sword*, Knopf, pp. 75–82, 95–101.

142 **"all the laws but one to go unexecuted":** Abraham Lincoln, Special Session Message (July 4, 1861), reprinted in Richardson, ed., *Papers of the Presidents*, vol. VII–VIII, pp. 3221–32. **Lincoln was never fully comfortable:** Wilson, *Lincoln's Sword*, pp. 82–86. **final message even promised:** Abraham Lincoln, Special Session Message (July 4, 1861), reprinted in Richardson, ed., *Papers of the Presidents*, vol. VII–VIII, pp. 3221–32.

143 **"legal sanction":** Abraham Lincoln, Special Session Message (July 4, 1861), Richardson, *Papers of the Presidents*, vol. VII, p. 3227; John Bruce Robertson, "Lincoln and Congress" (Ph.D. diss., University of Wisconsin, 1967), p. 256. **And so, as planned:** *Cong. Globe*, 37th Cong., 1st Sess. (1861), pp. 11, 13; George Clarke Sellery, *Lincoln's Suspension of Habeas Corpus as Viewed by Congress* (Chicago: University of Chicago, 1907), p. 223. **Seward had warned:** Stahr, *Seward*, pp. 280–81.

143 **first few weeks:** *Cong. Globe*, 37th Cong., 1st Sess. (1861), pp. 11–400; Robertson, "Lincoln and Congress," pp. 243–57; Goodwin, *Team of Rivals*, p. 370; Goodheart, *1861*, pp. 364–66. **serious efforts:** Senator Trumbull, "Army Appropriations Bill" (July 15, 1861), 37th Congress, 1st Session, p. 120; Kenneth L. Deutsch and Joseph R. Fornieri, *Lincoln's American Dream: Clashing Political Perspectives* (Potomac Books, Inc., 2005), p. 280.

143 **Others in Congress:** *Cong. Globe*, (1861) 37th Congress, 1st Session, pp. 24–25. **The delays plagued:** Robertson, "Lincoln and Congress," pp. 17–39; *Cong. Globe*, 37th Cong., 1st Sess. (1861), pp. 24–26, 115, 224, 227. **Everything, it seemed:** Robertson, "Lincoln and Congress," pp. 17–39.

143 On July 29: "An Act to Provide for the Suppression of Rebellion Against and Resistance to the Laws of the United States" (July 29, 1861), *Cong. Globe*, 37th Cong., 1st Sess., p. 308. On July 31: "An Act Authorizing the Secretary of War to Reimburse Volunteers for Expenses Incurred in Employing Regimental and Other Bands, and for Other Purposes" (July 31, 1861), *Cong. Globe*, 37th Cong., 1st Sess., p. 336. "approve[,] and in all respects": "An Act to Increase the Pay of the Privates in the Regular Army and in the Volunteers in the Service of the United States, and for other purposes" (August 6, 1861), *Cong. Globe*, 37th Cong., 1st Sess., pp. 450–59.

144 more than a month: *Cong. Globe*, 37th Cong., 1st Sess. (1861), p. 1. In fact, Senator Henry Wilson: "S.1," *Cong. Globe*, 37th Cong., 1st Sess. (1861), p. 2. Even die-hard Republicans: *Cong. Globe*, 37th Cong, 1st Sess. (1861), pp. 452–52, 455–67; Robertson, "Lincoln and Congress," pp. 36–39.

144 bill to ratify: *Cong. Globe*, 37th Cong., 1st Sess. (1861), pp. 167, 275, 336–38, 342, 346, 381. Thaddeus Stevens: *Cong. Globe*, 37th Cong., 1st Sess. (1861), p. 444.

144 While still in Quincy: Orville Hickman Browning, 1861, reprinted in Pease, ed., *Diary of Orville Hickman Browning*, vol. I, pp. 621, 678–79; Robertson, "Lincoln and Congress," p. 62. urging passage of Wilson's ratification bill: *Cong. Globe*, 37th Cong., 1st Sess. (1861), pp. 2, 16, 21, 40–46, 144, 235, 391–93, 451–53; Robertson, "Lincoln and Congress," pp. 40–41.

145 argument made all the more compelling: Goodwin, *Team of Rivals*, p. 371; McPherson, *Tried by War*, pp. 39–40, 51. Making matters worse: Robertson, "Lincoln and Congress," p. 37.

145 Lincoln had come through: Robertson, "Lincoln and Congress," pp. 55–58; *Cong. Globe*, 37th Cong., 2d Sess. (1861), pp. 1–10. watched as the man: Orville Hickman Browning, 1861, reprinted in Pease, ed., *Diary of Orville Hickman Browning*, vol. I, p. 479. "Our Legislation has been hasty . . . when I came here": Ibid., p. 493.

146 "radicals" in Congress: Introduction, Records of the Probate Court in Quincy, Illinois, reprinted in Pease, ed., *Diary of Orville Hickman Browning*, vol. 1, p. 586.

146 "irrepressible conflict": Horace White, *Life of Lyman Trumbull* (Boston:

Houghton Mifflin, 1913), p. 106. **Lincoln had been careful:** Abraham Lincoln, First Inaugural Address (March 4, 1861), available at: http://www.bartleby.com/124/pres31.html; Abraham Lincoln, Special Session Message (July 4, 1861), Richardson, ed., *Papers of the Presidents*, vol. VII–VIII, pp. 3221–32; Robertson, "Lincoln and Congress," pp. 17–18, 89.

146 **bills to make inroads on the evil institution:** Robertson, "Lincoln and Congress," pp. 68–69.

146 **"March at once . . . done with them":** Orville H. Browning to Abraham Lincoln (April 30, 1861), Library of Congress Manuscript Division.

147 **In late May, three slaves:** James Oakes, *Freedom National: The Destruction of Slavery in the United States, 1861–1865* (New York: W. W. Norton & Company, 2012), pp. 95–96; Goodwin, *Team of Rivals*, pp. 368–69. **head of the Army of the Potomac:** Oakes, *Freedom National*, pp. 104, 113, 211–213. **"contraband":** Ibid., p. 104; Goodwin, *Team of Rivals*, pp. 368–369.

147 **"come within your lines":** Simon Cameron to Benjamin Butler, reprinted in Burrus Carnahan, *Act of Justice: Lincoln's Emancipation Proclamation and the Law of War* (University Press of Kentucky, 2007), p. 85; Oakes, *Freedom National*, pp. 91–94.

147 **Congress stepped in:** "Act of August 6, 1861" (August 6, 1861), 12 Stat. 319; *Cong. Globe*, 37th Cong., 2d sess. (1861), pp. 1, 18, 1077, 1136, 2917–21; White, *Life of Lyman Trumbull*, p. 173. **new law just endorsed:** Robertson, "Lincoln and Congress," pp. 63–65.

148 **Butler's background, as a Democrat:** Goodwin, *Team of Rivals*, pp. 368–71. **not all of Lincoln's officers:** White, *Life of Lyman Trumbull*, pp. 169–72; Goodwin, *Team of Rivals*, pp. 390–92.

148 **already declared martial law:** Goodwin, *Team of Rivals*, pp. 390–92. **"all persons who shall . . . hereby declared freemen":** John Frémont, "Proclamation of Gen. Fremont," *New York Times* (August 31, 1861), available at: http://www.nytimes.com/1861/09/01/news/important-from-missouri-proclamation-of-gen-fremont.html.

148 **All the caveats:** Goodwin, *Team of Rivals*, pp. 390–391; White, *Life of Lyman Trumbull*, p. 173. **So, too, was any acknowledgment:** *Cong. Globe*, 37th Cong., 2d Sess. (1861), pp. 1, 18, 1077; Oakes, *Freedom National*, pp. 163–65. "Act of August 6, 1861" (August 6, 1861), 12 Stat. 319.

149 **president was convinced the proclamation:** Robertson, "Lincoln and Congress," pp. 64–65, 76, 99; Goodwin, *Team of Rivals*, pp. 390–91.

149 **Put off by a midnight:** Thomas C. Mackey, *Documentary History of the American Civil War Era* (Knoxville: University of Tennessee Press, 2013), vol. 2, p. 103; Robertson, "Lincoln and Congress," pp. 64–65, 76, 99; Goodwin, *Team of Rivals*, pp. 390–91. **"cheerfully . . . not to transcend":** Abraham Lincoln, "To John C. Fremont" (September 11, 1861), reprinted in *The Collected Works of Abraham Lincoln* (Wildside Press, 2008), vol. IV, pp. 517–18.

149 **president's rebuke:** Oakes, *Freedom National*, pp. 163–65; Robertson, "Lincoln and Congress," pp. 64–65, 76, 99; Goodwin, *Team of Rivals*, pp. 390–91.

149 **moderate by nature:** Orville Hickman Browning, 1861, reprinted in Pease, ed., *Diary of Orville Hickman Browning*, vol. I, pp. 466–67. **Eager for Frémont to succeed:** Orville H. Browning to Abraham Lincoln (September 17, 1861), reprinted in Harlan Hoyt Horner, "Lincoln Rebukes a Senator," *Journal of the Illinois State Historical Society*, vol. 44 (1951), pp. 114–115; **"Frémont's proclamation":** Donald, *We Are Lincoln Men*, p. 126. **Then, six days later:** Orville H. Browning to Abraham Lincoln (September 24, 1861), reprinted in Horner, "Lincoln Rebukes a Senator," p. 115.

150 **"It is true . . . legal provisions":** Orville H. Browning to Abraham Lincoln (September 17, 1861), reprinted in Horner, "Lincoln Rebukes a Senator," vol. 44 (1951), pp. 114–15. **First Confiscation Act:** Oakes, *Freedom National*, pp. 163–65; Horner, "Lincoln Rebukes a Senator," pp. 114–15; Robertson, "Lincoln and Congress," pp. 63–65; "Act of August 6, 1861" (August 6, 1861), 12 Stat. 319.

150 **"astonished":** Abraham Lincoln to Orville H. Browning (September 22, 1861), reprinted in Horner, "Lincoln Rebukes a Senator," pp. 116–18. **Browning had recently but unsuccessfully lobbied:** Ibid., p. 110; David Chambers Mearns, *The Lincoln Papers* (New York: Doubleday, 1948), pp. 531–33.

150 **"purely political . . . of property by proclamation":** Lincoln to Orville H. Browning (September 22, 1861), reprinted in Horner, "Lincoln Rebukes a Senator," pp. 116–18.

151 **He followed Lincoln's reply:** Orville H. Browning to Abraham Lincoln (September 30, 1861), available at the Illinois State Historical Library;

Pease, ed., *Diary of Orville Hickman Browning*, vol. I, pp. 502; Horner, "Lincoln Rebukes a Senator," pp. 118–19.

151 **new legislative session convened:** Goodwin, *Team of Rivals*, pp. 403–08; Stahr, *Seward*, pp. 312–23; McPherson, *Tried by War*, pp. 85–87. **"greatest purpose seems":** Ward Hill Lamon, *Recollections of Abraham Lincoln* (Lincoln: University of Nebraska Press, 1994), p. 183.

151 **confided at one point to Browning:** Orville Hickman Browning, 1861, reprinted in Pease, ed., *Diary of Orville Hickman Browning*, vol. I, p. 523. **Lincoln was wary:** Goodwin, *Team of Rivals*, pp. 390–91; Oakes, *Freedom National*, pp. 163–65.

151 **Senator Lyman Trumbull:** *Cong. Globe*, 37th Cong., 2d Sess. (1861), pp. 501–02, 516–17, 2966–70; David P. Currie, "The Civil War Congress," *University of Chicago Law Review*, vol. 73 (2006), p. 1185; White, *Life of Lyman Trumbull*, p. 106; Oakes, *Freedom National*, pp. 238, 321–23, 324. **Browning took center stage:** *Cong. Globe*, 37th Cong., 2d Sess. (1861), pp. 502, 2921–28.

152 **"insure the speedy termination . . . the seizure":** "Act of July 17, 1862" (August 6, 1861), 12 Stat. 589; "Act of July 17, 1862" (August 6, 1861), 12 Stat. 591; **sweeping provision applied:** Silvana R. Siddali, *From Property to Person: Slavery and the Confiscation Acts, 1861–1862* (Baton Rouge: Louisiana State University Press, 2005), pp. 123–25.

152 **"There was no disagreement":** Hickman Browning, 1861, reprinted in Pease, ed., *Diary of Orville Hickman Browning*, vol. I, p. 512.

152 **Browning had grown fearful:** Horner, "Lincoln Rebukes a Senator," p. 119; Baxter, "Lincoln's Friend and Critic," pp. 448–49; *Cong. Globe*, 37th Cong., 2d Sess. (1862), p. 2923.

153 **Browning drew on the logic:** Orville H. Browning to Abraham Lincoln (September 17, 1861), reprinted in Horner, "Lincoln Rebukes a Senator," pp. 114–15.

153 **The Constitution, Browning believed:** Horner, "Lincoln Rebukes a Senator," pp. 113–19; Baxter, "Lincoln's Friend and Critic," pp. 18–19.

153 **With the legislative debate:** *Cong. Globe*, 37th Cong., 2d Sess. (1862), pp. 2921–28. **There was some sympathy:** *Cong. Globe*, 37th Cong. 2d Sess. (1862), pp. 501–02, 516–17, 2966–70.

154 **Browning's allies were few:** *Cong. Globe*, 37th Cong., 2d Sess. (1862), pp. 2966–70; Robertson, "Lincoln and Congress," pp. 49, 83–84.

154 "Congress may make": *Cong. Globe*, 37th Cong., 2d Sess. (1862), p. 2966. "In the Federal Convention": *Cong. Globe*, 37th Cong., 2d Sess. (1862), p. 2968.

154 "direct the movements": *Cong. Globe*, 37th Cong., 2d Sess. (1862), pp. 2966, 2970.

154 "Should the President . . . case is the Constitution": *Cong. Globe*, 37th Cong., 2d Sess. (1862), p. 2969.

155 "meet[ing] the question . . . shoot your prisoners": *Cong. Globe*, 37th Cong., 2d Sess. (1862), p. 2970.

155 "buzzing . . . harassments": Orville Hickman Browning, 1861, reprinted in Pease, ed., *Diary of Orville Hickman Browning*, vol. I, pp. 542–43.

156 "His general views . . . whether they were to control him": Orville Hickman Browning, 1861, reprinted in Pease, ed., *Diary of Orville Hickman Browning*, vol. I, p. 558; Stahr, *Seward*, pp. 340–41.

156 Second Confiscation Act was not: Stahr, *Seward*, pp. 341–42; Goodwin, *Team of Rivals*, pp. 460–61.

157 The very morning: Gideon Welles, *Diary of Gideon Welles: Secretary of the Navy Under Lincoln and Johnson* (New York: Houghton Mifflin, 1911), vol. I, p. 70.

157 "a military necessity": Welles, *Diary*, vol. I, p. 70.

158 Lincoln issued the preliminary emancipation proclamation: Abraham Lincoln, "Preliminary Emancipation Proclamation" (September 22, 1862), National Archives and Records Administration, available at: http://www.archives.gov/exhibits/american_originals_iv/sections/preliminary_emancipation_proclamation.html#.; Stahr, Seward, pp. 346–47; Oakes, *Freedom National*, p. 251.

158 proclamation's first references to abolition: Abraham Lincoln, "Preliminary Emancipation Proclamation" (September 22, 1862), National Archives and Records Administration, available at: http://www.archives.gov/exhibits/american_originals_iv/sections/preliminary_emancipation_proclamation.html#; Abraham Lincoln, "The Emancipation Proclamation" (January 1, 1863), National Archives and Records Administration, available at: www.archives.gov/exhibits/featured_documents/emancipation_proclamation/transcript.html.

159 at an earlier moment: Abraham Lincoln, "To John C. Fremont"

(September 11, 1861), reprinted in *Collected Works of Abraham Lincoln*, vol. IV, pp. 517–18.

159 **He should have, in Browning's view:** Orville Hickman Browning, 1861, reprinted in Pease, ed., *Diary of Orville Hickman Browning*, vol. I, pp. 562, 582, 625; Robertson, "Lincoln and Congress," p. 250. **"Act of Justice":** Abraham Lincoln, "A Proclamation," (January 1, 1863), 12 Stat. pp. 1268–1269.

Chapter 9
≡ *The War Ends*

161 **epigraph:** Mr. Fessenden, *Cong. Globe*, 39th Cong., 2d Sess. (1867), p. 1851.

161 **years out of the limelight:** Chester G. Hearn, *The Impeachment of Andrew Johnson* (Jefferson, NC: McFarland, 2000), p. 112; *Ex Parte Milligan*, 71 U.S. 2 (1866). **Supreme Court was assembled:** "Old Senate Chamber," Architect of the Capitol, available at: http://www.aoc.gov /capitol-buildings/old-senate-chamber. **Reflecting this shift:** Hearn, *Impeachment of Andrew Johnson*, p. 112.

161 **Much of what Black said:** Eric L. McKitrick, *Andrew Johnson and Reconstruction* (Chicago: The University of Chicago Press, 1960), p. 313; Hearn, *Impeachment of Andrew Johnson*, p. 112; Majorie Fribourg, *The Supreme Court in American History* (Avon Books, 1969), p. 98. **Black had made the legal case:** Frank Burr, "Judge Black's Answer," *Philadelphia Weekly Press* (September 13, 1883); Jeremiah Black, "Mr. Black to Mr. Wilson," *Galaxy*, vol. 11, Issue 2 (February 1871), pp. 264–66.

162 **Thus, Johnson:** McKitrick, *Johnson and Reconstruction*, pp. 3–6, 46–47; Hans L. Trefousse, *Andrew Johnson: A Biography* (New York: W. W. Norton & Company, 1991), p. 255. **legislative plan depended heavily:** David O. Stewart, *Impeached: The Trial of Andrew Johnson and the Fight for Lincoln's Legacy* (New York: Simon & Schuster, 2009), pp. 173–74.

163 **They would stitch the nation:** McKitrick, *Johnson and Reconstruction*, pp. 4–5.

163 **Johnson lacked Lincoln's unique:** Ibid., pp. 135–37. **Johnson had made a fool:** Stewart, *Impeached*, pp. 8–10; McKitrick, *Johnson and Reconstruction*, pp. 135–37.

163   **Johnson carried himself:** Trefousse, *Andrew Johnson*, pp. 193, 197, 207.
      He had the good sense: McKitrick, *Johnson and Reconstruction*, pp. 96–
      98; Stewart, *Impeached*, p. 17.

164   **With his popularity soaring:** Stewart, *Impeached*, pp. 5, 8; Trefousse,
      Andrew Johnson, pp. 207, 210–11.

164   **Johnson's tendency toward rigidity:** Stewart, *Impeached*, pp. 15–18;
      Annette Gordon-Reed, *Andrew Johnson: American President Series, The
      17th President, 1865–1869* (New York: Macmillan, 2011), pp. 5, 11–13,
      44, 124–129, 144.

164   **real problem for Johnson:** Eric Foner, *Reconstruction: America's Unfin-
      ished Revolution*, 1863–1877 (New York: HarperCollins, 2002), p. xvii;
      Gordon-Reed, *Andrew Johnson*, pp. 14, 96–104, 105–121, 122–140.
      "true fold": Trefousse, *Andrew Johnson*, p. 217; McKitrick, *Johnson and
      Reconstruction*, pp. 71–72.

165   **Black was contesting:** Curtis A. Bradley, "The Story of Ex Parte Mil-
      ligan: Military Trials, Enemy Combatants, and Congressional Autho-
      rization," in *Presidential Power Stories* (New York: Foundation Press,
      2009), pp. 109–11; Samuel Klaus, ed., *The Milligan Case* (New York:
      A.A. Knopf, 1929), pp. 67–73.

165   **Depending on the outcome of the case:** Klaus, *Milligan Case*, p. 121;
      Bradley, "Story of Ex Parte Milligan," pp. 109–11.

166   **Black was making the point:** Klaus, *Milligan Case*, pp. 121–25.

166   **By all accounts:** William Norwood Brigance, *Jeremiah Sullivan Black: A
      Defender of the Constitution and the Ten Commandments* (Philadelphia:
      University of Pennsylvania Press, 1934), p. vii; Mary Black Clayton, *Rem-
      iniscences of Jeremiah Sullivan Black* (Christian Publishing Company,
      1887), pp. 170–71. **"most magnificent":** Orville Hickman Browning,
      reprinted in Theodore Calvin Pease, ed., *The Diary of Orville Hickman
      Browning* (Springfield, IL: James G. Randall ed., 1925–1933), vol. II, p. 65.

166   **"people rose in their wrath . . . 'em hell":** Clayton, *Reminiscences of Jer-
      emiah Sullivan Black*, p. 134.

167   **president was by then making it well known:** Stewart, *Impeached*,
      pp. 16–20; Gordon-Reed, *Andrew Johnson*, pp. 14, 96–104, 105–121,
      122–140. **should have been no surprise:** Andrew Johnson, "A Proc-
      lamation by the President of the United States" (August 20, 1866) at
      http://www.presidency.ucsb.edu/ws/?pid=71992.

167 **"there no longer existed . . . State or Federal":** Ibid.

167 **new birth of freedom:** Abraham Lincoln, The Gettysburg Address (November 19, 1863), available at: www.abrahamlincolnonline.org/lincoln/speeches/Gettysburg.htm.

168 **Court announced its judgment:** *Ex Parte Milligan*, 71 U.S. (4 Wall.) 2 (1866). **ruling drew howls:** Bradley, "Story of Ex Parte Milligan," pp. 116–21; Mark Tushnet, ed., *The Constitution in Wartime: Beyond Alarmism and Complacency* (Durham, NC: Duke University Press Books, 2005), pp. 169–73.

168 **Court's ruling alarmed:** George Stanton Denison, ed., *Diary and Correspondence of Salmon P. Chase* (U.S. Government Printing Office, 1903), pp. 517–20; John Niven, ed., *The Salmon P. Chase Papers: Correspondence, 1865–73* (Kent, OH: Kent State University Press, 1998), p. 298; John Niven, *Salmon P. Chase: A Biography* (New York: Oxford University Press, 1995), pp. 387, 403–05; Frederick J. Blue, *Salmon P. Chase: A Life in Politics* (Kent, OH: Kent State University Press, 1987), p. 248.

168 **majority had held:** *Ex Parte Milligan*, 71 U.S. (4 Wall.) 2, 132–42 (1866); David J. Barron and Martin S. Lederman, "The Commander in Chief at the Lowest Ebb—A Constitutional History," *Harvard Law Review*, vol. 121 (2008), pp. 1017–18 n.246.

169 **Chase served as an informal advisor:** Niven, *Salmon P. Chase*, p. 382. **"conduct of campaigns":** Chief Justice Salmon P. Chase, concurrence in *Ex Parte Milligan*, 71 U.S. 2, 139 (1866); Niven, *Chase Papers*, pp. 66–69.

170 **"We are fast approaching":** H. W. Brands, *The Man Who Saved the Union: Ulysses Grant in War and Peace* (New York: Random House, 2013), p. 398.

170 **Grant was too circumspect:** Edward Smith, *Grant* (New York: Simon & Schuster, 2001), pp. 433–38; Brands, *Man Who Saved the Union*, p. 398.

170 **first sign of Grant's break:** Trefousse, *Andrew Johnson*, pp. 270–71; Smith, *Grant*, p. 434.

170 **Grant's refusal:** Brands, *Man Who Saved the Union*, pp. 407–08; Stewart, *Impeached*, pp. 71–72.

171 **Stanton thought that with their help:** George Sewall Boutwell, *Reminiscences of Sixty Years in Public Affairs* (MA: McClure, Phillips & Company, 1902), vol. II, pp. 107–108; Trefousse, *Andrew Johnson*, p. 291.

171 "I received a note from Mr. Stanton": Boutwell, *Reminiscences*, vol. II, pp. 107–108.

171 "had been more disturbed . . . through the aid of the Executive": Ibid., vol. II, p. 108.

172 "thought it necessary . . . dictation": Ibid., vol. II, p. 108.

172 "fixed at Washington . . . had been so issued": Ibid., vol. II, p. 108; Niven, *Salmon P. Chase*, pp. 411–12.

172 extraordinary bill: Edgar J. McManus and Tara Helfman, *Liberty and Union: A Constitutional History of the United States, Concise Editions* (London: Routledge, 2014), p. 231; Act of Mar. 2, 1867, ch. 170 §2, 14 Stat-485, 486–87.

172 Congress took up the measure: Niven, *Salmon P. Chase*, pp. 411–12. "Commander in Chief . . . Army shall do, or shall not do": *Cong. Globe*, 39th Cong., 2d Sess. (1867), p. 1851.

173 "I understand the honorable . . . command was concerned": *Cong. Globe*, 39th Cong., 2d Sess. (1867), p. 1852.

173 "Suppose the President of the United States": *Cong. Globe*, 39th Cong., 2d Sess. (1867), p. 1852.

174 "absolute power . . . Army of the United States": *Cong. Globe*, 39th Cong., 2d Sess. (1867), p. 1852.

174 "it has been the practice": *Cong. Globe*, 39th Cong., 2d Sess. (1867), p. 1854.

174 As the appropriations bill: Trefousse, *Andrew Johnson*, p. 281; Smith, *Grant*, pp. 433–34; John Y. Simon, ed., *The Papers of Ulysses S. Grant*, volume 17: January 1–September 30, 1867 (Carbondale, IL: Southern Illinois University Press, 1967), pp. 256–64.

175 With Jeremiah Black's help: Trefousse, *Andrew Johnson*, pp. 281–82; Edward McPherson, *The Political History of the United States During the Period of Reconstruction*, April 15, 1865–July 15, 1870 (Washington, D.C., 1870), pp. 178–81, 192–94; Jeremiah S. Black to Andrew Johnson, March 23, 1867, in Paul H. Bergeron, ed., *The Papers of Andrew Johnson*, vol. 12, February–August 1867 (Knoxville: The University of Tennessee Press, 1995), pp. 175–76; Andrew Johnson, *Veto Message* (July 19, 1867), available at, www.presidency.ucsb.edu/ws/?pid=72121.

175 "fitting end to all our controversy": Brands, *Man Who Saved the Union*, p. 401.

175 "Do not show what I said . . . in a public matter": Ibid.

175 much as Andrew Johnson hated: McManus and Helfman, *Liberty and Union*, p. 231; Brands, *Man Who Saved the Union*, pp. 400–01, 403; Howard K. Beale, ed., *Diary of Gideon Welles: Secretary of the Navy Under Lincoln and Johnson* (New York: W. W. Norton & Company, 1960), vol. III, pp. 48–49.

176 president did his best to undermine: Stewart, *Impeached*, pp. 83–86; Brands, *Man Who Saved the Union*, pp. 400–01, 403. Consistent with that resistance: Stewart, *Impeached*, p. 93; Brands, *Man Who Saved the Union*, p. 401.

176 Johnson thought Grant: William S. McFeely, *Grant: A Biography* (New York: W. W. Norton & Company, 2002), pp. 247–48. Secretary of War Stanton: Beale, ed., *Diary of Gideon Welles*, vol. III, pp. 45–46; Stewart, *Impeached*, pp. 93–94.

176 latter act made it a crime: Stewart, *Impeached*, pp. 93–96; Beale, ed., *Diary of Gideon Welles*, vol. III, pp. 131–32, 134; Tenure of Office Act, Ch. 154, §§1, 2, 9, 14, 430, 432 (1867); Against the advice of Grant: McKitrick, *Johnson and Reconstruction*, pp. 490, 494–495.

177 Similar rumors of such a takeover: Peter Carlson, "130 Years Ago, Parallels Up to a Boiling Point," *Washington Post* (December 13, 1998); McKitrick, *Johnson and Reconstruction*, pp. 289–91.

177 immediate trigger: Stewart, *Impeached*, pp. 114–15. scuttlebutt was that Johnson: L. David Norris, James C. Milligan, and Odie B. Faulk, *William H. Emory: Soldier-Scientist* (Tucson, AZ: University of Arizona Press, 1998), pp. 254–56.

177 In response to these reports: Stewart, *Impeached*, pp. 142–43, 148–49; Brands, *Man Who Saved the Union*, p. 401; Norris et al., *William H. Emory*, p. 255. "in disregard of the Constitution . . . commission of said Emory": *The American Annual Cyclopedia and Register of Important Events* (D. Appleton, 1869), vol. 8, p. 354.

178 "very calmly . . . they had put him": "Notes of Colonel W.G. Moore, Private Secretary to President Johnson, February 24, 1868" in *American Historical Review*, volume XIX (London: MacMillian and Co, 1914), p. 122.

178 Senate gathered: Stewart, *Impeached*, p. 169. instead, in offering: Edmund G. Ross, *History of the Impeachment of Andrew Johnson* (New York: Burt Franklin, 1868), pp. 82–83, 126–28, 132.

178   According to Emory: Ross, *Impeachment of Andrew Johnson*, pp. 82–83, 126–28, 132; *Cong. Globe*, 40th Cong., 2d Sess., Supp. (1868), pp. 78–80; Norris et al., *William H. Emory*, p. 256.

178   "Am I to understand": Ross, *History of the Impeachment of Andrew Johnson*, p. 127; *Cong. Globe*, 40th Cong., 2d Sess., Supp. (1868), pp. 78–80.

179   "object of the law": Emory, *Autobiography*; Ross, *History of the Impeachment*, p. 127.

179   Johnson was ultimately acquitted: McKitrick, *Johnson and Reconstruction*, pp. 4–5, 506–07. High on the list: Stewart, *Impeached*, pp. 197–98. rulings reflected Chase's concern: Chief Justice Salmon P. Chase, concurrence in *Ex Parte* Milligan, 71 U.S. 2, 139 (1866).

179   decades after the trial: Michael Les Benedict, *The Impeachment and Trial of Andrew Johnson* (New York: W. W. Norton & Company, 1973), pp. 9–25, 26–60; Stewart, *Impeached*, pp. 1–4, 177–79.

180   "conduct of Campaigns": Chief Justice Salmon P. Chase, concurrence in *Ex Parte Milligan*, 71 U.S. 2 (1866), p. 139; for the first time: John Norton Pomeroy, *An Introduction to the Constitutional Law of the United States* § 703 (1868), pp. 470–73; David J. Barron and Martin S. Lederman, "The Commander in Chief at the Lowest Ebb: A Constitutional History," *Harvard and Life Review* 121, pp. 941, 1018–21 (2008).

181   Grant, upon taking office: Ulysses S. Grant, "First Inaugural Address" (March 4, 1869); Brands, *Man Who Saved the Union*, p. 428.

181   Congressional government: Woodrow Wilson, *Congressional Government: A Study in American Politics* (Transaction Publishers, 1956); Arthur M. Schlesinger, *The Imperial Presidency* (Houghton Mifflin Harcourt, 2004), pp. 75–76.

Chapter 10
≡ *Imperialism*

183   epigraph: Elihu Root in Phillip C. Jessup, *Elihu Root*, vol. I (New York: Dodd, Mead + Company, 1938), pp. 342–43.

184   "genius of our institutions . . . entangling alliances with none": Grover Cleveland, "Inaugural Address" (March 4, 1885).

185 "large policy . . . imperialism": Christopher McKnight Nichols, *Promise and Peril: America at the Dawn of the Global Age* (Cambridge, MA: Harvard University Press, 2011), pp. 36–41, 84–86.

186 "Theodore is one of the most lovable": John A. Garraty, *Henry Cabot Lodge: A Biography* (New York: Knopf, 1953), pp. 86–87. "telepathy": Ibid., p. 222.

186 Darwinist theories of social progress: Nichols, *Promise and Peril*, pp. 50–57; 74–81; Evan Thomas, *The War Lovers: Roosevelt, Lodge, Hearst, and the Rush to Empire, 1898* (New York: Little, Brown and Company, 2010), pp. 62–73.

186 "fighting-fleet": Theodore Roosevelt, "The Influence of Seapower Upon History," *Atlantic Monthly* (October 1890).

187 "we want no wars of conquest": William McKinley, "Inaugural Address" (March 4, 1897).

187 "great democracy is moving onward": Thomas, *War Lovers*, p. 143.

187 president eventually gave in: Ibid., p. 150. tireless in bending the naval bureaucracy: Ibid., pp. 169–79.

188 American warship *Maine*: Gregg Jones, *Honor in the Dust: Theodore Roosevelt, War in the Philippines, and the Rise and Fall of America's Imperial Dream* (New York: New American Library, 2012), pp. 5–9; Thomas, *War Lovers*, pp. 205–08.

188 cause of the explosion: Ibid., pp. 210–11. Roosevelt and others effectively portrayed: Jones, *Honor in the Dust*, pp. 9–11. that moment on: "H.R. 10086: Declaration of War With Spain, 1898" (April 25, 1898).

188 "in confidence . . . policy that we both desire": Henry Cabot Lodge, "Letter from Lodge to Roosevelt, May 24, 1898," Massachusetts Historical Society, Lodge Roosevelt Correspondence: 1896–1898.

189 "Camp near San Antonio . . . something marvelous": Theodore Roosevelt, "Letter from Roosevelt to Lodge, May 25, 1898," Massachusetts Historical Society, Lodge Roosevelt Correspondence: 1896–1898.

189 "earnestly hope . . . taken away from Spain": Ibid.

189 treaty that the United States signed: Treaty of Peace between the United States of America and the Kingdom of Spain, 30 Stat. 1754 (December 10, 1898).

190 clearest sign of that reckoning: Nichols, *Promise and Peril*, pp. 86–89.

190 Roosevelt's supporters were not overly worried: Jones, *Honor in the Dust*, p. 168. as the insurrection persisted: Ibid., pp. 271–75, 279–80.

191　undertake a more focused inquiry: Ibid., pp. 270–75.

191　tensions between the commander in chief: Ibid., pp. 271, 274; Edmund Morris, *Theodore Rex* (New York: Random House, 2001), pp. 97–99.

191　He had miscalculated: Ibid., pp. 127–29.

192　he would resign: Jones, *Honor in the Dust*, pp. 296–99. "Act to make the President": "An Act to Make the President of the US a Military Dictator," *New York Evening Post* (August 23, 1902).

192　secret administration report: Morris, *Theodore Rex*, pp. 97–99. Lodge felt that he had no choice: Jones, *Honor in the Dust*, pp. 300–01.

192　Major Cornelius Gardener: Jones, *Honor in the Dust*, pp. 277–78.

192　Taft had appeared: Ibid., pp. 271–74.

193　"by reason of the conduct of the troops . . . making permanent enemies": "Friction in Philippines: Gov. Gardener Charges Army with Using Harsh Methods," *New York Times* (April 11, 1902).

193　Lodge gamely tried to: Jones, *Honor in the Dust*, p. 300; Henry Cabot Lodge, *Affairs in the Philippine Islands: Hearing Before the Committee on the Philippines of the United States Senate*, Doc. 331, 57th Congress, 1st Session (1902), p. 850.

193　"to kill and burn . . . Ten years": Jones, *Honor in the Dust*, pp. 292–93.

194　"simply held down . . . allowed to come to": *Affairs in the Philippine Islands*, p. 1767.

194　particularly bad day for the administration: Jones, *Honor in the Dust*, pp. 305–07.

195　"Great as the provocation . . . part of the American Army": Elihu Root in Jessup, *Elihu Root*, vol. I, pp. 342–43.

195　"practical statesmanship . . . centuries cannot eradicate": George F. Hoar, "Subjugation of the Philippines," *Speaker: A Quarterly Magazine*, vol. III (Pearson Brothers, 1908), pp. 182–86.

195　Roosevelt decided to speak out: Theodore Roosevelt, "On the Occasion of the Unveiling of the Soldiers' and Sailors' Monument at Arlington, Under the Auspices of the National Society of the Colonial Dames of America," in *Presidential Address and State Papers of Theodore Roosevelt*, vol. 1 (New York: P.F. Collier & Son, 1910), pp. 53–67.

196　final report of the Lodge inquiry: Affairs in the Philippine Islands. insurrection was in its last throes: Theodore Roosevelt, "Proclamation

483: Granting Pardon and Amnesty to Participants in Insurrection in the Philippines" (July 4, 1902). **Hoar turned out to be:** Jones, *Honor in the Dust*, p. 324.

196 **nod to the strength:** Jones, *Honor in the Dust*, p. 324.

197 **midst of his second term:** Mike McKinley, "The Cruise of the Great White Fleet," Naval History and Heritage Command, available at: history .navy.mil/research/library/online-reading-room/title-list-alphabetically /c/cruise-great-white-fleet-mckinley.html.

198 **days in office winding down:** Theodore Roosevelt, "Executive Order No. 969: Defining the Duties of the United States Marine Corps" (1908).

198 **amendment was quickly put forward:** "Act of March 3, 1909," 35 Stat. 753, pp. 773–74.

198 **reprising the role that he had played:** Lodge, *Cong. Record*, vol. 43, 60th Cong., 2nd Sess. (1909), p. 2447.

199 **"Suppose upon the occasion . . . bad man happens to be President":** Bacon, *Cong. Record*, vol. 43, 60th Cong., 2nd Sess. (1909), p. 2452.

199 **"fathers who framed the Constitution":** Borah, *Cong. Record*, vol. 43, 60th Cong., 2nd Sess. (1909), p. 2452.

199 **extended constitutional debate:** David J. Barron and Martin S. Lederman, "The Commander in Chief at the Lowest Ebb—A Constitutional History," *Harvard Law Review*, vol. 121 (2008), p. 1037.

199 **"Inasmuch as Congress has power . . . employed in some designated way":** "Appropriations-Marine Corps-Service on Battle ships, Etc.," 27 Op. Att'y Gen, (1909), pp. 259–60.

200 **"emergency making such action":** "Removal of Floating Dry Dock from Algiers, La., to Guantanamo, Cuba," 28 Op. Att'y Gen. (1910), pp. 511, 522. **"who is to determine the movements . . . votes in the market-place":** William Taft, *Our Chief Magistrate and His Powers* (New York: Columbia University Press, 1916), p. 129. **"we come to the power of the President":** William Taft, "Boundaries Between the Executive, the Legislative and the Judicial Branches of the Government," *Yale Law Journal*, vol. 25 (1916), p. 610.

Chapter 11
≡ *The Great War*

205 **epigraph:** Woodrow Wilson, Address to a Joint Session of Congress, February 26, 1917, in Arthur S. Link, ed., *The Papers of Woodrow Wilson* (Princeton, NJ: Princeton University Press, 1983), vol. 41, p. 285.

205 **"He Kept Us":** John Milton Cooper, Jr., *Woodrow Wilson* (New York: Random House, 2011), pp. 341–42. **constant attacks:** A. Scott Berg, *Wilson* (London: Simon & Schuster UK, 2013), pp. 411–13.

205 **a resigned Wilson:** Berg, *Wilson*, pp. 414–17.

206 **"future security":** Cooper, *Woodrow Wilson*, p. 369.

206 **make good on that commitment:** Link, ed., *Papers of Woodrow Wilson*, vol. 45, pp. 534–39. **"peace without victory":** Cooper, *Woodrow Wilson*, pp. 370–71.

207 **Prominent observers:** Berg, *Wilson*, pp. 422–26.

207 **even more worrisome:** Cooper, *Woodrow Wilson*, p. 372. **"every available weapon":** Note from Johann-Heinrich von Bernstorff to Robert Lansing, in Link, ed., *Papers of Woodrow Wilson*, vol. 41, pp. 74–76.

208 **"congressional government":** Woodrow Wilson, *Congressional Government* (New York: Houghton Mifflin, 1900), p. 284.

208 **his academic writings:** Woodrow Wilson, *Constitutional Government in the United States* (New York: Columbia University Press, 1908), pp. 58–59.

208 **keying off of Lincoln's:** Ibid., pp. 78–79.

209 **Throughout his first term:** Berg, *Wilson*, pp. 11–13; 433.

209 **German U-boat campaign:** Cooper, Woodrow Wilson, p. 375. **At a cabinet meeting:** David F. Houston, *Eight Years with Wilson's Cabinet: 1913–1920* (New York: Doubleday, 1926), vol. I, p. 234. **Wilson had been pondering a policy:** Correspondence from Robert Lansing to Wilson, February 21, 1917, in Link, ed., *Papers of Woodrow Wilson*, vol. 41, p. 263. **Wilson worried:** Houston, *Eight Years*, vol. I, p. 234.

210 **"one of the most animated":** Letter from Franklin Knight Lane to George W. Lane, February 25, 1917, in Link, ed., *Papers of Woodrow Wilson*, vol. 41, pp. 282–83. **"government would continue":** Houston, *Eight Years*, pp. 235–37.

210 **next day, Wilson drafted:** Memorandum to William Gibbs McAdoo, with

Enclosure, February 24, 1917, in Link, ed., *Papers of Woodrow Wilson*, vol. 41, pp. 279–80. **"No doubt I already possess . . . in their spirit"**: *Address to a Joint Session of Congress*, February 26, 1917, in ibid., vol. 41, pp. 283–87.

210 **Front-page reports the next day**: Cooper, *Woodrow Wilson*, pp. 377–78.

211 **Senate rules of that era**: Arthur S. Link, *Wilson: Campaigns for Progressivism and Peace, 1916–1917* (Princeton, NJ: Princeton University Press, 1965), pp. 360–62; Seward W. Livermore, *Politics Is Adjourned: Woodrow Wilson and the War Congress 1916–18* (Middletown, CT: Wesleyan University Press, 1966), pp. 216–17.

211 **waiting for Chief Justice Edward White**: Link, *Campaigns for Progressivism and Peace*, pp. 360–61.

211 **After taking the oath**: Cooper, *Woodrow Wilson*, p. 379; Link, *Campaigns for Progressivism and Peace*, p. 362. **"little group of willful men . . . unprecedented unanimity and spirit"**: in Link, ed., *Papers of Woodrow Wilson*, vol. 41, pp. 318–20.

212 *New York Times* **reported**: "Sharp Words by Wilson," *New York Times* (March 5, 1917).

212 **"even more grave"**: Ibid. **"discovery that . . . may nullify"**: "Supplementary Statement from the White House," *New York Times* (March 5, 1917); Link, ed., *Papers of Woodrow Wilson*, vol. 41, p. 320.

212 **"expressly provide[d] . . . at amity"**: *Cong. Record*, 64th Cong., 2d Sess. (1917), p. 4749.

213 **departing for the ceremonial inaugural events**: "President Requests Reply in 24 Hours on Right to Arm Vessels," *New York Times* (March 6, 1917).

213 **news of the obstacle out**: "Says Convoys are Legal; Princeton Professor Thinks Wilson Obscures the Issue," *New York Times* (March 6, 1917). **"only really effective method"**: "Wickersham Holds Wilson has Power," *New York Times* (March 5, 1917). **got it the next morning**: "Admits He Has Full Power," *New York Times* (March 10, 1917); see also "Gregory Asked for Opinion," *New York Times* (March 6, 1917). **"more or less technical"**: Memorandum from Robert Lansing to Wilson, March 6, 1917, in Link, ed., *Papers of Woodrow Wilson*, vol. 41, pp. 341–42.

213 **announced the action**: Link, ed., *Papers of Woodrow Wilson*, vol. 41, pp. 377–79; "Admits He Has Full Power."

213 **Wilson's strategy**: "Admits He Has Full Power."

214 **submarines began sinking:** Cooper, *Woodrow Wilson*, p. 381. **"neither right nor constitutionally . . . to be in the balance":** "An Address to a Joint Session of Congress," April 2, 1917, in Link, ed., *Papers of Woodrow Wilson*, vol. 41, p. 519–27.

214 **"I shall take the liberty . . . will most directly fall":** Ibid., p. 522.

214 **Before Congress declared war:** Cooper, *Woodrow Wilson*, pp. 390–92; *Cong. Record*, 65th Cong., 1st Sess. (1917), pp. 3258–65.

215 **"the argument . . . nor dot an 'i' ":** *Cong. Record*, 65th Cong., 1st Sess. (1917), p. 1376.

216 **Wilson had effectively won:** Livermore, *Politics Is Adjourned*, pp. 16 18.

216 **House and Senate prepared:** "Roosevelt Wins Army Bill Point," *New York Times* (May 16, 1917); Livermore, *Politics Is Adjourned*, p. 27. **Everyone knew this volunteer program:** "Senate Passes Draft Bill 65–8; Wilson May Proclaim it Tomorrow; New Army to Mobilize in September," *New York Times* (May 18, 1917).

216 **Roosevelt had even informed:** Letter from Roosevelt to Baker, February 2, 1917, in Appendix G of Theodore Roosevelt, *The Foes of Our Own Household* (New York: George H. Doran Co., 1917), pp. 304–05.

217 **Baker brushed Roosevelt off:** Ibid., pp. 306–38. **In one exchange:** Telegram from Baker to Roosevelt, March 20, 1917, in ibid., pp. 308–09. **"respectfully . . . eligible":** Letter from Roosevelt to Baker, March 23, 1917, in ibid., pp. 309–10.

217 **"one of the most extraordinary":** Memorandum from Wilson to Newton D. Baker, March 27, 1917, in Link, ed., *Papers of Woodrow Wilson*, vol. 41, p. 478.

217 **"So far as I am able":** Livermore, *Politics Is Adjourned*, p. 21, quoting Roosevelt letter to F.C. Walcott, March 7, 1917.

217 **He popped in unannounced:** John Joseph Leary, *Talks with T.R.: From the Diaries of John J. Leary, Jr.* (Boston: 1920), p. 94. **two men, archrivals:** Link, ed., *Papers of Woodrow Wilson*, vol. 42, p. 32 n.1. **during the twenty-five minutes:** Joseph P. Tumulty, *Woodrow Wilson as I Knew Him* (Garden City, NY: 1921), p. 288.

218 **Roosevelt's expeditionary force:** Cooper, *Woodrow Wilson*, pp. 393–95.

218 **"There is but one Theodore Roosevelt . . . no other American is known":** *Cong. Record*, 65th Cong., 1st Sess. (1917), pp. 1437–38, 1492; "Senate Debate Spirited," *New York Times* (April 29, 1917).

218 **"any feature that would embarrass"**: Letter from Wilson to Rep. Stanley Hubert Dent, Jr., May 11, 1917, in Link, ed., *Papers of Woodrow Wilson*, vol. 42, p. 274. **"tenacity . . . in his veins"**: *Cong. Record*, 65th Cong., 1st Sess. (1917), p. 2454 (statement of Sen. Johnson). **"Roosevelt Wins"**: "Roosevelt Wins Army Bill Point," *New York Times* (May 16, 1917).

218 **Roosevelt immediately sent a telegram**: Telegram from Roosevelt to Wilson, May 18, 1917, in Roosevelt, *Foes of Our Own Household*, p. 338.

219 **"with a view to providing . . . not avail [him]"**: "Will not Send Roosevelt: Wilson Not to Avail Himself of Volunteer Authority at Present," *New York Times*, May 19, 1917.

219 **Wilson sent a telegram**: Letter from Wilson to Roosevelt, May 19, 1917, in Link, ed., *Papers of Woodrow Wilson*, vol. 42, p. 346. **"men who have volunteered . . . American Army and Navy"**: Letter from Roosevelt "[t]o the men who have volunteered for immediate service on the firing line in the divisions which Congress authorized," May 21, 1917, in Roosevelt, *Foes of Our Own Household*, pp. 340–47.

219 **"make a special study . . . branches of the Government"**: *Cong. Record*, 65th Cong., 1st Sess. (1917), p. 459.

220 **"render my task . . . executive work of the administration"**: Letter from Woodrow Wilson to Asbury Francis Lever, July 23, 1917, in Link, ed., *Papers of Woodrow Wilson*, vol. 43 p. 245. **"We are jointly the servants"**: Letter from Robert Latham Owen, August 2, 1917, in ibid., vol. 43, pp. 348–50.

220 **"criticism and publicity . . . not efficiency"**: Letter from Wilson to Robert Latham Owen, August 3, 1917, in ibid., vol. 43, pp. 357–58.

221 **"any other matters"**: Livermore, *Politics Is Adjourned*, pp. 129–30; *Cong. Record*, 65th Cong., 2d Sess. (1918), p. 6238.

221 **"These are serious times . . . of the constituted Executive"**: Letter from Wilson to Thomas Staples Martin, May 14, 1918, in Link, ed., *Papers of Woodrow Wilson*, vol. 48, pp. 10–11.

221 **president would assign**: Letter from Edward Mandell House to Wilson, May 9, 1918, in Link, ed., *Papers of Woodrow Wilson*, vol. 47, p. 584.

221 **"the command of forces"**: Charles Evans Hughes, "War Powers Under the Constitution," Address to the Fortieth Annual Meeting of the American Bar Association (Saratoga Springs, NY: September 4, 1917).

221 **"damned piker"**: Diary entry of Col. Edward M. House, May 17, 1918,

in Link, ed., *Papers of Woodrow Wilson*, vol. 48, p. 50. **Wilson's appointment:** Livermore, *Politics Is Adjourned*, p. 133 (citing New York World, May 23, 1918).

222 **American effort . . . was hamstrung:** Ibid., pp. 62–63. **Back in the States:** Ibid., pp. 73–76.

222 **Members of both parties:** Ibid., p. 64. **Chamberlain again led the effort:** George E. Chamberlain, "Defects of the U.S. War Machine," *New York Times* (January 13, 1918); "A Bill To Create a Department of Munitions," S.3327, 65th Cong., 2d Sess. (January 4, 1918).

222 **"upon high patriotic grounds":** "Munitions Reform to be a Party Issue," *New York Times*, January 13, 1918. **"we would not only be disappointed":** Letter from Wilson to George Earle Chamberlain, January 11, 1918, in Link, ed., *Papers of Woodrow Wilson*, vol. 45, p. 566.

223 **"three distinguished citizens":** *Cong. Record*, 65th Cong., 2d Sess. (1918), pp. 1077–78. **"inefficiency in every bureau":** Letter from George Earle Chamberlain to Wilson, January 21, 1918, in Arthur S. Link, ed., *Papers of Woodrow Wilson*, vol. 46, p. 54.

223 **"President has his blood . . . nerve any man needs":** Entry from the Diary of Josephus Daniels, January 19, 1918, in Link, ed., *Papers of Woodrow Wilson*, vol. 46, p. 41. **Taking on Chamberlain:** Livermore, *Politics Is Adjourned*, p. 101.

223 **"Senator after Senator has appealed":** Letter from Wilson to Lee Slater Overman, March 21, 1918, in Link, ed., *Papers of Woodrow Wilson*, vol. 47, p. 94.

223 **"frank amazement . . . lawmaking power":** "President Seeks Blanket Powers for War Period," *New York Times* (February 7, 1918). **in May, Congress enacted:** 40 Stat. 556 (May 20, 1918).

224 **"way in which . . . Politics is adjourned":** "An Address to a Joint Session of Congress," May 27, 1918, in Link, ed., *Papers of Woodrow Wilson*, vol. 48, pp. 162–65.

224 **first German peace note:** "Translation of Communication from German Government to the President of the United States, as transmitted by the Chargé d'Affaires a.i. of Switzerland," October 6, 1918, in Link, *Papers of Woodrow Wilson*, vol. 51, p. 253. **Wilson responded cautiously:** "Communication from Robert Lansing to Friedrich Oederlin," October 8, 1918, in ibid., vol. 51, pp. 268–69.

224 **"general association . . . Abyss of Internationalism"**: Livermore, *Politics Is Adjourned*, p. 216.

225 **"to the dreamers"**: Ibid., p. 210. **"we are not internationalists . . . duty-performing family life"**: Theodore Roosevelt, "Yankee Blood Versus German Blood," speech delivered at Springfield, IL, August 26, 1918, in *Chicago Tribune* (August 27, 1918); Livermore, *Politics Is Adjourned*, p. 212. **"poisonous peace propaganda"**: *Cong. Record*, 56th Congress (1917), pp. 9392–94.

225 **"Let us dictate peace"**: "Roosevelt Assails 14 Peace Points," *New York Times*, October 25, 1918.

225 **Wilson had been drafting the statement**: Link, ed., *Papers of Woodrow Wilson*, vol. 51, pp. 317–18, 343–44, 353–55. **final written appeal**: "An Appeal for a Democratic Congress," October 19, 1918, in ibid., vol. 51, pp. 381–82.

225 **"occur in the most critical period . . . of their own choosing"**: "An Appeal for a Democratic Congress," in ibid., vol. 51, pp. 381–82.

226 **November, the electorate delivered**: Livermore, *Politics Is Adjourned*, pp. 225–26. **"one of the worst mid-term defeats"**: Letter from Lodge to Lord Bryce, November 16, 1918, Henry Cabot Lodge Papers, Massachusetts Historical Society.

227 **barnstormed the country**: Richard L. Merritt, "Wilson and the 'Great and Solemn Referendum,'" *Review of Politics*, vol. 27, no. 1 (Jan. 1965), p. 89.

Chapter 12
≡ *Preparing for World War II*

229 **epigraph**: Robert H. Jackson, Draft Autobiography, Robert H. Jackson Papers (on file with the Library of Congress, Washington, D.C.).

229 **president neared the end**: David J. Barron and Martin S. Lederman, "The Commander in Chief at the Lowest Ebb—A Constitutional History," *Harvard Law Review*, vol. 121, no. 4 (February 2008), p. 1041.

229 **"President should not be"**: Memorandum from President Franklin Roosevelt for the Att'y Gen. (July 1, 1939) (on file with the Harvard Law School Library). **"would be amply justified . . . does not have"**: Memorandum from Harold L. Ickes, Sec'y of the Interior, to President Franklin Roosevelt (July 1, 1939) (on file with the Harvard Law School Library).

230 **"'If we fail to get . . .'"**: Memorandum from President Franklin Roosevelt for the Att'y Gen. (July 1, 1939) (on file with the Harvard Law School Library).

230 **"a great nation in a world"**: Cordell Hull, Letter to the Chairman of the Committee on Foreign Relations (May 27, 1939) (on file with the Harvard Law School Library).

231 **"violations of the law"**: Thomas Jefferson to James Wilkinson, Feb. 3, 1807, reprinted in Andrew A. Lipscomb and Albert Ellery Bergh, eds., *The Writings of Thomas Jefferson*, (Washington, D.C.: Thomas Jefferson Memorial Association of the United States, 1905), vol. XI, pp. 147–50.

231 **"this instance . . . is quite another thing"**: Memorandum from Edward Kemp, Special Assistant to the Att'y Gen., to Frank Murphy, Att'y Gen. (July 7, 1939) (on file with the Harvard Law School Library).

232 **"Apart from the legal side . . . tendencies and purposes"**: Ibid.

232 **Supreme Court had frustrated Roosevelt**: Jeff Shesol, *Supreme Power: Franklin Roosevelt vs. the Supreme Court* (New York: W. W. Norton & Company, 2010), pp. 2–4; Robert H. Jackson, *That Man: An Insider's Portrait of Franklin D. Roosevelt* (Oxford: Oxford University Press, 2003), pp. 50–54.

232 **Court-packing plan imploded**: Jackson, *That Man*, p. 54. **because these criminal prohibitions**: David J. Barron and Martin S. Lederman, "Commander in Chief at the Lowest Ebb," pp. 1041–42.

233 **"legalism"**: James R. Holmes, *Theodore Roosevelt and World Order: Police Power in International Relations* (Dulles, MD: Potomac Books, 2006), p. 22; Jack Goldsmith, *The Terror Presidency: Law and Judgment Inside the Bush Administration* (New York: Norton, 2009), p. 48. **at the same time**: Richard Moe, *Roosevelt's Second Act* (Oxford: Oxford University Press, 2013), pp. 51–52. **comfort with ambiguity**: Barron and Lederman, "Commander in Chief at the Lowest Ebb," p. 1042; Franklin Roosevelt, Fireside Chat (May 26, 1940); Franklin D. Roosevelt, Address on Constitution Day (Sept. 17, 1937), available at: www.presidency.ucsb.edu/ws/?pid=15459.

233 **"wretched little bob-tailed . . . chuckle-headed"**: Joseph Alsop and Robert Kintner, *American White Paper: The Story of American Diplomacy and the Second World War* (New York: Simon & Schuster, 1940), pp. 41–42.

233   **Congress finally relented:** Moe, *Roosevelt's Second Act*, pp. 77–79.

233   **The president initially wanted:** William R. Casto, "Advising Presidents: Robert Jackson and the Destroyers-For-Bases Deal," *American Journal of Legal History*, vol. 52, no. 2 (2012), pp. 70–71.

234   **"In carrying out our neutrality laws":** Harold L. Ickes, *The Secret Diary of Harold L. Ickes* (Cambridge, MA: Da Capo Press, 1974), vol. II, p. 474.

234   **underlying war bureaucracy:** Kenneth S. Davis, *FDR: Into the Storm* (New York: Random House, 1993), p. 548. **"err on the side":** Sidley Fine, *Frank Murphy: The Washington Years* (Ann Arbor, MI: University of Michigan Press, 1984), p. 109.

234   **"untimely and unwise":** Fine, *Frank Murphy*, p. 110.

234   **Planes and other matériel:** Davis, *Into the Storm*, pp. 513–14, 548.

235   **middle of May:** Moe, *Roosevelt's Second Act*, pp. 122–24.

235   **"scene has darkened . . . astonishing swiftness":** Conrad Black, *Franklin Delano Roosevelt: Champion of Freedom* (New York: Public Affairs, 2005), pp. 550–51.

235   **"specific authorization":** Philip Goodhart, *Fifty Ships that Saved the World* (London: Heinemann, 1965), pp. 22–23; Moe, *Roosevelt's Second Act*, p. 124.

235   **mosquito boats were different:** Casto, "Advising Presidents," pp. 31–33.

236   **still wanted the destroyers:** Ibid., p. 35.

236   **Picking up on news reports:** Ibid., p. 36.

236   **Senate committee convened:** Committee Hearing, 86 *Cong. Record*, 8775 (June 21, 1940); Michael Korda, *With Wings like Eagles* (New York: Harper, 2009), pp. 93–119.

236   **outraged senators listened:** Casto, "Advising Presidents," pp. 37–38; Committee Hearing, 86 *Cong. Record*, 8775 (June 21, 1940).

237   **Jackson became the nation's top lawyer:** Davis, *Into the Storm*, p. 530. **thanks to a long association:** Jackson, *That Man*, p. 136. **It was rumored:** Conrad Black, *Franklin Delano Roosevelt: Champion of Freedom* (New York: Public Affairs, 2005), p. 443.

237   **White House meeting in early June:** Casto, "Advising Presidents," pp. 32–34.

237   **turned to Newman Townsend:** Ibid., pp. 38–40; Newman A. Townsend to Attorney General, June 20, 1940, Robert H. Jackson Papers (on file with Library of Congress, Washington, D.C.)

237 controversy over the deal: Ibid., p. 41. decision caused some concern: Jackson, *That Man*, p. 94. White House issued a statement: "Torpedo Boat sale to British Halted: President Acted on Jackson's Opinion That 1917 Law Would Be Violated," *New York Times*, June 25, 1940, p. 10. Walsh had already informed: Casto, "Advising Presidents," pp. 41–42 n.216.

238 "glad that Bob Jackson": Goodhart, *Fifty Ships*, p. 89.

238 By their terms: 18 U.S.C. §33 (1940 codification) states that "during a war in which the United States is a neutral nation, it shall be unlawful to send out . . . of the United States any vessel built, armed, or equipped as a vessel of war . . . with any intent . . . that such vessel shall be delivered to a belligerent nation"; Act of 1794, ch. 50, sec. 3 (June 5, 1794).

238 impact of Jackson's ruling: Casto, "Advising Presidents," pp. 44–46.

239 "use[d] . . . to the defense of the United States": An Act to expedite national defense, and for other purposes, 76th Cong., 3d Sess., ch. 440, §14(a), 54 Stat. 676, 681.

239 "fit" for use: Act of July 19, 1940, 76th Cong., 3d Sess., ch. 644, §7, 54 Stat. 780, codified at 34 U.S.C. §493a (1940 codification).

240 prospect of England falling: Davis, *Into the Storm*, p. 558.

240 Henry Stimson: Henry Lewis Stimson, The Henry Lewis Stimson Diaries, available in the Yale University Library, vol. 30, p. 41. "hook or crook": Harold L. Ickes, *The Secret Diary of Harold L. Ickes: The Lowering Clouds, 1939–1941* (New York: Simon & Schuster, 1954), vol. III, p. 233.

240 "long history of the world": Telegram from Joseph Kennedy, U.S. Ambassador to the United Kingdom, to Cordell Hull, Sec'y of State (Aug. 15, 1940) in 3 *Foreign Relations: Diplomatic Papers* 1940, pp. 66, 67. Moe, *Roosevelt's Second Act*, pp. 255–56.

240 "strong-man": Ibid., p. 331.

241 Frankfurter advised: Ibid., pp. 191–94.

241 yet, at the very same time: Ibid., pp. 262–64.

241 journalist Joseph Alsop: Casto, "Advising Presidents," pp. 53–54.

242 Cohen knew he would need: Casto, "Advising Presidents," pp. 55–56.

242 "relative . . . absolute": William Lasser, *Benjamin V. Cohen: Architect of the New Deal* (New Haven, CT: Yale University Press, 2002), p. 228.

242 As for the neutrality laws: Ibid., p. 224.

243 **"congressional opinion":** Ibid., p. 222.

243 **Roosevelt was impressed:** Robert Shogan, *Hard Bargain* (Boulder, CO: Westview Press, 1999), p. 183; Jackson, *That Man*, p. 90.

243 **conviction was bolstered:** Jackson, *That Man*, pp. 82–89.

243 **cabinet meeting the afternoon:** Ibid., p. 87. **"too serious":** Stimson, *Diaries*, vol. 30, p. 57.

244 **"The matter involves . . . the President and Mr. Wilkie":** Stimson, *Diaries*, vol. 30, p. 57.

244 **"there was no chance":** Ibid., p. 81.

244 **Cohen was in regular contact:** Shogan, *Hard Bargain*, pp. 187–90. **He had even resigned:** James Chace, *Acheson: The Secretary of State Who Created the American World* (New York: Simon & Schuster, 2008), p. 67.

244 **Acheson immediately saw promise:** Chace, *Acheson*, pp. 79–80; **appeared in the *New York Times*:** "No Legal Bar Seen to Transfer of Destroyers," *New York Times*, August 11, 1940.

245 **"The enclosed idea may have a germ . . . limit his constitutional discretion":** Letter from Murry Nelson to Franklin Delano Roosevelt, August 12, 1940, President's Secretary's File, Franklin D. Roosevelt Library, Hyde Park, New York.

245 **The following January:** Stimson, *Diaries*, vol. 32, pp. 129, 131. **"speck of light . . . gloomy":** Ibid, vol. 30, p. 80.

246 **Acheson and Cohen called:** Moe, *Roosevelt's Second Act*, pp. 263–64. **Frankfurter was telling Stimson:** Stimson, *Diaries*, vol. 30, p. 91.

246 **"in view of the Jackson opinion":** Ickes, *Secret Diary*, vol. III, p. 271.

246 **"I think he feared . . . he was without it":** Jackson, *That Man*, p. 95.

246 **help, and perhaps assurance:** Ibid., pp. 79–82.

246 **Townsend agreed:** William R. Casto, "Attorney General Robert Jackson's Brief Encounter with the Notion of Preclusive Presidential Power," *Pace Law Review*, vol. 30, No. 2 (2010), pp. 372–374; Newman A. Townsend, Memorandum for the Attorney General, August 13, 1940, Robert H. Jackson Papers (on file with the Library of Congress, Washington, D.C.).

247 **Vinson's July amendment:** Casto, "Jackson's Brief Encounter," pp. 374–76; Newman A. Townsend, Memorandum for the Attorney General, August 13, 1940, Robert H. Jackson Papers (on file with the Library of Congress, Washington, D.C.).

247 still not convinced: Jackson, *That Man*, pp. 96–98; Shogan, *Hard Bargain*, p. 234.

247 "it may be possible": Black, *Champion of Freedom*, p. 578.

248 chief of naval operations was willing: Shogan, *Hard Bargain*, pp. 217–19.

248 Back at the Justice Department: Shogan, *Hard Bargain*, p. 218. "In view of your constitutional power": Robert H. Jackson, Draft Opinion Regarding the Sale of Over-Age Destroyers to Great Britain, Robert H. Jackson Papers (on file with the Library of Congress, Washington, D.C.), quoted in Casto, "Jackson's Brief Encounter," p. 366 n.8.

248 "The opinion—not rest on Stimson": Casto, "Jackson's Brief Encounter," p. 376 n.75. Jackson chose to rely: Robert J. Delahunty, "Robert Jackson's Opinion on the Destroyer Deal and the Question of Presidential Prerogative," *Vermont Law Review* (2013), p. 87.

248 "very good . . . out in the open": Stimson, *Diaries*, vol. 30, p. 93.

249 still some concern: Shogan, *Hard Bargain*, pp. 232–33.

249 "should actually have been put forward": Stimson, *Diaries*, vol. 30, p. 108.

249 Roosevelt had been assured: Shogan, *Hard Bargain*, p. 178. Jackson and his lawyers: Moe, *Roosevelt's Second Act*, pp. 265–66.

249 Roosevelt set up a phone call: Moe, *Roosevelt's Second Act*, pp. 265–66.

250 An earlier version: Robert H. Jackson, Draft Opinion Regarding the Sale of Over-Age Destroyers to Great Britain, Robert H. Jackson Papers (on file with the Library of Congress, Washington, D.C.) quoted in Casto, "Jackson's Brief Encounter," p. 376 n.75. "So far as concerns this statute . . . certain restrictions thereon": Robert H. Jackson, "United States Attorney General: Opinion on Exchange of Over-Age Destroyers for Naval and Air Bases," *American Journal of International Law*, vol. 34 (August 27, 1940), pp. 728–37.

251 "fait accompli": Shogan, *Hard Bargain*, p. 238; Moe, *Roosevelt's Second Act*, pp. 267–68.

251 "method by which": James A. Hagerty, "Willkie Condemns Destroyer Trade," *New York Times* (September 7, 1940).

251 famous Princeton historian: Edward Corwin, "Executive Authority Held Exceeded in Destroyer Deal," *New York Times* (October 13, 1940). "endorsement of unrestrained autocracy . . . Attorney General of the United States": Corwin, "Executive Authority."

251 "very little patience . . . when action is imperative": Chace, *Acheson*, p. 80.

252 "chief hold of the Congress . . . don't know enough": Casto, "Advising Presidents," vol. 52, no. 1 (2012), p. 97 n.527; Henry Stimson, Diaries of Henry L. Stimson (September 9, 1940), at Henry L. Stimson Papers, Yale University.

252 Jackson's final opinion had even reaffirmed: Robert Jackson, "Acquisition of Naval and Air Bases in Exchange for Over-Age Destroyers," 39 U.S. Op. Atty. Gen. 484 (August 27, 1940); Shogan, *Hard Bargain*, p. 247.

253 "The fact was that the opinion . . . authority notwithstanding": Robert H. Jackson, Draft Autobiography, Robert H. Jackson Papers (on file with the Library of Congress, Washington, D.C.).

253 "Your president says": Thomas Fleming, *The New Dealers' War* (New York: Basic Books, 2001), pp. 2–5. "The turning point": Stimson, *Diaries*, vol. 30, p. 99.

253 heels of that historic transaction: Moe, *Roosevelt's Second Act*, pp. 325–27.

254 before war was declared: "Roosevelt Due to Order Army To Take Over Factory Today: Coast Strikers Refuse to Go Back to Work," *Washington Post* (June 9, 1941).

254 wake of the Japanese bombing raid: "U.S. Carries Out Seizure of Peabody-Salem Tanneries," *Christian Science Monitor* (November 24, 1943). declared martial law: "Hawaii Under Martial Law, Islands Quiet; Blackout Enforced, Violators Punished," *New York Times* (December 11, 1941). following spring: Rennie Taylor, "Resettlement of Japanese Involves Unusual Problems," *Washington Post* (May 4, 1942). Congress supported: An Act to Provide a Penalty for Violation of Restrictions or Orders with Respect to Persons Entering, Remaining in, Leaving, or Committing Any Act in Military Areas or Zones, March 21, 1942, 18 U.S.C.A. §97(a), 56 Stat. 173.

255 arrest of two groups: "Military Court Named to Try Saboteur Cases: F. D. Proclamation Denies Access to Civil Courts," *Boston Globe* (July 3, 1942).

Chapter 13

≡ *Total War*

257 epigraph: Felix Frankfurter, J., Letter to Justice Black regarding the Saboteur Cases, in Papers of Hugo L. Black, Supreme Court Case File, Special Term, July 1942, Box 269 (July 1942).

257 "back eddy": Robert H. Jackson, *That Man: An Insider's Portrait of Franklin D. Roosevelt* (New York: Oxford University Press, 2003), p. 107. "marble mausoleum": David M. Kennedy, *Freedom from Fear: The American People in Depression and War*, 1929–1945 (New York: Oxford University Press, 1999), pp. 629–30.

257 Justice Byrnes coped: Jackson, *That Man*, p. 110. at Roosevelt's request: Ibid., p. 177; James F. Byrnes, "Opinion on President's Power to Evade Congressional Law on Price Administration Act," Letter to Major Luther Brice, Clemson University Libraries, 8020634 (August 8, 1942).

258 "there were a good many men": Jackson, *That Man*, p. 107.

258 "work on the Court . . . permanent importance": Ibid., p. 107.

258 The case: *Ex Parte Quirin*, 317 U.S. 1 (1942).

259 "conduct of campaigns": Chief Justice Salmon P. Chase, concurrence in *Ex Parte Milligan*, 71 U.S. 2, 139 (1866).

259 Emergency Price Control Act of 1942: 50 U.S.C. §901 (1942).

260 first four German operatives: Michael Dobbs, *Saboteurs: The Nazi Raid on America* (New York: Alfred A. Knopf, 2004), pp. 82–83. They hit the sand: Ibid., pp. 82–83. landed at Ponte Vedra Beach: Ibid., p. 129.

260 large amounts of cash: Edward S. Corwin, *Total War and the Constitution* (Freeport, NY: Books for Libraries Press, 1970), p. 117. tasked with blowing up: Pierce O'Donnell, *In Time of War: Hitler's Terrorist Attack on America* (New York: The New Press, 2005), p. 6. "Jewish-owned": Ibid., p. 7.

261 end of June: O'Donnell, *In Time of War*, p. 84.

261 men were in federal custody: Ibid., p. 303.

261 defendants did not submit quietly: Ibid., pp. 190–192. went to the home: Ibid., pp. 193–94. He took the lead: Ibid., p. 202.

262 Roosevelt had personally suggested: Ibid., p. 213; Dobbs, *Saboteurs*, p. 238.

262 **military commission met:** Dobbs, *Saboteurs*, p. 210; O'Donnell, *In Time of War*, p. 141.

262 **Most recently the solicitor general:** O'Donnell, *In Time of War*, pp. 72–74.

262 **Biddle came to that view:** Ibid., p. 121. **"Hanging would afford":** William D. Hassett, *Off the Record with F.D.R., 1942–1945* (Chicago: Academy Chicago Publishers, 2001), p. 83.

263 *Ex Parte Milligan:* 71 U.S. (4 wall.) 2 (1866).

263 **After burying their sabotage materials:** O'Donnell, *In Time of War*, p. 63; **whisked off the streets:** Ibid., p. 77.

263 **"during time of war":** *Ex Parte Quirin*, 317 U.S. 1, 22–23 (1942).

264 **when Kenneth Royall decided:** O'Donnell, *In Time of War*, p. 190. **"win the Supreme Court":** Ibid., p. 128. **"You're damned right":** Alexander Biddle, *In Brief Authority* (New York: Doubleday and Co., 1962), p. 331.

264 **Douglas had to fly:** Dobbs, *Saboteurs*, p. 238. **Murphy recused himself:** Ibid., p. 239. **Two other justices:** O'Donnell, *In Time of War*, p. 265.

264 **The proceedings began at noon:** Dobbs, *Saboteurs*, p. 239. **"total war":** Ibid., p. 243; "Ex Parte Quirin (1942) Oral Arguments," Landmark Briefs and Arguments of the Supreme Court of the United States: Constitutional Law (1975), vol. 39, pp. 495, 599, 601, 666.

264 **The justices seemed convinced:** Ibid., vol. 59, pp. 505–25.

265 **The justices seemed less clear:** Ibid., pp. 526–34.

265 **justices made a point of asking . . . "an invading force":** Ibid., vol. 39, p. 510.

265 **He argued the defendants:** Ibid., vol. 39, pp. 520–23.

265 **"hair" of the *Milligan* precedent:** Ibid., vol. 39, p. 611.

266 **Under the Articles of War:** Articles of War, Bul. No. 25, W.D., 66th Cong., 2d Sess., Art. 43 (1920). **Those rules:** "Order Establishing a Military Commission to Try Eight Captured German Saboteurs," July 2, 1942. **Nor did the commission require:** Articles of War, Bul. No. 25, W.D., 66th Cong., 2d Sess., Art. 46, 50 1/2 (1920).

266 **"exercise of his great authority":** "Ex Parte Quirin (1942) Oral Arguments," Landmark Briefs and Arguments of the Supreme Court of the United States: Constitutional Law (1975), vol. 39, p. 607.

266 **"[did] not have to come to that":** Ibid., vol. 39, p. 608. **"modified by Congress . . . is not bound by a statute":** Ibid., vol. 39, pp. 635–36.

266 "Commander in Chief": Ibid., vol. 39, p. 636.

267 the Court issued: *Ex Parte Quirin*, 317 U.S. 1, 18 n.1 (1942)

267 "not surprised": Hassett, *Off the Record*, p. 97-98; Dobbs, *Saboteurs*, p. 253. In short order: Ibid., p. 254-57. commuted the sentences: Ibid., p. 257.

267 Stone announced: *Ex Parte Quirin*, 317 U.S. 1 (1942); O'Donnell, *In Time of War*, p. 234.

267 origins could be traced: Kenneth S. Davis, *FDR: The War President: 1940-1943* (New York: Random House, Inc., 2001), p. 458.

268 April, prices were rising: Nancy Beck Young, *Why We Fight: Congress and the Politics of World War II* (Lawrence, KS: University Press of Kansas, 2013), p. 67. a seven-pronged blueprint: Davis, *War President*, p. 462.

268 lengthy message to Congress: Davis, *War President*, pp. 462-63.

268 "president did not consider . . . privately or publicly": Samuel S. Rosenman, *Working with Roosevelt* (New York: Harper and Brothers, 1952), p. 333.

268 "greatly increased cost . . . his time and thought": Ibid., p. 333.

268 Despite these concerns: Ibid., p. 339. farm lobby's influence: Ibid., p. 339.

269 Pressed hard by his closest aides: Robert E. Sherwood, *Roosevelt and Hopkins* (New York: Enigma Books, 2001), p. 604.

269 days leading up to the deadline: Ibid., pp. 604-05.

270 In one camp were those aides: Ibid., p. 604.

270 "There were unquestionably . . . which might be unpopular": Ibid., pp. 604-05.

270 Other aides argued: Ibid., p. 604-05.

270 "in favor of an arbitrary": Ibid., p. 605. "possibly announcing a proposal . . . fully realizes it": Hassett, *Off the Record*, p. 115.

271 "hard . . . his proposal to Congress": Hassett, *Off the Record*, p. 115. "a weekend consideration . . . and the toughest": Ibid., p. 117.

271 "with no announcement": Ibid., p. 118. "huge task": Ibid., p. 117.

271 "elaborate forecasts": Ibid., p. 118.

271 "virtually unanimous in saying": Ibid., p. 118.

271 "The president told me a number . . . Congress Monday": Ibid., p. 118.

272 **"strongly recommended"**: Sherwood, *Roosevelt and Hopkins*, p. 605.

272 **"didn't want to see it . . . no Executive Order"**: Hassett, *Off the Record*, p. 121.

272 **address to the nation over the radio:** Franklin D. Roosevelt, Fireside Chat 22, On Inflation and Food Prices (September 7, 1942), available at: millercenter.org/president/fdroosevelt/speeches/speech-3328. **his congressional message:** Message to Congress on Stabilizing the Economy (September 7, 1942), available at www.presidency.ucsb.edu /ws/?pid=16302.

273 **"doctrine that is asserted . . . so revolutionary":** Young, *Why We Fight*, pp. 68–69, Frederick R. Barklely, "Roosevelt Stirs Congress by Threat to Act on Prices," *New York Times* (September 18, 1942). **If Roosevelt could impose:** Ira Katznelson, *Fear Itself: The New Deal and the Origins of Our Time* (New York: Liveright, 2013), p. 337.

273 **"It came as a shock . . . never get to an issue"':** Thomas I. Emerson, *Young Lawyer for the New Deal* (Savage, MD: Rowman and Littlefield Publishers, 1991), p. 189.

273 **claiming unchecked constitutional powers:** Hassett, *Off the Record*, p. 122.

273 **"President has the powers . . . any previous war":** Russell D. Buhite, *FDR's Fireside Chats* (Norman, OK: University of Oklahoma Press, 1992), pp. 234–35.

273-74 **"if we were invaded . . . those powers belong":** Buhite, *FDR's Fireside Chats*, p. 235.

274 **"under the Constitution":** Ibid., p. 234.

274 **"responsibility of the government . . . is popularly supposed":** mimeographed address to Society for the Advancement of Management (August 13, 1942), The Papers of Oscar S. Cox, Box 69 (on file with the Franklin D. Roosevelt Presidential Library and Museum, Hyde Park, N.Y.).

275 **latitude in this case:** Second World Powers Act, 1942, 50 U.S.C. §633 (1942).

275 **Cox began sketching:** Oscar S. Cox, "Wage and Agricultural Price Control under Existing Law," Letter to James F. Byrnes (July 23, 1942), The Papers of Oscar S. Cox, Box 63 (on file with the Franklin D. Roosevelt Presidential Library and Museum, Hyde Park, N.Y.).

275 **"not believe that the President . . . by the average citizen":** James F. Byrnes, "Opinion on President's power to evade Congressional law on Price Administration Act," Letter to Major Luther Brice, Clemson University Libraries, 8020634 (August 8, 1942).

275 **Second War Powers Act:** Oscar Cox, "Legality of proposed Executive Order 'Providing for the Stabilizing of the National Economy,'" Letter to President Franklin D. Roosevelt (September 3, 1942), The Papers of Oscar S. Cox, Box 63 (on file with the Franklin D. Roosevelt Presidential Library and Museum, Hyde Park, N.Y.).

276 **"Stabilization Administrator . . . price conditions":** Oscar Cox, "Control of farm prices by allocation of agricultural commodities," Memorandum to the Attorney General (August 31, 1942), The Papers of Oscar S. Cox, Box 63.

276 **When Roosevelt last pulled:** Jackson, *That Man*, pp. 97–98.

277 **congressional debate that followed:** *Cong. Record*, 77th Cong., 2d Sess. (1942), pp. 7338–99. **To cap off the bold move:** Davis, *War President*, p. 624.

278 **"Just how the opinion in these cases . . . I invite your attention":** Memorandum to the Court from Chief Justice Stone, in *Ex Parte Quirin* (Sept. 25, 1942), Box 69, Harlan Fiske Stone Papers, Manuscript Division, Library of Congress.

278 **"the fact . . . relied to secure petitioners' liberty":** Ibid.

278 **"proposition of law . . . advisory opinion":** Ibid.

279 **Jackson was convinced:** Memorandum to the Court from Justice Jackson, in *Ex Parte Quirin* (October 16, 1942) (on file with the Robert H. Jackson Papers, Library of Congress).

279 **For that reason, Jackson proposed:** Ibid.

280 **"We should not only be slow . . . his constitutional functions":** Ibid.

280 **"You shock me":** O'Donnell, *In Time of War*, pp. 193–94.

280 **Black was happy to rule:** Opinion of Justice Black on the Saboteur Cases, in *Ex Parte Quirin* (October 2, 1942) (on file with the Hugo Black Papers, Library of Congress). **As Black's law clerk explained:** John Frank, "Memo to Mr. Justice Black: Ex Parte Quirin: The Jackson Memo" (on file with the Hugo Black Papers, Library of Congress).

281 **"completely . . . executive for the future":** Ibid.

281 **two men traded letters:** Max Freedman, *Roosevelt and Frankfurter,*

Their Correspondence 1928–1945 (Boston MA: Little, Brown and Company, 1967), p. 660.

281 **"merely because some of the matters":** Ibid., p. 669.

281 **"judicial lockjaw":** Ibid., p. 669. **"need to go . . . Court can limit":** Felix Frankfurter, J., Letter to Justice Black regarding the Saboteur Cases, in Papers of Hugo L. Black, Supreme Court Case File, Special Term, July 1942, Box 269 (July 1942).

282 **He urged his brethren:** Felix Frankfurter, J., Letter to Justice Black regarding the Saboteur Cases, Opinion of Felix Frankfurter, J. (October 29, 1942) (on file with the Felix Frankfurter Papers, Library of Congress). **"F.F.'s Soliloquy":** Felix Frankfurter Soliloquy: Felix Frankfurter, F.F.'s Soliloquy (Oct. 23, 1942) (on file with the Felix Frankfurter Papers, Library of Congress).

282 **"could not for the life of me":** Ibid.

282 **"requires no poet's imagination . . . a judge's tongue":** Ibid.

282 **"What in hell do you fellows think . . . constitutional discussion":** Ibid.

283 **"Just relax":** Ibid.

283 **Court instead unanimously declared:** *Ex Parte Quirin*, 317 U.S. 1, 22–23 (1942).

286 **wake of the president's victory:** Davis, *War President*, pp. 627–630; Andrew H. Bartels, "The Office of Price Administration and the Legacy of the New Deal, 1939–1946," *Public Historian*, vol. 5 (Summer, 1983), p. 16.

Chapter 14
≡ *Korea and Absolute War Powers*

289 **epigraph:** Secretary Acheson, Assignment of Ground Forces of the United States to Duty in the European Area: Hearings Before the Committee on Foreign Relations and the Committee on Armed Services (Washington: United States Government Printing Office, 1951), p. 109.

289 **though Truman had risen:** David McCullough, *Truman* (New York: Simon & Schuster, 1992), p. 333.

289 **voracious reading:** Ibid., p. 463.

290 **popularity soared:** Ibid., p. 398.

290 **"silly . . . window dressing":** Dean Acheson, *Present at the Creation: My*

Years in the State Department (New York: W.W. Norton & Company, 1969), p. 224.

292 **"nations not set":** *Cong. Record*, 79th Cong., 1st Sess. (1945), p. 11085.

292 **midst of the Korean War:** *Youngstown Sheet & Tube Co. v. Sawyer*, 343 U.S. 579, 589 (1952). **judicial opinion Jackson wrote:** Ibid., p. 634 (Jackson, J., concurring).

292 **"moon, the stars":** Harry S. Truman, *Memoirs of Harry S. Truman: Year of Decisions*, vol. 1 (New York: Signet Book, 1955), p. 31. **some sobering news:** McCullough, *Truman*, p. 376.

292 **Truman had heard rumors:** Garry Wills, *Bomb Power: The Modern Presidency and the National Security State* (New York: Penguin Press, 2010), p. 12. **Stimson needed him to know:** McCullough, *Truman*, p. 376.

293 **Within the week:** Ibid., pp. 377–78; Henry Lewis Stimson, The Henry Lewis Stimson Diaries, available in the Yale University Library, vol. 51, pp. 68–72.

293 **tactical advantage it offered:** McCullough, *Truman*, p. 378; Stimson, *Diaries*, vol. 51, p. 68–72.

293 **decide against using the bomb:** Wills, *Bomb Power*, pp. 25–26; Stimson, *Diaries*, vol. 51, pp. 149–51.

293 **two resulting blasts:** McCullough, *Truman*, p. 456–57; George McKee Elsey, *An Unplanned Life: A Memoir* (Columbia: University of Missouri Press, 2005), pp. 90–93.

294 **"If we do not have . . . many fine boys in our air force":** Telegram, Richard Russell to Harry S. Truman, August 7, 1945, Official File, Truman Papers.

294 **one man to make a judgment:** Bert Andrews, "Should One Man Decide Atomic Bomb Future? Senator Questions It," *Washington Post* (October 7, 1945), p. B1. **"terrible responsibility":** Henry Lewis Stimson, Memorandum of Conference with the President, August 8, 1945, at 10:45 A.M., in the Papers of Henry Lewis Stimson, Yale University Library. **"humane feeling . . . in the same manner":** Telegram, Harry S. Truman to Richard Russell, August 9, 1945, Official File, Truman Papers.

295 **In fact, with Stimson's backing:** Harry S. Truman, "Special Message to the Congress on Atomic Energy," October 3, 1945, The American Presidency Project, available at http://www.presidency.ucsb.edu

/ws/?pid=12327; Scott Ritter, *Dangerous Ground: America's Failed Arms Control Policy, from FDR to Obama* (New York: Nation Books, 2010), p. 22; George L. Harrison, Memorandum for the Secretary, September 11, 1945, in Papers of Henry Lewis Stimson, Yale University Library; Wills, *Bomb Power*, pp. 30–31.

295 **even under the new law:** An Act for the Development and Control of Atomic Energy, Pub. L. 79-585, 60 Stat. 755 (enacted August 1, 1946); Wills, *Bomb Power*, pp. 31, 45.

295 **It was no real surprise:** McCullough, *Truman*, p. 763.

295 **Truman's closest aides:** James Chace, *Acheson: The Secretary of State Who Created the American World* (New York: Simon & Schuster, 1998), p. 234; McCullough, *Truman*, p. 757. **"Even if the Soviet Union":** Chace, *Acheson*, pp. 234–35.

296 **"Can the Russians do it . . . Let's get on with it":** Chace, *Acheson*, p. 235.

296 **Rather than first going to Congress:** Larry Wayne Blomstedt, "Truman, Congress and the Struggle for Korea" (Ph.D. Dissertation, Texas A&M University, 2008), pp. 231–40.

296 **Congress expressed little concern:** Ibid., pp. 120–21, 240–42, 247. **"most of the members":** Meeting at Blair House, July 3, 1950, Document 72, p. 2, in Papers of Dean Acheson, Department of State; Blomstedt, "Truman, Congress and the Struggle for Korea," p. 247. **Congress did quietly appropriate:** Mutual Defense Assistance Act of 1950, Pub. L. No. 447, 64 Stat. 5 (1950); Far Eastern Assistance Act of 1950, Pub. L No. 447, 64 Stat. 5 (1950); Selective Service Extension Act of 1950, Pub. L. No. 599, 64 Stat. 318 (1950).

297 **"They are all with me":** Blomstedt, "Truman, Congress and the Struggle for Korea," p. 266; *Public Papers of President of the United States: Harry Truman, 1950* (Washington: U.S. Government Printing Office, 1965), p. 513. **There was some concern:** Blomstedt, "Truman, Congress and the Struggle for Korea," pp. 241–42, 261.

297 **"special agreements":** Blomstedt, "Truman, Congress and the Struggle for Korea," pp. 241–42, 261–63; United Nations Participation Act, December 20, 1945, The Avalon Project at Yale Law School at http://avalon.law.yale.edu/20th_century/decad031.asp.

298 **"police action . . . war":** Harry S. Truman, "The President's News Conference," June 29, 1950, The American Presidency Project, available at

http://www.presidency.ucsb.edu/ws/?pid=13544. **skirting the Constitution:** Blomstedt, "Truman, Congress and the Struggle for Korea," p. 266.

298 **provoke the new Communist regime:** Blomstedt, "Truman, Congress and the Struggle for Korea," p. 266. **"many atomic bombs":** W.H. Lawrence, "President Warns," *New York Times* (May 8, 1951), p. 1.

298 **secretary of state began pushing:** Acheson, *Present at the Creation*, pp. 414–15.

299 **"appear to be trying":** Blomstedt, "Truman, Congress and the Struggle for Korea," p. 248; Meeting at Blair House, July 3, 1950, Document 72, in Papers of Dean Acheson, Department of State.

299 **"he did not think Congress . . . events in Korea":** United States Department of State, *Foreign Relations of the United States, 1950, Korea* (Washington: United States Government Printing Office, 1950), p. 291.

299 **"under active consideration":** Harry S. Truman, "The President's News Conference," November 30, 1950, The American Presidency Project, available at http://www.presidency.ucsb.edu/ws/?pid=13673; Acheson, *Present at the Creation*, pp. 478–79; Wills, *Bomb Power*, pp. 105, 114.

300 **Truman was oblivious:** McCullough, *Truman*, pp. 821–22.

300 **administration spokesman:** McCullough, *Truman*, p. 822; Acheson, *Present at the Creation*, pp. 478–79.

300 **Attlee sought assurances:** Blomstedt, "Truman, Congress and the Struggle for Korea," pp. 139–42; Acheson, *Present at the Creation*, pp. 479–84.

302 **"send troops anywhere":** Harry S. Truman, "The President's News Conference," January 11, 1951, The American Presidency Project, available at http://www.presidency.ucsb.edu/ws/?pid=14050.

302 **Korea as a backdrop:** Acheson, *Present at the Creation*, pp. 488; 491–96.

302 **key witness:** Assignment of Ground Forces, p. 77.

303 **Truman had stood by Acheson:** Acheson, *Present at the Creation*, pp. 354–68; Blomstedt, "Truman, Congress and the Struggle for Korea," pp. 4–5, 22–23, 38–41.

303 **president's standing in the polls:** George Gallup, "Truman Popularity at New Low," *Washington Post* (December 30, 1951), p. B5.

304 **more than willing to push:** Assignment of Ground Forces, pp. 88–93, 110–11.

304 Acheson explained to the members of Congress: Ibid., pp. 92–93.

304 "Not only has the President the authority . . . under the Constitution": Dean Acheson, "Memorandum," January 6, 1951, in ibid., p. 92. "direction of the armed forces": *Powers of the President to Send the Armed Forces Outside the United States* (Washington: United States Government Printing Office, 1951), p. 16.

305 "trying to split legal hairs": Assignment of Ground Forces, p. 99. "We are in a position . . . ought to do it": Ibid., p. 93.

305 "the whole business . . . carry on this great task": Ibid., p. 109.

305 the hearing had been framed: Ibid., p. 8. Wherry's proposed resolution: Ibid., p. 38.

306 Truman had put off: McCullough, *Truman*, pp. 896–900.

306 When pressed at a news conference: Harry S. Truman, "The President's News Conference," April 17, 1952, The American Presidency Project, available at http://www.presidency.ucsb.edu/ws/index.php?pid=14471; McCullough, *Truman*, pp. 899–900; "Publishers Assail President's Claim," *Los Angeles Times* (April 24, 1952), p. 8.

306 calm things down: Harry S. Truman, "The President's News Conference," May 1, 1952, The American Presidency Project, available at http://www.presidency.ucsb.edu/ws/index.php?pid=14101. "cannot even review": *The Steel Seizure Case, Briefs for the Government*, Part I, 82nd Cong., 2nd Sess. (Washington: United States Government Printing Office, 1952), pp. 371–72.

307 Pine ruled the government's position "alien": *Youngstown Sheet & Tube Co. v. Sawyer*, 103 F. Supp. 569, 576 (D.D.C 1952). At a specially called emergency session: *Youngstown Sheet & Tube Co. v. Sawyer*, 343 U.S. 579, 589 (1952). In probably the most famous war powers opinion: Ibid., pp. 638–42 (Jackson, J., concurring).

307 drive home the point: Ibid.

308 "I should indulge the widest latitude": Ibid., p. 645.

308 "dreams Joseph was called": Ibid.

308 He had been privately assured: James St. Clair and Linda C. Gugin, *Chief Judge Fred M. Vinson of Kentucky: A Political Biography* (Lexington: University Press of Kentucky, 2002), pp. 195, 217. agreed to join the justices: McCullough, *Truman*, p. 901.

309 blanketed with newspaper editorials: "The Divine Right of Presidents?"

Los Angeles Times (April 19, 1952), p. A4; "The Only Remedy," *Chicago Daily Tribune* (April 21, 1952), p. 18; "Government by 'Intuition,'" *Los Angeles Sentinel* (April 24, 1952), p. A8; "Harry Truman Makes it Worse," *Los Angeles Times* (April 25, 1952), p. A4; "The Presidential Powers," *New York Times* (April 27, 1952), p. E8; "Harry Truman's Distorted Picture," *Los Angeles Times* (April 29, 1952), p. A4; "Adm. Gehres Lauds Judge Pine Ruling," *Los Angeles Times* (May 1, 1952), p. 11; Lawrence E. Davies, "Drift to Dictator Feared by Warren," *New York Times* (May 8, 1952), p. 23; "Truman's Steel Seizure Ripped by Sen. Martin," *Chicago Daily Tribune* (May 12, 1952), p. B14; Raymond Moley, "Now They Know Welfare is the Father of Tyranny," *Los Angeles Times* (June 7, 1952), p. A4; Marquis Childs, "Steel and the Seizure Power," *Washington Post* (June 10, 1952), p. 14; "Taft and the Law," *Chicago Daily Tribune* (June 15, 1952), p. 24; "The Constitution vs. Dictatorship," *Chicago Daily Tribune* (June 22, 1952), p. 24. **key member of his team resigned:** "Truman Broke Word, Wilson Says," *Los Angeles Times* (March 31, 1952), p. 1.

309   **spent the last weeks on the stump:** John Fisher, "Truman Storms at 'Fanaticism' of Eisenhower," *Chicago Daily Tribune* (October 18, 1952), p. 8; "Truman Charges Dictator Tactics," *Los Angeles Times* (October 19, 1952), p. 27; John Harris, "Truman Calls Ike Drive 'Low, Gutter' Campaign," *Daily Boston Globe* (October 19, 1952), p. C1.

309   **"usurpations . . . socialism":** "National Affairs: Against Trumanism," Time (October 27, 1952), p. 27; Blomstedt, "Truman, Congress and the Struggle for Korea," p. 90.

309   **in office, Eisenhower aimed:** Robert H. Ferrell, ed., *The Diary of James C. Hagerty: Eisenhower in Mid-Course, 1954–1955* (Bloomington: Indiana University Press, 1983), p. 174; Stephen E. Ambrose, *Eisenhower: Soldier and President* (New York: Simon & Schuster, 1991), p. 374.

310   **Testifying as a top military commander:** Assignment of Ground Forces, pp. 10–11.

310   **"I do think that the Congress . . . with both feet":** Ibid., p. 34. **"should like to see a certain degree . . . to our normal senses":** Ibid., p. 11.

311   **bound to disappoint them:** John W. Malsberger, *The General and the Politician: Dwight Eisenhower, Richard Nixon, and American Politics* (Lanham, MD: Rowman & Littlefield, 2014), pp. 36–38.

311 **sending troops here and there:** Wills, *Bomb Power*, pp. 177–82; Tim Weiner, *Legacy of Ashes: The History of the CIA* (New York: Doubleday, 2007), pp. 76–77; Evan Thomas, *Ike's Bluff: President Eisenhower's Secret Battle to Save the World* (New York: Little, Brown, 2012), pp. 137–44.

Chapter 15
≡ *War in Indochina and Congressional Resurgence*

313 **epigraph:** Leonard Garment, Memorandum for Bryce Harlow (May 26, 1970).

313 **May of 1970:** Tom Huston, "The Assault on the Constitutional Power of the Presidency," Memorandum to Bryce Harlow, John Ehrlichman, H.R. Haldeman, William Timmons, and Henry Kissinger (May 23, 1970).

313 **Huston wrote, in unusually blunt terms:** Ibid.

314 **The Nixon administration had worked hard:** Elizabeth Drew, *Richard M. Nixon: The American Presidents Series: The 37th President, 1969–1974* (New York: Times Books, 2007), p. 30. **memo showed that:** Huston, "Assault on the Constitutional Power of the Presidency."

314 **Just as Huston predicted:** Ibid.

314 **summed up by an evocative phrase:** Arthur M. Schlesinger, Jr., *The Imperial Presidency* (New York: Houghton Mifflin, 1973).

315 **height, the nation's commitment:** Stanley Karnow, *Vietnam: A History* (New York: Penguin Books, 1983), p. 683. **Even after the most recent round:** Ibid., pp. 684–85.

315 **second run for the White House succeeded:** Ibid., pp. 581–82.

316 **first year alone:** Department of Defense, Office of the Under Secretary of Defense for Personnel and Readiness, Defense Human Resources Activity, Defense Manpower Data Center, "DCAS Vietnam Conflict Extract File record counts by INCIDENT OR DEATH DATE," Defense Casualty Analysis System: Vietnam Casualties, Record Group 330, National Archives Identifier 2163536 (April 2008).

316 **thanks to a leaked report:** William Beecher, "Raids in Cambodia by U.S. Unprotested," *New York Times* (May 9, 1969); Karnow, *Vietnam*, p. 592.

316 **Nixon was drawing down the troops:** Karnow, *Vietnam*, pp. 608, 644–46.

317 **regular demonstrations in Washington:** Rick Perlstein, *Nixonland* (New York: Simon & Schuster, 2008), p. 418.

317 **through it all, Congress:** Ibid., p. 428; Karnow, *Vietnam*, p. 615. **sweeping law had been followed:** Tonkin Gulf Resolution: Southeast Asia Resolution, Pub. L. No. 88-408 (1964); Measures following Gulf of Tonkin: An Act to authorize certain construction at military installations, and for other purposes, Pub. L. No. 90-110 (1967); An Act to authorize appropriations during the fiscal year 1967 for procurement of aircraft, missiles, and tracked combat vehicles, and research, development, test, evaluation, and military construction for the Armed Forces, and for other purposes, Pub. L. No. 90-5 (1967); An Act to authorize certain construction at military installations, and for other purposes, Public Law 90-408 (1967).

317 **Huston had picked up signs:** Bo Burlingham, "Paranoia in Power," *Harper's Monthly* (October 1974).

318 **Seated at his desk in the Oval Office:** Perlstein, *Nixonland*, p. 478; Karnow, *Vietnam*, p. 685.

318 **Nixon knew that by publicly ordering:** Perlstein, *Nixonland*, pp. 477–79.

318 **Some of the secrecy:** Schlesinger, *Imperial Presidency*, p. 256; **"madman theory":** Perlstein, *Nixonland*, pp. 419–20.

319 **"go to the heart of the trouble":** Richard Nixon, "139—Address to the Nation on the Situation in Southeast Asia," *Public Papers of the Presidents of the United States: Richard Nixon* (April 30, 1970), p. 407.

319 **"If the North Vietnamese . . . of our American men":** Ibid., p. 408.

320 **The lead editorial: "Gulf of Tonkin Resolution fulfilled":** Thomas Geoghegay, "Congress: The Laos Watch," *The Harvard Crimson* (March 3, 1970).

320 **"any time then or later . . . failure of constitutional mechanisms":** Ibid.

321 **"legislative independence":** Ibid.

321 **"For the first time":** Huston, "Assault on the Constitutional Power of the Presidency," p. 1.

321 **"a major revolution":** Ibid., pp. 2–3.

322 **series of steps:** Perlstein, *Nixonland*, pp. 545–46; "Hearing before the Select Committee to Study Governmental Operations with Respect to

Intelligence or Activities of the United States Senate, Houston Plan," 94th Congress, 1st Session (1975).

322 **Outrageous as the Huston plan was:** Paul Clancy, *Just a Country Lawyer: A Biography of Senator Sam Ervin* (Don Mills, Ontario: Indiana University Press, 1974), p. 281; "The Nation, In Summary Mr. Nixon," *New York Times* (May 22, 1977); **"When the President does it, that means":** Richard Nixon, "Frost/Nixon Interview, Part 3" (May 19, 1977).

323 **Through this outreach effort:** Huston, "Assault on the Constitutional Power of the Presidency."

323 **Three days after Huston's memo:** Leonard Garment, Memorandum for Bryce Harlow (May 26, 1970).

323 **memo summarized the views:** Ibid.

323 **"President does not need . . . fight in Cambodia":** Ibid.

324 **secret opinion signed a week earlier:** William Rehnquist, "Presidential Authority to Permit Incursion into Communist Sanctuaries in Cambodia-Vietnam Border Area," Memorandum for Charles W. Colson (May 14, 1970).

324 **president, Rehnquist concluded:** Ibid.

324 **Rehnquist agreed there had to be some limit:** William H. Rehnquist, "Hearings before the Subcomm. on National Security Policy and Scientific Developments of the H. Comm. on Foreign Affairs," 91st Cong. 235 (1970).

325 **antiwar bills then pending:** Perlstein, *Nixonland*, pp. 495–96. **This one, by contrast:** Eugene Dvorin, ed., *The Senate's War Powers* (Chicago, IL: Markam Publishing Company, 1971), p. 12.

325 **Cooper was a tall, thin:** Randall B. Woods, ed., *Vietnam and the American Political Tradition: The Politics of Dissent* (Cambridge, UK: Cambridge University Press, 2003), pp. 327–38. **Frank Church, by contrast:** Ibid., pp. 106, 122–23.

325 **while it was far from clear:** LeRoy Ashby and Rod Gramer, *Fighting the Odds: The Life of Senator Frank Church* (Pullman, WA: Washington State University Press, 1994), p. 307–08.

325 **"Unctuous . . . *Sieg Heil*":** Ibid., pp. 307–08.

326 **fuming on May 1:** Ibid., p. 308–09.

326 **"want to take out . . . blow the hell out of them":** Perlstein, *Nixonland*, p. 482.

326 "boy orator": Ashby and Gramer, *Fighting the Odds*, p. 81.

326 The earliest of those measures: Amy Belasco, et al. "Congressional Restrictions on US Military Operations in Vietnam, Cambodia, Laos, Somalia, and Kosovo: Funding and Non-Funding Approaches," Congressional Research Service Report (January 16, 2007), pp. 6–21.

326 Church correctly judged: Ashby and Gramer, *Fighting the Odds*, p. 295. "bugout resolutions": Richard Reeves, *President Nixon: Alone in the White House* (New York: Simon & Schuster, 2001), p. 133.

327 Church's middle way: Ashby and Gramer, *Fighting the Odds*, p. 315.

327 "could 'properly manifest' . . . responsibility for American lives": William Safire, *Before the Fall: An Inside View of the Pre-Watergate White House* (Garden City, NY: Doubleday & Company, 2005), p. 193.

327 The president's challenge at that meeting: Dvorin, *Senate's War Powers*, pp. 38–45.

328 seemed like they were saying: Ibid., pp. 38–45.

328 critics charged Church and company: Ibid., p. 30.

328 tweak would ensure: Ibid., p. 30.

328 "dispatch of American troops . . . American intervention in Indochina": Ibid., p. 9.

328 Cooper-Church also began: Ibid., pp. 10–11.

329 Church conceded: Ibid., p. 111.

329 "constitutional power and authority": Ibid., pp. 190, 192.

330 Javits was so concerned: Ibid., pp. 193–97.

330 language also passed: Ibid., pp. 198, 237.

330 "pattern was clear . . . flexibility for negotiations": Henry A. Kissinger, *The White House Years* (New York: Little, Brown, and Company, 1979), p. 512.

330 Cooper-Church finally passed: An act to provide additional foreign assistance authorizations, and for other purposes, Pub. L. No. 91-652, Sec. 7 (1971).

331 Not long after Cooper-Church became law, Congress at last: Foreign Military Sales Act of 1971, Pub. L. No. 91-672, 84 Stat. 2053 (1971), p. 2055.

Chapter 16
≡ *The Imperial Presidency and the End of the President's War*

333 **epigraph:** Arthur M. Schlesinger, Jr., *The Imperial Presidency* (New York: First Mariner Books Edition, 2004), p. 421.

334 **"remember a crowd":** Arthur M. Schlesinger, Jr., to Arthur Goldberg, November 9, 1972, box 262, folder 262.20, Arthur M. Schlesinger, Jr., Papers, New York Public Library. **"year comes to an end . . . tragic thing in American history":** Arthur Schlesinger, Jr., Journals, box 314, December 29, 1972; Andrew and Stephen Schlesinger, eds., Arthur M. Schlesinger, J., *Journals, 1952–2000* (New York: Penguin, 2007), eds., p. 366.

334 **"tough hombre":** Arthur Schlesinger, Jr., Journals, Box 314, December 29, 1972.

335 **"drumfire of pressure":** Arthur Schlesinger, Jr., Journals, box 314, December 29, 1972.

335 **get the drumfire rolling:** Arthur Schlesinger, Jr., Journals, box 314, December 29, 1972. **"war at presidential pleasure":** Arthur Schlesinger, Jr., "Presidential War," *New York Times Magazine* (January 7, 1973), p. 12.

335 **"invent[ed] . . . this writer among them":** Ibid.

335 **Schlesinger assured his readers:** Ibid., pp. 12–13.

335 **True, Lincoln had responded unilaterally . . . protect Americans in distress:** Ibid., pp. 13, 26–27.

336 **"unlimited right of the American chief":** Ibid., p. 12.

336 **"unwritten checks":** Ibid., pp. 27–28, 30. **"organize consent":** Arthur Schlesinger, Jr., to Richard McAdoo, March 6, 1973, box 285, 285.2.

337 **concluded his article:** Schlesinger, "Presidential War," p. 29.

337 **"only [thing] . . . hard-hitting book":** Richard McAdoo to Arthur Schlesinger, Jr., January 9, 1973, box 285, folder 285.2.

337 **"discuss not only . . . good guys":** Richard McAdoo to Arthur Schlesinger, Jr., January 9, 1973, box 285, folder 285.2.

338 **Schlesinger had already written:** Arthur M. Schlesinger, Jr., *A Thousand Days: John F. Kennedy in the White House* (New York: Houghton Mifflin Co., 1965). **At that very moment he was working:** Arthur Schlesinger, Jr., *Robert Kennedy and His Times* (New York: Houghton Mifflin Co., 1978). **Together, these works would make fitting complements:** Arthur

Schlesinger, Jr., *The Crisis of the Old Order: 1919–1933, The Age of Roosevelt*, Vol. I (New York: Houghton Mifflin Co., 1957); Arthur M. Schlesinger, Jr., *The Coming of the New Deal: 1933–1935, The Age of Roosevelt*, Vol. II (New York: Houghton Mifflin Co., 1958); Arthur M. Schlesinger, Jr., *The Politics of Upheaval: 1935–1936, The Age of Roosevelt*, Vol. III (New York: Houghton Mifflin Co., 1960); Arthur M. Schlesinger, Jr., *The Age of Jackson* (New York: Little Brown & Co., 1946).

338 **"I am interested . . . should be considerable":** Arthur Schlesinger, Jr., to Richard McAdoo, January 12, 1973, box 285, folder 285.2.

339 **"coming home to roost":** Arthur Schlesinger, Jr., *Journals: 1952–2000* (New York: Penguin, 2007), p. 352.

340 **"The Almighty Presidency":** Arthur Schlesinger, Jr., to Kenneth Galbraith, March 23, 1973, box 285, folder 285.3.

340 **"The Omnipotent Presidency":** Arthur Schlesinger, Jr., to Richard McAdoo, April 10, 1973, box 285, folder 285.2, Arthur Schlesinger Collection; Richard McAdoo to Arthur Schlesinger, Jr., April 19, 1973, box 285, folder 285.2. **"The Runaway Presidency":** Arthur Schlesinger, Jr., to Richard McAdoo, March 6, 1973, box 285, folder 285.2.

340 **Schlesinger seemed to come upon:** Arthur Schlesinger, Jr., to Richard McAdoo, April 10, 1973, box 285, folder 285.2.

340 **America's rise to power:** Arthur M. Schlesinger Jr., *The Imperial Presidency* (Boston, MA: Houghton Mifflin Co., 1973).

341 **decide whether to use military force:** Ibid.

341 **reviewers praised him:** Gary Wills, "A pattern of rising power: The Imperial Presidency," *New York Times* (November 18, 1973); Arthur G. Hansen, "The Imperial Presidency," *Saturday Evening Post* (May 1, 1974). **"last half century . . . imperial Presidency":** Schlesinger, *Imperial Presidency*, p. 421.

342 **"no more embarrassment . . . or the misuse of it":** Henry Steel Commager to Arthur Schlesinger, Jr., November 1, 1973, box 262, folder 262.20.

342 **In 1951, he had publicly defended:** Arthur Schlesinger, Jr., "Presidential Powers: Taft Statement on Troops Opposed, Actions of Past Presidents Cited," *New York Times* (Jan. 9, 1951). **"police action":** News Conference of President Harry S. Truman, June 29, 1950, reprinted in *Public Papers of the Presidents*, January 1 to December 31, 1950 (Washington,

D.C.: US GPO, 1965), p. 504. **Now, writing with the conviction:** Arthur Schlesinger, *The Imperial Presidency*, pp. 323–25, 458–62.

343 **"in high-flying":** Arthur Schlesinger, Jr., to Henry Steel Commager, October 26, 1973, box 285, folder 285.3.

343 **Congress passed a series:** Making supplemental appropriations for the Fiscal Year ending June 30, 1973, Pub. L. No. 93-50 (1973); The second Supplemental Appropriations Act for FY1973, Pub. L. No. 93–52 (1973); Richard F. Grimmett, "Congressional Use of Funding Cutoffs Since 1970 Involving U.S. Military Forces and Overseas Deployments," Congressional Research Service Report (January 10, 2001), p. 2.

344 **"My problem is . . . the Congressional opposition":** Henry Kissinger, *Ending the Vietnam War: A History of America's Involvement in and Extrication from the Vietnam War* (New York: Simon & Schuster, 2003), p. 469.

344 **passed the War Powers Resolution:** War Powers Resolution, Pub. L. No. 93-148 (1973).

344 **Congress renewed the funding limits:** Grimmett, "Congressional Use of Funding Cutoffs."

Chapter 17
≡ *The New Normal*

347 **epigraph:** Gerald Ford, "Remarks and a Question-and-Answer Session With Reporters in Atlantic City, New Jersey, October 27, 1976," in *Public Papers of the Presidents of the United States: Gerald R. Ford, 1976–1977,* Book III (Washington D.C.: United States Government Printing Office, 1979), p. 2720.

347 **For a quarter century:** James Cannon, *Gerald R. Ford: An Honorable Life* (The University of Michigan Press, 2013), p. 9. **Even as a representative:** Gerald Ford, "Ford on War Powers" in *Cong. Record,* vol. 119, 93rd Cong., 1st Sess. (1973), pp. 35682, 36204.

348 **"Eisenhower without medals":** Jerald F. terHorst, *Newsweek* (October 18, 1976), p. 36.

348 **banned the playing:** Yanek Mieczkowski, *Gerald Ford and the Challenges of the 1970s* (Lexington, KY: The University Press of Kentucky, 2005), p. 43.

349 **"It's hard for politicians":** David S. Broder, " 'Civil War' within the GOP," *Washington Post* (March 12, 1975).

350 **despite the Paris peace accords:** Henry Kissinger, *Ending the Vietnam War: A History of America* (New York: Simon & Schuster, 2003), pp. 497–99.

350 **president and his top national security advisor:** P. Edward Haley, *Congress and the Fall of South Vietnam and Cambodia* (East Brunswick, NJ: Associated University Presses, 1982), pp. 159–62.

350 **Congress had passed measures:** Haley, *Congress and the Fall*, p. 40.

351 **president and his team took up the prospect . . . Cambodia was lost:** "Document 211: Memorandum of Conversation, April 8, 1975, 9:00 a.m." in *Foreign Relations of the United States, 1969–1976*, vol. X (U.S. Department of State, Office of the Historian), pp. 760–61.

351 **Vietnam was a different story. . . . would not agree to a settlement:** Ibid., p. 761.

351 **"vicious in these things":** Ibid.

351 **Ford chose the Johnson model:** "Document 211:" ibid., pp. 762–63; Haley, *Congress and the Fall of South Vietnam*, pp. 95–97. **America had a moral obligation:** Kissinger, *Ending the Vietnam War*, p. 535; Haley, *Congress and the Fall of South Vietnam*, pp. 90–91; "Interview with Gerald R. Ford," WGBH (Apr. 29, 1982), https://www.digitalcommon wealth.org/search/commonwealth-oai:sx61f638t.

352 **"require violation of the law . . . this will require U.S. forces":** "Document 212: Minutes of National Security Council Meeting, April 9, 1975, 11:25am–1:15pm," in *Foreign Relations of the United States, 1969–1976*, vol. X, pp. 775–76.

352 **"innate" authority . . . "use U.S. Forces for this purpose":** Ibid., p. 776.

353 **"would lie offshore . . . humanitarian":** War Powers: A Test of Compliance Relative to the Danang Sealift, the Evacuation of Phnom Penh, the Evacuation of Saigon, and the Mayaguez Incident, Hearings before the Subcommittee on International Security and Scientific Affairs, 94th Cong., May 7 and June 4, 1975 (Washington, D.C.: U.S. Government Printing Office, 1975), p. 3.

353 **Ford asked hopefully:** "Document 212," p. 776.

353 **"politically acceptable . . . we who are in trouble":** Ibid., pp. 776–77.

353 **evacuation would be very hard to justify legally:** Ibid., p. 776.

354 "think that we should ask . . . to their advantage": Ibid., pp. 776–77.

354 Ford resolved to ask: Ibid., pp. 778–79; Gerald Ford, "Address on U.S. Foreign Policy" (April 10, 1975).

355 "by what authority . . . Khmer evacuation is incidental": "Document 226: Memorandum of Conversations, April 11, 1975, 4:30pm," in *Foreign Relations of the United States, 1969–1976*, vol. X, p. 804.

355 "stretching the law . . . we might be vulnerable": "Document 226," p. 804.

355 Ford reported the evacuation operation: "Letter to the Speaker of the House and the President of the Senate Transmitting Proposed Legislation to Assist the Republic of Vietnam, April 11, 1975," in *Public Papers of the Presidents of the United States: Gerald R. Ford, 1975* (Washington, D.C.: United States Government Printing Office, 1977), pp. 474–75.

356 During that meeting, Kissinger explained: "Document 232: Memorandum of Conversations, April 14, 1975, 3:30pm," in *Foreign Relations of the United States, 1969–1976*, vol. X, pp. 817–22.

356 "large sums for evacuation . . . in an enclave for a long period": Ibid., p. 820.

356 "envisaged": Ibid., p. 820. "I feel put upon . . . getting the Vietnamese out": Ibid., p. 821. "idea here is very different": Ibid., p. 822.

357 "reiterate our previous request . . . Congress work its will": "Memorandum of Conversation, April 15, 1975, 9:23–10:04am," from National Security Adviser's Memoranda of Conversation Collection at the Gerald R. Ford Presidential Library. "My experience on Vietnam . . . chance for Vietnam in Congress": Ibid.

357 "don't think they will pass anything . . . let it go at that": "Memorandum of Conversation, April 15, 1975, 9:23–10:04am," from National Security Adviser's Memoranda of Conversation Collection at the Gerald R. Ford Presidential Library.

357 Even then, Kissinger found: Henry Kissinger, *Ending the Vietnam War: A History of America's Involvement in and Extrication from the Vietnam War* (New York: Simon & Schuster, 2003), pp. 505–13.

358 the president made his case: Gerald R. Ford, "Address Before a Joint Session of the Congress Reporting on United States Foreign Policy 1 PUB. PAPERS 464 (Apr. 10, 1975); David J. Barron & Martin S. Lederman,

"The Commander in Chief at the Lowest Ebb—Framing the Problem, Doctrine, and Original Understanding," *Harvard Law Review*, vol. 121 (2008), pp. 1071–72.

358 **Unable to find legislative language:** Ibid., pp. 1071–72.

358 **South Vietnamese could be spirited away:** *War Powers*, p. 26.

358 **"Congress would surely":** Kissinger, *Ending the Vietnam War*, p. 535.

359 **"final American withdrawal":** Lou Cannon and Michael Getler, "Deciding on the Final Withdrawal," *Washington Post* (April 30, 1975), p. A1.

359 **went to the Residence:** Ibid., p. A29.

359 **With Ford's approval:** Ibid.

359 **"fact is we did not panic":** Ibid.

360 **security advisor informed him:** Roy Rowan, *The Four Days of Mayaguez* (New York: W. W. Norton & Company, 1975), pp. 67–68.

360 **"would have to be scrutinized:** "Document 285: Minutes of National Security Council Meeting, May 12, 1975, 12:05–12:50pm," in *Foreign Relations of the United States, 1969–1976*, vol. X, p. 978. **"would be hamstrung . . . irrespective of the Congress":** Ibid., p. 983.

360 **"have to state the problems":** "Document 295: Minutes of National Security Council Meeting, May 13–14, 1975, 10:40pm–12:25am," in *Foreign Relations of the United States, 1969–1976*, vol. X.

360 **Ford—after asking Buchen:** "Document 298: Minutes of National Security Council Meeting, May 14, 1975, 3:52–5:42pm," in *Foreign Relations of the United States, 1969–1976*, vol. X.

361 **As a congressman, Ford had pressed:** *Cong. Record*, 119th Congress (1973), pp. H36204–05. **"We cannot be that concerned":** "Document 295," p. 1014. **Ford even declined:** Ralph Wetterhahn, *The Last Battle: The Mayaguez Incident and the End of the Vietnam War* (New York: Carroll & Graf Publishers, 2001), pp. 122–24; Rowan, *Four Days of Mayaguez*, p. 176. **emphasized in his memoirs:** Gerald R. Ford, *A Time to Heal: The Autobiography of Gerald R. Ford* (New York: Harper & Row, 1979), pp. 279–80.

361 **rescue operation was carried out:** Ford, *Time to Heal*, p. 281; Peter Goldman, "Ford's Rescue Operation," *Newsweek* (May 26, 1975).

361 **"It went perfectly":** Ibid.

362 **"hopelessly naïve":** Ford, *Time to Heal*, p. 283.

362 **"it puts the epaulets back on":** Goldman, "Ford's Rescue Operation."

"he is that 'strong president'": David Nyham, "Ford's Strategy for Election," *Boston Globe* (July 9, 1975).

362 **Ford tried to head them off:** Gerald R. Ford, Executive Order 11,905, "United States Foreign Intelligence Activities" (Jan. 24, 1978). **proposal to place limits . . . of the same view:** Barron and Lederman, "Commander in Chief at the Lowest Ebb," pp. 1075–76; Philip Buchen, "Re Legislation on Electronic Surveillance for Foreign Intelligence Purposes," Memorandum for President Gerald Ford (Mar. 15, 1976).

363 **internal opposition:** Neil A. Lewis, "Edward H. Levi, Attorney General Credited With Restoring Order After Watergate, Dies at 88," *New York Times* (March 8, 2000). **Ford had sought him out:** Ford, *Time to Heal*, pp. 236–237.

363 **Levi strongly believed:** "Restoring Justice: The Legacy of Edward H. Levi," *Bulletin of the American Academy of Arts & Sciences* (Winter 2002), p. 22. **had even drawn up:** Foreign Intelligence Surveillance Act, H.R. 12750 & S. 3197 (proposed Mar. 23, 1976); Statement by the Honorable Edward H. Levi, Attorney General of the United States, before the Senate Select Committee on Intelligence (Washington, D.C., July 1, 1976), http://www.justice.gov/sites/default/files/ag/legacy/2011/08/23/07-01-1976.pdf. **ensured his contrary view was noted:** Philip Buchen, "Re Legislation on Electronic Surveillance for Foreign Intelligence Purposes," Memorandum for President Gerald Ford (Mar. 15, 1976).

363 **"the bill does it . . . this bill does that":** Edward H. Levy, Attorney General of the United States, Foreign Intelligence Surveillance Act of 1976, Hearings before the Subcommittee on Criminal Laws and Procedures, 94th Cong., May 29, 30, 1976 (Washington, D.C.: U.S. Government Printing Office, 1976), p. 20.

364 **"difference between the Ford Administration . . . our Founding Fathers believed":** Gerald Ford, "Remarks and a Question-and-Answer Session With Reporters in Atlantic City, New Jersey, October 27, 1976," in *Public Papers of the Presidents of the United States: Gerald R. Ford, 1976–1977*, Book III (Washington D.C.: United States Government Printing Office, 1979), p. 2720.

364 **"cooperated with the Senate Judiciary Committee . . . virtually**

noncontroversial": Gerald Ford, "Attorney General Edward H. Levi," *University of Chicago Law Review*, vol. 52 (1985), pp. 286–87.

Chapter 18
≡ *Post–Cold War*

367 **epigraph:** Griffin Bell, Attorney General of the United States, Foreign Intelligence Electronic Surveillance: Hearings on H.R. 5794, H.R. 9745, H.R. 7308, and H.R. 5632 Before the Subcomm. on Legis. of the H. Permanent Select Comm. on Intelligence, 95th Cong. 26 (1978), at 38.

367 **But Bush sought:** Authorization for Use of Military Force Against Iraq Resolution, Pub. L. No. 102-1, 105 Stat. 3 (1991).

369 **He had tried to avoid its taint:** Gerald Ford, "Statement and Response to Questions from Members of the House Judiciary Committee Concerning the Pardon of Richard Nixon" (October 17, 1974), available at: presidency.ucsb.edu/ws/?pid=4471.

369 **word "humble":** Jimmy Carter, "Inaugural Address," January 20, 1977, The American Presidency Project, available at http://www.presidency .ucsb.edu/ws/?pid=6575. **Carter got out of the presidential limousine:** James T. Patterson, *Restless Giant: The United States from Watergate to Bush v. Gore* (New York: Oxford University Press, 2005), p. 109; Sean Wilentz, *The Age of Reagan: A History, 1974–2008* (New York: Harper Perennial, 2008), p. 74. **"They're walking":** Associated Press, "Presidential strut is now iconic inaugural moment," Fox News (Jan. 14, 2013).

369 **keeping with a campaign promise:** Ethics in Government Act of 1978, Pub. Law 95-521, 92 Stat. 1824 (1978), p. 1867.

370 **"appropriate reduction":** Jimmy Carter, " 'Ask President Carter' Remarks During a Telephone Call-in Program on the CBS Radio Network," CBS Radio (March 5, 1977), available at http://www.presidency .ucsb.edu/ws/?pid=7119. **formal legal opinion:** John Harmon, "4a Opinion: Presidential Power to Use the Armed Forces Abroad Without Statutory Authorization," Office of Legal Council (1980).

370 **to end the era:** Foreign Intelligence Surveillance Act, Pub. Law 95-511, 92 Stat. 1783 (1978), p. 1785.

370 **top constitutional lawyer had already testified:** "Memorandum from

John M. Harmon, Assistant Att'y Gen., Office of Legal Counsel, to Hon. Edward P. Boland, Chairman, House Permanent Select Comm. on Intelligence," Foreign Intelligence Electronic Surveillance: Hearings Before the Subcommittee on Legislation of the Permanent Select Committee on Intelligence House of Representatives on H.R. 5794, H.R. 9745, H.R. 7308, and H.R. 5632 (1978), pp. 26–31.

370   "two Presidents in a row": "Testimony of Attorney General Griffin Bell," Foreign Intelligence Electronic Surveillance: Hearings Before the Subcommittee on Legislation of the Permanent Select Committee on Intelligence House of Representatives on H.R. 5794, H.R. 9745, H.R. 7308, and H.R. 5632 (1978), p. 38.

370   "we know the Constitution": "Statement of Representative Henry Hyde," 124 *Cong. Record*, 28,3999 (1978).

370   although the House approved: David J. Barron and Martin S. Lederman, "The Commander in Chief at the Lowest Ebb—Framing the Problem, Doctrine, and Original Understanding," *Harvard Law Review*, vol. 121 (2008), p. 1077. "exclusive means by which electronic surveillance": Foreign Intelligence Surveillance Act, Pub. Law 95-511, 92 Stat. 1783 (1978), p. 1797.

371   "crisis of confidence": Jimmy Carter, "Crisis of Confidence" (July 15, 1979).

371   November 4, 1979: Patterson, *Restless Giant*, p. 125.

371   military plan called for a rescue: Ibid., pp. 125–26.

372   By Election Day 1980: Douglas Brinkley, *The Unfinished Presidency: Jimmy Carter's Journey Beyond the White House* (New York: Penguin Books, 1998). returns finally came in: Ibid. "promised you four years ago . . . say it doesn't hurt": Jimmy Carter, "1980 Presidential Election: Remarks on the Outcome of the Election," *Public Papers of the Presidents of the United States: Jimmy Carter, 1980–1981* (November 4, 1980), p. 2687.

372   president spent his last forty-eight hours: Hamilton Jordan, *Crisis: The Last Year of the Carter Presidency* (New York: G.P. Putnam's Sons, 1982), pp. 390–92.

373   "Restore power & auth": Charlie Savage, *Takeover: The Return of the Imperial Presidency* (New York: Little Brown & Co., 2007), p. 43

373   Reagan sent a significant contingent: Steven F. Hayward, *The Age*

of Reagan: The Conservative Counterrevolution, 1980–1989 (New York: Three Rivers Press, 2009), pp. 268–70; Patterson, *Restless Giant*, p. 206.

374 **limited nature of the projection:** Ronald Reagan, Letter to the Speaker of the House and the President Pro Tempore of the Senate Reporting on the United States Participation in the Multinational Force in Lebanon (September 29, 1982); Ronald Reagan, Statement on Signing the Multinational Force in Lebanon Resolution (October 12, 1983). **The thinking was that:** Ibid.

374 **April of 1983:** Patterson, *Restless Giant*, p. 198.

374 **Congress passed a joint resolution:** Multinational Force in Lebanon Resolution, Pub. L. No. 98-119, 97 Stat. 805 (1983).

374 **Congress did agree, however:** Multinational Force in Lebanon Resolution, Pub. L. No. 98-119, 97 Stat. 805 (1983).

374 **"Impermissibl[e] infringements":** Ronald Reagan, "Statement on Signing the Multinational Force in Lebanon Resolution" (October 12, 1983) at http://www.presidency.ucsb.edu/ws/?pid=40624.

375 **"Our problem is . . . Syrians to pull back":** Douglas Brinkley, ed., *Reagan Diaries*, vol. 1 (New York: HarperCollins e-books, 2010), pp. 272–74.

375 **"Navy guns turned loose":** Ibid., p. 276.

375 **late October, a car bomb:** Savage, *Takeover*, p. 51. **Congress moved to require:** Steven Roberts, "Beirut Gives Congress Some Second Thoughts," *New York Times* (December 18, 1983).

375 **two days after the barracks bombing:** Savage, *Takeover*, p. 51; Patterson, Restless Giant, pp. 205–06.

376 **"another Vietnam":** Ronald Reagan, *An American Life: The Autobiography* (New York:) pp. 451–52.

376 **Dramatically, and with little warning:** Wilentz, *Age of Reagan*, pp. 350–51.

377 **"Before we commit our troops":** Reagan, *American Life*, p. 466.

377 **secret program also seemed to have involved:** Patterson, *Restless Giant*, pp. 208–10.

377 **resulting uproar led to the appointment:** Ibid., pp. 211–13; Wilentz, *Age of Reagan*, p. 540.

378 **"Congressional actions to limit the president":** "Minority Report," in

Report of the Congressional Committees Investigating the Iran-Contra Affair, NO. 100-433, S. REP. NO. 100-216 (1987), p. 457; Savage, *Takeover*, pp. 55–56.

378 **slew of signing statements:** Barron and Lederman, "Commander in Chief at the Lowest Ebb," pp. 1083–87. **Bush, like Reagan:** Patterson, *Restless Giant*, p. 226.

378 **faced with the biggest military decision:** Patterson, *Restless Giant*, pp. 232–33; Jon Meacham, *Destiny and Power: The American Odyssey of George Herbert Walker Bush* (New York: Random House, 2015), pp. 451–56.

379 **prospect that he privately feared:** Meacham, *Destiny and Power*, p. 453. **president's approval rating soared:** Ibid., p. 466.

379 **last months of the Bush administration:** Derek Chollet and James Goldgeier, *America Between the Wars: From 11/9 to 9/11* (New York: Public Affairs, 2008), p. 53.

380 **"I'm not asking you . . . out of there by inauguration day":** Ibid., p. 53.

380 **"We can get in":** Christopher D. O'Sullivan, *Colin Powell: A Political Biography* (Lanham, MD: Rowman & Littlefield Publishers, 2009), p. 108.

380 **horrific images:** Chollet and Goldgeier, *America Between the Wars*, pp. 75–76; Patterson, Restless Giant, p. 338.

381 **"people who are dragging American bodies":** Clifford Krauss, "The Somalia Mission; White House Tries to Calm Congress," *New York Times* (Oct. 6, 1993).

381 **Gramm's assessment was widely shared:** Ibid. **"To authorise the mission":** Ibid.

381 **Congress codified that commitment:** Department of Defense Appropriations Act, 1994, Pub. L. No. 103-139, 107 Stat. 1418, (1993), p. 1476.

381 **Congress enacted statutes:** Barron and Lederman, "Commander in Chief at the Lowest Ebb," pp. 1088–90.

382 **president instead targeted a proposed law:** "Placing of United States Armed Forces Under United Nations Operational or Tactical Control," 20 Op. Off. Legal Counsel 182 (1996).

382 **he also scuttled:** Barton Gellman, "U.S. Reconsiders Putting GI's Under U.N.," *Washington Post* (Sept. 22, 1993), pp. A1, A32.

382 **accepted a provision:** Department of Defense Appropriations Act, 1994, Pub. L. No. 103-139, 107 Stat. 1418, (1993), pp. 1476–78.

382 **He asserted his authority to organize:** National Defense Authorization Act for Fiscal Year 1998, Pub. L. No. 105-85, 111 Stat. 1629 (1997); Department of Defense Appropriations Act, 1994, Pub. L. No. 103-139, 107 Stat. 1418 (1993).

Chapter 19
≡ *The Global War on Terrorism*

385 **epigraph:** John C. Yoo, Deputy Assistant Attorney General, "The President's Constitutional Authority to Conduct Military Operations Against Terrorists and Nations Supporting Them," Opinions of the Office of Legal Counsel, vol. 25 (September 25, 2001), p. 214.

385 **make some cursory remarks:** Peter Baker, *Days of Fire: Bush and Cheney in the White House* (New York: Anchor Books, 2013), pp. 120–22.

385 **"evil, despicable acts":** George W. Bush, "Address to the Nation on the Terrorist Attacks" (September 11, 2001).

386 **"acts of war":** George W. Bush, "Remarks Following a Meeting with the National Security Team" (September 12, 2001).

386 **even thanked Congress:** Bush, ibid., Authorization for Use of Military Force, Pub. L. No. 107-40, 115 Stat. 224 (2001).

386 **talks were conducted by representatives:** David Abramowitz, "The President, the Congress, and Use of Force: Legal and Political Considerations in Authorizing Use of Force Against International Terrorism," *Harvard International Law Journal*, vol. 43 (2002), pp. 71–72.

387 **"unnecessary and even undesirable":** Ibid., p. 73 n.5.

387 **"to deter and pre-empt":** Ibid., p. 73.

387 **"particularly breathtaking":** Ibid., p. 74 n.8. **"would have authorized the President":** Ibid., p. 73.

388 **"Given the breadth of activities":** Ibid.

389 **political risk:** Jon Meacham, *Destiny and Power: The American Odyssey of George Herbert Walker Bush* (New York: Random House, 2015), pp. 451–57.

390 **"another Tonkin Gulf Resolution":** Abramowitz, "President, the Congress, and Use of Force," p. 73 n.6.

391 **"necessary and appropriate":** Authorization for Use of Military Force,

Pub. L. No. 107-40, 115 Stat. 224 (2001). **"with this language, Congress denied":** Tom Daschle, "Power We Didn't Grant," *Washington Post* (December 23, 2005).

391 · **"ties the President's hands":** *Cong. Record*, vol. 147, 107th Cong., 1st Sess. (2001), p. H5654.

391 **speech after speech:** "Authorizing Use of United States Armed Forces against those Responsible for Recent Attacks Against the United States," *Cong. Record*, vol. 147, 107th Cong., 1st Sess. (2001), pp. H5638–81, S9459–60.

392 **"in the United States":** Daschle, "Power We Didn't Grant."

392 **"dumbfounded":** Richard W. Stevenson, "Congress Never Authorized Spying Effort, Daschle Says," *New York Times* (December 23, 2005).

393 **"clear away":** *Cong. Record*, vol. 147, 107th Cong., 1st Sess. (2001), p. H5682.

393 **Those harboring such concerns:** "Authorizing Use of Military Force in Response to Terrorist Attachs," *Cong. Record*, vol. 147, 107th Cong., 1st Sess. (2001), pp. H5632-34.

394 **"shock and rage we all felt . . . unprecedented grant of authority":** Daschle, "Power We Didn't Grant."

394 **Daschle formally asked:** *Cong. Record*, vol. 147, 107th Cong., 1st Sess. (2001), pp. S9411–13. **"all necessary and appropriate force . . . such nations, organizations or persons":** Authorization for Use of Military Force, Pub. L. No. 107-40, 115 Stat. 224 (2001).

395 **all ninety-eight senators:** *Cong. Record*, vol. 147, 107th Cong., 1st Sess. (2001), p. S9421. **Later that day, the House:** *Cong. Record*, vol. 147, 107th Cong., 1st Sess. (2001), p. H5683.

395 **"Both Houses of Congress . . . threat to our peace and security":** George W. Bush, "Statement on Signing the Authorization for Use of Military Force" (September 18, 2001), available at http://www.presidency.ucsb.edu/ws/?pid=64595.

395 **"Ambition must be made":** James Madison, "The Federalist No. 51: The Structure of the Government Must Furnish the Proper Checks and Balances Between the Different Departments," *Independent Journal* (February 6, 1788).

395 **"part of an ongoing dialogue . . . separate and distinct powers":** Abramowitz, "President, the Congress, and Use of Force," p. 79.

396 **"have to work . . . to achieve our objective"**: Dick Cheney, "Interview with Vice President Cheney conducted by Tim Russert, host of NBC's Meet the Press" (September 16, 2001).

396 **"restrictions placed . . . to assist in intelligence gathering"**: Ibid.

396 **"Will we lift"**: Ibid.

396 **"Well, I think so . . . accomplishing their mission"**: Ibid.

397 **"have to check with the lawyers . . . this is a war"**: Ibid.

397 **"government, working with Congress"**: George W. Bush, "Remarks Following a Meeting with Congressional Leaders and an Exchange with Reporters," (September 19, 2001), available at http://www.presidency.ucsb.edu/ws/index.php?pid=65080. **"leadership at such an important time"**: George W. Bush, "Address Before a Joint Session of the Congress on the United States Response to the Terrorist Attacks of September 11," (September 20, 2001), available at http://www.presidency.ucsb.edu/ws/index.php?pid=64731.

397 **six days later, on September 25**: John C. Yoo, "The President's Constitutional Authority," pp. 188–214.

398 **"ultimate question of law"**: Peter M. Shane, "Learning McNamara's Lessons: How the War Powers Resolution Advances the Rule of Law," *Case Western Reserve Law Review*, vol. 47 (1997), p. 1281. **"full-scale war"**: Yoo, "President's Constitutional Authority," p. 202.

398 **"can place any limits . . . for the President alone to make"**: Yoo, "President's Constitutional Authority," p. 214.

398 **memo to the White House counsel**: John C. Yoo and Robert J. Delahunty, "Authority for Use of Military Force to Combat Terrorist Activities Within the United States" (October 23, 2001), available at http://nsarchive.gwu.edu/torturingdemocracy/documents/20011023.pdf. **opinion from another deputy**: Patrick F. Philbin, "Legality of the Use of Military Commissions to Try Terrorists: Memorandum Opinion for the Counsel to the President," Opinions of the Office of Legal Counsel, vol. 25 (November 6, 2001), pp. 1–38. **memorandum from the head**: Jay S. Bybee, "Memorandum for William J. Haynes, II General Counsel, Department of Defense, Re: The President's power as Commander in Chief to transfer captured terrorists to the control and custody of foreign nations" (March 13, 2002), available at http://nsarchive.gwu.edu/torturingdemocracy/documents/20020313.pdf.

399   **first suggested that a statute passed:** John C. Yoo, "Memorandum for
      Daniel J. Bryant, Assistant Attorney General, Office of Legislative Af-
      fairs-Re: Applicability of 18 U.S.C. 4001(a) to Military Detention of
      United States Citizens," (June 27, 2002), available at https://www.justice
      .gov/sites/default/files/olc/legacy/2009 /08/24/memodetentionuscitizens
      06272002.pdf. **second defended his constitutional authority:** Jay S.
      Bybee, "Legal Constraints to Boarding and Searching Foreign Vessels
      on the High Seas" (June 13, 2002).

399   **"Congress can no more interfere with the President's conduct . . . pre-
      vent attacks upon the United States":** Jay S. Bybee, "Memorandum for
      Alberto R. Gonzales, Counsel to the President, Re: Standards of Conduct
      for Interrogation under 18 U.S.C. 2340–2340A," (August 1, 2002), p. 39,
      available at http://nsarchive.gwu.edu/NSAEBB/NSAEBB127/02.08.01
      .pdf.

400   **One of the August memos:** Jay S. Bybee, "Memorandum for Alberto R.
      Gonzales, Counsel to the President-Re: Standards of Conduct for In-
      terrogation under 18 U.S.C. 2340–2340A" (August 1, 2002), available
      at http://nsarchive.gwu.edu/NSAEBB/NSAEBB127/02.08.01.pdf. **Pen-
      tagon applied:** John C. Yoo, "Memorandum for William J. Haynes II,
      General Counsel of the Department of Defense, Re: Military Interro-
      gation of Alien Unlawful Combatants Held Outside the United States,"
      (March 14, 2003), available at http://nsarchive.gwu.edu/torturing
      democracy/documents/20030314.pd f.

400   **"could render specific conduct":** U.S. Dep't of Defense Working
      Group, "Working Group Report on Detainee Interrogations in the
      Global War on Terrorism: Assessment of Legal, Historical, Policy, and
      Operational Considerations" (Apr. 4, 2003), p. 20. **president issued:**
      President's Statement on Signing of H.R. 2863, "Department of De-
      fense, Emergency Supplemental Appropriations to Address Hurricanes
      in the Gulf of Mexico, and Pandemic Influenza Act, 2006" (Dec. 30,
      2005); Detainee Treatment Act of 2005, Pub. L. No. 109–148, 119 Stat.
      3136 (2005).

400   **classified memorandum:** John C. Yoo, "Memorandum for the Attorney
      General" (November 2, 2001), available at https://www.justice.gov/sites
      /default/files/olc/legacy/2011 /03/25/johnyoo-memo-for-ag.pdf.

401   **"strangled by law":** Jack Goldsmith, *The Terror Presidency: Law and*

Judgment Inside the Bush Administration (New York: W. W. Norton & Company, 2009), p. 69.

402   **when the administration confronted that question:** Ibid., pp. 81–90.

402   **most important war powers case:** *Hamdan v. Rumsfeld*, 548 U.S. 557 (2006).

402   **"not going to overrule":** Baker, *Days of Fire*, p. 469.

402   **administration announced:** Ibid., pp. 469–70; Linda Greenhouse, "Justices, 5–3, Broadly Reject Bush Plan to Try Detainees," *New York Times* (June 30, 2006).

Chapter 20
≡ *Iraq*

405   **epigraph:** Norm N. Levey, "Congress Unleashes Anti-war Proposals: A Senate Resolution Opposes Bush's Troop Increase. A House Plan Calls for Withdrawal," *Los Angeles Times* (January 18, 2007).

405   **president wanted to know:** Peter Baker, *Days of Fire: Bush and Cheney in the White House* (New York: First Anchor Books, 2014), pp. 135–36.

406   **most prominent contenders:** Barack Obama, "Remarks of Illinois Sen. Barack Obama Against Going to War with Iraq" (October 2, 2002).

406   **no-fly zone:** Bob Woodward, *Plan of Attack: The Definitive Account of the Decision to Invade Iraq* (New York: Simon & Schuster Paperbacks, 2004), pp. 9–12.

407   **"As the President said":** Condoleezza Rice, "September 11, 2001: Attack on America—Remarks By the National Security Advisor Condoleezza Rice to the Conservative Political Action Conference" (January 31, 2002).

407   **"the Imperial Option":** Woodward, *Plan of Attack*, p. 297.

408   **editorial that appeared:** Brent Scowcroft, "Don't Attack Saddam," *Wall Street Journal* (August 15, 2002).

409   **president told his top people:** Woodward, *Plan of Attack*, p. 167.

409   **"a call for 21st century imperialism":** Ted Kennedy, "Remarks on Iraq," *Cong. Record*, vol. 148 (October 7, 2002), p. S19201.

409   **UN resolution in hand:** "Resolution 1441 (2002): Adopted by the Security Council at its 4644th meeting, on 8 November 2002," S/Res

/1441 (2002) available at http://www.un.org/Depts/unmovic/documents /1441.pdf; Woodward, *Plan of Attack*, pp. 182–84.

409 **a credible threat:** Ibid., p. 203; Johanna Neuman, "2 Parties, 2 Paths, 1 Concern," *Los Angeles Times* (October 10, 2002).

409 **Congress approved a broad authorization:** Authorization for Use of Military Force Against Iraq Resolution of 2002, Pub. L. No. 107-243, 116 Stat. 1498 (2002); Woodward, *Plan of Attack*, pp. 169, 203–04.

409 **Polling showed:** Pew Research Center, "Most Americans Support War with Iraq, Shows New Pew/CFR Poll—Commentary by Lee Feinstein," Council on Foreign Relations (October 10, 2002).

410 **war on Iraq had begun:** George W. Bush, "Address to the Nation on Iraq" (March 19, 2003), available at http://www.presidency.ucsb.edu /ws/index.php?pid=63368.

410 **"Mr. President, bring some troops home":** Baker, *Days of Fire*, p. 487. **"I will not withdraw":** Ibid.

411 **in a televised address:** George W. Bush, "Address to the Nation on Military Operations in Iraq" (January 10, 2007), available at http://www .presidency.ucsb.edu/ws/index.php?pid=24432. **"I respect you . . . give it a chance":** George W. Bush, "Address Before a Joint Session of the Congress on the State of the Union" (January 23, 2007), available at http://www.presidency.ucsb.edu/ws/index.php?pid=24446.

411 **Congress had all but ordered:** Thomas L. Friedman, "The Somalia Mission; Clinton Sending More Troops to Somalia," *New York Times* (October 7, 1993); Michael R. Gordon and Thomas L. Friedman, "Details of U.S. Raid in Somalia: Success So Near, a Loss So Deep," *New York Times* (October 25, 1993). **leading the administration to scramble:** Randolph Moss, "Authorization for Continuing Hostilities in Kosovo: Memorandum Opinion for the Attorney General" (December 19, 2000), available at: justice.gov/sites/default/files/olc/opinions/2000/12/31/o p-olc-v024-p0327.pdf

411 **Within days of the president's speech:** Baker, *Days of Fire*, pp. 524–29; Brian Kowlton, "Democrats Step Up Criticism of Iraq Plan," *New York Times* (January 7, 2007); Carl Hulse, "Measure in Senate Urges No Troop Rise in Iraq," *New York Times* (January 18, 2007); John O'Neil, "Senators Assert Right to Block Bush on Iraq," *New York Times* (January 30, 2007). **proposals with the best shot:** Jeff Zeleny and Michael Luo, "A divided

House Denounces Plan for More Troops," *New York Times* (February 17, 2007).

412 **leading Democratic contenders:** Stephen Braun, "Hillary Clinton opposes buildup," *Los Angeles Times* (January 18, 2007); Elana Schor, "Senate Dems to Try Again on the 'Surge,'" *Hill* (February 7, 2007).

412 **"I cannot believe":** Noam N. Levey, "Congress unleashes antiwar proposals: A Senate resolution opposes Bush's troop increase. A house plan calls for withdrawal," *Los Angeles Times* (January 18, 2007).

412 **"never to cut off":** Nancy Pelosi, "Exclusive: Pelosi Says Bush 'Has to Answer for This War,'" ABC News with Diane Sawyer (January 19, 2007); Baker, *Days of Fire*, p. 538.

413 **"won't stop us":** Baker, *Days of Fire*, p. 530.

413 **In April, the Senate and the House attached:** H.R. 1591: U.S. Troop Readiness, Veterans' Care, Katrina Recovery, and Iraq Accountability Appropriations Act, 2007; George Bush, Message to the House of Representatives Returning Without Approval the "U.S. Troop Readiness, Veterans' Care, Katrina Recovery, and Iraq Accountability Appropriations Act, 2007," 43 Weekly Comp. Pres. Doc. 560 (May 1, 2007). **urgent White House discussions:** Ibid., pp. 556–57.

Epilogue

415 **epigraph:** Stephen G. Bradbury, Memorandum for the Files, Re: Status of Certain OLC Opinions issued in the Aftermath of the Terrorist Attacks of September 11, 2001 (U.S. Department of Justice, Office of Legal Counsel, January 15, 2009), p. 4.

415 **spent the better part:** David J. Barron and Martin S. Lederman, "The Commander in Chief at the Lowest Ebb—Framing the Problem, Doctrine, and Original Understanding," *Harvard Law Review*, vol. 121 (2008).

417 He had made that clear: Barack Obama, "Renewing American Leadership," *Foreign Affairs* (July/August 2007); Charlie Savage, *Power Wars: Inside Obama's Post-9/11 Presidency* (New York: Little, Brown and Co., 2015), p. 61.

418 **issued an executive order:** Barack Obama, Executive Order 13491: Ensuring Lawful Interrogations (January 22, 2009), available at https://

www.whitehouse.gov/the_press_office/EnsuringLawfulInterrogations. **had told the courts:** Michael Hertz et al., Respondents' Memorandum Regarding the Government's Detention Authority Relative to Detainees Held at Guantanamo Bay, In re: Guantanamo Bay Detainee Litigation, Misc. No. 08-442 (Washington, D.C.: United States District Court for the District of Columbia, March 13, 2009). **he had shepherded through:** Military Commissions Act of 2009, Pub. L. No. 111-84, 123 Stat. 2574 (2009).

419 **his campaign in Libya:** Caroline D. Krauss, "Authority to Use Military Force in Libya: Memorandum Opinion for the Attorney General" (April 2011), available at http://www.justice.gov/sites/default/files/opinions /2011/04/31/authority-military-use-in-libya.pdf. Charlie Savage, "2 Top Lawyers Lost to Obama in Libya War Policy Debate," *New York Times* (June 17, 2011).

420 **Through a series of legislative restrictions:** Savage, *Power Wars*, pp. 125–30, 326–28.

421 **"poverty of useful":** , 343 U.S. 579, 589 (1952) (Jackson, J., concurring).

421 **"must be divined from materials":** Ibid. (Jackson, J., concurring).

423 **"purpose of this memorandum . . . remaining opinions identified below":** Steven G. Bradbury, Memorandum for the Files, p. 1.

423 **"issued in the wake of the atrocities . . . extraordinary time pressure":** Ibid.

423 **"perhaps . . . the views of OLC":** Ibid.

423 **"advanced a broad assertion . . . supported by the President":** Ibid., p. 2.

424 **"A law that is constitutional . . . are not sustainable":** Ibid., p. 4.

ACKNOWLEDGMENTS

I began thinking about these ideas more than a decade ago. At the time, I was preparing for a presentation at an academic conference on executive power at Duke Law School. My focus then was on a legal question: What limits does the Constitution let Congress place on the president's power to wage war? In continuing to think about these ideas in the years since—as I have made the switch from law professor to executive branch legal advisor to judge—my focus has shifted. My aim is no longer to make a legal argument about what wartime presidents are allowed to do when Congress tries to check them. My aim is to tell the story of what they actually have done.

Along the way, I have received help from too many people to name: students, academic colleagues, librarians, lawyers with whom I have had the privilege to work, friends, and family. I also have had the benefit of the vast body of scholarship—both historical and legal—that addresses this subject.

My first agent, Scott Moyers, encouraged me to write this as a story rather than an argument. He then helped me find a publisher before I left my teaching post at Harvard to join the Obama Administration in January 2009. My second agent, the incomparable Andrew Wylie, helped me revive the project when I came back to Harvard in 2010. The final version of this book exists due to the guidance, patience, and encouragement of my wonderful editor, Alice Mayhew. Thanks are due as well to her excellent assistant, Stuart Roberts.

I benefited over the course of many years from the research assistance of a fleet of incredibly talented and thoughtful students at Harvard Law School: Adam Lebovitz, Joshua Matz, Lauren Moxley, Jacob Reisberg, Andrew Rubenstein, Shivan Sarin, Kyle Wrshba, and David Zimmer. Adam went above and beyond by reading the whole manuscript and by offering excellent suggestions. I have had great and generous help as well from Nancy Katz and George Tauoltsides of the Harvard Law School Library, and from my faculty assistants, Mindy Eakin and Patricia Fazzone.

I have been talking about the limits of the president's power with my (now former) faculty colleagues at Harvard ever since I first arrived there as an assistant professor in the summer of 1999. I want to give special thanks to Dan Meltzer, who passed away too soon, but who taught me, as he taught all who knew him, how to provide advice; Elena Kagan, who, as my dean, (among her many other kindnesses over so many years), provided the research support that enabled me to write so much of this; John Manning, who invited me to present a version of this book at the public law workshop that he runs with my other former dean, Martha Minow; Martha herself, who helped me think through the idea for this book during a late night walk in New York City; Larry Tribe, who offered some crucially approving words when what became this book was just a draft law review article looking for a journal to accept it; and Jack Goldsmith, one of the great former heads of the Office of Legal Counsel and a generous reader and critic of this manuscript. Thanks are in order, too, to Jerry Frug, who did so much to bring me to Harvard Law School way back when and with whom I have discussed this book and so much else.

My former colleagues at the Office of Legal Counsel have taught me as much as anyone about the challenges of offering legal advice concerning the president's legal powers. They have been a source of support and inspiration since I first began practicing law. One of those former colleagues deserves special mention: Marty Lederman. We have been in conversation about law generally, and these ideas in particular, for more hours than either of us—or our families—would care to count. Together,

Marty and I wrote two lengthy law review articles about this very topic, served together at OLC in the Clinton and Obama administrations, and, for a time, worked on this book together, before Marty had to step away to pursue his own scholarly work as a law professor at Georgetown. His research and thinking inform every page, and most especially the chapter on World War I (though any errors are mine). I could not be more grateful for his friendship.

Three former colleagues from my time in government—Bob Bauer, Dawn Johnsen, and Chris Schroeder—also deserve special recognition. Each kindly and carefully commented on drafts of the book. I am indebted to them for the time they took to do so.

I also want to thank Mallory Heath. A great friend (along with her husband, Brian) of our family, a nanny to our children, and a master research librarian, Mallory has, with her love of the past and deep attention to detail, helped get the notes, pictures, and the text into fighting shape.

The real instigation for this book is my father, Jerry Barron. He was a professor of constitutional law for more than fifty years until he recently retired. He has been my truest teacher of the subject. When I first mentioned to him that I was working on an article about the president's power in war, he casually said, "I guess you will need to figure out what every president did." He was, as usual, right. Together, he and my mother, Myra—as careful a reader and legal thinker as there is—have been steadfast in encouraging me in this project, as in all things. They also were instrumental in supporting me, and my then very young family, when we went to Washington in January 2009 to work on some of these issues for real.

I have been blessed as well to have the support of my indefatigable in-laws, Bob and Milly Kayyem. They moved into our house to take care of the kids for a month in the winter of 2008 so that my wife, Juliette, and I could work on the presidential transition—my first introduction to the real-time pressures of advising a wartime president.

My sister, Jen, and my brother, Jon, have been, for this project—as for everything I have done—not only enthusiastic supporters but also great sources of insight.

For Cecilia, Leo, and Jeremiah—my greatest source of joy—there is no longer any need to ask when I will finish it. I am sorry that it took so long. I wrote it with the idea that it might help, in some small way, to ensure that you inherit a future in which the system of checks and balances that we are so fortunate to live under remains up to the task.

And then there is Juliette. I have now known her longer than I have not, though I felt like I had known her forever when I first met her more than twenty-five years ago. There is no one whose judgment about what makes sense and what does not that I trust more. There is also no one who writes more beautifully. And so, there is no one whom I would rather have had read this manuscript, which, amazingly, she did, again and again, draft chapter after draft chapter. There is not much romance in this book. That makes it hard to draw on its themes to close on a proper note. But if this book does have a single message, it is this: It is better to do things together than alone. Thanks to Juliette, I believe that message with all my heart.

ILLUSTRATION CREDITS

INDEX

ABOUT THE AUTHOR

David J. Barron is a federal judge on the United States Court of Appeals for the First Circuit. He was previously the S. William Green Professor of Public Law at Harvard Law School, where he still teaches as a visiting professor. He served as the acting assistant attorney general for the Office of Legal Counsel in the United States Department of Justice during the first term of the Obama administration. He was a law clerk to Associate Justice of the United States Supreme Court John Paul Stevens and to Judge Stephen Reinhardt of the United States Court of Appeals for the Ninth Circuit.